David Boddy
University of Glasgow

MANAGEMENT

An Introduction
Seventh Edition

 Pearson

Harlow, England • London • New York • Boston • San Francisco • Toronto • Sydney • Dubai • Singapore • Hong Kong
Tokyo • Seoul • Taipei • New Delhi • Cape Town • São Paulo • Mexico City • Madrid • Amsterdam • Munich • Paris • Milan

Pearson Education Limited
Edinburgh Gate
Harlow CM20 2JE
United Kingdom
Tel: +44 (0)1279 623623
Web: www.pearson.com/uk

First published 1998 under the Prentice Hall Europe imprint (print)
Second edition published 2002 (print)
Third edition published 2005 (print)
Fourth edition published 2008 (print)
Fifth edition published 2011 (print)
Sixth edition published 2014 (print and electronic)
Seventh edition published 2017 (print and electronic)

The Financial Times. With a worldwide network of highly respected journalists, The Financial Times provides global business news, insightful opinion and expert analysis of business, finance and politics. With over 500 journalists reporting from 50 countries worldwide, our in-depth coverage of international news is objectively reported and analysed from an independent, global perspective. To find out more, visit www.ft.com/pearsonoffer.

ISBN: 978–1–292–08859–4 (print)
    978-1-292-08862-4 (PDF)
    978-1-292-17766-3 (ePub)

British Library Cataloguing-in-Publication Data
A catalogue record for the print edition is available from the British Library

Library of Congress Cataloguing-in-Publication Data
Names: Boddy, David, author.
Title: Management : an introduction / David Boddy.
Description: Seventh Edition. | New York : Pearson, 2016. | Revised edition
    of the author's Management, 2014.
Identifiers: LCCN 2016030939 | ISBN 9781292088594
Subjects: LCSH: Management.
Classification: LCC HD31 .B583 2016 | DDC 658—dc23
LC record available at https://lccn.loc.gov/2016030939

10 9 8 7 6 5 4 3 2 1
22 21 20 19 18 17

Cover image © Lisa-Blue/Getty Images

Print edition typeset in 10.5/12.5 pt Minion by SPi Global
Printed and bound by L.E.G.O. S.p.A., Italy

NOTE THAT ANY PAGE CROSS REFERENCES REFER TO THE PRINT EDITION

BRIEF CONTENTS

PART 5 LEADING

PART 6 CONTROLLING

CONTENTS

PART 1
AN INTRODUCTION TO MANAGEMENT

PART 2
THE ENVIRONMENT OF MANAGEMENT

PART 5
LEADING

CHAPTER 14
INFLUENCING

CHAPTER 15
MOTIVATING

CHAPTER 16
COMMUNICATING

CHAPTER 17
TEAMS

PART 6
CONTROLLING

PREFACE TO THE SEVENTH EDITION

This seventh edition takes account of helpful comments from staff and students who used the sixth edition, and the suggestions of reviewers (please see below). The book retains the established structure of six parts, and the titles of the 20 chapters also remain the same. Within that structure each chapter has been updated where necessary, with many new and current examples both in the narrative and in the 'Management in practice' features. New empirical research maintains the academic quality. The main changes of this kind are:

Chapters

Chapter 1 (Managing in organisations) – introduces the new 'Develop a skill' feature in Sections 1.0 and 1.8, and the 'triple bottom line' in assessing business performance.

Chapter 4 (Managing internationally) – new chapter case study, Carlsberg, and introduces the idea of contextual intelligence, which is also cited as a useful skill to develop.

Chapter 5 (Corporate responsibility) – more structured view of corporate responsibility from work by Rangan (2015), including the idea of shared value.

Chapter 6 (Planning) – develops distinction between rational and creative approaches to planning and decision making.

Chapter 7 (Decision making) – new 'Management in practice' feature based on McDonald's, to illustrate how different types of decision require different methods; the relation between planning and decision making is now explained more clearly and consistently in Chapters 6 and 7.

Chapter 11 (Human resource management) – outlines empirical studies of how HRM practice affects performance; and use of social media in recruitment.

Chapter 12 (Information systems and e-business) – two new 'Management in practice' features (Topshop and ASOS) showing the use of social media in retailing.

Chapter 13 (Creativity, innovation and change) – new chapter case study, Dyson, Appliances and a new 'Key ideas' feature on Stephen Johnson's book about the sources of innovation.

Chapter 14 (Influencing) – includes 'Key ideas' feature on Heimans and Timms' distinction between 'old' and 'new' sources of power – and another on Sir Alex Ferguson's talents in this department.

Chapter 15 (Motivating) – last section outlines flexible and high-performance work systems respectively, with empirical studies of how they affect organisational outcomes.

Academic content This has been extended and updated where appropriate, with over 90 new references, mostly reporting empirical research to enable students to develop the habit of seeking the empirical evidence behind management ideas. Examples include new research on the effects of management on outcomes in Chapter 1, an attempt to change the culture at a Premier League club in Chapter 3, the concepts of shared value and the triple bottom line respectively in Chapters 1 and 5, the design of strategy workshops in Chapter 8 and the effects of high-performance work practices in Chapter 15.

Integrating themes The intention of this section is to provide a way for teachers to guide students with a particular interest in one or other of the themes to become familiar with some of the academic literature on the topic, and to see how each theme links in a coherent way to all of the topics in the text. The section aims to relate aspects of the chapter to each theme, bringing each chapter to a consistent close.

Teachers may want to use this feature by, for example, setting a class project or assignment on one of the themes (such as sustainable performance) and inviting students to draw on the multiple perspectives on the topic that each chapter provides. For example:

Chapter 3 (Section 3.8) provides material on sustainability from the Stern report.

Chapter 6 (Section 6.9) shows how one company is planning to work more sustainably.

Chapter 10 (Section 10.9) shows how sustainability can be supported by a suitable structure.

Chapter 15 (Section 15.8) links motivation to sustainability and illustrates it with a company that includes measures of sustainability in its management reward system.

Chapter 18 (Section 18.8) argues that all waste is the result of a failure in operations, which therefore needs to be the focus of improving sustainable performance.

Case studies These have been revised and updated where appropriate, and three are completely new – BBC (Chapter 3), Carlsberg (Chapter 4) and Dyson Appliances (Chapter 13).

Revel for *Management* by David Boddy is based on this textbook and is an interactive learning environment, seamlessly blending world-class content, interactive learning activities, assessments and analytics to enable students to learn, apply and develop critical thinking skills in one interactive experience. Delivered online, via mobile and iPad, REVEL presents content in manageable pieces with integrated quizzing, so students can read a little, do a little and check their understanding at regular intervals on concepts to yield a higher impact on learning. REVEL gives educators access to student and class performance information and can be integrated into teaching in a various ways to improve engagement, comprehension, application and critical thinking.

Features Many of the 'Management in practice' features have been updated and renewed, as have some 'Key ideas'. There are over 90 new references and additional suggestions for the 'Read more' section. Several of the case questions and activities have been revised to connect more closely with the theories being presented. The learning objectives provide the structure for the 'Summary' section at the end of each chapter, and for the 'Test your understanding' feature.

Test your understanding As before, there is a set of questions at the end of each chapter to help students assess their progress towards the learning objectives.

Think critically A section at the end of the first chapter presents the components of critical thinking – assumptions, context, alternatives and limitations. These themes structure the 'Think critically' feature at the end of each chapter.

Develop a skill This is the major innovation in this edition, introduced in response to the belief that students and employers are seeking more connections between academic work and employment. The feature is consistently based on two theoretical structures: (1) a theoretical model in the chapter showing the underlying rationale for developing this skill; and (2) an established model of skill development, which informs the structure of the 'Develop a skill' feature at the end of each chapter. Both ideas are explained in Chapter 1 – in Sections 1.0 and 1.8 respectively. The skills are listed here by chapter:

Chapter 1 – Networking

Chapter 2 – Self-awareness

Chapter 3 – Presenting a reasoned case

Chapter 4 – Mindfulness

Chapter 5 – Clarifying values

Chapter 6 – Defining a problem rationally

Chapter 7 – Defining a problem creatively

Chapter 8 – Setting clear goals

Chapter 9 – Identifying customer needs

Chapter 10 – Coordinating work

Chapter 11 – Preparing for an interview

Chapter 12 – Setting a project agenda

Chapter 13 – Identifying stakeholders and their interests

Chapter 14 – Setting goals to influence others

Chapter 15 – Designing a motivating job

Chapter 16 – Presenting ideas to an audience

Chapter 17 – Observing team processes

Chapter 18 – Understanding what customers mean by quality

Chapter 19 – Monitoring progress on a task

Chapter 20 – Reading a Profit and Loss Statement

I do not envisage that many will work on the skills in every chapter – it is a resource to be used as teachers think best. The 'Instructors manual' includes a suggestion on how it could complement the academic content of a course.

Read more For students who want to read more about the topic. The format varies, but usually includes a mix of classic texts, one or two contemporary ones and a couple of academic papers that represent good examples of the empirical research that underlies study of the topic.

Go online Each chapter concludes with a list of the websites of companies that have appeared in it, and a suggestion that students visit these sites (or others in which they have an interest) to find more information related to the chapter. This should add interest and help retain topicality.

Part case studies The Part case studies are intended to help students engage with text material throughout the Part. The common principle is to encourage students to develop their 'contextual awareness' by seeing how organisations act and react in relation to, among other things, their environment. The common structure therefore is:

- The company – material on the company and major recent developments.
- Managing to add value – some ways in which managers appear to have added value.
- The company's context – identifying between three and five contextual factors.
- Current management dilemmas – drawing on the previous sections to identify pressing issues.
- Part case questions – now in two groups – the first looking back to the material in the text, the second more focused on the company, and so perhaps offering a link to 'employability skills' – see below.

As well as supporting individual learning, these extended cases could be suitable for group assignments and other forms of assessment.

Employability skills Each Part continues to conclude with a section on 'Employability skills – preparing for the world of work'. This is a response to the growing expectations that universities and colleges do more to improve the employability of their students. The organising principle is to provide a structured opportunity for the student to develop and record evidence about six commonly cited employability skills:

- Business awareness
- Solving problems
- Thinking critically
- Team working
- Communicating
- Self-management.

To help do this, students are asked to work through tasks that link the themes covered in the Part to the six skills (sometimes called capabilities and attributes) that many employers value. The layout should help students to record their progress in developing these skills, and articulate them to employers during the selection processes.

The basis of these tasks is the enlarged Part case study described above. The Employability section builds on this by setting alternative tasks relating to the Part case study (to be chosen by the student or the instructor as preferred). That task in itself relates to the business awareness theme – and concludes by asking the student to write a short paragraph giving examples of the skills (such as information gathering, analysis and presentation) they have developed from this task, and how to build this into a learning record.

The other skills are developed by successive tasks that ask them to reflect on how they worked on the 'Business awareness' task – solving problems, thinking critically and so on.

I do not envisage that many will work through all of these tasks in every Part – it is a resource to be used as teachers and their students think best. I hope that teachers and students find this new feature valuable, and look forward to feedback and comments in due course.

List of reviewers We would like to express thanks to the original reviewers and review panel members who have been involved in the development of this book. We are extremely grateful for their insight and helpful recommendations.

PREFACE TO THE FIRST EDITION

This book is intended for readers who are undertaking their first systematic exposure to the study of management. Most will be first-year undergraduates following courses leading to a qualification in management or business. Some will also be taking an introductory course in management as part of other qualifications (these may be in engineering, accountancy, law, information technology, science, nursing or social work) and others will be following a course in management as an element in their respective examination schemes. The book should also be useful to readers with a first degree or equivalent qualification in a non-management subject who are taking further studies leading to Certificate, Diploma or MBA qualifications.

The book has the following three main objectives:

- to provide newcomers to the formal study of management with an introduction to the topic;
- to show that ideas on management apply to most areas of human activity, not just to commercial enterprises;
- to make the topic attractive to students from many backgrounds and with diverse career intentions.

Most research and reflection on management has focused on commercial organisations. However, there are now many people working in the public sector and in not-for-profit organisations (charities, pressure groups, voluntary organisations and so on) who have begun to adapt management ideas to their own areas of work. The text reflects this wider interest in the topic. It should be as useful to those who plan to enter public or not-for-profit work as to those entering the commercial sector.

European perspective

The book presents the ideas from a European perspective. While many management concepts have developed in the United States, the text encourages readers to consider how their particular context shapes management practice. There are significant cultural differences that influence this practice, and the text alerts the reader to these – not only as part of an increasingly integrated Europe but as part of a wider international management community. So the text recognises European experience and research in management. The case studies and other material build an awareness of cultural diversity and the implications of this for working in organisations with different managerial styles and backgrounds.

Integrated perspective

To help the reader see management as a coherent whole, the material is presented within an integrative model of management and demonstrates the relationships between the many academic perspectives. The intention is to help the reader to see management as an integrating activity relating to the organisation as a whole, rather than as something confined to any one disciplinary or functional perspective.

While the text aims to introduce readers to the traditional mainstream perspectives on management, which form the basis of each chapter, it also recognises that there is a newer body of ideas that looks at developments such as the weakening of national boundaries and the spread of information technology. Since they will affect the organisations in which readers will spend their working lives, these newer perspectives are introduced where appropriate. The text also recognises the more critical perspectives that some writers now take towards management and organisational activities. These are part of the intellectual world in which management takes place and have important practical implications for the way people interpret their role within organisations. The text introduces these perspectives at several points.

Relating to personal experience

The text assumes that many readers will have little, if any, experience of managing in conventional organisations, and equally little prior knowledge of relevant evidence and theory. However, all will have experience of being managed and all will have managed activities in their domestic and social lives. Wherever possible the book encourages readers to use and share such experiences from everyday life in order to explore the ideas presented. In this way the book tries to show that management is not a remote activity performed by others, but a process in which all are engaged in some way.

Most readers' careers are likely to be more fragmented and uncertain than was once the case and many will be working for medium-sized and smaller enterprises. They will probably be working close to customers and in organisations that incorporate diverse cultures, values and interests. The text therefore provides many opportunities for readers to develop skills of gathering data, comparing evidence, reflecting and generally enhancing self-awareness. It not only transmits knowledge but also aims to support the development of transferable skills through individual activities in the text and through linked tutorial work. The many cases and data collection activities are designed to develop generic skills such as communication, teamwork, problem solving and organising – while at the same time acquiring relevant knowledge.

ACKNOWLEDGEMENTS

This book has benefited from the comments, criticisms and suggestions of many colleagues and reviewers of the sixth edition. It also reflects the reactions and comments of students who have used the material and earlier versions of some of the cases. Their advice and feedback have been of immense help.

Most of the chapters were written by the author, who also edited the text throughout. Chapter 11 (Human resource management) was created by Professor Phil Beaumont and then developed by Dr Judy Pate and Sandra Stewart: in this edition it was revised by the author. Chapter 18 (Managing operations and quality) was created by Professor Douglas Macbeth and developed in the fourth edition by Dr Geoff Southern and in the fifth edition by Dr Steve Paton: in the sixth and in this edition it was revised by the author. In the fifth edition Dr Steve Paton contributed new material to Chapters 13 and 19. In the sixth and in this edition both chapters were revised by the author. Chapter 20 (Finance and budgetary control) was created by Douglas Briggs: in the fifth edition it was revised by Dr Steve Paton, in the sixth edition by Janan Sulaiman and in this edition by Tom Ellsworth. I also thank Dickon Copsey, Employability Officer in the College of Social Sciences, University of Glasgow, for his advice on the employability material at the end of each Part. Errors and omissions are my responsibility.

David Boddy
University of Glasgow, March 2016

Publisher's acknowledgements

We are grateful to the following for permission to reproduce copyright material:

Figures

Figure 2.2 from *Becoming a Master Manager: A Competency Framework*, 3rd edn, Wiley, New York (Quinn, R.E., Faerman, S.R., Thompson, M.P. and McGrath, M.R. 2003) p. 13, reproduced with permission of John Wiley & Sons Inc.; Figure 4.4 from Clustering countries on attitudinal dimensions – A review and synthesis, *Academy of Management Review*, vol. 10, no. 3, pp. 435–54 (Ronen, S. and Shenkar, O. 1985), © 1985, Academy of Management; Figure 5.2 adapted from *adapted from Business and Society: Ethics and Stakeholder Management*, 9th edn, Cengate Learning (Carroll, A.B abd Buchholz, A.K., 2015) © 2015 Cengage Learning, Inc., reproduced by permission, www.cengage.com/permissions; Figure 5.3 from Corporate social responsibility: evolution of a definitional construct, *Business & Society*, vol. 38(3), p. 268-295 (Carroll, A.B 1999), © 1999 by Sage Publications, reprinted by permission of Sage Publications; Figure 5.5 from Does it pay to be green? A systematic overview, *Academy of Management Perspectives*, vol. 22, no. 4, pp. 45–62 (Ambec, S. and Lanoie, P. 2008), © 2008 by Academy of Management (NY); Figure 5.6 from 'Implicit' and 'Explicit' CSR: A Conceptual Framework for a Comparative Understanding of Corporate Social Responsibility, *Academy of Management Review*, vol. 33, no. 2, pp. 404–24 (Matten, D. and Moon, J. 2008), © 2008 by Academy of Management (NY); Figure 6.7 from *Managing Information Systems:Strategy and Organisation*, 3rd edn, FT/Prentice Hall, Harlow (Boddy, D., Boonstra, A, and Kennedy, G. 2009) p. 258, Figure 9.5, © Pearson Education Ltd 2002, 2005, 2009; Figure 11.1 from How does Human Resource Management Influence Organisational Outcomes? A Meta-Analytic investigation of mediating mechanisms, *Academy of Management Journal*, vol. 55, no. 6, pp. 1264–94 (Jiang, K., Lepak, D.P., Jia J. and Baer, J.C. 2012), Academy of Management; Figure 14.4 from How to choose a leadership pattern:should a manager be democratic or autocratic - or something in between?, *Harvard Business Review*, Vol. 37(2), pp. 95–102 (Tannenbaum, R and Schmidt, W.H 1973), © 1973 Harvard Business School Publishing Corporation, all rights reserved, reprinted by permission of Harvard Business Review; Figure 15.3 from The psychology of the employment relationship; an analysis based on the psychological contract, *Applied Psychology*, Vol. 53(4), pp. 541–55 (Guest, D.E 2004), © 2004 John Wiley & Sons, reproduced with permission of Blackwell Scientific in the format Republish in a book via Copyright Clearance Center; Figure 15.5 from One more time:how do you motivate employees?, *Harvard Business Review*, Vol.65(5), pp. 109–20 (Herzberg, F 1987), ©1987 Harvard Business School Publishing Corporation, all rights reserved, reprinted by permission of Harvard Business Review; Figure 16.4 from The selection of communication media as an executive skill, *Academy of Management Executive*, Vol. 11(3), pp. 225–32 (Lengel, R.H and Daft, R.L 1988), © 1988 by Academy of Management (NY), Academy of Management; Figure 18.4 adapted from Link manufacturing process and product lifecycles, *Harvard Business Review*, Vol. 57(1), pp. 133–40 (Hayes, R.H and Wheelwright, S.C 1979), © 1979 Harvard Business School Publishing Corporation, all rights reserved, reprinted by permission of *Harvard Business Review*.

Tables

Table 1. from Ryanair profits take off to beat expectations, *Financial Times* 26/05/2015 (Nathalie Thomas and Peter Wells); Table 13.1 from Assessing the work environment for creativity, *Academy of Management Journal*, Vol. 39(5), pp. 1154–84 (Amabile, T.M, Conti, R., Coon, H., Lazenby, J and Heron, M 1996), p. 116, Academy of Management; Table 17.1 from *Groups that Work (and Those that Don't)*, Jossey-Bass, San Francisco, CA (Hackman, J.R) p. 489, reprinted with permission of John Wiley & Sons, Inc; Table 17.3 from *Team Roles at Work*, 2nd edn, Butterworth/Heinemann, Oxford (Belbin, R.M 2010) p. 22, Table 3.1, with permission of Belbin Associates.

Text

p. 188 from *Financial Times*, 29/04/2013, p. 25, © The Financial Times Limited. All Rights Reserved.

Photographs

(Key: b – bottom; c – centre; l – left; r – right; t – top)
123RF.com: hxdbzxy; **Alamy Images:** Action Plus Sports Images 271, Elly Godfroy 191*tr*, geogphotos 191*br*, Jack Sullivan 445, 562, Matthew Chattle 191*bl*, Mike Booth 653, Philip Dubois 473, Prisma Bildagentur AG 5, Tim Ayers 430, tony french 191*tl*, vario images GmbH & Co.KG 633; **Co-operative Group:** 143; **Edificio Inditex:** 577; **Getty Images:** Ben Stansall/AFP 313, Chris Ratcliffe/Bloomberg 183, 239, Christopher Furlong 608, David Paul Morris/Bloomberg 298, Gisela Schober 347, Josh Edelson/AFP 507, Kim Kulish/Corbis 373, Mario Proenca/Bloomberg 537, Sean Gallup 70, Susana Gonzalez/Bloomberg 168; **IKEA Ltd:** 207; **innocent drinks:** 37; **James Dyson Foundation:** 403; **Shutterstock.com:** A.Zhernosek.FFMstudio.com, Eric Broader Van Dyke, Gilmanshin, gyn9037, Zastolskiy Victo.

All other images © Pearson Education

PART 1

AN INTRODUCTION TO MANAGEMENT

Introduction

This Part considers why management exists and what it contributes to human wealth and well-being. Management is both a universal human activity and a distinct occupation. We all manage in the first sense, as we organise our lives and deal with family and other relationships. As employees and customers we experience the activities of those who manage in the second sense, as members of an organisation with which we deal. This Part offers some ways of making sense of the complex and contradictory activity of managing.

Chapter 1 clarifies the nature and emergence of management and the different ways in which people describe the role. It explains how management is both a universal human activity and a specialist occupation. Its purpose is to create wealth by adding value to resources, which managers do by influencing others – the chapter shows how they do this. It begins and ends with ideas about using the material throughout the book to begin developing practical management skills, which should help you approach graduate recruiters with confidence.

Chapter 2 sets out the main theoretical perspectives on management and shows how these complement each other despite the apparently competing values about the nature of the management task. Be active in relating these theoretical perspectives to real events as this will help you to understand and test the theories.

The Part Case study is Apple Inc., one of the world's most valuable and innovative companies, which illustrates how those managing it have been able to add value so successfully over many years – and also the challenges it now faces from new competitors.

CHAPTER 1
MANAGING IN ORGANISATIONS

Aim

To introduce the tasks, processes and context of managerial work in organisations.

Objectives

By the end of your work on this chapter you should be able to outline the concepts below in your own terms and:

1   Understand that this text provides an opportunity to develop management skills as well as management knowledge

2   Explain that the role of management is to add value to resources

3   Give examples of management as a universal human activity and as a distinct role

4   Compare the roles of general, functional, line, staff and project managers, and of entrepreneurs

5   Compare how managers influence others to add value to resources through:

   a. the process of managing;

   b. the tasks (or content) of managing; and

   c. the contexts within which they and others work

6   Explain the elements of critical thinking and understand how to use these to develop your networking skills

7   Suggest the implications of the integrating themes of the book for managing

Key terms

This chapter introduces the following ideas:

management skills	functional manager
organisation	line manager
tangible resources	staff manager
intangible resources	project manager
competences	entrepreneur
value	stakeholders
management as a universal human activity	networking
manager	management tasks
management	critical thinking
management as a distinct role	sustainability
role	triple bottom line
general manager	corporate governance

Each is a term defined within the text, as well as in the glossary at the end of the book.

Case study   Ryanair   www.ryanair.com

In 2015 Ryanair, based in Dublin, reported that it had carried over 90 million passengers in the 12 months to the end of March, 11 per cent more than in the previous year. Revenue had grown by 12 per cent and profit by 66 per cent. It believed this growth reflected managers' efforts to improve passengers' experience, such as renewing the website and allowing them to take on board an extra small item.

Tony Ryan (1936–2007) founded the company in 1985 with a single aircraft flying passengers from Ireland to the UK. Ryan, the son of a train driver, left school at 14 to work in a sugar factory, before moving in 1954 to work as a baggage handler at Aer Lingus, the state-owned Irish airline. By 1970 he was in charge of the aircraft leasing division, lending Aer Lingus aircraft and crews to other airlines. This gave him the idea, which he quickly put into practice, to create his own aircraft leasing company. As Guinness Peat Aviation this became a world player in the aviation leasing industry, and is now part of GE Capital.

In 1985 he founded Ryanair, to compete with his former employer. Southwest Airlines in the US inspired this move by showing that a new business could enter the industry to compete with established, often state-owned, airlines. Tony Ryan turned Ryanair into a public company in 1997 by selling shares to investors.

In the early years the airline changed its business several times – initially competing with Aer Lingus in a conventional way, then a charter company, and at times a freight carrier. The Gulf War in 1990 discouraged air travel and caused the company financial problems. Rather than close the airline he and his senior managers (including Michael O'Leary, who is now Chief Executive) decided it would be a 'no-frills' operator, discarding conventional features of air travel such as free food, drink, newspapers and allocated seats. It would serve customers who wanted a functional and efficient service, not luxury.

In 1997 changes in European Union regulations enabled new airlines to enter markets previously dominated by national carriers such as Air France and British Airways. Ryanair management saw this as an opportunity to open new routes between Dublin and continental Europe, which they did very quickly. Although based in Ireland, 80 per cent of its routes

© Prisma Bildagentur AG/Alamy Images

are between airports in other countries – in contrast to established carriers, which depend on passengers travelling to and from the airline's home country (Barrett, 2009, p.80). The company has continued to grow, regularly opening routes to destinations it thinks will be popular. It refers to itself as 'the world's largest international scheduled airline', and continues to seek new bases and routes.

In May 2015 the chairman of the board presented the company's results for the latest financial year.

Measures of financial performance in recent financial years (ending 31 March)

	2015	2014
Passengers (millions)	90.6	81.7
Revenue (millions of Euros)	5,654	5,037
Profit after tax (millions of Euros)	867	523
Earnings per share (Euro cents)	62.59	36.96

Sources: *Financial Times*, 27 May 2015; Kumar (2006); Doganis (2006); company website.

Case questions 1.1

- Identify examples of the resources that Ryanair uses, and of how managers have added value to them (refer to Section 1.2)
- Give examples of three points at which managers changed the focus of the company and how it works.

1.0	Management knowledge and management skill

Knowing management theory can help your career, but will not in itself bring success or satisfaction. Putting what you know into practice – using it to add value to resources – depends on skill. A good degree will show potential employers that you understand the theory, but they expect you to demonstrate some of the skills required to use that theory to deal with practical problems. **Management skills** are identifiable sets of actions that individuals perform to produce an outcome they value. They show the person has expertise, dexterity – the reliable ability to do something to an acceptable standard. Jiang et al. (2012) reviewed the evidence from over one hundred studies of the link between skill and performance, and found, as they expected, that practices to enhance employees' training and education had a positive effect on their skills, including management skills. That, in turn, had a positive effect on organisational performance.

> **Management skills** are identifiable sets of actions that individuals perform to produce an outcome they value.

Henry Mintzberg (1975), an influential management teacher and scholar, advocated including skills development in management courses at universities. He proposed that while potential managers must learn substantial amounts of *academic theory* through reading and attending lectures, this does not make them managers. They should also be given the opportunity to begin developing core *management skills,* to prepare for employment.

Employers seek employees who can work independently and cope with complex and difficult situations. Their representative body, the Confederation of British Industry (CBI) (CBI and Universities UK, 2009) consistently identifies two broad types of management skill that new graduates require – *business awareness* and *social awareness* – Section 1.8 explains these.

A person's competence in each of these areas – academic theory, business awareness, social awareness – is enhanced by the skill of critical thinking. This is essential to developing theoretical knowledge: it is equally essential to developing business and social awareness, which are easy to state but challenging to apply in complex conditions. Figure 1.1 shows this relationship.

This text includes material to help you develop these skills – in 'Develop a skill' at the end of each chapter, and in the 'Employability skills' sections at the end of each part.

Key ideas   How we develop skill

Whetten and Cameron (2011) show that individuals develop skill through five steps:

- **Assessment.** To show learners their present level of skill, and to motivate improvement.
- **Learning.** To know the theory and research showing why the skill is valuable.
- **Analysis.** To help learners see links between skills used and results achieved.
- **Practice.** To give learners the chance to practice and adapt skills to suit the way they work, and to local circumstances. Feedback enables further improvement.
- **Application.** To give learners the chance to use new skills in practical situations (Whetten and Cameron, 2011, pp. 35–7).

In a training course designed to develop skills, learners repeat these steps many times to gain confidence in using them. In a degree course designed to develop theoretical knowledge, there is not time for that. However, the 'Develop a skill' feature at the end of each chapter uses this model to help you to begin connecting one piece of theory to a management skill. It also helps you to understand how you can begin to develop any skill by following these five steps.

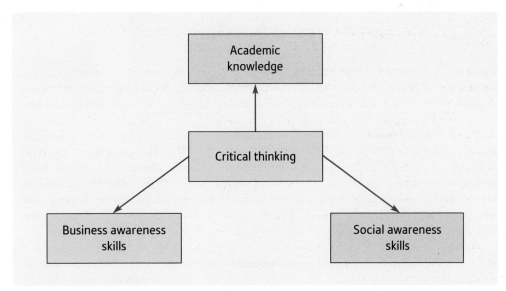

Figure 1.1
Critical thinking
helps to develop
knowledge and skill

1.1　Introduction

Ryanair illustrates several aspects of management. Entrepreneur Tony Ryan, who had already created one business, saw a further opportunity and created an organisation to take advantage of it. He persuaded others to provide resources – especially money for the aircraft and the costs of operating it – and organised these into a service that he sold to customers. The business changed frequently in the early years, and under the current chief executive, Michael O'Leary, it has continued to be innovative in how it operates, quick to identify new routes and imaginative in identifying new sources of revenue.

Entrepreneurs thrive on innovation as they try to make the most of opportunities. Managers in established businesses often face the different challenge of how to meet more demand with fewer resources. Those managing the United Nations World Food Programme struggle to raise funds from donor countries: aid is falling while hunger is increasing. In almost every public healthcare organisation, managers face a growing demand for treatment, but fewer resources with which to provide it.

All organisations – from new ones like Facebook to established ones such as Royal Dutch Shell or Marks & Spencer – depend on people at all levels who can run the current business efficiently, and also innovate. This book is about the knowledge and skills that enable people to meet these expectations, and so build a satisfying and rewarding career.

Figure 1.2 illustrates the themes of the chapter. It represents the fact that people draw resources from the external world and transform them into outputs, which they pass back to the environment. The value they obtain in return (money, reputation, goodwill, etc.) enables them to attract new resources to continue in business (shown by the feedback arrow from output to input). If the outputs do not attract sufficient resources, the enterprise will fail.

The chapter begins by examining the significance of managed organisations in our world. It then outlines what management means and introduces theories about the nature of managerial work. It introduces four integrating themes, which conclude each chapter of the book – entrepreneurship, sustainability, internationalisation and governance. Finally, it explains how the book will help you understand how you can develop the skills you need for a rewarding and satisfying career.

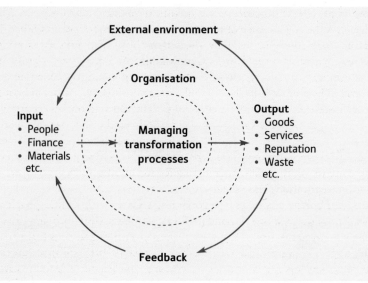

Figure 1.2
Managing
organisation and
environment

What is 'management'?

Record a few notes summarising what you think 'management' means.

● Think of instances in which you have encountered 'management' – such as when you have been managed in your school, university or job.
● Alternatively, reflect on an occasion when you have managed something, such as a study project. Keep the notes so you can refer to them.

1.2   Managing to add value to resources

An organisation is a
social arrangement for
achieving goals that
create value.

We live in a world of managed **organisations**. We experience many every day – domestic arrangements (family or flatmates), large public organisations (the postal service), small businesses (the newsagent), large businesses (the jar of coffee), or a voluntary group (the club we attended). They affect us and we judge their performance. Did the transaction work smoothly or was it chaotic? Was the service good, reasonable or poor? Will you go there again?

Key ideas   **Joan Magretta on the innovation of management**

What were the most important innovations of the past century? Antibiotics and vaccines that doubled, or even tripled, human life spans? Automobiles and aeroplanes that redefined our idea of distance? New agents of communication, such as the telephone, or the chips, computers and networks that are propelling us into a new economy?

All of these innovations transformed our lives, yet none of them could have taken hold so rapidly or spread so widely without another. That innovation is the discipline of management, the accumulating body of thought and practice that makes organisations work. When we take stock of the productivity gains that drive our prosperity, technology gets all of the credit. In fact, management is doing a lot of the heavy lifting.

Source: Magretta (2013), p. 1.

Bloom et al. (2012) provide strong quantitative evidence to support Magretta's view (Key ideas) on the significance of management. Using interview and other data from 8000 manufacturers in 20 countries, they show that those who adhered consistently to three management practices (targets, incentives, monitoring) performed significantly better (on criteria of productivity, growth in sales, return on capital and company survival) than those that did not. The authors' studies in public organisations (schools and hospitals) provided similar evidence that good management adds value throughout an economy.

Good managers make things work – aid is delivered, roads are safe, shops have stock, mobile devices work, hospitals function. They don't do the work themselves, but build an organisation with the resources *and* competences to deliver goods and services. **Tangible resources** are physical – plant, people, finance etc. **Intangible resources** are non-physical – information, reputation, knowledge etc.

To transform these resources into goods and services with a value, people work together. They need to know what to do, understand customers, deal with enquiries and generally make the transaction work. They seek to improve, innovate and learn from experience. Good managers bring out the best in others so that they willingly 'go the extra mile': together they develop effective ways of working that become second nature. These 'ways of working' are **competences** – skills, procedures or systems that enable people to use resources productively. Managers' role is to obtain the resources, and develop the competences to use them, so that the organisation adds **value** – by producing things that are more valuable to customers than the cost of the resources used.

Well-managed organisations create value by delivering goods and services that make the customer feel better in some way – a punctual flight, a bright and well-equipped gym, a trendy phone, clothes that enhance their image. Others value good service or clear instructions. Good managers understand this, and invest resources (build an organisation) to satisfy them. They add value through the performance of the product AND through the quality of the relationship between the customer and the organisation (O'Cass and Ngo, 2011).

Tangible resources are the physical assets of an organisation such as plant, people and finance.
Intangible resources are non-physical assets such as information, reputation and knowledge.

Competences are the skills and abilities that an organisation uses to deploy resources effectively, such as systems, procedures and ways of working.

Value is added to resources when they are transformed into goods or services that are worth more than their original cost plus the cost of transformation.

| Management in practice | Creating value at the Southbank Centre |

www.southbankcentre.co.uk

Jude Kelly was appointed Artistic Director of London's Southbank Centre in 2005. This is the UK's largest arts centre, receiving (in 2014–15) 42 per cent of its income from public funds, and the rest from ticket sales, commercial activities and sponsorship. In 2014–15 over 6 million visitors engaged with their onsite activities, offered by more than 3000 artists. Are there any special challenges in managing creative people?

People who are confident about their creativity are confident about asking questions . . . So you have to be flexible and excited about a variety of solutions. . . The best leaders of creative projects are those who are excited by other people's imagination and not just their own.

Ms Kelly stresses that artists are aware of practicalities:

To finish a piece of work an artist [has to know] to marshall the material [in time for an audience] coming through the door. Good arts organisations have to be highly entrepreneurial and flexible and make a little go a long way.

Source: *Financial Times*, 16 September 2013, p. 16; Southbank Centre Annual Review, 2014–2015.

Commercial organisations of all kinds (business start-ups, small and medium-sized enterprises and large private-sector businesses, often operating internationally) create wealth by adding value to resources. In financial terms, they aim to invest capital to generate cash flows that generate an acceptable rate of return on the investment to the owners: they can only do this by offering goods and services that customers want. Co-operatives (in 2016 there were

7000 co-operative enterprises in the UK, compared to 4,800 in 2009, according to their trade body, Co-operatives UK – www.uk.coop) do the same, though with a different ownership structure. Some (like retail co-operatives, of which the largest is the Co-operative Group) are owned by customers, who receive a share of the profits as a dividend. Others are owned by their employees – the John Lewis Partnership (www.johnlewispartnership.co.uk) is the most prominent example. Smaller examples include Circle (www.circlepartnership.co.uk), a healthcare company founded and owned by clinicians; and Suma (www.suma.coop) a worker-owned distribution business.

Voluntary and charitable organisations aim to add value by educating people, counselling the troubled or caring for the sick. The British Heart Foundation (www.bhf.org) raised over £142 million from legacies, fundraising activities and the retail business in 2014–15, enabling it to deliver its mission of curing and preventing heart disease. Raising the income, and ensuring that the research and other projects give value for money, is a formidable management task – with over 700 shops, it is the largest charity retailer in the UK. Managing this is at least as demanding a job as running a commercial business – to add value to limited resources (see **Part 5 Case**).

Glastonbury, Tate Modern and Yorkshire Sculpture Park create value by offering inspiration, new perspectives or unexpected insights. Other organisations add value by serving sectional interests – such as Unison, a trade union that represents workers in the UK public sector, or the British Medical Association, the doctors' trade union. Private companies create trade organisations to protect their interests.

While organisations aim to add value, many do not do so. If people work inefficiently they use more resources to make a product than customers will pay for, and so destroy value – as does pollution and waste. Motorways create value for drivers, residents of bypassed villages and shareholders – but deplete value for some people if the route destroys ancient woodland rich in history and wildlife. Deciding if managers have created value can be subjective and controversial.

Some management issues (setting targets, motivating staff, monitoring performance) arise in all organisations, while others are unique to their setting (charities must retain the support of donors). Table 1.1 illustrates this diversity, and their (relatively) unique, additional challenges.

The value an organisation creates depends on how well people understand their situation, and use that knowledge to develop the right resources and competences. Within each

Table 1.1 Where people manage

Setting – industry or type	Examples in this book	'Unique' challenges
Business start-ups	innocent drinks in the early days **(Chapter 2 Case)**	Securing funding to launch, and enough sales to sustain cash flow. Building credibility.
Small and medium-sized enterprises (SMEs)	Child Base Nurseries **(MIP feature in Chapter 15)**	Generating enough funds to survive, innovate and enter new markets.
Professional service firms	Hiscox (insurance) **(MIP feature in Chapter 11)**	Managing highly qualified staff delivering customised, innovative services.
Large private businesses, often working internationally	Virgin Group **(Part 3 Case)**	Controlling diverse activities, meeting shareholder expectations.
Voluntary, not-for-profit organisations and charities	Eden Project **(Chapter 15 Case)**	Providing quality visitor experience; fulfilling mission; retaining donors.
Co-operatives – customer – or employee-owned	The Co-operative Group **(Chapter 5 Case)**	Balancing democratic and commercial interests; raising capital.
Public-sector organisations	Crossrail **(Chapter 6 Case)**	Managing high-profile political and commercial interests.

broad 'setting' there is great variety – 'professional services' includes legal, auditing and engineering consultancy businesses, which differ in their knowledge base, degree of autonomy and the nature of their client relationships. So they need different resources and competences. Successful managers know their situation, and use their skills to suit the context.

Activity 1.2	Focus on diverse management settings

Choose ONE of the settings in Table 1.1 that interests you. Gather information about that type of organisation (using case studies in this book or someone you know who works there) so you can:

- name one organisation in that setting;
- identify how it adds value to resources, and the management challenges it faces;
- compare your evidence with someone who has gathered data about a different setting, and summarise similarities and differences.

1.3	Meanings of management

Management as a universal human activity

As individuals we run our lives and careers: in this respect we are managing. Family members manage children, elderly dependants and households. Management is both a **universal human activity** and a distinct role. In the first sense, people manage an infinite range of activities:

> When human beings 'manage' their work, they take responsibility for its purpose, progress and outcome by exercising the quintessentially human capacity to stand back from experience and to regard it prospectively, in terms of what will happen; reflectively, in terms of what is happening; and retrospectively, in terms of what has happened. Thus management is an expression of human agency, the capacity actively to shape and direct the world, rather than simply react to it. (Hales, 2001, p. 2)

Rosemary Stewart (1967) expressed this idea when she described a **manager** as someone who gets things done with the aid of people and other resources, defining **management** as the activity of getting things done with the aid of people and other resources. So described, management is a universal human activity in domestic, social and political settings, as well as in organisations.

In pre-industrial societies people typically work alone or in family units, controlling their time and resources. They decide what to make, how to make it and where to sell it, combining work and management to create value. Self-employed craftworkers, professionals in small practices and those in a one-person business do this every day. We all do it in household tasks or voluntary activities in which we do the work (planting trees or selling raffle tickets) and the management activities (planning the winter programme).

Management as a universal human activity occurs whenever people take responsibility for an activity and consciously try to shape its progress and outcome.

A manager is someone who gets things done with the aid of people and other resources.

Management is the activity of getting things done with the aid of people and other resources.

Activity 1.3	Think about the definition

Choose a domestic, community or business activity you have undertaken.

- What, specifically, did you do to 'get things done with the aid of people and other resources'?
- Decide if the definition accurately describes 'management'.
- If not, how would you change it?

Management as a distinct role

Human action can also separate the 'management' element of a task from the 'work' element, thus creating 'managers' who are in some degree apart from those doing the work. **Management as a distinct role** emerges when external parties, such as a private owner of capital, or the state, gain control of a work process that a person used to complete themselves. These parties may then decide what to make, how to make it and where to sell it. Workers become employees selling their labour, not the products of their labour. From about 1750 in the UK, factory production began to displace domestic and craft production in sectors such as textiles and iron production. Factory owners took control of the physical and financial means of production and tried to control the time, behaviour and skills of those who were now employees rather than autonomous workers.

The same evolution occurs when someone starts an enterprise, initially performing the *technical* aspects of the work – writing software, designing clothes – and also more *conceptual* tasks – deciding their markets, or how to raise money. If the business grows and the entrepreneur engages staff, he or she needs to work on *interpersonal* tasks such as training and supervision. The founder progressively takes on more management roles – a **role** being the expectations that others have about the requirements of a job, which someone holding it should do (or not do). If the business grows, the founder needs others to share the management role – and begins to build a management team. Levy (2011) traces how this proved controversial as Google grew. Founders Larry Page and Sergey Brin were not convinced that the hundreds of engineers they were recruiting needed managers – they could report to the head of engineering. The engineers disagreed:

> Page wanted to know why. They told him they wanted someone to learn from. When they disagreed with colleagues and discussions reached an impasse, they needed someone who could break the ties. (p. 159)

Google has since developed a robust system to measure managers' effectiveness and improve their skills (Garvin 2013; and see Chapter 12 Case).

This separation of management and non-management work is not inevitable or permanent. People deliberately separate the roles, and can also bring them together. As Henri Fayol (1949) (of whom you will read more in Chapter 2) observed:

> Management . . . is neither an exclusive privilege nor a particular responsibility of the head or senior members of a business; it is an activity spread, like all other activities, between head and members of the body corporate. (p. 6)

Management as a distinct role develops when activities previously embedded in the work itself become the responsibility not of the employee, but of owners or their agents.

A **role** is the sum of the expectations that others have about the responsibilities of a person occupying a position.

Key ideas	Tony Watson on separating roles

All humans are managers in some way. But some of them also take on the formal occupational work of being managers. They take on a role of shaping . . . work organisations. Managers' work involves a double . . . task: managing others and managing themselves. But the very notion of 'managers' being separate people from the 'managed', at the heart of traditional management thinking, undermines a capacity to handle this. Managers are pressured to be technical experts, devising rational and emotionally neutral systems and corporate structures to 'solve problems', 'make decisions', 'run the business'. These 'scientific' and rational–analytic practices give reassurance but can leave managers so distanced from the 'managed' that their capacity to control events is undermined. This can mean that their own emotional and security needs are not handled, with the effect that they retreat into all kinds of defensive, backbiting and ritualistic behaviour, which further undermines their effectiveness.

Source: Watson (1994), pp. 12–13.

Someone in charge of a production department will usually be treated as a manager, and referred to as one. Those operating the machines will be called something else. In a growing business like Ryanair the boundary between 'managers' and 'non-managers' will be fluid, with all being expected to perform many tasks, irrespective of their title.

1.4   Specialisation between areas of management

As an organisation grows, senior managers usually create functions and a hierarchy, so 'management' becomes divided (there are some rare exceptions).

Functional specialisation

General managers typically head a complete unit, such as a division or subsidiary, within which there will be several functions. The general manager is responsible for the unit's performance, and relies on the managers in charge of each function. A small organisation will have just one or two general managers, who will also manage the functions. At Shell UK the most senior general manager in 2016 was Eric Bonino, the Chairman.

General managers are responsible for the performance of a distinct unit of the organisation.

Functional managers are responsible for an area of work – either as line managers or staff managers. **Line managers** are in charge of a function that creates value directly by supplying products or services to customers: they could be in charge of a retail store, a group of nurses, a social work department or a manufacturing area. Their performance significantly affects business performance and image, as they and their staff are in direct contact with customers. At Shell, David Moss was (in 2016) General Manager of the UK retail business.

Functional managers are responsible for the performance of an area of technical or professional work.

Line managers are responsible for the performance of activities that directly meet customers' needs.

Management in practice   The store manager – fundamental to success

A manager with extensive experience of retailing commented:

> The store manager's job is far more complex than it may at first appear. Staff management is an important element and financial skills are required to manage a budget and the costs involved in running a store. Managers must understand what is going on behind the scenes – in terms of logistics and the supply chain – as well as what is happening on the shop floor. They must also be good with customers and increasingly they need outward-looking skills as they are encouraged to take high-profile roles in the community.

Source: Private communication from the manager.

Staff managers are in charge of activities such as finance, personnel or legal affairs that support the line managers, who are their customers. Staff in support departments are not usually in direct contact with external customers, and so do not earn income directly for the organisation. Managers of staff departments act as line managers within their unit. At Shell, Michael Coates was (in 2016) Head of Legal, and Jacky Freer was General Manager, External Relations.

Staff managers are responsible for the performance of activities that support line managers.

Project managers are responsible for a temporary team created to plan and implement a change, such as a new product or system. Mike Buckingham, an engineer, managed a project to install new machinery in a van factory. He still had line responsibilities for

Project managers are responsible for managing a project, usually intended to change some element of an organisation or its context.

Entrepreneurs are people who see opportunities in a market, and quickly mobilise the resources to deliver the product or service profitably.

manufacturing, but worked for most of the time on the project, helped by a team of technical specialists. When the change was complete he returned to his line job.

Entrepreneurs are people who are able to see opportunities in a market that others have overlooked. They secure resources and use them to build a profitable business. Simon Mottram is obsessed by cycling, and ten years ago regularly rode to work in London. The only snag was that he hated the poorly designed clothing available at the time – so set about creating Rapha (www.rapha.cc) to make and sell better kit. Raising capital was hard, requiring over 200 meetings to raise £140,000. It took over five years to begin making a profit, but the breakthrough came in 2013 when Team Sky, the Manchester-based professional cycling team, appointed Rapha as its kit supplier (*Financial Times*, 10 December 2014, p. 14).

Management hierarchies

Figure 1.3 shows the positions within a management hierarchy. The amount of 'management' and 'non-management' work within them varies, and their boundaries are fluid.

People doing the work

These are the people who do the manual and mental work needed to make and deliver products or services, ranging from low-paid cleaners or shop workers to highly-paid pilots at Ryanair or software designers at Apple. The activity is likely to contain some aspects of management work, though in lower-level jobs this will be limited. People running a small business combine management work with direct work to meet customer requirements.

First-line managers – supervising those doing the work

Sometimes called supervisors, first-line managers typically direct and support the daily work of a group of staff, framed by the requirement to monitor, report and improve work performance (Hales 2005, p. 484). They allocate and co-ordinate work, monitor the pace and help with problems, and sometimes work with middle managers on operational issues. Examples include the supervisor of a production team, the head chef in a hotel, a nurse in charge of a hospital ward, the manager of a bank branch. This role is especially challenging

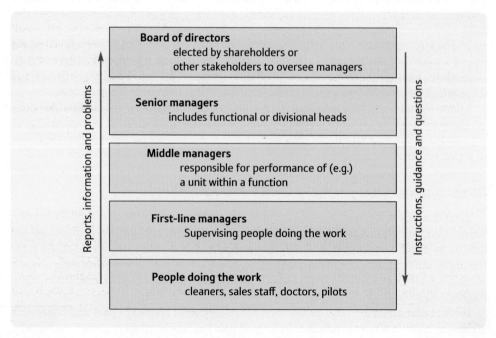

Figure 1.3
Generic levels within management hierarchies

when 'subordinates' are skilled professionals with strong views on how to do the work. First-line managers sometimes continue to perform direct operations with their staff: Lloyd and Payne (2014) show this is common in coffee shops, where managers perform many of the tasks of those they are supervising:

> Even for those . . . who spent more time on managerial tasks, it was still the case that 'everybody does everything' . . . and 'it's all hands on, even for management' (p. 477).

Management in practice   Leading an army platoon

In the British Army an officer in charge of a platoon is responsible for 30 soldiers. Captain Matt Woodward, a platoon commander, describes the job:

> As a platoon commander at a regiment you're looking after up to 30 soldiers, all of whom will have problems you have to deal with – helping them [sort out financial difficulties], one of them might need to go to court, and you might represent them, try and give them a character reference, help them as best you can. Or a soldier who has got a girl pregnant, or a soldier who has got family problems and needs some help. Somebody else may want to take a posting back to England if they're based in Germany, or indeed if they're in England they might want to go to Germany. That's your job to help them out as best you can, to find them the best job they can but also in the place they want to be. And, obviously, as well as these problems we lead soldiers in the field and on operations.

Source: Based on an interview with Matt Woodward.

Middle managers – supervising first-line managers

People in this role – such as an engineering manager at Ryanair – ensure that first-line managers work in line with company policies. This requires them to translate strategy into operational tasks, mediating between senior management vision and operational reality – and often interpreting and re-shaping higher policies to suit local conditions. They may also help develop strategy by presenting information about customer expectations to senior managers. Burgess and Currie (2013), show how this worked in a hospital, where 'hybrid' middle managers (those with a clinical training who had taken on middle managerial work) played a vital communication role between senior managers and professional staff. Those working for charities have the challenge of managing volunteers – ensuring they turn up, work effectively and don't annoy customers.

Middle-management work is often challenging, especially when they believe the decisions of senior managers are flawed, and/or they receive little recognition. Yet senior managers depend on competent middle managers to solve problems locally, and pass information upwards.

Senior managers – supervising middle managers

The senior management team is expected to ensure that middle managers, suppliers and other business partners work in ways that add value to resources – that they follow agreed plans, suggest innovations, deliver supplies as agreed and so on. The most senior of these is usually called the managing director (MD) or chief executive officer (CEO), and will be assisted by functional heads (such as the heads of engineering or marketing) or heads of the main product divisions. This senior team reports to the board of directors, the board of trustees in a charity such as the British Heart Foundation, or the equivalent in public sector organisations.

Board of directors – managing the business

Managing the business is the work of a small group, usually called the board of directors, the most senior of whom is usually called the chairman. They establish policy and have a particular responsibility for managing relations with people and institutions in the world outside – shareholders, media or elected representatives. At Marks & Spencer the board focuses on corporate culture, strategy and succession planning. A board needs to be aware of the work of senior managers, but spends most of its time looking to the future or dealing with external affairs. The CEO is usually a member of the board, and some of the senior team may also be. The board usually includes non-executive directors – senior managers from other companies who should bring a wider, independent view to discussions. Such non-executive directors can enhance the effectiveness of the board, and give investors confidence it is acting in their interests. They can

> both support the executives in their leadership of the business and monitor and control executive conduct (Roberts et al. 2005, p. S6)

by challenging, questioning, discussing and debating issues with the executive members.

1.5   Influencing through the process of managing

Stakeholders are individuals, groups or organisations with an interest in, or who are affected by, what the organisation does.

Whatever their role, people add value to resources by influencing others, including internal and external **stakeholders** – those parties who affect, or who are affected by, an organisation's actions and policies. The challenge is that stakeholders will have different priorities, so managers need to influence them to act in ways they believe will add value.

They do this directly and indirectly. Direct methods are the interpersonal skills (**Chapter 14**) that managers use – persuading a boss to support a proposal, a subordinate to do more work, or a customer to change a delivery date. Managers also influence indirectly through:

- the process of managing (this section);
- the tasks of managing (Section 1.6); and
- shaping the context (Section 1.7).

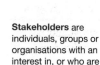

Key ideas   **Rosemary Stewart – how managers spend their time**

What are managers' jobs like? One of the best-known studies was conducted by Rosemary Stewart (1967) of Oxford University, who asked 160 senior and middle managers to keep a diary for four weeks. This showed that they typically worked in a fragmented, interrupted fashion. Over the four weeks they had, on average, only nine periods of 30 minutes or more alone, with 12 brief contacts each day. They spent 36 per cent of their time on paperwork (writing, dictating, reading, calculating) and 43 per cent in informal discussion. They spent the remainder on formal meetings, telephoning and social activities.

The research identified five profiles, based not on level or function but on how people spent their time:

- **Emissaries** spent most time out of the organisation, meeting customers, suppliers or contractors.
- **Writers** spent most time alone reading and writing, and had the fewest contacts.
- **Discussers** spent most time with other people and with their colleagues.
- **Troubleshooters** had a fragmented work pattern, with many brief contacts, especially subordinates.
- **Committee members** had most internal contacts, and spent much time in formal meetings.

Source: Stewart (1967).

Henry Mintzberg – ten management roles

Mintzberg (1973) observed how (five) chief executives spent their time, and used this data to create a model of management roles. Like Stewart (see 'Key ideas'), he noted that managers' work was varied and fragmented, and contained ten roles in three categories – informational, interpersonal and decisional. Managers use these to influence others to get things done. Table 1.2 describes them, and illustrates each with an example provided by the manager of a school nutrition project.

Informational roles

Managing depends on obtaining information about external and internal events, and passing it to others. The *monitor* seeks, receives and screens information to understand the organisation and its context, using websites, reports, chance conversations. Much of this information is oral (gossip as well as formal meetings), building on personal contacts. In the *disseminator role* the manager shares information by forwarding reports, passing on rumours or briefing staff. As a *spokesperson* the manager transmits information to people

Table 1.2 Mintzberg's ten management roles

Category	Role	Activity	Examples from a school nutrition project
Informational	Monitor	Seek and receive information, scan reports, maintain interpersonal contacts	Collect and review funding applications; set up database to monitor application process
	Disseminator	Forward information to others, send memos, make phone calls	Share content of applications with team members by email
	Spokesperson	Represent the unit to outsiders in speeches and reports	Present application process at internal and external events
Interpersonal	Figurehead	Perform ceremonial and symbolic duties, receive visitors	Sign letters of award to successful applicants
	Leader	Direct and motivate subordinates, train, advise and influence	Design and coordinate process with team and other managers
	Liaison	Maintain information links in and beyond the organisation	Become link person for government bodies to contact for progress reports
Decisional	Entrepreneur	Initiate new projects, spot opportunities, identify areas of business development	Use initiative to revise application process and to introduce electronic communication
	Disturbance handler	Take corrective action during crises, resolve conflicts amongst staff, adapt to changes	Holding face-to-face meetings with applicants when the outcome was negative; handling staff grievances
	Resource allocator	Decide who gets resources, schedule, budget, set priorities	Ensure fair distribution of grants nationally
	Negotiator	Represent unit during negotiations with unions, suppliers, and generally defend interests	Working with sponsors and government to ensure consensus during decision making

Source: Based on Mintzberg (1973), and private communication from the project manager.

outside the organisation – speaking at a conference, briefing the media or presenting at a company meeting. Michael O'Leary at Ryanair is renowned for flamboyant statements to the media about competitors or officials in the European Commission.

Interpersonal roles

Interpersonal roles arise directly from a manager's formal authority and status, and shape relationships with people within and beyond the organisation. As a *figurehead* the manager is a symbol, representing the unit in legal and ceremonial duties such as greeting a visitor, signing legal documents, presenting retirement gifts or receiving a quality award. The *leader role* defines the manager's relationship with other people (not just subordinates), including motivating, communicating and developing their skills and confidence. One commented:

> I am conscious that I am unable to spend as much time interacting with staff members as I would like. I try to overcome this by leaving my door open whenever I am alone as an invitation to staff to come in and interrupt me, and encourage them to discuss any problems.

Liaison refers to maintaining contact with people outside the immediate unit. Managers maintain networks in which they trade information and favours for mutual benefit with clients, officials, customers and suppliers. For some managers, particularly chief executives and sales managers, the liaison role takes much of their time and energy.

Management in practice   Strengthening interpersonal roles

A company restructured its regional operations, closed a sales office in Bordeaux and transferred the work to Paris. The sales manager responsible for south-west France was now geographically distant from her boss and the rest of the team. This caused communication problems and loss of teamwork. She concluded that the interpersonal aspects of the role were vital to the informational and decisional roles. The decision to close the office had broken these links.

She and her boss agreed these changes:

- A 'one-to-one' session of quality time to discuss key issues during monthly visits to head office.
- Daily telephone contact to ensure speed of response and that respective communication needs were met.
- Use of fax and email at home to speed up communications.

These overcame the break in interpersonal roles caused by the location change.

Source: Private communication.

Decisional roles

In the *entrepreneurial* role managers see opportunities and create projects to deal with them. Beamish Museum (www.beamish.org.uk) is England's biggest open-air museum, telling the story of working life in the north-east region in the 18th and 19th centuries. In 2008 the charity was in financial trouble as the number of visitors had stabilised, and government subsidy was declining. The director saw opportunities to attract visitors, create new attractions and devise new sources of revenue. In three years visitors increased by 70 per cent and revenue more than doubled – almost removing the need for subsidy. A manager becomes the *disturbance handler* when they deal with unexpected events, which draw their attention away from planned work. Surprise is a common feature of organisational life, so good managers devise systems to deal with it and limit disruption – Bechky and Okhuysen (2011) show how some organisations prepare for the unexpected.

The resource allocator chooses among competing demands for money, equipment, personnel and other resources. How much of her budget should the housing manager (quoted on page 24) spend on different projects? How much to spend on advertising? The manager of an ambulance service regularly decides between paying overtime to staff to replace an absent team member, or letting service quality decline until a new shift starts. This is close to the negotiator role, in which managers seek agreement with those on whom they depend. Managers at Ryanair regularly negotiate with airport owners to agree services and fees for a subsequent period.

Activity 1.4   **Gather evidence about Mintzberg's model**

Recall a time when you were responsible for managing an activity. Alternatively, draw on your experience of being managed and recall your manager at the time as the focus for the activity.

- Do the ten roles cover all of your/their work, or did you do things not on Mintzberg's list? What were they?
- Give examples of what you/they did under five of the roles.
- On reflection, were there any of these roles to which you/they should have given more time? Or less?
- If possible, compare your results with other members of your course.
- Decide if the evidence you have collected supports or contradicts Mintzberg's theory.

Mintzberg observed that every manager's job combines these roles, with their relative importance depending on the manager's personal preferences, position in the hierarchy and the type of business. Managers usually recognise that they use many of the roles as they influence others.

Case study   **Ryanair – the case continues**   www.ryanair.com

Michael O'Leary joined the company in 1988 (he was previously financial adviser to founder Tony Ryan) and became chief executive in 1994. He depends on securing agreements with airport operators, and on persuading authorities to allow Ryanair to open a route. This often leads him into public disputes with airport operators and/or with the European Commission. O'Leary takes a deliberately aggressive stance to these controversies, believing that:

> as long as it's not safety-related, there's no such thing as bad publicity.

He is outspokenly dismissive of traditional high-cost airlines, the European Commission, airport operators, and governments that subsidise failing airlines. Since 2013 the company has also adopted a friendlier approach to customers, which appears to have paid off, as passenger numbers have risen steadily since then.

Airline seats have no value if they are not filled on a flight, so companies aim to maximise the proportion sold, using a technique known as dynamic pricing – typically, fares rise the nearer the date is to that of departure, though if seats are empty near the flight date, fares will fall.

It earns revenue by charging for services such as checking baggage into the hold or booking by credit card, selling insurance, priority boarding and refreshments. Each time a passenger rents a car or books a hotel room on the Ryanair website, it earns a commission. The company expects revenue from ancillary activities will grow more rapidly than ticket sales, and in 2015 they brought in 25 per cent of total revenue.

Sources: *Financial Times*, 5 October 2015, p. 14; company website.

Case questions 1.2

- Make notes showing which of Mintzberg's management roles you can identify in the case. Support your answer with specific examples.

Two roles are missing from Mintzberg's list – *manager as subordinate* and *manager as worker*. Most managers have subordinates but, except for those at the very top, they are subordinates themselves. Part of their role is to advise, assist and influence their boss – over whom they have no formal authority. Managers often need to persuade people higher up the organisation of a proposal's value or urgency:

> This is the second time we have been back to the management team, to propose how we wish to move forward, and ask for the resources we need. It is worth taking the time to get all members fully supportive of what we are trying to do. Although it takes a bit longer we should eventually move the [top team] forward.

Many managers spend time doing the work of the organisation. A director of a small property company helps with sales visits, or an engineering director helps with difficult technical problems. A lawyer running a small practice performs both professional and managerial roles.

Key ideas   Managerial work in small businesses

O'Gorman et al. (2005) studied the work of ten owner–managers of small growing businesses to establish empirically if the nature of their work differs from those in the large businesses studied by Mintzberg. They concluded that it was in some ways similar to that in large organisations, finding brevity, fragmentation and variety; mainly verbal communication; and an unrelenting pace.

Managers also moved frequently between roles, switching from, say, reviewing financial results to negotiating prices with a customer. They were constantly receiving, reviewing and giving information, usually by telephone or in unscheduled meetings. They reacted immediately to live information by redirecting their attention to the most pressing issues, so that their days were largely unplanned, with frequent interruptions. Finally, the owners of these small businesses spent 8 per cent of their time in non-managerial activities – twice that in Mintzberg's study.

> Managerial work in small, growth-orientated businesses had the same brevity and fragmentation as in large organisations, but with much more informal communication.
>
> Source: O'Gorman et al. (2005).

Managers as networkers

Does the focus of a manager's influencing activities affect performance? Mintzberg's study gave no evidence on this point, but work by Luthans (1988) showed that the relative amount of time spent on specific roles did affect outcomes. The team observed 292 managers in four organisations for two weeks, recording their behaviours in four categories – communicating, 'traditional management', networking and human resource management They also distinguished between levels of 'success' (relatively rapid promotion) and 'effectiveness' (work-unit performance and subordinates' satisfaction). They concluded that *successful* managers spent much more time networking (socialising, politicking, interacting with outsiders) than the less successful. *Effective* managers spent most time on communication and human resource management.

Wolff and Moser (2009) confirmed the link between **networking** and career success, showing building, maintaining and using internal and external contacts was positively associated with current salary, and with salary growth. Good networks help entrepreneurs to secure resources, information and status – which then further extends their network. A manager who wants to understand society and markets will benefit from meeting socially with a broad circle of friends, from widely different backgrounds.

> **Networking** refers to behaviours that aim to build, maintain and use informal relationships (internal and external) that may help work-related activities.

Key ideas	**Networking skills**

Trought (2012) develops ideas on the practical values of networking, including being a way to find job opportunities. How you manage your network is unique to you – reflecting your personality and circumstances, including the networks of those who are in your network. She suggests several ways to build a more valuable network, including:

Face-to-face networks

- Find ways to attend formal networking events – perhaps through your careers service.
- Use casual conversations to seek out additional people with whom to network.
- Create events that others want to attend – which may in turn widen your network.
- Maintain, as well as build, your network – keep in touch with people, make opportunities and try to ensure they benefit from networking with you.

Social media networks

- Vital to build an active online network on professional sites such as LinkedIn.
- Ensure that the image you present there is the right one for the goals you have in mind.

Source: Trought (2012), pp. 88–91.

1.6   Influencing through the tasks of managing

> **Management tasks** are those of planning, organising, leading and controlling the use of resources to add value to them.

A second way in which managers influence others is when they manage the transformation of resources into more valuable outputs. Building on Figure 1.1, this involves the **management tasks** of planning, organising, leading and controlling the transformation process.

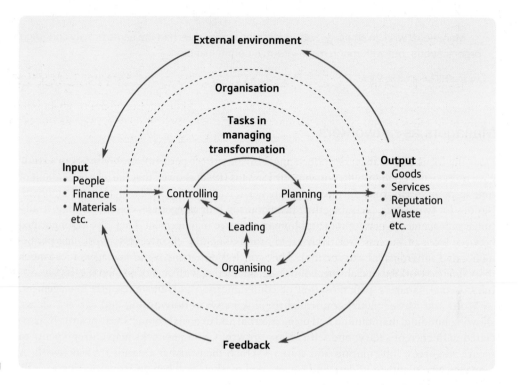

Figure 1.4 The tasks of managing

The amount of each varies with the job and the person, and they perform them simultaneously, switching as required.

Figure 1.4 illustrates the elements of this definition. It expands the central 'transformation' circle of Figure 1.2 to show the tasks that together make up the transformation process. People draw inputs (resources) from the environment and transform them through the tasks of planning, organising, leading and controlling. This results in goods and services that they pass as output into the environment. The feedback loop indicates that this output is the source of future resources.

External environment

Organisations depend on the external environment for the tangible and intangible resources they need to do their work. They also depend on people in that environment being willing to buy or otherwise value their outputs. Commercial firms sell goods and services and use the revenue to buy resources. Public bodies depend on their sponsors being sufficiently satisfied with their performance to provide their budget. Most managers face the challenge of using natural resources efficiently and sustainably. Part 2 of the book deals with the environment of management.

Planning

Planning sets out the overall direction of the work. It includes forecasting future trends, assessing resources and developing performance objectives. It means deciding on the scope of the business, the areas of work in which to engage and how to allocate resources between different projects or activities. Managers invest time and effort in developing a sense of direction for the organisation, or their part of it, and express these as goals. Part 3 deals with planning.

Geely plans for the long term   www.geely.com

Chinese billionaire Li Shufu, founder and chairman of Zhejiang Geely, made a bold move in 2010 when he bought Swedish car maker Volvo from Ford. But it was not a sudden move – he had been thinking about Volvo since 2002, even before he had established the Geely car business:

> **I just felt that with Ford owning all these brands, at some point it could give us an opportunity to get one of them, and Volvo was my favourite.**

Hakan Samuelson, Volvo's chief executive, says the Swedish group has prospered under Geely's ownership thanks to the stability and investment it has brought.

Mr Li believes there is much more the Swedish company could do in communication and marketing, particularly of its vaunted reputation for safety, a big asset in China. Talking about Volvo's brand and what he sees as its respect for the environment and human beings, he stresses that his investment is for the long term. The brand's image is in tune with the way in which the world is developing, he argues.

 Source: *Financial Times*, 7 April 2014, p. 16.

Organising

Organising moves abstract plans closer to reality by deciding how to allocate time and effort. It includes creating a structure for the enterprise, developing policies for HRM, deciding what technology people need and how to encourage innovation. Part 4 deals with organising.

Leading

Leading is the task of generating effort and commitment – influencing, motivating and communicating – whether with individuals or in teams. It is directed at the tasks of planning, organising and controlling, so is in the middle of Figure 1.4. Part 5 deals with this topic.

Controlling

Control is the task of monitoring progress, comparing it with plan and taking corrective action. Managers set a budget for a housing department, an outpatients' clinic, or for business travel. They ensure there is a system to collect information regularly on expenditure or performance – to check they are keeping to budget. If not, they decide how to bring actual costs into line with budget. Are the outcomes consistent with the objectives? If so, they can leave things alone. But if by Wednesday it is clear that staff will not meet the week's production target, the manager needs to act. They may deal with the deviation by a short-term response – authorising overtime. Control is equally important in creative organisations. Ed Catmull, cofounder of Pixar comments:

> Because we're a creative organisation, people [think that what we do can't be measured]. That's wrong. Most of our processes involve activities and deliverables that can be quantified. We keep track of the rates at which things happen, how often something had to be reworked, whether a piece of work was completely finished or not when it was sent to another department. . . Data can show things in a neutral way, which can stimulate discussion. (Catmull, 2008, p. 72).

That discussion to which Catmull refers is the way to learn from experience. Good managers create and use opportunities to learn from what they are doing. Part 6 deals with control.

The tasks in practice

Managers typically switch between tasks many times a day. They deal with them intermittently and in parallel, touching on many different parts of the job, as this manager in a not-for-profit housing association explains:

> My role involves each of these functions. Planning is an important element as I am part of a team with a budget of £8 million to spend on particular forms of housing. So planning where to spend it is very important. Organising and leading are important too, as staff have to be clear on which projects to take forward, clear on objectives and deadlines. Controlling is also there – I have to compare the actual money spent with the planned budget and take corrective action as necessary.

And a manager in a professional services firm:

> As a manager in a professional firm, each assignment involves all the elements to ensure we carry it out properly. I have to set clear objectives for the assignment, organise the necessary staff and information to perform the work, supervise staff and counsel them if necessary, and evaluate the results. All the roles interrelate and there are no clear stages for each one.

Activity 1.5   Gather evidence about the tasks of managing

Reflect on a time when you have been responsible for managing an activity.

- Do the four tasks of managing cover all of your work, or did you do things that are not included?
- Give an example of something that you did in each of the tasks.
- On reflection, were there any of these to which you should have given more time? Or less?
- If possible, compare your results with other members of your course.

Case study   Ryanair – the case continues   www.ryanair.com

Top management is organised by function. Under Michael O'leary as chief executive are two deputy chief executives who are also chief operating officer and chief financial officer respectively. There are executives in charge of pilots, customer service, engineering, legal affairs, ground operations and personnel/in-flight. The board of directors consists of the chief executive and eight non-executive directors – senior managers in other businesses.

Managers are responsible for delivering the strategy – to bring the benefits of flying to as many people as possible. They control costs rigorously by:

- using a single aircraft type (Boeing 737–800), which simplifies maintenance, training and crew scheduling;
- using secondary airports (away from major cities) with low landing charges and less congestion;

- staff typically preparing an aircraft for its next flight in 25 minutes (many airlines take an hour), which allows aircraft to spend more time earning revenue (11 hours a day compared to seven at others);
- not assigning seats simplifies administration, and passengers arrive in time to board early;
- flying directly between cities avoids transferring passengers and baggage between flights;
- cabin staff collecting rubbish from the cabin, saving costs.

Managers soon saw the benefits of online booking, and it now sells over 99 per cent in this way. It has tried to minimise staff costs by introducing productivity-based incentive payments – such as awarding a bonus to cabin staff based on in-flight sales, and to pilots based on the number of hours they fly, within the legal limits. Over 90 per cent of flights arrived on time in 2015–16, helped by a daily conference call between the company and airport personnel at each base airport. These record the reasons for any flight or baggage delays, and aim to identify their root causes to prevent them happening again.

Sources: *The Economist*, 20 July 2004; company website.

Case question 1.3

- Make notes showing examples of the tasks of management in the Ryanair case.
- What might Luthans' theory (**Section 1.5**) imply for staff selection criteria?

1.7   Influencing through shaping the context

A third way to influence others is by changing the context in which they work – the office layout, their reporting relationships, or the reward system. The context influences managers, and is a tool they use to influence others:

> It is impossible to understand human intentions by ignoring the settings in which they make sense. Such settings may be institutions, sets of practices, or some other contexts created by humans – contexts which have a history, within which both particular deeds and whole histories of individual actors can and have to be situated in order to be intelligible (Czarniawska, 2004, p. 4).

Managers aim to create contexts that will support their objectives.

Dimensions of context

Internal context

Figures 1.2 and 1.4 showed the links between managers, their organisation and the external environment. Figure 1.5 enlarges the 'organisation' circle to show more fully the elements that make up the internal context within which managers work. Any organisation contains these elements – they represent the immediate context of the manager's work. As Apple grew into a major business, the management team made decisions about structure, people, technology, business processes – and indeed to all the elements in the figure, which later chapters examine:

- **Culture** (Chapter 3) – norms, beliefs and underlying values of a unit;
- **Objectives** (Chapters 6 and 8) – a desired future state of an organisation or unit;
- **Structure** (Chapter 10) how tasks are divided and coordinated to meet objectives;
- **Technology** (Chapter 12) – facilities and equipment to turn inputs into outputs;
- **Power** (Chapter 14) – the amount and distribution of power with which to influence others;
- **People** (Chapter 15) – their knowledge, skills, attitudes and goals;
- **Business processes** (Chapter 18) – activities to transform materials and information; and
- **Finance** (Chapter 20) – the financial resources available.

Effective managers do not accept these as constraints or limitations – all can represent opportunity as well as threat. They also try to change the context to support their goals (Chapter 13).

Historical context

Managers work in the flow of history, as what people do reflects past events and future uncertainties. Managers typically focus on current issues, ensuring that things run properly. At the same time, history influences them, being the source of the structure and culture

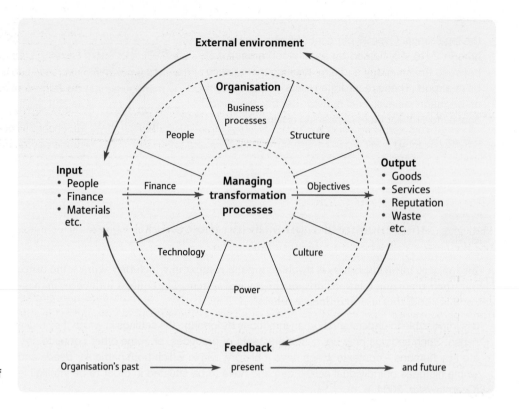

Figure 1.5 The internal and external context of management

within which they and others work. People at all levels welcome familiar ways, and resist attempts to change them.

Effective managers also look to the future, questioning systems and observing external changes. Are we wasting resources? What are others doing? The arrow at the foot of the figure represents the historical context.

External context

Chapter 3 shows that the external context includes an immediate competitive (micro) environment and a general (or macro) environment. These affect performance, and part of the manager's work is to identify, and adapt to, external changes. Managers in the public sector are expected to deliver improved services with fewer resources, so they seek to influence people to change the internal context (such as how staff work) to meet external expectations. They also seek to influence those in the external context to secure more resources and/or lower their expectations.

Table 1.3 summarises the last two sections and illustrates how managers can influence others as they perform tasks affecting internal, micro and macro contexts.

Table 1.3 Examples of influencing others by managing tasks in each context

	Internal (organisational)	Micro (competitive)	Macro (general)
Planning	Clarifying the objectives of a business unit, and communicating them clearly to all staff	Reducing prices in the hope of discouraging a potential competitor from entering the market	Lobbying for a change in a trade agreement to make it easier to enter an overseas market
Organising	Changing the role of a business unit and ensuring staff understand and accept it	Creating a new division to meet a competitive challenge more robustly	Lobbying government to simplify planning laws to enable more rapid business development

	Internal (organisational)	Micro (competitive)	Macro (general)
Leading	Redesigning tasks and training staff to higher levels to improve motivation	Arranging for staff to visit customers so that they understand more fully what they need	Sending staff to work in an overseas subsidiary to raise awareness of cultural differences
Controlling	Ensuring the information system keeps an accurate output record	Implementing an information system directly linked to customers and suppliers	Lobbying for tighter procedures to ensure all countries abide by trade agreements

Managers and their context

Managers use one of three theories (even if subconsciously) of the link between their context and their action – determinism, choice or interaction.

Determinism

This describes the assumption that factors in the external context determine an organisation's performance – micro and macro factors such as the industry a company is in, the amount of competition, or the country's laws and regulations. Managers adapt to external changes and have little independent influence on the direction of the business. On this view, the context is an independent variable – as in Figure 1.6(a).

Choice

An alternative assumption is that people influence events and shape their context. Those in powerful positions choose which businesses to enter or leave, and in which countries they will operate. Managers in major companies lobby to influence taxation, regulations and policy generally to serve their interests. On this view, the context is a dependent variable – shown in Figure 1.6(b).

Interaction

The interaction approach expresses the idea that people are influenced by, and themselves influence, the context. They interpret the existing context and act to change it to promote personal, local or organisational objectives. A manager may see a change in the company's external environment, and respond by advocating that it enters the market with a product to meet a perceived demand. Others interpret this proposal in the light of *their* perspective – competitors may lobby government to alter some regulations to protect them. All try

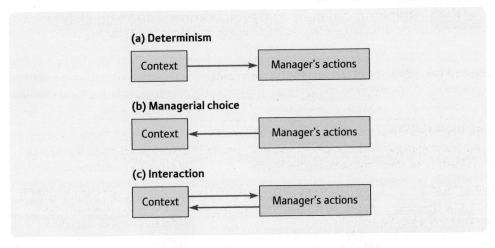

Figure 1.6
Alternative models of managers and their context

to influence decisions to suit their interests. The outcomes from these interactions affect the context (the company enters the market, or the regulations deter them) – which now provides the historical background to future action. The essential idea is that the relationship between manager and context works both ways – Figure 1.6(c). People shape the context, and the context shapes people.

Case study

Ryanair – the case continues   www.ryanair.com

International Air Transport Association statistics showed that Ryanair carried over 76 million passengers on international scheduled flights in 2011 – ahead of Lufthansa (49 million), easyJet (42 million), Air France (32 million), Emirates (32 million) and British Airways (29 million). In that year it received less than one complaint for every 2000 passengers.

In 2013 the company (Europe's largest low-cost carrier by revenue) launched a policy to attract more business passengers, admitting that it had allowed rival easyJet to gain a lead in this market sector. The company's finance director said that the airline

was considering several facilities to help business travellers, such as offering (at a charge) quicker security clearance, and purchasing flights with an American Express card. It would also upgrade its website and mobile phone applications (perhaps to enable passengers to download boarding passes to a smartphone).

For several years the company had been trying to acquire Aer Lingus, despite opposition from the Irish Government and the European Commission. In 2015 International Airlines Group (in which British Airways is the largest company) acquired Aer Lingus.

 Source: *Financial Times*, 26 September 2013, p. 22.
© The Financial Times 2013. All Rights Reserved.

Case questions 1.4

- Which aspects of the external general environment have affected the company (including some mentioned earlier)?
- How has the company affected these environments?
- Considering the case as a whole, identify three ways in which effective networking has probably helped Ryanair's managers to add value.
- In early 2016 the company was continuing the strategy of widening its appeal to business travellers, and improving the experience of all passengers. Visit the website or other news sources to discover the outcome on these issues, and what management lessons, if any, may be drawn from that.

1.8   Thinking critically to develop knowledge and skill

Managers continually receive data, information and knowledge – but cannot take it at face value. They must test it by questioning the underlying assumptions, relating them to context, considering alternatives and recognising limitations. These are the skills of critical thinking.

Critical thinking

Brookfield (1987) stresses the benefits of thinking critically, in that it:

> involves our recognising the assumptions underlying our beliefs and behaviours. It means we can give justifications for our ideas and actions. Most important, perhaps, it means we try to judge the rationality of these justifications . . . by comparing them to a range of varying interpretations and perspectives. (p. 13)

Critical thinking is a positive activity that enables people to see several possibilities, not a single path. Critical thinkers 'are self-confident about their potential for changing aspects of their worlds, both as individuals and through collective action' (p. 5). He identifies four components.

Critical thinking identifies the assumptions behind ideas, relates them to their context, imagines alternatives and recognises limitations.

Identifying and challenging assumptions

Critical thinkers look for the assumptions that underlie ideas, beliefs and values, and question their accuracy. They discard those that no longer seem valid in favour of more suitable ones. A manager who presents a well-supported challenge to a marketing idea that seems unsuitable to the business, or who questions the assumptions used to justify a new venture, is thinking critically.

Recognising the importance of context

Critical thinkers are aware that context influences thought, actions and results. Thinking uncritically means assuming that ideas and methods that work in one context will work in others. What we regard as an appropriate way to deal with staff reflects a specific culture: people in another culture – working in another place or at a different time – will have other expectations. Critical thinkers look for ideas and methods that seem suitable for the context.

Imagining and exploring alternatives

Critical thinkers develop the skill of imagining and exploring alternative ways of managing. They ask how others have dealt with a situation, and seek evidence about the effectiveness of different approaches. This makes them aware of realistic alternatives, and so increases the range of ideas that they can adapt and use.

Seeing limitations

Critical thinking alerts people to the limitations of knowledge and proposals. They recognise that because a practice works well in one situation it will not necessarily work in another. They are sceptical about research whose claims seem over-sold, asking about the sample or the analysis. They are open to new ideas, but only when supported by convincing evidence and reasoning.

Thinking critically will deepen your understanding of management. It is not 'do-nothing' cynicism, 'treating everything and everyone with suspicion and doubt' (Thomas, 2003, p. 7). Critical thinking is part of a successful career, as it helps to ensure that proposals reflect reasonable assumptions, suit their context, take account of alternatives and acknowledge limitations. It helps you develop both knowledge and skills.

Developing knowledge

At the end of each chapter a 'Think critically' feature encourages you to deepen your understanding of the knowledge presented in the chapter.

Developing skill – business and social awareness

The critical thinking skills that help you to acquire theoretical knowledge also help you develop employability skills, using the same disciplines of considering assumptions, contexts, alternatives and limitations. Figure 1.1 illustrated this.

At the end of each chapter there is a 'Develop a skill' feature, which gives you an opportunity to begin to develop a management skill (adding to your business or social awareness), using a theory or idea from the chapter. It shows how theory can guide practice.

> ### 1.9   Integrating themes

Entrepreneurship

Managers depend on others to get things done, and entrepreneurs must be able to build and use informal networks. Shaw (2006) studied six advertising and design companies (less than ten employees), and showed (as have other studies) that informal networking is vital to entrepreneurs in this intensely competitive sector. She worked closely with the firms' owners and staff for eighteen months to trace the pattern of their informal contacts, their focus and why they used them.

The networks typically built upon the owners' personal networks, and those of their families and people they knew in non-competing firms. Most encouraged staff to use *their* personal networks to gather evidence about competitor moves or new entrants to the market. Such information (as well as that about legal, tax or financial matters) was the most common reason for the network contacts, as it was a significant addition to the resources available to these small firms – who rarely used official business support agencies. Their personal networks also generated new business. Finally, the study showed that entrepreneurs are selective – only networking with people they think can contribute directly, or indirectly by reputation and referral, to their client base and revenue.

The theme of entrepreneurship recurs throughout the book, and this recurring section links the topic to the theme of that chapter.

Sustainability

Sustainability refers to economic activities that meet the needs of the present population while preserving the environment for the needs of future generations.

Management decisions traditionally focused on creating economic value, but many now expect them to take account of social and economic criteria. Writers such as Hawken *et al.* (1999), who drew on years of advisory experience at the Rocky Mountain Institute, maintain that companies who achieve **sustainability** in their performance – who make productive use

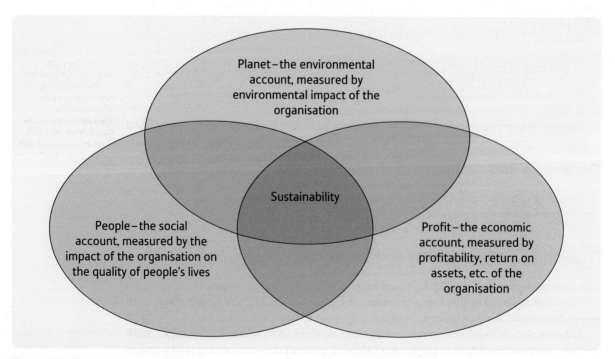

Figure 1.7 The triple bottom line

not just of financial and physical resources, but also of human and natural ones – do well. They turn waste into profit – for example by taking a radical approach to energy efficiency in buildings, processes and vehicles, by designing products and services to avoid waste, and by designing working practices that are more satisfying for employees.

A term that sums up this approach is the **triple bottom line** – the idea that performance has social and environmental dimensions as well as financial ones. This is sometimes expressed as 'people, planet and profit', as shown in Figure 1.7. Chapter 5 develops sustainability as one aspect of corporate responsibility, and this recurring section links it to the theme of each chapter.

The **triple bottom line** is the idea that organisations can assess their performance on social and environmental criteria as well as financial ones.

Internationalisation

Developments in communications technology and changes in the regulations governing international trade have led to an increase in the amount of trade that crosses national borders. Managing the international activities of an organisation has become a common feature of the work of many managers – whether working as an expatriate manager in another country or being part of an international team with colleagues from other countries.

This has many implications for managing, since those a manager is working with are increasingly likely to be from cultures with different values and ways of seeing the world. They will also be from countries with different political and institutional backgrounds, which shape the policies and practices they can adopt. Javidan and Bowen (2013) advise managers to develop the competence of having a global mindset – the ability to influence those who are unlike ourselves. Chapter 4 develops this, and gives the chance to develop a relevant skill.

Governance

High-profile corporate scandals and collapses have occurred despite the companies' annual reports giving the impression that all was well. There is much criticism of the pay and pensions of senior executives, especially in banks. These scandals have damaged investors and employees – and public confidence in the way managers were running these and other large companies.

Many questioned how such things could happen. Why could such apparently successful businesses get into such difficulties so quickly? Were there any warning signals that were ignored? What can be done to prevent similar events happening again? How can public confidence in these businesses be restored? These questions are all linked to **corporate governance**:

Corporate governance is concerned with ensuring that internal controls adequately balance the needs of those with a financial interest in the organisation, and that these are balanced with the interests of other stakeholders.

> a lack of effective corporate governance meant that such collapses could occur; good corporate governance can help prevent [them] happening. (Mallin, 2013, p.1)

Chapter 3 develops these issues and this section links them to the theme of each chapter.

Summary

1   **Explain that the role of management is to add value to resources**

- Managers create value by transforming inputs into outputs of greater value: they do this by developing competences within the organisation that, by constantly adding value (however measured) to resources, are able to survive and prosper. The concept of creating value is subjective and open to different interpretations. Managers work in an infinite variety of settings, and Table 1.1 shows how each setting raises unique challenges.

2 **Give examples of management as a universal human activity and as a distinct role**

- Management is an activity that everyone undertakes to some extent as they manage their lives. In another sense management is an activity within organisations, conducted in varying degrees by many people. It is not exclusive to those called 'managers'. People create the distinct role when they separate the work itself from the management of that work, and allocate the tasks to others. The distinction between management and non-management work is fluid and the result of human action.

3 **Compare the roles of general, functional, line, staff and project managers, and entrepreneurs:**

- General managers are responsible for a complete business or a unit within it. They depend on functional managers who can be either in charge of line departments meeting customer needs, such as manufacturing and sales, or in staff departments such as finance that provide advice or services to line managers. Project managers are in charge of temporary activities usually directed at implementing change. Entrepreneurs create new businesses, or new ventures in existing ones, to exploit opportunities.

4 **Explain how managers influence others to add value to resources through:**

- The processes of managing. Rosemary Stewart drew attention to the fragmented and interrupted nature of management work, while Mintzberg identified ten management roles – grouped as informational, interpersonal and decisional. Luthans and more recently Moser found that successful managers were likely to be those who networked widely with people inside and outside of the organisation.
- The tasks (or content) of managing. Planning develops the broad direction of an organisation's work, to meet customer expectations, taking into account internal capabilities. Organising is the activity of deciding how to deploy resources to meet plans, while leading seeks to ensure that people work with commitment. Control monitors activity against plans, so that people can adjust either if required.
- The contexts within which people work. The internal context consists of eight elements that help or hinder the manager – objectives, technology, business processes, finance, structure, culture, power and people. The historical context also influences events, as does the external context of competitive and general environments.

5 **Explain the elements of critical thinking and understand how to use these to develop your networking skills:**

- Critical thinking is a positive approach to studying, as it encourages people to develop the skills of identifying and challenging assumptions, recognising the importance of context, imagining and exploring alternatives and seeing the limitations of an idea.
- Developing networking skills is likely to be more effective if a manager questions the assumption that networking is always appropriate, and whether or not their context encourages the practice or not. They are also likely to benefit more if they seek alternative ways to network, and are conscious of the possible limitations of the practice.

6 **Integrating themes – each chapter ends by relating the topic to four themes of management:**

- Entrepreneurship. Research by Shaw (2006) shows that entrepreneurs depend very heavily on a network of informal contacts to get things done.
- Sustainability. Adding value has traditionally been measured primarily in economic terms, but can also be measured by 'the triple bottom line' – profit, people, planet.
- Internationalisation is a pervasive theme in discussing management, and affects each aspect of the management role.
- Public criticism of corporate scandals and failures has increased interest in corporate governance methods, which are intended to oversee the activities of management.

Test your understanding

1 How do non-commercial organisations add value to resources?

2 What is the difference between management as a general human activity and management as a special-ised occupation? How has this division happened, and what are some of its effects?

3 What examples are there in the chapter of this boundary between 'management' and 'non-management' work being changed, and what were the effects?

4 Describe, with examples, the differences between general, functional, line, staff and project managers.

5 How does Mintzberg's theory of management roles complement that which identifies the tasks of management?

6 What is the significance to someone starting a career in management of Luthans' theory about roles and performance?

7 Give examples from your experience or observation of each of the four tasks of management.

8 How can thinking critically help managers do their job more effectively?

9 Review and revise the definition of management that you gave in Activity 1.1.

Think critically

- What **assumptions** about the role of management appear to guide the way you, or others, manage? Are these assumptions supported by the evidence – have they worked, or not? Does your observation support, or contradict, Luthans' theory on the effect of networking?

- What aspects of the historical or current **context** of the company appear to influence how you, and others, interpret the management role? Does it encourage networking, or not?

- Can you compare and contrast your role with that of colleagues on your course? Does this suggest **alterna-tive** ways of constructing your role – where you focus time and energy? This may also suggest alternative ways of networking.

- What **limitations** can you see in the theories and evidence presented in the chapter? For example, how valid is Mintzberg's theory (developed in large firms) for those in small businesses? Is networking always wise, or have you seen places where it would not work?

Develop a skill – networking

Networking skills can benefit someone's career progression, so this exercise is about them.

- **Assessment.** How good do you consider you are at networking? Thinking of one area of your life, how many people are in that 'network'? Do you actively try to extend your network, or do you prefer doing things alone or with a small number of people?

- **Learning.** Section 1.5 defined networking and reported research by Luthans and later by Wolff and Moser. This showed the implications of this practice for career success. Read that section again, paying special attention to the 'Key ideas' feature (page 21), which gives tips on networking. Summarise the principles about networking in these theories. How would you distinguish a good networker from a poor one? Why is networking likely to help career success?

- **Analysis.** Consider the possible implications for you of this evidence in Section 1.5. Identify someone (whom you know, or can read about) who seems to be a good networker. Consider what they do, what the effects seem to be and what you may be able to learn from them.

- **Practice.** Identify one way in which you may be able to improve your networking skills – see Trought (2012) for ideas (see 'Key ideas' on page 21). Identify a suitable opportunity to practice this for a few days. Then record the results, and reflect on what you can learn.

- **Application.** Following your reflection, identify how you will try to further improve your skill, and seek another opportunity to practice it within the next week.

Read more

Bloom, N., Sadun, R. and Van Reenen, J. (2012), 'Does management really work?', *Harvard Business Review,* vol. 90, no. 11, pp. 76–82.

A substantial empirical study assessing the extent to which management adds value.

Drucker, P. (1999), *Management Challenges for the 21st Century,* Butterworth/Heinemann, London.

Worth reading as a collection of insightful observations from the enquiring mind of this great management theorist.

Magretta, J. (2013), *What Management Is (How it works, and why it's everyone's business),* (2nd edn) Profile Books, London.

A new edition of this small book by a former editor at the *Harvard Business Review* offers a brief, readable and jargon-free account of the work of general management.

Timpson, J. (2010), *Upside Down Management: A Common Sense Guide to Better Business,* Wiley, Chichester.

Few successful entrepreneurs have the ability to explain what running a business entails: John Timpson, owner and chairman of the dominant chain of shoe-repair shops, does.

Go online

These websites have appeared in the chapter:

www.ryanair.com
www.southbankcentre.co.uk
www.uk.coop
www.johnlewispartnership.co.uk
www.circlepartnership.co.uk
www.suma.coop
www.bhf.org
www.rapha.cc
www.royalmail.com
www.geely.com

Visit two of the business sites in the list, or those of other organisations in which you are interested, and navigate to the pages dealing with recent news, press or investor relations.

- What are the main issues that the organisation appears to be facing?
- Compare and contrast the issues you identify on the two sites.
- What challenges may they imply for those working in, and managing, these organisations?

CHAPTER 2
MODELS OF MANAGEMENT

Aim

To present the main theoretical perspectives on management and to show how they relate to each other.

Objectives

By the end of your work on this chapter you should be able to outline the concepts below in your own terms and:

1. Explain the value of models of management, and compare unitary, pluralist and radical perspectives

2. State the structure of the competing values framework and evaluate its contribution to our understanding of management

3. Summarise the rational goal, internal process, human relations and open systems models and evaluate what each can contribute to a manager's understanding of their role

4. Use the model to classify the dominant form in two or more business units, and gather evidence on how this affects the roles of managers in those units

5. Consider which of the 'competing values' you feel most comfortable with, and use that to help develop the skill of self-awareness

6. Show how ideas from the chapter add to your understanding of the integrating themes

Key terms

This chapter introduces the following ideas:

model (or theory)	open system
self-awareness	system boundary
scientific management	feedback
operational research	subsystem
bureaucracy	socio-technical system
administrative management	contingency approach
human relations approach	complexity theory
system	non-linear system

Each is a term defined within the text, as well as in the glossary at the end of the book.

Case study

innocent drinks www.innocentdrinks.com

Richard Reed, Jon Wright and Adam Balon founded innocent drinks in 1998, having been friends since they met at Cambridge University in 1991. The business was successful, and in 2013 the founders sold most of their shares to Coca-Cola for an undisclosed amount, but which observers estimated at £100 million. They stressed the sale would not affect the character of the company, as Coca-Cola already owned a small stake in the company, which had helped to finance expansion and continues to enable the regular introduction of new products – such as the range of 'nutritionally-powered' smoothies in 2014. It now employs about 350 people.

After they graduated, Reed worked in advertising, while Balon and Wright worked in (different) management consultancies. They often joked about starting a company together, considering several ideas before deciding on 'smoothies' – which they built into one of the UK's most successful entrepreneurial ventures of recent years.

Smoothies are blends of fruit that include the pulp and sometimes contain dairy products such as yoghurt. They tend to be thicker and fresher than ordinary juice. Some are made to order at juice bars and similar small outlets, but the trio decided to focus on pre-packaged smoothies sold through supermarkets, and to offer a premium range. These contain no water or added sugar and cost more than the standard product.

Any new business requires capital and must also be assured of further cash for expansion. This is a challenge, as the product is usually unknown, and the business has no record to show whether the promoters can make a profit. If investors doubt that they will get their money back, they will not lend it. Even if the initial plan succeeds, growth will require more finds – launching a new product or entering a new geographical market inevitably drains cash before it becomes profitable. The founders eventually persuaded Maurice Pinto, a private investor, to put in £235,000 in return for a 20 per cent share.

The company succeeded and, as sales grew, Pinto advised the founders to consider expanding in Europe and/or extending the product ranges. They initially started selling the core range in continental Europe and are now active in 15 countries, mostly in Europe, but also Russia and Australia.

© innocent drinks

They also diversified the product range, which in 2016 included eight smoothies (including three 'nutritionally enhanced' varieties), juices, coconut water, bubbles (a mixture of fruit and spring water) and 'kids range'.

The founders knew that their success would depend on the quality and commitment of their staff, including professional managers from other companies. Reed says:

> we've always set out to attract people who are entrepreneurial – we want them to stay and be entrepreneurial with innocent. But the inevitable result is that some want to go and do their own thing by setting up their own new businesses. We help and support them with whatever we can. (Quoted in *Director*, June 2011)

The founders believe they are enlightened employers who look after staff well. All receive shares in the business, which means they share in profits.

Sources: Based on material from 'innocent drinks', a case prepared by William Sahlman (2004), Harvard Business School, Case no. 9-805-031; Germain and Reed (2009); company website.

Case questions 2.1

Visit the website and check on the latest news about developments in the company.

- In what ways are managers at innocent drinks adding value to the resources they use?

- As well as raising finance, what other issues would they need to decide once they had entered their chosen market?

2.1   Introduction

The story of innocent drinks illustrates three themes that run through this book. First, they were entrepreneurs who created a new business – which would only survive if it offered something that customers valued. Second, their personal values meant they wanted to leave the world a better place – by enabling staff to enjoy work (and supporting some to become entrepreneurs themselves), treating suppliers fairly and using sustainable production methods. Third, while based in the UK, they manage internationally – bringing materials from around the world, turning them into products and selling these throughout Europe.

To achieve this they created an organisation – securing resources from responsible suppliers, turning them into products that customers value, reinvesting profits to grow the business. Most managers cope with similar issues. All need to recruit willing and capable people and ensure they create value. Many share innocent's commitment to responsible business practice – sustainability is on the agenda of most management teams, as is the challenge of working internationally.

Managers approach their work using a mental model that represents, accurately or not, the situation they face, and suggests how to deal with it. In simple situations, a single familiar model may serve quite well, but in the complex situations that most managers face, this is not enough. Customers want innovation, but at low cost; they expect efficient and predictable working, while staff value varied and creative work. Others press firms to work transparently with open communications, while also expecting them to control customer and staff information very securely. Managers balance these conflicting expectations while also ensuring the organisation adds value and survives. Heracleous (2013) shows how Apple Inc. has balanced intense efficiency in operations with outstanding creativity in product design – see Part 1 Case). Someone aware of several models who can, depending on the situation, draw on the most suitable, is likely to perform better than someone limited to a single perspective.

The next section considers why management models are useful in practice. Section 2.3 presents the competing values framework – whose four theoretical perspectives (models) have different implications for a manager's skills. Subsequent sections outline each model.

2.2   Why study models of management?

A model (or theory) represents a complex phenomenon by identifying the major elements and relationships.

A **model (or theory)** represents a complex reality. Focusing on the essential elements and their relationship helps to understand that complexity, and how change may affect it. Most management problems can only be dealt with by using ideas from several models, as no one model offers a complete solution. Those managing a globally competitive business require flexibility, quality and low-cost production. Managers at Ford or DaimlerChrysler want models of the production process that help them to organise it efficiently from a technical perspective. Managers at GlaxoSmithKline want models that help them manage research programmes to create new pharmaceuticals at an acceptable cost. The management task is to use models to devise a solution that is acceptable in their situation. Good models save time and effort – they help identify relevant variables in a situation quickly, and so to act more confidently. Pfeffer and Sutton (2006) suggest why people frequently ignore such evidence: see 'Key ideas'.

Key ideas   Pfeffer and Sutton on why managers ignore evidence

In a paper making the case for evidence-based management, Pfeffer and Sutton (2006) observe that experienced managers frequently ignore new evidence relevant to a decision and suggest that they:

- trust personal experience more than they trust research;
- prefer to use a method or solution that has worked before;
- are susceptible to consultants who vigorously promote their solutions;
- rely on dogma and myth – even when there is no evidence;
- uncritically imitate practices that appear to have worked well for famous companies.

Source: Pfeffer and Sutton (2006).

Models identify variables

Models aim to identify the main variables in a situation, and the relationships between them. Since each situation is unique, some managers doubt the value of theory. Magretta answers:

> without a theory of some sort it's hard to make sense of what's happening in the world around you. If you want to know whether you work for a well-managed organisation – as opposed to whether you like your boss – you need a working theory of management (Magretta, 2013, p. 10).

We all use theory, acting on (perhaps implicit) assumptions about the relationships between cause and effect. The perspective we take reflects our assumptions as we interpret, organise and make sense of events – see 'Key ideas'.

Key ideas Alan Fox and a manager's frame of reference

Alan Fox (1974) studied the relationship between managers and employees, and proposed that the underlying assumptions a manager holds about this affects how they do their job. Those who take a:

- **unitary perspective** believe that organisations aim to develop rational ways of achieving common interests. Managerial work arises from a technical division of labour, and managers work to achieve objectives shared by all members.
- **pluralist perspective** believe that the division of labour in modern organisations creates groups with different interests. Some conflict over ends and/or means is inevitable, and managerial work involves gaining sufficient consent to meet all interests to a mutually acceptable extent.
- **radical perspective** challenge both unitary and pluralist models, believing that they ignore how the horizontal and vertical division of labour sustains unequal social relations within capitalist society. As long as these exist managers and employees will be in conflict.

Source: Fox (1974).

Managers influence others to add value by drawing on their mental model of the situation to decide where to focus effort. Zenger (2013) illustrates this in a study that relates Apple's success to Steve Jobs' enduring model of the company (see also Part Case), which was that

> consumers would pay a premium for ease of use, reliability and elegance in computing and other devices, and that the best means for delivering these was relatively closed systems, significant vertical integration and tight control over design (p. 76).

Figure 2.1 develops Figure 1.5 (the internal context within which managers work) to show some variables within each element: 'structure' could include more specific variables such as roles, teams, or control systems. In 2016 Willie Walsh, Chief Executive of British

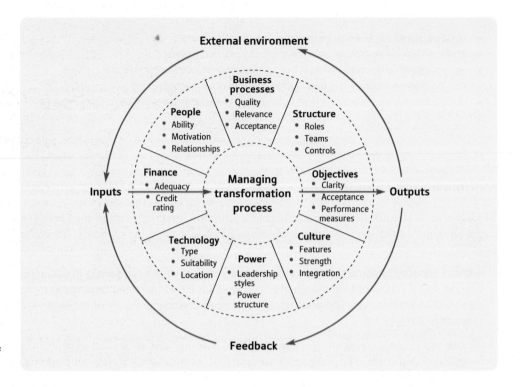

Figure 2.1 Some variables in the internal context of management

Airways (www.ba.com – now part of International Airlines Group, IAG), was continuing his long-standing objective to raise operating profits to 10 per cent of sales – sales themselves were 13 per cent higher than the previous year. Figure 2.1 suggests ways of meeting the profit objective:

- **objectives** – retaining a reputation for premium travel (a different market than Ryanair)
- **people** – continuing to reduce the number of employees
- **technology** – reducing fuel costs by using more fuel-efficient aircraft
- **business processes** – negotiating new working practices with cabin staff.

In each area there are theories about the variables and their relationships. A change in one element affects others – reducing staff may threaten the aim of providing a premium service. Any change would depend on available *finance* – and on the chief executive's *power* to get things done. External events (Chapter 3), such as rising fuel prices or changes in economic conditions, shape all of these internal factors.

Managers need to influence people to add value: people who are aware, thinking beings, with unique experiences, interests and objectives. The 'Management in practice' feature illustrates contrasting assumptions about how to deal with subordinates.

Management in practice

Practice reflects managers' theories

These examples illustrate contrasting theories about motivation.

- **Motivating managers:** Tim O'Toole became chief executive of London Underground in 2003 (in 2016 he was Chief Executive of FirstGroup – www.firstgroup.com) and put in a new management structure – appointing a general manager for each line to improve accountability.

Now there's a human being who is judged on how that line is performing and I want them to feel that kind of intense anxiety in the stomach that comes when there's a stalled train and they realise that it's their stalled train.

Source: From an article by Simon London, *Financial Times*, 20 February 2004.)

● **Supporting staff:** John Timpson, chairman of the shoe repair and key-cutting chain, believes the most important people in the company are those who cut customers' keys and re-heel their shoes:

You come back for the service you get from the people in the shops. They are the stars. . . we need to do everything to help them to look after you as well as possible. [A bonus based on shop takings] is fundamental to the service culture I want. It creates the adrenalin. That is the reason why people are keen to serve you if you go into one of our shops. And why they don't take long lunch breaks.

 Source: *Financial Times*, 3 August 2006.

Case questions 2.2

● Give examples of the variables in Figure 2.1 that innocent will deal with as it extends the product range.

● Which of the variables may have had a particularly strong influence on performance?

Models illuminate the manager's context

In 1974, *The New York Times* reported that sales of Peter Drucker's latest book, *Management: Tasks, Responsibilities, Practices,* (Drucker, 1974) had overtaken those of Alex Comfort's illustrated primer *The Joy of Sex*. For one brief moment, management was the hottest topic of all. Only Drucker could have achieved this. 'No other person has had the impact on the practice of management that he did,' according to one of today's leading authorities, C.K. Pralahad. (From an article by Stefan Stern in the *Financial Times*, 24 November 2009.)

Stern was writing on the occasion of a conference to celebrate the hundredth anniversary of Drucker's birth, and to debate his significance and continued relevance to managers, such as his advice to focus relentlessly on their purpose by remembering 'the five most important questions you will ever ask': What is our business? Who is our customer? What does the customer value? What are our results? What is our plan?

Managers have long valued such clear guidance but also find that, as Drucker acknowledged, they need to interpret these questions to suit their unique circumstances. Thousands of books offer advice: these are only useful if the manager understands (has a good model of) his or her context, and uses ideas in a way that reflects that.

A **metaphor** is an image used to signify the essential characteristics of a phenomenon.

Key ideas   Gareth Morgan's images of organisation

Managers look at problems from several perspectives, or viewpoints: each will illuminate one aspect – while obscuring others. Gareth Morgan (1997) shows how alternative mental images and **metaphors** can represent organisations. Metaphors are a way of thinking, by attaching labels to represent an image of the object. They can help understanding, but can distort understanding if we use the wrong image. Morgan explores eight ways of seeing organisations:

- **Machines** – mechanical thinking and the rise of bureaucracies
- **Organisms** – recognising how the environment affects their health
- **Brains** – an information-processing, learning perspective
- **Cultures** – a focus on beliefs and values
- **Political systems** – a focus on conflicts and power
- **Psychic prisons** – shows how people can become trapped by habitual ways of thinking
- **Flux and transformation** – a focus on change and renewal
- **Instruments of domination** – over members, nations and environments.

Critical thinking helps improve mental models

The ideas on critical thinking in Chapter 1 suggest that working effectively depends on being able and willing to test the validity of a theory (model), and to use the experience to:

- identify and challenge assumptions;
- recognise the importance of context;
- imagine and explore alternatives;
- see limitations.

As you work through this chapter, you will be able to practise these skills.

2.3   The competing values framework

Quinn et al. (2003) believe that successive models of management (see Kiechel, 2012, for a historical overview) complement, rather than contradict, each other. They are all:

> symptoms of a larger problem – the need to achieve organisational effectiveness in a highly dynamic environment. In such a complex and fast-changing world, simple solutions become suspect . . . Sometimes we needed stability, sometimes we needed change. Often we needed both at the same time (p. 11).

They identify four underlying philosophies – 'rational goal', 'internal process', 'human relations' and 'open systems' – proposing that while each adds to our knowledge, none is sufficient. They integrate them by highlighting their underlying values within a 'competing values' framework – see Figure 2.2.

The vertical axis represents the tension between flexibility and control. Managers seek flexibility to cope with rapid change. Others try to increase control – apparently the opposite of flexibility. The horizontal axis distinguishes an internal focus from an external one. Some focus on internal issues, others on the world outside. Most models of management correspond to the values of one of the four segments.

The labels within the circle indicate the criteria of effectiveness that are the focus of models in that segment, shown around the outside. In the human relations model, upper left in the figure, effectiveness is measured by criteria such as commitment, participation and openness. In the open systems model (upper right) the criteria relate to innovation, adaptation and growth. The rational goal model focuses on productivity, direction and goal clarity. The internal process model aims for stability, documentation and control, within a hierarchical structure.

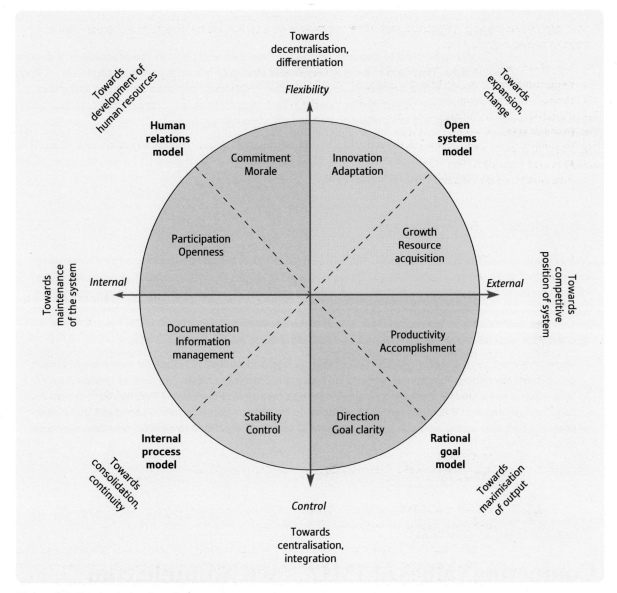

Figure 2.2 Competing values framework

Source: Quinn et al. (2003), p. 13.

Finally, the outer ring indicates the central beliefs and values associated with each model:

- **rational goal** – maximising output;
- **human relations** – developing people;
- **internal process** – consolidation, continuity; and
- **open systems** – expansion, change.

Competing values and management skills

Each value implies that a manager using that approach needs to use skills appropriate to the value. Using a 'rational goal' approach is likely to need skills in the areas of developing a vision, setting goals and working productively; a 'human relations' approach will need skills in areas of developing employees, encouraging participation and building teams; and so on. Quinn et al.:

> Managers tend to become trapped in their own style, and in the organisation's cultural values. They tend to employ very similar strategies in a wide variety of situations . . . Each model in the framework suggests value in different, opposite strategies [reflecting] the complexity confronted by people in real organisations. It . . . provides a tool to broaden thinking and to increase choice and effectiveness (p. 14).

Self-awareness refers to a person's understanding of their preferred reaction to people and situations.

Successive sections of the chapter outline theories corresponding with each value. The 'Develop a skill' feature helps you identify your 'preferred' model, and become more aware of how that may link to practice.

Key ideas   Self-awareness

A clear implication of the competing values idea is that we need to be aware of our preferred model of managing, AND that there are other possibilities. Those who are **self-aware** – in the sense of understanding their instinctive reaction to people and situations, are more likely to use the model effectively to guide what they say and do.

Quinn et al. (2003), having set out the four values in the competing values model, outline the skills associated with the respective quadrants. This includes the skill of being aware of self and others:

> Managers must have some understanding of themselves and others. Although all members of a work group have something in common, each individual is in some way unique. [As well as having different task-related skills people also differ] in their feelings, needs and concerns. People react differently to . . . situations, and it is important for managers to be able to perceive and understand these reactions . . . By being aware, you can better understand your own reactions to people, and their reactions to each other. (p.31)

Source: Quinn et al. (2003).

Management in practice

Competing values at IMI?   www.imiplc.com

When Martin Lamb took control of IMI (a UK engineering group, which in 2016 employed 12,000 staff in 75 countries) he introduced significant changes to make the company profitable. He decided to concentrate the business on five sectors of engineering, each associated with high-value products and a strong chance of growth. He moved much manufacturing to low-cost countries, encouraged close links with key customers and aimed to boost innovation. Mr Lamb says:

> This is a fundamental transition, aimed at moving IMI away from an old-established manufacturing enterprise to a company focused on product development and applications of knowledge.

Someone who knew the company well commented:

> I always had the feeling . . . that IMI was a bit introverted and anything that (makes) the company more aggressive on the sales side is to be applauded.

Mr Lamb left the company at the end of 2013, by which time it had become a major manufacturer, and one of the top 100 companies listed on the London Stock Exchange.

2.4 Rational goal models

Adam Smith (1776), the Scottish economist, had explained how pin manufacturers in Glasgow had broken a job previously done by one man into several small steps. A single worker now performed one of these steps repetitively, and this specialisation greatly increased their output. Smith believed this was one of the main ways in which the new industrial system was increasing the wealth of the country.

The availability of powered machinery during the Industrial Revolution enabled business owners to transform manufacturing and mining processes. These technical innovations encouraged, but were not the only reason for, the growth of the factory system. The earlier 'putting-out' system of manufacture, in which people worked at home on materials supplied and collected by entrepreneurs, allowed them great freedom over hours, pace and methods of work; those supplying the materials had little control over the quantity and quality of output. Entrepreneurs with capital found they could secure more control if they built a factory and brought workers into it. Having all workers on a single site meant that:

> coercive authority could be more easily applied, including systems of fines, supervision . . . the paraphernalia of bells and clocks, and incentive payments. The employer could dictate the general conditions of work, time and space; including the division of labour, overall organisational layout and design, rules governing movement, shouting, singing and other forms of disobedience. (Thompson and McHugh 2002, p. 22)

This still left entrepreneurs across Europe and later the United States with the problem of how to manage these new factories. Although domestic and export demand for manufactured goods was high, so was the risk of business failure. Similar problems still arise in rapidly growing manufacturing economies – see 'Management in practice'.

Management in practice

Pressure at Foxconn   www.foxconn.com

In September 2012 Foxconn Technology Group's plant in Taiyuan, China, was the setting for one of China's worst incidents of labour unrest in years. Forty people were arrested after a riot by more than 2000 workers. The company is the largest private employer in China, with more than 1 million workers making products for Apple, including most of the iPhones and iPads. A professor from the school of social sciences at Nanjing University:

> The nature of the Foxconn worker's job – the pressure, the monotony, the tediousness – has not changed. Therefore it is unavoidable that [despite the company awarding pay rises to the staff] incidents like this happen from time to time.

Such is the pressure on the company to meet demand that it planned to increase the workforce at its Zengzhou iPhone factory from 150,000 to 250,000 in four months.

 Sources: *Financial Times*, 25 and 26 September, 2012.
© The Financial Times 2012. All Rights Reserved.

Key ideas   Charles Babbage

Charles Babbage supported and developed Adam Smith's observations. He was an English mathematician better known as the inventor of the first calculating engine. During his work on that project he visited many workshops and factories in England and on the Continent. He then published his reflections on 'the many curious processes and interesting facts' that had come to his attention (Babbage, 1835). He believed that 'perhaps the most important principle on which the economy of a manufacture depends is the division of labour amongst the persons who perform the work' (p. 169).

Babbage also observed that employers in the mining industry had applied the idea to what he called 'mental labour':

> Great improvements have resulted . . . from the judicious distribution of duties . . . amongst those responsible for the whole system of the mine and its government' (p. 202).

He also recommended that managers should know the precise expense of every stage in production. Factories should also be large enough to secure the economies made possible by the division of labour and the new machinery.

Source: Babbage (1835).

Frederick Taylor

Scientific management was a school of management that attempted to create a science of factory production.

The fullest answer to the problems of factory organisation came in the work of Frederick W. Taylor (1856–1915), always associated with the ideas of **scientific management**. An American mechanical engineer, Taylor focused on the relationship between the worker and machine-based production systems:

> the principal object of management should be to secure the maximum prosperity for the employer, coupled with the maximum prosperity for each employee. The words 'maximum prosperity' . . . mean the development of every branch of the business to its highest state of excellence, so that the prosperity may be permanent.' (Taylor, 1917, p. 9)

He believed the way to achieve this was to ensure that each worker reached their state of maximum efficiency, by doing 'the highest grade of work for which his natural abilities fit him' (p. 9). This would follow from detailed control of the process, which would become the managers' primary responsibility: they should concentrate on understanding the production systems, and use this to specify every aspect of the operation. In terms of Morgan's images, the appropriate image would be the machine. Taylor advocated five principles:

- use scientific methods to determine the one best way of doing a task, rather than rely on traditional methods;

- select the best person to do the job so defined, by ensuring they had suitable physical and mental qualities;
- train, teach and develop the worker to follow the defined procedures precisely;
- provide financial incentives to ensure workers follow the prescribed method; and
- move responsibility for planning and organising from the worker to the manager.

Taylor's underlying philosophy was that scientific analysis and fact, not guesswork, should inform management. Like Smith and Babbage before him, he believed that efficiency rose if tasks were routine and predictable. He advocated techniques such as time and motion study, standard tools and individual incentives. Breaking work into small, specific tasks would increase control. Specialist managerial staff would design these tasks and organise the workers:

> The work of every workman is fully planned out by the management at least one day in advance, and each man receives in most cases complete written instructions, describing in detail the task which he is to accomplish, as well as the means to be used in doing the work . . . This task specifies not only what is to be done but how it is to be done and the exact time allowed for doing it. (Taylor, 1917, p. 39)

Taylor also influenced the development of administrative systems such as record keeping and stock control to support manufacturing.

Management in practice   Using work study in the 1990s

Oswald Jones recalls his experience as a work study engineer in the 1990s, where he and his colleagues were deeply committed to the principles of scientific management:

> Jobs were designed to be done in a mechanical fashion by removing opportunities for worker discretion. This had dual benefits: very simple jobs could be measured accurately (so causing less disputes) and meant that operators were much more interchangeable which [improved] efficiency. (p. 647)

Source: Jones (2000).

Managers in many industrial economies adopted Taylor's ideas: Henry Ford was an enthusiastic advocate. When he introduced the assembly line in 1914 the time taken to assemble a car fell from over 700 hours to 93 minutes. Ford also developed systems of materials flow and plant layout, a significant contribution to scientific management (Biggs, 1996; Williams et al.1992).

Increased productivity often came at human cost – more from the way managers implemented them than from the ideas themselves. Trade unions believed Taylor's methods increased unemployment and many people find that working on an assembly line is boring. Nevertheless, many modern industrial plants around the world use these ideas, especially those making clothing and consumer electronic goods, such as mobile phones.

Management in practice   Ford's Highland Park plant

Ford's plant at Highland Park, completed in 1914, introduced predictability and order 'that eliminates all questions of how work is to be done, who will do it, and when it will be done. The rational factory, then, is a factory that runs like a machine' (Biggs, 1996, p.6). Biggs provides abundant evidence of the effects of applying rational production methods:

> The advances made in Ford's New Shop allowed the engineers to control work better. The most obvious and startling change in the entire factory was . . . the constant movement, and the speed of that movement, not only the speed of the assembly line, but the speed of every moving person or object in the plant. When workers moved from one place to another, they were instructed to move fast. Labourers who moved parts were ordered to go faster. And everyone on a moving line worked as fast as the line dictated. Not only were workers expected to produce at a certain rate . . . to earn a day's wages but they also had no choice but to work at the pace dictated by the machine. By 1914 the company employed supervisors called pushers . . . to 'push' the men to work faster.

The 1914 jobs of most Ford workers bore little resemblance to what they had been just four years earlier, and few liked the transformation. . . . As early as 1912, job restructuring sought an 'exceptionally specialised division of labour [to bring] the human element into [the] condition of performing automatically with machine-like regularity and speed'. (Biggs, 1996, p. 132)

Frank and Lillian Gilbreth

Frank and Lillian Gilbreth (1868–1924 and 1878–1972) worked as a husband and wife team advocating scientific management. Frank Gilbreth had been a bricklayer, and knew why work was slow and output unpredictable. He filmed men laying bricks and used this to set out the most economical movements for each task. He specified exactly what the employer should provide, such as trestles at the right height and materials at the right time. Supplies of mortar and bricks (arranged the right way up) should arrive at a time that did not interrupt work. An influential book (Gilbreth, 1911) gave precise guidance on how to reduce unnecessary actions (from 18 to 5), and hence fatigue. The rules and charts would help apprentices:

> (They) will enable the apprentice to earn large wages immediately, because he has . . . a series of instructions that show each and every motion in the proper sequence. They eliminate the 'wrong' way [and] all experimenting (quoted in Spriegel and Myers, 1953, p. 57).

Lillian Gilbreth focused on the psychological aspects of management and workers' welfare, believing that scientific management, properly applied, would enable individuals to reach their potential. Through good systems, careful selection, well-planned training and proper equipment, workers would build their self-respect and pride. In *The Psychology of Management* (1914) she wrote that if workers did something well, and that was made public, they would develop pride in their work and in themselves. She believed workers had enquiring minds, and that management should explain the reasons for work processes:

> Unless the man knows why he is doing the thing, his judgment will never reinforce his work . . . His work will not enlist his zeal unless he knows exactly why he is made to work in the particular manner prescribed (quoted in Spriegel and Myers, 1953, p. 431).

Activity 2.2   What assumptions did they make?

What assumptions did Frederick Taylor and Lillian Gilbreth make about the interests and abilities of industrial workers?

Operational research

Another practice within the rational goal model is **operational research** (OR). This originated in the early 1940s, when the UK War Department faced severe management problems – such as the most effective distribution of radar-linked anti-aircraft gun emplacements, or the safest speed at which convoys of merchant ships should cross the Atlantic (see Kirby (2003) for a non-technical introduction). It formed operational research (OR) teams, with expertise mainly in mathematics and physics. These produced significant results: Kirby shows that while at the start of the London Blitz 20,000 rounds of ammunition were fired for each enemy aircraft destroyed:

> by the summer of 1941 the number had fallen . . . to 4,000 as a result of the operational research (teams) improving the accuracy of radar-based gun-laying (Kirby, 2003, p. 94).

After the war, managers in industry and government saw that operational research techniques could also help to run complex civil organisations. The scale and complexity of business was increasing, and required new techniques to analyse the many interrelated variables. Mathematical models could help, and computers supported increasingly sophisticated models. In the 1950s the steel industry needed to cut the cost of importing iron ore: staff used OR techniques to analyse the most efficient procedures for shipping, unloading and transferring it to steelworks.

The method is widely used in both business and public sectors, where it helps planning in areas as diverse as maintenance, cash flow, inventory and staff scheduling in call centres (e.g. Taylor, 2008). Willoughby and Zappe (2006) illustrate how a university used OR techniques to allocate students to seminar groups.

OR cannot take into account human and social uncertainties, and the assumptions built into the models may be invalid, especially if they involve political interests. The technique clearly contributes to the analysis of management problems, but is only part of the solution.

> **Operational research** is a scientific method of providing (managers) with a quantitative basis for decisions regarding the operations under their control.

Current status

Table 2.1 summarises principles common to rational goal models and their modern application.

Examples of rational goal approaches are common in manufacturing and service organisations – but a company will often use just one of the principles that suits its business. The 'Management in practice' feature gives an example from a service business with highly committed and involved staff – which wishes to give the same high-quality experience wherever the customer is. They use the principle of systematic work methods to achieve this.

Table 2.1 Modern applications of the rational goal model

Principles of the rational goal model	Modern applications
Systematic work methods	Work study and process engineering departments develop precise specifications for processes
Detailed division of labour	Where staff focus on one type of work or customer in manufacturing or service operations
Centralised planning and control	Modern information systems increase the scope for central control of worldwide operations
Low-involvement employment relationship	Using temporary staff as required, rather than permanent employees

> **Management in practice   Making a sandwich at Pret A Manger   www.pret.com**
>
> It is very important to make sure the same standards are adhered to in every single shop, whether you're in Crown Passage in London, Sauchiehall Street in Glasgow, or in New York. The way we do that is very, very detailed training. So, for example, how to make an egg mayonnaise sandwich is all written down on a card that has to be followed, and that is absolutely non-negotiable.
>
> When somebody joins Pret they have a ten-day training plan, and on every single day there is a list of things that they have to be shown, from how to spread the filling of a sandwich right to the edges (that is key to us), how to cut a sandwich from corner to corner, how to make sure that the sandwiches look great in the box and on the shelves. So every single detail is covered. At the end of that ten days the new team member has to pass a quiz, it's called the big scary quiz, it is quite big and it is quite scary, and they have to achieve 90 per cent on that to progress.
>
> Source: Interview with a senior manager at the company.

The methods are widely used in the mass-production industries of newly industri-alised economies such as China and Malaysia. Gamble et al. (2004) found that in such plants:

> Work organisation tended to be fragmented (on Taylorist lines) and routinised, with con-siderable surveillance and control over production volumes and quality (p.403).

Human resource management policies were consistent with this approach – the recruit-ment of operators in Chinese electronics plants was:

> often of young workers, generally female and from rural areas. One firm said its opera-tors had to be 'young farmers within cycling distance of the factory, with good eyesight. Education is not important' (p.404).

> **Activity 2.3   Finding current examples**
>
> Try to find an original example of work that has been designed on rational goal princi-ples. There are examples in office and service areas as well as in factories. Compare your examples with those of colleagues.

2.5   Internal process models

Max Weber

Bureaucracy is a system in which people are expected to follow precisely defined rules and procedures rather than to use personal judgement.

Max Weber (1864–1920) was a German social historian who noted that as societies became more complex, they concentrated responsibility for core activities in large administrative units. Government departments and large industrial or transport businesses were hard to manage, so those in charge created systems – rules and regulations, hierarchy, precise divi-sion of labour, detailed procedures. Weber observed that **bureaucracy** brought routine to office operations just as machines had to production – see 'Key ideas'.

Key ideas   The characteristics of bureaucratic management

- **Rules and regulations:** The formal guidelines that define and control the behaviour of employees. Following these ensures uniform procedures and operations, regardless of an individual's wishes. They enable top managers to coordinate middle managers and, through them, first-line managers and employees. Managers leave, so rules bring stability.
- **Impersonality:** Rules leads to impersonality, which protects employees from the whims of managers. Although the term has negative connotations, Weber believed it ensured fairness by evaluating subordinates objectively on performance rather than subjectively on personal considerations. It limits favouritism.
- **Division of labour:** Managers and employees work on specialised tasks, with the benefits originally noted by Adam Smith – such as that jobs are easier to learn.
- **Hierarchy:** Weber advocated a hierarchy in which jobs were ranked by the amount of authority to make decisions. Each lower position is under the control of a higher position.
- **Authority:** A system of rules, impersonality, division of labour and hierarchy forms an authority structure – the right to make decisions of varying importance at different levels.
- **Rationality:** This refers to using the most efficient means to achieve objectives. Managers should run their organisations logically and 'scientifically' so that all decisions help to achieve the objectives.

Activity 2.4   Bureaucratic management in education?

Reflect on your role as a student and how rules have affected the experience. Try to identify one specific example from your institution to add to those below:

- Rules and regulations – the number of courses you need to pass for a degree
- Impersonality – admission criteria, emphasising exam performance, not friendship
- Division of labour – chemists not teaching management, and vice versa
- Hierarchical structure – to whom your lecturer reports, and to whom they report
- Authority structure – who decides whether to recruit an additional lecturer
- Rationality – appointing new staff to departments that have the highest ratio of students to staff.

Compare your examples with those of other students and consider the effects of these features of bureaucracy on the institution and its students.

Weber was aware that, as well as creating bureaucratic structures, managers were using scientific management techniques to control production and impose discipline on factory work. The two systems complemented each other. Formal structures of management centralise power, and hierarchical organisation aids functional specialisation. Fragmenting tasks, imposing close discipline on employees and minimising their discretion ensures controlled, predictable performance (Thompson and McHugh, 2002).

Weber stressed the importance of a career structure linked to a person's position. This allowed them to move up the hierarchy in a predictable and open way, which would increase their commitment. Rules about selection and promotion brought fairness, when it was common practice to give preference to friends and family. He also believed that officials should work within a framework of rules – the right to give instructions derived from someone's position in the hierarchy. This worked well in large organisations such as government departments and banks. While recognising the material benefits of these methods, Weber saw their costs:

> Bureaucratic rationalisation instigates a system of control that traps the individual within an 'iron cage' of subjugation and constraint . . . For Weber, it is instrumental rationality, accompanied by the rise of measurement and quantification, regulations and procedures, accounting, efficiency that entraps us all in a world of ever-increasing material standards, but vanishing magic, fantasy, meaning and emotion (Gabriel, 2005, p. 11).

Activity 2.5   Gathering evidence on bureaucracy

Rules often receive bad publicity, and obstructive rules frustrate people. To evaluate bureaucracy, collect evidence. Think of a job that you or a friend has held.

- Do supervisors operate within a framework of rules, or do as they wish? What are the effects?
- Do clear rules guide selection and promotion? What are the effects?
- As a customer of an organisation, how have rules and regulations affected your experience?
- Compare what you have found with that prepared by others on your course. To what extent does your evidence illustrate the advantages, and the disadvantages, of bureaucracy?

Henri Fayol

Administrative management is the use of institutions and order rather than relying on personal qualities to get things done.

Managers were also able to draw on Henri Fayol's ideas of **administrative management**. While Taylor focused on production systems, Fayol (1841–1925) devised principles that would apply to the whole organisation. He was an engineer who, in 1860, joined Commentry–Fourchambault– Decazeville, a coal mining and iron foundry company. He earned rapid promotion and was managing director from 1888 until 1918, when he retired – widely seen as one of France's most successful managers (Parker and Ritson, 2005). Throughout his career he kept diaries and notes, which he used in retirement to stimulate debate about management. His book *Administration, Industrielle et Générale* became available in English in 1949 (Fayol, 1949).

Fayol credited his success to the methods he used, not to his personal qualities. He believed that managers should use the principles in the 'Key ideas' box. The term 'principles' did not imply they were rigid or absolute:

> It is all a question of proportion . . . allowance must be made for different changing circumstances . . . the principles are flexible and capable of adaptation to every need; it is a matter of knowing how to make use of them, which is a difficult art requiring intelligence, experience, decision and proportion. (Fayol, 1949, p.14)

In using terms such as 'changing circumstances' and 'adaptation to every need', Fayol anticipated the contingency theories that were developed in the 1960s (see Chapter 10). He was an early advocate of management education:

> Elementary in the primary schools, somewhat wider in the post-primary schools, and quite advanced in higher education establishments. (Fayol, 1949, p.16)

Key ideas	Fayol's principles of management

1 **Division of work:** If people specialise, they improve their skill and accuracy, which increases output. However, 'it has its limits which experience teaches us may not be exceeded'.

2 **Authority and responsibility:** The right to give orders derived from a manager's official authority or their personal authority. 'Wherever authority is exercised, responsibility arises.'

3 **Discipline:** 'Essential for the smooth running of business . . . without discipline no enterprise could prosper.'

4 **Unity of command:** 'For any action whatsoever, an employee should receive orders from one superior only' – to avoid conflicting instructions and resulting confusion.

5 **Unity of direction:** 'One head and one plan for a group of activities having the same objective . . . essential to unity of action, co-ordination of strength and focusing of effort.'

6 **Subordination of individual interest to general interest:** 'The interests of one employee or group of employees should not prevail over that of the concern.'

7 **Remuneration of personnel:** 'Should be fair and, as far as possible, afford satisfaction both to personnel and firm.'

8 **Centralisation:** 'The question of centralisation or decentralisation is a simple question of proportion . . . [the] share of initiative to be left to [subordinates] depends on the character of the manager, the reliability of the subordinates and the condition of the business. The degree of centralisation must vary according to different cases.'

9 **Scalar chain:** 'The chain of superiors from the ultimate authority to the lowest ranks . . . is at times disastrously lengthy in large concerns, especially governmental ones.' If a speedy decision was needed, people at the same level of the chain should communicate directly. 'It provides for the usual exercise of some measure of initiative at all levels of authority.'

10 **Order:** Materials should be in the right place to avoid loss, and the posts essential for the smooth running of the business filled by capable people.

11 **Equity:** Managers should be both friendly and fair to their subordinates – 'equity requires much good sense, experience and good nature'.

12 **Stability of tenure of personnel:** A high employee turnover is not efficient. 'Instability of tenure is at one and the same time cause and effect of bad running.'

13 **Initiative:** 'The initiative of all represents a great source of strength for businesses . . . and . . . it is essential to encourage and develop this capacity to the full. The manager must . . . sacrifice some personal vanity to grant this satisfaction to subordinates . . . a manager able to do so is infinitely superior to one who cannot.'

14 **Esprit de corps:** 'Harmony, union among the personnel of a concern is a great strength in that concern. Effort, then, should be made to establish it.' Fayol suggested doing so by avoiding unnecessary conflict, and using verbal rather than written communication when appropriate.

Source: Fayol (1949).

Current status

Table 2.2 summarises some principles common to the internal process models of management and indicates their modern application.

'Bureaucracy' has critics, who believe it stifles creativity, fosters dissatisfaction and hinders motivation. Others credit it with bringing fairness and certainty to the workplace, where it clarifies roles and responsibilities, makes work effective – and so helps motivation. Adler and Borys (1996) sought to reconcile this by distinguishing between bureaucracy that is:

- enabling – designed to enable employees to master their tasks; and that which is
- coercive – designed to force employees into effort and compliance.

Table 2.2 Examples of modern applications of the internal process model

Some principles of the internal process model	Modern applications
Rules and regulations	All organisations have these, covering areas such as expenditure, safety, recruitment and confidentiality
Impersonality	Appraisal processes based on objective criteria or team assessments, not personal preference
Division of labour	Setting narrow limits to employees' areas of responsibility – found in many organisations
Hierarchical structure	Most company organisation charts show managers in a hierarchy – with subordinates below them
Authority structure	Holders of a particular post have authority over matters relating to that post, but not over other matters
Centralisation	Organisations balance central control of (say) finance or online services with local control of (say) pricing or recruitment
Initiative	Current practice in many firms to increase the responsibility of operating staff
Rationality	Managers are expected to assess issues on the basis of evidence, not personal preference

They studied one aspect of bureaucracy – workflow formalisation (the extent to which an employee's tasks are governed by written rules, etc.) – in companies such as Ford, Toyota and Xerox. They concluded that if employees helped to design and implement a procedure, they were likely to accept it, knowing it would help them work effectively. 'Enabling bureaucracy' had a positive effect on motivation, while imposed rules ('coercive bureaucracy') had a negative effect.

Bureaucratic methods are widely used (Walton, 2005), especially in the public sector and in commercial businesses with geographically dispersed outlets – such as hotels, stores and banks. Customers expect a predictable service wherever they are, so management design centrally-controlled procedures and manuals – how to recruit and train staff, what the premises must look like and how to treat customers. If managers work in situations that require a degree of change and innovation that even an enabling bureaucracy will have trouble delivering, they need other models.

Case study   innocent – the case continues   www.innocentdrinks.com

Another early decision (after finance) was how to set up the roles to build the business. Reed, from advertising, took care of marketing. Balon, who had been selling Virgin Cola, took on sales, while Wright (who had studied manufacturing engineering) was in charge of operations. They agreed that rather than have one chief executive, all three would jointly lead the company. They had assumed they would build a factory but soon realised that it would be smarter to work with a manufacturing partner, as this would allow the founders to focus on the core tasks of growing the business and building the brand. The team found a UK supplier who was able to take on this work, enabling the company to increase sales rapidly with little capital.

Despite the fun image, they ran the business very firmly and everyone had to pull their weight. Staff work in functional teams such as people, finance, production, and fruit and ingredients. The latter is especially significant, as a core value at innocent is that products and production methods are as environmentally sustainable as possible – requiring growers and processing plants around the world to follow specified procedures. Fruit comes from thousands of farms, and the company tries to ensure they are certified by independent environmental and social organisations who certify their agricultural practices and treatment of staff: innocent only buy bananas from plantations with a Rainforest Alliance certificate.

To reduce the carbon footprint they process fruit near the farms, which avoids transporting waste. Packaging is designed for low environmental impact,

and all cartons use cardboard from sources certified by the Forestry Stewardship Council (FSC).

Sources: Based on material from 'Innocent Drinks', a case prepared by William Sahlman (2004), Harvard Business School, Case no. 9-805-031; Germain and Reed (2009); company website.

Case question 2.3

- What examples can you see in the case so far of elements of the 'competing values' framework?

2.6   Human relations models

In the early twentieth century, writers such as Follett and Mayo recognised the limitations of the scientific management perspective.

Mary Parker Follett

Mary Parker Follett (1868–1933) graduated with distinction from Radcliffe College (now part of Harvard University) in 1898, having studied economics, law and philosophy. She took up social work and quickly acquired a reputation as an imaginative and effective professional. She realised the creativity of the group process, and the potential it offered for truly democratic government – which people themselves would have to create.

She advocated replacing bureaucratic institutions with networks in which people themselves analysed their problems and implemented their solutions. True democracy depended on tapping the potential of all members of society by enabling individuals to work in groups to solve a problem and accept personal responsibility for the result. Modern-day community enterprises and tenants' groups are examples of these ideas in action.

Key ideas   Mary Parker Follett on groups

Follett saw the group as an intermediate institution between the solitary individual and the abstract society, and one that enabled people to organise cooperative action. In 1926 she wrote:

> Early psychology was based on the study of the individual; early sociology was based on the study of society. But there is no such thing as the 'individual', there is no such thing as 'society'; there is only the group and the group-unit – the social individual. Social psychology must begin with an intensive study of the group, of the selective processes which go on within it, the differentiated reactions, the likenesses and the unlikenesses, and the spiritual energy which unites them.

Source: Graham (1995), p. 230.

In the 1920s leading industrialists invited Follett to investigate business problems. She again advocated the self-governing principle that would support the growth of individuals and their groups. Conflict was inevitable if people brought valuable differences of view to a problem: the group must resolve the conflict to create what she called an integrative unity of members.

She acknowledged that organisations had to optimise production, but did not accept that the strict division of labour would achieve this (Follett, 1920), as it devalued human creativity. The human side should not be separated from the mechanical side. She believed that people, whether managers or workers, behave as they do because of reciprocal responses. If managers tell people to behave as if they are extensions of a machine, they will do so. She implied that effective managers would not manipulate their subordinates, but train them to use power responsibly:

> managers should give workers a chance to grow capacity or power for themselves.

Graham (1995) provides an excellent review of Follett's work.

Elton Mayo

Elton Mayo (1880–1949) was an Australian who taught logic, psychology and ethics at the University of Queensland. In 1922 he moved to the United States, and in 1926 became Professor of Industrial Research at Harvard Business School, applying psychological methods to industry. He was a good speaker, and his ideas aroused wide interest in academic and business communities (Smith, 1998).

In 1924 managers of the Western Electric Company initiated experiments at their Hawthorne plant in Chicago to discover the effect that changing the physical environment would have on output. The first studied the effects of lighting. The researchers established a control and an experimental group, varied the light level and measured the output. As light rose, so did output. More surprisingly, as light fell, output continued to rise: it also rose in the control group, where conditions had not changed. The team concluded that changing physical conditions had little effect, so set up a more comprehensive experiment to identify other factors.

They assembled a small number of workers in a separate room and systematically altered variables – working hours, length of breaks and providing refreshments. The experienced workers were assembling small relays for telephone equipment. A supervisor was in charge and an observer recorded how workers reacted to successive changes. The researchers took care to prevent external factors disrupting the effects of the variables – for example by explaining what was happening, ensuring workers understood what they should do and listening to their views.

They also varied conditions every two or three weeks, while the supervisor measured output regularly. This showed a gradual, if erratic, increase – even when the researchers returned conditions to those at an earlier stage, as Figure 2.3 shows.

Activity 2.6	**Explaining the trend**

Describe the pattern shown in Figure 2.3. Compare in particular the output in periods 7, 10 and 13. Before reading on, how would you explain this?

In 1928 the company invited Mayo to present the research to a wider audience (Smith, 1998; Roethlisberger and Dickson, 1939; Mayo, 1949). They concluded from the relay-assembly test room experiments that the increase in output was not related to the physical changes, but to changes in the social situation:

> the major experimental change was introduced when those in charge sought to hold the situation humanly steady (in the interests of critical changes to be introduced) by getting the co-operation of the workers. What actually happened was that 6 individuals became a team and the team gave itself wholeheartedly and spontaneously to co-operation in the environment. (Mayo, 1949, p. 64)

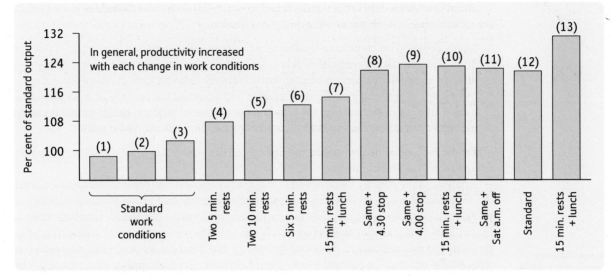

Figure 2.3 The relay-assembly test room – average hourly output per week (as percentage of standard) in successive experimental periods

Source: Based on data from Roethlisberger and Dickson (1939). From *Behaviour in Organisations*, 6th edition, Greenberg and Baron, © 1997. Reprinted by permission of Pearson Education, Inc. Upper Saddle River, NJ.

The group felt special: managers asked for their views, were involved with them, paid attention to them and they had the chance to influence some aspects of the work.

The research team also observed another part of the factory, the bank wiring room, which revealed a different aspect of group working. Workers were paid according to a piece-rate system, in which management pays workers a set amount for each piece they produce. This reflects the assumption that financial incentives will encourage effort, yet the researchers observed that employees regularly produced less than they could have done. They had developed a sense of a normal rate of output, and ensured that all members adhered to this, believing that if they produced, and earned, too much, management would reduce the rate for each piece. Workers exercised sanctions against colleagues who worked too hard (or too slowly), until they conformed. Members who did too much were 'rate-busters' while those who did too little were 'chisellers'. Anyone who told the supervisor was a 'squealer'. Sanctions included being 'binged' – tapped on the shoulder to show that what they were doing was wrong. Managers had little or no control over these groups.

Finally, the research team conducted an extensive interview programme. They began by asking employees about the working environment and how they felt about their job, and then about their life in general. The responses showed that work affected home life more than expected, and domestic circumstances affected their feelings about work. This implied that supervisors needed to think of a subordinate as a complete person, not just as a worker.

Activity 2.7   A comparison with Taylor

Compare this evidence with Frederick Taylor's belief that piece-rates would be an incentive to individuals to raise their performance. What may explain the difference?

Mayo's reflections on the Hawthorne studies drew attention to aspects of human behaviour that practitioners of scientific management had neglected. He introduced the idea of 'social man', in contrast to the 'economic man' at the centre of earlier theories. While financial rewards would influence the latter, group relationships and loyalties would influence the former. On financial incentives, Mayo wrote:

> Man's desire to be continuously associated in work with his fellows is a strong, if not the strongest, human characteristic. Any disregard of it by management or any ill-advised attempt to defeat this human impulse leads instantly to some form of defeat for management itself. In [a study] the efficiency experts had assumed the primacy of financial incentive; in this they were wrong; not until the conditions of working group formation were satisfied did the financial incentives come into operation. (Mayo, 1949, p. 99)

People had social needs that they sought to satisfy – and how they did so may support or oppose management interests.

Analysis of the data by Greenwood et al. (1983) suggested the team had underestimated the influence of financial incentives: being in the experimental group in itself increased a worker's income. Despite possibly inaccurate interpretations (see also a scholarly review by Hassard (2012) of the context in which the Hawthorne studies were conducted), the findings stimulated interest in social factors in the workplace. Scientific management stressed the technical aspects of work. The Hawthorne studies implied that management should give at least as much attention to human factors, leading to the **human relations approach**. Advocates of this believe that employees will work better if managers are interested in their well-being and supervise them humanely.

Human relations approach is a school of management that emphasises the importance of social processes at work.

Current status

The Hawthorne studies have been controversial, and the interpretations questioned. Also, the idea of social man is itself now seen as an incomplete picture of people at work. Providing good supervision and decent working environments may increase satisfaction, but not necessarily productivity. The influences on performance are certainly more complex than Taylor assumed – and also more than the additional factors that Mayo identified.

Other writers have followed and developed Mayo's emphasis on human factors. McGregor (1960), Maslow (1970) and Alderfer (1972) have suggested ways of integrating human needs with those of the organisation as expressed by management. Some of this reflected a human relations concern for employees' well-being. A stronger influence was the changing business environment, which has become less predictable. This encouraged scholars to develop open systems models.

2.7   Open systems models

The open systems approach builds on general systems theory, advocating that managers think of their organisation not as a **system**, but as an **open system**.

A **system** is a set of interrelated parts designed to achieve a purpose.

An **open system** is one that interacts with its environment.

The open systems approach draws attention to the links between the internal parts of a system, and to the links between the whole system and the outside world. The system is separated from its environment by the **system boundary**. An open system imports resources such as energy and materials, which are transformed within the system and leave as goods and services. It emphasises that organisations depend on their environment for resources – see Figure 2.4 (based on Figure 1.2).

A **system boundary** separates the system from its environment.

The figure shows input and output processes, transformation processes and feedback loops. The organisation must satisfy those in the wider environment well enough to ensure that they continue to provide resources. The management task is to sustain those links. **Feedback** refers to information about the performance of the system. It may be deliberate, through customer surveys, or unplanned, such as losing business to a competitor. Feedback can prompt remedial action.

Feedback (systems theory) refers to the provision of information about the effects of an activity.

Another idea is **subsystems**. A course is a subsystem within a department or faculty, the faculty is a subsystem of a university, the university is a subsystem of the higher education system. This, in turn, is part of the whole education system. A course itself has several subsystems – for quality, enrolment, teaching, assessment and so on. In terms of Figure 2.1, each organisational element is a subsystem – technical, people, finance – as Figure 2.5 shows.

Subsystems are the separate but related parts that make up the total system.

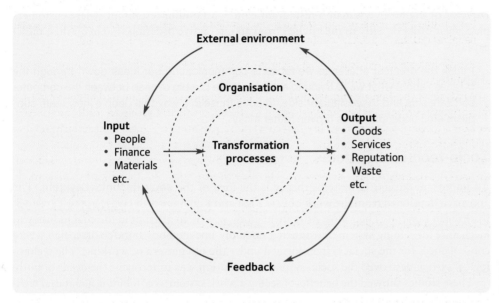

Figure 2.4 The systems model

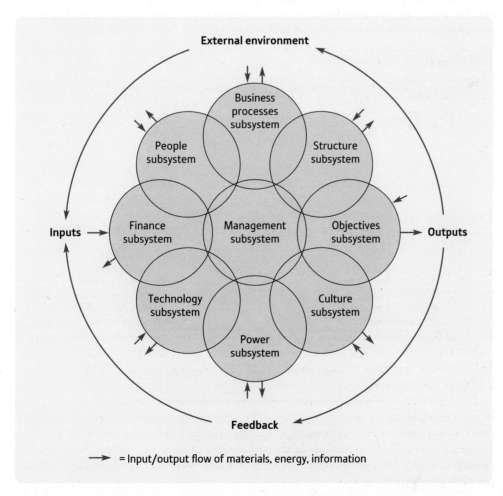

→ = Input/output flow of materials, energy, information

Figure 2.5 Interacting subsystems in organisations

These subsystems interact with each other, and how well people manage these links affects the functioning of the whole: when a university significantly increases the number of students admitted to a popular course, this affects many parts of the system – such as accommodation (*technology*), teaching resources (*people*) and examinations (*business processes*).

A systems approach emphasises the links between systems, and reminds managers that a change in one will have consequences for others. For example, Danny Potter, Managing Director of Inamo (www.inamo-restaurant.com – a London restaurant where customers place their order directly to the kitchen from an interactive ordering system on their table) explains:

> I think the greatest challenge we faced is communicating our ideas down through the business about what we're trying to achieve. There is a big overlap between the computer software side and the restaurant side, to unite those in a way that people [new staff, suppliers etc.] understand has proven rather tricky.

Socio-technical systems

A **socio-technical system** is one in which outcomes depend on the interaction of both the technical and social subsystems.

An important variant of systems theory is the idea of the **socio-technical system**. The approach developed from the work of Eric Trist and Ken Bamforth (1951) at the Tavistock Institute in London. Their most prominent study was of an attempt in the coal industry to mechanise the mining system. Introducing assembly-line methods at the coalface had severe consequences for the social system formed under the old pattern of working. The technological system destroyed the social system: the solution was to reconcile the needs of both.

These studies showed the benefits of seeing a work system as combining a material technology (tools, machinery, techniques) and a social organisation (people and relationships). Figure 2.6 shows an organisation has technical and social systems: it is a socio-technical system, implying that practitioners should aim to integrate both (Mumford, 2006).

Contingency management

A further part of the open systems view is the contingency approach (Chapter 10). This arose from the work of Burns and Stalker (1961) and Woodward (1965) in the United Kingdom, and of Lawrence and Lorsch (1967) in the United States. Their theme is that to

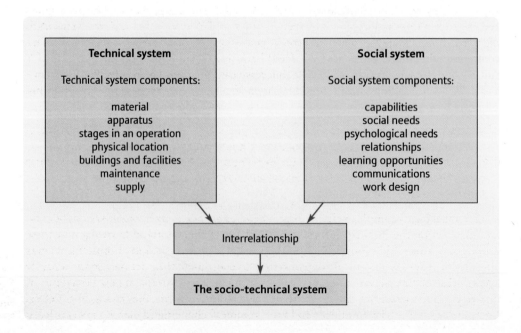

Figure 2.6 The organisation as a socio-technical system

perform well, managers must adapt the structure of the organisation to external conditions. The **contingency approach** tries to identify those aspects of the environment that managers take into account in shaping their organisation – see 'Management in practice' feature.

Management in practice   Hong Kong firms adapt to the environment in China

Child et al. (2003) studied the experience of Hong Kong companies managing affiliated companies in China, predicting that successful firms would be those that adapted their management practices to suit those conditions. Because the business environment at the time was uncertain and difficult for foreign companies, they proposed that a key aspect of management practice in these circumstances would be the extent to which affiliated companies are controlled by, and integrated with, the parent company.

Their results supported this – in this transitional economy successful firms kept their mainland affiliates under close supervision, maintained frequent contact and allowed them little power to make decisions.

Source: Child et al. (2003).

As their environment changes, managers can use contingency perspectives to examine what structure best meets the needs of the business. Contingency theorists emphasise creating organisations that can cope with uncertainty and change, using the values of the open systems model: they also recognise that some functions need to work in a stable and predictable way, using the values of the internal process model.

> **Contingency approaches** to organisational structure are those based on the idea that the performance of an organisation depends on having a structure that is appropriate to its environment.

Complexity theory

A popular theme in management thinking is that of managing complexity, which arises from feedback between the parts of linked systems. People in organisations, both as individuals and as members of a web of working relationships, react to an event or an attempt to influence them. That reaction leads to a further response – setting off a complex feedback process. Figure 2.7 illustrates this for three individuals, X, Y and Z.

If we look at the situation in Figure 2.7 from the perspective of X, then X is in an environment made up of Y and Z. X discovers what Y and Z are doing, chooses how to respond and then acts. That action has consequences for Y and Z, which they discover. This leads them to choose a response, which has consequences that X then discovers, and acts on. This continues indefinitely. Every act by X feeds back to have an impact on the next acts of Y and Z – and the same is true of Y and Z. Successive interactions create a feedback system – and the sequence shown for the individuals in the figure also occurs between organisations. These then make up complex systems:

> In contrast to simple systems, such as the pendulum, which have a small number of well-understood components, or complicated systems, such as a Boeing jet, which have many components that interact through predefined coordination rules. . . complex systems typically have many components that can autonomously interact through emergent rules. (Amaral and Uzzi, 2007, p. 1033)

In management, complex systems arise whenever agents (people, organisations or communities) act on the (limited) information available to them without knowing how these actions may affect other (possibly distant) agents, nor how the action of those agents may affect them. There is no central control system to coordinate their actions, so the separate agents organise themselves spontaneously, creating new structures and new behaviours as they respond to themselves and their environment: in other words, they change themselves. **Complexity theory** tries to understand how complex, changing (dynamic) systems learn

> **Complexity theory** is concerned with complex dynamic systems that have the capacity to organise themselves spontaneously.

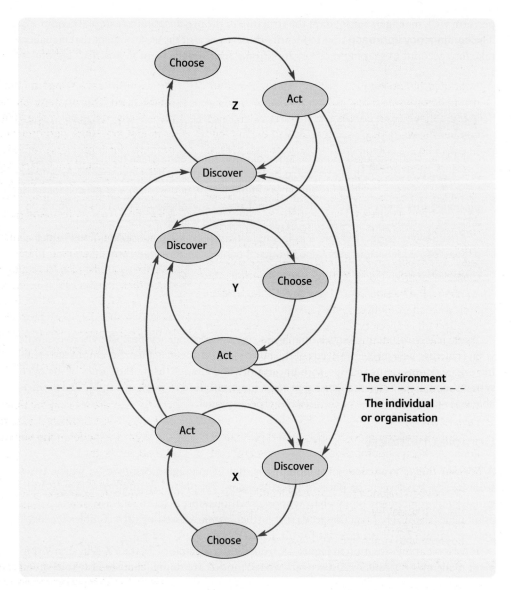

Figure 2.7 Feed-back in non-linear systems

and adapt from their internal experiences and from their interactions with similar systems.

These ideas on self-organising systems have implications for management, especially for how they cope with change and innovation. The management skill is to balance extremes. If an organisation is too stable it will stifle innovation, but if it is too unstable it will disintegrate.

Linear systems are those in which an action leads to a predictable reaction. If you light a fire in a room, the thermostat will turn the central heating down. **Non-linear systems** systems are those in which outcomes are less predictable. If managers reduce prices they will be surprised if sales match the forecast – they cannot predict the reactions of competitors, changes in taste, or new products. Circumstances in the outside world change in ways that management cannot anticipate, so while short-term consequences of an act are clear, long-run ones are not.

Linear systems are those in which an action leads to a predictable reaction.

Non-linear systems are those in which small changes are amplified through many interactions with other variables so that the eventual effect is unpredictable.

Case study   innocent – the case continues   www.innocentdrinks.com

Reed and his colleagues realised that while continental Europe was a major potential market, in each country they would compete with large established companies, who could spend heavily to defend their position. So in September 2008 they decided to raise more finance: Coca-Cola invested £30 million in return for 20 per cent of the shares. Some customers complained, believing that selling part of the business ran counter to its values. The founders reiterated that they remain in charge and that the deal enabled the company to continue growing, and spreading its values. Even though in 2016, after a further sale of the founders' shares, Coca-Cola now owns most of the company, the founders retain a minority shareholding and sit on an executive committee.

A friend, Dan Germain, joined the business in 1999 and suggested printing offbeat messages on the cartons, which became a brand 'hallmark' as the tone was offbeat, honest, irreverent and distinctly non-corporate. Germain became the unofficial voice of the brand – writing labels and a customer newsletter.

As the company grew it incorporated more traditional marketing approaches, such as bus and London Underground advertisements:

> We have to balance Big Brand with Little Brand – the former being a row of cartons on a supermarket shelf, the latter being an innocent fridge covered with grass in a café next door.

An experienced marketing consultant commented:

> They have a really astute understanding of what makes a young metropolitan audience tick. It's almost anti-marketing.

They want to prove that business can be a force for good:

> We want to leave things a little better than we found them. Our strategy for doing so is simple – firstly, only ever make 100% natural products that are 100% good for people. Secondly, procure our ingredients ethically. Thirdly, use ecologically sound packaging materials. Fourth, reduce and offset our carbon emissions across our entire business system. Fifth, lead by example at Fruit Towers by doing good things.

The company gives 10 per cent of annual profits to the innocent foundation, which supports charities around the world helping to reduce hunger, while in the UK it runs 'the big knit'. This invites people to knit woolly hats, which are placed on the bottles – and for each one sold, innocent gives 25p to Age UK. By 2015 this had raised £1.6 million for the charity.

innocent staff constantly communicate with customers – thousands of whom receive a weekly email. As one observer noted:

> Consumers are looking for businesses to trust, and they want to reward that trustworthiness. innocent is a model of the values all businesses should aspire to.

Sources: Based on material from 'Innocent drinks', a case prepared by William Sahlman (2004), Harvard Business School, Case no. 9-805-031; Germain and Reed (2009); company website.

Case questions 2.4

- What are the likely advantages and disadvantages to the innocent brand of being 90 per cent owned by Coca-Cola?
- Why might Coca-Cola have decided to invest in this small UK company?

2.8   Integrating themes

Entrepreneurship

From the perspective of the competing values model, entrepreneurs starting a new business are likely to take an open systems view, and focus on innovation, adaptation, growth and resource acquisition – though as the business develops other values will become significant.

They need to develop practices that help them do that: Genius, in the 'Management in practice' feature, illustrates this.

Management in practice

genius   www.geniusglutenfree.com

Lucinda Bruce-Gardyne created Genius in 2009 to supply gluten-free bread to people who have an allergy to gluten (a substance present in wheat). She had been a cookery writer, and when her son was found to be gluten intolerant she began baking gluten-free loaves at home, and was considering supplying local shops where she lived. This changed when Sir Bill Gemmell, who had the same condition, received one of her loaves by chance. He was an entrepreneur who had founded Cairn Energy, and was so impressed by the loaf that he offered his services, and financial backing, to help Ms Bruce-Gardyne create a much larger enterprise. In 2016 it was the UK's leading bakery brand within the 'free from' category.

Ms Bruce-Gardyne's 'model' for her success:

- **Find a backer who shares the vision** and is deeply familiar with the needs of the customers.
- **Surround yourself with the skills you lack,** so you can focus on where you can add value - in this case on product development and quality control.
- **Use social media to connect with customers,** and become aware quickly of any snags.
- **Listen and learn,** but stick to your instincts of what is right.

Source: *Financial Times,* 11 January 2012, p. 14.
© The Financial Times 2012. All Rights Reserved.

Successful entrepreneurs develop their models through experience and exchanging ideas.

Sustainability

Current attention to sustainability is an example of the values associated with the open systems model – recognising, in this case, that human and natural systems interact with each other in unpredictable ways. Senge et al. (2008) show how reducing a company's carbon footprint not only reduces environmental damage but also makes the business more efficient.

In 2002 General Electric began making alternative energy technologies (such as desalination systems) when oil was $25 a barrel. As oil prices rose, the company prospered as demand for non-oil energy systems increased. Customers, too, played a role – the authors quote the GE chief executive:

> When society changes its mind, you better be in front of it and not behind it, and this is an issue on which society has changed its mind. As CEO, my job is to get out in front of it, or you're going to get ploughed under.

Governments and other institutions are developing policies to try to limit the damage that human activity does to the planet. This work tends to reflect values of order, regulation and control – values associated with the internal process model. Others, like GE, work on the same problem, sustainability, from the values associated with the open systems model. Both perspectives help towards a more sustainable economy.

Internationalisation

The theories outlined here were developed when most business was conducted within national boundaries, although with substantial foreign trade. Hofstede's (1991) study increased awareness of differences in national cultures, and their implications for those managing internationally. There is much more about national cultures in Chapter 4. Theories of international management are still evolving and there is still uncertainty about whether, and in what ways, management models differ between countries.

Taras et al. (2011) review hundreds of empirical studies of culture, and conclude that while there are indeed observable differences in national culture, the evidence is unclear about their effect on management processes. They cite the example of a large US company that decided to expand the business in Europe, mainly by buying established companies. While theories of cultural difference imply that in such circumstances the acquiring firm should take account of local practices, the company did the opposite – rapidly imposing US practices and ways of working upon their (new) European employees. Cultural theorists would have predicted a disastrous outcome – but Taras et al. (2011) claim the venture succeeded – possibly beyond expectations. They contrast this with Walmart, which went on a similar route to expansion that was not a success.

Governance

Theories of corporate governance, like those of management, continue to evolve in response to evidence that current arrangements are no longer suitable for the job. Pfeffer and Sutton (2006) present the case for basing management actions on substantiated theories and relevant evidence. They acknowledge the difficulties of putting that into practice, in part because evidence-based management depends on being willing to put aside conventional ways of working.

Nevertheless they identify practices that could help those responsible for corporate governance to foster an evidence-based approach:

> If you ask for evidence of efficacy every time a change is proposed, people will sit up and take notice. If you take the time to parse the logic behind that evidence, people will become more disciplined in their own thinking. If you treat the organisation like an unfinished prototype and encourage trial programs, pilot studies, and experimentation – and reward learning from these activities, even when something new fails – your organisation will begin to develop its own evidence base. And if you keep learning while acting on the best knowledge you have and expect your people to do the same – if you have what has been called 'the attitude of wisdom' – then your company can profit from evidence-based management. (p.70)

Such an approach would bring substantial change to the way in which many organisations operate.

Summary

1 **Explain the value of models of management, and compare unitary, pluralist and radical perspectives:**
   - Models represent more complex realities, help to understand complexity and offer a range of perspectives on the topic. Their predictive effect is limited by the fact that people interpret information subjectively in deciding how to act.
   - A unitary perspective emphasises the common purpose of organisational members, while the pluralist draws attention to competing interest groups. Those who take a radical perspective believe that organisations reflect deep divisions in society, and attempts to integrate interests ignore persistent differences in the distribution of power.

2 **State the structure of the competing values framework and evaluate its contribution to our understanding of management**
   - A way of integrating the otherwise confusing range of theories of management. Organisations experience tensions between control and flexibility and between an external and

an internal focus. Placing these on two axes allows theories to be allocated to one of four types – rational goal, internal process, human relations and open systems.

3   **Summarise the rational goal, internal process, human relations and open systems models and evaluate what each can contribute to a manager's understanding of their role:**

- Rational goal (Taylor, the Gilbreths and operational research):
  - clear direction leads to productive outcomes, with an emphasis on rational analysis and measurement.
- Internal process (Weber, Fayol):
  - routine leads to stability, so an emphasis on defining responsibility, documentation and defined administrative processes.
- Human relations (Follett, Mayo):
  - people are motivated by social needs, and recognising these will secure commitment. Practices include considerate supervision, participation and seeking consensus.
- Open systems (socio-technical, contingency and chaos):
  - continual innovation secures external support, achieved by creative problem solving.

These theories have contributed to the management agendas in these ways:

- Rational goal – through techniques such as time and motion study, work measurement and a variety of techniques for planning operations; also the narrow specification of duties, and the separation of management and non-management work.
- Internal process – clear targets and measurement systems, and the creation of clear management and reporting structures. Making decisions objectively on the basis of rules and procedures, rather than on favouritism or family connections.
- Human relations – considerate supervision, consultation and participation in decisions affecting people.
- Open systems – understanding external factors and being able and willing to respond to them through individual and organisational flexibility. Non-linear systems are those in which actions may have unexpected consequences.

4   **Use the model to classify the dominant form in two or more business units, and to gather evidence about the way this affects the roles of managing in those units**

- You can achieve this objective by asking people (perhaps others on your course) to identify which of the four cultural types in the competing values framework most closely correspond to the unit in which they work. Ask them to note ways in which that cultural type affects their way of working. Compare the answers systematically, and review the results.

5   **Consider which of the 'competing values' you feel most comfortable with, and use that to help develop the skill of self-awareness**

- Becoming more aware of the values that lie behind actions helps clarify the links between the two, and so how to learn to act more consistently. Such self-awareness may also help relationships with those holding different values.

6   **Show how ideas from the chapter add to your understanding of the integrating themes**

- Entrepreneurship is inherently associated with the open systems model, but within that those starting a new business need to create a model of management that is suitable for them.
- Increased attention to sustainability is an example of the values associated with the open systems model, while attempts to regulate and control activities is perhaps associated with internal process values.
- The alternative models in the competing values framework remind us that values that shape management practice in one country do not necessarily have the same influence in others.
- Pfeffer and Sutton's ideas on evidence-based management offer a model that those seeking more effective governance and control could use – challenging managers to back up ideas with more rigorous evidence and analysis to reduce risk

Test your understanding

1 Name three ways in which theoretical models help the study of management.

2 What are the assumptions of the unitary, pluralist and critical perspectives?

3 Name at least four of Morgan's organisational images and give an original example of each.

4 Draw the two axes of the competing values framework, and then place the theories outlined in this chapter in the most appropriate sector.

5 List Taylor's five principles of scientific management and evaluate their use in examples of your choice.

6 What did Lillian Gilbreth advocate about the way managers should act towards staff?

7 What did Mary Parker Follett consider to be the value of groups in a community?

8 Compare Taylor's assumptions about people with those of Mayo. Evaluate the accuracy of these views by reference to an organisation of your choice.

9 Compare the conclusions reached by the Hawthorne experimenters in the relay-assembly test room with those in the bank wiring room.

10 Is an open system harder to manage than a closed system, and if so, why?

11 How does uncertainty affect organisations and how do non-linear perspectives help to understand this?

12 Summarise an idea from the chapter that adds to your understanding of the integrating themes.

Think critically

Think about the way your company, or one with which you are familiar, approaches the task of management.

- What **assumptions** about the nature of management appear to guide what people do? Which of the four models do they seem to prefer? Which of these is closest to your preference?

- What factors such as the history or current **context** may have affected that? Does the approach appear to be right for the company and stakeholders?

- From your work on this chapter, what **alternative** ways to manage the business might be suitable, as shown by evidence from other companies? May those be closer to your preferred values? What **limitations** can you see in the theories and evidence presented in the chapter? Can you see limitations in the model associated with your preferred values?

Develop a skill – self-awareness

Self-awareness is a useful attribute in building a satisfying career, and this exercise is intended to help you become more aware of the values that guide what you do.

- **Assessment:** Assess how self-aware you are – are you conscious of the ideas and beliefs that lie behind what you think or express? Are you conscious of people who seem to be more – or less – self-aware than you are?

- **Learning:** Section 2.3 outlined the competing values model, and the 'Key ideas' feature on page 44 introduced the benefits of self-awareness. Read both of these again. Summarise the main ideas in the framework. Why is knowing your preferred values likely to help you in what you do?

- **Analysis:** Decide which of the values corresponds most closely to how you prefer to relate to others, how you get things done, what gives you satisfaction.

  - Read again the section that outlines that model of management (e.g. if you preferred the rational goal model, re-read Section 2.4).

- Identify someone (whom you know, or can read about) who seems to use that approach to managing, or is close to it. Consider what they do, what the effects seem to be and what you can learn from them. Try to identify specific practices. Examples you may look for could be:
- *Rational goal* – setting clear goals, showing people exactly how to do a job.
- *Internal process* – making responsibilities clear, setting out how to check progress.
- *Human relations* – being a considerate supervisor, checking for good work–life balance.
- *Open systems* – identifying subsystems and how they affect each other, taking account of external changes.
- **Practice:** Identify one such practice associated with your values, which may help you become more skilful in applying those values to what you do. Identify a suitable opportunity or activity in which you can try to use it in the next week.
  - Practise it, and record the results to see what you can learn from the experience.
  - Ideally, discuss your work with a colleague who preferred different values, which led them to a different approach.
- **Application:** Decide on another opportunity to practise this, or another, technique linking values and practice in the next week.

Read more

Drucker, P. (1954), *The Practice of Management,* Harper, New York.

Still the classic introduction to general management.

Fayol, H. (1949), *General and Industrial Management,* Pitman, London.

The original works of these writers are short and lucid. Taylor (1917) contains illuminating detail that brings the ideas to life, and Fayol's (1949) surviving ideas came from only two short chapters, which again are worth reading in the original.

Heracleous, L. (2013), 'Quantum Strategy at Apple Inc', *Organisational Dynamics,* vol. 42, no. 2, pp. 92–9.

Shows how Apple's ability to follow two apparently conflicting models at the same time has been part of its success.

Kiechel, W. (2012), 'The Management Century', *Harvard Business Review,* vol. 90, no. 11, pp. 62–75.

A useful, illustrated, historical overview of management theory, prepared to mark the 90th anniversary of *Harvard Business Review.*

Shirley, S. and Askwith, R. (2013), Let IT Go: The story of the Entrepreneur Turned Philanthropist, Andrews UK Limited, Luton.

The autobiography of Dame Stephanie Shirley who came to the UK as a refugee in 1939, built a software business and gives most of her fortune to charities. An extraordinary and inspiring life.

Taylor, F.W. (1917), *The Principles of Scientific Management,* Harper, New York.

Go online

These websites have appeared in the chapter:

www.innocentdrinks.com
www.imiplc.com
www.foxconn.com
www.ba.com
www.firstgroup.com
www.pret.com
www.geniusglutenfree.com

Visit two of the sites in the list, or those of other organisations in which you are interested, and navigate to the pages dealing with recent news, press or investor relations.

What are the main issues that the organisations appear to be facing?

Compare and contrast the issues you identify on the two sites.

What models of management may be relevant for those working in, and managing, these organisations?

PART 1 CASE
APPLE INC.

www.apple.com

The company

In the 2015 financial year Apple sold 231 million iPhones, a 37 per cent increase on the previous year; it also sold 55 million iPads, a decline of 19 per cent on 2014. It received revenue of $155 billion and $23 billion respectively from these two products, together accounting for 76 per cent of total sales that year. In the intensely competitive market for computer electronics, Apple had had a good year – though in the management commentary with the financial results it cautioned investors about the difficulties it would face in maintaining that rate of growth.

The company began in 1976, designing and making personal computers. At the time these were a novelty: most computers then were 'mainframe' machines, operated by companies and public bodies. By 2013 the company's product range included the Apple Mac personal computer, iTunes (launched in 2001), iPod digital music player (also 2001), iPhone (the company's first move into mobile phones – 2007), MacBook (2008) and iPad tablet (2010). The iPhone success was especially significant as it showed the ability of a computer maker to succeed in the mobile phone sector. The attractive design enabled the company quickly to become the leading player in the industry, helped by the thousands of applications available for the iPhone through the online Apple Store – which competitors such as Nokia and Motorola could not match.

When the late Steve Jobs and Steven Wozniak set up the business in 1976, each invested $1300. They secured funds from private investors, and in 1980 rapid growth again required more finance – which they raised by selling 4.6 million shares in the company to the public, for $22 each. In early 2016 these were trading on the New York Stock Exchange at about $110. A measure of the value it was adding to resources is the operating profit margin – broadly the difference between its expenditure and income. In 2015 this was over 40.1 per cent (38.6 per cent the previous year), helped by strong sales of the iPhone and the declining cost of producing each one as sales increased.

The table shows some measures of performance in the two most recent financial years.

© Sean Gallup/Getty Images

Measures of performance to 30 September in each year

	2015	2014
Total net sales ($m)	233,715	182,795
Cost of sales ($m)	140,089	112,258
Gross margin ($m)	93,626	70,537
Gross margin% of sales	40.1	38.6
Net income before tax ($m)	72,515	53,483
Net income after tax ($m)	53,394	39,510
Earnings per share ($)	9.28	6.49
Dividend per share	1.98	1.82

Source: Apple Inc. Annual Reports filed with the United States Securities and Exchange Commission.

Managing to add value
Management style

Steve Jobs typified the distinctive business environment of 'Silicon Valley' – the area in California where many of the world's leading electronic businesses have their headquarters. He created a corporate culture characterised by an intense work ethic and casual dress code. Michael Moritz, who observed Jobs for many years, noted in his biography, published before Jobs' death:

Steve is a founder of the company [and the best founders] are unstoppable, irrepressible forces of nature. . . Steve has always possessed the soul of the questioning poet – someone a little removed from the rest of us who, from an early age, beat his own path. [He has a sharp] sense of the aesthetic – that influence is still apparent in all Apple products and advertising. Jobs' critics will say he can be wilfull, obdurate, irascible, temperamental and stubborn [which is true, but he is also a perfectionist]. There is also. . . an insistent, persuasive and mesmerising salesman. (Moritz, 2009, pp. 13–14)

In 1983 Jobs was chairman and Mike Markkula, who had joined the company at the start, was chief executive. Markkula had never intended to stay as CEO, and now wished to leave. The Board of Directors (including Jobs) decided to appoint John Sculley, an executive from Pepsi-Cola, to the post. The two men frequently disagreed and in 1985 Jobs (then aged 30) left the company. Apple did not perform well under Sculley, and in 1997 the Board persuaded Jobs to return to the company, and soon appointed him CEO.

He began to rebuild Apple by an insistent focus on a limited product range – cutting costs, staff and undistinguished products. The focus was the iMac – an immediate success since it delivered what consumers wanted by combining compelling designs with advanced technology. Apple again became known for sleek design and an elegant user interface. He also hired new senior managers with whom he had worked, skilled in software, hardware, retail and manufacturing. They included Jonathan Ive, a respected designer, and Tim Cook who joined in 1999. He became Chief Executive when Jobs died in 2012.

Jobs had insisted that a named individual be responsible for every task, however large or small: 'at Apple you can figure out exactly who is responsible'. This principle is enshrined in the 'Directly Responsible Individual' – DRI: this is the person the company calls to account if anything goes wrong:

The DRI is a powerful management tool, enshrined as Apple corporate best practice, passed on by word of mouth to new generations of employees. Any effective meeting at Apple will have an action list – next to it will be the DRI. (Lashinsky, 2012, pp. 67–8).

Functional structure

Apple is organised by function, so people are hired and promoted for their ability in that function, not for their general management skills. Steve Jobs explained:

[As companies grow large, they] lose their vision. They insert lots of layers of middle management between the people running the company and the people doing the work. They no longer have an inherent feel or passion about the products. The creative people, who are the ones who care passionately, have to persuade five layers of management to do what they know is the right thing to do (quoted in Lashinsky, 2012, p. 71).

When Jobs returned to Apple he found it had become like the companies he disparaged – good technical people had moved into general management roles.

What was wrong with Apple wasn't individual contributors . . . we had to get rid of about four thousand middle managers. (Lashinsky, 2012, p. 71)

At the top of the company is the CEO (since 2012, Tim Cook), supported by the executive team, whose purpose is to coordinate the business and set the tone for the company. It comprises the head of each function directly involved in Apple products – marketing, hardware and software engineering, operations, retail stores, internet services and design – together with heads of finance and legal. The team meets weekly to review the company's product plans – which it does in great detail. Teams throughout the company prepare material for their respective bosses to inform the presentation by their functional head:

Everybody is working towards these Monday presentations [says a former Apple designer]. There is executive review of every significant project. (Lashinsky, 2012, p. 71)

Product innovation

Jobs continually stressed the significance of products rather than profit – believing that if management focused on providing high-quality, innovative products, profit would follow (Isaacson, 2011). He believed that:

putting products ahead of profit was the quality . . . responsible for the success that made it the world's most valuable technology company, with a stock market value (in late 2011) two-thirds higher than its nearest competitor, Microsoft. (*Financial Times,* 25 October 2011, p. 18)

Apple engineers focus obsessively on the minutest details of how the customer will experience the product – including the box, the last thing the customer will see before the product:

Obsessing over details and bringing a Buddhist level of focus to a narrow assortment of offerings sets Apple apart from its competitors . . . good design subliminally telegraphs to consumers that the manufacturer cares about them. This, in turn, creates a bond between brand and consumer. The genesis of most Apple products is simply Apple's desire to make them. Not focus groups. Not reader surveys. Not a competitive analysis . . . The iPhone is a classic case in point. Prior to the device's introduction, Apple executives typically hated their smartphones. 'That's why we decided to do our own' said Jobs. (Lashinsky 2012, pp. 53–4)

This involved analysing the other products and adapting ideas from them to create the distinctive iPhone. Moritz (2009) writes:

> Jobs' achievement . . . was to ensure that a technology company employing tens of thousands of people could make and sell millions of immensely complicated yet exquisite products that were powerful and reliable, while also containing a lightness of being . . . [the achievement] is to steer, coax, nudge, prod, cajole, inspire, berate, organise and praise – on weekdays and at weekends – the thousands of people all around the world required to produce something that drops into pockets and handbags or . . . rests on a lap or sits on a desk. (pp. 339–40)

At Apple, the design philosophy is that products start with their industrial designers (led by Briton Jonathan Ive). Design is pre-eminent – everyone else must conform to the designer's vision.

Tight control

The company has traditionally used an 'integrated model', in the sense that it controllled the hardware and software components in its devices, as well as the services on which they rely. Jobs believed that integration is the only way to make 'perfect' products. As they design hardware and software, staff aim to give users an exceptionally good experience of the compatibility between all Apple devices and the applications that run on them (see below – Collaboration).

Once design is underway, the rest of the company moves in, especially engineering and supply-chain teams, working to the Apple New Product Process. This details each stage in a product's creation, prescribes who touches it, assigns functional responsibilities and shows when assignments will be completed (Lashinsky, 2012, p. 56).

The emphasis on control was extended when the company launched the Apple Stores. This was unusual, as manufacturers rarely become successful retailers. The Apple network of dealers and Apple Stores ensures that the image of the brand is closely dovetailed with the products themselves. The App Store has exceeded

expectations, with thousands of software developers offering their products on the site.

Secrecy

As well as investing heavily in R&D, the company is intensely secretive and protective of its intellectual property (IP) – the ideas and designs behind the products. Most companies protect these from outsiders, but Apple also has high internal secrecy. Staff do not discuss projects outside their immediate team, and new recruits are briefed on the strict security regime, including the penalty for revealing Apple secrets, intentionally or unintentionally: swift termination (Lashinsky, 2012, p. 36). When Apple launches a product, the secrecy creates curiosity and extensive media coverage – without heavy advertising.

It also helps to retain the 'start-up' mentality that the company values. As engineers work in isolated small teams they have little chance to contact those outside their team:

> By selectively keeping employees from concerning themselves with colleagues elsewhere in a giant company, Apple creates the illusion that [they] work for a start-up. (Lashinsky, 2012, p. 73)

Small teams have long been integral to the Apple way of working, and frequently major projects are assigned to very small teams – two engineers wrote the vast amount of code required for a feature of the iPad, which many companies would give to a team of ten. Small teams help foster the start-up mentality.

Collaboration

While internally Apple displays tight control and secrecy, it is the hub of a creative network. It excels at cooperating with partners and rivals when this will benefit customers – an early example being when Jobs saw the value of 'mouse' technology in another company's product, which his engineers then incorporated into the first Macs. The company recognised that in the rapidly developing mobile phone industry, Apple could never generate consistently strong products and services on its own, so encouraged selected independent developers to build applications for the iPhone. These sell through the App Store, earning revenue for both the developer and Apple, while the huge range of apps available reinforces the iPhone's appeal to customers. Developers can of course choose to work for other companies, if they appear to be moving ahead of Apple.

In 2014 it significantly extended the scope of collaboration by opening up more aspects of the iPhone operating system to independent developers. This will enable them, for example, to develop and sell their own keyboards, which customers can download to use with their iPhone. Analysts said this represented a big philosophical shift, as it will allow developers to design features for the iPhone, without Apple having to approve them.

In the same year it entered a partnership with IBM to sell iPads and iPhones to big corporate customers – a further sign that Apple is becoming more willing to work with other businesses.

It also collaborates in manufacturing, which it outsources to overseas suppliers, especially Foxconn, an immense Chinese supplier that meets most of Apple's requirements. Under Tim Cook, the company has committed to removing 'conflict minerals' (those from mines in conflict zones) from its products, and is seeking new agreements with suppliers like Foxconn to improve working conditions – even though this will increase costs. It claims to monitor supplier performance closely, and acts swiftly when it finds violation of its required labour standards.

Aspects of Apple's context

Apple has succeeded by offering products that appeal to consumers in previously separate industries. Its continued success will depend on how well it can do this, especially as competitors develop rival products.

Before Apple launched the iPhone the mobile phone industry was dominated by Nokia, with Sony Ericsson and Motorola having smaller but significant shares of the market. Apple's success with the iPhone has been challenged by devices using Google's Android software, notably Samsung and its Galaxy range. In 2012 Samsung had about 33 per cent of the global smartphone market and Apple 16 per cent: the rest of the market was fragmented among many companies.

Apple's launch of the iPad helped to transform personal computing – one estimate was that tablets would take almost a fifth of the global PC market by 2013 (data quoted in *Financial Times,* 31 May 2011, p. 21). By late 2012 Apple's share of the global tablet market had fallen from two-thirds to half since the middle of the year. Many lower-priced competitors such as Samsung and Amazon had entered the market.

In 2015 China was Apple's second-largest market after the US, with sales there valued at $59 billion (25 per cent of the total), 84 per cent more than 2014. It still faces tough competition in China from Asian suppliers such as Samsung and Huawei.

The many innovative companies in the industry vigorously defend their product patents. Apple is involved in many disputes in which it accuses others of stealing its intellectual property, especially Samsung which it regards as an especially serious competitor.

So-called 'cloud computing' is likely to become a significant feature of the industry, allowing, for example, iPhone users to float their music and apps on to an iPad or a TV and then back again. If Apple were to position itself as a cloud-services company it would be competing with Google, Microsoft and Amazon.

Current management dilemmas

In 2016 Apple was facing several issues to ensure that it retained its prominent position in the computing and telecommunications industry, especially ensuring that it continued the flow of innovations that its loyal customers and investors expected.

Strategic direction

A threat to the company's dominance could come from strong competitors such as Google and Microsoft, both of whom were targeting segments of Apple's market with new products. By 2015, over half of the company's revenue came from the iPhone. Apple appeared to some to be becoming a handset company, which is fickle and subject to sudden changes of fashion.

It is considering offering more services (such as cloud computing) but, as a hardware and software company, can it be equally successful in services?

Apple's shareholders have become used to high growth so they, and financial journalists, may have unrealistic expectations. They could begin to demand higher dividend payments, which would mean less money available to invest in the R&D essential for new products.

Innovation

In 2015 about $155 billion of Apple's revenue came from the iPhone, and another $23 billion from the iPad – neither of which existed eight years ago. This remarkable achievement serves as a reminder of the need to keep investing heavily in new products – able to earn equally large revenues in just a few years. In early 2015 there were reports of investors becoming restless at the lack of significant new launches.

An opportunity the company has been publicising is 'cloud computing', which would enable users to integrate all the information they have on their several Apple devices to be accessed at any time, often on other devices. This would enhance the user's experience, and also make it less likely that they would move to a rival device, since that would reduce easy access to their data. Apple may not have as strong a position in that market as companies that were created as services companies, such as Google or Amazon.

Management

By 2015 Tim Cook had emerged from Steve Jobs' shadow, and was imprinting the company with his values and priorities, bringing in new senior managers, opening Apple to more collaboration and paying more attention to social issues. He has added three women to what was previously a white-male-dominated executive team and changed Apple's Board charter to seeking out candidates from minorities when appointing directors.

In 2012 Cook appointed Jonathan Ive, the company's hardware designer, to be head of software as well. He became responsible for all the company's user interfaces, giving him final say in the design and 'feel' of products and services. This perhaps recreated the dominant role that Steve Jobs played in this regard, ensuring the deep integration typical of Apple products.

Sources: Moritz (2009); *The Economist,* 1 October 2009; Lashinsky (2012); Isaacson (2011); *Financial Times,* 27 August 2012, 31 October 2012, 21 December 2012, 23 April 2013, 3 June 2013, 4 June 2014, 12 December 2014, 9 March 2015, p. 16, 15 July 2016, p. 24.

Part case questions

(a) Relating to Chapters 1 and 2

1 Refer to Table 1.1, and the 'unique challenges' listed in the right-hand column. Identify examples of these challenges that Apple faced, as it evolved from 'business start-up' to 'international business'.

2 Refer to Table 1.2, and the 'Activity' suggested alongside each role. Identify as many examples as you can of managers in Apple having to perform these roles.

3 What examples of 'specialisation between areas of management' (Section 1.4) does the case mention?

4 What examples can you find in the case of Apple's management influencing people by shaping the contexts in which they work? (Section 1.7)

5 Which values and assumptions appear to be reflected in the company's practices? (Section 2.2)

6 What examples can you find in the case of Apple's management practices corresponding to one or more of the models in the 'competing values' framework? Which of these appears to dominate? (Section 2.3 and rest of Chapter 2)

(b) Relating to the company

1 Visit the company's website (and especially its latest Annual Report), and make notes about how, if at all, the dilemmas identified in the case are still current, and how the company has dealt with them.

2 What has been its relative market share of smartphones and tablets in the most recent trading period? Which competitors have gained and lost share? Access this information from the websites of *The Economist, Financial Times* or BBC News (Business and Technology pages).

3 What new issues appear to be facing the company that were not mentioned in the case?

4 Can you trace how one or more aspects of the history of the company, as outlined in the case, has helped or hindered it in dealing with a current issue?

5 For any one of those issues it faces, how do you think it should deal with it? Build your answer by referring to one or more features of the company's history outlined in the case.

PART 1

EMPLOYABILITY SKILLS – PREPARING FOR THE WORLD OF WORK

To help you develop useful skills, this section includes tasks that relate the themes covered in the Part to six employability skills (sometimes called capabilities and attributes) that many employers value. The layout will help you to articulate these skills to employers and prepare for the recruitment process you will encounter in application forms, interviews and assessment centres.

Task 1.1 Business awareness

If a potential employer asks you to attend an assessment centre or a competency-based interview, they may ask you to present or discuss a current business topic to demonstrate your business awareness. To help you to prepare for this, write an individual or group report on ONE of these topics and present it to an audience. Aim to present your ideas in a 750-word report and/or ten PowerPoint slides at most.

1 Using data from one or more websites or printed sources, outline significant recent developments affecting, and within, Apple, especially regarding:

- external changes affecting the company, including innovations that may affect their business, and significant moves by competitors;
- changes in Apple's product range; and
- relations with shareholders and other stakeholders.

Include a summary of commentators' views on Apple's recent progress.

2 Gather information on the interaction between Apple and their competitive environment in the consumer electronics industry, including specific examples of new challengers, or new moves by established competitors. What generally relevant lessons can you draw about competition in this sector? Use Chapter 3 (Section 3.4) to structure your answer.
3 Choose another company that interests you – and which you may be considering as a career option.

- Gather information from the website and other sources about its structure and operations.
- What unique challenges does it face? (Use Table 1.1 as a starting point)
- Look for clues suggesting which (possibly more than one) of the 'competing values' may be most dominant in the organisation. (Section 2.3)
- In what ways, if any, have governments and politics influenced the business?
- To what extent is it an international business?

Task 1.2   Thinking critically

Reflect on the way that you handled Task 1.1, and identify how you exercised the skills of thinking critically (Chapter 1, Section 1.8). For example:

1   Did you spend time identifying and challenging the **assumptions** implied in the reports or commentaries you read? Summarise what you found then, or do it now.
2   Did you consider the extent to which they took account of the **context** in which managers are operating? Summarise what you found then, or do it now.
3   How far did they, or you, go in imagining and exploring **alternative** ways of dealing with the issue?
4   Did you spend time outlining the **limitations** of ideas or proposals that you thought of putting forward?

When you have completed the task, record a short paragraph giving examples of the thinking skills you have developed from this task. You can transfer a brief note of this to the Table in Task 1.7.

Task 1.3   Solving problems

Chapter 6 includes ideas on planning to deal with a problem – such as that of completing Task 1.1. Refer to these if you need more guidance on this activity, which invites you to analyse how your team worked on a task.

Use the scales below to rate the way your team planned how it would work on Task 1.1 – circle the number that best reflects your opinion of the discussion.

1   The team used suitable methods to gather sufficient information to create a good plan to complete the task (Section 6.4).

1	2	3	4	5	6	7
Strongly disagree						Strongly agree

2   The team set SMART goals that gave focus to our work on the task (Section 6.5).

1	2	3	4	5	6	7
Strongly disagree						Strongly agree

3   The goals helped to motivate us to achieve the task (Section 6.5).

1	2	3	4	5	6	7
Strongly disagree						Strongly agree

4   The team made a full list of what had to be done to achieve the goals (Section 6.6).

1	2	3	4	5	6	7
Strongly disagree						Strongly agree

5 The team made a suitable implementation plan, and followed it (Section 6.7).

1	2	3	4	5	6	7
Strongly disagree						Strongly agree

6 The team monitored the progress of the plan, and adjusted it accordingly (Section 6.7).

1	2	3	4	5	6	7
Strongly disagree						Strongly agree

When you have completed the task, record a short paragraph giving examples of the planning skills you have developed from this task. You can transfer a brief note of this to the Table in Task 1.7.

Task 1.4   Team working

Chapter 17 includes ideas on team working. This activity helps you use these to analyse how your team worked on Task 1.1.

Use the scales below to rate the way your team worked on this task – circle the number that best reflects your opinion of the discussion.

1 The team was effective in obtaining and using necessary information.

1	2	3	4	5	6	7
Strongly disagree						Strongly agree

2 The team members took on complementary team roles (Section 17.4).

1	2	3	4	5	6	7
Strongly disagree						Strongly agree

3 The team progressed through the stages of team development (Section 17.5).

1	2	3	4	5	6	7
Strongly disagree						Strongly agree

4 The team developed effective working processes that suited the task (Section 17.6).

1	2	3	4	5	6	7
Strongly disagree						Strongly agree

5 The team used its time effectively.

1	2	3	4	5	6	7
Strongly disagree						Strongly agree

6 The team regularly reviewed the ways it was working, and changed these when it would improve performance (Section 17.6).

1	2	3	4	5	6	7
Strongly disagree						Strongly agree

Record three practices that you could use in your next task. If possible, compare your results and suggestions with other members of the team, and agree on practices that would help a team work better.

When you have completed the task, write a short paragraph giving examples of team working skills (such as observing the team to improve performance) that you have developed from this task. You can transfer a brief note of this to the Table in Task 1.7.

Task 1.5   Communicating

Chapter 16 includes ideas on communicating – and Sections 16.4 and 16.5 are especially relevant to this task. They will help you to analyse how well your team communicated as you worked on Task 1.1.

Use the scales below to rate the way your team communicated during Task 1.1 – circle the number that best reflects your opinion of the discussion.

1 The team handled face-to-face communication well during its meetings (Section 16.4).

1	2	3	4	5	6	7
Strongly disagree						Strongly agree

2 The team communicated effectively by phone, mobile, voicemail and other electronic systems (Section 16.4).

1	2	3	4	5	6	7
Strongly disagree						Strongly agree

3 The team communicated effectively by personal, written methods – letters, email, texting (Section 16.4).

1	2	3	4	5	6	7
Strongly disagree						Strongly agree

4 The team communicated effectively by impersonal written methods – newsletters, online communities (Section 16.4).

1	2	3	4	5	6	7
Strongly disagree						Strongly agree

5 The team adapted between centralised and decentralised communication networks according to the needs of the task (Section 16.5).

1	2	3	4	5	6	7
Strongly disagree						Strongly agree

6 The team communicated its report well to the chosen audience.

1	2	3	4	5	6	7
Strongly disagree						Strongly agree

7 The team experienced no significant barriers to communication, either internally or externally.

1	2	3	4	5	6	7
Strongly disagree						Strongly agree

Record three communication practices that you could use in your next task. If possible, compare your results and suggestions with other members of the team, and agree on practices that would help a team work better.

When you have completed the task, record a short paragraph giving examples of communication skills you have developed from this task. You can transfer a brief note of this to the Table in Task 1.7.

Task 1.6   Self-management

This activity helps you to learn more about managing yourself, so that you can present convincing evidence to employers showing, among other things, your willingness to learn, your ability to manage and plan learning, workloads and commitments, and that you have a well-developed level of self-awareness and self-reliance. You need to show that you are able to accept responsibility, manage time and use feedback to learn.

Reflect on the way that you handled Task 1.1, and identify how you exercised skills of self-management.

1 I effectively planned the time I would spend on each part of the task.

1	2	3	4	5	6	7
Strongly disagree						Strongly agree

2   I tried to balance my commitments and those of other team members across the work, so that all were reasonably busy.

1	2	3	4	5	6	7
Strongly disagree						Strongly agree

3   I think I used my time well.

1	2	3	4	5	6	7
Strongly disagree						Strongly agree

4   I tried to ensure that I and others took responsibility for distinct areas of work, to keep moving the task forward.

1	2	3	4	5	6	7
Strongly disagree						Strongly agree

5   I often reflected on how I was working on the task to identify possible ways to improve our performance.

1	2	3	4	5	6	7
Strongly disagree						Strongly agree

Write down three self-management practices that you could use in your next task. If possible, compare your results and suggestions with other members of the team, and agree on practices that would help a team work better.

When you have completed the task, write a short paragraph giving examples of the self-management practices you have developed from this task. You can transfer a brief note of this to the Table in Task 1.7.

Task 1.7   Recording your employability skills

To conclude your work on this Part, use the summary paragraphs above to record the employability skills you have developed during your work on these tasks, and in other activities. Use the format of the table below to create an electronic record that you can use to combine the list of skills you have developed in this Part, with those in other Parts.

Most of your learning about each skill will probably come from the task associated with it – but you may also gain insights in other ways, so include those as well.

Template for laying out record of employability skills developed in this Part

Skills/Task	Task 1.1	Task 1.2	Task 1.3	Task 1.4	Task 1.5	Task 1.6	Other sources of skills
Business awareness							
Thinking critically							

Skills/Task	Task 1.1	Task 1.2	Task 1.3	Task 1.4	Task 1.5	Task 1.6	Other sources of skills
Solving problems							
Team working							
Communicating							
Self-management							

To make the most of your opportunities to develop employability skills as you do your academic work, you need to reflect regularly on your learning and record the results. This helps you to fill any gaps, and provides specific evidence of your employability skills.

PART 2

THE ENVIRONMENT OF MANAGEMENT

Introduction

Managers work within a context, and try to influence it by lobbying powerful players, doing deals with competitors and shaping public opinion. Since the organisation depends on the external world for its resources, it needs to deliver goods and services well enough to persuade people in that environment to continue their support. This is equally relevant in the public service: if a department set up to deliver care or run public transport is managed badly it will not deliver those services to an acceptable standard. Taxpayers or clients will press their elected representatives to improve performance, and they in turn will demand improved performance from management and staff. If they do not, the enterprise will fail the public.

Chapter 3 examines the most immediate aspect of the manager's context – the culture of their organisation – and then offers tools for systematically analysing the competitive and general environments, and stakeholder expectations. Chapter 4 reflects the international nature of management, by examining international features of the general environment – political developments such as the European Union, international economic factors and differences in national culture.

Pressure from interest groups and some consumers has encouraged many companies to take a positive approach to corporate responsibility. There are conflicting interests here, and Chapter 5 presents some concepts and tools that help you consider these in a coherent and well-informed way.

The Part Case is BP – a leading player in the world energy business. The company is inherently international, being affected by political and economic developments around the world. The case also raises issues of responsibility in safety and environmental matters.

CHAPTER 3
ORGANISATION CULTURES AND CONTEXTS

Aim

To identify the cultures and contexts within which managers work, and to outline some analytical tools.

Objectives

By the end of your work on this chapter you should be able to outline the concepts below in your own terms and:

1 Compare the cultures of two organisational units, using Quinn's or Handy's typologies

2 Use Porter's five forces model to analyse an organisation's competitive environment

3 Collect evidence to make a comparative PESTEL analysis for two organisations

4 Compare environments in terms of their complexity and rate of change

5 Give examples of stakeholder expectations

6 Explain the meaning and purposes of corporate governance

7 Identify the PESTEL factors relevant to a specified organisation, and understand how to use that to develop the skill of presenting a reasoned case

8 Show how ideas from the chapter add to your understanding of the integrating themes

Key terms

This chapter introduces the following ideas:

internal environment
competitive environment
general environment
external environment
organisation culture
power culture
role culture

task culture
person culture
five forces analysis
PESTEL analysis
corporate governance
agency theory

Each is a term defined within the text, as well as in the glossary at the end of the book.

Case study | British Broadcasting Corporation (BBC) www.bbc.co.uk

In 2016 the British Broadcasting Corporation (BBC) is one of the world's leading media organisations, with nine TV channels, 15 network radio stations, local radio, an online presence and the World Service. The constitutional basis for the BBC is the Royal Charter, which sets out the public purposes of the BBC, guarantees its independence and outlines the duties of the BBC Trust and the Executive Board. A new Charter is expected to come into effect at the beginning of 2017.

Since the first Charter in 1926, the BBC has sought to combine editorial independence with a public service mission – expressed as 'to inform, educate and entertain'. These central aims of providing balanced information and encouraging debate sometimes extend, for example, to enhancing transparency and accountability in matters of public concern – a 'watchdog' function. This is contentious, and draws it into political controversy.

The BBC's main source of revenue is the licence fee: every household is expected to pay an annual fee, currently fixed until 2017, and set by negotiation with the government.

The corporation had a monopoly on TV broadcasting until 1955, when the government granted a licence to a competitor – ITV, and then to Channel 4 in 1982. In 1972 licences were issued to competing radio stations. The commercial companies' main income comes from advertising and/or subscriptions. They challenge the BBC's dominant position, and see the licence fee as an unfair subsidy.

In its early years the UK audience was less diverse than it is now, with many shared cultural reference points. The BBC at that time reinforced these by allying itself with the view that 'culture' is 'transcendent, evidence of the timeless unity of the human spirit [and] an oasis of agreed value in a quarrelsome world' (Hendy, 2013, p. 47). An alternative view of culture is that it represents a whole way of life – a quality that pervades everything and makes a person feel 'at home', or just 'ordinary'. This can be expressed in many ways – and the BBC now seeks to serve an audience by reflecting its culture back to itself as accurately as possible. In a culturally diverse society, this means a culturally diverse output (Hendy, 2013, pp. 48–9).

BBC staff work in many identifiable professional groups, in media (radio, TV, online) and in the regions and nations of the UK. Observers also note a contrast in cultural values between programme makers and those in management roles.

It closely monitors its audience, reporting that 97 per cent of UK adults used the BBC TV, radio or online services at least once during each week (Annual Report for 2014–15). It also reports that 48 per cent of the public supports the licence fee – up from 43 per cent in 2009, and 31 per cent in 2004 (though down from 53 per cent in 2013–2014). On average, these people spent 18.3 hours each week with the BBC, down from 18.5 the previous year.

Case questions 3.1

- Visit the BBC website, and read the statements by the Governor and the Director General in the most recent Annual Report. What have been the main developments in the last year?

- From what you know of the BBC, and the text above, what are the main challenges facing its managers?

Sources: BBC Annual Report and Accounts 2014–15; Hendy (2013).

3.1   Introduction

The BBC is a national institution with which almost everyone in the UK has some contact at least once a week. The power of broadcasting means that it is often at the centre of controversy, the most fundamental of which has been its relationship with government – which determines much of its income and, through the Royal Charter, the terms on which it exists. It competes with many more alternative sources of news, information and entertainment than hitherto, reflecting technological, legal and social changes. These have potentially severe implications for the corporation, which it is management's role to resolve in ways that retain wide public support.

All managers work within a context that both constrains and supports them. How well they understand, interpret and interact with that context affects their performance. Finkelstein (2003, especially pp. 63–8) shows how Motorola, an early market leader in mobile communications, failed, in the late 1990s, to see that consumers preferred digital to analogue devices. This oversight allowed Nokia to take a commanding lead in mobile devices. Years later, it was Nokia's turn to suffer when it failed to sense how quickly people would take to smartphones.

Figure 3.1 shows four environmental forces. The inner circle represents the organisation's **internal environment** (or context) – which is the manager's most immediate context. That includes its culture, which has a significant influence on managers' actions and

The **internal environment** (or context) consists of those elements of the organisation or unit within which a manager works, such as it people, culture, structure and technology.

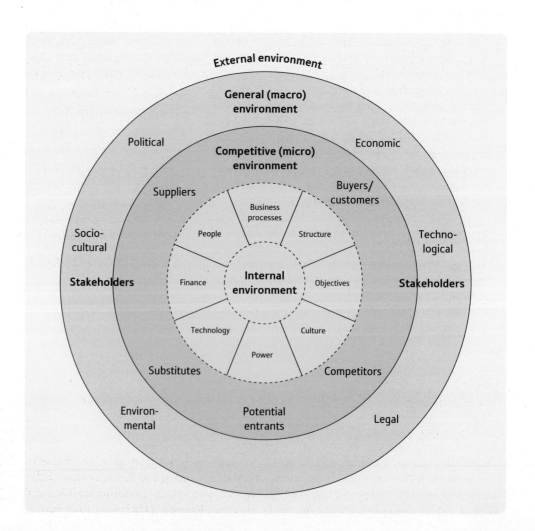

Figure 3.1
Environmental influences on the organisation

performance. Beyond that is the **competitive environment** (or context), sometimes known as the micro-environment. This is the industry-specific environment of customers, suppliers, competitors, potential entrants and substitute products. The outer circle shows the **general environment (or context)**, sometimes known as the macro-environment – political, economic, social, technological, (natural) environmental and legal factors that affect all organisations.

Together these make up an organisation's **external environment** (context) – a constantly changing source of threats and opportunities: how well people cope with these affects performance. Roeder (2011) gives many insights into the scale and likely effects of these external changes.

Forces in the external environment do not affect practice of their own accord. They become part of the agenda only when internal or external stakeholders act to place them on the management agenda. In terms of Figure 3.1, they are a fourth force. Managers (who are themselves stakeholders) balance conflicting interpretations of their context. They work within an internal context, and look outside for actual and potential changes that may affect the centre of Figure 3.1. The figure implies a constant interaction between an organisation and its external environment.

Managers do not passively accept their external environment, but actively shape it by persuading governments and other agencies to act in their favour (known as 'lobbying'). Car makers and airlines routinely ask governments for subsidies, cheap loans or regulations to help their businesses, while industry bodies (such as the National Farmers Union – www.nfuonline.org) do the same with national and international bodies such as the European Commission.

The next section presents ideas on organisational culture. Beyond that managers need to interact intelligently with their competitive and general environments. They can only do so if they have learned the skills of presenting a reasoned case to others about, for example, the potential threats or opportunities to their organisation of some external change. The chapter contrasts stable and dynamic environments, outlines stakeholder expectations and introduces ideas on governance and control.

> A **competitive environment** (or context) is the industry-specific environment comprising the organisation's customers, suppliers and competitors.

> The **general environment** (or context) (sometimes known as the macro-environment) includes political, economic, social technological, (natural) environmental and legal factors that affect all organisations.

> The **external environment** (or context) consists of elements beyond the organisation – it combines the competitive and general environments.

Activity 3.1   Which elements of the business environment matter?

Record some notes summarising aspects of a business environment of which you are aware. You may find it helpful to think of a manager you have worked with, or when you have been managing an activity.

- Identify two instances when they (or you) were discussing aspects of the wider context of the job – such as the culture of the organisation, or the world outside.
- How did this aspect of the context affect the job of managing?
- How did the way people dealt with the issue affect performance?

3.2   Cultures and their components

Developing cultures

Interest in **organisation culture** has grown as academics and managers have come to believe that it influences behaviour. Several claim that a strong and distinct culture helps to integrate individuals into the team or organisation, and so helps performance (Deal and Kennedy, 1982; Peters and Waterman, 1982). Deal and Kennedy (1982) refer to culture as

> **Organisation culture** is the set of values, beliefs, norms and assumptions that are shared by a group and that guide their interpretations of, and responses to, their environments. (Ogbonna and Harris 2014, p. 668)

'the way we do things around here' and Hofstede (1991) sees it as the 'collective programming of the mind', distinguishing one group from another. Mergers frequently experience disruption when management tries to integrate distinct cultures (Teerikangas and Very, 2006).

Someone entering a department or organisation for the first time can usually sense and observe the surface elements of the culture. Some buzz with life and activity, others seem asleep; some welcome and look after visitors, others seem inward looking; some work by the rules, while others are entrepreneurial and risk taking; some have regular social occasions while in others staff rarely meet except at work.

Management in practice   **An enduring culture in a Premier League club**

Ogbonna and Harris (2014) show how the long-established culture of a Premier League football club impeded attempts to introduce new management practices, which were intended to improve efficiency and financial performance.

The club had been run by a 'benevolent authoritarian' for 30 years, and this had coincided with the most successful on-field performance in its history – regularly winning major trophies. Respondents used words such as 'honesty', 'hard work', 'winning', 'trust', 'family' and 'togetherness' to describe the culture:

the bond, the sense of community and belonging that people have here, have remained the same. (p. 676)

The management team launched the cultural change plan at high-profile presentations, extolling the new values of efficiency, self-financing and being successful commercially as well as on the field. The CEO created new roles, such as a Brand and Marketing Director, and tried to ensure that new employees were sympathetic to these values.

No one openly opposed the plan, but four years after the launch it was generally accepted that it had not worked. Ogbonna and Harris' study of the episode concluded that this was due to the continued loyalty to symbols of the old values, and to the proud history of the club, which all employees, including new ones, valued and wanted to be part of.

These included, for example, the regular presence of former players in the club museum to greet visitors and help them celebrate that history, and bring it to life for new staff. It also included a tradition that the team (and those associated with it) is revered and respected: this continued, but with the unintended effect that it was then hard to persuade team-members to take part in promotional events, which were part of the plan for change. Their study shows how, in this case, the executives, though wanting to change parts of the culture, themselves valued and accepted symbols that encouraged continuity and thwarted the change effort:

organisations with a strong history of success and . . . cultural factors that promote and perpetuate existing values are more likely to develop enduring cultures that will be less susceptible to management control. (p. 683)

Source: Ogbonna and Harris (2014)

Figure 3.2 illustrates how a distinctive culture (such as that at the Premier League club) develops: as people form common values they use these to establish shared beliefs about how to behave towards each other and to outsiders. Positive outcomes reinforce their belief in the underlying values, which then become a stronger influence on how people should work and relate to each other. Should people have job titles? How should they dress at work? Should meetings be confrontational or supportive? A shared culture guides people on how they should contribute, and following this culture strengthens it and makes it hard to change.

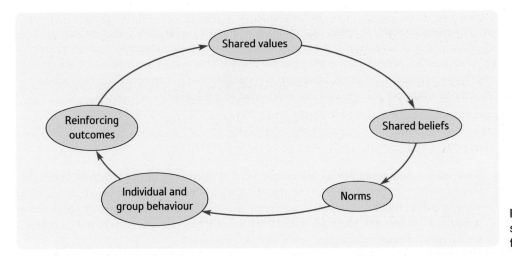

Figure 3.2 The stages of cultural formation

Components of cultures

Schein (2010) identifies three levels of a culture, 'level' referring to the degree to which the observer can see its components.

- **Artefacts** represent the visible level – elements such as the language or etiquette that someone coming into contact with a culture can observe:
  - Architecture (open-plan offices without doors or private space)
  - Technology and equipment (use of presentational technology)
  - Style (clothing, manner of address, emotional displays)
  - Rituals and ceremonies (leaving events, awards ceremonies, away days)
  - Courses (to induct employees in the culture as well as the content).

  While it is easy to observe artefacts, outsiders will have trouble understanding what they mean to the group, or the beliefs and values they represent.

- Beliefs and values are the accumulated ideas that members hold about their work. As a group develops, members refine their ideas about 'what works here': how people make decisions, how teams work, how they solve problems. Practices that work become acceptable behaviours:
  - 'Quality pays'
  - 'We should stick to our core business'
  - 'Take personal responsibility'
  - 'Work as a team'
  - 'Challenge a proposal – whoever made it'.

  Some companies (Ikea is an example) codify and publish their beliefs and values, to help induct new members and to remind current staff. The extent to which employees internalise these beliefs probably depends on whether they observe senior managers behaving in accordance with them.

Key ideas   **Values matter in management**

The beliefs and values that shape an organisation's culture affect the practice and ultimately the reputation of its managers. The financial crisis that began in 2008 was, in large part, due to cultures in banks and other financial institutions that encouraged greed and self-interest above honesty and customer service.

Companies who treat employees as self-interested opportunists who must be forced to do their job, tend to create employees who do just that. Conversely, managers who assume a reasonable degree of trust and cooperation create a system in which honest, cooperative people flourish. Prophecies are often self-fulfilling – so the prevailing values have a significant influence on how an organisation treats employees and customers, and for the reputation of those who work in it. As one observer noted to the author:

What matters most in management is not what you make, but what you believe.

- **Basic underlying assumptions** are deeply held by members of the group as being the way to work together. As they act in accordance with their values and beliefs, those that work become embedded as basic underlying assumptions. When the group holds these strongly, members will act in accordance with them, and reject actions based on others:
  - 'We need to satisfy customers to survive as a business'
  - 'Our business is to help people with X problem live better despite that'
  - 'People can make mistakes, as long as they learn from them'
  - 'We employ highly motivated and competent adults'
  - 'Financial markets worry about the short term: we are here for the long term'.

Difficulties arise when people with assumptions developed in one group need to work with people from another. King et al. (2012) show how this prevented two groups of healthcare professionals from using a shared information system. This would save time and improve patient care, but cultural beliefs meant that neither group would accept information prepared by the other.

Management in practice   **Culture as an asset at Bosch**   www.bosch.com

Franz Fehrenbach was (in 2009) chief executive of Bosch, Germany's largest privately owned engineering group, and the world's largest supplier of car parts. He said:

The company culture, especially our high credibility, is one of our greatest assets. Our competitors cannot match us on that because it takes decades to build up.

The cultural traditions include a rigid control on costs, an emphasis on team thinking, employees taking responsibility for their errors, cautious financial policies and long-term thinking. For example, to cope with the recession in 2009 Mr Fehrenbach explained that:

We have to cut costs in all areas. We will reduce spending in the ongoing business, but we will not cut back on research and development for important future projects.

Source: Based on an article by Daniel Schaefer, *Financial Times*, 2 March 2009, p. 16.

Activity 3.2   **Culture spotting**

- Identify as many components of culture (artefacts, beliefs and values, underlying assumptions) in an organisation or unit as you can.
- What may the artefacts suggest about the deeper beliefs and values, or underlying assumptions?
- Gather evidence (preferably by asking people) about how the culture affects behaviour, and whether people think it helps or hinders performance.

3.3 Types of culture

This section outlines three ways of describing and comparing cultures.

Competing values framework

Chapter 2 outlined the competing values model developed by Quinn et al. (2003). This reflects inherent tensions between flexibility or control, and between internal or external focus. Figure 3.3 (based on Figure 2.2) shows four cultural types.

Rational goal

Members value rationality and efficiency. They define effectiveness in terms of economic goals that satisfy external requirements. Motivating factors include competition and achieving goals. Examples are large, established businesses – mechanistic.

Internal process

Members focus on internal matters with the goal of making the unit efficient, stable and controlled. Tasks are repetitive, methods stress specialisation and rules. Motivating factors include security, stability and order. Examples include utilities and public authorities – dislike change.

Human relations

People emphasise the value of informal interpersonal relations. They try to nurture and support members, aiming for their well-being and commitment. Motivating factors include cohesiveness and membership. Examples include voluntary groups and small professional or creative firms.

Open systems

People see the external world as a vital source of ideas, energy and resources. They also sees it as turbulent, requiring entrepreneurial leadership and flexible, responsive behaviour. Motivators are creativity and variety. Examples are start-up firms and new business units – flexible.

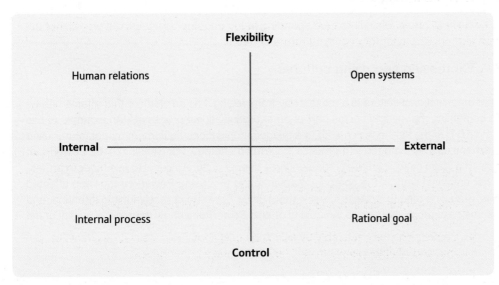

Figure 3.3 Types of organisational culture

Source: Based on Quinn et al. (2003).

A **power culture** is one in which people's activities are strongly influenced by a dominant central figure.

A **role culture** is one in which people's activities are strongly influenced by clear and detailed job descriptions and other formal signals as to what is expected of them.

A **task culture** is one in which the focus of activity is towards completing a task or project using whatever means are appropriate.

A **person culture** is one in which activity is strongly influenced by the wishes of the individuals who are part of the organisation.

Charles Handy's cultural types

Charles Handy (1993) distinguished four cultures – **power**, **role**, **task** and **person**.

Power

A dominant central figure holds power: others follow, and interpret new situations in the way the leader would. Many entrepreneurial firms are like this, with few rules but with well-understood codes on how to behave and work. It relies on the individual, not consensus.

Role

Typical of this culture are the job description or the procedure. Managers define what they expect, and select people for a job if they meet the requirements. Procedures guide how people and departments interact, and rules enable coordination. Position in the hierarchy determines power.

Task

People focus on completing the task regardless of formal role. They value each other for what they contribute and expect everyone to join in. The focus is on securing resources and people – and combining their diverse skills to a common purpose.

Person

The individual is at the centre and any structure or system is there to serve them. The form is unusual – small professional, communal and artistic organisations are probably closest. They exist to meet the needs of the professionals or members, rather than some larger organisational goal.

Activity 3.3   Cultural examples

For each of Handy's four cultural types, identify an example from within this text that seems to correspond with that form.

- What clues led you to that choice?
- Why do you think that culture is suitable for that organisation?
- Compare the 'competing values' and Handy models: where are they similar, and where different?

Key ideas   Expressing and using cultures

A theme in studies of organisational culture is a move away from seeing it as an element that affects behaviour, to seeing it as something that people use as part of other organisational processes. An example of this is a study by Kaplan (2011) of the way in which staff in a telecommunications equipment manufacturer used PowerPoint presentations as they engaged in a process to develop strategy. For Schein (2010), PowerPoint would be an example of a static cultural artefact representing a deeper cultural value – to use modern professional tools. From her empirical work in the company Kaplan found that using PowerPoint (or not) affected the strategy process. Staff who tried to express ideas without using PowerPoint received little attention, and Kaplan noted that some gave more attention to the quality of their PowerPoint show than to the quality of the ideas it contained.

Source: Kaplan (2011).

Multiple cultures

Martin (2002) proposed that large organisations (the BBC is an example) have multiple cultures, towards which observers take one of three perspectives:

- **Integration** – a focus on identifying consistencies, and acts that support a common goal.
- **Differentiation** – a focus on conflict, identifying different and possibly conflicting views.
- **Fragmentation** – a focus on the fluidity of organisations, and of changing views about events.

Ogbonna and Harris (1998, 2002) provided empirical support for this view, based on interviews with staff in a retail company. They found that a person's position in the hierarchy determined their perspective on the culture (see Table 3.1). As consensus on the culture was unlikely, the authors advised managers to recognise the subcultures, and only seek to reconcile those differences that were essential to policy. They observed that culture remains highly subjective, largely in the eye of the beholder:

> and is radically different according to an individual's position in the hierarchy. (p. 45)

Culture and performance

Peters and Waterman (1982) believed that an organisation's culture affected performance, and implied that managers should try to change their culture towards a more productive one. Klein (2011) takes a similar approach by tracing the relation between culture and performance in three successful companies. Others are more sceptical, questioning whether, even if a suitable culture has a positive effect, managers can consciously change it. Kotter and Heskett (1992) studied 207 companies to assess the link between culture and economic performance. Although they were positively correlated, the relationship was weaker than advocates of culture as a factor in performance had predicted.

Thompson and McHugh (2002), while critical of much writing on the topic, observe the potential benefits that a suitable culture can bring:

> Creating a culture resonant with the overall goals is relevant to any organisation, whether it be a trade union, voluntary group or producer co-operative. Indeed, it is more important in

Table 3.1 Hierarchical position and cultural perspectives

Position in hierarchy	Cultural perspective	Description	Example
Head office managers	Integration	Cultural values should be shared across the organisation. Unified culture both desirable and attainable	'If we can get every . . . part of the company doing what they should be doing, we'll beat everybody.'
Store managers	Differentiation	Reconciling conflicting views of head office and shop floor. See cultural pluralism as inevitable	'People up at head office are all pushing us in different directions. Jill in Marketing wants customer focus, June in Finance wants lower costs.'
Store employees	Fragmented	Confused by contradictory nature of the espoused values. See organisation as complex and unpredictable	'One minute it's this, the next it's that. You can't keep up with the flavour of the month.'

Source: Based on Ogbonna and Harris (1998).

such consensual groupings. Co-operatives, for example, can degenerate organisationally because they fail to develop adequate mechanisms for transmitting the original ideals from founders to new members and sustaining them through shared experiences. (pp. 208–9)

As managers work within an organisational culture, they also work within an external context – whose members have expectations of them. They need tools with which to analyse that context.

Case study   BBC – the case continues   www.bbc.co.uk

There are many local and professional BBC cultures, but two culturally distinct groups are evident – the programme-makers and the managers. In the earliest days, when the BBC was a monopoly with a growing audience and income, the emphasis was on production quality. This meant recruiting capable people, and giving them a high degree of professional autonomy. The programme-makers are a relatively small group of people, to whom most of the other staff provide support. Hendy points out:

> detailed oversight of day-to-day activity is impossible. In the last resort it is the programme producer who determines the quality and tone of what goes on air . . . they are trusted to 'get on with it' and exercise their own judgement. (Hendy, 2013, p. 71)

This is especially true of the outstanding individuals who create award-winning documentaries, comment on major sporting events, or host popular entertainment shows. They are well-known public figures and often have more frequent access to senior politicians and business leaders than senior BBC managers. Their focus is on the quality of the programme, with little interest in budgets, schedules or other routine considerations.

The managers – senior managers and their subordinates, staff working close to the top of staff functions and administrative staff – have other values.

They give more attention to external stakeholders and their interests and intentions towards the BBC. They value rules about budget compliance, consistency with salary policy, ensuring expenses claims are in line with the rules, productivity, coordination and stability. These values, as well as the public's concern that they get a good return for their licence fee, will inevitably constrain some areas of programme-makers' autonomy.

External change, especially more competition, has affected the relationship between the two. Marketing and scheduling became more vital to ensure the best chance of attracting mass audiences, greatly increasing the role of channel controllers, who decide what programmes to make, together with the content and timing of schedules. They are also able to commission work from external programme-makers working for independent production companies, who now provide about a quarter of total BBC output.

Source: Nissen (2014); Hendy (2013); BBC website.

Case questions 3.2

- Which of the four cultures expressed in the competing values model would you expect to find in these two groups?
- What might that imply for their management and the relationship between them?

3.4   The competitive environment – Porter's five forces

Five forces analysis is a technique for identifying and listing those aspects of the five forces most relevant to the profitability of an organisation at that time.

Senior managers face significant investment decisions about the scope and direction of their business – such as whether to diversify into a new industry, or to withdraw from one. Michael Porter (1980a, 1985) offered a model of the forces they should take into account to increase their chances of adding value. He proposed that the ability of a firm to earn an acceptable return depends on **five forces analysis** shown in Figure 3.4.

Porter (1980a) believes that the collective strength of the five forces determines industry profitability, through their effects on prices, costs and investment requirements. Buyer

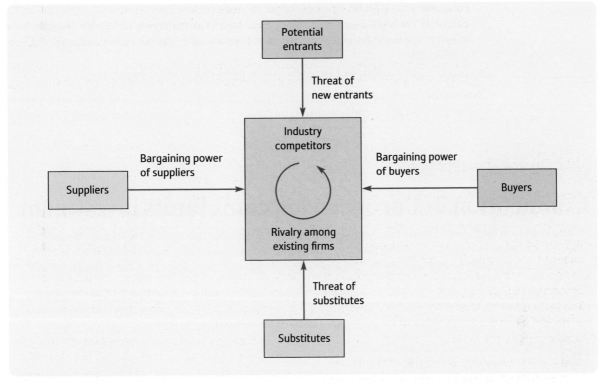

Figure 3.4 The five forces of industry competition
Source: Porter (1980a), p. 5.

power influences the prices a firm can charge, as does the threat of substitutes. The bargaining power of suppliers determines the cost of raw materials and other inputs. The greater the collective strength of the forces, the less profitable the industry: the weaker they are, the more profitable.

Threat of new entrants

Factors that affect how easily new entrants can enter an industry include:

- the need for economies of scale (to compete on cost), which are difficult to achieve quickly;
- the amount of capital investment required;
- available distribution channels;
- subsidies and regulations that benefit existing firms;
- need for tangible and intangible resources that existing firms control; and
- how loyal customers feel to existing firms.

China is accelerating its efforts to launch a commercial passenger plan that will challenge Airbus and Boeing. Analysts predict that China will buy about half of all commercial airliners produced over the next thirty years, and would prefer to buy some of them from themselves. They have easy access to capital, and most early sales will be within China.

Intensity of rivalry among competitors

Strong competitive rivalry lowers profitability, and occurs when:

- there are many firms in an industry;
- there is slow market growth, so companies fight for market share;

- fixed costs are high, so firms use capacity and overproduce;
- exit costs are high; specialised assets (hard to sell) or management loyalty (in old family firms) deter firms from leaving the industry, which prolongs excess capacity and low profitability;
- products are similar, so customers can easily switch to other suppliers.

The airline, print media and food retailing industries are examples of those with intense competitive rivalry – and low profitability.

Management in practice

Competition in European telecoms limits investment

The European telecoms industry has experienced strong competition, especially in mobiles, for several years. Consumers have enjoyed low tariffs but mobile revenues have fallen by 18 per cent since 2008. Profits . . . have been even worse, down 22 per cent. Return on capital employed has been almost halved.

The European Commission wants more investment by the industry, but this cannot happen unless companies have higher earnings with which to finance it. So it is encouraging mergers between some competitors, as this will allow the companies to raise earnings, and have more incentive to invest.

 Source: *Financial Times*, 19 November 2014, p. 9.
© The Financial Times 2014. All Rights Reserved.

Power of buyers (customers)

Buyers (customers) seek lower prices or higher quality at constant prices, thus forcing down prices and profitability. Buyer power is high when:

- the buyer purchases a large part of a supplier's output;
- there are many substitute products, allowing easy switching;
- the product is a large part of the buyer's costs, encouraging them to seek lower prices;
- buyers can plausibly threaten to supply their needs internally.

Management in practice   Small farmers and large retailers   www.nfuonline.org

Most milk in the UK is produced by small farmers and sold through large retailers, either as liquid milk or as dairy products. In 2015 their trade organisation, the National Farmers Union, ran a campaign to secure higher prices for milk. They pointed out that in June 2015 the average price that farmers received for their milk was about 24 pence a litre, while a year before the price had been 32 pence. The average cost to produce milk is about 30 pence a litre.

The power of farmers is further reduced by a world surplus of milk, which has reduced prices.

Source: NFU website.

Bargaining power of suppliers

Conditions that increase the bargaining power of suppliers are the opposite of those applying to buyers. The power of suppliers relative to customers is high when:

- there are few suppliers;
- the product is distinctive, so that customers are reluctant to switch;

- the cost of switching is high (e.g. if a company has invested in a supplier's software);
- the supplier can plausibly threaten to extend their business to compete with the customer;
- the customer is a small or irregular purchaser.

Aircraft manufacture (dominated by Boeing and Airbus), pharmaceutical companies with medicines protected (temporarily) by patents, or computer operating systems (Microsoft) could be examples of suppliers with high bargaining power.

Threat of substitutes

Substitutes are products in other industries that can perform the same function – such as using cans instead of bottles – and such close substitutes constrain the ability of firms to raise prices. This threat is high when:

- technological developments reduce the advantages of existing providers or open the way to new ones;
- buyers are willing to change their habits; and
- existing firms have no legal protection for their position.

Physical retailers and travel agents have lost market share to online substitutes suppliers, as have print media companies.

Analysing the five forces helps companies to assess their strengths and weaknesses when developing their strategies – the Virgin case illustrates this (see Part 3).

Case study   BBC – the case continues   www.bbc.co.uk

Hendy (2013) considers what differentiates a public broadcaster like the BBC from a commercial one. He suggests it is the daily struggle in public broadcasters' working lives:

> between two fundamental interpretations of what it means to serve the public: between giving the public what it asks for and [allowing privileged individuals, the broadcasters] to decide in advance on the public's behalf. It's a struggle . . . between reflecting public taste and shaping it; as a struggle between assuming that supply must follow demand and assuming that, on the contrary, [supply can shape demand]; or, as a BBC Chairman once posed the dilemma: is it the Corporation's role to lead or to follow?

He also notes a widely shared public assumption that:

> These predominantly middle-class and highly educated people will – viewed from the Left – invariably reflect 'establishment' thinking and values, or – viewed from the Right – consistently represent a progressive or permissive set of beliefs. (pp. 71–2)

BBC television was a monopoly until 1955, and radio until 1972. TV now competes with four independent channels, and many subscription channels – sometimes termed 'narrowcast' as they cater for specific interests, such as Sky Sports, BT or Virgin. Another option for viewers is to download videos or computer games, vastly widening the range of substitutes available to them.

Social media offers consumers new ways to engage with content, enabling them to create and share it as well as receive it. They can contribute blogs, write online reviews, share videos and belong to online communities designing and publishing content. The BBC has responded to this by investing heavily in BBC Online and in promoting the iPlayer, which it sees as central to its response to the digital revolution.

Case questions 3.3

- Which of the five forces can you identify in the BBC's environment (in the whole case so far)?
- What management challenges does this account of external change illustrate?

3.5   The general environment – PESTEL

PESTEL analysis is a technique for identifying and listing the political, economic, socio-cultural, technological, environmental and legal factors in the general environment most relevant to an organisation.

Forces in the wider world also shape management policies, and a **PESTEL analysis** (short for political, economic, socio-cultural, technological, environmental and legal) helps to identify these. It is easy to list many such forces in the context, but the management skill is to recognise which of these are likely to have a significant effect on the organisation's performance. Some will be obvious and pressing, while others can safely be given a lower priority. Figure 3.5 is an example of such a list: it is not a scientifically verified tool, but a compilation of the forces that affect organisations in varying degrees, as circumstances change. Managers rarely deal with them in isolation – they take account of the relevant forces in combination: pharmaceutical companies dealing with regulators who require costly trials, competitors offering cheap alternatives to patented drugs and governments trying to reduce the costs of health care. Figure 4.2 presents a similar compilation of factors that become significant when managers are doing business internationally.

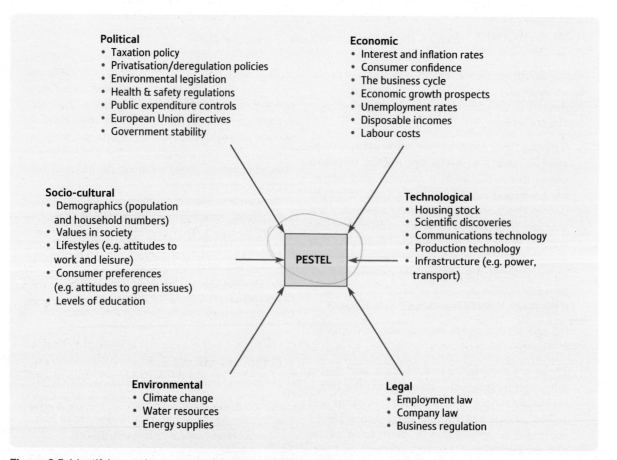

Figure 3.5 Identifying environmental influences – PESTEL analysis

Political factors

Political systems shape what managers can and cannot do. Most governments regulate industries such as power supply, telecommunications and transport by specifying, among other things, who can offer services, on what conditions, and what they can charge.

When the UK and most European governments altered the law on financial services, non-financial companies such as Virgin and Sainsbury's began to offer banking services. Deregulating air transport stimulated the growth of low-cost airlines, especially in the US (e.g. Southwest Airlines), Europe (easyJet), Australia (Virgin Blue) and parts of Asia (Air Asia).

Managers aim to influence these political decisions by employing professional lobbyists, especially at international institutions. The European Commission relies on ideas from interested parties to inform its decisions, and lobbying firms provide this to people who can influence decisions, such as Members of the European Parliament.

Economic factors

Economic factors – wage, inflation, interest rates, growth rates – affect an organisation's income and costs. Ikea reported increased sales in 2012 since, as people were short of money during the recession, more of them were choosing to shop at the Swedish company's large out-of-town stores because of their low prices. Other companies doing well were those employing low-skilled staff in service occupations, where wage costs were static.

The state of the economy also influences capital investment decisions. If economic forecasts predict slower growth, managers will delay some capital investments. As India has become richer, Tata (www.tata.com), the Indian conglomerate, has decided to launch a low-cost car, the Nano.

Socio-cultural factors

Demographic change such as an ageing population affects management in many ways – as older employees with special requirements, as customers for pharmaceuticals and private nursing homes and as those with age-related conditions – see 'Management in Practice'. Ethnic diversity also offers opportunities to meet different needs.

Management in practice　　**Better stores for people with Alzheimer's**

As people live longer, some businesses try to adapt services to help the frail. In research for the Alzheimer's Society, 23 per cent of people with dementia (a broad term for the progressive loss of mental ability, the most common form of which is Alzheimer's) said they had stopped shopping. This was mainly because they needed longer to organise themselves and feared other people's impatience. The society has made several recommendations to retailers:

- encourage customers with dementia to carry personal statements that staff can view, such as a reminder to staff to speak slowly, and details of their carer in case of a crisis;
- involve people with dementia and their carers in suggesting changes to retail layout, product design and customer service that would make their life easier; and
- train staff to recognise possible signs of confusion such as repetition, wandering from the point and agitation – and offer to help, preferably in a quiet area.

Source: Based on an article by Alicia Clegg, *Financial Times*, 26 May 2015, p. 14.

Changes in consumer habits open new business opportunities. Some food producers aim to satisfy preferences for healthy eating, while airBnB (www.airBnB.co.uk) enables those with spare accommodation, and those seeking it, to make a mutually-profitable transaction. Some want higher quality beers, and entrepreneurs have opened many new, often local, breweries. In the UK, Camra (www.camra.org.uk) reported in September 2015 that there were over 1,400 breweries, up 204 in the last 12 months – the most in living memory.

Key ideas — Grown Up Digital

In 2009 Don Tapscott reported on his study of how what he calls the 'net generation' – people born between 1977 and 1997 – sometimes called 'generation Y'– access and use information. His team interviewed thousands of 16-to-19 year olds in 12 countries, as well as doing comparative interviews with older people. He notes that the net generation grew up using a wider range of media than its parents: they typically spend hours on their computer – while also talking on the phone, listening to music, doing homework and reading. Technology is shaping their minds to access information in a different way. Rather than absorb information sequentially from a limited number of sources, they 'play' with information by clicking, cutting, pasting and linking to interesting material.

Tapscott suggests this challenges established educational methods. Media companies try to adapt established products to suit the way young people expect to interact with information.

Source: Tapscott (2009).

Technological factors

Companies pay close attention to the physical infrastructure – such as the adequacy of power supplies and transport systems. The rapid growth of shale oil production in the United States more than doubled the amount of oil carried by rail to coastal refineries in 2012 compared to 2011 – but the railway companies were aware that new pipelines would threaten this. Businesses monitor advances in information technology, which are dramatically changing their business environment. Computers traditionally handled data, while other systems handled voice (telephones) and pictures (film and video). Digitisation – the packaging of data, images and sounds into a single format – has profound implications, which Table 3.2 illustrates.

Bernoff and Li (2008) show how social networking (Facebook) and user-generated content sites (YouTube) change the technological context – to which companies respond.

Table 3.2 Examples of digital technologies affecting established businesses

Technology	Application	Businesses affected
DVDs	Store sound and visual images	Sales of stereophonic sound systems decline sharply
iPod, MP3 and smartphones	Digital downloads of music and films	Threat to retailers such as HMV
Broadband services delivering online content	Enables readers and advertisers to use online media rather than print or television	Threat to print newspapers – most now have online formats
Voice over Internet Protocol (VoIP)	Enables telephone calls over the internet at very low cost	Growth of new providers such as Skype
Digital photography	Enables people to store pictures electronically and order prints online	Threat to photographic retailers

Case study   BBC – the case continues   www.bbc.com

There is clear evidence from the United States that younger viewers watch less TV than older people – they are much more likely to watch YouTube, explore Facebook and other social media platforms rather than turn on TV. They are also watching on-demand services, and ignoring 'linear TV' with set times at which they can view content. This has led to a steady decline in the number of people watching scheduled TV production. They also watch content on smartphones and gaming consoles, which makes it hard to measure audiences. Young audiences are keen to be involved in creating programmes, suggesting that entertainment is no longer a matter of professionals creating content for an audience – at least part of the potential audience like to feel they have a say in the programme, and want to be involved in customising what is broadcast.

The BBC has responded to these technological and social changes by investing heavily in digital, and especially interactive, programming. However, these changes bring significant internal changes. Jackson (2014) studied two BBC participatory programmes, and shows the changes to management

and production practices that they require. For example, it may involve acknowledging and answering responses from thousands of participants – a radical change from the 'filter then publish' model of broadcasting. It became clear that

> Producers often dislike engaging with the public, believing such interaction is not part of their job or is a task for more junior production staff. Contributions from the public were usually framed as augmenting professionally produced content. From managers' perspective, user-generated content was [often seen to] be of low quality and opening the BBC to potential libel or defamation. (p. 244)

Source: Jackson (2014).

Case questions 3.4

- Which **three** PESTEL factors (throughout the case) are likely to have the most effect (positive or negative) on the BBC, and why?

Environmental factors

The natural resources available in an economy – minerals, land, climate – affect the businesses that entrepreneurs create. Most know that climate change has implications for their organisations, and are working out how best to respond. Some face serious risks from droughts, floods, storms and heat waves – less rainfall in some places, more in others. For some this is a threat – insurance companies, house builders and water companies are only the most visible examples. For others sustainability brings opportunities – alternative energy suppliers, emission control businesses and waste management companies are all experiencing rising demand for their products and services.

Management in practice

An advocate for sustainability at Unilever www.unilever.com

Paul Polman, chief executive of Unilever, is a strong advocate of sustainability in business:

> Our ambitions are to double our business, but to do that while reducing our environmental impact and footprint. We say this publicly and it causes some discomfort . . . But you see, you cannot go on in this world the way we're doing.
>
> But the road to well-being doesn't go via reduced consumption. It has to be done via more responsible consumption . . . So that's why we're taking such a stand on moving the world to sustainable palm

oil. That's why we go to natural refrigerants in our ice-cream cabinets. That's why we work with small farmers, to be sure that people who don't have sufficient nutrition right now have a change to have a better life. Because at the end of the day, I think companies that take that approach have a right to exist.

Legal factors

Competent governments assert their authority over the territory, creating a stable legal framework embodying the rule of law, commercial contracts and property rights (including intellectual property covering patents and inventions). Without these tools, organisations find it difficult and expensive to operate, which led the UK parliament to pass the Joint Stock Companies Act in 1862. Previously, investors were personally liable for the whole of a company's debts if it failed. The Act limited their liability to the value of the shares they held in the company – they could lose their investment, but not the rest of their wealth. This stimulated company formation and other countries soon passed similar legislation, paving the way for the countless 'limited liability' companies that exist today (Micklethwait and Wooldridge, 2003). Laws on employment and trade unions affect the way managers engage with employees.

Activity 3.5   Critical reflection on a PESTEL analysis

Conduct a PESTEL analysis for your organisation, or one with which you are familiar.

- Which of the external forces you have identified has most implications for the business?
- To what extent has the organisation's policy taken account of these forces?
- Compare your analysis with that which you did for the BBC, and present a summary of similarities and differences in the forces affecting the companies.

Key ideas   Presenting a reasoned case

To use the PESTEL model in practice depends not only on hard analysis, but also on being able to present a reasoned case or proposal to colleagues.

This is a fundamental part of a manager's job, since to get things done they need to present evidence for (or against) a proposal in a clear and reasoned way. Issues are usually more complex than they appear, the 'facts' are not always available and people make decisions on limited information. Effective managers are good at presenting a reasoned case.

Quinn et al. (2003) write that most proposals have three elements:

1. The claim or conclusion: the claim answers the question – 'what is this about?'.
2. The grounds or the facts and evidence to support the claim: the 'grounds' answers the question 'what leads you to say that?'.
3. The warrant, or bridge between the claim and the grounds: the 'warrant' answers the question 'How does your claim connect to the grounds you've offered?'.

This 'warrant' is the hardest of the three to deal with, as what seems like a strong link to you may not look that way to someone else, and vice versa. But developing an understanding of this link is a powerful tool for both creating and evaluating arguments. The 'Develop your skills' feature at the end of this chapter will help you to do this.

Source: Based on Quinn et al. (2003), p. 108.

3.6 Environmental complexity and dynamism

Perceptions of environments

The axes in Figure 3.6 show two variables (Duncan, 1972) that affect how people see their environment – the degree of complexity and the degree of dynamism. Complexity refers to the number and similarity of factors that people consider in a decision – the more of these, and the more different they are, the more complex the situation. Dynamism refers to the degree to which these factors remain the same or change.

To consider just the most contrasting cells in Figure 3.6, those who perceive themselves to be in a simple-static environment will experience stability. Competitors offer similar products, newcomers rarely enter the market and there are few technological breakthroughs. Examples could include routine legal work such as house sales and wills, or the work of local tradesmen such as joiners and builders. The information they need for a decision is likely to be available, so they can assess likely outcomes quickly and accurately, using the past to predict the future with reasonable confidence. Some aspects of health and education, where demand is driven largely by demographic change, may also fit this pattern: the capacity needed in primary and secondary schools is easy to predict several years ahead.

At the other extreme, those working in complex-dynamic environments face great uncertainty. They have to monitor many diverse and changing factors. Companies in the mobile

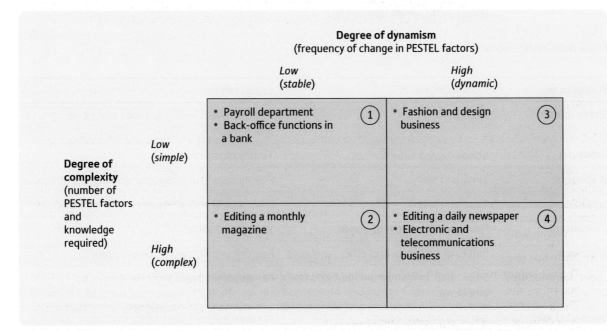

Figure 3.6 Types of environment

phone or entertainment industries are like this. Multinationals such as Shell and BP experience great complexity, operating across diverse political, legal and cultural systems. Eric Schmidt (until 2012 CEO of Google) said that in many high-tech industries:

> the environment is changing so fast that it requires improvisation in terms of strategy, products and even day-to-day operations. Just when you think you understand the technology landscape, you see a major disruption.

Activity 3.6   Critical reflection on type of environment

Use Figure 3.6 to analyse the environment in which your unit of the organisation works. Then try to do the same analysis for one or two other units of the organisation.

- Compare the nature of these environments.
- What are the implications of that for managing these departments, and the organisation?

Managers who work in dynamic and complex situations face such uncertainty that historical analysis is unlikely to be a useful guide to the future.

3.7   Stakeholders and corporate governance

Stakeholders

Stakeholders are those (individuals, groups or other organisations) with a legitimate claim on an organisation (Freeman, 1984). This legitimacy can arise from ownership, through holding a title to an asset (such as a share in a company); from legal rights to, say, privacy or security of tenure; from moral rights to, say, fair treatment; or from having an interest because they will be affected by a decision. They have usually contributed to the organisation, and seek something in return. Hill and Jones (1992) set out these mutual obligations for stakeholders, shown in Table 3.3.

Table 3.3 Contributions and expectations of stakeholders

Stakeholders	Contributions	Expectations
Shareholders	Capital	Adequate dividend payments and/or rising share value
Creditors	Loans	Timely repayment
Managers	Time and skill	Fair income and adequate working conditions
Employees	Time and skill	Fair income and adequate working conditions
Customers	Revenues from sale of goods	Value for money
Suppliers	Inputs of materials and other resources	Fair prices and dependable buyers
Local communities	Sites, local infrastructure, perhaps tax incentives	No damage to quality of life
General public	National infrastructure	No damage to quality of life and obey law

Source: Based on Hill and Jones (1992, p. 133).

Each stakeholder is part of a nexus of implicit and explicit contracts (of contributions and rewards) that make up the organisation.

However, as a group, managers are unique in this respect because of their position at the centre of the nexus of contracts. Managers are the only group of stakeholders who enter into a contractual relationship with all other stakeholders. Managers are also the only group of stakeholders with direct control over the decision-making apparatus of the firm (Hill and Jones, 1992, p. 134).

Since stakeholders provide the (diverse) resources, managers allocate the resources available in the hope of meeting expectations – which inevitably means some compromise when they conflict. Nutt (2002) shows the dangers: he studied 400 strategic decisions, and found that half of them 'failed' – in the sense that they were not implemented or produced poor results – largely because managers failed to attend to stakeholders.

Allocating resources to meet the interests of one stakeholder will often mean a loss to another. A topical example is the conflict between managers and shareholders over executive rewards, especially when business performance has been poor. One way to resolve such conflicts is through corporate governance.

Case questions 3.5

- Who are the stakeholders in the BBC?
- What are their interests in the success of the broadcaster?
- How can the BBC maintain the support of the most important stakeholders?

Corporate governance

Scandals and failures in prominent organisations lead people to question the adequacy of their systems of **corporate governance**. Berle and Means (1932) first raised the issue when they described the dilemma facing owners who become separated from the managers they appoint to run the business. The shareholders (principals) have financed, and own, the business, but delegate the work of running it to managers (agents). The principals then face the risk that managers may not act in their (the principals') best interests: they may take excessive investment risks, or withhold information so that the state of the business appears to be better than it is. The principals are then at a disadvantage to the agents (the managers), who may use this to personal advantage. Their observations led to what is now termed **agency theory**, which seeks to explain what happens when one party (the principal) delegates work to another party (the agent). Failures at major financial institutions, caused in part by lending money to risky borrowers in the hope of high returns, show that the separation of ownership from management, of principal from agent, is as relevant as ever.

Corporate governance refers to the rules and processes intended to control those responsible for managing an organisation.

Agency theory seeks to explain what happens when one party (the principal) delegates work to another party (the agent).

Management in practice   The interests of managers and shareholders

While senior managers often claim to be trying to align their interests with those of shareholders, the two often conflict. Mergers often appear to benefit senior managers and their professional advisers rather than shareholders. Acquiring companies often pay too much for the target, but executives inside the enlarged company receive higher pay. Professional advisers (investment bankers) make money on both the merger and the break-up.

Using company money to buy the company's shares in the market uses money that can't be spent on dividends. From the vantage point of many CEOs, paying dividends is about the last thing they would want to do with corporate earnings. In theory, a CEO is carrying out shareholder wishes. In practice, as the spate of recent scandals has shown, the interests of chief executives and their shareholders can widely diverge.

Source: Based on extracts from an article by Robert Kuttner, *Business Week,* 9 September 2002.

Widening recognition that managers have responsibilities not only to shareholders but to a wider group of stakeholders means that corporate governance now usually refers to arrangements designed to make senior managers formally accountable for their actions. Similar issues arise in the public sector, where elected members are nominally in charge of local authorities, health boards and other agencies – but who appoint professional managers to run the organisation on behalf of the citizens. Elected members face the risk that the people they appoint act in their personal interests, rather than the electors'. Hartley (2008):

> a new awareness of the social, economic and cultural contribution of government, public organisations and public services has resulted in a significant period of reform and experimentation. At the heart of these initiatives is the idea that improvements to the way public services can be governed, managed and delivered will produce improved outcomes for citizens. (p. 3)

Stakeholder theory is the term used for ideas trying to explain the evolving relationship between an organisation and its stakeholders. Governance systems are based on the principle that those managing an organisation are accountable for their actions, and create mechanisms to do that.

Mechanisms of corporate governance

Mallin (2013, p. 8) suggests that to provide adequate oversight, governance systems require:

- an adequate system of internal controls that safeguards assets;
- mechanisms to prevent any one person having too much influence;
- processes to manage relationships between managers, directors, shareholders and other stakeholders;
- the ability to balance the interests of shareholders and other stakeholders; and
- to encourage transparency and accountability, which investors and many external stakeholders expect.

This book examines governance as one of the integrating themes at the end of each chapter.

3.8   Integrating themes

Entrepreneurship

Barringer and Ireland (2010) stress the significance of opportunity recognition – the process of perceiving the possibility of a new business or a new product. They identify some of the characteristics shared by those who excel at recognising opportunities that others miss.

- **Prior experience.** The authors cite studies showing the effects of prior experience on opportunity recognition. One study of 500 entrepreneurs found that almost half got their new business idea while working for companies in the same industry – this enabled them to spot unsolved problems that represent opportunities, and to build a network of advice and information.
- **Cognitive factors.** Some believe that entrepreneurs have a sixth sense that allows them to notice things without engaging in deliberate search. Entrepreneurial alertness is a learned skill, and people who know an industry are more alert to opportunities and more able to assess a market.

- **Social networks.** People who build a substantial network of social and professional contacts are exposed to more opportunities and ideas than those with sparse ones. A survey of 65 startups showed that half of the entrepreneurs obtained their initial business idea from social contacts.
- **Creativity.** The fourth factor is the person's ability to generate a novel or useful idea from the information gleaned from the other factors.

Sustainability

Nicholas Stern (Stern, 2009) advises the UK government on climate change, and calls for urgent action to mitigate the effects. The paragraphs below summarise some of his points.

Climate change is not a theory struggling to maintain itself in the face of problematic evidence. The opposite is true: as new information comes in, it reinforces our understanding across a whole spectrum of indicators. The subject is full of uncertainty, but there is no serious doubt that emissions are growing as a result of human activity and that more greenhouse gases will lead to further warming.

The last 20 years have seen special and focused attention from the Intergovernmental Panel on Climate Change (IPCC) (www.ipcc.ch), which has published four assessments, the most recent in 2007. With each new report, the evidence on the strength and source of the effects, and the magnitude of the implications and risks, has become stronger. The basic scientific conclusions on climate change are very robust and for good reason. The greenhouse effect is simple science: greenhouse gases trap heat, and humans are emitting ever more greenhouse gases. There will be oscillations, there will be uncertainties. But the logic of the greenhouse effect is rock-solid and the long-term trends associated with the effects of human emissions are clear in the data.

In 2010 a report by the UK Meteorological Office (Stott, 2010) confirmed these conclusions, saying that the evidence was stronger now than when the Intergovernmental Panel on Climate Change carried out its last assessment in 2007. The analysis assessed 110 research papers on the subject, concluding that the earth is changing rapidly, probably because of greenhouse gases. The study found that changes in Arctic sea ice, atmospheric moisture, saltiness of parts of the Atlantic Ocean and temperature changes in the Antarctic are consistent with human influence on our climate.

Internationalisation

Models of national culture (see Chapter 4) are highly generalised summaries of diverse populations. Their value is to give some clues about broad differences between the places in which those managing internationally will be working. They encourage people to be ready to adapt the way they work to local circumstances.

The 'Management in practice' feature shows how Iris, a rapidly growing advertising agency with a very strong and distinctive company culture AND many global clients, seeks to gain the benefits of the diversity of its international staff and combine this to add more value for the client.

Management in practice   Gaining from cultural differences   www.irisnation.com

Iris was founded in 1999 and has established a distinctive position as an independent media and advertising agency, with a growing international business. An innovative technique that is very popular with global clients is 'Project 72'. Steve Bell, chief executive of Iris London, and one of the founding partners, explains:

Project 72 is a very simple concept, and probably the purest way of bringing different agencies in the group together as one with a common goal and a common vision. [Suppose] Iris Miami is working on a brief for a client: they say 'right, let's engage a Project 72 on this one'. So the brief will go to the other agencies around the world, it will be handed to London for example, we will work on it for twelve hours, we will then [hand the baton] to Sydney, they will work on it for twelve hours, baton change to Singapore, so you can see how within 72 hours we've got the best freshest brains working on a brief to the common goal of developing the best creative work that we possibly can do. It's been fantastic . . .

Project 72 benefits hugely from the cultural differences, and when I say cultural differences I don't mean within the agency but the societal cultural differences that happen within different areas around the world. So tapping into the fact that Singapore has a certain view around mobile telecomms enables us to look at things in a slightly different way, so it just allows fresh thinking, fresh outlooks, fresh cultures to inject some pace and some innovation around a particular brief at a given time.

Source: Interview with Steve Bell.

Governance

This chapter has examined the culture of organisations and their external contexts: governance links the two. There are many high-profile examples of organisations whose cultures have encouraged managers and staff to act in their interests, rather than in the interests of those they were expected to serve – usually shareholders but also customers or members of the public.

Barings Bank is one example (see also Mallin, 2013) – one of Britain's oldest banks when it collapsed in 1995. Nick Leeson, a trader based in Singapore, had built a reputation for gambling successfully on the stock market, and his senior managers in London were happy to provide him with funds to do this, as they were earning large profits. When his luck ran out he asked for more funds, which the bank continued to provide: he continued to invest in shares that then fell in value, making the situation worse. He was able to hide the losses from senior management for several months as he controlled the administrative processes – the trading and financial records – to conceal what was happening. The bank eventually collapsed, essentially because senior management had not imposed and enforced sufficiently robust controls, either through direct supervision or through transparent reporting procedures.

This illustrated the folly of trusting an apparently successful employee and being unwilling to scrutinise what they are doing. These lessons were ignored a decade later, when some senior traders in the investment division at The Royal Bank of Scotland engaged in very risky trading in securities derived from US home loans. Again the board (including the independent directors) was unable or unwilling to control the people who were making these trades, in part because they did not understand what they were doing – and were impressed by the profits they were earning.

Such cases (which happen in all sectors, though less spectacularly than in finance) draw attention to governance, which is part of the manager's context.

Summary

1 **Compare the cultures of two organisational units, using Quinn's or Handy's typologies:**
   - Quinn et al. (2003) – open systems, rational goal, internal process and human relations.
   - Handy (1993) – power, role, task and person.

2 **Use Porter's five forces model to analyse the competitive environment of an organisation:**
   - This identifies the degree of competitive rivalry, customers, competitors, suppliers and potential substitute goods and services.

3 Collect evidence to make a comparative PESTEL analysis for two organisations:
   - The PESTEL model of the wider external environment identifies political, economic, socio-cultural, technological, environmental and legal forces.

4 Compare environments in terms of their complexity and rate of change:
   - Environments can be evaluated in terms of their rate of change (stable/dynamic) and complexity (low/high).

5 Give examples of stakeholder expectations
   - These are shown in Table 3.3.

6 Explain the meaning and purpose of corporate governance
   - Corporate governance is intended to monitor and control the performance of managers, to ensure they act in the interests of stakeholders, not just of themselves.

7 Identify the PESTEL factors relevant to a specified organisation, and understand how to use that to develop the skill of presenting a reasoned case
   - Using the PESTEL model to guide a management decision depends on being able to present a convincing case to other people, and the chapter includes guidance on how to do that.

8 Show how ideas from the chapter add to your understanding of the integrating themes
   - Entrepreneurs depend on being quick to see opportunities, and research shows that this is increased by prior experience, cognitive factors (such as intuition) and wide social networks.
   - A major feature of the natural environment relevant to managers is the accumulating evidence that climate change is due to human activities, leading to pressure for organisations and people to work and live more sustainably.
   - While culture has a powerful effect on what people do in an organisation, when they operate internationally it provides an opportunity to benefit from diverse perspectives.
   - Some cultures encourage staff to take excessive risks, damaging companies and economies: this is leading stakeholders to press for tighter governance and control mechanisms.

Test your understanding

1 Describe an educational or commercial organisation that you know in terms of the competing values model of cultures.

2 What is the significance of the idea of 'fragmented cultures' for attempting cultural change?

3 Identify the relative influence of Porter's five forces on an organisation of your choice and compare your results with a colleague's. What can you learn from that comparison?

4 How should managers decide which of the many factors easily identified in a PESTEL analysis they should attend to? If they have to be selective, what is the value of the PESTEL method?

5 Since people interpret environmental forces from unique perspectives, what meaning can people attach to statements about external pressures?

6 Illustrate the stakeholder idea with an example of your own, showing their expectations of an organisation.

7 Explain at least two of the mechanisms that Mallin (2013) recommends should be part of a corporate governance system.

8 Summarise an idea from the chapter that adds to your understanding of the integrating themes.

Think critically

Think about the culture that seems to be dominant in your company (or another that interests you), and how managers deal with the business environment. Then make notes on these questions:

- What **assumptions** do people have about the culture, and whether it helps or hinders the business? How convincing is the evidence behind those views?
- What factors in their **context** have shaped the prevailing view about which PESTEL factors matter most to the business? What grounds are there for that claim?
- Compare your business environment with that of colleagues on your course. Does this show up **alternative** ways to see the context? What evidence would you expect in a convincing 'warrant' for adopting that alternative?
- What are the **limitations** of the PESTEL model?

Develop a skill – present a reasoned case

Part of many managers' role is to influence others to support proposals, so they need to develop the skill of presenting a reasoned case. This exercise is intended to help you do that.

- **Awareness.** Review how you usually present a proposal to someone whom you want to convince. How would you rate your ability to present a reasoned case? Review a presentation you have made (at work or during your course): how well do you think you did?
- **Learning.** Read again the 'Key ideas' feature (pp. 102–3, end of Section 3.5) including the elements of claim, grounds and warrants. Summarise the main ideas about presenting a reasoned case. How will being good at that help someone's career?
- **Analysis.** Identify someone (whom you know, or can read about) who is good at presenting a reasoned case. Consider what they do, what are the effects, and what you can learn from them.
- **Practice.** Recall the work you did on Case Question 3.4, and the 'Think critically' feature above. For ONE of the PESTEL factors you chose, summarise how you would claim that this factor matters for the BBC, by recording your notes under these headings:

PESTEL factor that you think matters for BBC	Your claim for why it is significant	Your explicit grounds for proposing that	Your warrant – does your claim connect to your grounds?

- Use your notes to prepare to present your claim to a listener.
- Create an opportunity to do this, record the results and reflect on what you can learn from the experience.
- **Application.** Decide on another opportunity to practise this skill within the next week.

Read more

Brown, L. (2010), *World on the Edge: How to prevent environmental and economic collapse,* Earthscan, London.

> Although it has flaws, this a useful introduction to some of the environmental issues businesses will face – especially the finite supplies of water and land.

Ogbonna, E. and Harris, L. C. (2014), 'Organisational cultural perpetuation: A case study of an English Premier League football club', *British Journal of Management,* vol. 25, no. 4, pp. 667–86.

A scientific study of organisational culture in a familiar industry: guess the club. . .

Pajunen, K. (2006), 'Stakeholder influences on organisational survival', *Journal of Management Studies,* vol. 43, no. 6, pp. 1261–88.

A theoretical background to case studies of stakeholder management.

Roeder, M. (2011), *The Big Mo: Why Momentum Now Rules Our World,* Virgin Books, London.

An account of how forces such as those discussed in the chapter sometimes gain progressively greater momentum, often with devastating results for businesses affected by them.

Tapscott, E. and Williams, A.D. (2006), *Wikinomics: How Mass Collaboration Changes Everything,* Viking Penguin, New York.

Best-selling account of the radical changes that convergent technologies bring to society, especially the relationship between producers and consumers.

Go online

These websites have appeared in the chapter:

www.bbc.co.uk
www.bosch.com
www.unilever.com
www.irisnation.com
www.ipcc.ch
www.tata.com
www.nfuonline.org
www.airBnB.co.uk
www.camra.org

Visit some of these, or any other companies that interest you, and navigate to the pages dealing with recent news, press or investor relations.

- What can you find about their culture?
- What are the main forces in the environment that the organisation appears to be facing?
- What assessment would you make of the nature of that environment?
- Compare and contrast the issues you identify on the two sites.
- What challenges may they imply for those working in, and managing, these organisations?

CHAPTER 4
MANAGING INTERNATIONALLY

Aim

To outline the factors shaping the work of those who manage internationally.

Objectives

By the end of your work on this chapter you should be able to outline the concepts below in your own terms and:

1 Contrast the ways in which organisations conduct international business

2 Explain, with examples, how PESTEL factors affect the decisions of those managing internationally

3 Summarise at least one aspect of EU policy (or of an international trade agreement) that is of interest to you for your career

4 Explain and illustrate the evidence on national cultures, and evaluate the significance of Hofstede's research for managers working internationally

5 Compare and contrast the features of national management systems

6 Summarise the forces stimulating the growth of international business

7 Use work related to Hofstede's cultural norms to understand how that can help you develop the skill of mindfulness

8 Show how ideas from the chapter add to your understanding of the integrating themes

Key terms

This chapter introduces the following ideas:

international management
offshoring
foreign direct investment
licensing
franchising
joint venture
multinational company
transnational company
global companies
theory of absolute advantage
political risk
ideology
pervasiveness (of corruption)

arbitrariness (of corruption)
high-context culture
low-context culture
cultural intelligence
mindfulness
power distance
uncertainty avoidance
individualism
collectivism
masculinity
femininity
globalisation

Each is a term defined within the text, as well as in the glossary at the end of the book.

Case study   Carlsberg   www.carlsberggroup.com

Carlsberg, based in Copenhagen, Denmark, is the world's fourth-largest brewer after ABinBev, SAB-Miller and Heineken. The main internationally marketed brands are the flagship Carlsberg, premium Kronenbourg 1664, Somersby cider and Tuborg. It manufactures, markets and sells 500 mainly local brands of beer from 85 breweries in more than 40 countries. In the financial year to the end of December 2015 its net revenue was 63.4 billion DKK, from which it generated an operating profit of 8.5 billion DKK, an operating margin of 13.4 per cent (down from 14.3 per cent the previous year). It employs 45,000 staff.

Beer consumption is falling in Western Europe and North America as people become more health-conscious, and many prefer to drink wine or spirits. Though founded in 1847, Carlsberg's first significant investment outside Denmark was in 1968 when it opened a brewery in Malawi. The following year it opened in Malaysia and, in 1981, Hong Kong; by the end of that decade it operated in many parts of the world. In 2001 management began a more determined overseas expansion – beginning with the acquisition of Norwegian brewer Orkla. This made Carlsberg the dominant player in the Nordic countries. In 2008 it acquired Kronenbourg (France) and Scottish and Newcastle in the UK, which also owned Baltic Beverages, market leader in Russia and the Baltics. These acquisitions gave it access to local brands, distribution networks and local knowledge of the beer market. It later acquired Chongqing Brewery in mainland China. This turned the company into a global business, which led to organisational change.

It has adopted a regional structure, in which local companies provide manufacturing, marketing and distribution expertise, reporting to regional management, while the centre manages support services such as IT and Finance. To internationalise its leadership and better support its strategy to be 'the fastest growing global beer company' it has hired managers from several global, fast-moving consumer goods (FMCG) companies. They were enthusiastic about moving the company rapidly in the direction of unified, centralised systems and brand, while simultaneously voicing respect for the belief that 'brewing will always be local'.

In 2015 the geographical distribution of sales by volume was: Western Europe 42 per cent; Eastern Europe 27 per cent; and Asia 31 per cent – the first year in which Asian sales have exceeded Eastern Europe. The Western Europe business is 'mature', with limited scope for growth, so it aims to improve profits by innovation and efficiency; in Eastern Europe the aim is to achieve rapid growth and higher earnings; while in Asia (especially China) it is to achieve long-term growth through building a strong market position. Carlsberg owns and manages breweries in each of these areas, and services the rest of the world through exporting and licensing arrangements. Western Europe also generates high profits, which Carlsberg uses to pay for expansion in Eastern Europe and Asia, or to pay dividends.

The Board also recognised the need for a cultural as well as structural change. A former CEO commented:

> The most important thing was to create a completely new winner culture, and to develop our staff so that they constantly take the lead in the market. (Søderberg, 2015, p. 239)

Sources: Søderberg (2015); company website.

Case questions 4.1

- What encouraged managers at Carlsberg to expand overseas, and what influenced their choice of countries in which to operate?
- What are the main risks that Carlsberg faces in expanding rapidly in overseas markets?
- What does the case so far suggest about the management issues it will face in operating internationally?

4.1 Introduction

Carlsberg's managers decided to expand the business overseas, and in doing so face common problems in managing around the world. These include where to focus investment, how to organise the overseas activities, how, if at all, to adapt to local tastes and how to ensure it adds value.

Retailers such as Tesco and Ikea face similar challenges of balancing the consistency of a global brand with what local customers expect. Manufacturers such as Ford and Coca-Cola are investing heavily in China, Brazil and India, where demand is growing rapidly. They have to manage relationships with local companies as partners or competitors, and work within their political and legal systems. They have to decide whether to work in a joint venture with a local company – in some countries the law requires this. Many overseas ventures fail, and so destroy value.

Managers consider not only economic aspects of growing overseas, but also whether the country's legal system will protect their investment, and its political stability. They face local sensitivities: when India's Tata Motors bought Jaguar and Land Rover they pledged to retain their UK identities, and to invest in modern equipment.

There has been international trade since the earliest times, dominated in recent centuries by Western economies. Now:

> China, India and the rest of the East, alongside [other] emerging economies, are beginning to challenge the West for positions of global industry leadership . . . By 2030, Asia's economy is estimated to be larger than that of the United States and the European Union combined . . . Asia is the world's most populous continent, [with 60 per cent of the world's population and is the fastest growing economic region] (Barkema et al., 2015, p. 461).

One-third of all trade takes place within transnational companies, part of the rapid growth in world trade – and of the shipping business – see 'Management in practice'.

Management in practice   Maersk and global trade   www.maersk.com

Maersk is the world's largest container shipping line, and its growth has reflected that of world trade. Doug Bannister, Managing Director of Maersk Line (UK and Ireland), explained:

> We're involved in the transportation sector, about 90 per cent of world trade is done by sea-borne transportation, it is an incredible industry to be associated with: our primary mission is to create opportunities in global commerce.
>
> The scale of containerised shipping is enormous. Container shipping has been around for 40 years, and it's had incredible growth, 8 to 10 per cent a year. The types of stuff we bring in are anything from lamps to furniture to bananas, about 90 per cent of anything that you'd see in any room was transported in by one of our ships.
>
> Several external factors have really played into Maersk Line's growth, globalisation probably being the primary one, and the explosion of world trade has been incredible. This is down to efficient transport solutions, and to companies moving production to low-cost countries.

Source: Interview with Doug Bannister.

International management is the practice of managing business operations in more than one country.

From a career point of view, **international management** (managing business operations in more than one country) can mean:

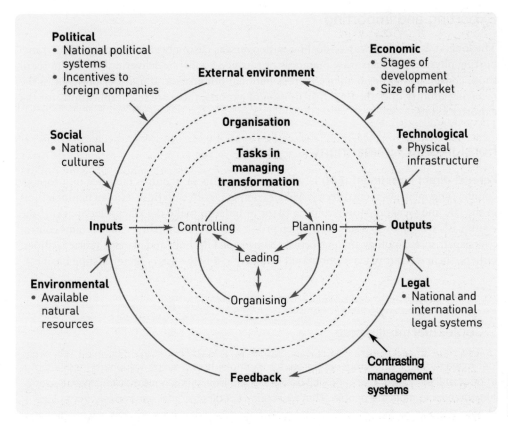

Figure 4.1 Themes in managing internationally

- working as an *expatriate manager* in another country
- joining or managing an *international team* with members from several countries
- managing in *a global organisation* whose employees, systems and structures are truly international in that they no longer reflect its original, national base.

The chapter begins by showing how companies conduct business internationally, and then turns to the context of international business (PESTEL), with sections on trade agreements and national cultures. Being 'mindful' when dealing with people from other cultures is a valuable skill, and there is an opportunity to begin to develop that. Finally, it contrasts national management systems and examines the forces driving globalisation. Figure 4.1 illustrates the themes.

4.2   Ways to conduct business internationally

Companies that conduct international business do so by one or more of six methods. Whichever they use, their success will depend on how well they take account of the local context (see 'Key ideas').

Offshoring

Offshoring happens when managers decide to transfer activities to countries to add more value. This began when companies in developed Western economies transferred routine manufacturing activities to low-wage developing countries. The internet enables companies to transfer administrative activities (such as payroll or accounting) overseas.

Offshoring is the practice of contracting out activities to companies in other countries who can do the work more cost-effectively.

Exporting and importing

The longest established way of dealing with overseas customers and suppliers is by transporting physical products (raw materials or finished goods) or delivering services (a retail shop, consultancy or legal advice) across national boundaries. If a dealer or agent in the receiving country does the final distribution of exports, there are few implications for the exporter's staff.

Foreign direct investment

Foreign direct investment (FDI) is the practice of investing shareholder funds directly in another country, by building or buying physical facilities, or by buying a company.

Foreign direct investment (FDI) is when a firm builds or acquires facilities in a foreign country, and manages them directly. Motor companies often do this – Nissan manufactures in the UK and General Motors built a plant in India to make the Chevrolet Spark. If the venture is a wholly-owned subsidiary then profits stay in the company, which retains control over expertise, technology and marketing. Nissan and GM built and managed their facilities. Others, such as Kraft when it purchased Cadbury's, buy the assets of an existing business.

Key ideas   Contextual intelligence

Context matters. Most managers and entrepreneurs agree, for example, that creating value and motivating talent are at the heart of what they do. But once you drill below the homilies, differences quickly emerge over what constitutes value and how to motivate people. That's because conditions differ enormously from place to place, in ways that aren't easy to codify – conditions not just of economic development, but of institutional character, physical geography, educational norms, culture and language. Students of management once thought that best manufacturing practices (to take one example) were sufficiently established that processes merely needed tweaking to fit local conditions. More often, it turns out, they need radical rewriting – not because the technology is wrong, but because everything surrounding the technology changes how it will work. . . '

Khanna (2014) illustrates the theme with an example from the cement industry:

The technology for manufacturing cement is the same everywhere, but individual cement plants are located in specific contexts that vary widely. Corrupt material suppliers may adulterate the mixtures that go into cement. Unions may impede or support plant operations. Finished cement may be sold to construction firms in bulk or to individuals in bags. Such variables often outweigh the unifying effects of a common technology. (p. 81)

Source: Khanna (2014).

Licensing

Licensing is when one firm gives another firm the right to use assets such as patents or technology in exchange for a fee.

Franchising is the practice of extending a business by giving other organisations, in return for a fee, the right to use your brand name, technology or product specifications.

Licensing occurs when a business licenses (grants the right to) a firm (the licensee) in another country to produce and sell its products – such as the deal between Imperial Tobacco and a Chinese group to produce and distribute Imperial brands in the world's largest cigarette market. The licensing firm receives a payment for each unit sold (usually called a royalty payment), while the licensee takes the risk of investing in manufacturing and distribution. **Franchising** is similar, used by service businesses to expand rapidly. The expanding firm sells the right (the franchise) to a company, which allows it (the franchisee) to use the brand name and product design to build a business in the target market. The seller usually imposes tight conditions on quality, working procedures and customer service: franchisees run many fast-food outlets.

Joint ventures

Joint ventures enable firms in two or more countries to share the risks and resources required to do business internationally. Most joint ventures link a foreign firm with one in the host country to take advantage of the latter's facilities and/or knowledge of local customs, politics and ways of working. They agree their respective investment and how to share the profits. Imax has a joint venture with Wanda Cinema Line, China's largest cinema operator, to open 75 cinemas in the country. The hazards of joint ventures include cultural differences and misunderstandings.

> A **joint venture** is an alliance in which the partners agree to form a separate, independent organisation for a specific business purpose.

Wholly-owned subsidiary

Managers who want to retain close control over international activities create a subsidiary in another country. This is costly, but if the venture works then all profits stay in the company, which retains control over its expertise, technology and marketing. It secures local knowledge by employing local staff. The company may establish the subsidiary as a new entity or acquire an existing business.

Johnson and Tellis (2008) found that the success depended on how much control the lead company retained. Exporting (cheap) gives little control, as managers cannot decide how their products are finally distributed and sold. A wholly-owned subsidiary (expensive) gives high control, as the company can deploy finance or marketing knowledge if required. Firms with a high degree of control were consistently more successful than those without.

Companies also develop forms of organisation through which to conduct their international business – multinational, transnational and global.

Management in practice   Banco Santander   www.santander.com

In less than twenty years Banco Santander changed from being a Spanish regional bank into one of the world's largest. Parada et al. (2009) report that, unusually, international growth was profitable, due to the systematic way managers built their international presence, namely:

- **building capabilities** in the home market;
- **creating growth options** in foreign markets through small acquisitions (e.g. acquiring Alliance and Leicester in the UK) to become familiar with a country, and to identify possible larger acquisitions; and
- **large-scale foreign market entry** and rapid integration. If it decides to remain in the country it acquires local banks and quickly integrates them into its established ways of working.

The bank regards information systems as critical to its operations and invests heavily in them: for example in credit risk management. The system the bank developed in the home market enables it to assess risk better than competitors and also to act swiftly and insistently when a client falls into arrears. As soon as Santander acquires a foreign bank all its systems are rapidly integrated, bringing further cost savings.

Source: Based on Parada et al. (2009).

Multinational companies are based in one country, and have significant production and marketing operations in many others – perhaps over a third of sales. Managers in the home country make the big decisions.

Transnational companies also operate in many countries, but decentralise many decisions to local managers. The company uses their local knowledge to build the business, while still projecting a consistent company image.

> **Multinational companies** are managed from one country, but have significant production and marketing operations in many others.
> **Transnational companies** operate in many countries and delegate many decisions to local managers.

Global companies work in many countries, securing resources and finding markets in whichever country is most suitable.

Global companies work in many countries, securing resources and markets in the most suitable. Production or service processes are performed, and integrated, across many global locations – as are ownership, control and top management. Staff at Trend Micro (www. trendmicro.co.uk), a global leader in IT security, must respond rapidly to threats anywhere in the world. Trend's financial headquarters is in Tokyo; product development is in Taiwan (a good source of staff with a PhD); and the sales department is in California – inside the huge US market. Nestlé (www.nestle.com) is another example: although headquarters are in Switzerland, 98 per cent of sales and 96 per cent of employees are not. Such businesses are often organised by product, with those in charge of each unit securing resources from whichever country gives best value.

Activity 4.1   Choosing between approaches

Consider the different ways of expanding a business internationally.

- For each of the methods outlined above, note the advantages and disadvantages.
- Identify a company with international operations, and gather evidence to help you decide which method(s) it has used.
- Compare your research with colleagues on your course, and prepare a short presentation summarising your conclusions.

Case questions 4.2

- Which of the modes of entry outlined above has Carlsberg used?
- Using the definitions here, is Carlsberg a multinational, transnational or global firm?

4.3   The contexts of international business – PESTEL

People managing internationally pay close attention to the international aspects of the general business environment (Chapter 3), shown in Figure 4.2. This is similar to Figure 3.5, in the sense that it is a compilation of groups of factors that managers, to a greater or lesser degree, pay attention to when managing internationally. The factors are always present in their context, but are only likely to come to their attention, become part of their agenda, when they start doing business internationally. Section 4.3 outlines four of these (beginning, for clarity, with the economic context), and Sections 4.4 and 4.5 present the legal and socio-cultural contexts.

Economic context

The **theory of absolute advantage** is a trade theory that proposes that by specialising in producing goods and services that they can produce more efficiently than others, and then trading them, nations will increase their economic wealth.

One area of economic theory aims to understand why nations trade with each other, rather than being self-sufficient. The **theory of absolute advantage** states that by specialising in the production of goods that they can produce more cheaply than other countries, and then trading them, nations will increase their economic well-being. If countries use the resources in which they have an advantage (land, raw materials or efficient methods) to produce goods and services, and exchange them with countries for things in which *they* are most efficient, this will add more value than if everyone was self-sufficient. Self-sufficiency sounds attractive, but costs more than buying things from someone else. The theory is more complex (see Chapter 6 in Rugman and Hodgetts (2003) for a fuller treatment) – but even this simple account begins to explain why nations trade, even though each could make the goods themselves.

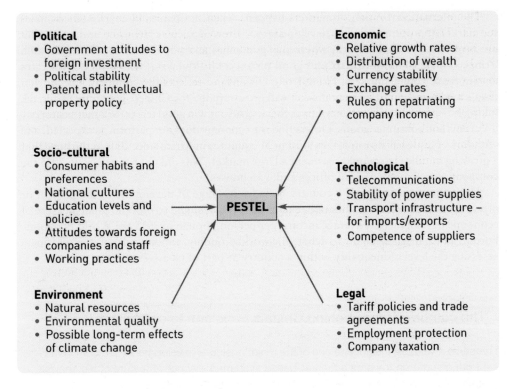

Political
- Government attitudes to foreign investment
- Political stability
- Patent and intellectual property policy

Economic
- Relative growth rates
- Distribution of wealth
- Currency stability
- Exchange rates
- Rules on repatriating company income

Socio-cultural
- Consumer habits and preferences
- National cultures
- Education levels and policies
- Attitudes towards foreign companies and staff
- Working practices

Technological
- Telecommunications
- Stability of power supplies
- Transport infrastructure – for imports/exports
- Competence of suppliers

PESTEL

Environment
- Natural resources
- Environmental quality
- Possible long-term effects of climate change

Legal
- Tariff policies and trade agreements
- Employment protection
- Company taxation

Figure 4.2 An international PESTEL analysis

The theory partly explains the rapid internationalisation of production since the 1960s. Firms in the developed world realised that labour-intensive manufacturing – especially in electrical goods, clothing, footwear and toys – costs more to make than to import. They quickly found suppliers in a small group of Asian countries – Taiwan, Hong Kong, South Korea and especially Singapore. These became major 'offshoring' centres, supplying goods and components to companies around the world. In 2015 Ford announced a $2.5 billion investment in Mexico, further enhancing the reputation of the nation as a manufacturing base. Carmakers from around the world have been attracted to Mexico by cheap labour and low tariffs on important materials to produce cars for the US market (*Financial Times*, 17 April 2015). Table 4.1 gives other examples.

Companies sometimes find that remote operations require more management time than they are worth (they add little value), so they 'repatriate' the outsourced activities.

Table 4.1 Examples of the internationalisation of production

Company	Work transferred	Reasons given
BT www.bt.com	Opened call centres in India, replacing the jobs of 2,000 staff in the UK	To meet cost-saving targets and remain competitive
Gillette www.gillette.com	Closed three factories (two UK and one German) and transferred work to new factory in Eastern Europe	Significantly reduce costs and improve operating efficiency
Dyson www.dyson.co.uk	Moved production of vacuum and cleaners and washing machines from UK to Malaysia	Reduce manufacturing costs to protect UK jobs in design and development

The internationalisation of markets happens when companies in developed countries see market opportunities in less developed ones. Brewers such as Heineken and SABMiller are investing heavily in Africa, where rising incomes and population stimulate demand. Tobacco maker Phillip Morris sees good prospects in Malaysia, whose high birth rates ensure more young smokers. Hong Kong Disneyland reflects the company's belief that Asia's media and entertainment market will grow rapidly: the Chinese government agreed, taking a 57 per cent stake. Disney hopes this will help it win good terms for other ventures – TV, films and consumer goods. Others find the economy does not perform as expected, and withdraw. Nestlé has invested over $1bn in 21 countries in Africa since 2008 in the hope that a growing middle class would represent a large market. This did not happen, so in 2015 the company closed many African offices and warehouses.

The economic context of a country includes its stage of development, the growth or otherwise of a middle class, inflation, exchange rates, debt and so on. The usual measure of economic development is average income per person, though in 2015 the World Economic Forum, which meets annually to debate the world economy, announced that it would begin assessing the level of inequality within a country as part of its assessment.

Key ideas	**The complex forces behind China's transition to capitalism**

Doug Guthrie (2006) presents a valuable insight into one of the major business developments in recent years – the transition of China from a state-run towards a market-based system. A distinctive feature of his analysis is the emphasis he places on the links between political, social, cultural and economic forces:

Economic institutions and practices are deeply embedded in political, cultural and social systems, and it is impossible to analyse the economy without analysing the way it is shaped by politics, culture and the social world. The perspective is essential for understanding the complex processes of economic and social reform in any transforming society, but it is especially critical for understanding China's reform path and trajectory. This position may seem obvious to some, but . . . for years, economists from the World Bank, the IMF, and various reaches of academia have operated from a different set of assumptions: they have assumed that a transition to markets is a simple and, basically, apolitical process . . . In other words, 'don't worry about the complexities of culture or pre-existing social or political systems; if you put the right capitalist institutions in place (i.e. private property), transition to a market economy will be a simple process'. The perspective I present here is that the standard economic view of market transitions that defined a good deal of policy for the IMF and the World Bank in the late twentieth century could not be more simplistic or more wrong.

Source: Guthrie (2006), pp. 10–11.

Political context

Whatever economic theory predicts about the patterns of trade, political factors – such as governmental arrangements, political involvement with business, and corruption – also affect a country's attractiveness to investment. They shape the **political risk** facing an investor – the risk of losing assets, earning power or managerial control due to political events or the actions of host governments. Those considering overseas investment try to take account of the stability of the regime, the rule of law (or not) and the risks of terrorism.

The political system in a country influences business, and managers adapt to the prevailing **ideology**. Political ideologies are closely linked to economic philosophies and attitudes towards business. In the United States the political ideology is grounded in a constitution guaranteeing property rights and freedom of choice. These are the foundations of a capitalist economy favourable to business. Australia and the UK are equally capitalist in outlook, while others such as Brazil or France have ideologies favouring social considerations.

Political risk is the risk of losing assets, earning power or managerial control due to political events or the actions of host governments.

Ideology is a set of integrated beliefs, theories and doctrines that helps to direct the actions of a society.

There are close links between political and economic systems – especially in how they allocate resources and deal with property ownership. Governments set rules that establish what commercial activity can occur, and how people conduct it – in a capitalist way, a centrally-controlled way, or a mix. Political systems affect business life through:

- the balance between state-owned and privately-owned enterprises;
- the amount of state intervention through subsidies, taxes and regulation;
- policies towards foreign companies trading in the country, with or without local partners (the Indian government has developed strict and complex rules governing foreign retailers to discourage them from entering the market: a government can prevent such acquisitions by buying shares in a threatened company, enabling the state to block the deal);
- policies towards foreign companies acquiring local firms;
- policies on employment practices, working conditions and job protection. In 2015 *The New York Times* began to increase its presence in London at the expense of its long-established European headquarters in Paris. The company . . . acknowledged that French Government laws had played a part in the decision: 'There is more labour flexibility in London compared with Paris' it said. (*Financial Times*, 8 June 2015, p. 19)

Management in practice   Guarded globalisation

Bremmer (2014) notes the emergence of what he terms 'guarded globalisation', in the sense that:

> Governments of developing nations have become wary of opening more industries to multinationals and are zealously protecting local interests. They choose the countries or regions with which they want to do business, pick the sectors in which they will allow capital investment, and select the local, often state-owned, companies they wish to promote. That's a very different flavour of globalisation: slow-moving, selective, and with a heavy dash of nationalism and regionalism. (p. 104)

Source: Bremmer (2014).

Corruption

All states experience some degree of **corruption** – which Transparency International (www.transparency.org) defines as the use of entrusted power for private gain. Coping with this is part of the job of international managers, but Rodriguez et al. (2005) point out:

> while corruption is everywhere . . . it is not the same everywhere. (p. 383)

They introduce a framework to analyse the implications of corruption for business – based on its **pervasiveness** and **arbitrariness**. Pervasiveness is the extent to which a firm is likely to encounter corruption during transactions with officials. Arbitrariness is the degree of ambiguity associated with corrupt transactions. When corruption is arbitrary, officials apply rules haphazardly – perhaps enforcing them strictly in some areas but ignoring them elsewhere. Figure 4.3 illustrates this.

Corruption is the use of entrusted power for private gain.

Pervasiveness (of corruption) represents the extent to which a firm is likely to encounter corruption in the course of normal transactions with state officials.

Arbitrariness (of corruption) is the degree of ambiguity associated with corrupt transactions.

Technological context

Infrastructure includes all of the physical facilities that support economic activities – ports, airports, surface transport, electricity and telecommunications. Companies operating abroad, especially in less developed countries, are closely interested in the quality of this aspect of a country as it has a huge effect on the cost and convenience of conducting business in the area.

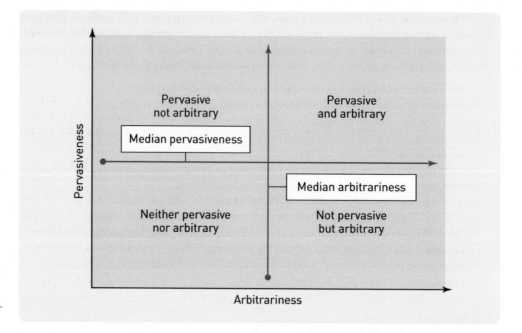

Figure 4.3 Two dimensions of corruption: pervasiveness and arbitrariness

Source: Based on Rodriguez et al. (2005).

Management in practice   **Power shortages benefit Aggreko**   www.aggreko.com

Many developing economies regularly experience severe shortages of power as demand for electricity exceeds their generating capacity. This provides opportunities for Aggreko, a UK company with about 2,000 staff, which rents power generation and temperature control equipment to businesses and governments. One division in the company is International Power Projects, which provides long-term power generation capacity to countries without sufficient installed capacity. For example, the company provides almost half of Uganda's electricity, and also supplies Bangladesh and Kenya.

Source: Company website.

A poor infrastructure is an opportunity for those supplying such facilities. European water companies have won contracts to provide water and sanitation to many developing countries.

Developments in information technology stimulate international trade in two ways. The electronics industry requires billions of high-value, low-weight components, produced in globally-dispersed factories and assembly plants – from which finished products are in turn transported around the world. These movements are a major source of growth in world trade. The internet makes it easier for managers to control international operations, and so encourages trade.

Environmental context

One aspect of the environment is an economy's natural resources – oil, coal and other minerals, land and the prevailing climate. Some resources are renewable but many are not. Water is scarce in many countries, and a major concern not only to local residents but to international food production companies. Many industries in China depend on water from the Yellow River – economic growth is making it harder to ensure adequate supplies.

These considerations affect the kind of businesses that people create in a country, and the pattern of world trade. Technological developments reveal previously unknown resources (new oil reserves in Central Asia) and allow the use of some that were uneconomic (shale oil in North America). This benefits the country, and the companies who extract the resources.

The process is also controversial, as when foreign mining or oil companies come into conflict with local populations whose land they occupy, or over the commercial terms of the concessions.

Some object to the environmental degradation associated with timber or mineral exploitation, whose effects spread widely (such as when rivers are polluted in one country before flowing to another). Economic development itself causes pollution – a problem for people in the area, and an opportunity for companies that clean up the environment.

Activity 4.2   Reflecting on contexts

- Go to the website of a large company (such as BAE systems, **www.bae.com**) and see what examples you can find of managers responding to ONE of the factors in this section.
- Alternatively, if you have worked in a company operating internationally, which of the contextual factors in this section had most effect on the management of the business?

4.4   Legal context – trade agreements and trading blocs

Managers planning to enter an overseas market ensure they are familiar with local laws and regulations affecting business practice: they also seek to satisfy themselves that the local legal system will protect them in the event of disputes with customers or suppliers. Beyond conditions in an individual country, companies work within trade agreements and economic alliances.

GATT and the World Trade Organization

The General Agreement on Tariffs and Trade (GATT) reduces the tendency of national governments to put tariffs on physical goods to protect domestic companies. Its main tool is tariff concessions, whereby member countries agree to limit the level of tariffs they impose on imports. GATT has also sponsored a series of international trade negotiations aimed at reducing restrictions on trade – one of which established the World Trade Organization (www.wto.org). This monitors international trade and arbitrates in disputes between countries over the interpretation of tariffs and other barriers to trade. It is also seeking a world agreement on rules governing foreign investment.

European Union

Since the leaders of the original member states signed the Treaty of Rome in 1959, the aim of the European Union (EU) (http://europa.eu) has been to eliminate tariffs and other restrictions that governments use to protect domestic industries. The European Commission (responsible for proposing and implementing policy) is encouraging European trade by proposing changes in national laws to make it easier. Car companies such as BMW have plants in several countries, each specialising in a few components or models. They import and export these between them as part of a European production system.

The Single European Act of 1986 aimed to create a single internal market. Introducing the euro as a common currency for many of the members encouraged further changes in the European economy by unifying capital markets and making price comparisons more transparent. It is the world's biggest exporter and the second biggest importer. The EU continues to deepen integration to enable the free movement of goods and services and so improve efficiency by:

- harmonising technical regulations between member states;
- creating a common industrial policy (e.g. eliminating subsidies for businesses);
- liberalising services (such as mail) across the EU;
- harmonising rules on employment and environmental protection;
- facilitating cross-border mergers; and
- recognising professional qualifications to enable freer movement.

The EU is developing common policies on monetary and political matters, so that it can speak with a single voice on (for example) interest rates and financial regulation. The Lisbon Treaty (2009) aims to enable the EU to work more effectively by extending Qualified Majority Voting (QMV) to streamline decisions in technical areas (e.g. appointments to the European Central Bank's board). The UK insists on maintaining national control in areas of justice, home affairs, social security, tax, foreign policy and defence: the Lisbon Treaty clarified this.

Enlargement has long been a feature of the EU agenda, the greatest event being in 2004 when ten members (many from Eastern Europe) joined. In 2016 a majority of the British electorate voted in favour of Britain leaving the EU, and negotiations will begin to bring that about.

Management in practice

Competition for the Polish Post Office

Jerzy Jozkowiak, head of the Polish national postal operator, is unsparing in his criticism of the company he has led since March 2011:

> Our efficiency is four or five times lower than in western Europe. The Polish Post Office is one of the most inefficient post offices in the European Union.

The Polish operator earns about €18,000 per worker, while the EU average is €72,600. Polish postal workers handle an average of 17,000 letters per year, while the European average is 63,600.

That is a problem because, from this month, the Polish postal market has been deregulated and letter deliveries have been opened to competition. Finally buckling to pressure from Brussels, Poland is one of the last EU countries to undertake this step, but the long resistance to change has left the post office very vulnerable. Mr Jozkowiak says:

> This is the largest market in this part of Europe. If someone has already gone through the privatisation process then this is a natural market for them.

Source: *Financial Times*, 11 January 2013.
© The Financial Times 2013. All Rights Reserved.

Activity 4.3   Access the European Union website http://europa.eu

- Access the European Union website, and navigate to areas that interest you, such as those on European Policies, or on Jobs at the Commission.
- Alternatively, gather information from the site that provides you with specific examples or evidence about one of the topics in this chapter, which you could use in an essay or assignment.
- Record notes on what you have found, and compare them with a colleague on your course.

4.5   Socio-cultural context

Culture is distinct from human nature (features that human beings have in common) and from an individual's personality (their unique way of thinking, feeling and acting). It is a collective phenomenon, which people learned and shared in a common social environment. Hofstede and Hofstede (2005) describe it as:

> the collective programming of the mind which distinguishes one group or category of people from others (in which 'group' means a number of people in contact with each other, and a 'category' means people who have something in common, such as people born before 1940). (p. 4 and p. 377)

While humans share common biological features, those in a particular society, nation or region develop a distinct culture. As a business becomes more international, managers balance the possible benefits of unified ways of working across the world with the unique local cultures in which they operate. Many now train managers in how to work with people from many cultures.

Cultural diversity and evolution

Hofstede and Hofstede (2005) note the diversity of cultures between human societies, even though people have evolved from common ancestors. There are recognisable differences between people in geographically separate areas in how they communicate, how they respond to authority, when they go to work – and in countless other aspects of social life. Societies develop these practices as they adapt to their environment, experience military or religious conquest, or exploit scientific discoveries. These are overlaid by the more recent creation of nations:

> strictly speaking, the concept of a common culture applies to societies, not to nations . . . yet rightly or wrongly, properties are ascribed to the citizens of certain countries: people refer to 'typically American', 'typically German', 'typically Japanese' behaviour. Using nationality is a matter of expediency. (pp. 18–19)

Nations develop distinct institutions – governments, laws, business systems and so on. Some believe these in themselves account for national differences in behaviour, implying that institutions (such as a legal system) that work in one country will do so elsewhere. A counter view is that institutions reflect their culture – something that works in one country, may fail in another:

> Institutions cannot be understood without considering culture, and understanding culture presumes insight into institutions. (p. 20)

Culture and managing internationally

Managers working internationally are aware of the benefits of understanding and managing cultural differences. This is most evident when one company acquires, or enters into a joint venture with, a company in a country with a different culture. These often take much longer to add value than expected – such as the merger between two telecoms-equipment makers – French company Alcatel and US company Lucent. Insiders claimed the two were never properly integrated, with damaging culture clashes wasting energy – it lost about four-fifths of its market value in the following eight years. One observer:

> A lot of companies are struggling to find the middle way. As a global company they would like to impose their view of the world. But being aware of cultural differences, you can't manage Chinese or Japanese employees the same way you manage Americans.

Cultural intelligence is when a person is skilled and flexible about understanding a culture, and learns as they interact with it.

Mindfulness is the ability to pay attention in a reflective and creative way to cues in cross-cultural situations.

Another noted how one company trying to build an overseas business had made considerable efforts to understand the local culture in new markets:

It's a very thoughtful company, the way it sees culture is continually evolving. It has had executives stay in people's homes in new markets, to stay with families to see their relationship with food.

It had also tried to import foreign knowledge, bringing overseas managers to the UK to observe and document the company's culture here, and helping to build a more blended management team. (*Financial Times*, 25 August 2011, p. 10)

Such practices are examples of being 'mindful' – paying attention to context. It means using our senses as we listen to others, viewing situations with an open mind, and being aware of our assumptions as we communicate across cultures. Activity 4.4 helps you with this.

Key ideas	Cultural intelligence

Thomas and Inkson (2009) advocate that those working across cultures should develop **cultural intelligence** – being skilled and flexible about understanding a culture, and learning about it as they interact with it.

We must learn to be flexible enough to adapt to each new cultural situation . . . with knowledge and sensitivity. Cultural intelligence consists of three parts.

First, the culturally intelligent person requires knowledge of culture and of the fundamental principles of cross-cultural interaction. This means knowing what culture is, how cultures vary, and how culture affects behaviour.

Second, the culturally intelligent person needs to practice **mindfulness**, the ability to pay attention in a reflective and creative way to cues in the cross-cultural situations encountered and to one's own knowledge and feelings.

Third, based on knowledge and mindfulness, the culturally intelligent person develops cross-cultural skills and becomes competent across a wide range of situations. These skills involve choosing the appropriate behaviour from a well-developed repertoire of behaviours that are correct for different intercultural situations. (p. 16)

Acquiring the skill of cultural intelligence is not about becoming more skilled in a particular . . . set of behaviours, but about building general skills that extend the range, or repertoire, of skilled behaviours and knowing when to use each one . . . The general skills that . . . relate to cross-cultural interactions are relational skills, tolerance for uncertainty, empathy, perceptual acuity and adaptability. The specific behavioural skills required to manage across cultures [are the familiar range of interpersonal skills – including empathy, listening, expressing ideas, or working together]. (pp. 57–60)

Source: Thomas and Inkson (2009).

Activity 4.4	Becoming mindful while comparing cultures

Form a group among your student colleagues made up of people from different countries.

- Identify the main characteristics of the respective cultures in your group.
- Do group members think the differences in cultures will affect the work of managing?
- Compare your evidence on cultural differences with that from Hofstede's research (Section 4.6).

• As you work on this, be mindful of how the group works: pay attention to the way you interact with each other, and try to note contrasts. Continue practising mindfulness whenever you are with people from different cultures.

High-context and low-context cultures

Hall (1976) distinguished between high- and low-context cultures. In a **high-context culture** information is implicit, and can only be fully understood by those with the benefit of shared experience, assumptions and verbal codes. This happens when people live closely together, developing deep mutual understandings that provide a rich context for communication. In a **low-context culture** information is explicit and clear. These cultures occur where people are psychologically distant, and so depend more on explicit information to communicate:

> Japanese, Arabs and Mediterranean people, who have extensive information networks among family, friends, colleagues and clients and who are involved in close personal relationships, are examples of high context cultures. Low context peoples include Americans, Germans, Swiss, Scandinavians and other northern Europeans; they compartmentalise their personal relationships, their work and many aspects of day-to-day life. (Tayeb, 1996, pp. 55–6)

High-context cultures are those in which information is implicit and can only be fully understood by those with shared experiences in the culture.

Low-context cultures are those where people are more psychologically distant so that information needs to be explicit if members are to understand it.

Attitude to conflict and harmony

Disagreements and conflict arise in all societies. The management interest is in how societies vary in how people deal with it. Individualistic cultures such as the United States or the Netherlands see conflict as healthy, as everyone has a right to express their views. People bring disagreements into the open and discuss them. Other cultures place greater value on social harmony and on not disturbing the peace:

> The notion of harmony is central in almost all East Asian cultures, such as Korea, Taiwan, Singapore and Hong Kong, through their common Confucian heritage. In . . . Korea the traditional implicit rules of proper behaviour provide appropriate role behaviour for individuals in junior and subordinate roles. (Tayeb, 1996, p. 60)

Several scholars have developed survey instruments to classify and compare national cultures, notably Trompenaars (1993), House et al. (2004) and Hofstede and Hofstede (2005). Hofstede's work has been widely used (Kirkman et al. 2006), and the next section outlines it.

4.6   Hofstede's comparison of national cultures

Geert Hofstede conducted widely quoted studies of national cultural differences. The second edition of his research (Hofstede and Hofstede, 2005) extends and refines the conclusions of his original work, which was based on a survey of the attitudes of 116,000 IBM employees, one of the earliest global companies. The research inspired many empirical studies with non-IBM employees in both the original countries in which IBM operated and in places where they did not. Kirkman et al. (2006) reviewed these and concluded that 'most of the country differences predicted by Hofstede were supported' (p. 308). Hofstede and Hofstede (2005, pp. 25–8) make a similar point and also provide an accessible account of the research method.

Hofstede saw culture as a collective programming of people's minds, which influences how they react to events. He identified five dimensions of culture and used a questionnaire to measure how people vary between countries in their attitudes to them.

Power distance

Power distance is the extent to which the less powerful members of organisations within a country expect and accept that power is distributed unevenly.

Power distance (PD) is 'the extent to which the less powerful members of ... organisations within a country expect and accept that power is distributed unevenly' (Hofstede and Hofstede, 2005, p. 46). Countries differ in how they distribute power and authority, and in how people view the resultant inequality. Some see inequality in boss/subordinate relationships as undesirable, while other people see it as part of the natural order. The questionnaire allowed the researchers to calculate scores for PD – high PD showing people accepted inequality. Those with high scores included Malaysia, Mexico, Venezuela, Arab countries, China, France and Brazil. Those with low PD scores included Denmark, Germany, Great Britain, Sweden and Norway.

Uncertainty avoidance

Uncertainty avoidance is the extent to which members of a culture feel threatened by uncertain or unknown situations.

Uncertainty avoidance is 'the extent to which the members of a culture feel threatened by ambiguous or unknown situations' (Hofstede and Hofstede, 2005, p. 167). People in some cultures are reluctant to move without clear rules or instructions – they avoid uncertainty. Others readily tolerate uncertainty and ambiguity – if things are not clear they improvise or use their initiative. Uncertainty avoidance scores were high in Russia, France, Latin American and Mediterranean countries, and for Japan and Korea. Low UA (happy with ambiguity) scores were recorded in China and most Asian countries, and in most of the Anglo and Nordic countries – United States, Great Britain, Sweden and Denmark.

Activity 4.5   Implications of cultural differences

- Consider the implications of differences on Hofstede's power distance and uncertainty avoidance dimensions for management in the countries concerned. For example, what would Hofstede's conclusions lead you to predict about the method that a French or Venezuelan manager would use if he or she wanted a subordinate to perform a task, and what method would the subordinate expect his or her manager to use? (Note: France is part of the Latin European cluster in Figure 4.4.)
- How would your answers differ if the manager and subordinates were Swedish?

Individualism/collectivism

Individualism pertains to societies in which the ties between individuals are loose.

Collectivism 'describes societies in which people, from birth onwards, are integrated into strong, cohesive in-groups which ... protect them in exchange for unquestioning loyalty.' (Hofstede, 2005, p. 76)

Hofstede and Hofstede (2005) distinguish between **individualism** and **collectivism**:

> Individualism pertains to societies in which the ties between individuals are loose: everyone is expected to look after himself or herself and his or her immediate family. Collectivism as its opposite pertains to societies in which people, from birth onwards, are integrated into strong, cohesive in-groups which throughout people's lifetime continue to protect them in exchange for unquestioning loyalty. (2005, p. 76)

Some people live in societies that emphasise the individual, and his or her responsibility for their position in life. Others value the group, placing more emphasis on collective action, mutual responsibility, and on helping each other through difficulties. High individualism scores occurred in the United States, Australia, Great Britain, France and Canada. Low scores occurred in less developed South American and Asian countries, including China.

Masculinity/femininity

A society is called **masculine** when emotional gender roles are clearly distinct: men are supposed to be assertive, tough and focused on material success, whereas women are supposed to be more modest, tender and concerned with the quality of life. A society is called **feminine** when emotional gender roles overlap (i.e. both men and women are supposed to be modest, tender and concerned with the quality of life). (Hofstede and Hofstede, 2005, p. 120)

Masculinity pertains to societies in which social gender roles are clearly distinct.

Femininity pertains to societies in which social gender roles overlap.

The research showed that societies differ in the desirability of assertive behaviour (which he labels as masculinity) and of modest behaviour (femininity). Many expect men to seek achievements outside the home while women care for things within the home. Masculinity scores were not related to economic wealth: 'we find both rich and poor masculine countries, and rich and poor feminine countries' (p. 120). The most feminine countries were Sweden, Norway, the Netherlands and Denmark. Masculine countries included Japan, China, Austria, Germany, Great Britain and the United States.

Integrating the dimensions

These dimensions describe the culture of a society, and each is unique. They also have similarities – UK, Canada and the US all have high individualism, moderate masculinity, low power distance and low uncertainty avoidance. In these nations managers expect workers to take the initiative and assume responsibility (high individualism), rely on the use of individual rewards to motivate staff (moderate masculinity), treat their employees as valued people whom they do not treat officiously (low power distance) and keep bureaucracy to a minimum (low uncertainty avoidance). An analysis of the data revealed that most countries (exceptions being Brazil, Japan, India and Israel) fall into a particular cultural cluster. Figure 4.4 illustrates this.

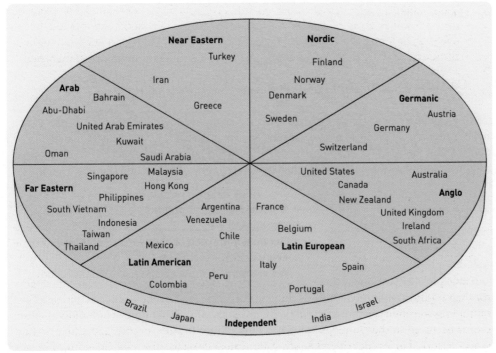

Figure 4.4
A synthesis of country clusters

Source: Ronen and Shenkar (1985).

Long-term and short-term orientation

In their 2005 work Hofstede and Hofstede added this fifth dimension:

> Long-term orientation (LTO) stands for the fostering of virtues orientated towards future rewards – in particular perseverance and thrift. Its opposite pole, short-term orientation, stands for the fostering of virtues related to the past and present – in particular respect for tradition, preservation of 'face', and fulfilling social obligations. (Hofstede and Hofstede, 2005, p. 210)

Countries with high LTO scores include China, Hong Kong, Taiwan and Japan. Great Britain, Australia, New Zealand, the United States and Canada have a short-term orientation, in which many people see spending, not thrift, as a virtue.

Current status

Hofstede's work has limitations, including:

- the small (and so possibly unrepresentative) number of respondents in some countries;
- reducing a phenomenon as complex as a nation's culture (whose population includes many class, social, ethnic and religious divisions) to five dimensions;
- basing the original sample on the employees of one global company;
- the likelihood of differences of culture within IBM.

Others, like Thomas Friedman in his book *The World is Flat* (2005) believe that deep and persistent changes – globalisation, communications technologies such as social networking, spread of market economies – are diminishing differences in national values and beliefs. Managers are also aware that national culture is just one factor affecting the performance of overseas operations.

Despite its limitations, the work provides a widely recognised starting point for those working internationally. They can use it to think about the culture in which they operate, reflect on their cultural biases and begin to develop the skill of cross-cultural working. The 'Key ideas' feature on cultural intelligence, and the 'Develop a skill' feature at the end of this chapter, will help this.

Case study — Carlsberg – the case continues   www.carlsberg.com

Top management believed Carlsberg should nurture 'a winning culture' with the attributes of being innovative, ambitious, responsible and honest. The strategic work to spread these values across the company ran into difficulties at events and workshops after the takeover of S&N in 2008. Not all of the acquired companies found them useful, among them the French Kronenbourg and the Russian Baltica, whose general managers did not want Carlsberg to impose what they saw as Danish values.

Carlsberg therefore decided to start again and develop a common strategic concept with the active participation of the new acquisitions, as well as the existing foreign subsidiaries. This activity resulted in the 2009 'Winning behaviours' concept – five beliefs 'guiding the way we work within the Carlsberg Group' (p. 240):

Together we are stronger
We want to win
Our customers and consumers are at the heart of every decision we make
We are each empowered to make a difference
We are engaged with society

Top management believes that Winning Behaviours incorporates the company's global strategy (a focus on optimising, centralising and standardising procedures across the group), while respecting the strengths of local brands, initiatives and interests.

Sources: Soderberg (2015).

Case questions 4.3

Consider what Hofstede's theory predicts about how managers and staff in any two of the countries shown would tend to react to the beliefs that:

- 'together we are stronger'
- 'we are all empowered to make a difference'.

Key ideas   Overemphasising diversity?

This section has illustrated the diversity of national cultures. There is another view that the underlying fundamentals of management outweigh cultural variations in detailed processes. One powerful constraint on diversity is the economic context of an essentially capitalist economic system. This places similar requirements on managers wherever they are. They have to provide acceptable returns, create a coherent organisational structure, maintain relations with stakeholders and try to keep control.

Further, if managers work in a multinational organisation that has developed a distinctive corporate culture (Chapter 3), will that influence their behaviour more than the local national culture?

Another constraint is the use of integrated information systems across companies (and their suppliers) operating internationally, which can place common reporting requirements on managers irrespective of their location. This ties units more closely together, and may bring more convergence in the work of management.

These are unresolved questions: look for evidence as you work on this chapter that supports or contradicts either point of view, and Activity 4.6 is also relevant.

Activity 4.6   Critical reflection on cultural differences

If you have worked in an organisation with international operations, reflect on whether your experience leads you to agree or disagree with the ideas in this section. For example:

- Can you recognise the differences in national cultures identified by Hofstede?
- If so, how did they affect how people worked and communicated?
- How did company culture and national culture interact, if at all?

4.7   Contrasting management systems

Despite the growth of international trade and the growing interdependence of business across the world, countries vary substantially in the way they organise economic activities. There are major differences in the way businesses are organised in different countries – even though all are capitalist economies. Whitley (1999):

Different patterns of industrialisation developed in contrasting institutional contexts and led to contrasting institutional arrangements governing economic processes becoming established in different market economies . . . Partly as a result, the structure and practices

Table 4.2 Contrasting business systems of the United States and Europe

	United States	Europe
Power of state	Relatively limited, with more scope for discretion by companies to provide employee and social benefits	Relatively strong, with more engagement in economic activity through state-owned companies
Financial system	Stock market central source of finance for companies, with shareholdings dispersed. Corporations expected to be transparent and accountable to investors	Corporations in network of relations with small number of larger investors. Non-shareholders often play equal role to shareholders
Education and labour system	Corporations have developed policies; relatively local and decentralised labour relations and collective bargaining	Publicly led training and labour market policies, in which corporations participated; national collective bargaining
Cultural systems	Traditions of participation, philanthropy, wary of government, moral value of capitalism; ethic of giving back to society	Preference for representative organisations – political parties, trade unions, trade associations, state

Source: Based on Whitley (1999 and 2009).

of state agencies, financial organisations and labour-market actors (in different) countries continue to diverge and to reproduce distinctive forms of economic organisation. (p. 5)

Table 4.2 illustrates Whitley's ideas in relation to the United States and Europe. There are significant differences between countries within Europe, and in some respects the UK is closer to the United States model than to the rest of Europe.

He also examines the Japanese model with networks of interdependent relations, and a tradition of mutual ownership between different, but friendly, business units. Companies have close financial and obligational links with each other, and the Ministry of Industry actively supports and guides the strategic direction of major areas of business. Firms create a network of mutually dependent organisations and decide strategy by negotiation with other companies and financial institutions.

At the other extreme, firms in the United States and United Kingdom are more isolated, raising most of their funds from the capital markets. Some observers believe that investors in US and UK companies expect steadily increasing returns from the companies they invest in, which in turn leads those managing the companies to focus on short-term profits at the expense of the long-term health of the business. The collapse of some financial institutions in 2008 was in part blamed on executives taking excessive risks to meet market expectations.

Management in practice   The evolving Japanese management system

A special issue of *Long Range Planning* in 2009 outlined both continuity and change in what has become known as the Japanese management system. A brief summary provides a point of comparison with other systems – while acknowledging that the system is most prevalent among large firms, so that many Japanese workers do not benefit. Stiles (2009) noted the main features:

- **Corporate governance and ownership** – large corporations have cooperative relationships with each other across industries and along the supply chain.
- **Culture** – a collectivist society values attaining cooperation and trust with others in the workplace.
- **Permanent employment** – core staff have high security of employment.

- **Seniority wages** – pay and promotion are largely based on education level and years with the employer.
- **Enterprise unions** – most firms have one union, and make changes in consultation with it.
- **Production methods** – a relentless focus on quality and continuous improvement.

Many of these practices are being challenged by intense competition from other Asian countries, and by dissenting views within Japan – from, for example, women and non-core workers, who are often denied the benefits of this system.

Source: Stiles (2009).

4.8   Forces driving globalisation

The globalisation of markets?

If you travel to another country, you immediately see many familiar consumer products or services – examples of the idea that global brands are displacing local products. In several industries identical products (Canon cameras, Sony Walkman, Famous Grouse whisky) are sold across the globe. Theodore Levitt observed this trend towards **globalisation** – see 'Key ideas'.

Globalisation refers to the increasing integration of internationally dispersed economic activities.

Key ideas   The globalisation of markets

Theodore Levitt, a Professor at Harvard Business School, believed that advances in communications technology were inspiring consumers around the world to want the same things.

The world's needs and desires have been irrevocably homogenised. This makes the multinational corporation obsolete and the global corporation absolute (p. 93).

He advised international companies to cease acting as 'multinationals' that customised their products to fit local markets and tastes. Instead they should become 'global' by standardising production, distribution and marketing across all countries. Sameness meant efficiency and would be more profitable than difference. Economies of scale would bring competitive advantage.

Source: Based on Levitt (1983).

Practice in many global businesses soon appeared to support Levitt's theory. In the mid-1980s British Airways developed an advertisement ('The world's favourite airline') and (after dubbing it into 20 languages) showed it in identical form in 35 countries with a developed TV network. Consumer companies such as Coca-Cola and McDonald's began promoting themselves as identical global brands, with standard practices and a centralised management structure.

What had led to this increasingly global business world? Yip (2003) developed a model (Figure 4.5) of the factors that drive globalisation in particular industries. Market factors were probably the most significant in Carlsberg – such as the transferability of the brand and advertising, and the ability to develop international distribution channels. In other industries cost factors are more prominent – car companies can benefit from economies of scale in manufacturing, and the ability to buy components around the world. In other cases government incentives for companies to relocate facilities away from their home

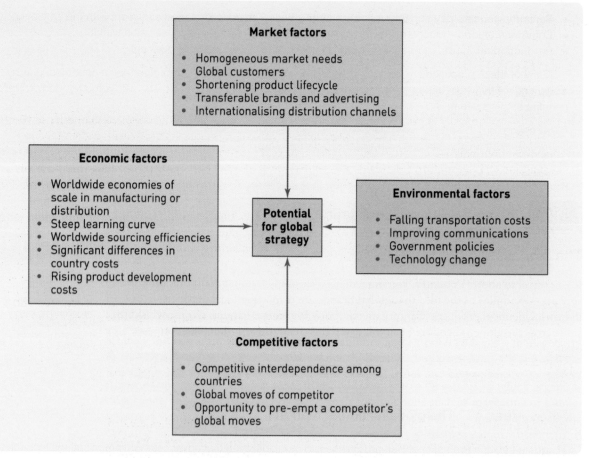

Figure 4.5 Factors driving globalisation in an industry
Source: Based on Yip (2003).

base have encouraged globalisation. Developments in communication technologies also drive globalisation, by enabling the efficient flow of data on which international operations depend.

There is resistance to the apparent inevitability of Yip's model. Local companies develop new products that may offer better value than global brands: so rather than 'going global' companies began to 'go local' – Coca-Cola now owns not one brand but 200, many of them in only one or two markets; Starbucks and McDonald's vary their offerings to suit local tastes; Nestlé has about 200 varieties of instant coffee. Government policies often block globalisation:

As for the digitalised world, the idea that everyone, everywhere, should have access to the same information has fallen foul of authoritarian politics and concerns about privacy. China, Russia, Turkey and others have thrown roadblocks across the digital highway to stifle dissent. Europeans want to protect themselves from US intelligence agencies and the monopoly capitalism of the digital giants . . . The web is heading for Balkanization. [Interest in global free trade agreements is waning, and] the advanced economies are looking instead to regional coalitions and deals.

 Source: (from an article by Philip Stephens, *Financial Times*, 5 September 2014, p. 13)
© The Financial Times 2014. All Rights Reserved.

The 'Management in practice' feature shows contrasting approaches in the motor industry.

Contrast Ford www.Ford.com with VW www.VW.com

In 2008 Ford announced that it was trying to break down the 'regional fiefdoms' which managers of the company's businesses around the world had developed. Designers, engineers and marketing staff focused primarily on their parts of the world producing, for example, a Ford Focus in Europe that was quite different from that sold in the United States. Alan Mulally, Ford's chief executive (who had joined the company from Boeing) saw this as inefficient:

We didn't make different 737s for France and China.

Under his plan, by 2015 all cars of each model would share a common platform, irrespective of where they are sold, believing this would produce great economies of scale for it and its suppliers.

In the same year Martin Winterkorn, then Chief Executive of Volkswagen, said that the days of building one car for the whole world were over:

We will make the VW group the world's most international car maker. The days of a 'world car' are dead and buried. Our customers in China or India expect us, as a global player, to offer entirely different solutions than we do in the US or western Europe.

 Source: *Financial Times*, 14 March 2008, and 25 July 2008.
© The Financial Times 2008. All Rights Reserved.

Alan Rugman has noted that rather than becoming globalised, the world has divided into three regions – North America, the European Union and Japan/East Asia – see 'Key ideas'. He notes that almost three-quarters of exports from EU members went to other EU countries, concluding that what we are seeing is not globalisation but regionalisation:

Only in a few sectors is globalisation a successful firm strategy . . . For most manufacturers and all services, regionalization is much more relevant than globalisation.' (p. 18)

Alan Rugman – the myth of globalisation

It is widely accepted that multinationals drive globalisation. The top 500 multinationals dominate international business, accounting for over 90% of the world's FDI and nearly half its trade. But globalisation, as commonly understood, is a myth. Far from taking place in a single global market, business activity by most large multinationals takes place within any one of the world's three great trading blocks – North America, Europe, and Asia-Pacific.

Of the world's 500 multinationals in 2001, 428 were in the USA, the EU, and Japan. Only [nine] were by my definition truly global. These took at least a fifth of their sales from each of the three regions, but less than half from any one region. Most – 320 out of 380 – were stay-at-home multinationals, deriving on average four-fifths of their sales from their home regions.

Source: Rugman (2005), p. 6.

Concerns about globalisation

Supporters of more world trade cite the benefits that wider access to markets brings to both consumers and workers by encouraging innovation and investment. It gives many consumers a wide choice of goods from suppliers around the world, often more cheaply than those produced locally. Others are critical, believing that agreements reached in bodies such as the WTO serve the interests of multinational businesses and richer economies rather than indigenous local producers.

Case study   Carlsberg – the case continues   www.carlsberggroup.com

Soderberg's (2015) account of how Carlsberg implemented the new values continues:

> The presentation of the concept on the Group website includes this statement from the CEO: 'What sets us apart from our competitors is that we strive to find the right balance – working closely together at a global level whilst allowing local brands and initiatives to flourish'. (pp. 240–41)

The company worked with local subsidiaries to help them articulate the meaning of the phrases (such as 'we are empowered to make a difference') in words that aligned with their cultural values. Thus, when it was introduced to the Malaysian subsidiary the local HR staff organised events for local managers who would then pass the ideas on to their staff.

Two of the five winning behaviours had special attention at this workshop, and the themes were presented to managers, and discussed with them, in these terms:

- We are empowered to make a difference
  - Take ownership of challenges when opportunity arises
  - Do not let fear of failure overcome the desire to succeed
  - We learn from failure when we made wrong steps
- Together we are stronger
  - Good leadership skills are vital for success
  - Leaders with correct and clear instructions can win faster

- Team spirit is important to work in harmony

What is notable to Western observers is how much emphasis senior management put on the widespread fear of failure among local employees, and thereby their sense of shame and fear of losing face. [They tried to overcome this by adding the idea] that 'we must learn from mistakes when we make wrong steps' and thereby learn to think and act in a more Western way.

> In Malaysia, avoiding loss of face is a major concern, so the managerial emphasis on 'clear instructions' is notable. However, while 'clear instructions' may collide with great concern about not losing face (if they go wrong), it also resonates with a desire at the shop-floor level for a direct and nurturing leadership, and for clear and unambiguous instructions that are moderately prescriptive.' (p. 244)

Source: Soderberg (2015); company website.

Case questions 4.3

- What does the case suggest about the challenges managers face in ensuring that staff from different cultures fully 'buy in' to organisational policies?
- What may be the effects of not acknolwedging and respecting local differences as thoroughly as Carlsberg appears to have done?

Activity 4.7   Debating globalisation

Arrange a debate or discussion on one or more of these questions:

- Has globalisation increased people's power as consumers, or diminished their power as employees?
- Has it lifted millions out of poverty, or has it widened the gap between rich and poor?
- Has it widened consumer choice, or has it encouraged levels of industrialisation and consumption that make unsustainable demands on the earth's natural resources?

- Does globalisation heighten aesthetic awareness of different cultures, or does it expose people to a stream of superficial images?
- Does it enable more people to experience diversity, or does it lead to a bland homogenisation of local cultures into a global view?

All of these developments imply much greater patterns of contact between managers in different countries. Legislative changes and treaties remove some barriers to trade, but they do not solve the management problems of making those economic activities work efficiently. Above all, they bring many managers face to face with the need to manage cultural differences.

4.9   Integrating themes

Entrepreneurship

Entrepreneurial businesses, especially those in high-tech sectors such as software or bio-medicine, face an early decision on whether to focus on their home market or to expand overseas. Many (possibly most) international ventures fail, which makes them a risky move for a small company, since an overseas failure could wipe out their limited reserves.

Research by Coeurderoy et al. (2012) identified factors in the success or failure of international ventures by small high-tech firms. They studied 600 such firms in the UK and Germany over six years, to assess what they did to make a success of their international expansion. Survival rates were improved by:

- **High knowledge intensity**: firms whose products had a high research and development content, and who were able to learn fast as they met unexpected problems did well. Firms inevitably meet hazards in a new market – and need to be able to think and act quickly to survive.
- **Close relations with specified customers**: high-tech products will be challenging to make and use, and overcoming early snags will be done most effectively if there are close relations between the supplier and their customer. Both benefit – the customer from close working with those who designed the product, and the designer from learning how the customer uses it.
- **Scale of international exposure**: the more a company has engaged in international ventures, the more likely it is that subsequent ones will succeed. While the first occasion will involve learning the first two factors, later ventures will be easier and less costly.

The authors suggest that underlying all these is an early decision by the entrepreneur to become an international business, and to devote resources to it. Without that commitment, they will lack the capacity to support these factors in success.

Sustainability

Bondy and Starkey (2012) studied the extent to which local concerns and culture were incorporated into the corporate social responsibilities (CSR) of 37 UK-based multinational corporations (MNCs). They found that the companies followed an integrated approach to their CSR policies, implying that practices formulated and agreed at HQ would be applied across all the jurisdictions in which the company operated. They acknowledge that CSR policy inevitably involves balancing cultural and ethical priorities of home and host nations. More involvement by managers in the host countries in formulating and implementing the CSR policies of MNCs would align more closely with the 'localisation' philosophy often expressed within CSR discussions.

Internationalisation

As business becomes increasingly international, do managers respond passively to aspects of the environment in the countries where they do business, or do they also try to shape it? The first view stresses how features of the political or other environments can constrain choice, especially in economies with a tradition of significant government involvement in business. It sees managers as having a passive role, reacting to pressures from their environment. An alternative view regards managers as proactive, influencing policies that are part of their context: the 'Management in practice' feature reports a study that gives some empirical support for the proactive view.

Management in practice   MNCs and environmental policy in China and Taiwan

In a study of the interaction between companies and government institutions over environmental policy, Child and Tsai compared the experience of companies in China and Taiwan. They examined three multinational corporations (MNCs) in the chemicals sector, each with plants in China and Taiwan – which have different environmental policies. In examining how these policies affected companies, and how companies affected the policies, they found that:

- MNCs took a broad view of the stakeholders to whom they paid attention, including suppliers, customers, local communities and especially non-governmental agencies (NGOs) who could affect public opinion.
- Non-governmental organisations (NGOs) played a major role in mobilising public concerns.
- MNCs engaged in proactive political action, often in conjunction with NGOs, to influence environmental policy.

Source: Based on Child and Tsai (2005).

Governance

Mallin (2013) notes that while Berle and Means' (1932) work on the implications of separating ownership from control in modern corporations influenced laws to protect shareholders, countries' legal systems mean they achieve this aim in different ways.

The US and the UK have legal systems that generally give good protection to shareholders, encouraging a diversified shareholder base. Other countries have different ownership systems – family firms, or a small number of large dominant shareholders, are more common in Continental Europe than in the UK. Banks often play a bigger role in financing companies, which they control by being members of the board. This implies that governance arrangements will fit the local institutional arrangements.

Mallin (2013) summarises the arrangements in many parts of the world, noting signs of convergence on some features, for example on the need for:

> more transparency and disclosure, accountability of the board, and the independence of at least a portion of the directors. (p. 182)

Summary

1 **Contrast the ways in which organisations conduct international business**

- Offshoring, exporting, licensing, joint ventures, wholly owned subsidiaries.
- Multinational (independent operations in many countries, run from centre); transnational (independent operations in many countries, decentralised); global (linked and interdependent operations in many countries, closely coordinated).

2 **Explain, with examples, how PESTEL factors affect the decisions of those managing internationally**

  - This would involve gathering data and information about how one or more of the political, economic, socio-cultural, technological, environmental and legal factors had affected a company's policies and practices.

3 **Summarise at least one aspect of EU policy (or of an international trade agreement) which is of interest to you for your career**

  - The chapter outlined several EU policies and practices relevant to management, especially in the areas of freer trade and common industrial policies.

4 **Explain and illustrate the evidence on differences in national cultures, and evaluate the significance of Hofstede's research for managers working internationally**

  - Early work distinguished between low-context and high-context cultures. In the former, information is explicit and clear while in the latter it is more implicit, and can only be understood through shared experience, values and assumptions.

  - Hofstede distinguished between cultures in terms of power distance (acceptance of variations in power); uncertainty avoidance (willingness to tolerate ambiguity); individualism/collectivism (emphasis on individual or collective action); masculinity/femininity (preferences for assertive or modest behaviour); and long-/short-term orientation. Case question 4.3 encouraged you to identify how cultural differences could affect attitudes and behaviours towards some management practices.

5 **Compare and contrast the features of national management systems:**

  - These shape the way people interpret generic activities of management:
    - US – individualistic, rational approach, contingent design of organisations
    - Europe – collective, rational approach, pragmatic
    - Japan – collective responsibility, secure employment, consensus building.

6 **Use work related to Hofstede's cultural norms to understand how that can help you develop the skill of mindfulness**

  - The chapter explained how the ability to pick up clues about cultural differences is a valuable part of cultural intelligence, and the 'Develop a skill' feature provides an opportunity to practise this.

7 **Summarise the forces stimulating the growth of international business**

  - Yip proposes that these factors are market, economic, environmental and competitive.

8 **Show how ideas from the chapter add to your understanding of the integrating themes**

  - Research has identified management practices that support the survival of small high-tech firms wanting to expand internationally.

  - Reducing global emissions of greenhouse gases depends on regulations by governments and international bodies; while the shape of these is still uncertain, managers should plan their long-term investments in ways that anticipate these changes.

  - Managers are often active in influencing government policy and regulations in the countries in which they want to do business.

  - Governance arrangements vary between countries, reflecting the evolution of distinctive national systems.

Test your understanding

1 What factors are stimulating the growth in world trade?

2 Compare internationalisation and globalisation. Give a specific example of a company of each type about which you have obtained some information.

3 Identify three PESTEL factors that have affected Carlsberg.

4 Outline the difference between a high- and a low-context culture and give an example of each.

5 Explain accurately to another person Hofstede's five dimensions of national culture. Evaluate his conclusions on the basis of discussions with your colleagues in Activity 4.4.

6 Name two distinct features of Japanese, European and US management systems respectively.

7 Compare the implications, if any, of globalisation for (a) national governments, (b) their citizens.

8 Summarise Yip's theory about the forces driving globalisation.

9 What is Rugman's contribution to perceptions about the spread of globalisation?

10 Summarise an idea from the chapter that adds to your understanding of the integrating themes.

Think critically

Think about the way managers in your company, or one with which you are familiar, deal with the international aspects of business. Then make notes on these questions:

- What **assumptions** appear to guide the way people manage internationally? Do they assume that cultural factors are significant or insignificant? Which of those views do you share?

- What aspects of the historical or current **context** of the company appear to influence your company's approach to international business? Do any of these contextual factors threaten the international operation?

- Can you compare your organisation's approach with those that colleagues on your course know about? Does this suggest plausible **alternative** ways of managing internationally?

- What **limitations** can you see in the theories and evidence presented? For example, is it always worth investing time to understand the subtleties of cultural differences?

Develop a skill – mindfulness

The skill of mindfulness enables people to work better across cultures.

- **Awareness:** Make an assessment of how mindful you are (such as paying attention to cues in cross-cultural situations, and to your own knowledge and feelings). Explore the assumptions you make about people from other cultures, and consider them critically. Use the ideas in this chapter to view situations through the eyes of others.

- **Learning:** Read the 'Key ideas' feature on cultural intelligence (in Section 4.5, p. 126), and recall your work on Activity 4.4 and Case questions 4.3. Summarise the main ideas. How can being mindful help a manager?

- **Analysis:** Consider the possible implications for you of the theories in Sections 4.5 and 4.6.

- Identify someone (whom you know, or can read about) who seems to be 'mindful' (or generally good at interacting with people from other cultures). Consider what they do, what the effects are and what you can learn from them.

- **Practice:** Identify one thing (perhaps from Activity 4.4) they do which you can try, and identify an opportunity to practise that mindfulness skill. Practise one of them, and record the results so that you can learn from the experience.

- **Application:** Decide on another opportunity to practise this skill within the next week.

Read more

Clissold, T. (2014), *Chinese Rules: Mao's Dog, Deng's Cat and Five Timeless Lessons from the Front Lines in China,* Harper Collins, London.

> Valuable insights, based on the author and entrepreneur's many years experience of doing business in China.

Friedman, T. (2005), *The World is Flat: A Brief History of the Globalised World in the 21st Century,* Penguin/Allen Lane, London.

> A best-selling account of the forces that drive globalisation – noting that they also assist terrorist networks.

Mahajan, V. (2012), *The Arab World Unbound: Tapping into the power of 350 million consumers,* Jossey-Bass, San Francisco, CA.

> An overview of the deep diversity within the region's many countries, which discards many stereotypes – valuable for anyone wishing to know about its markets and peoples.

Taras, V., Steel, P. and Kirkman, B. L. (2011), 'Three decades of research on national culture in the workplace: Do the differences still make a difference?', *Organisational Dynamics,* vol. 40, no. 3, pp. 189–198.

> A clear overview of Hofstede's work, and of later studies developing the idea. It also traces implications for practice.

Go online

These websites have appeared in the chapter:

> **www.carlsberggroup.com**
> **www.maersk.com**
> **www.aggreko.com**
> **www.wto.org**
> **http://europa.eu**
> **www.ford.com**
> **www.vw.com**
> **www.transparency.org**

Visit two of the sites in the list, or others that interest you, and navigate to the pages dealing with recent news, press or investor relations.

- What signs are there of the international nature of the business, and what are the main issues in this area that the business appears to be facing?
- Compare and contrast the issues you identify on the two sites.
- What challenges may they imply for those working in, and managing, these organisations?

CHAPTER 5
CORPORATE RESPONSIBILITY

Aims

To introduce the dilemmas of ethical and responsible behaviour, and offer some analytical tools.

Objectives

By the end of your work on this chapter you should be able to outline the concepts below in your terms and:

1 Give examples of corporate malpractice and of philanthropy
2 Distinguish the values people use to evaluate individual and corporate actions
3 Use a model of ethical decision making to explain behaviour
4 Show how stakeholders, strategies and responsible behaviour interact
5 Evaluate an organisation's methods for managing corporate responsibility
6 Identify the values underlying action, and understand how this can help you develop the skill of clarifying your values
7 Show how ideas from the chapter can add to your understanding of the integrating themes

Key terms

This chapter introduces the following ideas:

philanthropy
enlightened self-interest
corporate responsibility
social contract
ethical decision-making models

ethical relativism
ethical investors
ethical consumer
ethical audit

Each is a term defined within the text, as well as in the glossary at the end of the book.

Case study
The Co-operative Group   www.co-operative.coop

The Co-operative Group (the Co-op) is the UK's largest mutual business, owned by the 6 million customers who chose to become members. It is the fifth-largest food retailer (with about 8 per cent of the market) and the leading convenience store operator. It employs about 70,000 people, and annual sales are £10 billion. As well as financial goals it also sets social goals. Unless it meets the financial and profit targets, it will become harder to meet the social targets. The interim report for the six months to July 2015 showed a profit before tax of £64 million, compared with a loss of £1 million the previous year. Chief Executive – Richard Pennycook – said the group had made a good start on the journey to rebuild the Co-op – putting in place new leadership teams and providing the investment to support the strategy.

© Co-operative Group

The Co-operative began in mid-19th century Yorkshire, when groups of workers in the new industrial towns decided to set up shops, rather than depend on those owned by others (often linked to the mine or factory where they worked). The idea spread rapidly and by 1900 there were over 1,400 co-operative societies, many of which gradually merged into regional groups.

This process of consolidation was largely completed in 2000 when the Co-operative Wholesale Society and Co-operative Retail Services merged to become The Co-operative Group. This controls 80 per cent of all co-operative retail outlets in the UK, with independent societies controlling the rest.

It has expanded the retailing activity by buying stores from other companies and is the UK's fifth-largest food retailer (measured by market share). It faces tough competition from 'the big four' (Tesco, Sainsbury's, Morrisons and Asda), and from aggressive discounters such as Aldi and Lidl.

The Co-op has had several turbulent years, during which it experienced financial losses, a major scandal, lost control of the Co-operative Bank, changed senior management and implemented new governance structures. Until 2010 the group was expanding both in retailing and banking (see later). It has more small stores than the 'big four' – but these are now opening more. Some are very close to a Co-op.

The collapse of The Co-op Bank left the group with a debt of £1.5 billion. It has begun to repay this by selling 'non-core' assets such as farms and a pharmacy chain. It now focuses on convenience food retail (about three quarters of turnover), alongside the remaining funeral care, insurance and legal businesses. The plan is to open 100 convenience shops annually, and sell larger outlets.

As well as sharing profits with members, it aims to meet the needs of customers and communities. An example of this was when members proposed that the group should stock more Fairtrade goods as part of their social aims. These are products where growers (usually in poorer countries) who meet specified environmental and labour standards receive a certificate. In return they receive higher prices than they would in the open market, and other benefits.

Sources: Company website; Company Interim Report, 2015.

Case questions 5.1
- Go to the Co-op website and find out about recent developments in the business.
- As a store manager responsible for meeting tough sales targets, what questions would you raise about the proposal to stock Fairtrade products?
- How would the success or otherwise of the Fairtrade idea help the group meet its current challenges?

5.1   Introduction

Managers at the Co-op balance two objectives – to make a profit, and to meet social goals. These continue to express the founders' vision of a fairer and more democratic society. Making the profit necessary to meet the social objectives is challenging in the intensely competitive retail sector. Following Co-op principles by meeting social objectives will not in itself ensure the business survives.

While some customers are consistently loyal to, and support, the social principles, others are not: they compare the Co-op offer with others and can easily switch. Stocking Fairtrade (www.fairtrade.org.uk) products supports the social aims, but not necessarily the business ones. Before the 2013 crisis many customers of other banks had moved to the Co-op Bank in which, since the crisis, it is now only a minority shareholder.

Many managers acknowledge that the financial wealth their activities generate comes at a price. The waste of resources in the economic system threatens the high living standards the system has created in the developed world. So companies respond – retailers work to limit their packaging; airlines buy aircraft that use less fuel; public bodies use less space and energy.

Spectacular examples of corporate malpractice are hard to defend, and examples of spectacular generosity are hard to criticise. Between such extremes are countless examples of ambiguous corporate behaviour:

> There is no consensus on what constitutes virtuous corporate behaviour. Is sourcing overseas to take advantage of lower labour costs responsible? Are companies morally obligated to insist that their contractors pay a 'living wage' rather than market wages? Are investments in natural resources in poor countries with corrupt governments always, sometimes or never irresponsible? (Vogel, 2005, pp. 4–5)

The chapter begins with examples of corporate malpractice and responsibility. It then outlines universal prescriptions for responsible behaviour, one of which is about identifying the values used to justify an action. A valuable skill in managing is to develop the habit of checking the values that lie behind actions – this may help build a person's confidence and authority, as clear values bring greater consistency to behaviour. The chapter helps develop this skill. It then offers three 'contextual' perspectives on behaviour – ethical decision making models, stakeholders and strategy. It concludes by showing how organisations try to manage their CR policies.

5.2   Corporate malpractice

Controversial issues of malpractice arise when:

- organisations give generous rewards to senior staff;
- banks sell customers unnecessary insurance; and
- retailers source goods from factories that pay little attention to workers' safety.

These practices erode trust and damage reputation – which can lead investors, potential employees and customers to withdraw their support. The 'Management in practice' feature gives one example, and Table 5.1 lists others.

| Management in practice | Bernard Madoff – the biggest fraud ever? |

In 2009 Bernard Madoff (aged 71) was sentenced to 150 years in prison for running a fraudulent investment scheme in the United States that took £40 billion from thousands of investors around the world. He attracted investors by offering unusually large returns and by cultivating an image of competence and trustworthiness – clients were eager for him to accept their money. Instead of investing it, he used it to pay dividends to earlier investors – so the scheme depended on continually attracting new ones. When economic decline began in 2008 some investors asked for their money back: it was no longer there.

A remarkable feature of the story was that regulatory bodies set up to prevent fraud failed to do so. The agency responsible for regulating that part of the financial services industry was understaffed, and never inspected his accounts.

Sources: *Financial Times* 24 June 2009, 17 December 2010; Henriques (2011).

Table 5.1 notes examples of corporate malpractice.

5.3   Corporate responsibility

Corporate responsibility (CR) refers to the awareness, acceptance and management of the wider implications of corporate decisions. Building on work by Rangan et al. (2015) this section distinguishes three broad forms of CR – philanthropy and enlightened self-interest; improving processes; and creating shared value.

> **Corporate responsibility (CR)** refers to the awareness, acceptance and management of the wider implications of corporate decisions.

Philanthropy and enlightened self-interest

It is often hard to distinguish between these two practices.

There is a long tradition of individual **philanthropy**, when people who have made money in business give part of their wealth to charities, including universities. They do not expect

> **Philanthropy** is the practice of contributing personal or corporate wealth to charitable or similar causes.

Table 5.1 Recent examples of corporate malpractice

Company	Incident	Outcome
Barclays Bank, 2015, UK bank	For five years, traders added secret mark-ups to the prices they charged for foreign exchange trades	Bank pleaded guilty, and US and UK regulators fined Barclays $2.32 billion. Traders dismissed
Volkswagen, 2015, German car maker	Fitted illegal software into diesel-powered cars, which turned off emissions controls except during official tests	Chief executive resigns, and other executives suspended. Company faces prosecutions and large fines
The Royal Bank of Scotland, 2008, UK bank	Used short-term borrowing to fund high-risk investments. These failed, and the company almost collapsed	UK Government bought majority stake. Fred Goodwin, chief executive, retired with £800,000 annual pension
Enron, 2001, a US trading company	Company collapsed in 2001, after discovery of accounting practices that inflated earnings and share prices, to benefit top managers	Employees lost jobs, directors received large financial benefits. Founder Ken Lay and CEO Jeff Skilling convicted of fraud in May 2006
Arthur Andersen, 2002, accounting and consulting firm, worked for Enron	Shredded thousands of documents to hide malpractice at Enron	Found guilty of obstructing justice, CEO resigns, firm collapses

this to increase sales or profits: it as a goodwill gesture to activities they support. Notable examples include:

- **Bill Gates** (founder of Microsoft) and his wife Melinda have given very large sums to health and education;
- **Jeff Skoll** (ex-president of eBay) gave £5 million to the Said Business School at Oxford University;
- **Lord Sainsbury** (former head of Sainsbury's) has given £400 million to his Gatsby Charitable Foundation and plans to give another £600 million before he dies.

They recognise their business success was in part due to the society in which they work, and choose to return some of their wealth. They experience the intrinsic pleasure of giving, and enhance their status and reputation.

Enlightened self-interest is the practice of acting in a way that is costly or inconvenient at present, but which is believed to be in one's best interest in the long term.

Some corporations give substantial sums to charities, make gifts in kind (donating free drugs to health programmes, or free software to universities and schools), encourage employee volunteering and generally try to be a good neighbour. They hope this will improve their reputation, brand image or access to government. It may also reduce the risks of bad publicity if they are in mining and construction businesses – a form of insurance. Acts like this are not philanthropy but are probably better described as **enlightened self-interest**.

Improving operations

This is the responsible corporate activity of working on business processes to improve efficiency – reduce waste, enhance employee working conditions etc. These are likely to benefit the company by lowering costs, and also bring benefits to society by reducing emissions, noise or pollution. Table 5.2 gives examples.

Creating shared value

Shared value is creating economic value in a way that also creates value for society by addressing its needs and challenges (Porter and Kramer, 2011, p. 64)

This refers to situations where the company and the community work together to adapt part of the company's operating system to create **shared value** – which benefits both. Porter and Kramer (2011) refer to it as creating economic value in a way that also creates value for society by addressing their needs. Rangan et al. (2015) give the example of a Unilever Hindustan company that traditionally distributed products to remote villages through wholesalers and retailers. It now recruits village women, gives them access to microfinance (a very small loan) and trains them to sell soap and other products door to door. More than 65,000 women entrepreneurs now participate, doubling their income; the community benefits from better hygiene and health; and the company sells more soap.

Table 5.2 Common ways to improve operations

Content (or substance) of corporate responsibility	
Topics	Examples
Inputs and resource supplies	Dealing fairly with producers and suppliers, sustainably sourcing raw materials and supplies, discouraging suppliers in developing countries from exploiting labour
Workforce activities	Promoting diversity, equality, health and safety, work–life balance, and other elements of the employment relationship; fair pay, bonus and pension schemes
Operations	Reducing materials and energy used in production and transport, using resources efficiently to reduce waste (e.g. less packaging)
Product and service impacts	Responsible customer relations, including advertising and promotion ('Drink responsibly'), protecting children, limiting harmful ingredients, clear and accurate labels, product accessibility

Another example is the Globe, the reconstructed Elizabethan theatre in London. There are several collaborations between the theatre and corporate sponsors: accounting firm PwC recently sent 12 of its young potential leaders to work with the Globe on a corporate training programme, which the Globe could then develop into a separate stream of income. The collaboration also brings intangible benefits – someone closely involved:

> 'As accountants, we're known as "pale, male and stale" – but to be surrounded by a totally multicultural experience (as happens at the Globe) is quite inspiring'. (*Financial Times,* 27 March 2014, p. 14)

Philanthropy and enlightened self-interest imply limited interaction between donor and recipient – beyond perhaps putting the company logo on the charity's publicity. Improving operations will involve mainly staff in the company, perhaps with some suppliers and customers. Creating shared value implies intense and continuing interaction between the parties. Many companies deal with these issues in partnership with Business in the Community (www.bitc.org.uk), whose website gives examples.

Activity 5.1   Looking for responsible business activity

Collect two examples of organisations that seem to be taking responsible business seriously by introducing policies on environmental, social or ethical matters. Check company or BITC websites for examples and links (**www.bitc.org.uk**)

- What aspects of the business (e.g. inputs, transformation, outputs, communities) does the policy cover?
- How did management develop the policy (e.g. which people or groups took part in forming it)?
- How do they ensure that people follow the policy, and that it has the expected effects?
- Compare what you find with colleagues on your course and present a short summary, and questions this has raised.

5.4   Perspectives on individual responsibility

Before looking at tools to help analyse these issues, use Activity 5.2 to locate your ethical position.

Activity 5.2   Reflecting on your ethics

You are walking down the street. There is no one nearby and you see: (a) a 50 pence piece, (b) a £5 note, (c) a £50 note, (d) a £100 note, (e) £1,000.

- Do you keep it? Yes or no?
- The money you find was in a wallet with the owner's name and address. Does this make a difference?
- That name shows it belongs to: (a) a wealthy person, (b) a pensioner of modest means, (c) a single parent. Does this make a difference?
- Suppose there were some people nearby. Does this make a difference?

Consider your reasons for each decision.

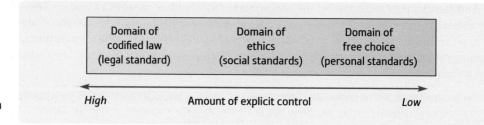

Figure 5.1 Three domains of human action

Three domains of human action

'Ethics' refers to a code of values that guide human action by setting acceptable standards. This becomes clearer if we compare ethics with actions that are governed by law and by free choice (see Figure 5.1). Some actions are the subject of laws that can be enforced in the courts: it is illegal to steal. Other actions are in the domain of free choice – anyone can apply for a job.

In between are acts that have an ethical dimension. Laws do not prohibit them, but shared values constrain people. An ethically acceptable action is legal and meets a society's ethical standards. This raises the question of how people form those standards: you may respect a standard that others ignore. People face these issues when someone offers them a favour – see 'Management in practice'.

Management in practice   Accepting hospitality in business

Companies offer hospitality of many kinds to people with whom they do business – and those who receive it do so as part of accepted practice. Common forms include:

- inviting customers or suppliers to prestigious events such as test cricket or The Grand National
- inviting journalists on free visits to exotic locations to hear company presentations
- inviting local government or health-service-elected members of staff to ostensibly 'professional' conferences, held in luxurious overseas venues.

Many businesses, especially those involved in high-value international deals, make such arrangements and expect staff to take part. The difficulty is to know when 'hospitality' becomes 'bribery'.

The UK government issued guidance when Parliament passed the Bribery Act in 2011. The guidance warns that hospitality can bribe people, but recognises that companies using it in a 'reasonable and proportionate' way to improve their image, better present their products or 'establish cordial relations' should not be punished automatically. The Justice Secretary wrote:

Under this law, no-one is going to try to stop businesses taking clients to Wimbledon, or a Grand Prix.

Yet for individual managers the risks of crossing the line are considerable, especially when they are competing internationally against companies whose governments take a more relaxed view.

Source: Based on an article in the *Financial Times*, 5 April 2011, p. 14.

Four criteria for evaluating an action

Philosophers have identified four principles that people use to evaluate whether an action is ethical – moral principle, utilitarianism, human rights and individualism – which may help to understand some behaviours. Being clear about values may bring greater consistency and confidence.

- **Moral principle** People use this criterion when they evaluate an action against a moral principle – the rules that societies develop, and which members generally accept as valid guides to action (such as that people do not steal, cheat or deliberately injure each other). If someone acts in a way that conforms to accepted principles, it is right: if not, it is wrong.
- **Utilitarianism** People use this criterion when they evaluate an action on the total balance of pleasure and pain in society. An act is right if it brings pleasure to more people than it hurts. An act is wrong if the amount of pain is greater than the amount of pleasure.
- **Human rights** People use this criterion when they evaluate an action against its effect on human rights that a society recognises (such as privacy, free speech or fair treatment). An act is right if it supports the human rights of those whom it affects, and wrong if it damages them.
- **Individualism** People use this criterion when they evaluate an action against its effect on their interests. An act is right if they can show that it serves a person's interests. This seems strange but Adam Smith used it in his book *The Wealth of Nations* (1776) to justify a free enterprise economy, on the grounds that apparently selfish behaviour would help society as a whole: entrepreneurs acting selfishly would only benefit if their actions benefitted others – by producing things they wanted to buy.

Activity 5.3   Justifying actions

Think of actions that you have justified on the grounds that:

- it was fair to those affected;
- it was the right thing to do;
- it was the best option for yourself;
- more people gained than lost.

Explain which of the four criteria outlined above matches each reason.

These tools from moral philosophy may show the reasoning behind someone's decision on an ethical issue – though Table 5.3 shows that others could challenge these criteria.

Figure 5.2 shows why people can disagree on whether a decision is ethical. Those (B, C, D . . .) who observe an action by A, and the criteria that A uses to justify it, will themselves be evaluating the action and the criteria. Diverse personalities, backgrounds and experiences mean they are likely to attach different meanings to what they see, and reach different conclusions.

Table 5.3 Questions within each philosophy

Philosophy	Questions
Moral principle	Who determines that a moral principle is 'generally accepted'? What if others claim that a principle leading to a different decision is equally 'accepted'?
Utilitarianism	Who determines the majority, and the population of which it is the greatest number? Is the benefit assessed over the short term or the long term?
Human rights	Actions usually involve several people – what if the decision would protect the rights of some, but breach the rights of others? How to balance them?
Individualism	Whose self-interest comes first? What if the action of one damages the self-interest of another?

Figure 5.2 Making ethical judgements

Source: Adapted from *Business and Society: Ethics and Stakeholder Management*, (9th edn.), Cengage Learning (Carroll, A. B. and Buchholtz, A. K. 2015). Copyright © 2015 Cengage Learning, Inc. reproduced by permission, www.cengage.com/permissions.

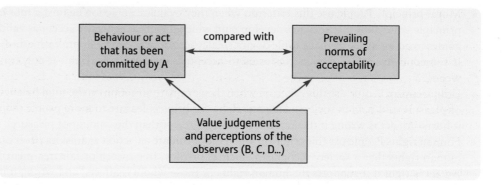

5.5 Perspectives on corporate responsibility

Figure 5.3 shows four responsibilities that may guide managers' actions. It builds on Figure 5.1 by adding economic responsibilities, reflecting the value-adding function of business.

Economic responsibilities

Milton Friedman believed that managers should satisfy shareholders.

> [In a free economy] there is one and only one social responsibility of business – to use its resources and engage in activities designed to increase its profits so long as it stays within the rules of the game, which is to say, engages in open and free competition, without deception or fraud. (Friedman, 1962, p. 133)

As an economist, Friedman believed that operating business 'without deception or fraud' provided social benefit by creating wealth. In terms of Figure 5.3, managers should concern themselves only with the legal and economic responsibilities. Giving money to charity is self-imposed taxation. The directors should concentrate on generating wealth, and distributing it to shareholders – so they can decide how to use it.

Many agree, claiming that environmental or other regulations increase costs, and make a business less competitive. When Burberry, the luxury goods retailer, decided to close a UK factory the finance director said:

> Ultimately if a factory isn't commercially viable you have to take the decision to close . . . that's what your obligations to your shareholders dictate. When you know you've made the right decision commercially, you have to stay true to that. These are the facts – commercial realities reign. (*Financial Times,* 15 February 2007, p. 3)

Figure 5.3 Four corporate responsibilities

Source: Carroll (1999).

Legal responsibilities

Society expects managers to obey the law – by not misleading investors, exploiting staff or selling faulty goods. Some companies take these responsibilities seriously – but go no further. They do what is legal: as long as a decision meets that test they will take it, even if others question the morality. When Starbucks, Google and other multinationals admitted paying very little UK tax, they claimed (correctly) that their tax payments were within the law at the time.

Ethical responsibilities

While society depends on business for products, business in turn depends on society. It requires inputs – employees, capital and physical resources – and the socially created institutions that enable business to operate, such as legal and education systems. Part of the moral case for CR is that society and business have mutual obligations within a **social contract**.

> The **social contract** consists of the mutual obligations that society and business recognise they have to each other.

Ethical actions are not specified by law, and may not serve a company's narrow economic interests. Managers may do things that support a wider social interest, such as discouraging waste or protecting the natural environment. They may also believe it will help them meet their economic responsibilities by enhancing their reputation – it is enlightened self-interest.

Discretionary responsibilities

This covers areas of behaviour that are entirely voluntary, independent of economic, legal or ethical considerations. They include anonymous donations with no possibility of a payback, sponsorship of local events, or contributions to charity – the actions are entirely philanthropic.

Those advocating an inclusive view of corporate responsibility believe that recognising wider interests is enlightened self-interest, in the sense that it can satisfy both economic and moral expectations. Managers may serve their shareholders better if they meet ethical and discretionary responsibilities, in ways that benefit the business.

Management in practice

Does business care?

The width and depth of corporate commitment to responsible behaviour is hard to measure, and anecdotes point both ways. A report in 2014 found that 85 per cent of companies in the FTSE 100 [the 100 largest companies, by market value, whose shares are traded on the London Stock Exchange] include a section on their corporate responsibility work in their Annual Report. Companies are aware that Governments expect them to publish a CR strategy.

Governments are enthusiastic about the idea, but this may not be matched by directors or investors. A survey for a United Nations body found that few world business leaders believed that their company's share price reflected its responsible business initiatives. The number who thought [such] initiatives would be very important to the success of their business had fallen over the past few years to fewer than half of those surveyed.

 Source: From an article in a *Financial Times* Supplement on Responsible Business, 8 July 2014.

Activity 5.4   Gathering views on the role of business

Gather information from people you know who work in a business, about which of the four views expressed in Figure 5.3:

- they personally favour;
- they believe has most influence on practice in their company.

If you work in an organisation:

- Which of the views in Figure 5.3 guides policy?
- Use Table 5.2 to gather examples of topics on which the organisation has deliberately acted as part of a corporate responsibility agenda.

Compare your examples with colleagues on your course.

Case study   The Co-op – the case continues   www.co-operative.coop

For many years Fairtrade products were available mainly through charity shops, churches and other small outlets: major retailers showed little interest. The Co-op board of directors decided to respond positively to members' suggestion that it would support their social aims. The challenge would be to do it in a way that supported commercial success.

The managers responsible for implementing the plan faced difficult decisions since:

- the food retail sector is intensely competitive;
- the Co-op is focussed on small stores – stocking Fairtrade means not stocking something else;
- stocking Fairtrade versions of existing products may mean a store sells less of the latter – which does not help meet sales targets;
- Fairtrade products cost more than standard ones: will enough customers (even those who had supported the idea) pay the higher prices?
- half of Co-op customers are in socio-economic group C1/C2 (not well-off financially), and

are less likely to buy Fairtrade than wealthier customers;
- this implied they would need to retain cheaper products, or risk losing some customers.

Despite the difficulties, managers were able to resolve these issues in some areas of the business, and soon converted all of their own-brand hot beverages to Fairtrade. They also sell Fairtrade products in more stores than any other retailer.

Sources: Company website; Company Annual Report, 2011; *Financial Times,* 19 March 2010.

Case questions 5.2

- How is the Co-op balancing the four responsibilities set out in Figure 5.3?
- In what ways might the Fairtrade initiative help meet economic responsibilities?
- How might it make them harder to meet?

5.6   An ethical decision-making model

Trevino and Weaver (2003) note that comments on modern scandals often take a universal, normative view – prescribing what people should and should not do in all circumstances:

> Important as it is to engage in the normative study of what is, and is not, ethically proper in business, it is just as important to understand the organisational and institutional context within which ethical issues, awareness and behaviour are situated. (p. xv)

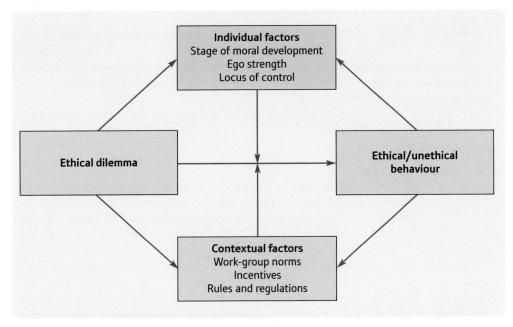

Figure 5.4 A simple model of ethical decision making

Figure 5.4 shows a simple **ethical decision-making model**. The figure predicts that someone's response to an ethical dilemma depends on individual and contextual factors. The individual factors:

Ethical decision-making models examine the influence of individual characteristics and organisational policies on ethical decisions.

- **Stage of moral development** – the extent to which the person can distinguish between right and wrong; the higher this is, the more likely the person will act ethically.
- **Ego strength** – the extent to which the person can resist impulses and follow their convictions; the greater this is, the more likely the person will do what they think is right.
- **Locus of control** – the extent to which the person believes they control their life; the more they see themselves as having control, the more likely they will act ethically.

The contextual factors:

- **Work-group norms** – beliefs within the work group about right and wrong behaviour.
- **Incentives** – management policies on rewards and disciplines.
- **Rules and regulations** – management policies about acceptable behaviour.

The figure also shows a feedback loop – behaviour has consequences for the individual and their context, which may shape future responses. Other factors could be added, but the purpose of the figure is to show that individual and contextual factors influence choices. Management values shape that context. In 2013 a US court fined GlaxoSmithKline for offences committed between 2005 and 2008, when it sold medicines to groups of people for which they had not been approved. The incentive system in the US division at that time had encouraged the practice.

Pierce and Snyder (2008) illustrate this by showing that the willingness of staff to commit fraud varied with their employer's policy. They analysed US state vehicle testing records over two years, during which time some testers moved between employers (typically small workshops). Testers' leniency varied with their employer – norms of behaviour and incentives at their current workshop encouraged them to behave ethically (making decisions in line with regulations) or unethically (passing vehicles that should fail).

Figure 5.4 also illustrates the dilemma people face when working in countries with different views on bribery. On the universal perspective they would act ethically wherever they are, **ethical relativism** suggests they would acknowledge the context, and incorporate local norms and values in their decision: if local and home country norms conflict, they would follow local ones. For international companies ethical relativism is a convenient philosophy, but causes difficulties for individuals if their views are more universal than relative.

Ethical relativism is the principle that ethical judgements cannot be made independently of the culture in which the issue arises.

5.7   Stakeholders and corporate responsibility

Stakeholder priorities – balancing trade-offs

Chapter 3 (Table 3.3) introduced the idea that stakeholders contribute to, and have expectations of, organisations. Table 5.4 extends this by showing their likely expectations in relation to CR.

Table 5.4 Stakeholders and their likely interests towards CR

Stakeholders	Likely interests towards corporate responsibility
Shareholders	Financially-centred investors: high return on investment **Ethical investors**: strong CR policies, reputation, long-term financial return
Creditors	Prompt payment
Managers	Fair income and career prospects, positive reputation for acting responsibly and sustainably
Employees	Employment, security, safe working conditions, rewarding work, fairness in promotion, security and pay
Customers	Majority – price, quality, durability and safety Minority (ethical consumers) – Fairtrade sources, fair treatment of staff, care for environment
Suppliers	Fair terms, prompt payment, long-term relationships
Local communities	Employment; income; limits on pollution and noise
Government	Pay taxes, obey laws, provide economic development, policies that support (e.g.) government renewable energy targets
Environmental campaigners	Minimise pollution, emissions, waste, and assist recycling. Use Fairtrade sources when possible

Ethical investors are people who only invest in businesses that meet specified criteria of ethical behaviour.

Some stakeholders share common interests, but the table implies many potential conflicts between and within the groups identified. Scottish and Southern Energy wants to generate power from wind farms, supporting government renewable energy targets. Some communities claim wind farms damage landscapes, endanger migrating birds and require subsidies. Local authorities wish to dump less waste and build incinerators, but nearby residents object.

In many areas of CR, managers can satisfy one group of stakeholders only at the expense of another. Devinney (2009) addresses this, believing that some advocates of CR ignore the conflicts between the virtues and vices of organisations – see 'Key ideas'.

Key ideas   **Timothy Devinney – the myth of the socially responsible firm**

Devinney (2009) questions the feasibility of the completely 'socially responsible firm' since, in his view:

> CSR is no free lunch [as] corporations, by their very nature, have conflicting virtues and vices that ensure that they will never be truly socially responsible by even the narrowest of definitions.

He is not saying that people and organisations do not have values and incentives to encourage ethical action. His point is that:

> any position taken by a firm and its management, social, ethical or otherwise, has trade-offs that cannot be avoided. Corporations can be made more 'virtuous' on some dimensions . . . but this will inevitably involve a price on other dimensions . . . [CR], like most aspects of life, has very few, if any, win/win outcomes.

Source: Devinney (2009).

Any major decision involves trade-offs, and this requirement to reach an acceptable balance between interests applies as much to CR as to any area of business.

Stakeholders influence managers

If the most powerful stakeholders expect a company to follow a Friedmanite position, managers will deliver that, perhaps with a public commitment to socially acceptable practice. Other companies have powerful shareholders who, while expecting a financial return, also believe managers can best deliver long-term returns by accommodating stakeholders' expectations.

> Firms with this perspective will invest in social initiatives because they believe that such investments will result in increased profitability. (Peloza, 2006)

Many companies differentiate themselves less by their products than by the ideas, emotions and images that their brand conveys – they value their reputation. Adopting responsible practices imbues the brand with a positive reputation that has value:

> precisely because (developing one) takes considerable time and depends on a firm making stable and consistent investments. (Roberts and Dowling, 2002)

If activists (Greenpeace) target the company this may damage the brand, so it may be wise to engage with them – see the 'Management in practice' feature about GAP (pp. 158–9).

Managers influence stakeholders – the lobbying business

Companies invest substantial resources to lobby governments to alter laws in their favour – see 'Management in practice' feature.

Facebook lobbies US government
www.facebook.com

Facebook increased its lobbying spending by almost 200 per cent in 2012 as it waged battles with Washington policy makers over consumer privacy, data collection, and immigration. The social networking company paid $3.99 million to influence US regulations according to forms filed with the government. Facebook said:

> Our presence and growth in Washington reflect our commitment to explaining how our service works, the actions we take to protect the billion plus people who use our service, the importance of preserving an open internet, and the value of innovation to our economy.

Facebook was joined by Google and Microsoft in its lobbying efforts, with those technology giants increasing spending by 70 per cent and 10 per cent respectively. Alan Webber, an analyst with the Altimeter Group said:

> There's a lot more potential regulation and laws coming out about how these companies do business. They're all very concerned about that, and they're all thinking, 'We want to influence the law from our perspective.'

The lobbying increase in the US is mirrored by efforts in the European Union. Jeff Chester, executive director of the Centre for Digital Democracy, was . . . in Brussels earlier this week, where he said lobbying by Silicon Valley companies . . . of EU officials around privacy laws was 'very intense'.

Source: *Financial Times*, 24 January 2013.
© The Financial Times 2013. All Rights Reserved.

5.8   Corporate responsibility and strategy

Unless a manager can align CR issues with wider corporate strategy it will remain a minority and marginal interest, with little chance of success. This raises the challenging question that David Vogel raised (see 'Key ideas') – 'will responsible behaviour pay? If it does not, how will the responsible organisation survive?' Vogel (2005) believes that responsible action is only sustainable if it yields a financial return – otherwise less responsible players will gain a competitive advantage.

David Vogel on responsibility and strategy

Vogel (2005) examines the claims for and against the idea that corporations should act responsibly, by analysing the forces driving CR. He concludes that while those managers who are prominent advocates of CR (Unilever, for example) are motivated by a commitment to social goals, CR is only sustainable if 'virtue pays off'. Not every policy needs to directly increase shareholder value, and many benefits of CR are difficult to quantify. But ultimately responsible action is made possible, and constrained, by market forces.

Encouraging forces include demand for responsibly made products, enhanced reputation, ethical investors and the values of managers and employees. These lead many firms to acknowledge they are accountable to a broad community of stakeholders. Virtuous behaviour can make business sense for some firms in some areas in some circumstances, but is also constrained:

> Many of the proponents of (CR) mistakenly assume that because some companies are behaving more responsibly in some areas, (more) firms can be expected to behave responsibly in more areas.

This assumption is misinformed. There is a place in the market economy for responsible firms. But there is also a large place for their less responsible competitors. (p. 3)

Some companies will benefit from acting responsibly, but this will not prevent others from acting in less responsible ways, and profiting from doing so.

Source: Vogel (2005).

Adapting the Rangan (2015) model in Section 5.3, there are four ways in which CR can contribute to the wider strategy: corporate mission; philanthropy and enlightened self-interest; improving operations; and creating shared value.

Corporate mission

Some companies position CR at the heart of their business, reflecting the beliefs and values of founders and senior managers. An early example was The Body Shop (founded by the late Anita Roddick), which became a major retailing group by, among many other things, taking a strong ethical position on issues such as testing cosmetics on live animals. Its unique position was gradually eroded – partly by its own success – and the company is now owned by the French cosmetics group, L'Oréal. The Co-op is a longer-lived example of combining economic and social aims: many small social enterprises do the same. All face the same challenge – to make a profit from their activities (or raise money in other ways) so that they survive.

Case study   The Co-op – the case continues   www.co-operative.coop

In 2010 the Co-op tripled the size of its banking business through a merger with the Britannia Building Society, and in 2012 the Board decided to bid for 630 branches of the Lloyds Banking Group. This would triple the size of the bank again, to almost 1,000 branches. Many commentators welcomed the deal as it would mean a stronger competitor for established banks. However, the expansion would be challenging as the company was still integrating the Britannia, and bank computing systems are troublesome to integrate. The Lloyds deal collapsed when the Co-op found it had insufficient capital to buy it – and that there were even bigger problems arising with Britannia: the Co-op Bank had £1.5 billion less capital than it had thought. A report into this calamity found that The Co-op Bank itself had been negligent – being over-optimistic about bad loans (frequently giving borrowers 'the benefit of the doubt'), paying insufficient attention to capital requirements, mis-selling insurance and failing to upgrade an old IT system. Many managers in senior positions lacked experience, while it described the (elected) bank chairman as a 'totally unsuitable' choice.

The Co-op Group owned 100 per cent of the bank before these events. It could not find the £1.5 billion capital shortfall itself, so a group of investors put in the money, in exchange for 70 per cent of the Co-op's stake in the Bank – leaving it with 30 per cent. It remains the largest single shareholder, and the bank retains its name. The bank now focuses on individual and small business customers.

In March 2014 the Bank revealed it needed to raise a further £400 million to cover potential compensation to customers for bank misconduct and other mistakes.

Sources: Company website; *Financial Times*, 22 October 2013; 25 March 2014; 1 May 2014.

Case questions 5.3

- What would this shift in the Co-op's stake in the bank imply for its governance structures, and for the ability of members to influence policy?

- Does it strengthen or weaken the Co-op's distinctive position as an ethical company?

Philanthropy and enlightened self-interest

Though donors are unlikely to expect or receive any direct business benefits from these activities, it still may make sense for managers to consider how they relate to their strategy – if only to ensure they do not evidently contradict each other. Jones et al. (2014) suggest another benefit of 'enlightened self-interest', by showing that a positive reputation for responsible behaviour makes a company more attractive to potential employees.

Improving operations

Table 5.2 implies that most activities can be re-designed to use fewer resources and make less waste. Many companies follow responsible practices towards resources – see, for example an account of Marks & Spencer's Plan A 2020 in Chapter 6 (pp. 201–2) showing how it aims to become the world's most sustainable retailer by 2020. Using energy efficiently, avoiding waste and treating staff with respect are established practice in many companies – which contributes towards their reputation for responsible practices. Mars, the world's biggest confectioner, is working with the Rainforest Alliance to produce all its cocoa sustainably by 2020. The company has good business reasons for this – they will not be able to buy enough cocoa unless they invest now. Others cite, for example, that the Forest Stewardship Council (www.fsc-uk.org) certifies their wood or the Rainforest Alliance (www.rainforest-alliance .org) their fruit. Companies hope this reassures customers and brings repeat purchases.

Others focus on meeting the needs of **ethical consumers** – those who consider ethical issues and try to avoid buying products from companies with a poor environmental record. Such consumers usually support Fairtrade products. Sales of products with sustainability attributes still represent a small fraction (often estimated at around 5 per cent) of total demand. There is a gap between consumers' expressed attitudes and their behaviour. A UN Environment Programme study found that while 40 per cent of people say they are willing to buy 'green' products, only 5 per cent do so (quoted in Luchs et al. 2010, p. 5). Ethical intentions may not match ethical buying at the checkout.

Ethical consumers are those who take ethical issues into account in deciding what to purchase.

Creating shared value

Porter and Kramer (2011) propose that companies are likely to perform well if they aim to create shared value, by balancing the interests of many stakeholders – see Section 5.10, in 'Sustainability'. They envisage business and society converging by finding ways to create economic value that also creates value for wider parts of society: Gap, in the 'Management in practice' feature, is an example.

Management in practice   **Gap redesigns the supply chain**   www.gap.com

Gap built an extensive worldwide supply chain, transporting raw materials and finished goods from many of the world's poorest countries to sell in the wealthier countries. By the early 1990s the company was receiving sustained attacks by human rights activists, who accused it of using sub-contractors with poor working conditions and child labour in their factories.

The company's first step was to create systems for monitoring the factories and ensuring compliance with labour standards. This helped, but the company realised that it could achieve more by engaging with the stakeholders to see if there were fundamentally better ways to do the work in the chain linking factories dealing with successive stages of making a particular garment.

The third stage was to consider the even more complex issues of how to make the whole supply chain more responsive to changes in fashion and demand.

The final stage was to consider how it can apply the lessons learned from this work on the supply chain, to redesign the way the company itself operates. Can those working on design, planning or packaging interact more with external stakeholders, to improve established company practices?

Source: Worley et al. (2010).

Rangan et al. (2015) stresses that whichever of these approaches a company chooses, it is essential that they also construct appropriate monitoring systems to ensure that the venture delivers the benefits it is expected to: otherwise there is no way to know if it has been worthwhile.

Activity 5.6   Gather information about CR policies and practices

Visit a company website and go to the section about CR. Gather information on these questions:

- Does the site explain the aims of the CR policies? Do they relate to these headings?
- What issues (e.g. waste, community projects) feature most prominently?
- Does it make any claims about the effects of the policies?

Does responsible action affect performance?

The evidence is unclear. Orlitzky et al. (2003) found a positive relationship between responsible behaviour and financial performance, while Ambec and Lanoie (2008) show seven mechanisms that enable firms to improve environmental and economic performance – see Figure 5.5.

Their research appears to show that companies can act responsibly and perform well economically. Eccles et al. (2014) offer empirical evidence through their analysis of the long-term relation between sustainable polices, internal processes and performance – see 'Key ideas'.

Key ideas   Does sustainability enhance performance?

Robert Eccles and his colleagues identified 90 US companies (which they termed high-sustainability companies) with a substantial number of environmental and social policies (on environment, employees, community, products and customers) adopted since the early 1990s. They also identified 90 comparable companies that adopted none or few of these policies – the low-sustainability companies. They found that the high-sustainability companies were more likely to:

- assign responsibility for sustainability to a specific Board committee;
- make executive pay depend on environmental, social and reputational measures;
- establish a more comprehensive and engaged stakeholder management process; and to
- measure and disclose information related to employees, customers and suppliers.

Routine auditing increased the credibility of the data, which also included much non-financial material. They comment:

> Our findings suggest that, to a large extent, the adoption of these sustainability policies reflects their underlying institutionalisation within the companies, rather than 'greenwashing' and 'cheap talk'.

Importantly. . . we find that high-sustainability companies outperform low-sustainability companies both in stock market as well as accounting performance . . . this outperformance is most pronounced in companies that sell products directly to individuals, compete on the basis of brand and reputation, and make substantial use of natural resources.

Source: Eccles et al. (2014).

Some people prefer to work for responsible organisations. Jones et al. (2014) show that those active in their community and with pro-environment policies were significantly more attractive to potential employees than companies without them. Three mechanisms supported this link:

- the job-seekers' anticipated pride in being associated with such a firm;
- their perception of a close fit between their and the company's values; and
- their expectations that such companies would treat staff well.

Vogel (2005) is sceptical. He found studies showing a positive relationship between, for example, lower greenhouse gas emissions and financial performance, but the direction of

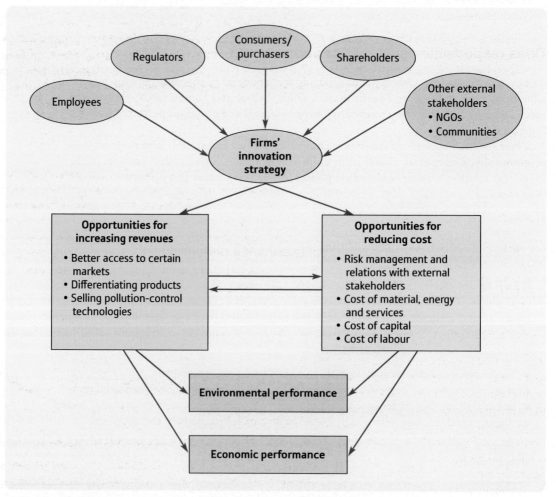

Figure 5.5 Positive links between environmental and economic performance
Source: Ambec and Lanoie (2008).

causality was unclear – perhaps profitable firms could afford better equipment. Another possibility was that factors not included in the research affected both variables. He concluded:

> just as firms that spend more on marketing are not necessarily more profitable than those that spend less, there is no reason to expect more responsible firms to outperform less responsible ones. (p. 33)

5.9 Managing corporate responsibility

Leading by example

Senior managers set the tone for an organisation by their actions. If others believe they are acting in line with stated principles, their credibility will rise and others are likely to follow. Leaders known to be engaging in malpractice will encourage others to do the same.

Management in practice Strict ethics at Wipro www.wipro.com

Wipro is one of India's leading high-tech businesses, and from its earliest days its founder, Azim Premji, has taken a firm stand on ethics. Steve Hamm (2007) writes:

> In the late 1960s and early 1970s corruption was rampant in the Indian economy. Government officials asked for kickbacks. Farmers bribed clerks to tamper with weighing machines . . . Premji set a zero-tolerance policy for bribes and any form of corruption or corner-cutting – from top managers to labourers . . . 'We said anybody committing a breach of integrity would lose their job. It's open and shut and black and white,' Premji says. It took several firings before people believed it. But finally they did. The company stood out, and not just from the local Indian outfits. Some of the multinationals had fallen into the trap of paying bribes as well. (p. 35)

Source: Hamm (2007).

Codes of practice

A code of practice is a formal statement of the company's values, setting out general principles on matters such as quality, employees or the environment. Others set out procedures for situations – such as conflicts of interest or the acceptance of gifts. Their effectiveness depends on whether top management supports them by example, and with sanctions and rewards.

Corporate responsibility structures and reporting

These are the formal systems and roles that companies create to support responsible behaviour – such as staff with direct responsibilities for CR policies and practices, and formal regular monitoring and reporting systems. Most companies now include a CR statement in their Annual Report, and may include in this an **ethical audit** profiling current practice.

Ethical audits are the practice of systematically reviewing the extent to which an organisation's actions are consistent with its stated ethical intentions.

The challenge facing all such practices is how robust they are against personal opportunism, when individuals pursue an immediate, short-term individual advantage, while ignoring considerations of principle and long-term advantage. If unchecked, this will spread and disfigure the business. The most important lesson to come from stories of corporate malpractice is that financial success without an ethical foundation leads to disaster. To avoid that, the governance of public and private organisations requires relentless attention by their directors to their personal ethical discipline, and to that of executives who are accountable to them.

Case study   The Co-op: the case continues   www.co-operative.coop

The traditional governance structure was that members (customers) elect area committees and regional boards that influence local policy: the regional boards in turn elected some of their members to the national board of directors. At each level these bodies held management accountable for the extent to which they are living up to co-operative values – self-help, self-responsibility, democracy and social responsibility. Those with experience of area committees claim that some vocal members place more emphasis on social goals (such as advocating that the Co-op should provide cheap food for disadvantaged groups) than on the business goals that would pay for it.

The review of the 2013 crisis was highly critical of this governance structure. Most of those elected to the national board lacked the experience required to guide an organisation of this scale, and some were openly hostile to professional managers. This discouraged them from working for the Co-op.

In 2014, after long debate, the members agreed to changes proposed by those advocating reform. These included a much smaller eleven-member Board, composed of two executives, six non-executive directors with wide business experience, and three elected by the members. This new Board structure is believed to have persuaded the current (in 2015) CEO, Richard Pennycook, to take the job. Members elect a new 100-member Council, to set strategy and monitor social performance.

Some members believe that these changes go against the Co-op tradition, and will make it harder to distinguish it from retail competitors. One commented that the ethical dimension had traditionally been driven by members, not management. A survey commissioned by the Co-op in 2014 gives some insight into customer's preferences: over 53 per cent said lower prices would be the incentive most likely to make them shop more with the business.

Source: *Financial Times*, 5 September 2014; 2 December 2014; Company website.

Case questions 5.4

- Go to the Co-op website and then to the 'Sustainability report' for the most recent year.
- Choose one sustainability topic that interests you and read that section of the report carefully so that you can explain to someone else what the Co-op has done in that area.

5.10   Integrating themes

Entrepreneurship

New businesses inherently have less experience, fewer systems and less money. Wang and Bansal (2012) suggest that this diminishes the benefits they gain from acting responsibly, while amplifying the negatives. Acting responsibly can add value to a company by, among other things, introducing environmentally-friendly products that appeal to customers, developing positive relationships with stakeholders and generally improving reputation. It also brings costs, including additional investments and the management time required, for example, to reorganise processes to reduce pollution – which they find hard to finance.

Wang and Bansal suggest that entrepreneurial businesses could offset these disadvantages if top management had a long-term, rather than a short-term, orientation. They proposed that having that outlook would help new ventures to avoid the trap of focusing on immediate crisis but to manage for the long term – even if this costs more at first. Their empirical work with 149 new ventures confirmed their hypotheses – that responsible behaviour did have a negative effect on the financial performance of new ventures. This effect was moderated by those whose founder or president was sufficiently well-funded to be able to take a long-term orientation: in their companies, responsible actions appeared to have positive financial effects.

Sustainability

Porter and Kramer (2011) recently wrote that business is widely perceived as the cause of most social and environmental problems, and that this begins to threaten their legitimacy in the eyes of many citizens. Part of the problem, the authors suggest, is that many managers still see the role of business as being to create a very narrowly defined form of value – that of short-term financial performance, almost regardless of the costs this may have for other people and institutions. This narrow focus means they ignore the most important customer needs (including sustainability) and the broader influences on long-term success.

They advocate business and society becoming closer by focusing on shared value – creating economic value in a way that also creates value for society by addressing its needs. Social and economic progress can connect if companies rethink their products and markets, redefine productivity in the value chain and enable local clusters to form.

> Shared value is . . . about expanding the total pool of economic and social value. A good example of this difference is the fair trade movement [which] aims to increase the proportion of revenue that goes to poor farmers by paying them higher prices. Though this may be a noble sentiment, fair trade is mostly about redistribution, rather than expanding the total amount of value created. A shared value perspective, instead, focuses on improving growing techniques and on the local cluster of supporting suppliers and institutions . . . to increase farmers' efficiency, yields, product quality and sustainability. That leads to [more revenue and profits for the farmers and the companies that buy from them]. Studies in the Cote d'Ivoire conclude that while fair trade can increase farmers' incomes by 10% to 20%, shared value investments can increase them by more than 300% (Porter and Kramer, 2011, p. 65).

Internationalisation

Matten and Moon (2008) observed that activity relating to corporate responsibility is much more visible in the United States than in Europe. They note:

> Comparative research in CSR between Europe and the United States has identified remarkable differences between companies on each side of the Atlantic. (p. 404)

These included evidence that:

- US companies were significantly more likely than French or Dutch companies to mention CSR explicitly on their websites;
- of 15 voluntary codes of conduct established by corporations in the coffee industry, only two were from Europe, with 13 from the US; and
- the value of voluntary community contributions by US companies was more than ten times greater than their UK counterparts.

They explain the apparent difference by using Whitley's (1999) model of differences in national business systems (Chapter 4, Section 4.7). This shows how differences in national systems lead to differences in the nature of firms, in how markets are organised and how companies are governed. Matten and Moon (2008) show that in the United States CR is embedded in a culture of individualism and democratic pluralism – corporations have more discretion, and often incentive, to engage publicly in CR. In Europe, CR is embedded in processes of industrial relations, labour law and governance.

Figure 5.6 illustrates their suggestion that countries that encourage individualism and favour private economic activities in liberal markets would encourage CR as an explicit aspect of corporate policies – as is the case in the United States. In contrast, European institutions have a more coordinated approach to economic and social governance through a partnership of representative actors led by government.

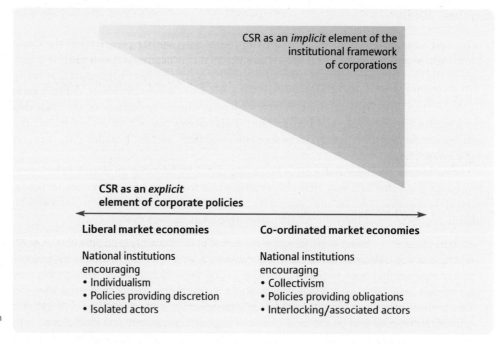

Figure 5.6 Implicit and explicit CR

Source: Matten and Moon (2008).

Governance

People expect a responsible organisation to introduce policies and ways of working that make its activities more sustainable. Many do so, such as by investing in equipment to reduce emissions or by signing up to certification schemes that monitor their environmental performance.

A valid question about such schemes is whether they actually affect sustainability. Schaefer (2007) studied the experience of three water companies as they introduced environmental management schemes (EMS) – sets of standards that specify the procedures and practices an organisation must follow to achieve and retain accreditation. Managers have several motives for introducing such systems, such as maintaining the goodwill of customers or improving performance (on cost or environmental measures).

Her long-term study showed that being keen to maintain the goodwill of customers was the main motivation, while improving environmental performance played a small role. Although this had improved, there was no evidence that this was due to introducing EMS: it was just as likely to have been due to more capital spending on equipment. Schaefer concludes:

> If one is to take the sustainability challenge seriously the implications are worrying. The adoption of a management innovation that improves companies' environmental legitimacy without doing much to tackle their (wider) environmental performance may give a false sense of achievement and [inhibit] more far-reaching improvement. (p. 531)

Boiral (2007) reached a similar conclusion in a study of the use of [an environmental] standard by nine Canadian companies. Boiral concluded:

> daily management practices remained decoupled from the prescriptions of the ISO 14001 system, of which employees generally had only a vague understanding. (p. 127)

Summary

1 **Give examples of corporate malpractice and of philanthropic business practices**

- Negative examples include poor treatment of suppliers or staff, wasteful uses of energy and other resources, and unfair treatment of customers. Reputations are also damaged by cases of senior management fraud and high compensation to failed managers.

- In contrast there are many examples of philanthropy and enlightened self-interest, in which people act with little or no expectation of a specific benefit in return.

2   **Distinguish criteria that people use to evaluate individual and corporate actions**
Individual

- Moral principle – is the decision consistent with generally accepted principles?
- Utilitarianism – does the decision benefit the greatest number of people?
- Human rights – does the decision support one of several human rights?
- Individualism – does the decision serve the individual's self-interest?

Corporate

- Legal responsibilities – obey the law.
- Economic responsibilities – the function of business is to act legally for shareholders.
- Ethical responsibilities – business has responsibility to the society on which it depends.
- Discretionary – actions that are entirely philanthropic.

3   **Use a model of ethical decision making to explain behaviour**

- Figure 5.4 shows a simple model of individual and contextual factors that shape ethical or unethical behaviour.

4   **Show how stakeholders, strategies and responsible behaviour interact**

- Stakeholders' expectations and relative power will influence how managers interpret responsible behaviour, bearing in mind Vogel's point that this is only sustainable if it supports strategy. The chapter showed how this happens – when CR is part of the mission, meets customer needs, or otherwise supports strategy.

5   **Evaluate an organisation's methods for managing corporate responsibility**

- These include leading by example, codes of practice and CR structures and reporting mechanisms.

6   **Identify the values underlying action, and understand how these can help you develop the skill of linking actions to values**

- Being clear about the values that guide your action is a valuable skill in being able to work consistently and with authority, and the chapter offered tools to help develop that.

7   **Show how ideas from the chapter add to your understanding of the integrating themes**

- Wang and Bansal (2012) show that while small companies appear to be at a disadvantage in developing responsible practices, those that have a long-term orientation to their business are able to do so without damaging their performance.
- The idea of creating shared value proposed by Porter and Kramer offers a way of re-establishing the legitimacy of business if managers can focus on activities that bring social as well as economic value.
- Variations in CR reporting between countries may have more to do with the traditions of national management systems than with differences in practice.
- There is evidence that some companies use environmental management schemes, intended to act as a form of governance and control, more to impress customers and regulators than to change daily practice.

Test your understanding

1   Identify two recent examples of corporate malpractice (including one from the public sector) and two of philanthropic behaviour. What were their effects?

2 Describe in your own terms each of four schools of ethical theory mentioned in the chapter, and illustrate each with an example of how it has been used to justify a decision.

3 Summarise the four responsibilities that corporations may choose to meet (or not), illustrating each with an example.

4 Sketch the ethical decision-making model, including as many of the variables as you can.

5 How can managers take account of the diverse interest of stakeholders?

6 Why is it important, in Vogel's view, to link corporate responsibility to strategy?

7 Illustrate each of the ways in which organisations do this with a current example.

8 Visit a website of your choice, and try to find out which practices the organisation uses to promote and monitor corporate responsibility.

9 Summarise an idea from the chapter that adds to your understanding of the integrating themes.

Think critically

Think about the way your company, or one with which you are familiar, approaches issues of corporate responsibility, and record your answers to these questions:

- What examples of the issues discussed in this chapter are currently relevant to your company?

- In responding to these issues, what **assumptions** about the role of business in society appear to have guided what people have done? What are *your* assumptions?

- What factors such as the history or **context** of the company appear to have influenced the prevailing view? Does the prevailing view match yours, or differ from it?

- Have people put forward **alternative** ways of dealing with these issues, based on evidence about other companies? What alternatives would you propose?

- What **limitations** do you find in the ideas and theories presented here? For example, can you find evidence for and against Vogel's view?

Develop a skill – clarifying values

How managers approach issues of corporate responsibility reflects their values: proposals that reflect clearly thought-out values are likely to be confident and coherent. This exercise is intended to help you clarify your values, and use that to guide what you do.

- **Awareness:** Assess how conscious you are of the values that lie behind what you think or do. Are you conscious of knowing people who you feel are more or less self-aware than you?

- **Learning:** Recall Section 5.4, including Activities 5.2 and 5.3. Summarise the main ideas presented. How is knowing about these likely to help a manager?

- **Analysis:** Which of the four ethical principles, if any, corresponds most closely to your personal preferences about how to respond to a situation (e.g. utilitarianism)?

  - Read again the description in the text of that principle, and also Section 5.4.

  - Identify someone (whom you know, or can read about) who uses your preferred ethical principle (e.g. utilitarianism) to guide their approach. Consider what they do (for example, they may stress the number of people a proposal will benefit, and minimise the number who will be worse off). What seem to be the effects of how they use the principle, and what may you be able to learn from them? Try to identify a specific practice.

- **Practice:** Identify ways in which you may be able to try one of these in the next few days. Create an opportunity to do this, record the results, and reflect on what you can learn from the experience.
- **Application:** Decide on another opportunity to practise this skill within the next week.

Read more

Ambec, S. and Lanoie, P. (2008), 'Does it pay to be green? A systematic overview', *Academy of Management Perspectives,* vol. 22, no. 4, pp. 45–62.

Clear analysis of how companies have acted to reduce their impact on the environment, and to become more profitable. The paper contains many examples of successful practice.

Clarke, F.L. (2003), *Corporate Collapse: Accounting, Regulatory and Ethical Failure,* Cambridge University Press, Cambridge.

Details the Enron collapse, which also destroyed accountants Arthur Andersen.

Germain, D. and Reed, R. (2009), *a book about innocent,* Penguin, London.

Shows how the enterprise combined responsible behaviour with profitable business.

Simms, A. and Boyle, D. (2010), *Eminent Corporations: The Rise and Fall of Great British Brands,* Constable, London.

Thorough analysis of eight major companies, this traces the underlying reasons for the widespread loss of trust in business.

Go online

These websites have appeared in the chapter:

www.co-operative.coop
www.bitc.org
www.facebook.com
www.wipro.com
www.gap.com
www.fairtrade.org.uk
www.rainforest-alliance.org

Visit two of the sites in the list (or others that interest you) and navigate to the pages dealing with corporate responsibility, sustainability or corporate governance.

- What are the main concerns upon which they report?
- What information can you find about their policies?
- Compare and contrast the concerns and policies expressed on the sites. What dilemmas does that imply that managers in these companies are dealing with?

PART 2 CASE

BP

www.bp.com

The company

In 2016 BP is the world's fourth-largest oil and natural gas producer (after ExxonMobil, Chevron and Royal Dutch Shell), with over 65,000 employees. The company is an 'integrated' oil company, in the sense that it has both 'upstream' (exploration and production) and 'downstream' (refining and marketing) operations. In this respect it is similar to other integrated oil companies, such as ExxonMobil and Total. This case is about the company's upstream activities.

The company is registered in Britain, but 40 per cent of its assets are in the United States, and it is that country's largest gas producer. It does 80 per cent of its business outside the UK, and is inherently engaged in international business, needing to succeed in many diverse political, economic and technological environments. In one recent year its sources of oil and gas (measured in 'barrels of oil equivalent per day') were:

- Europe 201,000;
- United States 778,000;
- Russia 985,000;
- Rest of world 1,478,000 (including Iraq).

The company expects that world demand for energy will continue to grow, possibly by as much as 40 per cent over 2010 levels by 2030. Advances in surveying and drilling technology mean that oil reserves previously out of reach can be recovered – such as those in deep oceans or beneath the Arctic ice cap. The company's future depends on being able to secure access to sufficient oil reserves to at least replenish what it extracts, and to meet growing demand. Securing these resources is competitive, as all of the world's major oil companies are seeking new sources. To access oil reserves BP must obtain permission from the country's government, and often the exploration and production is through a

joint venture with a local oil company that usually has close links with the national government.

BP faces issues of corporate responsibility throughout the business, especially in exploration and production. Oil production inevitably brings some environmental damage and the 2010 explosion on a production rig working for BP in the Gulf of Mexico vividly demonstrated the hazards of deep-water production.

© Susana Gonzalez/Bloomberg/Getty Images

Environmental groups challenge oil exploration in sensitive areas, and a task for BP's corporate governance is to ensure that these concerns are given adequate consideration alongside commercial interests.

It also has a large presence in the United States, where it both extracts and sells large quantities of oil. Relationships have been damaged by the company's safety record, and it has had to pay significant compensation to individuals and businesses affected by these events, as well as fines to the US government.

The company's financial performance affects many stakeholders, as most pension funds hold shares in the company, using the dividend income they receive to pay their pensioners. Financial returns have been affected in recent years by the recession reducing demand, while production costs have risen. The company has also had to meet the costs of compensation and US Government fines following the Gulf of Mexico accident. The directors decided to pay a dividend to shareholders of 40 cents a share for 2015. The table shows the main financial indicators of performance in the two most recent years.

Measures of financial performance in financial years ending 31 December

	2015	2014
Total revenues ($m)	43,235	65,424
Profit (loss) before interest and tax ($m)	(7,918)	6,412
Profit (loss) after taxation ($m)	(6,482)	3,780
Dividend per ordinary share (cents)	40.00	39.00

Source: BP Annual Report, 2014, 2015.

Managing to add value

Securing oil reserves

A central preoccupation for management is to secure new oil supplies. The company has invested heavily to acquire licenses to search for oil itself and by acquiring, or creating joint ventures with, companies that already own such licenses. Since 2010 it has become more focused on building the upstream business, by acquiring 400,000 sq km of oil fields – more than double the acreage secured in the previous nine years.

It draws supplies from new oil fields in Azerbaijan and Indonesia, and in 2009 reached an agreement with Iraq to rehabilitate the giant Rumaila oil field, which it did successfully, well within the time allowed. This deal gave the company a presence in a country with the world's third-largest known oil reserves. In 2011 the Indian government approved a $7.2 billion oil and gas investment, which gave BP a 30 per cent stake in a large but technically difficult natural gas field off India's east coast. This positioned the company as the first oil major to gain a foothold in a country where demand for oil is growing rapidly. Its collaborator in the deal is Reliance Industries, a major Indian company with a good reputation for project delivery and strong political connections. A year later there were signs of difficulty, with administrative delays to investment plans, and evidence that output from the field (which has been operating for several years) was declining more rapidly than expected.

The company has to face the political risks that these ventures entail, especially in politically unstable countries where power conflicts among ruling elites can, directly or indirectly, threaten commercial ventures.

Joint ventures and governments

The company's most significant joint ventures have been with Russian companies. For several years its business in Russia was conducted by TNK-BP (set up in 2003), in which it had a 50 per cent share. BP saw this as a strategically important deal, providing about 29 per cent of its annual oil production. It also opened the way for further deals, giving it access to Russia's large oil and gas reserves in Siberia, and fitted a wider political strategy of reducing dependence on Middle Eastern supplies. By 2012 it was clear that there were severe differences between BP and the Russian partners in the joint venture – over strategic direction and how to manage it – and soon afterwards BP sold its share of the venture to Rosneft, a state-owned Russian oil group. As part of the deal BP received a 20 per cent stake in Rosneft, giving it preferential access to resources, and a close alignment of their interests with those of the Russian government.

Culture and structure

During John Browne's tenure as chief executive (from 1992 to 2007), the company became decentralised, in the sense that managers responsible for a business unit faced tough financial targets but had considerable autonomy in how they met them. Senior managers believed this helped to reduce administrative costs and enabled unit managers to use their local knowledge and contacts to best advantage.

When Tony Hayward replaced Browne in 2007 he began to change the style, requiring managers to develop more common working processes across the business, to reduce complexity and cut costs. In an email to staff in October 2007 the head of exploration and production claimed that recent safety lapses in the US had shown that the decentralised approach had dangers. Many business units that had enjoyed considerable autonomy under Browne would be eliminated, and the company would 'standardise more of what we do'.

That decentralised structure contrasted sharply with that at ExxonMobil, the acknowledged global leader in the industry for safety and engineering excellence. Exxon is organised on functional lines, so the worldwide exploration operation, for example, is a single division. This helps spread best practice and new technology rapidly around the company:

Wherever you travel in the ExxonMobil world, you will hear consistent strategies and approaches, consistent expectations for the high standards for safety and operational performance. Senior management also takes a hands-on approach. [One recent CEO] would every morning review the progress of every well the company was drilling anywhere in the world. If he did not like what he saw, he would call the manager responsible.

 Source: From an article by Ed Crooks, *Financial Times*, 24 July 2007, p. 21. © The Financial Times 2007. All Rights Reserved.

Safety

The company's reputation had suffered in March 2005 when an explosion at the Texas City refinery, its biggest in the US, killed 15 people and injured about 500, making it the deadliest US refinery accident in more than a decade. An investigation by the Department of Labour uncovered more than 300 violations at the refinery. An internal BP report found that senior managers at the plant had ignored advice to spend money on safety, though the plant was very profitable.

There was further damage in 2006 when a pipeline spilt 270,000 gallons of crude oil into Alaska's Prudhoe Bay. The Alaska Department of Environmental Conservation blamed corrosion, which BP denied on the grounds that expenditure on corrosion maintenance was higher than it had ever been. When Tony Hayward took over as CEO in 2007 he stressed his priority:

BP had to implement strategy by focusing like a laser on safe and reliable operations.

This ambition received a severe blow when, on 20 April 2010, the Deepwater Horizon – a production rig – exploded in the Gulf of Mexico while taking oil from the Macondo well, which BP owned. The safety arrangements intended to cap the well in such circumstances failed to work, and oil flowed into the sea for many months, polluting it and the nearby coastline. The explosion killed 11 workers and the ensuing pollution caused economic damage to fishing and tourism, and widespread public criticism of the company in the United States. The company pointed out that it neither owned nor operated the production rig – but agreed to pay compensation to businesses and communities affected by the accident. It set aside $45 billion to meet likely costs, and the fines for breaching US safety and environmental laws. To meet this cost it suspended

dividend payments to shareholders (which resumed in 2011) and sold several oil fields and refineries. In July 2015 it announced an agreed settlement for civil penalties and damages with US authorities – meaning that it had resolved one of the few remaining uncertainties arising from the disaster.

The company also made many internal changes – including the resignation of the chief executive, Tony Hayward. He was replaced by Bob Dudley, an American citizen who had previously been chief executive of TNK-BP. His immediate task in handling the massive disturbance of the spill was to ensure the leak was plugged. The company's engineers did so in August 2010 – a remarkable feat of engineering, as the well was over 5,000 feet below sea level. Then he had to (among other things):

- meet claims for damages without letting the costs run out of control;
- stabilise BP's financial position by selling assets;
- establish the cause of the incident in conjunction with US government agencies;
- reform relevant internal practices;
- restore the company's reputation in the US; and
- develop a new strategy for the business.

Inquiries identified technical and managerial failures that had caused the accident – including inadequate maintenance and inaccurate interpretation of data from the well. BP acknowledged its own failings, but also argued that other companies were partially responsible, including Transocean, which owned and operated the rig, and Haliburton, a contractor working on it: Haliburton had supplied the faulty cement intended to seal the leak. BP sought substantial damages from both companies – alleging that Transocean workers failed to spot evidence of oil and gas escaping, and did not respond effectively when the escape became evident.

Although the well had been sealed in late 2010, the event was continuing to affect the company's performance in 2012. The well had not yet resumed production, losing valuable output and income, while continuing uncertainty over the legal liabilities limited the dividends payable, and lowered the share price – adding to shareholders' dissatisfaction.

In June 2009 the company appointed a new Chairman – Carl-Henric Svanberg. He was previously chief executive of the Swedish company Ericsson, where he developed a deep knowledge of the world's emerging countries. He also believes that the pace of growth of car ownership and air travel are unsustainable:

With a normal growth rate, the world's gross domestic product will triple by 2050, and we will

probably see another 2 billion people in the world. If we continue to do things in the same way, it will not be easy for this planet to cope with that. So we have to find more intelligent solutions, and the energy industry is in the centre of that. BP is actively searching for alternative energy sources.

Aspects of BP's context

Oil demand and supply

In early 2016 oil prices were about half the level they had been three years earlier. This severely affects the viability of new wells, so the energy groups had been cutting exploration investment – one estimate was that over $100 billion of planned investment had been cancelled or deferred by June 2015. All oil companies responded to the falling price by cutting costs – not only in exploration, but also improving operational efficiency – it changed from 'chasing barrels to chasing efficiency.'

Apart from this fall in prices, new fields that have been discovered are often in challenging areas – the rocks below the Arctic Ocean are believed to hold vast amounts of oil and gas, but which will be very expensive to extract.

Another technological change is the growing use of shale oil, especially in the United States, where oil production is (2015) at its highest level since 1979. One observer has predicted it may be self-sufficient in oil by 2025.

Governments with oil reserves on their territory often depend on the technical resources of the world's major oil companies to recover these reserves profitably. While the oil majors are eager to work there, they acknowledge that this requires them to work with business partners with different political and legal systems, including how they deal with human rights, democracy and bribery.

Oil exploration and production evidently affects the environment – even in normal working it can disrupt wildlife, damage indigenous communities, and pollute air and water. The production process itself contributes to carbon dioxide emissions when gas is flared from oil fields. Dealing with the industry's impact on the environment was a prominent feature of John (now Lord) Browne's leadership of BP prior to 2007, when it made significant investments in alternative sources of energy such as biofuels, wind farms and solar power.

Current management dilemmas

Major shareholders have been pressing management to improve performance – since the low dividend payments in recent years, and the continuing doubt about Gulf of Mexico costs has damaged share price: in 2007 they were trading at 600 pence, and in early 2016 they were around 400 pence – with a yield of about 5 per cent. The company's owners expect managers to improve this performance. They want clarity about strategic direction on issues like new sources of supply, relations with partners and safety.

New energy sources

One strategic issue is how BP strikes the balance between investing in oil and alternative non-oil sources of energy, such as bio-mass or wind. During the tenure of John Browne these were a prominent feature of the company, but appear not to have been so significant in recent years. These alternative investments could bring environmental benefits, but may not help with the pressure from shareholders for better returns on their investments. The fall in oil price from late 2014 meant that it had cut investment in exploration.

Relations with partners

The company relies heavily on joint ventures with other companies, but they are hard to manage. The stake in Rosneft earns about 16 per cent of BP's profits: some investors worry that this investment will be endangered if relations between Russia and the West deteriorate due to differences over conflicts in Ukraine and the Middle East. A feature of the Gulf of Mexico accident was that the field was being developed in partnership with other companies. As these will be prominent in the company's future it relies heavily on the associated arrangements for oversight and governance. In each case governments – Russia and the United States respectively – played a significant part in the outcomes. Coll (2012) shows how rival ExxonMobil exerts influence over the companies and governments with which it has to deal.

Producing oil safely

Soon after taking over as CEO, Dudley made structural changes to reduce the autonomy of the powerful exploration and production division. This had had a high degree of autonomy, partly because it accounted for most of BP's profit. Dudley split it into three units responsible for exploration, development and production respectively: the heads of these units will report directly to the chief executive, giving him direct insight into their working. He also created a separate safety unit whose staff are embedded in the operating units, and whose head reports directly to the CEO.

Sources: Coll (2012); *Financial Times,* 26 June 2009, 27 July 2010, 30 April 2014, 29 January 2015, 1 April 2015; 23 July 2012, 19 October 2012, 16 November 2012, 2 January 2013, 18 March 2013, 26 April 2013; BP website; and other sources.

Part case questions

(a) Relating to Chapters 3 to 5

1 The case mentions 'culture' at several points. What subcultures can you identify, and what may this imply for senior management's attempts to establish a unified image of the business? (Section 3.3)

2 Consider which of Porter's five forces are likely to be affecting BP most seriously. Do they represent threats or opportunities? (Section 3.4)

3 Construct a PESTEL analysis to establish the main aspects of the environment that affect BP (Section 3.5)

4 Which stakeholders is management dealing with in the case? (Section 3.7)

5 In what ways will managing in BP, with such an international exposure, be different from managing in a national company with no international business? List the three most significant. (Sections 4.3, 4.5, 4.6)

6 Visit the BP website and gather examples of its corporate responsibility activities. How do the examples relate to the headings in Table 5.2?

7 From what you read in the case, and your wider knowledge, in what ways is BP fulfilling the four responsibilities of business? (Section 5.5)

(b) Relating to the company

1 Visit the BP website, including the pages on 'investor relations' and 'sustainability review'. Note recent events that add to material in this case. Make notes on which, if any, of the dilemmas identified in the case are still current, and how the company has dealt with them.

2 How prominent are safety issues in the company's report, and what has been the outcome of the legal proceedings brought by the US Government after the Gulf of Mexico disaster?

3 What is BP's relative share of world oil production in the most recent trading period? Which competitors have gained and lost share? Access this information from the websites of *The Economist*, *Financial Times* or BBC News (Business and Technology pages).

4 What new issues appear to be facing the company that were not mentioned in the case?

5 For any one of those issues it faces, how do you think it should deal with it? Build your answer by referring to one or more features of the company's history outlined in the case.

PART 2
EMPLOYABILITY SKILLS – PREPARING FOR THE WORLD OF WORK

To help you develop useful skills, this section includes tasks that relate the themes covered in the Part to six employability skills (sometimes called capabilities and attributes) that many employers value. The layout will help you to articulate these skills to employers and prepare for the recruitment process you will encounter in application forms, interviews and assessment centres.

Task 2.1   Business awareness

If a potential employer asks you to attend an assessment centre or a competency-based interview, they may ask you to present or discuss a current business topic to demonstrate your business awareness. To help you to prepare for this, write an individual or group report on *one* of these topics and present it to an audience. Aim to present your ideas in a 750-word report and/or 10 PowerPoint slides at most.

1   Using data from one or more websites or printed sources, outline significant recent developments in BP, especially regarding its:
   ● exploration and production activities;
   ● safety performance; and
   ● internal governance.

Finally, present a summary of the contrasting views of commentators on BP's progress towards restoring its safety reputation and generating dividends for shareholders.

2   Gather information on the interaction between BP and its political and regulatory context, including specific examples of interventions by regulators to influence the company, and vice versa. What generally relevant lessons can you draw from this example of business–government interaction?
3   Choose another energy company that interests you – and which you may consider as a career option. Gather information from the website and other sources about its structure and operations.
   ● How have technological developments affected the main players in the industry – and how has management responded?
   ● What competitive challenges does it face?
   ● In what ways, if any, have governments and politics influenced the business?
   ● In what ways, if at all, does sustainability and corporate responsibility feature in its activities and reporting?

When you have completed the task, record a short paragraph giving examples of the skills (such as information gathering, analysis and presentation) you have developed from this task. You can transfer a brief note of this to the Table at Task 2.7.

Task 2.2 Thinking critically

Reflect on the way that you handled Task 2.1, and identify how you exercised the skills of thinking critically **(Chapter 1, Section 1.8)**. For example:

1 Did you spend time identifying and challenging the assumptions implied in the reports or commentaries you read? Summarise what you found then, or do it now.
2 Did you consider the extent to which they took account of the context in which managers are operating? Summarise what you found then, or do it now.
3 How far did they, or you, go in imagining and exploring alternative ways of dealing with the issue?
4 Did you spend time outlining the limitations of ideas or proposals which you thought of putting forward?

When you have completed the task, record a short paragraph giving examples of the thinking skills you have developed from this task. You can transfer a brief note of this to the Table at Task 2.7.

Task 2.3 Solving problems

Chapter 6 includes ideas on planning to deal with a problem – such as that of completing Task 2.1. Refer to these if you need more guidance on this activity, which invites you to analyse how your team worked on a task.

Use the scales below to rate the way your team planned how it would work on Task 2.1 – circle the number that best reflects your opinion of the discussion.

1 The team used suitable methods to gather sufficient information to create a good plan to complete the task **(Section 6.4)**.

1	2	3	4	5	6	7
Strongly disagree						Strongly agree

2 The team set SMART goals, which gave focus to our work on the task **(Section 6.5)**.

1	2	3	4	5	6	7
Strongly disagree						Strongly agree

3 The goals helped to motivate us to achieve the task **(Section 6.5)**.

1	2	3	4	5	6	7
Strongly disagree						Strongly agree

4 The team made a full list of what had to be done to achieve the goals **(Section 6.6)**.

1	2	3	4	5	6	7
Strongly disagree						Strongly agree

5 The team made a suitable implementation plan, and followed it **(Section 6.7).**

1	2	3	4	5	6	7
Strongly disagree						Strongly agree

6 The team monitored the progress of the plan, and adjusted it accordingly **(Section 6.7).**

1	2	3	4	5	6	7
Strongly disagree						Strongly agree

When you have completed the task, record a short paragraph giving examples of the planning skills you have developed from this task. You can transfer a brief note of this to the Table at Task 2.7.

Task 2.4   Team working

Chapter 17 includes ideas on team working. This activity helps you use these to analyse how your team worked on Task 2.1.

Use the scales below to rate the way your team worked on this task – circle the number that best reflects your opinion of the discussion.

1 The team was effective in obtaining and using necessary information.

1	2	3	4	5	6	7
Strongly disagree						Strongly agree

2 The team members took on complementary team roles **(Section 17.4).**

1	2	3	4	5	6	7
Strongly disagree						Strongly agree

3 The team progressed through the stages of team development **(Section 17.5).**

1	2	3	4	5	6	7
Strongly disagree						Strongly agree

4 The team developed effective working processes that suited the task **(Section 17.6).**

1	2	3	4	5	6	7
Strongly disagree						Strongly agree

5 The team used their time effectively.

1	2	3	4	5	6	7
Strongly disagree						Strongly agree

6 The team regularly reviewed the ways it was working, and changed these when it would improve performance (Section 17.6).

1	2	3	4	5	6	7
Strongly disagree						Strongly agree

Record three practices that you could use in your next task. If possible, compare your results and suggestions with other members of the team, and agree on practices that would help a team work better.

When you have completed the task, write a short paragraph giving examples of team working skills (such as observing the team to improve performance) you have developed from this task. You can transfer a brief note of this to the Table at Task 2.7.

Task 2.5 Communicating

Chapter 16 includes ideas on communicating – and Sections 16.4 and 16.5 are especially relevant to this task. It will help you to analyse how well your team communicated as you worked on Task 2.1.

Use the scales below to rate the way your team communicated during Task 2.1 – circle the number that best reflects your opinion of the discussion.

1 The team handled face-to-face communication well during its meetings (Section 16.4).

1	2	3	4	5	6	7
Strongly disagree						Strongly agree

2 The team communicated effectively by phone, mobile, voicemail and other electronic systems (Section 16.4).

1	2	3	4	5	6	7
Strongly disagree						Strongly agree

3 The team communicated effectively by personal, written methods – letters, email, texting (Section 16.4).

1	2	3	4	5	6	7
Strongly disagree						Strongly agree

4 The team communicated effectively by impersonal written methods – newsletters, online communities (Section 16.4).

1	2	3	4	5	6	7
Strongly disagree						Strongly agree

5 The team adapted between centralised and decentralised communication networks according to the needs of the task **(Section 16.5).**

1	2	3	4	5	6	7
Strongly disagree						Strongly agree

6 The team communicated its report well to the chosen audience.

1	2	3	4	5	6	7
Strongly disagree						Strongly agree

7 The team experienced no significant barriers to communication, either internally or externally.

1	2	3	4	5	6	7
Strongly disagree						Strongly agree

Record three communication practices that you could use in your next task. If possible, compare your results and suggestions with other members of the team, and agree on practices that would help a team work better.

When you have completed the task, record a short paragraph giving examples of communication skills you have developed from this task. You can transfer a brief note of this to the Table at Task 2.7.

Task 2.6   Self-management

This activity helps you to learn more about managing yourself, so that you can present convincing evidence to employers showing, among other things, your willingness to learn, your ability to manage and plan learning, workloads and commitments, and that you have a well-developed level of self-awareness and self-reliance. You need to show that you are able to accept responsibility, manage time and use feedback to learn.

Reflect on the way that you handled Task 2.1, and identify how you exercised skills of self-management.

1 I effectively planned the time I would spend on each part of the task.

1	2	3	4	5	6	7
Strongly disagree						Strongly agree

2 I tried to balance my commitments and those of other team members across the work, so that all were reasonably busy.

1	2	3	4	5	6	7
Strongly disagree						Strongly agree

3 I think I used my time well.

1	2	3	4	5	6	7
Strongly disagree						Strongly agree

4 I tried to ensure that I and others took responsibility for distinct areas of work, to keep moving the task forward.

1	2	3	4	5	6	7
Strongly disagree						Strongly agree

5 I often reflected on how I was working on the task to identify possible ways to improve our performance.

1	2	3	4	5	6	7
Strongly disagree						Strongly agree

Write down three self-management practices that you could use in your next task. If possible, compare your results and suggestions with other members of the team, and agree on practices that would help a team work better.

When you have completed the task, write a short paragraph giving examples of the self-management practices you have developed from this task. You can transfer a brief note of this to the Table at Task 2.7.

Task 2.7   Recording your employability skills

To conclude your work on this Part, use the summary paragraphs above to record the employability skills you have developed during your work on these tasks, and in other activities. Use the format of the table below to create an electronic record that you can use to combine the list of skills you have developed in this Part, with those in other Parts.

Most of your learning about each skill will probably come from the task associated with it – but you may also gain insights in other ways – include those as well.

Template for laying out record of employability skills developed in this Part

Skills/Task	Task 2.1	Task 2.2	Task 2.3	Task 2.4	Task 2.5	Task 2.6	Other sources of skills
Business awareness							
Thinking critically							
Solving problems							

Skills/Task	Task 2.1	Task 2.2	Task 2.3	Task 2.4	Task 2.5	Task 2.6	Other sources of skills
Team working							
Communicating							
Self-management							

To make the most of your opportunities to develop employability skills as you do your academic work, you need to reflect regularly on your learning and record the results. This helps you to fill any gaps, and provides specific evidence of your employability skills.

PART 3
PLANNING

Introduction

This Part examines the generic management activities of planning and decision making, and then two substantive applications of these ideas – to strategy and marketing respectively. Both depend on understanding the environment of the business and the stakeholders within it. They also depend on building an internal capability to deliver whatever direction management decides upon.

Chapter 6 provides an overview of planning in organisations, setting out the purposes of planning, the types of plan and the generic elements in a plan. The shape of these elements will always depend on the circumstances (context) of the plan.

Decision making is closely linked to planning, made necessary by finite resources and infinite demands. People in organisations continually decide on inputs, transformation processes and outputs – and the quality of these decisions affects performance. Chapter 7 therefore introduces the main decision-making processes, and several theories of decision making.

Chapter 8 outlines the strategy process, and introduces techniques that managers use to analyse the options facing all forms of business. This analysis can then lead to clearer choices about future direction.

Central to that is the market the organisation chooses to serve, so Chapter 9 presents some marketing methods. Like strategy, marketing uses external and internal analysis to establish a way forward. And, like strategy, it depends on the support of other units to meet customer expectations profitably.

The Part Case is Virgin Group, illustrating the interaction of the external environment with the developing corporate and marketing strategies of this unique venture capital firm.

CHAPTER 6
PLANNING

Aim

To describe how plans help to solve problems, and what a plan can contain.

Objectives

By the end of your work on this chapter you should be able to outline the concepts below in your own terms and:

1　Explain five iterative tasks in planning, why people plan and the content of several types of plan

2　Outline the core activity of gathering information, and some common techniques

3　Explain the significance of setting goals, and a theory of their motivational effects

4　Describe a model to help specify what has to be done to achieve the goals

5　Show how context affects the ability of managers to implement and monitor a plan

6　Contrast rational and creative planning processes

7　Outline a rational approach to planning and understand how this may help you develop the skill of defining problems

8　Show how ideas from the chapter can add to your understanding of the integrating themes

Key terms

This chapter introduces the following ideas:

planning
goal (or objective)
business plan
strategic plan
strategic business unit
operational plans
enterprise resource planning
SWOT analysis

critical success factor
optimism bias
strategic misrepresentation
sensitivity analysis
scenario planning
stated goal
real goal
organisational readiness

Each is a term defined within the text, as well as in the glossary at the end of the book.

Crossrail is a new railway for London and the South East of England, which will connect the City, Canary Wharf, the West End and Heathrow Airport to commuter areas east and west of the capital. It aims to be a world-class railway, with frequent services across the capital. It is intended to:

- relieve congestion on many Underground and rail lines;
- provide new connections and services on modern trains;
- provide eight new stations in central London.

It will add 10 per cent to London's transport capacity and provide 40 per cent of the extra rail capacity London needs. Main construction of the railway began in 2010, with services planned to begin in 2017. Crossrail will use mainline-size trains, each carrying more than 1,500 passengers.

It is the largest construction project in Europe and the largest single addition to the London transport network for over 50 years. It will run 118km from Maidenhead and Heathrow in the west to Shenfield and Abbey Wood in the east, joining the Great Western and Great Eastern railway networks. 21 km of the route will be in new twin tunnels under Central London.

The project was first proposed in 1990, but amidst considerable opposition it was cancelled in 1996. Supporters, especially national and London business groups, continued to advocate the line as a contribution to London's transport, and eventually gained sufficient political support. Parliament passed the Crossrail Act in July 2008 giving authority to build the railway, and in December of that year the government and the Mayor of London signed funding agreements.

The Crossrail website points out that it is a multiple worksite programme with construction works running concurrently across the route. It depends on cooperation among many organisations including Crossrail Central, London Underground, Network Rail, Docklands Light Railway, Canary Wharf Group and Berkeley Homes. Major construction tasks include:

- using eight tunnelling drives to bore the tunnels under central London;
- shipping seven million tonnes of excavated material to Wallasea Island in Essex, to form a nature reserve;
- building eight new Underground stations to connect with the Underground and rail network; and

© Chris Ratcliffe/Bloomberg /Getty Images

- building four overground lines from the central section, including one to Heathrow Airport.

The tunnel section needs to cross above the Jubilee Line and below the Central and Circle Lines, weaving around buried utilities and deep building foundations. The Chairman of Crossrail:

> It's a huge engineering challenge to protect the assets around us. St Paul's Cathedral, for instance, has no foundations. But the Gherkin has very deep foundations, to precisely the depth at which we want to tunnel (*Financial Times*, 25 June 2013, p. 3).

The Learning & Skills Council agreed to provide £5 million towards the cost of a Tunnelling and Underground Construction Academy, which opened in October 2011, increasing the supply of the skilled workers the project requires. In 2015 the tunnelling was complete, and work was continuing on building the new stations, laying track and signalling, and the trains.

Source: Company website; *Financial Times*, 25 June 2013, p. 3.

Case questions 6.1
Visit the Crossrail website (see above).

- What are the main items of recent news about the progress of the project?
- What kind of environment do you think the company is operating in (Chapter 3, Section 3.6)?
- What are the main planning challenges that Crossrail managers face?

6.1   Introduction

Crossrail is an example of a major project that managers can only achieve by dealing with an infinite number of problems – before, during and after the visible construction. Those charged with delivering the project decide on the plans that will best overcome these problems. From the early political processes to secure support from many interested parties (Glaister and Travers, 2001) – some in favour of the project, some against – then raising capital and securing public consent, managers have continually been developing plans to guide the project towards completion in several years' time. That continues during construction, with work guided by the very detailed plans required to drive a railway beneath the centre of a capital city. The complex organisation of clients, main contractors and subcontractors also needs to be planned, so that Crossrail can be sure that the hundreds of firms working on the project have the right staff in place to do the work. The case will illustrate how Crossrail's managers solve these problems – some of which only appear as the work proceeds.

This chapter on planning is very closely linked to the next, on decision making. A plan is usually (not always) a distinct written entity that sets out how an organisation plans to deal with a problem. This plan is the outcome of decisions that people have made about how best to manage that problem (or opportunity) – a plan cannot exist unless people have made decisions to commit resources to support the elements, or actions, within it.

Figure 6.1 shows five generic elements in planning how to solve a problem: gathering information; setting goals; specifying what has to be done to achieve the goals; implementing what has to be done; and monitoring progress. To make such a plan, those working on it need to make decisions about each element – deciding what information to use and how to interpret it, what goals to set, what has to be done to achieve them and so on. The content of the plan is shaped as people decide these elements: they do so iteratively, reconsidering an earlier stage when new information suggests that, say, they should change the goals, or some aspect of how to achieve them.

A 'problem' in management arises when something out of the routine occurs or when something out of the routine is needed. It is a skill we need in almost every aspect of

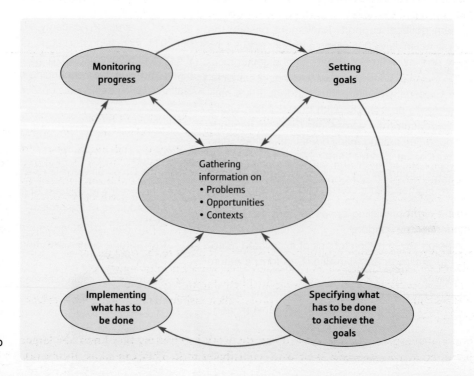

Figure 6.1 Five generic elements in planning how to solve a problem

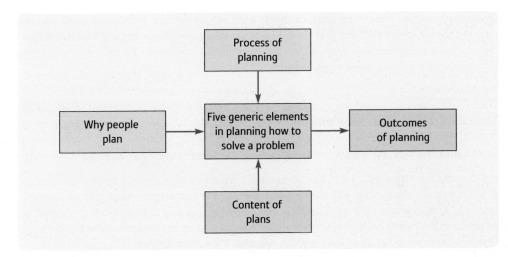

Figure 6.2
An overview of planning

life – every day we meet problems – often minor, sometimes major – which we try to solve. Managing is inherently about solving problems – which we try to do by making a plan.

Becoming aware of a problem creates uncertainty, and making a plan motivates us to try to solve the problem by gathering information to clarify goals, specify how to achieve them, implement that and monitor progress. Plans include both ends (why?) and means (how?).

Informal, unwritten plans work perfectly well in many situations – but as more people become involved they need some guidance. When two entrepreneurs decided to create the City Inn hotel chain they planned in detail the kind of hotels they would be – contemporary, city-centre, newly built, 'active and open' atmosphere, and a consistent room design across the group. They communicated their plan to those working on the project to ensure they acted consistently.

Figure 6.2 provides an overview. At the centre are the five generic elements in planning how to solve a problem. The chapter outlines why people plan, the issues (content) for which they plan and how they plan (process). One significant distinction is the degree to which the processes combine rational and creative methods, depending on the context. This chapter explains both, and provides an opportunity to begin developing the skill of a rational approach; Chapter 7 does the same for a creative approach.

6.2   Why people plan

A planner is an individual contemplating future actions: the activity of **planning** involves thinking and acting to gather relevant information about the task and its context. It requires deciding which **goals (or objectives)** to set, which have priority, and showing how to achieve them, including how to cope with distractions when time is limited. It involves implementing the plan and monitoring progress. Goals are the desired future state of an activity or unit: achieving the end requires deciding the means – what needs to be done, by when and by whom?

A plan, if done well:

- clarifies direction, so that people give attention and effort to the right tasks;
- motivates people, by letting them see where their work fits into the whole;
- uses resources efficiently by estimating the likely duration of tasks; and
- increases control, by enabling people to protect their task from interference and to measure progress against targets.

Good plans give direction to those doing the work by ensuring they know the larger purpose of an activity and how their work contributes to it. They can adjust their work

Planning is the iterative task of setting goals, specifying how to achieve them, implementing the plan and evaluating the results.

A **goal (or objective)** is a desired future state for an activity or organisational unit.

intelligently (sometimes suggesting changes) with others so that everyone knows who is responsible for each task, and that they do not overlook any. Knowing the end result (the big picture) means they can respond to changes without waiting to be told, see their contribution and may take more responsibility.

Management in practice   **Maersk – planning key to strategy**   www.maersk.com

The shipping company Maersk depends on planning. Mark Cornwall, Operations Manager, explains:

Maersk operates 470 container ships with 1.9 million individual containers that are all travelling around the world, and our job is to build efficiencies into the system – moving the cargo to the customer on time.

Part of our strategy is to deliver unmatched reliability, and operations is key to that. From the top of the company right down to the clerks on the desk, everybody's focussed on meeting deadlines and the requirements of the customer every step of the way. So whether it's a ship arriving in a port on time, or a container loading on a ship on time, or a truck delivery to a warehouse, everybody's focussed all the way through the chain on making sure that everything happens against the deadline as planned.

Efficiency's all about making the best use of your assets, so whether it's putting as many containers as possible on a ship, or maximising your utilisation of a particular train, or getting as many miles out of a truck as you can during a shift, it's all about planning your assets to get the biggest use out of them during that period.

Source: Interview with Mark Cornwall.

Setting intermediate goals towards the final destination lets people follow progress, so that they can change the goal, seek help, or change the way they are working. This is the monitoring component of plans – helping to complete the task efficiently and to learn from the experience.

The content of a plan is the subject – what aspect of business it deals with: strategic, business unit, operational, tactical or special purpose. The next section deals with those topics, and that which follows focuses on how – the problem-solving process that leads to the plan.

6.3   The content of plans

A **business plan** is a document describing the markets or users a business intends to serve, how it will do so and what finance is required.

People starting a new business or expanding an existing one prepare a **business plan** – a document that sets out the markets the business intends to serve, how it will do so and what finance is required (Sahlman, 1997; Blackwell, 2008). It probably does so in considerable detail as it needs to convince potential investors to lend money. Managers seeking capital investment or other corporate resources need to convince senior managers to allocate them – so they, too, make a convincing plan. Public sector managers do the same – a director of roads (for example) needs to present a plan to convince the chief executive or elected members that investing in roads will be a good use of resources – knowing that (say) the director of social services will be presenting a competing plan. Service managers inevitably compete with each other for limited resources, and develop business plans to support their case.

A **strategic plan** sets out the overall direction for the business, is broad in scope and covers all the major activities.

Strategic plans apply to the whole organisation. They set out the overall direction and cover major activities – markets and revenues, together with plans for marketing, human resources and production. Strategy is concerned with deciding what business an organisation should be in and how it is going to get there. These decisions involve major resource commitments and usually require convincing plans showing how the decision will be put into effect. In a large business there will be divisional plans for each major unit. If subsidiaries operate as autonomous **strategic business units** (SBUs), they develop plans with limited inputs from the rest of the company.

A **strategic business unit** consists of a number of closely related products for which it is meaningful to formulate a separate strategy.

Shell plans to remove Brent structures
www.shell.com

In 2015 Shell began to consult on its plan to decommission the UK's biggest oilfield – Brent, in the North Sea. The initial work is a disposal plan for the 'topside' of one of the four platforms on the Brent field. Engineers will cut through the concrete legs supporting the 23,500 tonne steel superstructure – incorporating the drilling rig and the accommodation block – and lift it onto a ship – the Pieter Schelte.

This will take the structure to Teesside to be broken up and recycled. Shell planned to do this part of the job during 2016, though they had not yet decided how to remove the huge concrete legs and the oil storage tanks on the sea bed, that were never designed to be taken away.

Shell believes that the method chosen will substantially reduce the risk, cost and environmental impact of the operation, and is preferable to taking the structure apart piece by piece in the North Sea.

However, David Santillo of Greenpeace warns that the second stage of the process, involving the platform's concrete legs and underwater storage tanks, is key: Shell should take full responsibility for the waste they have generated and not leave anything on the seabed that it is possible for them to recover.

Strategic plans usually set a direction for several years, though in businesses with long lead times (energy production or aircraft manufacture) they look perhaps 15 years ahead. Ryanair plans to increase its share of the European short-haul passenger market from 12 per cent in 2012–13 to 18 per cent by 2022. That implies increasing the fleet from 300 aircraft to 450: replacing older aircraft means it will probably buy about 300 new ones. It will have plans showing the implications – for finance, maintenance, recruitment, scheduling and so on. Such plans are not fixed: managers update them to reflect new conditions, so they are sometimes called 'rolling plans'.

Operational plans detail how managers will achieve their strategy, by showing what each department or function will do. They create a hierarchy of related plans – a strategic plan for the organisation and main divisions, and operational plans for departments or teams – the 'Management in practice' feature about Shell's Brent platforms is an example. In 2014 Vodafone announced a plan to open 150 new stores in the UK as part of a £1 billion investment to improve retail services, itself part of a broader plan for the UK division. Within the stores plan will be others to deliver lower-level goals, becoming progressively more specific down to the work needed in each store. Table 6.1 shows this hierarchical arrangement, and how the character of plans changes at each level.

Operational plans detail how the overall objectives are to be achieved, by specifying what senior management expects from specific departments or functions.

Crossrail – the case continues   www.crossrail.co.uk

The company has published its outline plans for stations and tunnels – the schedule below lists a small selection. At some locations enabling works (diverting utilities such as gas mains and demolishing buildings) need to be scheduled before main works. Plans also need to cover fitting out the structures ready for use.

Stations

The table gives examples of the planned start of station enabling works, and of the start and completion dates of the stations themselves (correct at 2016).

Location	Enabling works started	Construction started	Works complete
Canary Wharf	December 2008	May 2009	Third quarter 2017
Tottenham Court Road	January 2009	January 2010	Fourth quarter 2016
Farringdon	July 2009	July 2011	Third quarter 2017
Custom House	January 2013	January 2013	Fourth quarter 2015

Tunnel portals and shafts

With tunnelling complete, shafts need to be constructed linking the platforms with the surface. Fit out will take place beyond these dates. Only the last three shafts to be constructed are shown here.

Location	Enabling works started	Construction started	Works complete
Mile End shaft	October 2012	October 2012	2016
Eleanor Street shaft	April 2012	September 2012	2018
Limmo Peninsula	May 2010	December 2010	2016

'On network' works

Network Rail is doing the work required on existing stations and tracks that Crossrail will use.

Other works

Press releases about contracts awarded give further insight into the scale and diversity of the plans. They included contracts for:

- design and construction of 13 stations on the western section of the line;
- signalling enabling works;
- ensuring the tunnel meets EU legislation on inter-operability, as several train companies will use the line;
- shipping material excavated from the tunnels to Wallasea Island in Essex, to create a nature reserve.

Trains

In early 2013 the company began the process to select the company to run the trains. In September 2015 the first test train carriage left the assembly line at Bombardier's plant in Derby.

Source: Company website; *Financial Times,* 29 April 2013, p. 25.

Case questions 6.2

- Visit the company website and look for information about progress on these (or other) plans.
- Can you identify any plans on the website that are clearly at strategic, operational or activity levels?
- While on the website, identify and list three other pieces of work for which plans will have been made – especially any involving other organisations.

Table 6.1 A planning hierarchy

Type of plan	Strategic	Operational	Activity
Level	Organisation or business unit	Division, department, function or market	Work unit or team
Focus	Direction and strategy for whole organisation	Functional changes or market activities to support strategic plans	Actions needed to deliver current products or services

Nature	Broad, general direction	Detail on required changes	Specific detail on immediate goals and tasks
Timescale	Long term (2–3 years?)	Medium (up to 18 months?)	Very short term (hours to weeks?)

Most organisations prepare annual plans that focus on finance and set budgets for the coming year – these necessarily include sales, marketing, production or technology plans as well. Activity plans are short-term plans that deal with immediate production or service delivery – a sheet scheduling which orders to deliver next week, or who is on duty tomorrow. Standing plans specify how to deal with routine, recurring issues such as recruitment or customer complaints. Some use a method called **enterprise resource planning** to integrate the day-to-day work of complex production systems – Chapter 12 describes this technique in Section 12.5.

Figure 6.3 contrasts specific and directional plans. Specific plans have clear, quantified objectives with little discretion in how to achieve them. When Tesco opens a new store, staff follow defined procedures detailing the tasks required to ensure it opens on time and within budget. Where there is uncertainty about what needs to be done, managers may use a directional plan, setting the objective but leaving staff to decide how to get there. Ed Smith, the former England cricketer, recalls that his experience as a cricket captain taught him that too much planning could be harmful and it was better to trust his players to react to what they found on the field:

> The same is true in business: If you are committed to over-prescriptive, over-predictive . . . courses of action then you are unable to react to [chance events]. (*Financial Times,* 9 October 2012, p. 14)

Enterprise resource planning (ERP) is a computer-based planning system that links separate databases to plan the use of all resources within the enterprise.

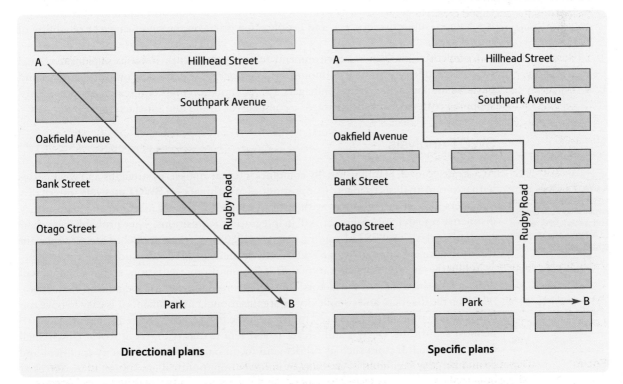

Figure 6.3 Specific and directional plans

Wise managers plan to deal with unexpected disasters such as product failures, accidents and explosions. Online communication implies that organisations need plans to counter cyber crime, and for what to do if hackers enter their systems. This requires not only having a recovery plan but training people every few months in how to use it, and ensuring it is instantly available online.

Activity 6.1   Make a learning plan

- Identify a short task that you will need to complete in your studies – an essay, assignment or presentation. Write a plan showing how you will do this.
- Identify and list the smaller tasks.
- Decide the likely order in which you will do them (you will usually work on them iteratively) and when you plan to finish each.
- Estimate how long you can spend on each, bearing in mind when you have to complete your chosen task.
- Show the plan visually, listing tasks down the left side of a grid and time along the top (see Figure 6.7 for an example).
- Use the plan to guide your work, noting deviations as you go. When you have finished the work, reflect on the experience, what you have learned about planning and monitoring progress, and how you may use that.

6.4   Gathering information

Any plan depends on information – including informal, soft information gained from casual encounters with colleagues, as well as formal analyses of economic and market trends. This is a human, subjective process, and people often differ on the significance or reliability of information.

Competitive and general environments feature prominently in business plans. External sources include government economic and demographic statistics, industry surveys and business intelligence services. Managers also commission market research on individuals' shopping patterns, attitudes towards a company or brand and satisfaction with services.

SWOT analysis

A **SWOT analysis** is a way of summarising the organisation's strengths and weaknesses relative to external opportunities and threats.

At a strategic level, planning usually combines internal analysis of strengths and weaknesses with external analysis to identify opportunities and threats – a **SWOT analysis**. Internally, managers look at the resources within, or available to, the organisation – skilled staff, a distinctive research capability, or skill in integrating acquisitions. They probably base their external analysis on PESTEL and/or Porter's (1980) five forces model to identify relevant trends. Figure 6.4 summarises a SWOT analysis made in 2015 for a successful café chain.

While the method appears rational, it is a human representation, so participants will differ about the weight of the factors: that debate may add value (Hodgkinson et al. 2006).

Given the diversity and complexity of organisational environments it is easy to have too much information. Managers need to focus on the few trends and events that are likely to be most significant. De Wit and Meyer (2004) report that planners at Royal Dutch Shell focus on critical factors such as oil demand (economic), refining capacity (political and economic), the likelihood of government intervention (political) and alternative sources of fuel (technological).

Strengths

❍ A popular brand at a time when casual dining spend continues to rise
❍ Caters for a range of food experiences, from breakfast to lunch and even dinner
❍ Strong brand identity that chairman Mr Johnson says can have customers queuing round the block

Threats

❍ Strong competition from scores of other food and coffee chains including Pret, Greggs and Browns
❍ A potential EU exit could hit business in terms of labour and import costs
❍ Sluggish UK growth continues to weigh on consumer spend

Paul May
Chief executive

Weaknesses

❍ Operates in a typically low-margin business, with costly overheads and high stock costs
❍ Rising rent costs have already forced the business to scale back growth in London
❍ Has previously lacked a significant digital presence

Opportunities

❍ Limited stores in parts of the UK including Wales and Scotland, giving the chain plenty of room to grow
❍ The company aims to open 20 new stores a year
❍ Typically a high street business, the company is increasing web sales and could branch out overseas

Figure 6.4 A SWOT analysis for a café chain

Source: *Daily Telegraph*, 21 May 2015

Activity 6.2   **Conducting a SWOT analysis**

Choose one of the companies featured in the text (or any that interests you).

- Gather information from their website and other public data to prepare a SWOT analysis.
- Compare your analysis with that of a colleague on your course.
- Identify any differences between you in terms of the factors identified, and the significance given to them. What do those differences tell you about the value of the SWOT method?

Critical success factors analysis

In considering whether to enter a new market, a widely used planning technique is to assess the **critical success factors** (Leidecker and Bruno, 1984) in that market. These are the things that customers in that market most value about a product or service – useful information for someone planning to enter it. Some value price, others quality, others some of the product's features – but in all cases they are things that a company must do well to succeed.

Critical success factors are those aspects of a strategy that must be achieved to secure competitive advantage.

Forecasting

Optimism bias refers to a human tendency to judge future events in a more positive light than is warranted by experience.

Forecasts or predictions usually analyse trends in relevant factors, and assumptions about things that may change, to try to foresee the future. In stable environments people can reasonably assume that past trends will continue, but in uncertain ones they have to consider radical alternatives. Newspaper publishers face a difficult problem planning how much (if any) print capacity to retain as more readers obtain news online.

Forecasting is big business, with companies selling analyses to business and government, using techniques such as time-series analysis, econometric modelling and simulation. Some believe that uncertain conditions reduce the value of detailed forecasts, and forecasts in public projects are notoriously unreliable – see 'Key ideas'.

Strategic misrepresentation is where competition for resources leads planners to underestimate costs and overestimate benefits, to increase the likelihood that their project gains approval.

Key ideas	The planning fallacy in large projects

Large infrastructure projects regularly cost more and deliver less than their promoters promised: Flyvbjerg (2008) shows that the average cost inaccuracy for rail projects is 44 per cent, for bridges and tunnels 34 per cent and roads 20 per cent. He then draws on work by Lovallo and Kahneman (2003), which identified a systematic fallacy in planning, whereby people underestimate the costs, completion times and risks of planned actions, whereas they overestimate their benefits. This 'planning fallacy' has two sources:

- **optimism bias** – a human tendency to judge future events more positively than experience warrants; and
- **strategic misrepresentation** – where planners underestimate costs and overestimate benefits to make their proposal more attractive than competing ones.

These biases lead planners to take an 'inside view', focusing on the constituents of their plan, rather than an 'outside view' – guided by information about the outcomes of similar, completed plans.

Source: Flyvbjerg (2008).

Sensitivity analysis

A **sensitivity analysis** tests the effect on a plan of several alternative values of the key variables.

One way to test assumptions is to make a **sensitivity analysis** of key variables in a plan. If this assumes a new product will gain (say) a 10 per cent market share within a year, a sensitivity analysis calculates what the effect on returns would be if they secure 5 per cent, or 15 per cent. What if interest rates rise, increasing the cost of financing the project? Planners can then compare the options and assess the risks. Johnson et al. (2014) give a worked example (pp. 380–1).

Scenario planning

An alternative to forecasting is to consider possible scenarios. Cornelius et al. (2005) note:

Scenario planning is an attempt to create coherent and credible alternative stories about the future.

> scenarios are not projections, predictions or preferences; rather they are coherent and credible stories about the future.

Scenario planning typically begins by considering how external forces such as the internet, an ageing population, or climate change might affect a company's business over the next five to ten years. The exposure management team at Lloyds of London spends their time thinking about worst-case scenarios – such as an oil tanker sinking in the Arctic, calculating the likelihood of it happening, and estimating the costs to the insurance industry. Advocates claim that it discourages managers from relying on a single view of the future, and encourages them to develop plans to cope with several possible outcomes. The chief executive of BASF (a German chemical maker):

> We don't think you can get to grips with uncertainty through long-term planning; rather you have to have scenarios. If something happens with Greece, for example, we have a plan A, plan B and plan C. (*Financial Times,* 15 January 2013, p. 12)

Few companies use the technique regularly as it is time consuming and costly, but Shell is an exception (report in *Financial Times,* 30 November 2010):

> Scenario thinking . . . underpins the established way of thinking at Shell. It has become a part of the culture, such that people throughout the company, dealing with significant decisions, normally will think in terms of multiple, but equally plausible futures to provide a context for decision making (Van der Heijden, 1996, p. 21).

A combination of PESTEL and five forces analysis should ensure that managers recognise major external factors. Forecasting and scenario planning can help them to consider possible implications for the business – and help them set plausible goals.

6.5   Setting goals (or objectives) – the ends

A clear plan depends on being clear about the intended goal (or objective) – whether for an organisation or a unit. This seems obvious, but managers favour action above planning (Stewart, 1967) – especially the ambiguities of agreeing on goals. Yet until people clarify these they make little progress.

Goals (or objectives)

Goals give a task focus – what will we achieve, by when? Setting goals is difficult as people need to look beyond a relatively known present to an unknown future. Bond et al. (2008) asked people to set objectives for a personally-relevant task (finding a good job) – and they consistently omitted nearly half of the objectives they later identified as important when these were drawn to their attention. The researchers secured the same results in a software company.

Goals, with a set timetable in which to meet them, provide the reference point for other decisions, and the criteria against which to measure performance. At the business level they usually include quantified financial objectives – earnings per share, return on shareholders' funds and cash flow. Others use non-economic measures, such as employee satisfaction, involvement with a community, or environmental performance – see 'Management in practice' for an example.

Management in practice   Environmental target at Heathrow Terminal 5

Building Terminal 5 was an opportunity to embed environmentally sustainable practices into every aspect of the terminal's operation. An environmental assessment group identified several sustainability focus areas, which evolved into the project requirements and then into environmental targets such as:

Aspect	Key performance indicator	Target
Water	Potable water use	70% cut
	Water consumption	25 litres/passenger

Aspect	Key performance indicator	Target
Pollution control	Total harmful emissions to water	Capture 25% of surface water runoff for re-use
Waste	Waste recycled/composted	40% by 2010, 80% by 2020
Resource use	Compliance with T5 materials	40% of coarse aggregate in concrete to be recycled

Source: Lister (2010).

Activity 6.3   Developing goals

- Go to the websites of companies that interest you and collect examples of planning goals.
- Gather examples of planning goals from organisations you know or can find out about, at organisational, operational or activity levels. If you can, ask about the process of setting them, and what, if any, are the effects.

A hierarchy of goals

A way of relating goals to each other is to build them into a hierarchy, in which organisational goals are transformed into specific goals for functions such as marketing or human resources. Managers in those areas develop plans defining what they must do to meet the overall goal. Figure 6.5 illustrates this using Ikea's plan to expand in Japan – itself part of a wider plan to sell more in Asia. That evolved into a plan for their probable location, and then into a precise plan for two stores near Tokyo. Managers then developed progressively more detailed plans for the thousands of tasks that needed to be complete to support the high-level goal.

Plans like this need to be flexible to cope with changes in conditions between design and completion. Managers may be committed to achieving high-level goals – but leave staff to decide on intermediate goals that they will meet.

Effective goal setting (producing goals that guide action) involves balancing multiple goals, ensuring they are SMART and evaluating how they affect motivation.

Single or multiple goals?

Statements of goals – whether long term or short – are usually expressed in the plural, since a single measure cannot indicate success or failure. Emphasis on one goal, such as growth, ignores another, such as dividends. Managers balance multiple, possibly conflicting goals: Gerry Murphy, who became chief executive of Kingfisher (a UK DIY retailer), recalled:

> Alan Sheppard, my boss at Grand Metropolitan and one of my mentors, used to say that senior management shouldn't have the luxury of single point objectives. Delivering growth without returns or returns without growth is not something I find attractive or acceptable. Over time we are going to do both. (*Financial Times*, 28 April 2004, p. 23)

Stated goals are those that are prominent in company publications and websites.

Real goals are those to which people give most attention.

As senior managers try to take account of a range of stakeholders they balance diverse interests. This can lead to conflict between **stated goals**, as reflected in public announcements, and the **real goals** – those to which people give most attention. The latter reflect senior managers' priorities, expressed through what they say and how they reward and discipline managers.

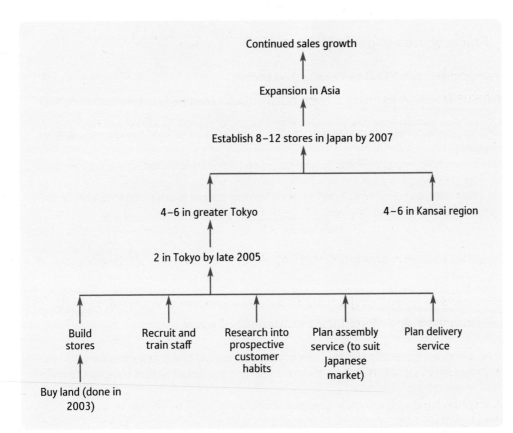

Figure 6.5
Developing a plan
for Ikea (Japan)

Criteria for assessing goals

The SMART acronym summarises some criteria for assessing a set of goals. What form of each is effective depends on circumstances.

- **Specific** Does the goal set specific targets? People who are planning a meeting can set specific goals for what they hope to achieve, such as:

  By the end of the meeting we will have convinced them to withdraw their current proposal, and to have set a date (within the next two weeks) at which we will start to develop an alternative plan.

  A clear statement of what a meeting (or any other activity) should achieve helps to focus effort.

- **Measurable** Some goals may be quantified ('increase sales of product X by 5 per cent a year over the next three years') but others, equally important, are more qualitative ('to offer a congenial working environment'). Quantitative goals are not inherently more useful than qualitative ones – what can be measured is not necessarily most important. What matters is that people define goals precisely enough to measure progress.

- **Attainable** Goals should be challenging, but not unreasonably difficult, or so easy as to seem trivial. Goal-setting theory (see 'Key ideas') predicts the motivational effects of targets.

- **Rewarded** If people know that if they attain a goal they will receive a reward they will be more committed.

- **Timed** Does the goal specify the time over which it will be achieved, and is that also a reasonable and acceptable standard?

Key ideas   **Practical uses of goal-setting theory**

Goal-setting theory has practical implications for those making plans:

- **Goal difficulty:** set goals for work performance at levels that will stretch employees but are just within their ability.
- **Goal specificity:** express goals in clear, precise and if possible quantifiable terms, and avoid setting ambiguous or confusing goals.
- **Participation:** where practicable, encourage staff to take part in setting goals to increase their commitment to achieving them.
- **Feedback:** provide information on the results of performance to allow people to adjust their behaviour and perhaps improve their achievement of future plans.

Source: Locke and Latham (2002).

Activity 6.4   **Evaluate a statement of goals**

- Choose a significant plan that someone has produced in your organisation within the last year. Is it SMART? Then try to set out how you would amend the goals to meet these criteria more fully.

6.6   **Specifying what has to be done to achieve the goals – the means**

This part of a plan sets out what needs to be done, who will do it, by when – and communicating that to all concerned. In a small activity, such as planning a project in a club, this would mean listing the tasks and dividing them clearly among able and willing members. At the other extreme, Crossrail's plans will have run to many thousands of pages.

Identifying what has to be done, by whom

Figure 1.2 (reworked as Figure 6.6) helps to specify systematically what has to be done to achieve a goal. It reflects the organisational context – the range of easily-overlooked factors that may need including in a list of things to be done.

If the goal is to launch a new product, the plan could identify which parts of the organisation will be affected (structure), what investment is needed (finance), how production will fit with existing lines (business processes), and so on. New technology projects often fail because planners pay too much attention to technology and too little to context – structure, culture and people (Boddy et al. 2009a). Each main heading will include further actions that people can identify and assign.

Communicating the plan

In a small organisation, or where the plan deals with only one area, formal communication is probably unnecessary, as those who have been involved in developing the plans will probably be implementing it. In larger enterprises managers will probably invest time to

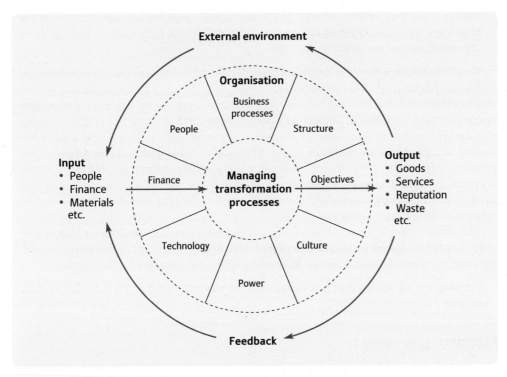

Figure 6.6
Possible action areas in a plan

communicate the goals and the actions required throughout the areas affected. They do this to:

- ensure that everyone understands the plan;
- allow them to resolve any confusion and ambiguity;
- communicate the judgements and assumptions that underlie the plan;
- ensure that activities around the organisation are coordinated in practice as well as on paper.

6.7   Implementing what has to be done, and monitoring progress

Implementing the plan

However good the plan, nothing worthwhile happens until people implement it, by making visible, physical changes to the organisation and the way people work. This is often challenging when the plan comes into contact with the processes and people affected. Those promoting the plan may encounter objections – and perhaps find that some of their assumptions are incorrect.

Organisations are slower to change than plans are to prepare – so events may overtake the plan. Miller et al. (2004) tracked the long-term outcomes of 150 strategic plans to establish how managers put them into action and how that affected performance. They defined implementation as:

> all the processes and outcomes which accrue to a strategic decision once authorisation has been given to . . . put the decision into practice. (Miller et al. 2004, p. 203)

They concluded that success was heavily influenced by:

- managers' experience of the issue, and
- **organisational readiness** for a change.

Organisational readiness refers to the extent to which staff are able to specify objectives, tasks and resource requirements of a plan appropriately, leading to acceptance.

> Having relevant experience of what has to be done . . . enables managers to assess the objectives [and to] specify the tasks and resource implications appropriately, leading [those affected to accept the process]. (p. 206)

Readiness means a receptive organisational climate that enables managers to implement the change within a positive environment.

They illustrated the statistical results with cases showing, for example, how managers in one company were able to implement a plan to upgrade their computer systems because they had experience of many similar changes. They were 'able to set targets, detail what needed doing and allocate the resources . . . That is, they could plan and control the implementation effectively'. In another illustration, a regional brewer extending into the London area had no directly relevant experience, and so was not able to set a specific plan. But people in the organisation were very receptive to new challenges, and could implement the move with little formal planning.

The authors concluded that the activities of planning do not in themselves lead to success, but are a means for gaining acceptance of what has to be done when it is implemented. Planning gives people confidence in the process, leading to high levels of acceptability:

> Planning is a necessary part of this approach to success, but it is not sufficient in itself. (p. 210)

Monitoring progress

The final stage in planning is to set up a system that allows people to monitor progress towards the goals. This happens at all levels – from a Crossrail project manager monitoring whether a supplier delivered material today, to the board at The Co-op Bank monitoring progress on its recovery plan. In complex projects such as that, monitoring focuses mainly on the interdependencies between the many smaller plans that make up the whole.

Project plans define and display every task and activity, but someone managing a programme of linked projects would soon become swamped with such detail. The programme manager needs to maintain a quick-to-understand snapshot of the programme. This should show progress to date, the main events being planned, interdependencies, issues and expected completion dates. This also helps the programme manager to communicate with senior executives and project managers. One way to do this is to create a single chart (sometimes called a Gantt chart) with a simplified view of each project on a timeline. Figure 6.7 illustrates this. Details vary but the main features are usually:

- a timeline, showing its passage;
- a list of the tasks or sub-projects, with symbols showing planned and actual completions or major milestones in each project;
- indications of interdependencies between projects.

Case study Crossrail – the case continues   www.crossrail.co.uk

An article in *Civil Engineering* explained how a construction company and its client used unusual planning practices to increase the speed and reduce the cost of building Canary Wharf Station.

Crossrail had developed outline designs for every station, but this one was on land owned by Canary Wharf Group (CWG) – a property company that had developed on 30 nearby sites. CWG offered to

contribute £150 million towards the cost if they were given full responsibility for design and construction. Crossrail agreed and those managing the project claimed that:

- involving the designers (Arup) of the station and the client (CWG) in early discussions enabled significant improvements to the original plan – reducing the size of the station without any loss of function, and adding a retail outlet;

- using CWG's local experience enabled radical innovations – such as changing the original Crossrail plan to fill in a dock before building the station. CWG believed this solution was costly and environmentally damaging so, using their knowledge of groundwater conditions, solved the problem in a way that avoided filling the dock and so cost less;
- commissioning a trial of a new piling machine, which provided valuable data about the time required for that work. The trial cost £250,000 but saved many times that during construction;
- good communications between client and designers enabled them to adapt the design as work progressed, using the experience gained during implementation.

Crossrail claimed these arrangements reduced the cost of the station to 58 per cent of the original budget, and reduced construction time by one year.

Source: Yeow et al. (2012).

Case questions 6.3

- This part of the case gives examples of which approach to planning (refer to Section 6.4)?
- What examples do you see here of managers acting to reduce 'optimism bias' (refer to Section 6.4)?
- Consider the risks and benefits of radical innovation in one part of an unprecedented project such as this.

6.8   Rational and creative planning processes

Any plan, formal or informal, strategic or operational, at any level of an organisation is the outcome of a process, during which people made decisions about its content and nature. These processes take many forms depending on history and circumstances, and it is convenient here to distinguish between 'rational' and 'creative' approaches. The labels are broad, and similar terms that others use for each are:

- **rational** – economic, formal, quantitative, analytic, objective;
- **creative** – intuitive, informal, qualitative, subjective.

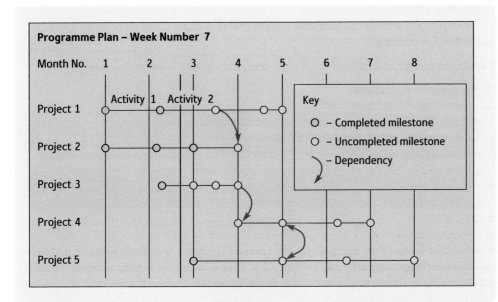

Figure 6.7
A programme overview chart
Source: Boddy et al. (2009a).

Though the methods and underlying values of the approaches are quite different, most of our plans are the result of using both approaches in some combination. Both are better suited to some situations than others, so effective managers learn to use either as appropriate.

Rational approaches

A **problem** is a deviation from an expected standard of performance.

People make decisions to commit time and resources when they recognise (become aware of) a problem or opportunity. A major risk is to move too quickly from awareness to action – the urge to 'do something'. This wastes resources unless people take time to make some deeper analysis. The first step in a rational decision process is to define clearly what the problem is, a **problem** being defined as a deviation from an expected standard of performance. Competent managers constantly monitor what is happening within their area of responsibility, comparing 'what is' with 'what we expected'. If the deviation is minor the manager may safely ignore it. If the deviation is significant the manager needs to define the problem as precisely as possible, using terms such as the scale, time, or location. They also try to identify what else changed (internally or externally), before the deviation, as this may help to identify the likely cause(s).

This approach is appropriate where wider goals are clear and uncontroversial, where the processes are well-established (so cause and effect relations are clear) and where the environment is relatively stable (competitors are well-known and unlikely to disrupt plans). In such conditions it is a valuable tool – see 'Key ideas'. The 'Develop a skill' feature at the end of the chapter gives you an opportunity to develop the skill of defining a problem rationally.

| **Key ideas** | **Defining a problem rationally** |

Whetten and Cameron (2011) offer guidance on the skill of defining a problem, which they regard as fundamental to a rational approach. It:

> involves diagnosing a situation so that the focus is on the real problem, not just its symptoms. For example, suppose you must deal with an employee who consistently fails to get work done on time. Slow work might be the problem, or it might be only a symptom of another underlying problem such as bad health, low morale, lack of training, or inadequate rewards. Defining the problem, therefore, requires a wide search for information. The more relevant information that is acquired, the more likely it is that the problem will be defined accurately.

They go on to list attributes of a good approach to problem definition, of which five are:

1 differentiate fact from opinion or speculation;
2 ask widely for ideas – encourage broad participation;
3 state the problem explicitly and clearly, to avoid ambiguity and misunderstanding;
4 identify what standard or expectation has been violated; and
5 ensure the definition is not a disguised solution – it should describe the problem, not suggest an answer.

Source: Whetten and Cameron (2011), pp. 196–8.

Where these conditions are not met, the rational approach is unlikely to work. There are potential challenges at each task in Figure 6.6. People may find it hard to agree on defining the problem, on the goals for improvement, or on what to do. If a rational approach is unlikely to produce an acceptable plan, managers can try a more creative approach.

Creative approaches

Whetten and Cameron (2011) identify several common blocks to creativity, including a tendency to ignore alternative ways of defining the problem, defining the problem too narrowly and not being sufficiently curious about its underlying causes.

They point out that while creative problem solving involves four steps, the first (preparation) embodies the greatest contrast with rational approaches: creative problem solvers are more flexible and fluid in how they gather information, define the problem and generate alternatives. They are typically less constrained in how they approach the tasks in Figure 6.6. The authors offer suggestions on how to develop these skills – see an example in 'Key ideas'.

Key ideas   **Defining a problem creatively**

Whetten and Cameron (2011) state that a creative way to define a problem is:

to use a question checklist. This is a series of questions designed to help you think of alternatives to an initial definition. Several creative managers have shared with us some of their most fruitful questions:

- Is there anything else that might be affecting the situation?
- Is this a symptom of a more general problem?
- Who sees it differently, and why might that be?

These questions offer an insight into the techniques of creative methods of problem solving, and feature in 'Develop a skill' in Chapter 7.

Source: Whetten and Cameron (2011).

6.9   Integrating themes

Entrepreneurship

In dynamic contexts (Chapter 3) plans to deal with problems must be provisional, with managers adapting them as circumstances change or new information appears. Brinckmann et al. (2010) note that entrepreneurs necessarily work in highly uncertain (dynamic) settings, with little information about how to solve the novel problems that arise in a new business. They probably make do with only the most basic plan, using their limited resources to create enough value for the business to survive. This experience should enable them to gather the information and knowledge they need to build a plausible business plan to raise money to expand.

Sustainability

Many companies are responding to the challenges posed by climate change, and are developing policies to reduce carbon emissions and other environmentally damaging practices. Such policy statements depend on the quality of the plans that managers develop – unless they make detailed plans, they will be no more than good intentions.

In 2007 Marks & Spencer announced 'Plan A' – and in 2010 extended this into a programme to become the world's most sustainable retailer by 2015. It achieved 94 of the 100 commitments in Plan A, and launched Plan A 2020. This has 100 revised and extended commitments, in four areas:

- **Inspiration** – 11 commitments that inspire customers to live a more sustainable lifestyle and encourage other businesses to take a lead on sustainability;

- **In touch** – 29 commitments that connect M&S employees and suppliers to local communities to improve employment opportunities and create shared value;
- **Integrity** – 24 commitments to lead the sector in sustainable consumption and production, covering product sourcing and operating to highest environmental and social standards;
- **Innovation** – 36 commitments that invest in the products, services and operations of the future.

The company produces regular reports and progress, with many examples of how the Plan A 2020 is making a difference. (www.marksandspencer.com).

Activity 6.5   Progress towards the goals of Plan A 2020

- Visit the M&S website and navigate to the Plan A 2020 pages. That explains the plan fully, and includes current information on progress.
- Identify a theme that interests you and find out what progress has been made on the plan.

Internationalisation

As managers engage in internationalisation they inevitably begin to work with colleagues from other national cultures in planning new products, joint ventures or merging information systems. The contrasts in national cultures that Hofstede and Hofstede (2005) observed (see Chapter 4) implies that some combinations of cultural types in cross-national teams may work better than others. A manager working on a project at EADS (the European consortium that included BAE Systems until 2006) studied the relations between British, French and German staff working on the A380 project. He considered how the dimensions of 'power distance' and 'uncertainty avoidance' differed among team members, and how this affected the way they worked together in planning.

French managers tended to be distant from their subordinates, while British and German employees felt they had greater freedom to talk back. Indeed, the British and German 'power distance' scores were identical. By contrast, the British had higher tolerance for uncertainty than the Germans or the French. While the French and German scores differed, they both showed less comfort with ambiguity and a greater desire for procedures. The British were good at contributing ideas to the planning process, but weaker at implementation.

Governance

Glaister and Travers (2001) describe the range of interests who invested significant capital or other resources in Crossrail, and who are closely interested in its progress. Decisions that those driving the project have to make could have serious consequences for one or more parties. They have therefore put in governance arrangements to ensure that, as far as possible, the project team acts in the interests of all the Crossrail sponsors.

The most obvious of these mechanisms is the company structure. Crossrail Limited is the company charged with delivering Crossrail. It was created in 2001 to promote and develop new lines and is a wholly owned subsidiary of Transport for London (TfL). The ten members of the Crossrail Board include representatives of the project sponsors and partners, as well as those appointed for their relevant expertise in, say, finance or law. Sponsors are the Mayor of London (through Transport for London) and the Department of Transport. Other partners are Network Rail, British Airports Authority (BAA), The City of London, Canary Wharf Group (property developers) and Berkeley Homes (residential property developers). The executive team managing the project report regularly to the Main Board.

Among the issues that they will seek regular reassurance on is the financial control of the project. Section 6.5 showed the common tendency of public infrastructure projects to cost more than expected. A function of the Main Board will be to monitor how executives manage the project to ensure it stays within budgeted costs, especially as public funds to cover any excess costs will be very hard to secure in the current financial climate.

Summary

1 **Explain five iterative tasks in planning, why people plan and the content of several types of plan**

- Planning involves the tasks of gathering information, setting goals, specifying what has to be done to achieve them, implementing the plan and monitoring progress.
- Effective plans can clarify direction, motivate people, use resources efficiently and allow people to measure progress towards objectives.
- Plans can be at strategic, tactical and operational levels, and in new businesses people prepare business plans to secure capital. Strategic business units also prepare plans relatively independently of the parent. There are also project plans and standing plans.

2 **Outline the core activity of gathering information, and some common techniques**

- Planners draw information from the general and competitive environments using tools such as Porter's five forces analysis. They can do this within the framework of a SWOT analysis, and also use forecasting, sensitivity analysis, critical success factors and scenario planning techniques.

3 **Explain the significance of setting goals, and a theory of their motivational effects**

- Goal-setting theory predicts that goals can be motivational if people perceive the targets to be difficult but achievable.
- Goals can also be evaluated in terms of whether they are specific, measurable, attainable, rewarded and timed.

4 **Evaluate whether a plan is sufficiently comprehensive about how to achieve the goals**

- Figure 6.6 provides a model for recalling the likely areas in an organisation that a plan should cover, indicating the likely ripple effects of change in one area on others.

5 **Show how aspects of context affect the ability of managers to implement a plan**

- The value of a plan depends on people implementing it, but Miller's research shows this depends on their experience, and the receptivity of the organisation to change.

6 **Contrast rational and creative planning processes**

- People can solve problems by combining, in varying degrees, rational and creative approaches, and the chapter outlined both.

7 **Outline a rational approach to planning, and understand how this may help you develop the skill of defining problems**

- The chapter outlined the features of a rational approach, and offers the opportunity to begin developing the skill of defining a problem rationally.

8 **Show how ideas from the chapter can add to your understanding of the integrating themes**

- All entrepreneurs can benefit from taking the time to write a business plan.
- Long-term sustainability depends on organisations making equally long-term plans, which many organisations now do.
- Companies operating internationally usually try to customise their products for local markets to reflect customer preferences. This affects not only the product but also

product advice, packaging and distribution methods – and is a significant planning activity in such firms.

- Complex, one-off projects, such as those in construction, require governance and control systems to help ensure that conflicting interests work together.

Test your understanding

1 What types of planning do you do in your personal life? Describe them in terms of whether they are (a) strategic or operational, (b) short or long term, (c) specific or directional.

2 What are four benefits that people in organisations may gain from planning?

3 What are the main sources of information that managers can use in planning? What models can they use to structure this information?

4 What are SMART goals?

5 In what ways can a goal be motivational? What practical things can people do in forming plans that take account of goal-setting theory?

6 What is meant by the term 'hierarchy of goals'?

7 Explain 'organisational readiness', and how people can use the idea during implementation.

8 What are the main ways of monitoring progress on a plan, and why is this so vital a task in planning?

9 Summarise an idea from the chapter that adds to your understanding of the integrating themes.

Think critically

Think about the way your company, or one with which you are familiar, makes plans. Review the material in the chapter, and perhaps visit some of the websites identified. Then record you responses to these questions:

- What **assumptions** about the nature of planning appear to guide the dominant approach? Do you share the prevailing assumption?

- What factors in the organisation's **context** appear to shape the approach to planning? Do you believe this is a correct interpretation of the environment, or is relevant information being ignored?

- Have you compared your planning processes with those in other organisations, to find out about **alternative** methods? Do you think these alternatives may be more suitable, and why?

- What **limitations** can you see in some of the ideas presented here? Can you envisage a situation in which a rational approach is inappropriate?

Develop a skill – defining a problem rationally

Being able to define a problem accurately is a valuable skill when making decisions rationally, and this exercise should help you develop that.

- **Awareness:** Assess how well you 'define the problem' when faced with a dilemma or decision. Do you, for example, prefer to act quickly to find a solution, rather than spend time going into detail? Do you accept at face value what others claim to be the problem? Or do you prefer to spend time digging a bit deeper?

- **Learning:** Read again Section 6.8, especially 'Key ideas' (p. 200). Summarise the main ideas of the **rational** approach. Why is this likely to help a manager?

- **Analysis:** Identify someone (whom you know, or can read about) who appears to use a rational approach well. Consider what they do, what the effects are and what you may be able to learn from them – try to identify a specific practice.

- **Practice:** Identify (on your own or with colleagues) a problem that is troublesome, and about which you can find some information. It could be something about your study group, sports team, or a tricky situation in your accommodation.
  - Record what you believe is the problem.
  - Then follow the steps outlined in 'Key ideas' (p. 200) to define the problem rationally.
  - Evaluate how that definition of the problem compares with your initial one. How may it be more useful in dealing with the problem?
  - Record your conclusions and reflect on what you have learned.
  - If possible, compare your work with that of others to see what else you can learn.
- **Application:** Decide on another opportunity to practise this skill within the next week.

Read more

Latham, G. P. and Locke, E.A. (2006), 'Enhancing the benefits and overcoming the pitfalls of goal setting', *Organisational Dynamics,* vol. 35, no. 4, pp. 332–40.

> An article cited in the chapter that is worth reading in its entirety, not just for the subject of the citation.

Leidecker, J.K. and Bruno, A.V. (1984), 'Identifying and using critical success factors,' *Long Range Planning,* vol. 17, no.1, pp. 23–32.

> This useful article identifies eight possible sources for identifying critical success factors, gives examples and suggests ways of assessing their relative importance.

Sahlman, W. A. (1997), 'How to write a great business plan', *Harvard Business Review,* vol. 75, no. 4, pp. 98–108.

> Valuable guidance by an experienced investor, relevant to start-ups and established businesses.

Whittington, R., Molloy, E., Mayer, M. and Smith, A. (2006), 'Practices of strategising/organising: Broadening strategy work and skills', *Long Range Planning,* vol. 39, no. 6, pp. 615–29.

> An article cited in the chapter that is worth reading in its entirety, not just for the subject of the citation.

Go online

These websites have appeared in the chapter:

> www.crossrail.co.uk
> www.shell.com
> www.merck.com
> www.marksandspencer.com
> www.maersk.com

Visit two of the sites in the list, and navigate to the pages dealing with corporate news, or investor relations.

- What planning issues can you identify that managers in the company are likely to be dealing with?
- What kind of environment are they likely to be working in, and how will that affect their planning methods and processes?

CHAPTER 7
DECISION MAKING

Aims

To show that decisions shape how management adds value (or not) to resources, and to outline alternative ways to make decisions.

Objectives

By the end of your work on this chapter you should be able to outline the concepts below in your own terms and:

1 Outline the (iterative) stages in a rational process for making decisions
2 Explain, and give examples of, programmed and non-programmed decisions
3 Distinguish decision-making conditions of certainty, risk, uncertainty and ambiguity
4 Contrast rational, administrative, political and 'garbage can' decision models
5 Give examples of common sources of bias
6 Explain the contribution of Vroom and Yetton, and of Irving Janis, to our understanding of decision making
7 Outline a creative approach to making decisions and understand how this may help you develop the skill of defining problems
8 Show how ideas from the chapter add to your understanding of the integrating themes

Key terms

This chapter introduces the following ideas:

decision
decision making
decision criteria
decision tree
programmed (or structured) decision
procedure
rule
policy
non-programmed (or unstructured) decision
certainty
risk
uncertainty
ambiguity

rational model of decision making
administrative model of decision making
bounded rationality
satisficing
incremental model
political model
heuristics
prior hypothesis bias
representativeness bias
illusion of control
escalating commitment
groupthink

Each is a term defined within the text, as well as in the glossary at the end of the book.

Case study   Ikea   www.ikea.com

In early 2016 Ikea employed 172,000 co-workers and had over 375 home furnishing stores in 28 countries: in the 2015 financial year it had generated sales of almost €34 billion. Online sales in the UK had grown by 21 per cent over the previous year, though this service is not available in all countries. Peter Agnefjall, CEO, said the company was satisfied with the group's sales and profit – up 5 per cent on 2014.

The Ikea vision 'to create a better everyday life for the majority of people' developed from a decision by Ingvar Kamprad, a Swedish entrepreneur, to sell home furnishing products at prices so low that many people could afford them. He aimed to achieve this not by cutting quality, but by applying simple cost-cutting solutions – products are designed, manufactured, transported, sold and assembled to support the vision. This has evolved into the 'Ikea Concept', elements of which include:

- focus on younger people and young families, and on modern innovative design;
- large stores on the outskirts of cities;
- customers serve themselves and assemble the furniture at home;
- purchase 90 per cent of stock from global suppliers;
- buy the land and build the store; and
- emphasise responsible and sustainable operations.

The first showroom opened in 1953 and until 1963 all stores were in Sweden. International expansion began with a store in Norway – it has entered one new country in almost every year since, and is now planning to open three stores in China every year.

The Ikea Group manages the worldwide stores and associated businesses. It is owned by Stichting INGKA Foundation, based in the Netherlands: Ingvar Kamprad and a family member have two of the five board seats. They also control the Interogo Foundation in Liechtenstein, which has links with the company. Inter Ikea, based in Luxembourg, manages arrangements with franchisees.

The company calls its employees 'co-workers', and aims to enable them to grow individually and

© Ikea Ltd

professionally, taking care to recruit people who share the company's values. The website explains that it seeks people with personal qualities such as a strong desire to learn, the motivation to continually do things better, common sense, ability to lead by example, efficiency and cost-consciousness:

These values are important to us because our way of working is less structured than at many other organisations.

Ikea gives a substantial amount of money to charities, mostly focused on women and children in South Asia. It is one of the biggest donors to child welfare in India, where it expects that within four years about 100 m people will have received support worth 125 million. It is also a major donor to Unicef and Save the Children, and in 2010 gave 47 million euros to charity.

Sources: Ikea Annual Report, 2015; *Financial Times*, 1 January 2011, (p. 23).

Case questions 7.1

- Make a note of the decisions in the story so far.
- How are they, and other decisions in the case, likely to have affected the development of the business?
- Visit the company's website, and note examples of recent decisions shaping the company.

7.1 Introduction

The case introduces one of Europe's biggest and most successful companies, now a global player in the home furnishing market. To move a small Swedish general retailer to its present position, senior managers at Ikea needed to decide where to allocate time, effort and other resources. Over the years their decisions paid off and they now face new issues, such as how to attract customers and well-qualified staff against competition from other retailers. They also face questions from environmental campaigners about their sources of timber (they are the world's third-largest user), and need to decide how to respond: this will shape Ikea's future.

Choice creates tension as we worry about 'what if' we had selected the other option (Schwartz, 2004). Good decisions add value, poor ones do the opposite: Tesco's decision to enter the US market destroyed about £1 billion of the company's value before it withdrew in 2014. Hewlett-Packard, the computer company, appears to destroy value regularly by deciding to buy other companies – including EDS, Palm and Autonomy – and then finding that they are less valuable than the purchase price. These three acquisitions alone are believed to have lost HP shareholders some $20 billion (*Financial Times*, 22 November 2012, p. 13).

The complexity of decision making in organisations arises from structural divisions. People at all levels and in all units make (often independent) decisions about problems that need fixing, and opportunities that may be worth taking. They arise throughout the management task: inputs (how to raise capital, who to employ), outputs (what to make, how to distribute them) and transformations (how to make a new product, how to control the costs). Decisions shape the plans that guide action throughout the organisation, and so have a direct influence on whether they add value or not. If the choices are coherent this may be due to luck, but it is more likely to be because the company has a good decision process – the routines people have learned to use when they make decisions. These give guidance on matters such as who to consult, what information to seek and how to check local decisions against wider policy.

Pentland (2013) claims his research shows the value of seeking ideas from a wide range of people, and testing them with an extensive network (see Chapter 1). He finds that good decision makers continuously engage with new people and ideas – and not just leaders in their field, or well-known names. Instead, they engage with people from many backgrounds to gain exposure to unconventional views – enabling them to combine their own ideas with those reflecting the 'wisdom of crowds'. The choice of decision-making process (see Section 7.7) influences the decision itself, and whether people implement it.

Figure 7.1 illustrates the themes of the chapter, showing that each of the generic elements in solving a problem (see Figure 7.2) involves deciding:

- whether the issue is 'programmed' or 'non-programmed';
- the nature of the surrounding conditions (risk, uncertainty etc);
- which model should shape the process;
- which style(s) to use; and
- how to guard against bias.

The central theme is that there are alternative ways to reach a decision, depending on how people see the context. 'Deciding how to decide' affects the success of an organisation. One such choice is how to balance rational and creative methods. Which works best depends on the context (circumstances), so effective managers have learned the necessary skills. This chapter provides an opportunity to practise the skill of a creative approach.

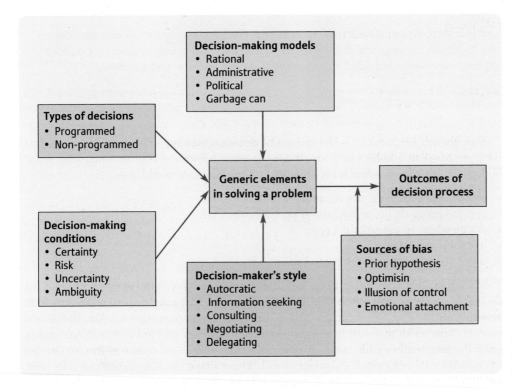

Figure 7.1 An overview of the chapter

7.2   Managing decisions

A **decision** is a specific commitment to action (usually a commitment of resources), in the form of a plan to deal with a problem. As Chapter 6 showed, these arise throughout the organisation, so deciding the form and content of these plans is an equally universal activity.

A **decision** is a specific commitment to action (usually a commitment of resources).

costs; whether to invest in emerging markets with high growth, high risks and few synergies with established businesses; or whether to acquire other global drinks brands, in the hope that greater marketing power will bring a good return on the investment – but good opportunities to do this are rare, and expensive.

Source: *Financial Times*, 12 January 2011, p. 17; company website.

Decision making is the process of identifying and defining problems and opportunities, and making plans to resolve them.

Such choices are part of a wider process of **decision making** – through which organisations create a plan to solve a problem. It involves effort before and after the immediate issue. In deciding whether to select Jean, Bob or Rasul the manager would also:

- identify the need for a new member of staff;
- perhaps persuade his or her boss to authorise the budget;
- decide where to advertise the post;
- interview candidates;
- select the preferred candidate, and so on.

Managers deal with these tasks iteratively, or divert their efforts to another set of decisions – such as who will be on the selection panel. Samsung's decision about which new models to offer follows many earlier decisions about the target market, the design concept, how much to invest in design, production volumes and price. A manager makes small but potentially significant decisions all the time – which of several urgent jobs to do, whose advice to seek, which customer to call. These shape the way people use their time and the plans they make.

Figure 7.2 repeats Figure 6.1, showing information at the centre of the process, which feeds to and from each of the elements in a continuous, iterative fashion. As we deal with one element we find new information, reconsider, revisit an earlier element and perhaps decide on a new route to our goal. People may miss an element, give too much attention to one or too little to others.

Others move quickly, and perhaps intuitively (see Section 7.5), from problem awareness to decision without formal analysis. For familiar or routine decisions this makes sense, as they know the situation and have the relevant information. Some decide major, very uncertain, issues this way.

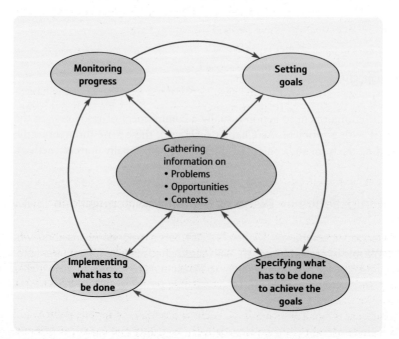

Figure 7.2 Five generic elements in planning how to solve a problem

Key ideas	Paul Nutt on 'idea discovery' and 'idea imposition'

Paul Nutt studied over 400 decisions involving major commitments of resources. He distinguished between an 'idea discovery process,' which usually led to success, and an 'idea imposition process,' which usually led to failure. Decision processes correspond to one or other of these alternatives.

Those following a discovery process spend time at the start looking beyond the initial claim that 'a problem has arisen that requires a decision': they spend time understanding the claims – by talking to stakeholders to judge the strength of their views. This leads to a clearer view of the "arena of action" on which to take a decision. They also identify at the outset the forces that may block them from implementing the preferred idea, as this helps to understand the interests of stakeholders whose support they need.

These early actions enable decision makers to set a direction – an agreed outcome of the decision. Dealing thoroughly with these three stages makes the remaining stages – uncovering and evaluating ideas – comparatively easy, as they help build agreement on what the decision is expected to achieve.

Those following an idea imposition process

skip some stages . . . jump to conclusions and then try to implement the solution they have stumbled upon. This bias for action causes them to limit their search, consider very few ideas, and pay too little attention to people who are affected, despite the fact that decisions fail for just these reasons. (Nutt, 2002, p. 49)

Analysis of more decisions (Nutt, 2008) confirmed that decision makers were as likely to use the failure-prone 'idea imposition process' as they were to use the (usually more successful) 'discovery process'.

Source: Nutt (2002, 2008).

Defining the problem precisely gives a better focus for the next step – deciding how to solve it. Start by setting a goal(s), and the criteria you will use to decide between solutions.

Setting goals (or objectives) – the ends

The goals (or objectives) of the decision(s) may seem obvious in view of the problem, but it is worth spending time to ensure that everyone is clear about which bit of the problem is being decided. The main issue is probably to clarify the scope of the decision, by asking what other factors should be included and what left to one side. Continuing the selection decision, earlier in the process the management team may have asked:

- do we need to replace the person who has left?
- shall we alter the terms of the job before we recruit?

Both are valid questions but it is worth being clear which bit of the problem a particular discussion is intended to solve: this is clarified by setting a goal for a decision such as it being:

- to decide if we need to appoint a replacement and, if so, at what grade?

That is separate from other decisions, such as

- which recruitment agency shall we appoint?

Spending time clarifying this may prevent people talking at cross purposes, or discussing issues that logically only arise once other decisions are known.

People also need to agree **decision criteria** – factors relevant to the decision – as without these they cannot sensibly choose between options. Rational approaches stress economic criteria, so that may imply stressing factors such as likely effects of a decision on costs, process, profitability and so on. Those favouring creative approaches may prefer criteria such as innovation or novelty.

Decision criteria define the factors that are relevant in making a decision.

If the decision concerns a small internal issue such as buying new mobile devices for staff, criteria could include useful features, price, delivery, warranty and ease of use. Some criteria are more important than others, and the decision process can represent this by (say) assigning 100 points between the factors depending on their relative importance. We can measure some criteria (price or delivery) objectively, while others (ease of use) are subjective.

People differ over the factors to include, their relative weight, and may also have private and unexpressed criteria – such as 'will cause least trouble', 'will help my career'. Changing the criteria or their weights will change the decision.

Specifying what has to be done to achieve the goals – the means

In some decisions, such as which flight to choose, this would be to list the available options. In more complex problems alternatives need to be developed, which may be costly. Too few limit choice, too many add to the cost. Schwartz (2004) found that giving people too many choices brings stress, frustration and anxiety about making the wrong decision – there is an example in Key ideas. A rational approach, having specified the goals in economic or financial terms, may do the same with this part of the plan. They may want to:

- set goals (using economic or non-economic criteria);
- set and weight the criteria (see above);
- identify alternatives routes to achieve the goal;
- gather hard information on the benefits and costs of each (economic or non-economic);
- compare alternatives against the criteria using this information;
- choose which route to recommend.

It will usually be valuable to seek ideas widely from those who know about the situation. This requires skill to integrate possibly conflicting ideas, but may be preferable to ignoring people who want to help. Consultation may also make implementation easier – but take time.

Key ideas   Too many jams to choose

Iyengar and Lepper (2000) demonstrated that consumers protect themselves from the stress of too much choice by refusing to purchase. In an experiment conducted in a food store, they set up a tasting booth offering different types of jam. When 24 types were on display, about 60 per cent of passers-by stopped at the booth, compared with just 40 per cent when only six jams were shown. But when it came to choosing a pot of jam to buy, the proportions changed. Only 3 per cent of visitors to the 24-jam booth made a purchase, while 30 per cent of those visiting the smaller display did so. The limited selection was the most effective in converting interest into sales.

Source: Iyengar and Lepper (2000).

A **decision tree** helps someone to make a choice by progressively eliminating options as additional criteria or events are added to the tree.

Sometimes people use a **decision tree** to structure a decision. This helps to assess the relative suitability of the options by assessing them against identified criteria – successively eliminating the options as each relevant factor is introduced – there is an example at Figure 7.7. The main challenge in using the technique is to identify the logical sequence of intermediate decisions and how they relate to each other.

Implementing what has to be done

This is often a problematic stage as it is here that the plan commits scarce resources – and perhaps meets new objections. So implementation often takes longer than expected, and depends on people making other decisions. It also shows the effects of the decision process: if the promoter involved others they may be more willing to cooperate with the consequential changes – such as in the way they work.

Management in practice

Entrepreneurial decisions – data or intuition?

Luke Johnson is a successful entrepreneur who runs Risk Capital Partners (www.riskcapitalpartners.co.uk), a private equity firm. Reflecting on how entrepreneurs reach decisions he wrote:

Do highly rational individuals make better entrepreneurs? I'm not so sure. I think a strong emotional quotient can matter more. Successful business builders know that for most companies, the core of any achievement will depend on personal relationships – with employees, customers, bankers, shareholders, suppliers and others. Managing these interactions is more dependent upon charisma than calculation.

Statistical analysis cannot handle the multiple issues involved in a start-up. One can get lost in the hundreds of pages of verbiage and spreadsheets and forget about critical issues such as culture and the big picture. [One company which I bought] was barely profitable at the time, but the brand and business model felt valuable. On strict criteria it was hard to justify the purchase price. Yet it has turned into one of the best investments I've ever made.

Source: *Financial Times*, 3 October 2012, p. 18.

Monitoring progress

The final stage is monitoring – looking back to see if the decision has resolved the problem, and what can be learned. It is a form of control, which people are often reluctant to do formally, preferring to turn their attention to future tasks, rather than reflect on the past. That choice inhibits their ability to learn from experience.

This is one formal model of the decision-making process: remember that while, if used flexibly and sensibly, it will work well in some conditions, it will not work well in all conditions. People need to use their knowledge and judgement of the circumstances when deciding how to decide. The following sections show these different circumstances.

Activity 7.2   Practice using a rational process to make a decision

Identify a problem that you need to deal with – such as how to make a presentation, complete a group project or course assignment – or organising a social event.

Use Figure 7.2 to guide you. Gather as much information as you can to work through the early tasks: make notes of ideas and suggestions under each heading:

- setting goals (or objectives) – the ends;
- how to achieve the goals – the means;
- implementing – how will you do it;
- monitoring – some ideas on how you will check and judge progress.

Work on this for about ten minutes, and then compare what you have done with a couple of course members, and consider these questions:

- Did working through these steps affect your views about the task?
- Are you better organised to deal with it?
- May spending time gathering information on the first two stages help you with the later ones?

7.3   Programmed and non-programmed decisions

Many decisions that managers face are straightforward and need not involve intense discussion.

Programmed decisions

A programmed (or structured) decision is a repetitive decision that can be handled by a routine approach.

A procedure is a series of related steps to deal with a structured problem.

A rule sets out what someone can or cannot do in a given situation.

A policy is a guideline that establishes some general principles for making a decision.

Programmed (or structured) decisions (Simon, 1960) deal with problems that are familiar, and where the information required is easy to define and obtain – the situation is well structured. If a store manager notices a product is selling well they use a simple, routine **procedure** to decide how much new stock to order. Decisions are 'structured' if they arise frequently and people deal with them by following a set procedure – a series of steps, often online, to deal with that problem. They may use a **rule** setting out what to do, or not do, in a given situation or refer to a **policy** – which sets out general principles to follow.

Programmed decisions deal with routine matters – ordering supplies, appointing a junior member of staff, lending money to a retail bank customer. Once managers formulate procedures, rules or policies, others can usually make the decisions. Computers handle many decisions of this type – the checkout systems in supermarkets link to systems recording sales and ordering stock.

Non-programmed decisions

A non-programmed (unstructured) decision is a unique decision that requires a custom-made solution when information is lacking or unclear.

Simon (1960) also observed that people make **non-programmed (unstructured) decisions** to deal with situations that are novel or unusual, and so require a unique solution. The issue has not arisen in quite that form, and the information required is unclear, vague or open to several interpretations. Major management decisions are of this type – such as the choice that managers at Marks & Spencer faced in 2010 in deciding whether to launch their programme to become the world's most sustainable retailer by 2015. Whatever benefits this may bring, it will be challenging and time-consuming to introduce as it involves changing the way suppliers work. While the company will have done a lot of research before making the decision, they could not know how customers and competitors would respond, or how long any benefit would last. Most issues of strategy are of this type, as they involve great uncertainty and many interests.

| Management in practice | Inamo – choosing a designer   www.inamo-restaurant.com |

Inamo is a London restaurant where customers place their order directly to the kitchen from an interactive ordering system on their table. Selecting the designer for such a novel idea was a big step. Noel Hunwick, Chief Operating Officer:

An early and crucial decision we had to make was to select our interior design company. The way we've always worked is to make sure that we always [have] options from which to choose so, based on recommendations and on web research, and going to various shows and events, I put together a large portfolio of work . . . to get a rough price per square foot that these companies generally charged.

We then selected eight companies to give us a full design brief, and then cut that down to three – who came out with three entirely different concepts so I think that then allowed us to narrow it down to two and have a final showdown. [Given our ordering system was so novel] I think that was a crucial decision – we had to make sure it wasn't an overload on the customer, so I think that was a very delicate and difficult business decision. We always want options. Every single decision, whether it's the cleaning company that we use, everything, we want three options at least. I think that's very important.

Source: Interview with Noel Hunwick.

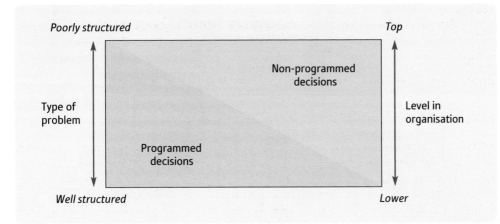

Figure 7.3 Types of decision, types of problem and level in the organisation

Source: Robbins, Stephen P., Coulter, Mary, *Management*, 8th edition, © 2005. Reprinted by permission of Pearson Education, Inc. Upper Saddle River, NJ.

While analytical techniques are good for programmed decisions, non-programmed decisions depend on judgement and intuition. Many decisions have elements of each type – complex non-programmed decisions probably contain elements that can be handled in a programmed way.

Figure 7.3 relates the type of decision to the levels of the organisation. People at lower levels typically deal with routine, structured problems by applying procedures. As they move up the hierarchy they face more unstructured decisions – junior staff hand decisions that do not fit the rules to someone above them, while the latter pass routine matters to junior staff.

Activity 7.3   Programmed and non-programmed decisions

Identify examples of the types of decision set out above. Try to identify one example of your own to add to those below or that illustrates the point specifically within your institution:

- **Programmed decision** – whether to reorder stock.
- **Non-programmed decision** – whether to launch a new service.

Compare your examples with those of other students and consider how those responsible made each decision. How easy is it to distinguish decisions as fitting one or other of these categories?

7.4   Decision-making conditions

Decisions arise within a context whose nature, measured by the degree of **certainty**, risk, uncertainty and ambiguity, materially affects the decision process. Figure 7.4 relates the nature of the problem to the type of decision. Whereas people can deal with conditions of certainty by making programmed decisions, many situations are both uncertain and ambiguous. Here people need to be able to use a non-programmed approach.

Certainty describes the situation when all the information the decision maker needs is available.

Certainty

Certainty is when the decision maker has all the information they need – they are fully informed about the costs and benefits of each alternative. A company treasurer wanting to place reserve funds can easily compare rates of interest from several banks, and calculate

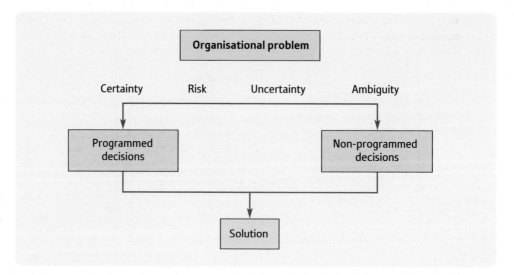

Figure 7.4 Degree of uncertainty and decision-making type

exactly the return from each. Few decisions are that certain, and most contain risk and/or uncertainty.

Risk

Risk refers to situations in which the decision maker is able to estimate the likelihood of the alternative outcomes.

Risk refers to situations where the decision maker can estimate the likelihood of the alternative outcomes, possibly using statistical methods. Banks have developed tools to assess credit risk, and so reduce the risk that the borrower will not repay the loan. The questions on an application form for a loan (home ownership, time at this address, employer's name, etc.) enable the bank to assess the risk of lending money to that person. Yet after the 2008 financial crisis much blame was attributed to banks misjudging credit and market risks, and making bad loans:

> A move away from professional exams in favour of narrow quantitative and sales data has . . . created a cultural inability by some banks to recognise and [deal with] risk (Carolyn Williams, technical director at the Institute of Risk Management, quoted in *Financial Times*, 28 April 2015, 'Special Report on Risk Management', p. 2).

Uncertainty

Uncertainty is when people are clear about their goals, but have little information about which course of action is most likely to succeed.

Uncertainty means that people know what they wish to achieve, but do not have enough information about alternatives and future events to estimate the risk confidently. Factors that may affect the outcomes of deciding to launch a new product (future growth in the market, changes in customer interests, competitors' actions) are impossible to predict. Entrepreneurs live with very high levels of uncertainty: they cannot know if their venture will succeed, nor is it in their nature to allow that to deter them.

Managers at GlaxoSmithKline, the pharmaceutical group, experience great uncertainty in allocating research funds. Scientists who wish to develop a range of vaccines have to persuade the board to allocate resources to the project. Uncertainties include rapid change in the relevant science, what competitors are doing and how many years will pass before the vaccines begins to earn revenue (if any).

Ambiguity

Ambiguity is when people are uncertain about their goals and how best to achieve them.

Ambiguity describes a situation in which the intended goals are unclear, and so the alternative ways of reaching them are equally fluid – leading to stress. Students would experience ambiguity if their teacher created student groups, told each group to complete a project, but gave them no topic, direction, or guidelines. Ambiguous problems are often associated with rapidly changing circumstances, and unclear links between decision elements – see 'Management in practice'.

Management in practice   **Different conditions, different ways to decide**
www.mcdonalds.co.uk

Rosenzweig (2013) shows how the context of a decision affects how to reach it, by contrasting two decisions (among many) that McDonald's, and similar fast-food outlets, faces.

- **Where to locate a new outlet.** They have done this many times, and have developed sophisticated database of the factors that affect the profitability of a store – traffic patterns, incomes, demography and many more. These data are readily available, and it is a routine calculation to compare which of several possible locations would be most profitable. This decision is in a 'certain' context, which routine calculations will answer.
- **How to respond to obesity.** The public is critical of the fast-food industry's role in obesity, and is expecting it to respond. But McDonald's has little or no information on how the public will respond to new, healthier products, nor about competitor responses. It cannot anticipate medical advances that may allay, or aggravate, health concerns, nor the lawsuits it may face if litigants claim that by offering new products it is admitting there was something wrong with the old ones. This a highly ambiguous and uncertain context, requiring a very different approach to decisions.

Source: Rosenzweig (2013).

Dependency

Another way to categorise decisions is by their dependency (or not) on other decisions. People make decisions in a historical and social context and so are influenced by past and possible future decisions, and by events in other parts of the organisation. Legacy computer systems (the result of earlier decisions) frequently constrain how quickly a company can adopt new systems.

Some decisions have few implications beyond their immediate area, but others have significant ripples around and beyond the organisation. Changes in technology usually require consistent, supportive changes in structures and processes if they are to be effective – but decisions on these areas are harder to make than those on technology. Figure 7.5 illustrates this.

Case study   **Ikea – the case continues**   www.ikea.com

Overseas expansion has been especially rapid in China, where in 2015 it had ten stores, making it the company's fastest-growing market. It is also active in Indonesia, Japan and Russia (its second-fastest-growing market) as well as in Western Europe and the United States. Many governments want to attract the revenues and modernising influences of international companies, but also face pressure from domestic retailers trying to protect their interests. Ikea's Asia-Pacific retail manager:

> We still face a very high level of uncertainty. It is a very sensitive political issue in India and it may

take a new government more time to negotiate with the different parties and agree the changes that are required to open up and develop the retail sector.

In 2014 Ikea opened its first store in Indonesia – attracted by the growing consumer class in Southeast Asia's biggest economy, and undeterred by the travails of doing business there. The government has banned foreign investment in the retail sector, so the store is operated under licence by an Indonesian business. The company had to have all its plates made in Indonesia because of a stringent safety standard, effectively aimed at curbing imports from China.

The stores have a common design around the world, intended to reflect the company values – and also to encourage people to stay there for a long time. Any outlet that wishes to organise the store in a particular way has to obtain permission from head office. The company spent five years planning its entry into the Japanese market, before opening the first store in 2006. It wanted to reduce the risks of the decision by understanding Japanese culture as it relates to the home – how people use their home, who has most influence on purchases, and how parents and their children spend time.

Ikea made quite significant changes to the concept to suit the needs of Japanese customers; indeed [these] have been greater than in any other country that Ikea has entered in recent years (Edvardsson and Enquist, 2009, p. 73).

In 2013 the company decided to slow the rate of overseas expansion to about 10 stores a year, down from a previous target of about 20 a year. The founder had criticised that target, advocating the company should put more investment into existing stores.

Sources: Edvardsson and Enquist (2009); *Financial Times*, 23 January 2013, p. 20; 2 September 2013, p. 15; 17 October 2014, p. 18.

Case questions 7.2

- Reflect on Ikea's decision to invest in Russia, China and now Indonesia. What risks, uncertainties, ambiguities or dependencies were probably associated with these situations? Use Figure 7.5 to structure your answer on dependencies.

- The company's decisions on the location, and rate, of expansion will have been informed by significant rational analysis. Identify examples of the questions managers probably considered under the first three headings of Activity 7.2.

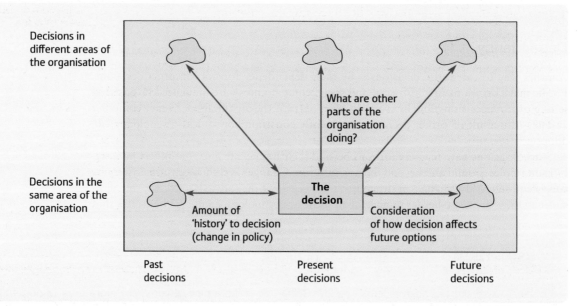

Figure 7.5 Possible relationships between decisions
Source: Cooke and Slack (1991), p. 24.

7.5 Decision-making models

James Thompson (1967) distinguished decisions on two dimensions – agreement or disagreement over goals, and the beliefs that decision makers hold about the relationship between cause and effect. Figure 7.6 shows that a decision can be positioned on these two dimensions, and suggests an approach to making decisions that seems best suited to each cell.

Agreement on goals?

	High	Low
Certainty	I Computational strategy Rational model	III Compromise strategy Political model
Uncertainty	II Judgemental strategy Administrative, incremental and intuitional models	IV Inspirational strategy Garbage-can model

Beliefs about cause-and-effect relationships

Figure 7.6 Conditions favouring different decision processes

Source: Based on Thompson (1967), p. 134.

Computational strategy – rational model

The **rational model of decision making** is sometimes called the 'economic model of rationality' because economists use it to analyse pricing, investment or other decisions in conditions where the goal is clear, and there are several ways to achieve it. The model prescribes that managers should make a decision by structuring the problem:

* specify the goal and the intended economic outcome;
* gather information about the likely costs and benefits of each route to the goal; and
* select the route that will probably bring the greatest economic return.

The model depends on the assumption that the decision maker is rational and logical in setting preferences, assigning values to costs and benefits and evaluating alternatives.

The rational model is normative, in that it defines how a decision maker should act – it does not necessarily describe how managers do act. It aims to help people to act more rationally, rather than relying on intuition and personal preferences. If they are able and willing to gather the required information and to agree criteria for choice, the approach is likely to add value – see 'Management in practice'.

> The **rational model of decision making** assumes that people make consistent choices to maximise economic value within specified constraints.

Management in practice   How Google decides between features   www.google.com

Google depends on the brilliance of its engineers to create search features that will enhance users' experience. They work in small teams and typically have a technical lead (the smartest engineer) and an Assistant Product Manager (APM), who is intended, in the broadest sense, to connect the team with the market. The company had great difficulty clarifying the APM role as the founders believed that engineers did not want to be managed. Others insisted they did – even if only to have someone to go to if they reached an impasse over a decision – most often over whether to develop, and then include, a new search feature.

> A product manager . . . did not give orders. His (or her) job was to charm the engineers into a certain way of thinking . . . The way to do that, of course, was by hard numbers. Information was a great leveller at Google. [APMs] can only gain authority over senior, experienced engineers if they gather the data, lobby the team, and win them over by data.

That process became an asset for Google, by making sure that data was at the centre of decision making. An APM:

could order up a 1 per cent A/B experiment (in which one out of a hundred users gets a version of the product with the suggested change), then go to the team and say, 'users with this new experience are doing 11 per cent more page views and clicking on ads 8 per cent more'. With ammunition like that, a decision to include the new feature in the product wouldn't be based on a power struggle but on a mathematical calculation. Nothing personal. It was data.

Source: Based on Levy, 2011, pp. 161–2.

Davenport and Harris (2005) describe how computer-based decision support systems analyse large quantities of data, with complex relationships – such as in power supply, transport management and banking. Automated decision systems:

sense online data or conditions, apply codified knowledge or logic and make decisions – all with minimal amounts of human intervention. (Davenport and Harris, 2005, p. 84)

Table 7.1 gives examples.

Such applications give objective, quantitative methods to deal with some significant decisions. Many other decisions in life, and in management, do not fit into that box in Figure 7.7: people are uncertain about the cause and effect relationships, and/or there is disagreement about goals. So managers need another decision strategy, of which there are at least three.

Judgemental strategies – administrative, incremental and intuitional

Administrative models

The **administrative model of decision making** describes how people make decisions in uncertain, ambiguous situations.

Simon's (1960) **administrative model of decision making** describes how managers make decisions in situations that are uncertain and ambiguous. Many management problems are unstructured (goals, and routes to achieve them, are unclear) and so not suitable for the

Table 7.1 Examples of automated decision systems by types of decision

Type of decision	Example of automated decision systems
Solution configuration	Mobile phone operators who offer a range of features and service options: an automated programme can weigh all the options, including information about the customer, and present the most suitable option to the customer
Yield optimisation	Widely used in the airline industry to increase revenue by enabling companies to vary prices depending on demand; spreading to other transport companies, hotels, retailing and entertainment
Fraud detection	Credit card companies, online gaming companies and tax authorities use automated screening techniques to detect and deter possible fraud
Operational control	Power companies use automated systems to sense changes in the physical environment (power supply, temperature or rainfall), and respond rapidly to changes in demand, by redirecting supplies across the network

Source: Based on Davenport and Harris (2005).

precise quantitative analysis of the rational model. People rely on judgement to resolve such issues.

Simon based the model on two concepts – bounded rationality and satisficing. **Bounded rationality** expresses the fact that people have mental limits, or boundaries, on how rational they can be. We cannot comprehend all the options, so select from what is available – so our selection represents a limited part of the whole. We cannot then make a rational decision, so instead we decide by **satisficing** – choosing the first solution that is 'good enough'. Searching for other options may produce a better return but identifying and evaluating them would cost more than the benefits. Suppose you are in a strange city and need coffee before a meeting. You look for the first acceptable coffee shop that will do the job – you satisfice. In a similar fashion, managers seek solutions only until they find one they believe will work.

> **Bounded rationality** is behaviour that is rational within a decision process that is limited (bounded) by an individual's ability to process information.
>
> **Satisficing** is the acceptance by decision makers of the first solution that is 'good enough'.

Key ideas   A behavioural theory of decision making

Richard Cyert, James March and Herbert Simon (Simon, 1960; Cyert and March, 1963; March, 1988) developed an influential model of decision making. It is sometimes referred to as the behavioural theory of decision making since it treats decision making as an aspect of human behaviour. Also referred to as the administrative model, it recognises that in the real world people are restricted in their decision processes, and therefore have to accept what is probably a less than perfect solution. It introduced the concepts of 'bounded rationality' and 'satisficing' to the study of decision making.

The administrative model focuses on the human and organisational factors that influence decisions. It is more realistic than the rational model for non-programmed, ambiguous decisions. According to the administrative model, managers:

- have goals that are typically vague and conflicting, and are unable to reach a consensus;
- have different levels of interest in the decision, and interpret information subjectively;
- rarely use rational procedures fully;
- limit their search for alternatives;
- accept satisficing rather than maximising solutions.

The administrative model is descriptive, showing how managers decide complex issues.

Management in practice   Satisficing in e-health projects

Boddy et al. (2009b) studied the implementation of several 'e-health' projects, in which modern information and communication technologies assist clinicians in delivering care. These include applications such as remote diagnostic systems, in which a consultant, assisted by video-conferencing equipment, examines the condition of a patient in a clinic hundreds of miles away. Such methods offer significant savings in patient travel time, and make better use of consultants' time, especially in remote parts of the country. Despite this, the health service has been slow to use e-health systems on a national scale.

To secure the fullest benefits, managers and staff also need to make significant changes throughout the organisation. The processes for interacting with patients change, as does the work of consultants, nurses and other medical staff. These changes are harder to implement than a decision to buy the technology. Pilot projects are producing modest benefits, but nothing like those that could flow from a national programme. A reasonable conclusion is that managers have unconsciously decided to satisfice – they are trying the new methods and producing benefits: securing their full potential would require more effort than they wish to give.

Source: Boddy et al. (2009b).

Incremental models

People use an **incremental model** of decision making when they are uncertain about the consequences. They search for a limited range of options, and policy unfolds from a series of cumulative small decisions.

Charles Lindblom (1959) developed an **incremental model,** which people use when they are uncertain about the consequences of their choice. He built on Simon's idea of bounded rationality to show that people typically make only a limited search until they find an option that is reassuringly close to what already exists. Current choices are heavily influenced by past choices.

On this view, policy unfolds not from a single event, but from the accumulation of small decisions. These help people to minimise the risk of mistakes, and they can reverse the decision if necessary. He called this incrementalism, or the 'science of muddling through'. Lindblom contrasted what he called the 'root' method of decision making with the 'branch' method. The root method required a comprehensive evaluation of options in the light of defined objectives. The branch method involved building out, step by step and by small degrees, from the current situation. He claimed that the root method is not suitable for complex policy questions, so the practical person follows the branch approach – the science of muddling through. The incremental model (like the administrative one) recognises human limitations.

Intuitional models

Klein (1997) studied how effective decision makers work, including those working under extreme time pressure such as surgeons, fire fighters and nurses. He found they rarely used classical decision theory to weigh the options: instead they used pattern recognition to relate the situation to their experience. They acted on intuition – a non-conscious mental process of basing decisions on experience and accumulated judgement – sometimes called 'tacit knowledge'. Klein concluded that effective decision makers use their intuition as much as formal processes – perhaps using both as the situation demands. Experienced managers act quickly on what seems like very little information – they rely on judgement. Hodgkinson et al. (2009) quote the co-founder of Sony, Akio Mariata, the driving force behind one of the great innovations of the 20th century:

> Creativity requires something more than the processing of information. It requires human thought, spontaneous intuition and a lot of courage. (p. 278)

They stress that intuition is not the same as instinct (autonomous reflex actions or inherited behaviour patterns), nor is it a random process of guessing.

Creative approaches

Whetten and Cameron (2011) point out that while creative problem solving involves four steps, the first (preparation) embodies the greatest contrast with rational approaches. Creative problem solvers are more flexible and fluent in data gathering, problem definition, alternative generation and examining options. Two techniques can improve creative problem-solving abilities: one helps people define problems more creatively; the other helps them generate more alternative solutions. The authors suggest ways to develop these skills – see 'Key ideas' in Chapter 6 (p. 201), and these make up the 'Develop a skill' feature at the end of this chapter.

Compromise strategy – political model

The **political model** is a model of decision making that reflects the view that an organisation consists of groups with different interests, goals and values.

The **political model** examines how people make decisions when, in terms of Figure 7.7, those involved are reasonably certain about cause and effect relationships (they understand how the situation they are dealing with works), but have a low level of agreement on their goals: they want different things (Pfeffer, 1992b; Buchanan and Badham, 1999). It recognises that while an organisation is a working system, it is also a political system that establishes the relative power of people and functions. A decision will enhance the power of some and limit that of others. People pursue goals supporting personal and sub-unit interests, as well as those of the organisation, evaluating a decision in terms of its likely effects on these interests.

They will often support their position by building a coalition with those who share their interest. This gives others the opportunity to contribute their ideas and enhances their commitment if the decision is adopted.

The political model assumes that:

- organisations contain groups with diverse interests, goals and values. Managers disagree about problem priorities and may not understand or share the goals and interests of other managers;
- information is ambiguous and incomplete. Rationality is limited by the complexity of many problems as well as personal interests; and
- managers engage in the push and pull of debate to decide goals and discuss alternatives – decisions arise from bargaining and discussion.

Inspirational strategy – garbage-can model

Cohen et al. (1972) suggested that decisions are made when four independent streams of activities meet – usually by chance. The four streams are:

- **Choice opportunities:** occasions at which people make decisions – such as budget or other regular management meetings, and chance encounters
- **Participants:** a stream of people who are able to decide
- **Problems:** a stream of problems that people recognise as significant – a lost sale, a new opportunity, a vacancy
- **Solutions:** a stream of potential solutions seeking problems – ideas, proposals, information – that people continually generate.

In this view, the choice opportunities (scheduled meetings and chance encounters) act as the container (garbage can) for the mixture of participants, problems and solutions. One combination of the three may be such that enough participants are interested in a solution that they can match to a problem – and take a decision accordingly. Another group of participants may not have made those connections, so would not have reached that decision.

This may at first sight seem an unlikely way to run a business, yet creative businesses depend on a rapid interchange of ideas, not only about specific, known problems but also about new discoveries, research at other companies, what someone heard at a conference. They depend on people bringing these solutions and problems together – but will lose opportunities if chance meetings don't happen. So it makes sense to create a context that increases the likelihood of creative exchange – which companies do when they construct buildings that give many opportunities for face-to-face contact, and build a culture that can make decisions quickly if necessary.

Table 7.2 summarises these four models – which are complementary in that a skilful manager or a well-managed organisation will use all of them, depending on the decision and the context. A new product idea may emerge from a process resembling the garbage can – but someone then needs to be able to build a rational case to persuade the board to invest resources in it.

Table 7.2 Four models of decision making

Features	Rational	Administrative/incremental	Political	Garbage can
Clarity of problem and goal	Clear problem and goals	Vague problems and goals	Conflict over goals	Goals and solutions independent
Degree of certainty	High degree of certainty	High degree of uncertainty	Uncertainty and/or conflict	Ambiguity

(continued)

Table 7.2 (*continued*)

Features	Rational	Administrative/incremental	Political	Garbage can
Available information on costs and benefits	Much information about costs and benefits	Little information about costs and benefits of alternatives	Conflicting views about costs and benefits of alternatives	Costs and benefits unconnected at start
Method of choice	Rational choice to maximise benefit	Satisficing choice – good enough	Choice by bargaining among players	Choice by accidental merging of streams

---

Activity 7.4 **Decide which approach to making decisions is most suitable**

Here are some decisions that Virgin (see Part Case) has faced:

- What fare structure to set for the unregulated services it operates (where it is free to set fares without involving the rail regulator).
- Whether to bid to retain its railway franchise to run the UK West Coast Main Line.
- Whether to bid for about 300 branches that the EU requires RBS to sell.
- Whether to order further airliners for Virgin Atlantic.

In each case, decide which of the four decision models best describes the situation, and explain why.

Compare your answers with colleagues on your course, and prepare a short report summarising your conclusions from this activity.

7.6 **Biases in making decisions**

Heuristics are simple rules or mental short cuts that simplify making decisions.

Since people have a limited capacity to process information they use **heuristics** – simple rules, or short cuts, that help us to overcome this constraint (Khaneman and Tversky, 1974). While they help us to make decisions, they bring the danger of one or more biases – prior hypothesis, representativeness, optimism, illusion of control, escalating commitment and emotional attachment.

Prior hypothesis bias

Prior hypothesis bias results from a tendency to base decisions on strong prior beliefs, even if the evidence shows that they are wrong.

People who have strong prior beliefs about the relationship between two alternatives base their decisions on those beliefs, even when they receive evidence that their beliefs are wrong. This is the **prior hypothesis bias**, which is strengthened by paying more attention to information that supports their beliefs, and ignoring what is inconsistent.

Representativeness bias

Representativeness bias results from a tendency to generalise inappropriately from a small sample or a single vivid event.

This is the tendency to generalise from a small sample or a single episode, and to ignore other relevant information. Examples of this **representativeness bias** are:

- predicting the success of a new product on the basis of an earlier success;
- appointing someone with a certain type of experience because a previous successful appointment had a similar background.

Optimism bias

Lovallo and Kahneman (2003) believe that a major reason for poor decisions is because people systematically underestimate the costs and overestimate the benefits of a proposal. This is **optimism bias** – a human tendency to exaggerate their talents and their role in success. Hodgson and Drummond (2009) give an example of a brewery whose senior managers were overconfident about their ability to acquire and rebuild a brewery that had closed down. What seemed like a good way to increase capacity turned out to be a poor decision, as the property required more expenditure than expected, which led to the failure of the purchasers' business.

Optimism bias is a human tendency to see the future in a more positive light than is warranted by experience.

Case study   Ikea – the case continues   www.ikea.com

Managers in Ikea have placed great emphasis on developing a strong culture, transmitting this to new employees and reinforcing it for existing ones. They believe that if co-workers develop a strong sense of shared meaning of the Ikea concept, they deliver good service wherever they work. Edvardsson and Enquist (2002):

> The strong culture in Ikea can give Ikea an image as a religion. In this aspect the Testament of a Furniture Dealer [written by Kamprad and given to all co-workers] is the holy script. The preface reads: 'Once and for all we have decided to side with the many. What is good for our customers is also good for us in the long run.'

After the preface the Testament is divided into nine points:

> (1) The Product Range – our identity, (2) The IKEA Spirit. A Strong and Living Reality, (3) Profit Gives us Resources, (4) To Reach Good Results with Small Means, (5) Simplicity is a Virtue, (6) The Different Way, (7) Concentration of Energy – Important to Our Success, (8) To Assume Responsibility – A Privilege, (9) Most Things Still Remain to be Done. A Glorious Future! (p. 166)

In 2013 Peter Agnefjall became chief executive, having for several years been assistant to the company's influential founder. The latter still gives advice, but senior executives manage the business – some in functional roles, others leading one of the overseas operations.

The company is committed to operate sustainably. Examples of the projects it has launched include a new form of board used in many of its products, made entirely from recycled paper. The stores only sell energy-saving LED lightbulbs, and many have solar systems on their roofs to supply their energy needs. It has also committed to spending 1 billion on research into climate change and renewable energy sources through the Ikea charitable foundation.

Sources: Edvardsson and Enquist (2002); *Financial Times,* 23 January 2012, p. 21; 14 November 2012, p. 14; 2 September 2013, p. 12.

Case questions 7.3

- How may the culture described here affect decision-making processes in Ikea?
- The company has been slow to promote online shopping across the group. This is a major decision – which of the decision-making models appears to best reflect the nature of this choice?

Illusion of control

The **illusion of control** is the human tendency to overestimate our ability to control activities and events. Those in senior positions with a record of success overestimate their chances of future success. The Part 4 Case on the Royal Bank of Scotland shows how several profitable acquisitions encouraged Fred Goodwin to bid for ABN-Amro Bank. Some questioned the value of the deal anyway, but a wider financial crisis (beyond Goodwin's control) ensured that it became a major cause of the RBS collapse.

The **illusion of control** is a source of bias resulting from the tendency to overestimate one's ability to control activities and events.

Escalating commitment

Escalating commitment is a bias that leads to increased commitment to a previous decision despite evidence that it may have been wrong.

Managers may also fall into the trap of **escalating commitment**, which happens when they decide to increase their commitment to a previous decision despite evidence that it may have been wrong (Drummond, 1996 – see 'Management in practice'). People are reluctant to admit mistakes, and rather than search for a new solution they increase their commitment to the original decision.

Management in practice   A study of escalation – Taurus at the Stock Exchange

Helga Drummond studied the attempt by management at the London Stock Exchange to implement a computerised system to deal with the settlement of shares traded on the Exchange. The project was announced in May 1986 and was due to be completed by 1989 at a cost of £6 million. After many crises and difficulties, the Stock Exchange finally abandoned the project in March 1993. By that time the Exchange had spent £80 million on developing a non-existent system. Drummond interviewed many key participants to explore the reasons for this disaster – which occurred despite the skill and willing efforts of the system designers.

She concluded that the project suffered from fundamental structural problems, in that it challenged several powerful vested interests in the financial community, each of whom had their own idea about what should be done. Each new demand, reflecting this continuing power struggle, made the system more complicated. However, while many interests needed to work together, structural barriers throughout the organisation prevented this. There was little upwards communication, so that senior managers were largely unaware of staff concerns about the timetable commitments being made.

Senior managers continued to claim the project was on track, and to invest in it, until a few days before it was finally, and very publicly, terminated. The lack of proper mechanisms to identify pressing issues lulled those making decisions into a false sense of security about the state of the project.

Source: Drummond (1996).

Guler (2007) found evidence of the same phenomenon in the venture capital industry – firms that lend money to entrepreneurs to start and build a business. They typically provide money in instalments over several years, which limits their risk: yet the study showed that investors became less likely to terminate an investment as they paid further instalments, despite evidence that returns were declining. Three factors caused this – social (losing face among colleagues), political (pressure from other investors) and institutional (damage to the firm's reputation if it pulled out).

Emotional attachment

Finkelstein et al. (2009) note that people are frequently influenced by emotional attachments to:

- family and friends;
- communities and colleagues;
- objects – things and places that have meaning for us.

These attachments (negative or positive) bring us meaning and happiness and are bound to influence our decisions. Most of the effects are insignificant, but sometimes a manager's emotional attachments can lead them to make bad business decisions. They give examples such as Samsung's disastrous investment in car manufacturing (widely opposed as a poor use of resources, but initiated and supported by a chairman who liked cars); and the chairman who justified the retention of a small and unprofitable design consultancy because:

I like it! It's exciting. I enjoy it . . . So I'm keeping it! (Finkelstein et al. 2009a, p. 87).

> **Key ideas** **Daniel Kahneman and the danger of biases**
>
> Nobel Prize-winning psychologist Daniel Kahneman has demonstrated the effects of cognitive biases on decisions, such as an aversion to loss that makes us cautious, and a tendency to anchor decisions on certain assumptions that may no longer be relevant. We fear being contradicted, so seek out information that confirms our established opinions. In his book *Thinking, Fast and Slow*, Prof. Kahneman recommends that managers create a form of quality control a round important decisions to avoid the negative effect of these biases, as well as the self-interest and political considerations of everyone involved. The goal is to liberate decision makers from wrong-headed bias, mistaken analogies and emotional attachment. Since human judgement is so badly flawed, the aim is to find ways to limit its worst consequences.
>
> Source: Kahneman (2011).

> **Activity 7.5** **Examples of bias**
>
> - List the six sources of bias.
> - Try to identify one example of each that you have personally experienced in your everyday discussions with friends, family or colleagues.
> - What (be specific) did they (or you) say that led you to label it as being of that type?
> - Compare your results, so that, if possible, you have a clear example of each type of decision bias.

7.7 Group decision making

While people often make decisions as individuals, they also do so within the context of a group. This section looks at two ideas – Vroom and Yetton's decision model and Irving Janis' identification of groupthink.

Vroom and Yetton's decision model

The idea behind Vroom and Yetton's (1973) contingency model of decision making is to influence the quality and acceptability of decisions. This depends on the manager choosing how best to involve subordinates in making a decision – and being willing to change their style to match the situation. The model defines five leadership styles and seven characteristics of problems. Managers can use these characteristics to diagnose the situation. They can find the recommended way of reaching a decision on that problem by using the decision tree shown in Figure 7.7. The five leadership styles defined are:

- **AI** (**Autocratic**) You solve the problem or make the decision yourself using information available to you at that time.
- **AII** (**Information-seeking**) You obtain the necessary information from your subordinate(s), then decide on the solution to the problem yourself. You may or may not tell your subordinates what the problem is in getting the information from them. The role played by your subordinates in making the decision is clearly one of providing the necessary information to you rather than generating or evaluating alternative solutions.
- **CI** (**Consulting**) You share the problem with relevant subordinates individually, getting their ideas and suggestions without bringing them together as a group. Then *you* make the decision that may or may not reflect your subordinates' influence.

- **CII (Negotiating)** You share the problem with your subordinates as a group, obtaining their collective ideas and suggestions. Then you make the decision that may or may not reflect your subordinates' influence.
- **G (Group)** You share the problem with your subordinates as a group. Together you generate and evaluate alternatives and attempt to reach agreement (consensus) on a solution. Your role is much like that of a chairperson. You do not try to influence the group to adopt 'your' solution, and you are willing to accept and implement any solution that has the support of the entire group.

The idea behind the model is that no style is in itself better than another. Some believe that consultative or delegating styles are inherently preferable to autocratic approaches, as being more in keeping with democratic principles. Vroom and Yetton argue otherwise. In some situations (such as when time is short or the manager has all the information needed

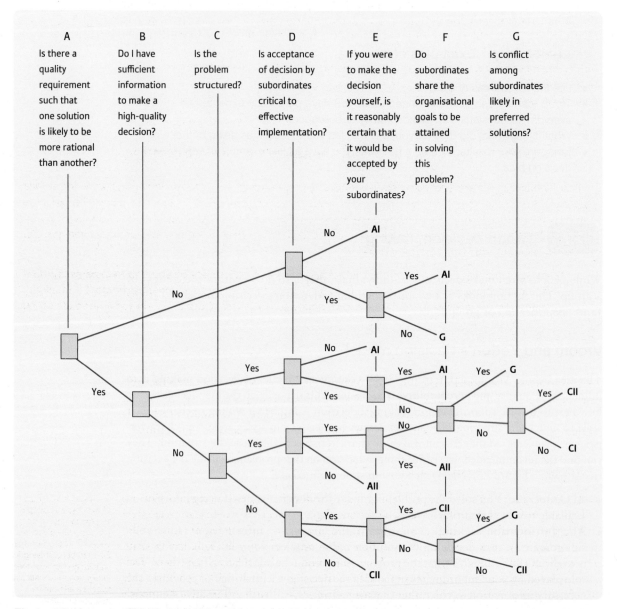

Figure 7.7 Vroom and Yetton's decision tree

Source: Reprinted from Vroom and Yetton (1973), p. 188 by permission of the University of Pittsburgh Press, copyright © 1973 by University of Pittsburgh Press.

for a minor decision) going through the process of consultation will waste time and add little value. In other situations, such as where the subordinates have the relevant information, it is essential to consult them. The point of the model is to make managers more aware of the range of factors to take into account in using a particular decision-making style.

The problem criteria are expressed in seven diagnostic questions:

- Is one solution likely to be better than another?
- Does the manager have enough information to make a high-quality decision?
- Is the problem structured?
- Is acceptance of the decision by subordinates critical to effective implementation?
- If the manager makes the decision alone, is it likely to be accepted by subordinates?
- Do subordinates share organisational goals?
- Is conflict likely among subordinates over preferred solutions?

The Vroom–Yetton decision model implies that managers need to be flexible in the style they adopt. The style should be appropriate to the situation rather than consistent among all situations. The problem with this is that managers may find it difficult to switch between styles, perhaps several times a day. Although the approach appears objective, it still depends on the manager answering the questions. Requiring a yes or no answer to complex questions is too simple, and managers often want to say 'it all depends' – on other historical or contextual factors.

Management in practice   Decision making in a software company

This Swedish company was founded in 1998, and now concentrates on developing software for mobile phones, such as an application that sends text messages from a computer to a mobile. It sells the products mainly to the operating companies who use them to add value to their services. The business depends on teams of highly skilled software developers, able to produce innovative, competitive products very rapidly. The Chief Technology Officer commented:

> As well as technical decisions we regularly face business decisions about where to focus development effort, or which customers to target. In this highly industrialised technocratic environment I am highly influenced by the experts in the team, and routinely consult them about the preferred course of action.

Source: Private communication from the Chief Technology Officer.

Nevertheless, the model is used in management training to alert managers to the style they prefer to use and to the range of options available. It also prompts managers to consider systematically whether that preferred style is always appropriate. They may then handle situations more deliberately than if they relied only on their preferred style or intuition.

Irving Janis and groupthink

Groupthink is a pattern of biased decision making that occurs in groups that become too cohesive – members strive for agreement among themselves at the expense of accurately and dispassionately assessing relevant, and especially disturbing, information. An influential analysis of how it occurs was put forward by the social psychologist Irving Janis. His research (Janis, 1972) began by studying major and highly publicised failures of decision making, looking for some common theme that might explain why apparently able and intelligent people were able to make such bad decisions – such as President Kennedy's decision to have US forces invade Cuba in 1961. One common thread he observed was the inability of the groups involved to consider a range of alternatives rationally, or to see the likely consequences of the choice they made. Members were also keen to be seen as team

Groupthink is 'a mode of thinking that people engage in when they are deeply involved in a cohesive in-group, when the members' striving for unanimity overrides their motivation to realistically appraise alternative courses of action' (Janis, 1972).

players, and not to say things that might end their membership of the group. Janis termed this phenomenon 'groupthink', and defined it as:

> . . . a mode of thinking that people engage in when they are deeply involved in a cohesive in-group, when the members' striving for unanimity overrides their motivation to realistically appraise alternative courses of action. (Janis, 1972, p. 9)

He identified eight symptoms of groupthink, shown in 'Key ideas'.

Key ideas   Irving Janis on the symptoms of groupthink

Janis (1977) identified eight symptoms that give early warning of groupthink developing – and the more of them that are present, the more likely it is that the 'disease' will strike. The symptoms are:

- **Illusion of invulnerability** The belief that any decision they make will be successful.
- **Belief in the inherent morality of the group** Justifying a decision by reference to some higher value.
- **Rationalisation** Playing down the negative consequences or risks of a decision.
- **Stereotyping out-groups** Characterising opponents or doubters in unfavourable terms, making it easier to dismiss even valid criticism from that source.
- **Self-censorship** Suppressing legitimate doubts in the interest of group loyalty.
- **Direct pressure** Strong expressions from other members (or the leader) that dissent to their favoured approach will be unwelcome.
- **Mindguards** Keeping uncomfortable facts or opinions out of the discussion.
- **Illusion of unanimity** Playing down any remaining doubts or questions, even if they become stronger or more persistent.

Source: Based on Janis (1977).

Management in practice   Groupthink in medicine

An experienced nurse observed three of the symptoms of groupthink in the work of senior doctors:

- **Illusion of invulnerability** A feeling of power and authority leads a group to see themselves as invulnerable. Traditionally the medical profession has been very powerful and this makes it very difficult for non-clinicians to question their actions or plans.
- **Belief in the inherent morality of the group** This happens when clinical staff use the term 'individual clinical judgement' as a justification for their actions. An example is when a business manager is trying to reduce drug costs and one consultant's practice is very different from those of his colleagues. Consultants often reply that they are entitled to use their clinical judgement. This is never challenged by their colleagues, and it is often impossible to achieve change.
- **Self-censorship** Being a doctor is similar to being in a very exclusive club, and none of the members wants to be excluded. Therefore doctors will usually support each other, particularly against management. They are also extremely unlikely to report each other for mistakes or poor performance. A government scheme to encourage 'whistle-blowing' was met with much derision in the ranks.

Source: Private communication.

When groupthink occurs, pressures for agreement and harmony within the group have the unintended effects of discouraging individuals from raising issues that run counter to the majority opinion (Turner and Pratkanis, 1998). An often-quoted example is the Challenger disaster in 1986, when the space shuttle exploded shortly after take-off. Investigations showed that NASA and the main contractors, Morton Thiokol, were so anxious to keep the Shuttle programme on schedule that they ignored or discounted evidence that would slow the programme down. On a lighter note, Professor Jerry Harvey tells the story of how members of his extended family drove 40 miles into town on a hot day, to no obvious purpose – and everyone was miserable. Discussing the episode with the family later, each person admitted that they had not wanted to go, but went along to please the others. Harvey (1988) coined the term 'Abilene paradox' to describe this tendency to go along with others for the sake of avoiding conflict.

7.8   Integrating themes

Entrepreneurship

Small entrepreneurial firms lack the resources of larger firms to support their decision-making process, so the question arises of how they make strategic decisions. Liberman-Yaconi et al. (2010) studied this in the software industry, wanting to know what patterns small firms followed in making decisions, what factors shaped their decision processes and what methods they used to gather and process data. Their research in 14 very small firms in web design or IT support enabled them to develop a model that synthesised their findings with earlier research.

The challenge facing the small firm is that any strategic decision, such as to develop a new product, will use significant resources. The entrepreneur cannot know the outcome: failure could destroy the firm. Yet by definition they do not have the resources to gather relevant information. The authors concluded that strategic decision making in these firms had these characteristics:

- more centralised and less formalised than is typical in larger firms;
- examples of iterative and garbage-can models;
- indicated bounded rationality and an intuitive process rather than a rational one; and
- gathered information from sources external to the firm, especially through informal business and social relationships.

Sustainability

In 2015 Ikea committed to spending €1 billion on renewable energy and other measures to tackle climate change – a move that exceeds what many countries are doing to tackle fossil fuel pollution. This included €500 million on wind power and €100 million on solar energy, over the next five years. It will also give 400 million to help people in regions most affected by climate change.

This continues a sustainability policy begun in 2012, in which it tries to give concrete targets for several green undertakings, such as producing as much renewable energy as it consumes by the end of the decade. Steve Howard, Chief Sustainability Officer, said it was keen to 'close the loop' in the supply chain where possible and encourage customers to return products at the end of their useful life to be reused.

> Some things are best recycled by local authorities. But others, we can help, like kitchens, wardrobes, mattresses. Maybe we should have low-cost leasing of kitchens and see a product offering become a service one. We want a smarter consumption, and maybe people are less attached to ownership. People have needs to be met – they need wardrobes, sofas, kitchens. The most important thing is to meet those needs in the most sustainable way possible.

In some countries the company already collects certain products from customers to get the raw materials back into its production system –there is a factory in France where 50 per cent of the wood comes from former products that are ground down to make new bookshelves or tables.

It has also decided to encourage consumers to use light-emitting diodes, and will stop selling other kinds of light bulbs by 2016. The company claims LEDs give a better quality of light, cost less to use over their 20-year life and do not contain the harmful chemical mercury.

There is, however, debate in green circles about whether a company such as Ikea, one of the world's largest users of wood, as well as other raw materials including leather and cotton, can be classed as sustainable. Critics believe the low-priced furniture encourages a 'throw-away' mentality. (Based on articles in the *Financial Times*, 23 October 2012, p. 23 and 4 June 2015, p. 19)

Internationalisation

The structure of decision-making processes changes as companies become international. Decisions will cross the boundaries between managers at global headquarters and those in local business units. Neither of the extreme possibilities is likely to work. If decision making tilts too far in favour of global managers at the centre, local preferences are likely to be overlooked, and local managers are likely to lack commitment to decisions in which they have had no say. Leaving too many decisions to local managers can waste opportunities for economies of scale or opportunities to serve global clients consistently.

A solution may be to identify the major ways in which the company adds value to resources, and align the decision-making processes to make the most of them. For example, if procurement is a critical factor and can best be done on a global scale, that implies that those at the centre should make these decisions. Once supply contracts are agreed, however, responsibility for operating them could pass back to local level. Conversely, they might leave decisions on pricing or advertising expenditure to local managers. The central issue is to spend time on the difficult choices about the location of each set of decisions, to achieve an acceptable balance between global and local expectations.

Governance

Several themes in this chapter highlight the traps that await decision makers, and at the time show how good governance arrangements can help to protect them and the organisation. The top-level strategic decisions that shape an organisation's future are inherently unprogrammed, unstructured decisions that no one has dealt with in quite that form. Senior managers make these decisions in conditions of risk, uncertainty and ambiguity – further placing at risk the assets and resources of the business. They are prone to any and all of the biases the chapter set out: a good example is the failure of the Taurus project at the London Stock Exchange, where those in charge continued to commit additional resources to the project, despite evidence that the project would not be able to deliver a solution acceptable to the main players. This was as much as anything a failure of governance.

More generally, the evidence on groupthink shows the delusions to which powerful senior managers are susceptible, as they come to believe in the soundness of their decisions and are dismissive of those who question their views. This was evident in the 2008 banking crisis, where not enough, if any, of the non-executive directors were able and willing to provide the necessary challenges to the over-enthusiasm of executives taking too many risky decisions. Put another way, these companies had, on the face of it, put in place suitable governance procedures – but those with the power to invoke them did not exercise those responsibilities.

Summary

1 Outline the (iterative) tasks in a systematic, rational decision-making process and the tasks required in each

Decisions are choices about how to act in relation to organisational inputs, outputs and transformation processes. The chapter outlined on pages 212 and 219 the main tasks in rational computational approaches, and Chapter 6 offered an opportunity to develop skill in this area.

Most decisions affect other interests, whose response will be affected by how the decision process is conducted, in matters such as participation and communication.

2 Explain, and give examples of, programmed and non-programmed decisions

- Programmed decisions deal with familiar issues within existing policy – recruitment, minor capital expenditure, small price changes.
- Non-programmed decisions move the business in a new direction – new markets, mergers, a major investment decision.

3 Distinguish decision-making conditions of certainty, risk, uncertainty, ambiguity and dependence

- Certainty – decision makers have all the information they need, especially the costs and benefits of each alternative action.
- Risk – where the decision maker can estimate the likelihood of the alternative outcomes. These are still subject to chance, but decision makers have enough information to estimate probabilities.
- Uncertainty – when people know what they wish to achieve, but information about alternatives and future events is incomplete. They cannot be clear about alternatives or estimate their risk.
- Ambiguity – when people are unsure about their objectives and about the relation between cause and effect.
- Dependence – when a decision affects, and is affected by, decisions by others around the organisation.

4 Contrast rational, administrative, political and garbage-can decision models

- Rational models are based on economic assumptions that suggest that the role of a manager is to maximise the economic return to the firm, and that they do this by making decisions on economically rational criteria.
- The administrative model aims to describe how managers actually make decisions in situations of uncertainty and ambiguity. Many management problems are unstructured and not suitable for the precise quantitative analysis implied by the rational model.
- The political model examines how people make decisions when conditions are uncertain, information is limited and there is disagreement among managers over goals and how to pursue them. It recognises that an organisation is not only a working system, but also a political system, which establishes the relative power of people and functions.
- The garbage-can model identifies four independent streams of activities that enable a decision when they meet. When choice opportunities, participants, problems and solutions come together in a relevant forum (a 'garbage can'), then a decision will be made.

5 Give examples of common sources of bias in decisions

Sources of bias stem from the use of heuristics – mental short cuts that allow us to cope with excessive information. Six biases are:

- Representativeness bias – basing decisions on unrepresentative samples or single incidents.

- Optimism bias – overconfidence in own abilities.
- Prior hypothesis bias – basing decisions on prior beliefs, despite evidence they are wrong.
- Illusion of control – excessive belief in one's ability to control people and events.
- Escalating commitment – committing more resources to a project despite evidence of failure.
- Emotional attachment – to people or things'

6 **Explain the contribution of Vroom and Yetton, and of Irving Janis, to our understanding of decision making in groups**

- Vroom and Yetton introduced the idea that decision-making styles in groups should reflect the situation. Which of the five ways of involving subordinates in a decision (autocratic, information-seeking, consulting, negotiating and delegating) to use depended on identifiable circumstances – such as whether the manager has the information required.
- Irving Janis observed the phenomenon of groupthink, and set out the symptoms which indicate that it is affecting a group's decision-making processes.

7 **Outline a creative approach, and understand how this may help you develop the skill of defining problems**

- People can solve problems by combining, in varying degrees, rational and creative approaches. This chapter outlined a creative approach, and offers the opportunity to begin developing this skill.

8 **Show how ideas from the chapter add to your understanding of the integrating themes**

- Liberman-Yaconi et al. (2010) showed that strategic decision making in small firms is boundedly rational and intuitive in nature, relying heavily on informal business and social contacts for information.
- Ikea is an example of the ways in which many companies are changing the way they operate to make them more sustainable.
- Those managing internationally constantly search for the best balance between central and local decision making.
- The chapter shows the many traps and biases that afflict decision makers – good governance can protect them and their organisations from these, by subjecting them to close external scrutiny. Groupthink is likely to have been a factor when management teams made bad decisions which damaged their firms and the economy.

Test your understanding

1 List three decisions you have recently observed or taken part in. Which of them were programmed, and which non-programmed?

2 How does the type of decision tend to vary with a person's level in the organisation?

3 Paul Nutt noted the difference between 'idea imposition' and 'idea discovery'. What are the main features of 'idea discovery'?

4 Explain the difference between risk and ambiguity.

5 What are the major differences between the rational and administrative models of decision making?

6 What is meant by satisficing? Can you illustrate the concept with an example from your experience? Why did those involved not try to achieve an economically superior decision?

7 List and explain three common biases in making decisions.

8 The Vroom–Yetton model describes five styles. How should the manager decide which style to use?

9 Recall four symptoms of groupthink, and give an example to illustrate each of them.

10 Summarise an idea from the chapter that adds to your understanding of the integrating themes.

Think critically

Think about how your organisation, or one with which you are familiar, makes decisions, and record your responses to these questions:

- Do those concerned deal mainly with programmed or non-programmed decisions? What **assumptions** about the nature of decision making appear to guide their approach? Does the evidence appear to support those assumptions?

- What factors in the history or **context** of the organisation may have influenced the way they reach decisions? Does this affect views on rational and creative approaches respectively?

- Have people put forward **alternative** approaches to decision making, based on evidence from other companies? Does this tend to support, or discourage, the use of a creative approach?

- Can you identify **limitations** in the ideas and theories presented here – for example, what are the limitations of a creative approach?

Develop a skill – defining a problem creatively

Thinking widely about the definition of a problem is a valuable skill in creative approach, and this exercise should help you develop that.

- **Assessment:** Assess how well you 'think creatively' when faced with a dilemma or decision. Do you, for example, prefer to act quickly to find a solution, rather than spend time going into detail? Do you accept at face value what others claim to be the problem? Or do you prefer to spend time digging a bit deeper?

- **Learning:** Read again Section 6.8 especially 'Key ideas' (p. 201). Summarise the main points made in this section. Why is knowing about these ideas expected to help managers in their work?

- **Analysis:** Identify someone (whom you know, or can read about) who appears to use a creative approach to solving problems. Consider what they do, what the effects are and what you may be able to learn from them – try to identify a specific practice.

- **Practice:** Identify (on your own or with colleagues) a problem that is troublesome, and about which you can find some information. It could be something about your study group, sports team, or a tricky situation in your accommodation.

  - Write down now what you believe is the problem.

  - Then follow the suggestions in 'Key ideas' in Chapter 6 (p. 201) about questions that may help to define the problem in a creative way, exploring ideas beyond those that immediately came to mind.

  - Record what you find, and reflect on what you have learned.

  - If possible, compare your work with that of others to see what else you can learn.

- **Application:** Decide on another opportunity to practise this skill within the next week.

Read more

Finkelstein, S., Whitehead, J. and Campbell, A. (2009), 'How inappropriate attachments can drive good leaders to make bad decisions', *Organisational Dynamics,* vol. 38, no. 2, pp. 83–92.

Revealing insights into this source of bias in decision making.

Harvey, J. B. (1988), 'The Abilene Paradox: The management of agreement', *Organisational Dynamics,* vol. 17, no. 1, pp. 17–43.

First published in the same journal in 1974, this reprint also includes an epilogue by Harvey, and further commentaries on this classic paper by other management writers.

Heath, C. and Heath, D. (2012), *Decisive: How to Make Better Choices in Life and Work,* Penguin, Random House, London.

The authors show convincingly how frequently people make bad decisions, explains their common causes, and so how to avoid them – not only in management, but throughout life.

Hodgson, J. and Drummond, H. (2009), 'Learning from fiasco: what causes decision error and how to avoid it', *Journal of General Management,* vol. 35, no. 2, pp.81–92.

An accessible account of the topic that draws on the authors' extensive knowledge of, and research into, the hazards of making decisions in organisations.

Nohria, N. and Stewart, T. A. (2006), 'Risk, uncertainty, and doubt', *Harvard Business Review,* vol. 84, no. 2, pp. 39–40.

A short article showing how 'doubt' is a common affliction for those faced with big decisions.

Go online

These websites have appeared in the chapter:

www.ikea.com
www.diageo.com
www.mcdonalds.co.uk
www.riskcapitalpartners.co.uk
www.google.com
www.inamo-restaurant.com

Visit two of the business sites in the list, or any other company that interests you, and navigate to the pages dealing with recent news or investor relations.

- What examples of decisions that the company has recently had to take can you find?
- How would you classify those decisions in terms of the models in this chapter?
- Gather information from the media websites (such as **www.FT.com**) that relate to the companies you have chosen. What stories can you find that indicate something about the decisions the companies have faced, and what the outcomes have been?

CHAPTER 8
MANAGING STRATEGY

Aim

To describe and illustrate the processes and content of managing strategy.

Objectives

By the end of your work on this chapter you should be able to outline the concepts below in your own terms and:

1 Explain why the process, content and context of strategy matters, and how the issues vary between sectors

2 Compare planning, learning and political views on strategy

3 Summarise evidence on how managers develop strategies

4 Explain how tools for external and internal analysis help managers develop strategy

5 Use the product/market matrix to compare corporate-level strategies

6 Use the generic strategies matrix to compare business-level strategies

7 Illustrate the alternative ways in which managers deliver a strategy

8 Summarise evidence that clear goals benefit strategy workshops, and understand how you can use this to develop your skill of setting clear goals

9 Show how ideas from the chapter add to your understanding of the integrating themes

Key terms

This chapter introduces these ideas:

strategy
competitive strategy
emergent strategy
relational resources
unique resources
strategic capabilities
dynamic capabilities

value chain
mission statement
cost leadership strategy
economies of scale
differentiation strategy
focus strategy

Each is a term defined within the text, as well as in the glossary at the end of the book.

Case study   GKN   www.gkn.com

GKN is an internationally successful engineering company based in the UK's West Midlands. It supplies components to automobile and aircraft manufacturers around the world, employing about 40,000 people at over 35 locations. In 2015 the company reported sales of £7,231 million, and profit before tax of £245 million – both higher than the year before. A strategically important decision in 2015 was the acquisition by the Aerospace Division of Fokker Technologies, which, after the earlier purchase of Volvo's aircraft engineering division, further strengthened the company's position in that market.

In 1759 nine entrepreneurs built a blast furnace at Dowlais, high in a Welsh valley, powered by water from a stream. Eight years later they appointed John Guest to manage their business, which he did successfully, being followed by his son, Thomas, and grandson Josiah John Guest – whose wife Charlotte led the business for several years after his death in 1852. They and their successors continued to invest in modern technology and to enter new markets – such as a steam engine in place of water in 1798, a transport link to Cardiff docks and a mill that allowed it to supply large quantities of iron rails for the rapidly growing railway network – including those in Russia and the US (Lorenz, 2009, p. 9).

In 1900 the iron company that Guest had founded merged with a major customer – Arthur Keen's nut and bolt company – to form Guest, Keen and Co. In 1902 this company acquired Nettlefold's to create the company that traded for many years as Guest, Keen and Nettlefolds.

By 1963 the company was mainly a steel producer, though also making semi-finished castings and forgings and huge quantities of screws, nuts and bolts. In 1967 the Labour government nationalised the UK steel industry, including the part owned by GKN. Senior management assumed that when the Conservatives returned to power they would denationalise the industry and the company would buy back the steel plants.

Trevor Holdsworth had recently joined the company in a senior finance role, and believed that returning to steel would be a serious strategic error. He saw the potential value of a resource the company had acquired a few years earlier – Birfield, an engineering company supplying components to the motor

© Chris Ratcliffe/Bloomberg /Getty Images

industry. This in turn owned a minority stake in Uni-Cardan – a German supplier to Volkswagen and other European car manufacturers. Holdsworth concluded the company should not return to the UK commodity steel business but instead should focus on supplying high-technology components to the international motor industry.

Lorenz (2009) shows it was only with great difficulty that Holdsworth, a courteous man who led by reason rather than charisma, persuaded the then Chairman to change his mind. Holdsworth prevailed: the board of directors decided not to return to steel, but instead to increase their stake in Uni-Cardan. Over the next 20 years GKN was able to establish a powerful position in Europe's strongest motor industry. Holdsworth had a clear idea of what sectors GKN should be in, and what it should leave.

Source: Lorenz (2009).

Case questions 8.1

Visit the company website and note recent events and developments in the company.

- Note the sales and profit performance in the most recent period compared to an earlier one.

- What do the chairman and chief executive write about the company's current strategy?

- What challenges do they say the company is facing?

8.1   Introduction

GKN illustrates the value of managing strategy. At successive periods in its long history it has faced major decisions about where to allocate financial resources – replacing water power with steam, investing in a mill to meet rising demand for rails, deciding to merge with other businesses to create GKN and, in more recent times, deciding not to buy back former steel assets, but instead to enter the business of supplying advanced components to the European car industry. These strategic investment decisions re-shaped the company.

All organisations face these issues of where to allocate effort and resources, and depend on senior management providing strategic leadership – see 'Management in practice'. The focus of strategy at the World Wildlife Fund (WWF) is where to allocate funds to bring most benefit to endangered species. A second strand is to use its conservation expertise to help global businesses ensure their strategies are sustainable (Roberts, 2014). Strategic issues at Virgin often focus on whether to extend the brand into more areas of activity and, if so, which will offer the best return.

Management in practice

A new strategist at easyJet   www.easyJet.com

Carolyn McCall became chief executive of easyJet in 2010 when the company was in disarray. She quickly stabilised the immediate problems, and embarked on a strategy to improve core operations and rebuild a demoralised management team with new appointments. The company has since reduced capacity in line with economic conditions, and worked hard to attract a wider range of customers, including business travellers from BA. By early 2013 the share price had risen, and the company was on the verge of entering the FTSE 100 index. One observer said:

> Before Carolyn arrived, the easyJet team were very nervous and reactive to what Ryanair did. Now you see them doing their own thing – and you see Ryanair even following easyJet. The world really has changed.

 Source: *Financial Times*, 19 February 2012, p. 21.
© The Financial Times 2012. All Rights Reserved.

Strategic management enables companies to be clear about how they will add value, as their context changes. Strategy links the organisation to the outside world, where changes in the competitive (micro) and general (macro) environment bring opportunities and threats. Table 8.1 gives examples of strategy changes.

Table 8.1 Examples of organisations making strategic changes

Organisation and strategic issue	Strategic decisions or moves
Reckitt Benckiser (UK consumer goods company) – to focus on areas of strength to increase growth (www.rb.com)	In 2014 CEO decides to sell the pharmaceuticals unit, to concentrate on personal care products (toothpaste) and health products that can be sold without a prescription
Lloyds Banking Group (UK's largest retail bank) – how to create a 'multi-channel' bank, able to meet the needs of online customers and those who use branches (www.lloydsbankinggroup.com)	Closing 200 branches that few customers use, and reinvesting the saving to develop new digital services and more automated administration
BT – how to offer retail customers fixed and mobile telecoms, broadband, TV on a single platform, to become a dominant player in UK Telecoms (www.bt.com)	Acquires EE, UK's largest mobile network for £12.5 billion to strengthen its position in the mobile sector

The first sections of the chapter outline the strategy process, how managers develop strategy and the tools they use for external and internal analysis. Two sections focus on corporate and business unit strategies respectively, followed by one on how managers deliver strategy. A widely used technique to develop strategy is the workshop, whose effectiveness depends on clear goals. The chapter offers an opportunity to begin to develop this skill, which is useful in all aspects of managing.

8.2 Strategy – process, content and context

What is strategy?

Strategy is about how people organise major resources to enhance the performance of an enterprise. These resource decisions are large, long-term, expensive and visible – with matching implications for performance: decisions that are not strategic are operational or tactical. Elaborating on the definition:

> **Strategy** is about how people decide to organise major resources to enhance performance of an enterprise.

- **People** – strategy is typically the responsibility of senior management, but some advocate engaging more people in the process.
- **Decide** – in formal planning processes and/or informal conversations among managers.
- **Organise** – how to divide and coordinate activities to add most value.
- **Major** – significant, expensive, visible – decisions with long-term implications.
- **Resources** – inputs the enterprise needs – including those in other organisations.
- **To enhance performance** – the intended outcome of strategic decisions.
- **Enterprise** – all types of organisation can benefit from managing their strategy.

The definition is consistent with the view of Johnson et al. (2007),who suggest that strategy is something people do (strategy process) and that organisations have (strategy content).

Process

People, usually senior managers, talk and email and argue about present and future strategy – their strategy process. In this sense, strategy is something that people do (Johnson et al. 2007). Understanding this perspective implies finding out who creates strategy, what information they gather, what tools they use and how they organise it. Sections 8.3 and 8.4 introduce ideas on strategy processes.

Content

The current strategy is the starting point of, and a new one emerges from, the strategy process – so in this sense strategy is something that organisations have (Johnson et al. 2007). Something stimulates managers to question current strategy, such as a hostile takeover bid or an idea for a new service. They then try to identify what can give their enterprise an edge, to redefine their **competitive strategy** and support it with suitable resources. This includes deciding what to offer, to which markets, using what resources. Sections 8.5 and 8.6 will deal with these topics.

Competitive strategy explains how an organisation (or unit within it) intends to achieve competitive advantage in its market.

Context

The organisation's context affects the issues those managing strategy will face. Not-for-profit (NFP) or public-sector organisations share some characteristics with commercial businesses (they need to attract and retain enthusiastic and capable staff) and differ in others (their performance criteria and sources of funding). Table 8.2 illustrates these differences.

Whatever their context, strategists hope to enhance performance by clarifying and unifying purpose, linking short-term actions to long-term goals and measuring performance.

Activity 8.2   Think about the definition

Reflect on an organisation you have worked in, or ask a friend or relative who works in an organisation to help.

- Can you identify people there whose jobs included some or all of the items in the definition?
- Did any of them mention tasks that they saw as part of strategy that the definition leaves out?
- Decide if the definition accurately describes 'strategy'.
- If not, how would you change it?

Table 8.2 Examples of strategic issues in different settings

Type of organisation	Distinctive strategic issues	Examples in this text
Large multinational corporations (MNCs)	Structure and control of global activities; allocating resources between units	Proctor & Gamble (this chapter); BP (Part 2 Case)
Small and medium enterprises (SMEs)	Strongly influenced by founders or owners; lack of capital limits choices	innocent drinks (Chapter 2)
Manufacturing	Relative contribution to competitive advantage of the manufacturing (physical product) or service aspect (delivery, customer support) of the offer	BMW (Chapter 11)
Firms in innovative sectors	Adding value depends on rapid innovation, so strategy aims to create a culture of questioning and challenge	Dyson (Chapter 13)

Public sector	Competing for resources, and so aim to demonstrate best value in outputs; most problems require co-operation between agencies, complicating strategy	Crossrail (Chapter 6)
Voluntary and NFP sector	Balancing ideology and values with interests of funding sources; balancing central control (consistency) with local commitment (volunteers and local staff)	The Eden Project (Chapter 15)

8.3   Planning, learning and political perspectives

Table 8.3 shows three perspectives on the strategy process, comparing their approach, content, nature and outcomes – and the context in which they may be suitable.

Planning

The 'planning view' is prescriptive, based on the idea that strategic decisions require a formal approach to guide managers through the process. Ansoff (1965) presented it as a systematic process, following a prescribed sequence and using many analytical tools and techniques – shown in Figure 8.1. Those favouring this method assume that events and facts can be expressed objectively, and that people respond rationally to such information.

Table 8.3 Alternative perspectives on the strategy process

	Planning	Learning	Political
Approach	Prescriptive; assumes rationality	Descriptive; based on bounded rationality	Descriptive; based on bounded rationality
Content	Analytical tools and techniques; forecasting; search for alternatives, each evaluated in detail	Limited use of tools and techniques, limited search for options, as time and resources are limited	As learning view, but some objectives and options disregarded as politically unacceptable
Nature of process	Formalised, systematic, analytical; top down – centralised planning teams	Adaptive, learning by doing; top down and bottom up	Bargaining; use of power to shape strategies; top down and bottom up
Outcomes	Extensive plans made before work begins; plans assumed to be achieved with small changes	Plans are made but not all are 'realised'; some strategies are not planned but emerge in course of 'doing'	Plans may be left ambiguous to secure agreement; need interpretation during implementation; compromises
Context/environment	Stable environment; assumption that future can be predicted; if complex, use of more sophisticated tools	Complex, dynamic, future unpredictable	Stable or dynamic, but complex; stakeholders have diverging values, objectives and solutions

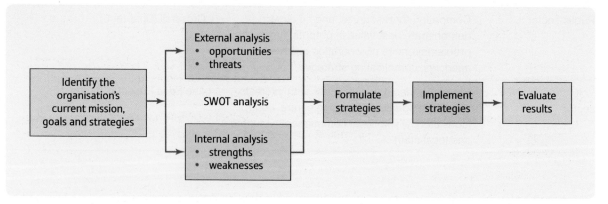

Figure 8.1 The planning view of strategy

Those who challenge these assumptions of objectivity and rationality advocate two alternative views – the learning and the political.

Learning

Mintzberg (1994) regards formal strategic planning as a system developed in stable times to suit the central bureaucracies typical of Western manufacturing industry in the mid-twentieth century. It worked well then, but rather less so when events require a quick response.

He therefore distinguished between intended and **emergent strategy** (Figure 8.2). This shows an intended plan, some parts of which are realised (deliberate strategy) – but also that some parts are not (unrealised strategy). Other moves or investments occur that were not intended when the plan was made – local managers deal with local problems, and their solutions become established as the way to do things. Mintzberg describes these as 'emergent strategies', which result from:

> actions taken one by one, which converged in time in some sort of consistency or pattern. (p. 25)

The realised strategy is a combination of surviving parts of the intended strategy, and of the emergent strategy.

Emergent strategies are those that result from actions taken one by one that converge in time in some sort of consistent pattern.

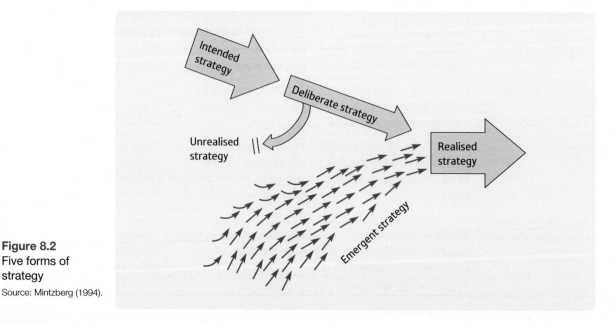

Figure 8.2
Five forms of strategy

Source: Mintzberg (1994).

> ### Management in practice   Emergent strategy at Ikea   www.ikea.com
>
> Barthélemy (2006) offers an insight into the strategy process at Ikea. Their strategy has clearly been successful, but how did it come about? The company's history shows that many elements of the strategy were not brought about through deliberate formulation followed by implementation:
>
> **Instead, the founder, Ingvar Kamprad started with a very general vision. Ikea's specific strategy then emerged as he both proactively developed a viable course of action and reacted to unfolding circumstances. (p. 81)**
>
> Examples include:
>
> - The decision to sell furniture was an adaptation to the market, not a deliberate strategy – furniture was initially a small part of the retail business, but was so successful that he soon dropped all other products.
> - The flat-pack method, which symbolises the group, was introduced to reduce insurance claims on the mail-order business – its potential became clear when the company started opening stores, and realised that customers valued this type of product.
> - The company only began to design its own furniture because other retailers put pressure on established furniture companies not to sell to Ikea.
>
> Source: Barthelemy (2006).

This view of strategy recognises that:

the real world inevitably involves some thinking ahead of time as well as some adaptation en route. (p. 26)

The essence of the learning view is adaptation, reacting to unexpected events, experimenting 'on the ground'. Mintzberg gives the example of a salesperson coming up

with the idea of selling an existing product to some new customers. Soon all the other salespeople begin to do the same, and one day, months later, management discovers that the company has entered a new market. (p. 26)

This was not planned but learned, collectively, during implementation. While advocating a learning view, Mintzberg notes the value of planning:

Too much planning may lead us to chaos, but so too would too little, more directly. (Mintzberg, 1994).

Political view

While the learning view reflects the logic that planning can never give complete foresight, the political view adds dimensions of power, conflict and ambiguity.

Drawing on his experience in the public sector, Lindblom (1959) drew attention to political influences on strategy, especially as value judgements influence policy, and how stakeholders' conflicting interests frustrate attempts to agree strategy. He concluded that strategic management is not scientific, comprehensive or rational, but an iterative, incremental process with much bargaining between the players. He notes 'successive limited comparisons' whereby 'new' strategy is made by marginal adjustments to existing strategy that are politically acceptable:

Policy is not made once and for all; it is made and remade endlessly . . . [through] . . . a process of successive approximation to some desired objectives.

Activity 8.3   **Gather evidence about the three perspectives**

Read one of these case studies – Crossrail (Chapter 6), Apple (Part 1 Case) – or any other organisation suitable for this activity.

- Identify two or three strategic moves made by the company, and record a brief note of each.
- Can you find evidence to show which of the three perspectives on strategy they used – planning, learning or political?
- Compare answers with other students on your course, and look for common themes.

Case study   GKN – the case continues   www.gkn.com

Commenting later on his disagreement over strategy with the then chairman, Trevor Holdsworth said:

> Thank goodness he gave in, or the constant velocity technology – which became central to our strategy – would have been lost (Lorenz, p. 140).

This decision to invest in Uni-Cardan was the basis of GKN's future in driveline systems (equipment to control vehicle steering) and also changed the company's geographical balance. It was previously confined mainly to the British Commonwealth, but the new business brought new customers and locations. By the mid-1980s the automotive business made 68 per cent of group profits.

For several years the company invested time and energy to build close links with the Japanese motor industry. To reduce their reliance on the only significant local driveline supplier, they invited GKN to supply these. Rather than build a plant in Japan, the company offered Toyota, Nissan and then Honda the right to make the components they required under licence, on condition that if they started to produce outside of Japan, they would buy these components from GKN.

As demand for Japanese cars grew in the US, each company built factories there – which GKN then supplied. This process was repeated in the UK when Nissan set up a plant in Sunderland, followed by Honda in Swindon. Both honoured their commitment to buy drivelines from GKN. By 1984, 75 per cent of GKN's auto component sales were to non-UK customers: it was becoming an international company making innovative engineering products (Lorenz, 2009, pp. 225–39).

The group was also implementing an earlier strategic decision to diversify into services, such as auto parts distribution and wooden pallet supply.

Source: Lorenz (2009).

Case questions 8.2

- What external developments have affected the company's strategy?
- What examples are there in the case of the three perspectives on strategy?

8.4   How do managers develop strategies?

Grant's (2003) study in eight oil companies shows how their strategy process changed. Previously they all followed a similar formal process – shown in Figure 8.3. In the relatively stable conditions of the 1970s the common practice was that staff at corporate HQ analysed economic trends, forecast energy demand and price and set the overall direction, within which business unit staff developed their strategy proposals. They discussed these with corporate staff, and the revised plans shaped the annual budget and corporate plan. After board approval, this plan provided the context for setting and monitoring annual performance targets.

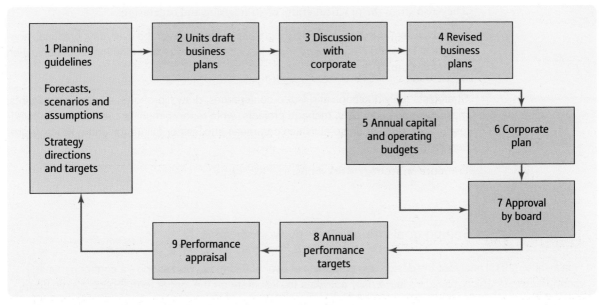

Figure 8.3 The generic strategic planning cycle among the oil majors
Source: Grant (2003), p. 499.

All the companies had changed the process as the business environment became more uncertain, so there was now:

- less detailed forecasting, more scenario planning (see below);
- less formality and documentation, more face-to-face discussion;
- shorter planning meetings; and
- responsibility had moved from corporate staff to business unit line management.

The plans now covered shorter periods, dealt with direction not detail, and set:

- financial targets;
- operating targets;
- safety and environmental targets;
- strategic mileposts; and
- capital expenditure limits.

Grant concluded that strategic planning now meant coordinating strategies emerging from the business units, and monitoring their implementation:

> Strategic planning has become less about strategic decision making and more a mechanism for coordination and performance managing . . . permitting increased decentralisation of decision making and greater adaptability and responsiveness to external change. (p. 515)

Eight oil companies are not typical – but studies in other sectors confirm that contemporary strategic planning combines elements of formality and informality, and of demanding targets used with intelligent flexibility. This is reflected by Whittington et al. (2006) who see 'strategy as practice', drawing on qualitative research in ten organisations. They found that the activities of formulating strategy and designing organisation are conducted as linked practical activities, by using three tools – strategy workshops, strategic change projects and symbolic artefacts (things that people develop to represent and communicate strategy). The research also showed the transitory nature of strategies and organisational forms, implying that two verbs ('strategising' and 'organising' respectively) capture the nature of the work people do in 'strategy'.

They also stress the practical crafts of strategising and organising:

Formal strategy can be renewed by a greater appreciation of the everyday, practical, non-analytical skills required to carry it out [especially those of coordination, communication and control]. (p. 616)

Strategists run workshops and video-conferences, draw flip-charts, design PowerPoints, manipulate spreadsheets, manage projects, write reports, monitor metrics and talk endlessly: their skills at these activities can mean success or failure for entire strategy processes. (p. 625)

For more on strategy workshops, see 'Key ideas'.

Key ideas | **Setting goals helps strategy workshops**

Healey et al. (2015) analysed the design and outcomes of over 650 strategy workshops – a common management practice in which managers leave daily activities to deliberate on the longer term. These events commonly use tools of SWOT analysis, stakeholder analysis, scenario planning, PESTEL and Value Chain Analysis. This study was designed to identify which design features of the workshops had most effect on the outcomes.

In designing the study, they noted evidence that workshops frequently fail because those designing them do not clarify sufficiently clearly the outcomes required from the workshop. They therefore fail to focus and guide discussion in that direction, leaving participants unclear about what they should focus on, and how to progress their analysis. Goal-setting theory (see Chapters 6 and 15) predicts that having clear goals at the outset of any group task is vital to focus effort on desired outcomes, energise participants and maintain persistence. Clear goals also help group identity and cohesion.

Healey et al. (2015) designed their research to test, among other things, the effects of clear goals on workshop outcomes. The results showed that the single most significant influence on outcomes was the clarity with which organisers clarified workshop goals, and communicated these to participants. Developing clear goals is evidently a valuable skill, and the 'Develop a skill' feature at the end of this chapter is an opportunity to do just that.

Source: Healey et al. (2015).

Sull (2007) believes that since volatile markets mean a steady stream of opportunities and threats, managers cannot predict their form, magnitude or timing. This makes the planning view of strategy inadequate, as it may deter people from taking account of new information. He sees the strategy process as iterative – a loop instead of a line:

According to this view, every strategy is a work in progress that is subject to revision in light of ongoing interactions between the organisation and its environment. To accommodate [this], the strategy loop consists of four major steps: making sense of a situation, making choices on what to do (and what not to do), making those things happen and making revisions based on new information. (p. 31)

Figure 8.4 shows the strategy loop, the most important feature of which is the implication that managers incorporate and use new information as it becomes available, closely linking formation and implementation.

Sull stresses the importance of conversations – formal and informal, short and long, one-on-one and in groups – as the key mechanism for coordination. To put the strategy loop into practice, managers at every level must be able to lead discussions about the four steps. The following sections provide ideas and examples about each:

● making sense – external and internal environments;
● making choices – strategy at corporate and business unit levels;

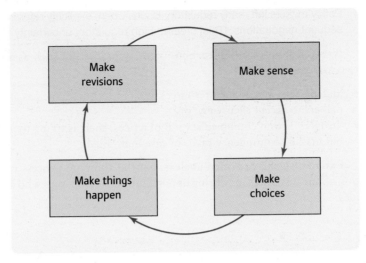

Figure 8.4 The strategy loop

Source: Sull (2007), p. 33.

- making things happen – delivering strategy; and
- making revisions – reflecting on results, and taking in new information.

8.5   Making sense – external analysis

Chapter 3 outlined Porter's five forces model, showing the forces that affect the profitability of an industry – see 'Key ideas'.

Key ideas   Using Porter's five forces in strategic analysis

Analysing the likely effects on a company of the five forces (Porter, 1980; 2008) can show potential action points.

- **Threat of entry**: what are the barriers that new entrants need to overcome if they are to compete successfully?
- **Threat of substitutes**: what alternative products and services may customers choose?
- **Power of buyers**: if buyers have bargaining power they force down prices and reduce profitably.
- **Power of suppliers**: if suppliers have few competitors they can raise prices.
- **Competitive rivalry**: the four forces combine to affect the intensity of rivalry in a sector.

The model remains popular, and Porter published a revised version in 2008 – mainly by adding current examples; the five forces remain the same. They help strategists to understand the fundamental conditions of their industry, and to work out how to make their company less vulnerable and more profitable.

Source: Porter (1980, 2008).

The PESTEL framework (Chapters 3 and 4) also helps companies to identify relevant factors in the general environment. Cuts to local authority budgets have encouraged many to outsource services to private companies, hoping they will save money: Care UK runs many care homes for the elderly for local authorities.

Engau and Hoffmann (2011) illustrate the diversity in the way companies respond to external change, in a study of the 1997 Kyoto Protocol. This is an international agreement setting national targets for lowering greenhouse gas emissions, but

Policy makers left many regulatory issues open, explicitly referring their resolution to subsequent negotiations. [This] created high regulatory uncertainty for firms. (p. 43)

Firms' responses (all in carbon-intensive industries, such as airlines) ranged between two extremes:

- 'daredevils' – put all their resources into one response, such as influencing national policy makers to accept their view; or
- 'hedgers' – who combined several practices, such as trying to influence national policy, but making contingency plans in case that failed.

External signals are often unclear, but the ability to process vast amounts of information about customers may bring opportunities to companies who are able to use it: see 'Key ideas'.

Key ideas

Opportunities in 'big data'?

'Big data' describe the large volumes of data generated about business activities from new sources such as social media. It includes data from point-of-sale terminals, cash machines, Facebook posts and YouTube videos. Companies use sophisticated software to analyse it, looking for patterns or trends they can use to make products more attractive to customers.

Companies and governments have been doing this for years with 'structured data' that is already well-organised, like sales records, but they now have access to 'unstructured data' – like Facebook posts. The lack of structure make this data harder to analyse – but potentially give insights into what people and their friends think of a brand, or their intentions towards a new product.

Analytical companies are developing models to capture and process this data, which they believe will be valuable to businesses in areas such as consumer goods, insurance and consumer loans, who want to understand consumers' decisions. The biggest gainers will be those who make the computer systems and software that do the analysis, such as IBM, Oracle and SAP.

 Source: From an article by Richard Waters in the *Financial Times*, 10 December 2012, p. 19.
© The Financial Times 2012. All Rights Reserved.

Strategy links an organisation's external relationships with its internal capabilities, so managers need an internal analysis to show how they may cope with external changes.

Activity 8.4 Using Porter's five forces to analyse a competitive environment

- Identify an industry that features in one of the cases in this book, such as airlines or retailing.
- Gather evidence and examples of each of the five forces, and of how it has affected competition.
- Try to identify how one company in the industry has changed its strategy to take account of this change in one or more of the five forces.

8.6 | Making sense – internal analysis

Resources, competences and dynamic capabilities

Managers analyse the internal environment to identify strengths and weaknesses – what the organisation does well, where it might do better and where it stands in relation to competitors.

Chapter 1 introduced the idea of strategic capability as the ability to perform at the level required to survive and prosper, and showed how this depends on the resources available to the organisation, and its competence in using them. Tangible resources are physical – buildings, equipment, people or finance; intangible resources include relational resources and reputation – see Figure 8.5.

Relational resources arise as a firm interacts with the environment – building relations with influential customers, government agencies, media or research centres provides valuable information. Reputation among other players is also a resource – a reputation for quality, trust or innovation will be more useful than one for sharp practice and poor delivery. A firm also gains from having **unique resources** that others cannot obtain – a powerful brand, access to raw material or a distinctive culture. Joe Morris, operations director at TJ Morris (www.tjmorris.co.uk), a rapidly growing chain of discount stores (trading as Home Bargains), claims its IT system (which his brother Ed designed) gives it a competitive advantage:

> It is our own bespoke product. It is extremely reliable and simple. We can do what we want to do very quickly.

Successful firms add value to resources by developing competences – activities and processes that enable them to use resources effectively. If staff develop higher skills, cooperate better, are innovative and creative, the company is likely to perform better than one where they do not. Johnson et al. (2014) show that resources and competences combine to provide capabilities – the things that an organisation is able to do in a reliable, efficient way. They define **strategic capabilities** as those that contribute to long-term survival or competitive advantage – combining resources ('what we have') and competences ('what we do well').

Ryanair has prospered not just because it has resources (a fleet of modern, standard aircraft) – other airlines have similar resources, but are unprofitable. The difference is that Ryanair has developed competences – such as quick turn a rounds that enable it to use aircraft more efficiently. GlaxoSmithKline has a strategy to acquire half of its new drugs

Relational resources are intangible resources available to a firm from its interaction with the environment.

Unique resources are resources that are vital to competitive advantage, and which others cannot obtain.

Strategic capabilities are the capabilities of an organisation that contribute to its long-term survival or competitive advantage.

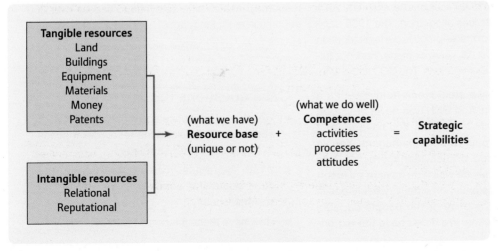

Figure 8.5
Resources, competences and capabilities

from other organisations; for this to work, it will develop a competence of identifying and working with suitable partners.

Management's task in internal analysis is to identify capabilities that customers value. At the *corporate level*, this could be the balance of activities that it undertakes – the product or service portfolio. Does it have sufficient capabilities in growing rather than declining markets? Are there useful synergies between the different lines of business? At the *divisional or strategic business unit level*, performance again depends on capabilities – adequate resources (physical, human, financial) and competences (such as in design or innovation).

A company may need to create new capabilities as the context changes – maybe to bring new products to the market more rapidly, or to develop alliances. These are **dynamic capabilities** – which enable it to renew and recreate itself. As described by Teece (2009) they include:

> the capacity (1) to sense and shape opportunities and threats, (2) to seize opportunities, and (3) to maintain competitiveness through enhancing, combining, protecting, and when necessary, reconfiguring the business enterprise's intangible and tangible assets. (p. 4)

These capabilities may be relatively formal, such as systems for sensing and responding to market opportunities or for identifying and acquiring firms with valuable skills or products. They may also be informal, such as the ability to reach decisions quickly when required, or the ability of staff to work well in constantly changing multi-professional teams.

Dynamic capabilities are an organisation's abilities to renew and recreate its strategic capabilities to meet the needs of a changing environment.

Case study   GKN – the case continues   www.gkn.com

One unexpected benefit of close, long-term links with the Japanese motor industry was that the driveline operation developed a cultural affinity with Japanese ways of working. This includes the concept of kaizen – continuous, incremental improvement in production processes.

> By the early 1980s GKN's drivelines operations had ingrained into their modus operandi a culture of continuous improvement [and] invested consistently in incremental improvements to both the joints themselves and their methods of manufacture (Lorenz, 2009, p. 231).

In 1995 the company decided to leave one significant part of its industrial services business (and by 2001 had left industrial services altogether). The 1995 decision was to dispose of the automotive parts distribution business, which, after 16 years of trying, had not fulfilled the company's expectations. The CEO at the time:

> Autoparts was like steel stock holding – it's a branch operation. And GKN was never any good at running branch operations. You have to do it by numbers through branch managers. You've got to have good branch managers . . . and reward them if they do well. You have to be monitoring them constantly, on a daily, weekly basis. We never had the drive or the people capable of running branches. We didn't have the experience, frankly. . .

Reflecting on the original decision to diversify, and to overestimate the company's ability to manage a different kind of business:

> Possibly we also had a slight delusion of grandeur. With the benefit of hindsight, that was a pretty bad mistake (Lorenz, 2009, pp. 281–2).

The company's website reports that it seeks to recruit talented individuals with the skills and energy to become leaders of the future. Each employee's role is related to the group strategy and the job purpose and its business context is explained. In 2015 it recruited over 100 graduates, and employed over 800 apprentices. GKN Academy, an online training resource, enables all employees to access over 360 courses in eight languages.

Sources: Lorenz (2009); GKN website.

Case questions 8.3

- Visit the GKN website and look for information about how it develops the resources it needs to deliver the current strategy.
- What examples have you seen in the case about the company's resources and competences?
- How have these interacted with strategy?

Value chain analysis

The concept of the **value chain**, introduced by Porter (1985), is derived from an accounting practice that calculates the value added at each stage of a manufacturing or service process. Porter applied this idea to the activities of the whole organisation, as an analysis of each activity could identify sources of competitive advantage.

Figure 8.6 shows primary and support activities. Primary activities transform inputs into outputs and deliver them to the customer:

- **inbound logistics**: receiving, storing and distributing inputs; also stock control etc;
- **operations**: transforming inputs into the product, by machining, mixing and packing;
- **outbound logistics**: storing and moving products to buyers:
- **marketing and sales**: activities to make customers aware of the product;
- **service**: enhancing or maintaining the product – installation, training, repairs.

These depend on four *support* activities:

- firm infrastructure – organisational structure, and planning, financial and quality systems;
- human resource management – recruitment, training and rewards;
- technology development – relate to inputs, operational processes, outputs; and
- procurement – acquiring materials and other resources.

Value chain analysis enables managers to consider which activities benefit customers, and which are troublesome – perhaps destroying value rather than creating it. It might, say, be good at marketing, outbound logistics and technology development – but poor at operations and human resource management. Managers can then consider which the business should do itself, and which it should outsource. Each activity can contribute to a firm's relative cost position and create a basis for differentiation (Porter, 1985) – the two main sources of competitive advantage. Analysing the value chain helps management to consider:

- Which activities have most effect on reducing cost or adding value? If customers value quality more than costs that implies a focus on quality of suppliers.
- What linkages do most to reduce costs, enhance value or discourage imitation?
- How do these linkages relate to cost and value drivers?

> A **value chain** 'divides a firm into the discrete activities it performs in designing, producing, marketing and distributing its product. It is the basic tool for diagnosing competitive advantage and finding ways to enhance it'. (Porter, 1985).

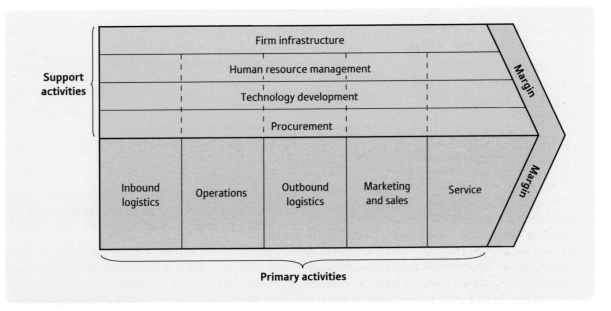

Figure 8.6 The value chain

Management in practice

Tough Science at Du Pont

In 2014 Ellen Kullman, chief executive at Du Pont, the largest US chemical company by market value, was continuing to reposition it as a 'science-based' business that can meet the needs of the 'growing global middle class': consumers in emerging economies who have rising demand for food, energy and security. The repositioning has included the $6.4 billion acquisition of a Danish enzyme technology company, and the $4.9 billion sale of its business making paints for cars and other industrial uses.

Ms Kullman said the strategy had been to shift to higher-margin and higher growth businesses where 'science makes a difference'. The company spends about 6 per cent of sales on Research and Development, ahead of competitors Dow and Monsanto. She acknowledges that 'science is tough' – but that being able to manage tough science is what gives the company a competitive advantage.

SWOT analysis

Strategy follows a 'fit' between internal capabilities and external changes – managers try to identify key issues from each and draw out the strategic implications. A SWOT analysis (see Chapter 6) summarises the internal and external issues and helps identify potentially useful developments – shown schematically in Figure 8.7.

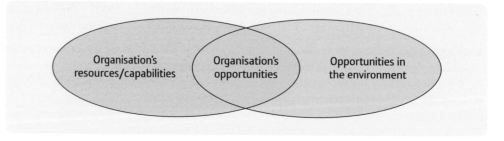

Figure 8.7
Identifying the organisation's opportunities

Hodgkinson et al. (2006) found that managers often use the technique in strategy workshops, though like any technique the value depends on how thoroughly they do so – by, for example, taking time to gather evidence about the relative significance of factors, rather than simply listing them.

If the SWOT analysis is done thoroughly, it is useful to managers as they develop and evaluate strategic alternatives, aiming to select those that make the most of internal strengths and external opportunities. Managers in large enterprises develop strategies at corporate, business and functional levels, though in smaller organisations there will be less complexity. Figure 8.8 shows this.

8.7 Making choices – deciding strategy at corporate level

At corporate level the strategy reflects the overall direction of the organisation, and the part which the respective business units will play. What is the overall mission and purpose? Should it focus on a small range of activities or diversify? Should it remain a local or national business, or seek to operate internationally? These decisions establish the direction of the organisation.

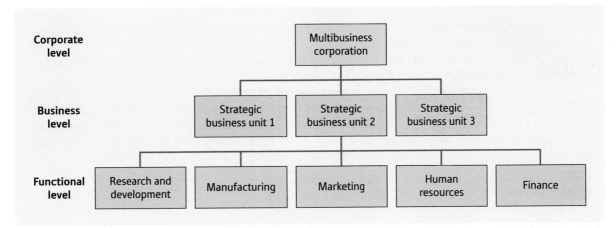

Figure 8.8 Levels of strategy

The corporate mission

A useful **mission statement** expresses the organisation's underlying beliefs and values, which staff can refer to. Some are more idealistic aspirations than guides to action, but if people see that senior managers respect the mission, they are more likely to do so – see 'Management in practice'.

> **A mission statement** is a broad statement of an organisation's scope and purpose, aiming to distinguish it from similar organisations.

Management in practice   **Examples of mission statements**

IKEA (www.ikea.com): "A better everyday life"
Google (www.google.com): "To organise the world's information"
Royal Society for the Protection of Birds (www.rspb.org.uk): "Saving nature"
Cancer Research UK (www.cancerresearchuk.org): "Together we will beat cancer"

Setting a strategic direction

Strategies can aim for growth, stability or renewal. Growth strategies try to expand the number of products offered or markets served. Stability is when the organisation offers the same products and services to much the same group of customers. Renewal often follows a period of trouble and involves significant changes to the business to secure the required turnaround.

Management in practice

BT takes aim at the mobile market   www.bt.com

In 2015 BT was seeking to re-establish a leading position in the UK mobile market. It had launched one of the UK's first networks in 1986, but sold that business in 2002, relying instead on networks provided by operators such as Vodafone. CEO Gavin Patterson wants to rebuild the company's mobile presence – and bought a majority stake in EE from Deutsche Telecom. That company was a willing seller, as it wanted to work with BT in a market where fixed and mobile telecoms are converging with TV and broadband.

Mr Patterson is described as being fiercely determined and with a ruthless eye on costs. But he is also credited with bringing an open-minded approach to a company with a risk-averse culture. Insiders say he delegates successfully, seeking opinions before making decisions and often passing on key tasks to independent teams, rather than 'micromanaging'.

Under the new approach BT will offer households TV, broadband, and fixed and mobile telecoms on a combined tariff – the so-called 'quad play' that is becoming popular in Europe. Analysts see the move as partly defensive, as offering an additional service strengthens customer loyalty. For mobile companies, the strategy raises the prospect of BT's strong telecoms brand offering disruptively low prices to entice customers to its premium broadband packages.

 Source: *Financial Times*, 1 April 2014, 26 November 2014, 5 February 2015.
© The Financial Times 2014, 2015. All Rights Reserved.

Managers can decide how to achieve their chosen option by using the product/market matrix, shown in Figure 8.9 They can achieve growth by focusing on one or more of the quadrants, stability by remaining with existing products and services and renewal by leaving some markets followed by entry into others.

Existing markets, existing product/service

Choice within this segment depends on whether the market is growing, mature, or in decline. Each box shows several possibilities:

- Market penetration aims to increase market share, which will be easier in a growing market. It could be achieved by reducing price, increasing advertising or improving distribution.
- Consolidation aims to protect the company's share in existing markets. This could mean improving efficiency and/or service. In declining markets it may mean acquiring competitors.
- Withdrawal adds value when competition is intense and the organisation cannot match rivals: staying in that line of business would destroy value, not create it.

	Existing products/services	New products/services
Existing markets	Market penetration Consolidation Withdrawal	Product/service development
New markets	Market development: • new territories • new segments • new uses	Diversification: • horizontal • vertical • unrelated

Figure 8.9
Strategy development directions – the product/market matrix

Source: As adapted in Johnson et al. (2014) from Chapter 6 of H. Ansoff (1988) *Corporate Strategy,* Penguin, London.

Existing markets, new products/services

A strategy of product or service development allows a company to retain the relative security of its present markets while altering products or developing new ones. In fashion, consumer electronics and financial services, companies continually change products to meet perceived changes in consumer preferences. Car manufacturers compete by adding features and extending their model range. Some new products, such as 'stakeholder pensions' in the United Kingdom, arise from government policy. Most new products fail commercially, so this is risky and costly.

New markets, existing products/services

Market development aims to find new outlets by:

- extending geographically – China's most rapidly growing smartphone maker is expanding aggressively into the Indian market;
- targeting new market segments (groups of customers, by age, income or lifestyle); or
- finding new uses for a product (a lightweight material developed for use in spacecraft is also used to make golf clubs).

Management in practice   P&G targets poorer customers   www.pg.com

Proctor & Gamble, the world's largest consumer goods company, has built its success on selling detergent, toothpaste and beauty products to the world's wealthiest 1bn consumers. Some years ago a new chief executive declared that from now on they would aim to serve all the world's consumers – poor as well as rich.

This surprised the company's staff as they did not have the product strategy or the cost structure to be effective in serving lower-income consumers. This began a significant transformation of the business, in which all the functions focus on meeting the needs of poorer consumers. For example, it now devotes 30 per cent of the annual research and development budget to low-income markets – which are expected to grow twice as fast as developed markets. The transformation has been evident in three areas:

- how the company finds out what customers want;
- how this affects R&D; and
- manufacturing facilities.

Source: Company website.

New markets, new products/services

Often described as diversification, this can take three forms:

- **Horizontal movement** Developing related or complementary activities, such as when mortgage lenders extend into the insurance business, using their knowledge of existing customers to offer an additional service. Kwik-Fit used its database of depot customers to create a motor insurance business.
- **Vertical integration** Moving backwards or forwards into activities related to the organisation's products and services. A manufacturer might decide to make its own components rather than buy them from elsewhere. Equally, it could develop forward into distribution.
- **Unrelated diversification** Developing into new markets outside the present industry. Virgin has used its strong brand to create complementary activities in sectors as diverse as airlines, media and banking. Amazon has diversified far beyond books and online retailing, into owning national newspapers, streaming videos and producing films.

These directions are not mutually exclusive: companies can follow several at the same time. Apple has moved very far from its origins as a computer manufacturer. One observer predicted, at the time of the iPad launch:

> Get on any train in five years' time, and people will be reading the newspaper (downloaded at home or automatically when they walk through Waterloo Station on the way home), books, watching TV, playing games (quite possibly with fellow passengers!) on their iPads.

8.8	Making choices – deciding strategy at business unit level

At the business unit level, firms face a choice about how to compete. Porter (1985) identified two types of competitive advantage: low cost or differentiation. From this he developed the idea that firms can use three generic strategies: cost leadership, differentiation and focus, which Figure 8.10 shows. The horizontal axis shows the two bases of competitive advantage. Competitive scope, on the vertical axis, shows whether a company's target market is broad or narrow.

Cost leadership

A **cost leadership** strategy is one in which a firm uses low price as the main competitive weapon.

Economies of scale are achieved when producing something in large quantities reduces the cost of each unit.

Cost leadership is when a firm aims to compete on price rather than, say, advanced features or excellent customer service. They will typically sell a standard product and try to minimise costs. This requires **economies of scale** in production and close attention to reducing operating costs – including the benefits of what is known as the experience curve – the tendency for the unit cost of making a product to fall as experience of making it increases. Low costs alone will not bring competitive advantage – consumers must see that the product represents value for money. Retailers that have used this strategy include Wal-Mart (Asda in the UK), Argos and Superdrug; Dell Computers is another example, as is Ryanair (Chapter 1 Case).

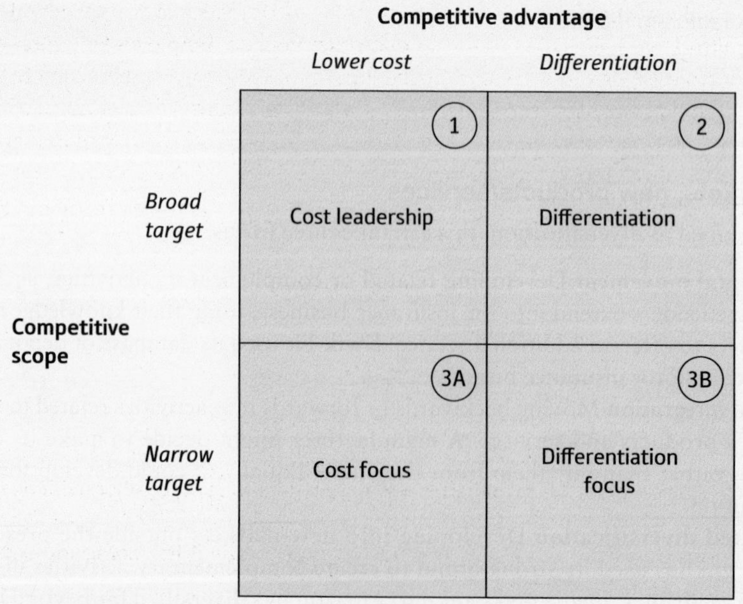

Figure 8.10
Generic competitive strategies

Source: Porter (1985), © 1985 Michael E Porter, reprinted with permission of The Free Press, a division of Simon & Schuster.

Differentiation

A **differentiation strategy** is seen when a company offers a service that is distinct from its competitors, and which customers value. It is 'something unique beyond simply offering a low price' (Porter, 1985) that allows firms to charge a high price or retain customer loyalty. Methods of differentiation include:

Differentiation strategy consists of offering a product or service that is perceived as unique or distinctive on a basis other than price.

- Apple offers innovation and an exceptional customer experience;
- Sony offers superior reliability, service and technology;
- BMW stresses a distinctive product/service image;
- Coca-Cola differentiates by building a widely recognised brand.

The focus of differentiation is unique to each sector: firms selling construction equipment will stress durability and rapid service, while in cosmetics differentiation relates to images of sophistication, exclusivity and eternal youth. Cities compete by stressing their cultural facilities, available land or superior transport links.

Focus

A **focus strategy** (sometimes called a 'niche' strategy) targets a narrow market segment, either by consumer group (teenagers, over-60s, doctors) or geography. The two variants – cost focus and differentiation focus – are simply narrow applications of the broad strategies. Examples include:

A focus strategy is when a company competes by targeting very specific segments of the market.

- Saga (www.saga.co.uk) offers travel and insurance for those over 50;
- Croda (www.croda.com) produces speciality chemicals used in other products, including cosmetics;
- NFU Mutual (www.nfumutual.co.uk)offers insurance for farmers.

Management in practice   Strategic focus at Maersk   www.maersk.com

I think because of the size of our organisation now, our strategy is really targeted to focus on certain segments. One of the things we did this year was start a brand new service from Costa Rica to the UK, specifically bringing in bananas. That was a new service for us and provided a different service for the customer. They've always been shipped in bulk vessels, and now we've containerised them. Once the customer has committed, we have small teams of customer service people looking after each one, all over the world.

Once we've locked them into the customer experience, we then want to build a long-term relationship with them, get to know the business, get to know where we can improve it. Not just on service but also from a cost point of view, because obviously cost is very important in this market. So we like to go into partnerships. Some of the biggest retailers in the UK for instance we have long-term relationships with, where we've been able to take a lot of costs out of their supply chain by giving them a personalised service by actually knowing their business.

Source: Interview with Brian Godsafe, Customer Services Manager.

Activity 8.5   Critical reflection on strategy

- Select two companies you are familiar with, and in each case gather evidence to help you decide which generic strategy they are following.
- Then consider what features you would expect to see if the company decided to follow the opposite strategy.

Porter initially suggested that firms had to choose between cost leadership and differentiation. Many disagreed, observing how companies often appeared to follow both strategies at the same time. By controlling costs, companies can reinvest the savings in features that differentiate them. Porter (1994) later clarified his view:

> Every strategy must consider both relative cost and relative differentiation . . . a company cannot completely ignore quality and differentiation in the pursuit of cost advantage, and vice versa . . . Progress can be made against both types of advantage simultaneously.' (p. 271)

However, he notes there are trade-offs between them and that companies should 'maintain a clear commitment to superiority in one of them'.

Functional level strategy

Business level strategies need the support of suitable functional level strategies – Chapters 9 (marketing), 11 (human resources) and 12 (information systems) give examples.

8.9   Making things happen – delivering strategy

Organisations deliver their strategies using internal development, acquisition, or alliance – or a combination: the choice affects the success of the strategy.

Internal development

The organisation delivers the strategy by expanding or redeploying relevant resources that it has or can employ. This enables managers to retain control of all aspects of the development of new products or services – especially where the product has technologically advanced features. Microsoft develops its Windows operating system in-house. Wanda, China's biggest property developer by sales, aims to triple its annual turnover by 2020 (compared with 2014), by international property development. Their ambition is to turn the brand, very well-known in China and Asia, into a global brand. One of its moves has been to buy a site in London, where it plans to build 440 homes and a hotel.

Merger and acquisition

One firm merging with, or acquiring, another allows rapid entry into new product or market areas and is a quick way to build market share. It is also used where the acquiring company can use the other company's products to offer new services or enter new markets: Microsoft and Cisco Systems frequently buy small, entrepreneurial companies and incorporate their products within the acquiring company's range. In 2013 accountancy firm PwC bought consultancy firm Booz and Company, so that it could quickly build an advisory capacity – a rapidly growing and profitable business. Shell bought BG in 2015 to gain access to the smaller company's oil and gas reserves.

Mergers and acquisitions frequently fail, destroying rather than adding value. When Sir Roy Gardner took over as chairman of Compass (a UK catering company) at which profits and the share price had fallen rapidly, he was critical of the previous management:

> (They) concentrated far too much on growing the business through acquisition. They should have stopped and made sure (that) what they had acquired delivered the expected results. Compass was being run by its divisional mangers, which resulted in a total lack of consistency. (*Financial Times,* 19 January 2007, p. 19)

Case study   GKN – the case continues   www.gkn.com

Since the early 1990s the company had been build-ing a presence in aerospace, from an earlier invest-ment in Westland helicopters. Kevin Smith had joined the company in 1999 as head of the aero-space division and began to integrate a disparate group of companies and facilities. He had worked in the aircraft industry and knew Boeing managers well, soon learning they were about to outsource a large fabrication plant. Smith saw this as a major opportunity – but the board had banned further aerospace purchases. Smith persuaded them to lift the ban, bought the plant and persuaded Boeing to appoint GKN as a preferred supplier of aerostruc-tures – such as wings and fuselages (Lorenz, 2009, p. 315).

This meant that GKN now had a significant pres-ence in US military aerospace, and in 2012 it bought Volvo's aero-engine unit. Mr Stein, by then GKN's CEO, said the deal meant that GKN components would be fitted in engines made by all three main aero-engine companies (General Electric, Pratt and Whitney and Rolls-Royce). His ambition is to expand the aerospace part of the business: in 2015 the division accounted for 30 per cent of group turnover, and in that year the company bought Fokker Technol-ogies, which makes light aerostructures and electrical wiring systems.

It had earlier completed the purchase of Stromag, which makes components such as electromag-netic brakes and hydraulic clutches, and of Getrag Driveline, which supplies all-wheel drive transmis-sion systems. Chief executive Nigel Stein said that both high-margin businesses had been successfully integrated into the Driveline division and had already made a positive contribution.

Sources: Lorenz (2009); group website, *Financial Times*, 19 April 2012, 6 July 2012, 29 July 2015.

Case questions 8.4

- Review the other instalments of the case and list the ways it GKN has chosen to deliver strat-egy against each of the headings in this section.
- Combine your results with the work you have done on Activity 8.6.

Joint ventures and alliances

An attraction of joint ventures is that they limit risk. In early 2015 China's largest ship-builder announced it would build the country's first cruise vessels, which will be a new market for the company. It is doing so in a joint venture with cruise-ship operator Carnival, which will contribute its expertise in that market.

A second reason for joint ventures (JVs) is to learn about new technologies or markets. Alliances also arise where governments want to keep sensitive sectors, such as aerospace, defence and aviation, under national control. Airbus, which competes with Boeing in air-craft manufacture, was originally a JV between French, German, British and Spanish manu-facturers. Alliances – such as the Star Alliance led by United Airlines of the United States and Lufthansa of Germany – are common in the airline industry, where companies share revenues and costs over certain routes. As governments often prevent foreign ownership of airlines, such alliances avoid that barrier.

Other forms of joint development include franchising (common in retailing – such as Ikea), licensing and long-term collaboration with suppliers.

Alliances and partnership working have also become commonplace in the public sector. In many cities alliances or partnerships have been created between major public bodies, businesses and community interests. Their main purpose is to foster a coherent approach to planning and delivering services. Public bodies often act as service commissioners rather than as direct providers, developing partnerships with organisations to deliver services on their behalf.

> ### Activity 8.6 — Critical reflection on delivering strategy
>
> - Select two companies you are familiar with, and in each case gather evidence to help you decide which of the available options (or a combination) they have chosen to deliver their strategy.
> - What are the advantages of the route they have chosen compared to the alternatives?
> - Compare your evidence with other students on your course, and identify any common themes.

8.10 — Making revisions – implementing and evaluating

Implementation turns strategy into action, moving from corporate to operational levels. Many strategies fail to be implemented, or fail to achieve as much as management expected. A common mistake is to assume that formulating a strategy will lead to painless implementation. Sometimes there is an 'implementation deficit', when strategies are not implemented at all, or are only partially successful. The 'Key ideas' feature reports on recent research that offers valuable insights into why this can happen.

Key ideas — Why do companies fail to implement?

Sull et al. (2015) noted other research that over two thirds of large organisations struggle to implement their strategies, either in whole or in part. A survey of almost 8,000 managers in over 260 companies showed this was indeed the case, and also uncovered five possible reasons:

- **Poor horizontal coordination:** Middle managers frequently reported that the main obstacle they had experienced in implementing the strategy was that of securing the cooperation of colleagues in other departments or units.
- **Slow to reallocate resources:** Circumstances frequently change between planning and implementation, to the extent that adding value depends on changing the resource allocations in the strategy. Companies were frequently too slow to do this.
- **Too much top-down communication:** Half of middle managers interviewed could not recall one of their firm's strategic priorities: the authors found that senior managers relied on one-way, top-down communication – which does not bring understanding.
- **Inappropriate incentives distort implementation:** Rewarding performance alone (in the sense of meeting financial targets) can undermine other valuable aspects of performance, such as agility, responsiveness, flexibility and teamwork.
- **Too much top-down implementation:** Implementing a new strategy depends on countless informed decisions and actions at all levels – made by 'distributed leaders' in line and staff departments, acting intelligently in the light of local circumstances. This is impeded if senior managers interfere.

The authors overriding message is that rather than seeing implementation as being the unwavering implementation of a strategy agreed at the top, managers should instead see it as an opportunity to seize opportunities that align with strategy, while also coordinating with other parts of the organisation.

Source: Based on Sull et al. (2015).

Evaluate results

Managers, shareholders (current and potential) and financial analysts routinely compare a company's performance with its published plans. Only by tracking results can these and other interested parties decide if performance is in line with expectations or if the company needs to take some corrective action. Many targets focus on financial and other quantitative aspects of performance, such as sales, operating costs and profit.

Although monitoring is shown as the last stage in the strategy model, it is not the end of the process. This is continuous as organisations adjust to changes in their business environment. Regular monitoring alerts management to the possibility that they will miss a target unless they make some operational changes. Equally, and in conjunction with continuous scanning of the external environment, performance monitoring can prompt wider changes to the organisation's corporate and competitive strategies.

8.11	**Integrating themes**

Entrepreneurship

Strategic change in public organisations provides opportunities for private entrepreneurs. The National Health Service continues to have difficulty in achieving the standards of care expected within available budgets, and sometimes decides to outsource services. One such provider is Circle (www.circlehealth.co.uk). This is a private company founded in 2004, in which just under half of the shares are owned by the clinicians and staff who work there, with the remainder owned by private investors.

Circle's management believes its ability to take on the challenge of improving hospitals' performance is due in part to its ownership structure, which incentivises staff through a share-ownership scheme. One senior manager said:

> Without this model of ownership we couldn't do what we are doing. We brought in employee engagement and entrepreneurial drive. We empowered people to feel they could conquer the world and run the hospital. Companies do need capital, but you also need employee engagement. (*Financial Times,* 3 July 2012)

The company runs several day-surgery units within NHS hospitals, and has built a privately-funded hospital in Bath. Further expansion is planned, following a successful effort to raise additional funds from investors. In 2015 the company withdrew from a contract to run Hinchingbrooke Hospital in Cambridge. The reasons were complex, but the company believed that while it had improved patient care (recognised by several awards), maintaining this would require investment beyond what it was able to provide.

Sustainability

If managers are to enhance the sustainability of their activities, they need to ensure it becomes part of their strategic discussions. A perspective that can help to clarify the issue was suggested by Vogel (2005), namely that while advocates of corporate responsibility (in this context, sustainability) are genuinely motivated by a commitment to social goals, it is only sustainable if 'virtue pays off'. Responsible action is both made possible and constrained by market forces.

Virtuous behaviour can make business sense for some firms in some areas in some circumstances, but does not in itself ensure commercial success. Companies who base their strategy on acting responsibly may be commercially successful, but equally they may fail – responsible behaviour carries the same risks as any other kind of business behaviour. While some consumers or investors will give their business to companies that appear to be acting responsibly, others will not. Some customers place a higher priority on price, appearance or any other feature than they do on whether goods are produced and delivered in a sustainable way. As Vogel (2005) observes:

> There *is* a place in the market economy for responsible firms. But there is also a large place for their less responsible competitors. (p. 3)

While some companies can benefit from a strategy based on acting responsibly, market forces alone cannot prevent others from having a less responsible strategy, and profiting from doing so.

Internationalisation

As the business world becomes ever more international, companies inevitably face difficult strategic choices about the extent to which they develop an international presence, and the way in which they develop their international strategy. The nature of the challenge is shown by the fact that while many companies have done very well from international expansions, many overseas ventures fail, destroying value rather than creating it.

Chapter 4 outlined the nature of the challenges faced as companies respond to what they perceive to be international opportunities. They need, for example, to deal with complex structural and logistical issues when products are made and sold in several countries, ensure that there are adequate links between research, marketing and production to speed the introduction of new products, and facilitate the rapid transfer of knowledge and ideas between the national components of the business. These are complex enough issues in themselves, but the extra dimension is that solutions that work in one national context may not work as well in another. Differences in national culture mean that people will respond in perhaps unexpected ways to strategies and plans, especially if these are perceived in some way to be inconsistent with the local culture (as the examples cited in Chapter 4 testify).

The content of an international strategy will be shaped by the process of its production – and the extent to which different players in the global enterprise take part in it.

Governance

Pye (2002) sees a close link between what she terms the process of governing and strategising. Having conducted long-term research with the boards of several large companies she notes:

i. in 1987–89, no one talked of corporate governance, whereas now most contributors raise this subject of their own volition, implying greater awareness of and sensitivity to such issues; and

ii. relationships with major shareholders have changed considerably across the decade and directors now see accounting for their *strategic direction* as crucial in this context. (p. 154, emphasis added).

She distinguished between governance and governing:

> Corporate governance is often identified through indicators such as board composition, committee structure, executive compensation schemes, and risk assessment procedures etc, which offer a snapshot view of governance practice, rather than the dynamic process of governing. To explore governing, i.e. how governance is enacted, means unravelling the complex network of relationships amongst [the board] *as well as* relationships with 'outsiders' who observe [the board's governance]. (p. 156)

She refers to strategising as the process by which directors go about deciding the strategic direction of the organisation, though this is primarily shaped by the executive directors. She found that almost all directors agreed that what is crucial is not so much the words on paper as the process of dialogue and debate by which those words are created – the strategising process is more important than the final document.

Summary

1 **Explain the significance of managing strategy and show how the issues vary between sectors**
   - Strategy is about the survival of the enterprise; the strategy process sets an overall direction with information about the external environment and internal capabilities. Defining the purposes of the organisation helps to guide the choice and implementation of strategy.

2 **Compare planning, learning and political perspectives on the strategy process**
   - The planning approach is appropriate in stable and predictable environments; while the emergent approach more accurately describes the process in volatile environments, since strategy rarely unfolds as intended in complex, changing and ambiguous situations. A political perspective may be a more accurate way of representing the process when it involves the interests of powerful stakeholders. It is rarely an objectively rational activity, implying that strategy models are not prescriptive but rather frameworks for guidance.

3 **Summarise evidence on how managers develop strategies**
   - The evidence is accumulating that companies in turbulent environments follow a strategy process that is relatively informal, with shorter planning meetings and greater responsibility placed on line managers to develop strategy rather than on specialist planners.
   - Formulating strategy and designing the organisation appear to be done as closely linked practical activities.
   - Sull uses the 'strategy loop' to describe how managers continually develop and renew their strategy.

4 **Explain the tools for external and internal analysis during work on strategy**
   - External analysis can use Porter's five forces model and the PESTEL framework to identify relevant factors.
   - Internally, managers can use the value chain to analyse their current organisation.

The two sets of information can be combined in a SWOT diagram.

5 **Use the product/market matrix to compare corporate-level strategies**
   - Strategy can focus on existing or new products, and existing or new markets. This gives four broad directions, with options in each – such as market penetration, product development, market development or diversification.

6 **Use the concept of generic strategies to compare business-level strategies**
   - Strategic choices are cost leader, differentiation or a focus on a narrow market segment.

7 **Give examples of alternative methods of delivering a strategy**
   - Strategy can be delivered by internal (sometimes called organic) development by rearranging the way resources are deployed. Alternatives include acquiring or merging with another company, or by forming alliances and joint ventures.

8 **Outline evidence on the effects of having clear goals for strategy workshops, and understand how you can use this to develop your skill of setting clear goals**

- Goal-setting theory predicts that having clear goals affects the outcomes of a task, research on strategy workshops confirms this and the chapter offers an opportunity to develop the skill of setting clear goals.

9 **Show how ideas from the chapter add to your understanding of the integrating themes**

- Since entrepreneurs typically lack the resources they need, a common solution is to form alliances with other businesses.
- Sustainable performance in the environmental sense only works in the economic sense if it is part of the organisation's strategy: i.e., that it makes business sense as well as environmental sense. There are many examples of companies that have done this.
- International expansion and diversification strategies often fail, probably when managers underestimate the complexity of overseas operations.
- Pye (2002) found that directors were more likely to be taking responsibility for strategic direction of the business as well as for their narrower governance responsibilities – emphasising the benefits of the process as much as the final outcomes.

Test your understanding

1 Why do managers develop strategies for their organisation?

2 How does the planning view of strategy differ from the learning and political views respectively?

3 Describe what recent research shows about how managers develop strategy.

4 Draw Sull's strategy loop, and explain each of the elements.

5 Discuss with a manager from an organisation how his or her organisation developed its present strategy. Compare this practice with the ideas in the chapter. What conclusions do you draw?

6 What are the main steps to take in analysing the organisation's environment? Why is it necessary to do this?

7 Describe each stage in value chain analysis and illustrate them with an example. Why is the model useful to management?

8 The chapter described three generic strategies that organisations can follow. Give examples of three companies each following one of these strategies.

9 Give examples of company strategies corresponding to each box in the product/market matrix.

10 What are the main ways to deliver strategy?

11 Summarise an idea from the chapter that adds to your understanding of the integrating themes.

Think critically

Think about the way your organisation, or one with which you are familiar, develops and implements strategy. Then record your responses to these questions:

- What examples of the issues discussed in this chapter are currently relevant to your organisation – such as whether to follow a differentiation or focus strategy?

- In responding to these issues, what **assumptions** about the strategy process appear to have guided people? Are the goals of the strategy clearly stated, and widely known?

- What factors such as history or **context** may have influenced prevailing views about how to create strategy? Do you agree with this interpretation?

- Have people put forward **alternative** strategies, or alternative ways of developing strategy, based on evidence about other companies? Have they made the goals of their proposal clear?

- What **limitations** can you see in any of the ideas presented here? Can you envisage a situation in which clear spending time setting clear goals may not be worthwhile?

Develop a skill – setting clear goals

Setting clear goals is an essential management skill, and practising how to do this should help you while studying, and in later life.

- **Assessment:** Assess how well you set goals for a task. Do you routinely spend time clarifying the goals (objectives) of a task? Can you express them quickly if someone asks? Do you ever waste time by doing tasks that are not relevant to the goal?

- **Learning:** Section 8.4 introduced the way managers develop strategy, including strategy workshops. Read that section again, paying special attention to the 'Key ideas' (p. 248) which shows the value of setting clear goals. Also read Section 6.5 on setting goals, especially the sub-section 'criteria for assessing goals' (p. 195), which describes the SMART technique, and the 'Key ideas' feature (p. 196) on goal-setting theory. What are the likely effects of clear goals?

- **Analysis:** Do you have experience of working (on any task) with unclear goals (or with clear ones)? How did either condition affect the outcome? How do you distinguish a clear goal from an unclear one?

- **Practice:** Identify a task that you need to complete soon, such as an essay, report or group presentation. Use the SMART technique to set intermediate goals for what you want to achieve within, say, the next week. These could include three or four goals, such as identify topic, identify relevant literature, complete part of literature review, begin to plan data collection, and so on. Note each goal you want to achieve, and use the SMART technique to sharpen and clarify each of them.

  - Complete the task, bearing in mind your goals.

  - When you have completed the task, review whether you have achieved your goals.

  Also review how you worked, and whether the SMART goals you set helped you. Reflect on what you have learned, preferably sharing any insights with others on your course.

- **Application:** Decide on another opportunity to revise your approach and practise this skill again on the next stage of your work, or on another task.

Read more

Gaul, G. M. (2015), *Billion-Dollar Ball: A journey through the big-money culture of college football,* Viking, New York.

A well-researched account of the huge business of American college football – how it lobbies successfully to retain generous tax breaks, and how independent the teams are of their colleges.

Healey, M. P., Hodgkinson, G. P., Whittington, R. and Johnson, G. (2015), 'Off to plan or out to lunch? Relationships between design characteristics and outcomes of strategy workshops', *British Journal of Management,* vol. 26, no. 3, pp. 507–28.

An empirical study of the design and outcomes of strategy workshops, whose lessons apply to most types of management workshops and activities in which you are likely to become involved.

Hensmans, M., Johnson, G. and Yip, G. (2012), *Strategic Transformation: Changing While Winning,* Palgrave Macmillan, Basingstoke.

Uses extensive empirical data from three UK companies to find clues to their success.

Lorenz, A. (2009), *GKN: The Making of a Business,* Wiley, Chichester.

An account of how the company evolved over more than 250 years, with many examples of strategic decisions along the way.

Rumelt, R. P. (2011), *Good Strategy/Bad Strategy: The difference and why it matters,* Profile, London.

Described by a reviewer as the most interesting business book of 2011, the author stresses that the essence of strategy is to think carefully about business problems, to discover 'what is going on here', using tools described in this chapter.

Go online

These websites have appeared in the chapter:

www.gkn.com
www.ikea.com
www.pg.com
www.maersk.com
www.circlehealth.co.uk
www.easyJet.com
www.rb.com
www.lloydsbankinggroup.com
www.bt.com
www.tjmorris.co.uk

Visit two of these sites, or any other company that interests you, and navigate to the pages dealing with news or investor relations.

- What are the main strategic issues they seem to be facing?
- What information can you find about their policies?

CHAPTER 9
MANAGING MARKETING

Aims

To explain how marketing can add value, and to introduce some marketing techniques.

Objectives

By the end of your work on this chapter you should be able to outline the concepts below in your own terms and:

1 Define marketing and explain how it can add value in organisations of all kinds

2 Explain the importance of understanding customers and markets, and the sources of marketing information

3 Illustrate the practices of segmenting markets and targeting customer groups

4 Explain the meaning and significance of customer relationship management

5 Compare a marketing orientation with other orientations and explain its significance

6 Describe the components of the marketing mix

7 Explain the stages of the product life cycle

8 Explain the idea of market segments, and understand how you can use this to develop the skill of identifying customer needs

9 Show how ideas from the chapter add to your understanding of the integrating themes

Key terms

This chapter introduces the following ideas:

marketing
customer
customer satisfaction
needs
wants
demands
market offer
exchange
transaction
marketing information system
marketing

marketing environment
market segmentation
target market
customer relationship marketing
 (CRM)
marketing orientation
consumer-centred organisation
marketing mix
brand
product life cycle

Each is a term defined within the text, as well as in the glossary at the end of the book.

Case study

Manchester United FC   www.manutd.com

With over 50 million fans across the globe, Manchester United Football Club (MU) is one of the best-known soccer clubs. Founded in 1878, it rose to prominence in the early 1950s. Since then the club has never been out of the sports headlines, hiring a series of almost legendary managers (including Sir Matt Busby and, from 1986 to 2013, Sir Alex Ferguson) and buying or developing world-recognised players (including David Beckham, Ryan Giggs and Wayne Rooney).

Revenue comes almost equally from ticket sales, broadcasting rights and commercial activities. Some revenues are evidently football-related businesses (tickets, TV rights and sports clothes), while others relate to the 'MU brand' (mobiles, travel, financial services). In 2015 the club signed a ten-year kit deal with Adidas and began several joint ventures, including one with 20th Century Fox to help promote the film *Deadpool*.

In May 2005 American sports tycoon Malcolm Glazer bought the club for £790 million in a deal that was heavily financed by debt. Some fans object to this, believing that high-interest payments on the debt have prevented the club from spending more on new players. In 2012 the company's debt was £459 million, and to reduce it the Glazer family sold 16.7 million shares in the club to the public at $14 each. These shares are unlikely to pay dividends, and carry few voting rights: the Glazer family still control the club. *Forbes* magazine ranked it as the world's wealthiest club, valuing it $1870 million, well ahead of nearest rivals Real Madrid and Arsenal.

Manchester United Football Club (MU) is only a part of the worldwide operations. The holding company (Manchester United PLC) owns MU, Manchester United Catering and Manchester United Interactive. MUTV, the club's official channel, is a joint venture between Manchester United PLC, Granada and BSkyB.

The Club's ambition is to be the most successful team in football. Its business strategy is to do this by having the football and commercial operations work hand-in-hand, both in the UK and in the potential markets represented by the Club's global fan base, especially Asia. The marketing strategy is built on maintaining success on the field and building global brand awareness through new products

© Action Plus Sports Images/Alamy Images

and partnered services designed to appeal to MU's worldwide fans. Nike is a substantial partner who uses its marketing channels to generate new value from the MU trademarks by supplying replica kits (for example) to the millions of MU fans in the UK and Asia.

MU attempts to control and develop its own routes to market for media rights (for example, MUTV), thereby exploiting the club's own performance and reputation rather than relying on the collective appeal of competition football. The management believes this enhances the ability to deliver branded services to customers anywhere in the world. They rely strongly on IT-based CRM (customer relationship management) technology to convert fans to customers.

Sources: Based on material from Butterworth Heinemann Case 0181, "Manchester United and British Soccer: Beautiful Game, Brutal Industry;" *Financial Times* 17 April 2012, 30 April 2012, 24 October 2012, 9 May 2013, 12 February 2016.

Case questions 9.1

- Consider the marketing implications of MU's activities. What is it offering to customers?
- What groups would MU see as competitors? Are they simply other successful football clubs?
- What distinctive challenges do you think may arise in marketing a football club?

9.1   Introduction

Manchester United (MU) depends on good marketing to ensure the continued loyalty and support of its customers – who seek different things. An MU football fan might buy a season ticket to fulfil a psychological need as part of a group with a common purpose; someone with no interest in football might use an MU mobile phone because they trust a product backed by the MU reputation. Someone who buys a replica MU jersey is making a statement about their personality, and is not sensitive to price: they pay up to £40 for something that costs a fraction of that to supply.

How should the company manage the brand in these often-unrelated markets? How best to understand the needs of different stakeholders – owners, managers, players, fans, sponsors, broadcasters? How to manage relationships with customers to ensure long-term loyalty – even if the club does badly on the field? How to present its goods and services to earn as much as it can?

All organisations face the challenge of understanding what customers want, and of meeting their expectations. Successful firms often place marketing at the heart of strategy. Ikea found and refined a formula that appeals to its target market, growing in 40 years from a single

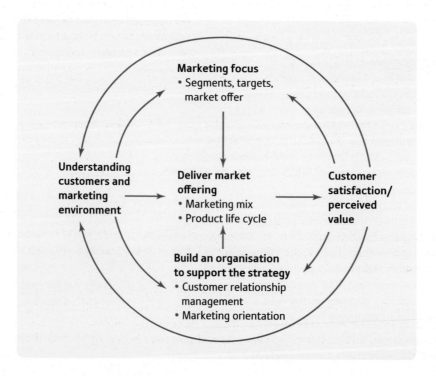

Figure 9.1 An overview of the chapter

store to an international brand. Virgin has done the same – like MU, offering a wide range of products to a global market. Successful not-for-profit organisations such as the Eden Project demonstrate the benefits of engaging with customers. All need to give value for money, by understanding customers' needs – which is the focus of this chapter's 'Develop a skill' feature.

The chapter clarifies 'marketing' and shows how it can add value to resources. It explains how marketers try to understand customers, the marketing environment, and to distinguish market segments. It explains the 'marketing mix' and 'product life cycle' ideas, before showing how managers try to develop close customer relations and build a marketing orientation. Figure 9.1 gives an overview.

9.2   Understanding customers and markets

We are all familiar with the techniques of advertising and selling, when companies:

- distribute brochures;
- offer promotional prices;
- sponsor television programmes;
- persuade celebrities to endorse their products; or
- send advertisements to mobiles.

These selling techniques are only the most visible part of a wider **marketing** process, through which organisations aim to identify and satisfy customer needs in a way that brings value to both parties. This depends on skills in researching customers and markets, designing products, setting prices, communicating the offer, ensuring delivery and evaluating responses. These activities bring marketing staff into contact with most parts of their organisation.

> **Marketing** is the process by which organisations create value for customers, to receive value from them in return.

The underlying idea is that if managers understand what current and potential **customers** value, they can develop products that ensure **customer satisfaction**. In commercial businesses this means customers are willing to pay a price that earns the company a profit. In public or not-for-profit organisations it means they are willing to make donations, use the service or otherwise support it. Managers can then secure the resources they need to maintain and grow the enterprise. Those who neglect marketing will not understand their customers, will not satisfy them and will have trouble securing resources. Organisations fail when staff do what they prefer, not what customers or service-users expect. Kotler et al. (2008) describe marketing as:

> **Customers** are individuals, households, organisations, institutions, resellers and governments that purchase products from other organisations.

> **Customer satisfaction** is the extent to which a customer perceives that a product matches their expectations.

> the homework which managers undertake to assess needs, measure their extent and intensity and determine whether a profitable opportunity exists. Marketing continues throughout the product's life, trying to find new customers and keep current customers by improving product appeal and performance, learning from product sales results and managing repeat performance (pp. 6–7).

Peter Drucker (1985) places the activity even more firmly at the centre of business:

> Because the purpose of business is to create and keep customers, it has only two central functions – marketing and innovation. The basic function of marketing is to attract and retain customers at a profit.

While many organisations have a designated 'Marketing Department', people throughout the enterprise can contribute by, for example, telling marketing staff what customers think of the product, or about competitors' activities. The more that employees understand what customers want, and the more that systems and processes help staff to meet those expectations, the more they will satisfy them.

Managers in any organisation can use marketing to increase the value they offer. Local government services such as libraries, museums or concert halls routinely survey samples of users about their satisfaction with services, and to assess likely demand for new ones. Mining companies such as Rio Tinto Zinc claim part of their skill is in matching ores to the right buyers. Iron ore has many variations in mineral content and purity, so by blending output from various mines the company tries to maximise the value of the ore. Speaking to investors, Sam Walsh, chief executive, said: 'Our marketing teams work very closely with our operations, so that [how we manage the mines] is fully aligned to the market' (*Financial Times*, 2 December 2014).

Management in practice — Marketing in the voluntary sector

Staff and volunteers in charities are sometimes uncomfortable with the idea that they are in marketing – preferring to see themselves as helpers or carers. Yet

. . . donors, local authorities, opinion formers, the media, all have the choice of whether or not to support a charity . . . They make up the markets within which the charity operates. Without knowledge and understanding of those markets, the charity . . . will fail . . . By knowing themselves and their mission, and by knowing the markets they . . . serve or work in, charities can match their activities to external needs and make sure that they achieve as much as possible for their beneficiaries. (p. 2)

The Part 5 Case is about the British Heart Foundation (**www.bhf.org.uk**), and shows the significance of marketing to a successful charity.

Source: Keaveney and Kaufmann (2001).

Customer needs, wants and demands

Needs are states of felt deprivation, reflecting biological and social influences.

Psychologists have developed theories of human **needs** – states of felt deprivation – that people try to satisfy. Chapter 15 presents several such theories (Maslow, 1970; McClelland, 1961), which identify needs ranging from basic necessities to those that are intangible – knowledge, achievement or public image. People vary in the strength of their needs – some are content to satisfy basic needs while others, once those are satisfied, seek opportunities to satisfy other needs – such as physical or intellectual challenge.

Wants are the form that human needs take as they are shaped by local culture and individual personality.

Wants are the form that human needs take, shaped by the person's personality and the culture in which they live. Everyone needs food, but satisfy the need in many ways – enabling the food industry to prosper by offering many varieties of basic products. A growing number of people want coffee 'on the go', which is attracting many new entrants to the sector: 'Wherever you go, specialist chains, fast-food operators, pubs, we're all offering coffee because customers want it' (chief executive of a fast-food operator, private communication).

Demands are human wants backed by the ability to buy.

People have limited resources, so needs and wants only become relevant to a supplier when the person can pay – when a want becomes a **demand**. Given their needs, wants and resources, people demand products to satisfy them. The better an enterprise understands these through customer research, the easier it will be to create an attractive market offering.

The market offer – products, services and experiences

A **market offer** is the combination of products, services, information or experiences that an enterprise offers to a market to satisfy a need or want.

Information about customers' wants and demands helps companies to develop a **market offer** – a combination of products, services and experiences they hope will satisfy them. While the features of a physical product are part of the value, service and experience also affect this: how staff treat the customer, their ability to answer questions, the quality of after-sales service. The experience of using the product also matters – both the thing itself (good to use?), and how others react (does it boost your image?). Effective marketers look beyond the product's attributes, aiming to create brands that mean something significant to customers, which they are willing to pay for.

Exchanges and transactions

People aim to satisfy needs and wants through **exchange** – the act of obtaining a desired object from someone by offering something in return. This process is at the core of many human activities: it only happens if both parties can offer something of value to the other, and if they can communicate this. Mutual agreement leads to a **transaction** in which they exchange things of value at a specified time and place. Countless transactions take place without further contact between buyer and seller – buying a newspaper or petrol during a journey. Some marketers are content if they sell enough to meet financial or other targets. Others aim to understand customers' needs and build long-term business relationships. Section 9.4 has more on this.

These transactions take place in a **market**, which in business usually means actual and potential customers with similar needs.

> **Exchange** is the act of obtaining a desired object from someone by offering something in return.
>
> A **transaction** occurs when two parties exchange things of value to each at a specified time and place.
>
> A **market** consists of all the actual and potential customers with similar needs.

9.3	The marketing environment

Marketers spend time and money identifying trends and events in the **marketing environment** that may influence consumer demands. Figure 3.1 (**Chapter 3**) showed the dimensions in the macro- and micro-environments respectively, partially repeated here as Figure 9.2.

> The **marketing environment** consists of the actors and forces outside marketing that affect the marketing manager's ability to develop and maintain successful relationships with its target consumers.

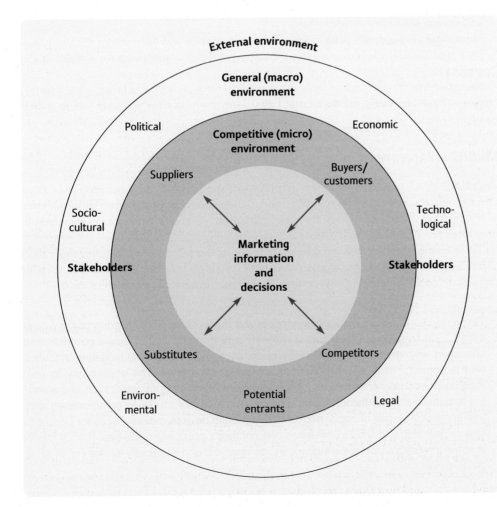

Figure 9.2
The marketing environment

Micro-environment

Each organisation has a unique competitive (micro) environment that managers can influence, in part through their marketing.

- **The company:** In developing a marketing plan, managers work closely with other units in their internal environment – R&D, finance, operations. These are all potential sources of marketing ideas, and it is through them that the company delivers.
- **Suppliers:** These provide many of the resources the company needs, so the quality of their work affects what it delivers.
- **Competitors:** Companies track what competitors offer, and try to distinguish themselves in a way that customers value. Apple, Samsung and other consumer electronics firms keep a close watch on competitor moves.
- **Customers:** The definition listed six broad types, and there is great diversity within each. This chapter focuses on individual and household consumers, especially the factors influencing what they decide to buy.
- **Substitutes:** E-cigarettes offer customers an alternative way of meeting the need they have traditionally met from cigarettes; watching TV is a substitute for a night at the cinema.
- **Potential entrants:** Uber, the innovative taxi operator, is active in large, often capital, cities. Taxi operators in other large cities wait anxiously for news on where it will open next.

Macro-environment

The macro-environment is similar for all players in an industry (consumer protection laws affect all businesses more or less equally), and organisations have little direct influence over it. It may have great significance for their marketing – Table 9.1 takes just one example from each PESTEL factor to illustrate the possible link.

Technological innovations are significant for marketers. People are spending more time on the internet, mobile services and video games than on traditional media (print, radio and scheduled TV), changing how companies communicate with customers. Kumar (2015) observed:

> The wide use of social media has encouraged many companies to advertise in social media, and to promote their brand through viral content, social media contests and consumer engagement efforts. Social media sites enable business to gather statistics on the impact, reach and progress of a product or service. The opportunity to gain insights into consumer behaviour, customer preferences, product penetration and branding is tremendous. Individuals and companies use social media to communicate with one another. Merging of social networks and mobile devices makes it easy for people to stay connected, and thus to influence one another's purchase decisions. [Social media is at the intersection between individuals, companies, and especially marketing] (Kumar, 2015, p. 5).

Table 9.1 Examples of the link between PESTEL factors and marketing

PESTEL factors	Marketing example
Political: Deregulation of civil aviation	Allowed low-cost airlines to enter, and grow, the market for 'no-frills' air travel
Economic: Growth in China, Russia and India creates great wealth for some of their citizens	Makers of luxury goods do well in this market – China is Rolls-Royce Motors' largest market
Social: Demographics – many well-off elderly people want easy-to-maintain dwellings	McCarthy and Stone create a business selling and managing blocks of retirement homes
Technological: Computing power enables new means of communicating at little cost	Wide use of social media transforms the way organisations and customers interact
Environmental: Effects of greenhouse gas emissions encourages use of cleaner energy	Suppliers of wind and solar energy systems see new opportunities
Legal: Government alters legislation to permit pubs to be open longer	Some pubs also vary the offer over the day, to cater for different customers' circumstances

Understanding consumer behaviour

Figure 9.3 shows that internal and external factors shape a consumer's purchase decision. Psychological theories of motivation help to identify internal factors. Some motivations are deep within someone's personality, while others are affected by their perception of events, their attitudes and how they respond to new ideas. Demographic factors also shape decisions.

Major external factors are the 'reference groups' to whom people feel an affinity, which affects what they buy. When retailers expand internationally they try to understand how the local culture affects buying habits. As societies become more ethnically diverse, consumer products companies introduce products adapted to these tastes. Figure 9.3 illustrates this, and Table 9.2 illustrates each of the factors influencing buying behaviour.

> ### Activity 9.3   What influenced you to buy?
>
> Identify a significant purchase you have made – either a physical product or a service.
>
> - Which, if any, of the factors in Table 9.2 affected your decision?
> - Can you identify influences that are not in the list?
> - Compare your lists with others on your course, and identify factors that appear most frequently. Do they vary between goods and services?

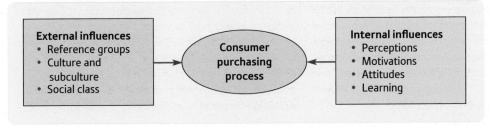

Figure 9.3
Influences on buyer behaviour

Table 9.2 Influences on buyer behaviour

Influence	Description	How marketers use this influence
Internal		
Motivation	Internal forces that shape purchasing decisions to satisfy needs	Design products to meet needs. Insurers remind people of dangers against which a policy will protect
Perception	How people collect and interpret information	Design promotional material so that the images, colours and words attract the attention of intended consumers
Attitudes	Opinions and points of view that people have of other people and institutions	Design products to conform. Increasing stress on environmental benefits of products and services
Learning	How people learn affects what they know about a product, and hence their purchasing decisions	Associate product with unique colours or images (Coke with red and white)
External		
Reference groups	Other people with whom the consumer identifies	Marketers establish the reference groups of their consumers, and allude to them in promotions – e.g. sponsoring athletes in return for product endorsement
Culture	The culture to which a consumer belongs affects their values and behaviour	Subcultures associated with music or cars influence buying behaviour – which marketers use in positioning products for those markets
Social class	People identify with a class based on income, education, or locality	Purchase decisions reaffirm class affinities or aspirations. Marketers design promotional material to suit

We make routine purchases without considering these factors, but for bigger items marketers are keen to influence our choice – and rely on information to do so.

Case study   Manchester United – the case continues   www.manutd.com

A football game is not a tangible product. A regular and significant intangible purchase by a Manchester United football fan is the cost of a ticket to see a home game at Old Trafford, or a pay-per-view TV package. There is no guarantee of satisfaction and no exchange or refund. No promotional advertising is needed and demand is 'inelastic' – prices can increase without sales volumes falling proportionately.

An important question for a marketing manager is 'how does a fan reach the decision to buy this experience and how is value measured?' The buyer behaviour framework in Table 9.2 can help: domestic UK fans are typically lifelong, acquiring perceptions of and loyalty to the club at school or in the home. Influencers would include peers and older pupils. Although football was formerly male-dominated, young females are an increasing part of the market. Most fans travel in groups of two or more, so this is an attribute that can be managed in raising awareness and favourability. Publicity photos can depict fans celebrating or commiserating together and the whole emphasis of attending a football match can be positioned away from 'did we win?' to 'did we have a good time?'. This approach is one of MU's declared marketing strategies.

Case questions 9.2

- What customer demands was Manchester United seeking to satisfy at the time of the case study?
- What other demands does the business have to satisfy?
- What marketing tools are mentioned in the case?

Marketing information systems

Marketing managers need a **marketing information system** – clear processes to collect and analyse information about customers and the macro and micro marketing environments, and to distribute it through the organisation. Figure 9.4 details the typical components. A marketing information system contains internal and external sources of data (see Table 9.3), and mechanisms to analyse and interpret the data so that marketing staff can use it.

The 'Management in practice' feature shows how Tesco used a sophisticated computer-based information system to gather data about customers. This aspect of marketing information is growing as companies gather ever more data about customers, and use sophisticated statistical methods to analyse it. Social media provides a new source of potentially valuable data, as users express and share their 'likes' about products. Consumer products companies spend heavily to find ways to access this data and target users with relevant promotions.

A marketing information system is the systematic process for the collection, analysis and distribution of marketing information.

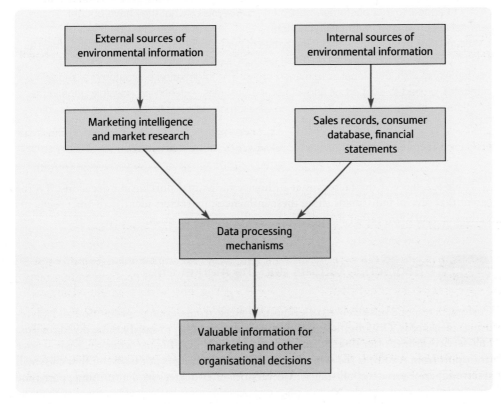

Figure 9.4
A marketing information system

Table 9.3 Sources of marketing information

Source	Description and examples
Internal records	Records of sales, costs, customer transactions, demographics, buyer behaviour, customer satisfaction, reports from the sales force
Marketing intelligence	Data on micro- and macro-environments – main competitors, potential new entrants, substitute products. What political, economic and social changes are likely to affect demand? Data is usually from secondary sources, often now from electronic sources and social-media tracking systems
Market research	Involves five tasks: 1 Defining the problem and research objectives (how many people with X income, living in place Y are aware of product Z?) 2 Developing hypotheses (is awareness higher or lower in area B, where the product has been advertised, than in C?) 3 Developing the research plan to collect data to refute or confirm hypotheses 4 Implementing the research plan – collecting and analysing the data 5 Interpreting and reporting the findings.

Management in practice   Market information from the Tesco Clubcard
www.tesco.com

The Tesco Clubcard scheme (Part 6 Case) has over 11 million active holders. Shoppers join the scheme by completing a simple form with some personal information about their age and where they live. Their purchases earn vouchers based on the amount they spend. Every purchase they make at Tesco is electronically recorded, and the data analysed to identify their shopping preferences. This is then used to design a package of special offers that are most likely to appeal to that customer, based on an analysis of what they have bought. These offers are sent to customers each quarter, with their vouchers.

The company analyses the data to identify the shopping habits of the Clubcard holder – whether they have a new baby, have young children, like cooking, and so on. Each product is given a set of attributes – expensive or cheap, ethnic recipe or traditional dish, own label or upmarket brand. The information on customers, shopping habits and product attributes is used to support all aspects of the business – identifying possible gaps in the product range, assessing the effect of promotional offers, noting variations in taste in different parts of the country.

Source: Part 6 Case.

Table 9.2 showed the factors that influence individual purchasing decisions. To the extent that several individuals share these influences, marketers identify distinct segments within a population, rather than seeing a market as homogenous.

9.4   Segments, targets and the market offer

Market segmentation is the process of dividing markets comprising the heterogeneous needs of many consumers into segments comprising the homogeneous needs of smaller groups.

Customers respond positively to offerings that meet (from design to promotion and advertising) their needs. Organisations use **market segmentation** to satisfy these diverse needs. Full-service airlines offer first, business, economy or budget flights: while the basic service (transport from A to B) is the same for all, the total offering is not (those in first class will receive superior service at all stages). Universities offer degrees by via full-time, part-time and distance-learning study. Mobile phone companies offer basic devices, those with many features and others for people wanting a luxury accessory.

Segmenting depends on identifying variables that distinguish consumers with similar needs:

- **Demography:** The easiest way to segment a consumer market is by demography. Magazine companies use gender and age to ensure that within their portfolio they have titles suitable for females, males and those of different ages. Councils use data on age and family structures to predict service demand.
- **Geography:** This segments markets by country or region, enabling multinational to 'think global but act local'. While maintaining uniform global standards of service and a common promotional theme, the product is varied to suit local tastes.
- **Socioeconomic:** This segments markets by variables such as income, social class and lifestyle. Lifestyle segmentation means identifying groups of consumers who share similar values about the ways in which they wish to live.
- **Behavioural:** Marketers can also divide buyers into groups on the basis of their attitude towards, or use of, a product. The Key ideas feature gives an example from the wine business.

The magazine *Marie Claire* uses age, gender, education, lifestyle and social class to attract a readership of educated, independently minded women between the ages of 25 and 35, in income brackets ABC1. Pubs aim for particular segments – sophisticated city-centre, food-led, urban community, country – to meet the distinct needs of each. Contemporary artist Damien Hirst (www.damienhirst.com) identified a group of wealthy art buyers who bought not only for artistic interest but also for fun, status, or investment. He designs his works for that segment.

Having segmented a market using these variables, marketers have to decide which to select as their **target market**, usually based on the criteria that it:

A **target market** is the segment of the market selected by the organisation as the focus of its activities.

- contains demands they can satisfy;
- is large enough to provide a financial return;
- is likely to grow.

Case questions 9.3

- Use the frameworks in this section to identify segments in the MU market.
- Visit the website to find specific examples of products the company offers to each segment.
- List your segments and examples, and exchange what you have found with other students.
- Can you identify any segments that may represent new target markets for the company?

9.5 Using the marketing mix

Marketing managers select the tools to satisfy the customers in their target market – everything they can do to influence demand. A widely-used technique to group these factors is the **marketing mix** – the 'four Ps' of product, price, promotion and place. Kotler and Keller (2014) propose a more complex model to reflect the circumstances of modern marketing, in which the 'four Ps' become People, Processes, Programmes and Performance. The 'Programmes' factor incorporates all the elements of the traditional marketing mix; as part of an introductory text, this chapter presents those elements in Figure 9.5.

The **marketing mix** is the set of marketing tools – product, price, promotion and place – that an organisation uses to satisfy consumers' needs.

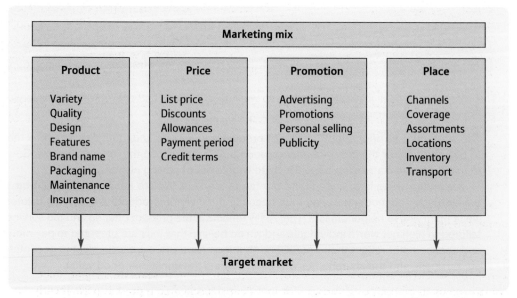

Figure 9.5 The four Ps in the marketing mix

| Key ideas | Marketing mix – strengths and limitations |

The marketing mix shows four 'levers' that marketing managers can control. The mix positions products in a way that makes them attractive to the target consumers. A product's position reflects what consumers think of it, in comparison with competitors – classy and desirable, cheap and affordable, pricey but reliable, and so on. Marketers aim to position their products within the minds of their target consumers as better able to satisfy their needs than competing products. To position products effectively, the marketing manager develops a coordinated, coherent marketing mix.

The 'four Ps' are an over-simplification, and it is easy to add other dimensions (see Kotler and Keller, 2014, cited above). However, the aim in an introductory text is to offer a usable framework showing how marketers can try to meet customer needs.

Product

Product refers to the range of goods and services that the company offers the target market. Some are physical products, others intangible services: most are a mixture of the two since the full experience of a product includes the services of delivery, advice and after-sales service. Some products achieve the status of a **brand** – 'a product or service whose [features] differentiate it in some way from other products or services designed to meet the same need' (Kotler et al. 2014, p. 263). Some customers identify strongly with the brand for functional (what it does) or emotional (what it represents) reasons. When people identify strongly with a brand, the company can charge more than for a functionally identical product – compare the prices for branded and generic aspirin, for example.

A **brand** is a product or service whose [features] differentiate it in some way from other products or services designed to meet the same need. (Kotler et al. 2014, p. 263)

| Management in practice | Swatch   www.swatch.com |

The development and introduction of Swatch is a classic example of marketing techniques being used by a traditional industry to launch a new product. Faced with competition from low-cost producers, SMH, an established Swiss watchmaker (whose brands include Longines and Omega), urgently needed a new product line. Its engineers developed a radically new product – the Swatch – which combined high quality with an affordable price. The company worked with advertising agencies in the United States on product positioning and advertising strategy. In addition to the name 'Swatch' (a snappy contraction of 'Swiss' and 'watch') this research generated the idea of positioning it not as a watch (that tells the time) but as a 'fashion accessory that happens to tell the time'. Swatch would be a second or third watch used in different situations without replacing the traditional 'status symbol' watch.

Swatch is now the world's largest watch company and continues to reposition itself through new products (such as Snowpass). It has been appointed official timekeeper of the Olympic Games until 2020.

Source: Based on 'Swatch', case no. 589-005-1, INSEAD-Cedep, Fontainebleau; and company website.

Services present particular challenges because they are perishable, intangible, heterogeneous and inseparable.

Perishable

Perishable services cannot be held in stock to sell later. Empty seats on a flight, unoccupied rooms in a hotel, or a vacant slot in a dentist's schedule represent permanently lost sales.

Intangible

Intangible services cannot usually be viewed, touched or tried before their purchase – so the customer cannot be sure what they are buying when they purchase a holiday or concert.

Heterogeneous and inseparable

Services rely on the skills, competences and experiences of the people who provide them, and this creates particular marketing challenges. Services are *heterogeneous* in that their personal nature means the customer may experience a slightly different product each time, even though they have arranged for essentially the same meal or dental treatment as they had before. Services are *inseparable* in that the customer interacts with the producer during delivery: it is consumed as it is produced, as in a medical appointment. Providers and consumers have personalities, opinions and values that make them unique, so the service delivered is always unique.

Organisations delivering services through branch systems (banks, fast-food outlets) have to ensure that staff deliver a consistent experience. Outlets such as Pizza Hut and UCI cinemas try to minimise differences by company uniforms, uniform premises and firm instructions to staff on how to deliver the service.

Consumer products (both goods and services) can be classified as convenience, shopping, specialty or unsought products. Each poses a different marketing challenge, which Table 9.4 summarises.

Price

Price is the value placed upon the goods, services and ideas exchanged between organisations and consumers. Money price is the commonest measure, though this part of the mix also includes discounts, trade-in allowances, payment periods and credit terms. Some airlines charge for elements of the service that others offer as part of an inclusive fare.

In selecting the price that will position a product competitively within consumers' minds, the marketing manager must be aware of the image that consumers have of the product. Jonathan Warburton (Chairman of Warburtons, the breadmaker (www.warburtons .co.uk)) recalls that when he joined the family firm at the age of 23 his job was to visit small supermarkets to make sure the bread was there and properly displayed. It was then that he

Table 9.4 Market challenges by type of product, using the marketing mix

Type of product	Examples	Marketing challenge
Convenience	Regular purchases, low price – bread, milk, magazines	Widely available, and easy to switch brands. Managers counter this by heavy advertising or distinct packaging
Shopping	Relatively expensive, infrequent purchase – washing machines, televisions, clothes	Brand name, product features, design and price are important and managers will spend time searching for best mix. Managers spend heavily on advertising and on training sales staff
Speciality	Less frequent, often luxury purchases – cars, jewellery, perfumes	Consumers need much information. Sales staff vital to a sale – management invest heavily in them, and in protecting image of product by restricting outlets. Also focused advertising and distinctive packaging
Unsought	Consumers need to buy – but don't get much pleasure from – insurance, a car exhaust	Managers need to make customers aware that they supply this need; use heavy advertising

realised his bread could be priced at a premium to the competitors. He tested this by raising the price in one of the shops – and sales went up.

> The premium made people stand back and judge it differently [to] the two [brands] that were alongside it. If we aren't worth [it] they wouldn't buy us again.

It is a philosophy they have adopted ever since (from an article in the *Financial Times*, 16 January 2012, p. 14).

Dynamic pricing was initially used by hotels and airlines, which face the problem that unsold capacity has no value, so they vary price to encourage demand when necessary. Some suppliers of clothing, mobile phones and consumer electronics now use the practice to dispose of fashionable stock whose value falls rapidly as time passes.

Promotion

Properly referred to as marketing communications, this element of the mix tells customers about the merits of the product to encourage a sale. New technologies offer many new and often very accurate ways to reach a target market, the goal always being to send the right ad to the right person at the right time. Common promotional methods are advertising, sales promotions, personal selling and publicity:

- **Advertising** has traditionally been used to transmit the same message to a large audience. This was impersonal, as there was no direct communication between advertiser and potential consumer. This is changing dramatically as social media enables advertisers to acquire data about individual consumer preferences, their friends and their current location, and much more. They can send highly personalised messages to the potential customer about a known preference, with, for example, a friend's recommendation, and name a nearby store, or a website, where they can buy it. More than 2 billion people now have smartphones, and advertisers are increasing what they invest in mobile phone advertising.
- **Sales promotions** encourage consumers who are considering a product to take the next step and buy it. They also use promotions to encourage repeat purchases and to try new products.
- **Personal selling** provides consumers with first-hand information before they buy. It is most useful for rarely purchased products – kitchens and cars are examples.
- **Publicity** or public relations (PR) aims to build a positive image of the company. It depends on good relationships with media companies to ensure positive coverage of events such as new product launches.

Management in practice   The internet and traditional media

The internet has posed significant challenges for traditional newspapers and magazines. Many consumers have substituted print content with online sources, and advertisers have followed suit. Some print media have tried to counter the loss of income by launching electronic versions of their print content, either on websites or as apps for mobile devices. These are often free, so tend to reduce revenue even more, unless they are able to attract significant advertising revenue.

Another reason for the decline in print media is that it is relatively inefficient at 'targeted advertising' – which reaches only the most receptive audiences. Online business can do this much more accurately than traditional media – making it more attractive to advertisers.

Source: Based on Chandra and Kaiser (2014).

Online communities enable users of a product to share experiences. Many form independently, but some companies sponsor them as a way to build relationships – especially by encouraging what is called 'user-generated content'. The most common type is when users provide product reviews. Negative comments may indicate genuine problems with a product that the company needs to deal with; good ones may be a signal to increase stocks to be ready for higher demand.

Advertise on mobile video or TV?

TV still receives the largest share of US marketing budgets, but internet advertising is catching up. Video in particular is taking a larger amount of marketing expenditure.

Digital media companies such as AOL, Yahoo and YouTube (owned by Google) are seeking those budgets by showing advertisers their ability to reach audiences of a size and demographic profile that television cannot, and promising a better return on the investment.

At a YouTube sales presentation, the Chief Executive, Susan Wokcicki claimed that her video site reaches more 18 to 49 year olds – the prime advertising demographic – than any cable network, and does so on mobile alone. The head of worldwide marketing at Universal pictures said his studio had used targeted YouTube ads to drive up awareness of some of its new films among their most likely viewers, 'while spending less than we ever thought possible'.

 Source: *Financial Times*, 5 May 2015, p. 16.
© The Financial Times 2015. All Rights Reserved.

Place

This refers to how products can best be distributed to the final consumer, either directly or through intermediaries. Some, especially those in luxury goods or fashion markets, take great care to ensure that products are only available through carefully controlled distributors, to help ensure consistent quality or promote their market image. Many companies debate how to combine online distribution with traditional channels – partly influenced by their understanding of why people buy the product. As one publisher observed:

> Music is only there to be listened to, but books are also shared, given as presents, used as furniture. (*Financial Times,* 13 April 2009, p. 17)

In developing a marketing mix that will place products competitively within the minds of consumers, marketing managers aim for coherence. In positioning a supermarket chain as, for example, value for money, they ensure that each part of the mix supports and reinforces this image. This means familiar product features, relatively low prices and promotion messages that stress the value for money. The stores should be simple, to avoid sending a message that the costs of creating a smart place will raise prices.

Case questions 9.4

- Use the frameworks in this section to identify how MU uses the marketing mix.
- Visit the website and identify two significant target markets for the company.
- For each market, analyse how the company has used the market mix to construct its market offering.
- List your markets and examples of the four Ps, and exchange what you have found with other students.
- Can you identify any significant aspects of the offering that are not covered by one of the 4 Ps?

9.6   The product life cycle

In managing the organisation's product decisions, marketing managers use a concept called the **product life cycle** (Levitt, 1965). The central assumption shown in Figure 9.6 is that measuring sales and profit over time shows that most products have a limited life, varying from months to decades. Depending on the stage reached in its life cycle, a known set of competitive conditions exists that can guide the marketing activities for that stage.

*The **product life cycle** suggests that products pass through the stages of introduction, growth, maturity and decline.*

Development

Pharmaceutical and electronics companies only survive if they show a steady stream of new products, a small proportion of which will be profitable. Sometimes they acquire already-developed products from other companies, as a way of quickly filling a perceived gap in their product range. Alternatively, they depend on their own R&D: this is expensive and brings no immediate return.

Introduction

Profits are still negative because sales from the early adopters have not reached the level needed to pay back investment in R&D. Few consumers are aware of the product and few businesses produce and distribute it. Marketing managers at this stage invest heavily in promotion to make as many potential consumers as possible aware of the product.

Growth

Consumers are buying the product, sales rise quickly and profits peak. More consumers become aware of the product and the high profits attract new competitors. The marketing manager's aim at this stage is to fight off existing competitors and deter potential entrants. This can be done by (a) encouraging consumer loyalty, (b) wide distributing to meet demand and (c) cutting prices – feasible as production costs fall as units produced increases. Competitors arriving later cannot do that, and this may deter them from entering the market.

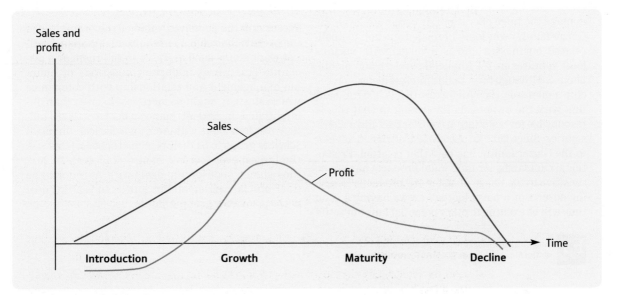

Figure 9.6 The product life cycle

Maturity

Profit and sales start to plateau and decline towards the end of this stage. Consumers know the product and there are probably more competitors. The marketing manager may react by reducing price again, or differentiating it in some way. Swatch continues to add value to its product in the later stages of its product life cycle with items such as the Infinity Concept watch. Product differentiation can sometimes reposition products to an earlier stage in their life cycle.

Decline

In the decline phase there is little demand and companies typically accept the inevitable, and reduce their investment – mainly by reducing advertising and other promotional costs. Certain products still generate profits in decline – spare parts for old cars.

Activity 9.4   Using the product life cycle

State the stage that you believe each of the following products to be in and comment on how long, in years, you believe their life cycle to be: drawing pins, iPods, umbrellas, hand soap.

Case study

Manchester United: the case continues
www.manutd.com

One of the challenges facing Manchester United is the best marketing structure through which to manage the huge operation. At corporate level, the Glazer family owns football-related and non-football-related businesses and is involved with various joint ventures in TV, financial services and mobile phones. Although most public interest focuses on the club's manager, the chief executive is a significant link with the owners, as the person in that role is responsible for negotiating transfer fees and players' salaries. Since 2013 Ed Woodward, a trusted adviser to the Glazer family, has held that position. Promotional campaigns for individual products have to be sensitive to the image of sister MU products. Hoarding adverts of a noisy football crowd having a good time will be exciting to other potential fans but could be off-putting for someone who has to produce their MU credit card at local stores.

Preserving the perceived value of the brand is also important: the replica jersey product manager will not want stores such as Tesco to sell them at a discount. This raises important questions of channel management and relationship with companies whose strategy might be more cost focused than differentiated. In 2009 MU signed a deal worth £80 million over four years with Aon, an American financial services group to be their principal sponsor: this was the largest-ever football sponsorship deal. In 2013 they signed sponsorship deals with Aeroflot to be their official carrier, and in 2015 a ten-year kit deal with sportswear group Adidas.

9.7   Customer relationship management

Some companies choose to focus on what they call **customer relationship management (CRM)** – aiming to develop long-term profitable relationships with customers in the hope that this will add more value to both parties. By increasing customer satisfaction they hope to build their loyalty to the product or service, so that they continue to make purchases over many years. This of course depends on understanding what features of the service will not only attract current purchasers, but also encourage return visits, which are quite different things.

Customer relationship management (CRM) is a process of creating and maintaining long-term relationships with customers.

A narrow interpretation of CRM is to gather data on individual customers and use that to build loyalty. Many hotels, airlines and retailers use loyalty schemes whereby every purchase earns points, which customers exchange for other benefits. Others use portable electronic devices that enable sales staff to create customer presentations, gather information during a call to prepare immediate quotations, share with colleagues and submit call reports.

CRM also has a broader meaning that includes all aspects of building and maintaining close relations with customers by understanding their needs, and delivering superior value to them. Techniques include:

- involving customers in product review and development;
- sponsoring consumer clubs and especially online communities;
- inviting customers to corporate sporting or cultural events;
- inviting online comments;
- sending promotional offers to customers' mobiles;
- encouraging staff to ask customers what they think of the service.

A CRM technique that is very popular with consumer-focused companies is to build collaboration with users – which Lego has done with great success: see 'Key ideas'.

Key ideas   Lego's collaboration with adult users   www.lego.com

Antorini et al. (2012) show how Lego has gained very substantial benefits by collaborating closely with thousands of adult users of the creative toy. Managers noted that many children continued to use the system as they grew up, so in 2005 the company created The Ambassador Programme. This provides a direct link for the company and its fans to get in touch with each other, and has been the source of many innovations – including new ways to customise designs, ideas about combining pieces in new ways and allowing thousands of users to upload their creations onto the site to benefit other builders.

Through trial and error the company has clarified four principles that have helped the relationship work well for both Lego and its fans:

- be clear about rules and expectations – e.g. that communication may sometimes be slow, as the fans have jobs and other commitments to attend to;
- ensure a win–win – the collaboration needs to bring rewards to both sides, and the fans value access to the company and contact with other fans more than financial rewards;
- recognise that outsiders are not insiders – fans are independent entities, not members of the company; and
- don't expect one size to suit all – different forms of communication are needed to suit the nature of the contribution the fan is making, and their communication preferences.

Source: Antorini et al. (2012).

> ### Activity 9.5 Examples of customer relationship management
>
> - Select an organisation in which you have an interest, ideally as a customer, that tries to build relationships with its customers.
> - Which of the tools mentioned in this section does it use?
> - How has this affected your attitude and behaviour towards the company?

9.8 A marketing orientation

Chapter 3 outlined the idea of organisational culture, and how it influences where people focus their efforts and attention. Four such cultures (or 'orientations') relevant in marketing are product, production, selling and marketing.

Four orientations

- **Product:** In units with a product orientation people focus on the design and perfection of the product itself. This could mean focusing on sophisticated products using the latest science – as Apple does, or delivering a familiar product or experience in a familiar way – as perhaps Marks & Spencer does. A risk in this approach is that of missing disruptive external changes in consumer preferences, and finding it hard to catch up. Burgers et al. (2008) show how Polaroid (which used to sell cameras cheaply to make money by selling the film) used their *technical* skills to develop digital cameras. Unfortunately they lacked the *market* skills to generate revenues from the new (film-free) cameras.
- **Production:** Here the aim is to produce large quantities of a limited range of products efficiently and economically. This works well when the low cost allows the firm to build a dominant position in that part of the market. A risk is that it loses the ability to work in other sectors, such as the needs of those who expect variety and change.
- **Sales:** Units with this orientation aim to turn available products into cash, often using aggressive sales techniques. This may be the only way to sell products ('distress purchases'), or where a concert has unsold seats a few days before the show. Companies also use this approach when they must raise cash urgently to pay a supplier or repay a debt.
- **Marketing:** Here the focus is on understanding and satisfying customer needs. This approach is useful when supply exceeds demand, so competition is intense. Some believe this is the situation most commonly facing modern organisations, and advocate that managers develop this approach in preference to the others. The next section outlines the features of the marketing orientation.

Marketing orientation

Marketing orientation refers to an organisational culture that encourages people to behave in ways that offer high-value goods and services to customers.

Most commercial organisations have a distinct marketing function, but a **marketing orientation** means much more than this: it refers to a situation where the centrality of marketing is embedded throughout the organisation. This means, among other things, that staff who are not in direct contact with customers nevertheless understand their needs, and give time and effort to satisfy them. While all the orientations in Table 9.5 work in some business conditions, many commentators believe that a marketing orientation is best suited to modern competitive environments (Morgan et al. 2009).

Table 9.5 Alternative organisational orientations

Organisational orientations	Focus	Benefits	Risks
Product	Technological skills and product features	High-quality, innovative products	Does not meet customer needs, so sales are poor
Production	Efficient, high-volume, low-cost production	Low price may build sales	Competition from lower cost producers, Inflexible
Sales	Sellers need to convert product into cash	May work for 'unsought goods' (insurance) and in cash-flow crises	Sales techniques may damage future sales prospects
Marketing	Understanding and meeting consumers' needs	Satisfying consumer needs improves firm performance	High costs of building and maintaining a marketing orientation

---

Key ideas   **Theodore Levitt and marketing myopia**

Levitt (1960) sets out with great clarity the case for a customer orientation. Beginning with the example of great industries that had suffered dramatic declines in demand, he claimed this was not because their market was saturated, but because their senior managers suffered from 'marketing myopia'. That is, they defined their businesses too narrowly: railway businesses saw themselves as providing railways, not transportation; Hollywood film companies saw themselves as producing films, not providing entertainment. In each case this prevented them from quickly seizing opportunities to enter new markets – road and air transport or TV production, respectively.

Levitt gives examples of companies that were indeed product focussed, but who prospered not because of their product focus, but because they also had a strong customer orientation. They constantly looked for opportunities to apply their acknowledged technical expertise to satisfy new customers. He concludes by proposing that managers must view the entire corporation as a customer-satisfying organism – not as producing products, but as providing customer satisfaction:

It must put this into every nook and cranny of the organisation, continuously, and with the flair that excites and stimulates the people in it. (p. 56)

Source: Levitt (1960).

Levitt (1960) drew attention to the danger of focusing on a product's features rather than on whether it could satisfy needs and wants – see 'Key ideas'. A marketing orientation is hard to achieve, as it depends on the culture encouraging appropriate behaviour in relation to:

- customers – understanding and anticipating their needs and demands;
- competitors – identifying and anticipating their marketing plans;
- coordination – ensuring all the separate functions work together to meet customer needs in a way that adds value.

It seems plausible that companies that pay attention to these factors will perform well, and a long-term study by Kumar et al. (2011) drawing on a panel of 261 managers between 1997 and 2005 confirmed this. Firms that had developed a marketing orientation among their staff experienced performance benefits over both short and long term, with early adopters gaining more than late. Morgan et al. (2009) show the specific processes by which firms deploy a marketing orientation. They were skilled at generating, disseminating and responding to market information, which they then put to good use through a familiar set of 'marketing mix' practices.

A **customer-centred organisation** is focused upon, and structured around, identifying and satisfying the demands of its consumers.

Concentrating on the market and being a **customer-centred organisation** enables managers to discover what consumers want – but as Homburg et al. (2009) note, generating knowledge about customers' needs often depends on the awareness and diligence of frontline employees. The team studied how such employees developed 'customer need knowledge' (CNK) – which they defined as 'the extent to which a frontline employee can correctly identify a given customer's hierarchy of needs' (p. 65). They found that an employee's customer orientation, training and the length of time they had known the customer increased CNK, though a large age difference between customer and employee decreased it. High levels of CNK were associated with high levels of customer satisfaction and with their willingness to pay.

Management in practice

Unilever reconnects with customers
www.unilever.com

After several years of performing less well than other consumer goods companies like Nestlé and Proctor & Gamble, Unilever appointed a new chief executive in 2009. Commenting on his task, Paul Polman said:

> We need to move increasingly from an efficiency-driven, manufacturing-driven supply chain. At the end what counts is to get the right product, at the right place, at the right price.

To help achieve that he is creating 'customer innovation centres' in the US, Europe and Asia as hubs for testing new products and conducting consumer research. Most exciting, potentially, is the new product pipeline. Mr Polman wants Unilever to develop fewer products, but to commercialise them faster.

Underpinning the reinvention of Unilever, Mr Polman is trying to create a more performance-based culture among staff, with six-monthly evaluations and bonus targets linked to volume growth and operating margins.

 Source: *Financial Times*, 7 May 2009.
© The Financial Times 2009. All Rights Reserved.

Activity 9.6   Gathering examples

- Select an organisation (or unit) with which you are familiar, or about which you can find out.
- Which of the four orientations in Table 9.5 most closely describes it?
- Describe briefly the features that best exemplify the way it works.
- If it has a marketing orientation, what examples can you give of the way people throughout the organisation work?

Compare what you have found with other students, and identify any common themes.

Developing a marketing orientation

While a marketing orientation is a desirable goal for companies in volatile markets, such cultural change is hard to achieve. All staff need to share a common commitment to work together in the interests of customers. It requires consistent and sustained effort by senior managers to clarify and implement the direction, sometimes replacing staff who are unable or unwilling to work in new ways. Gebhardt et al. (2007) give a comprehensive empirical analysis of the scale of the task.

9.9	Integrating themes

Entrepreneurship

Marketing in entrepreneurial firms is likely to be very different from that in the large firms that are the source of most marketing principles:

> Attempts to adapt and apply traditional marketing models to SMEs, based on the assumption that the basic principles of marketing . . . are universally applicable, have been unsuccessful (Jones and Rowley, 2011, p. 26).

These authors quote research into how small firms do their marketing, finding that what they call 'entrepreneurial marketing' has a distinctive style – being informal, simple, haphazard, reactive and opportunistic. This probably reflects the unique context in which it takes place, including:

- influence of the entrepreneur (who is rarely an expert in marketing);
- limited size and resources of the business;
- lack of formal structures; and
- few, if any, communication systems.

Marketing activities here tend to depend heavily on informal networking as sources of information and advice, as well as for generating customer contacts through personal networks. They are likely to have a high degree of customer orientation, as they can react quickly to customer needs, leading to high levels of customer satisfaction and loyalty (Jones and Rowley, 2011, p. 28).

Sustainability

Marketing is both part of the problem and part of the route to sustainability. Companies have used the skills of marketing to promote higher consumption, which has contributed to the current situation. It is possible that the discipline of marketing could also be part of the solution of achieving a sustainable economic system, since proposals about the significant lifestyle changes that may be needed depend on wide acceptance by the public. The scale of that challenge is illustrated by Heath and Chatzidakis (2012), who conducted a small survey of consumers' views on consumption. A clear majority agreed that there is excessive material consumption in developed societies, but few saw a link between that and environmental problems: respondents were aware of both phenomena, but few saw that one is a significant contributor to the other. When asked why people buy as much as they do

> the most common view was . . . that firms, and marketing in particular, are to blame for excessive consumption [and that] marketing techniques make people buy unnecessary things (p. 661).

Respondents took a different view of their own purchasing behaviour, most agreeing that when they went shopping they only bought what was essential – tending to distance themselves from any personal responsibility for over-consumption. The authors relate this to other work showing how individuals are unwilling to change their behaviour (including consuming less) while at the same time agreeing that social change was needed.

Internationalisation

Petersen et al. (2015) asked whether a consumer's national culture explained differences in their financial decision making, and whether it moderates the links between a bank's marketing efforts and their financial decision making. They used data from a bank based in the United Arab Emirates, which had customers in 33 countries, whose dominant culture was measured by Hofstede and Hofstede (2005). They found that a consumer's national culture has a direct impact on his or her financial decisions. Those from countries higher in long-term orientation are more likely to have a higher savings rate, those from countries higher in uncertainty avoidance are less likely to use credit and those from countries higher in masculinity are likely to spend more relative to their income.

They also noted that differences in national culture affected responses to the bank's marketing policies – for example, that promotion-focused efforts are more effective at increasing spending by customers from countries that are higher in masculinity.

Governance

One aspect of governance is that of assessing risks – indeed, it is one of the requirements of The Combined Code (2006) that boards appoint a risk assessment committee. While this would normally focus on the financial or perhaps technological risks potentially embodied in a strategy, reputational risk will sometimes also be worth evaluating as new products or services are developed. This is where a company acts in a way that many believe to be unethical, leading to long-term damage to its reputation. A clear example of this would be the way in which companies in financial services, in the years before the 2008 financial crisis, encouraged people to support their lifestyles on debt that they could not afford.

While governance has traditionally been concerned primarily with the immediate financial arrangements of a company, some now suggest that part of the governance process should include an assessment of the risks to which the company is exposed through the way it conducts the business. In some lines of business, especially financial services, governance and control could arguably include the role of marketing in shaping the risks to which the company is exposed.

Activity 9.7 Revising your definition

- Having completed this chapter, how would you now define marketing?
- Compare this definition with the one that you were asked to make in Activity 9.1 and comment on any changes.

Summary

1 **Define marketing and explain how it can add value in organisations of all kinds**

- Marketing is the activity of creating value for customers to receive value (resources) from them in return. All organisations depend on being able to attract inputs from the outside world, and need resources to do that.

2 **Explain the importance of understanding customers and markets, and the sources of information marketers can use**

- Understanding customers needs, wants and demands is the foundation of marketing, as only then can suppliers know how to satisfy them. They also aim to understand what influences buying behaviour.
- A marketing information system uses internal and external data, and also conducts marketing research to learn more about actual and potential customers.

3 **Illustrate the practices of segmenting markets and targeting customer groups**

- Understanding customer needs enables a company to segment the market according to groups of customers with different needs.

- Targeting is when the company decides which of the distinct segments of the market it will aim to serve to meet their distinctive needs.

4 **Describe the components of the marketing mix**

- Product, price, promotion and place. There are many other formulations, but a simple one such as this serves as a useful reminder of the tasks involved in shaping an offering.

5 **Describe the stages of the product life cycle**

- Development, introduction, growth, maturity, decline.

6 **Explain the meaning and significance of customer relationship management**

- The practice of building close long-term relationships with significant customers.
- A narrow interpretation of the term is when companies use information technology to manage data about customers, and perhaps use that to target special offers.
- A wider interpretation extends the idea to practices such as involving customers closely in product design and development, or creating online communities for customers.

7 **Compare a marketing orientation with other orientations and explain its significance**

- This is contrasted with product, production and sales orientations, which are suitable in certain circumstances.
- A marketing orientation implies that the organisation focuses all activities on meeting consumer needs and is organised with that in mind. It is especially useful in very competitive markets, where customers have a wide choice of suppliers.
- Adopting a marketing orientation makes the customer the centre of attention and is different from product, production and sales philosophies. It becomes a guiding orientation for the whole organisation.

8 **Explain the idea of market segments, and understand how you can use this to develop the skill of identifying customer needs**

- Understanding customer needs enables a company to segment the market according to groups of customers with different needs, and the chapter included an opportunity to develop that skill.

9 **Show how ideas from the chapter add to your understanding of the integrating themes**

- Jones and Rowley (2011) show that what they call 'entrepreneurial marketing' in small firms has a distinctive style, being informal, simple, haphazard, reactive and opportunistic.
- While many see marketing as part of the sustainability problem, others see it as part of the solution: customers as well as organisations need to change the way they behave to achieve a sustainable economy, and the skills of marketing can help to achieve that.
- Petersen et al. (2015) show how differences in national cultures affected responses to a bank's market activities.
- Innovative marketing practices, especially, but not solely, in financial services have exposed some companies to risks that threatened their existence. In sectors with this scale of risk, marketing practices could legitimately be part of an effective governance regime.

Test your understanding

1 Why do charities and local authorities need to devote resources to marketing?

2 Explain why understanding what customers want is a valuable investment.

3 Outline sources of marketing information and illustrate each with an example.

4   In what way is an organisation's micro-environment different from its macro-environment? How do these environments affect marketing activities?

5   What are the main stages in conducting a market research project?

6   What are the advantages of market segmentation and what variables do marketers typically use to segment consumer markets?

7   Illustrate each element in the marketing mix with an original example.

8   Use a product of your choice to illustrate all or part of the product life cycle.

9   What are the two broad approaches to customer relationship management?

10   Does the marketing orientation have advantages over product, production or sales philosophies?

11   Summarise an idea from the chapter that adds to your understanding of the integrating themes.

Think critically

Think about the ways in which your company, or one with which you are familiar, manages marketing. Then make notes on these questions:

- What examples of the marketing issues discussed in this chapter struck you as being relevant to practice in your company?

- Considering the people you normally work with, what **assumptions** about the customers appear to guide their approach – a production, sales or marketing orientation?

- What factors such as the history or current **context** of the company appear to influence the marketing approach used? What factors in the context seem to be shaping customer needs?

- Has there been any pressure to adopt **alternatives** – such as a more customer-focused approach, with more knowledge of their needs? Is there an evidence base for that idea?

- The chapter has stressed a marketing orientation, and a focus on understanding customers. What **limitations** can you identify with this? Is it always useful to identify customers' needs?

Develop a skill – identifying customer needs

Being able to understand customers' needs is vital to many aspects of management, and this exercise helps you begin to develop that skill.

- **Assessment:** Assess how aware you are of what people are seeking from familiar consumer products, such as wine, magazines or films – do you instinctively see differences between people when they buy something and how they judge it, or do you think all customers are the same?

- **Theory:** Section 9.4 introduced theories of market segmentation. Read that section again, paying special attention to the 'Key ideas' feature (p. 281), which gives an example of segmenting a market. Summarise the principles of market segments. Why do marketers do this?

- **Analysis:** Considering the example from the wine trade in 'Key ideas' (p. 281), identify three people you know who would each be representative of one or other of the segments. What observations led you to position them there?

- **Practice:** Identify three print wine advertisements. Decide which of the six segments of the wine market they are trying to attract. Then find three online wine advertisements. Decide which of the six segments of the wine market they are trying to attract.

- What customer needs are the marketers trying to satisfy in each case? Are there any differences between the needs the two media were trying to meet?
- Compare your conclusions with someone on your course, and summarise what you have learned about identifying customer needs.
- **Application:** Decide on another opportunity to practise this skill within the next week.

Read more

Antorini, Y. M., Muniz, A. M. and Askildsen, T. (2012), 'Collaboration with customer communities: Lessons from the Lego Group', *MIT Sloan Management Review,* vol. 53, no. 3, pp. 73–9.

Clear account of how Lego and their fans cooperate creatively in a customer community.

Heath, M. T. P. and Chatzidakis, A. (2012), 'Blame it on marketing: consumers' views on unsustainable consumption', *International Journal of Consumer Studies,* vol. 36, no. 6, pp. 656–7.

Insights into how consumers rationalise what they prefer to do.

Ogilvy, D. (2012), *Confessions of an Advertising Man,* Southbank Publishing, London.

For anyone planning to work in marketing or advertising, this new edition of the classic work by the man who ran a vast advertising agency is an essential book.

Schor, J.B. (2004), *Born to Buy: The commercialised child and the new consumer culture,* Schribner, New York.

A revealing account of the ploys that some marketers use to sell products to children – turning them, Schor argues, into miniature consumption machines.

Go online

These websites have appeared in the chapter:

www.manutd.com
www.swatch.com
www.tesco.com
www.unilever.com
www.hiscox.com
www.lego.com
www.bhf.org.uk
www.damienhirst.com
www.warburtons.co.uk

Visit two of the sites in the list (or that of another organisation in which you have an interest).

- What markets are they in? How have they segmented the market?
- What information can you find about their position in their respective markets, and what marketing challenges they face?
- Gather information from media websites (such as www.FT.com) that relate to the organisations you have chosen. What stories can you find that relate to the marketing decisions they have made, and the outcomes?

PART 3 CASE
THE VIRGIN GROUP
www.virgin.com

The company

Virgin Group is a venture capital organisation known all over the world, whose brand aims to offer value for money, quality, innovation and fun. Founded by Richard Branson, it has created hundreds of companies in many sectors of the economy, though senior management is said to pay close attention to only about twenty of these. They are distinguished by being part of the Virgin brand.

Branson opened his first record shop in 1971, followed by a recording business in 1973. Virgin Atlantic Airways began operating in 1984, quickly followed by Virgin Holidays and a joint venture offering financial services. By 1997 Virgin was an established international business with airline, retailing and travel operations: in 2013 the then chief executive, Stephen Murphy, was overseeing activities in six business sectors:

- Aviation and Tourism;
- Telecom and Media;
- Retail Financial Services;
- Health and Wellness;
- US Hotels;
- Special Situations (several unconnected businesses such as Virgin Trains and Virgin Galactic).

The original record business was launched shortly after the UK government abolished retail price maintenance, a practice that had limited competition and kept prices high. Richard Branson saw this as an opportunity to start a mail order business offering popular records for about 15 per cent less than shop prices. A postal strike encouraged him to open a retail outlet, which was an immediate success, and the start of Virgin Retail. He consolidated these interests into the Megastore concept, a joint venture with another retailer, selling home entertainment products – music, videos and books – in large stores in major cities across the world.

In the early 1980s the airline business was tightly regulated, with routes, landing rights, prices and service levels established and maintained by intergovernmental arrangements. These regulations were intended to protect inefficient state-owned, national 'flag carriers', which offered poor service at high prices. A change

© David Paul Morris/Bloomberg/Getty Images

in these regulations created an opportunity for new entrants and, after three months of intense activity, Branson and his business partner had gained permission to fly, arranged to lease an aircraft and recruited staff. Virgin Atlantic was a London-New York airline that offered 'first-class tickets at business-class prices': innovations included limousine pick-up for first class passengers and seat-back video entertainment systems for economy passengers.

In 1999 Virgin invested in telecommunications by launching Virgin Mobile in the UK. In 2006 this merged with a cable-television company and was rebranded as Virgin Media, in which Virgin has only a minority stake. It is important to the group because of the number of customers it reaches. Almost all Virgin businesses are joint ventures with other companies, using finance raised privately.

Managing to add value
Using the Virgin brand

Branson believed that the Virgin name, known for its consumer-friendly image and good service, would translate well across a range of businesses – 'Virgin isn't a company, it's a brand', commented one senior manager in the company. Market research demonstrated the impact of quirky advertising and publicity stunts: 96 per cent of UK consumers recognised the brand, and 95 per cent correctly identified Richard Branson as the company's founder. Respondents associated the Virgin name with fun, innovation, success and trust, and identified it with a range of businesses. This is unusual, as most strong consumer brands are associated with a single product or industry (such as Coke in beverages). Stephen Murphy (a former CEO):

> Virgin defies the usual 'rules' of brand limits. The brand has been successfully applied to businesses as diverse as music, airlines, trains, financial services, fitness centres, mobile telephony and the Internet. [The reason is that] the Virgin brand has some core features that are in all our companies – we try to do things differently, have fun, innovate, provide value for money, and provide great customer service. Every product we create emphasises or de-emphasises certain elements. We do not have to have equal elements in everything that we do. For example, in banking, consumers are looking mainly for value for money because they think they have been ripped off all along, then customer service, and finally a little bit of fun. They would probably not want too much innovation: people are conservative when it comes to money. In the media business, customers would mainly want fun and innovation. (Quoted in Pisano and Corsi (2012), p. 8.)

A director of the company:

> The Virgin brand helps recruitment . . . as the company is constantly rated as a good place to work. We attract great people, because talented entrepreneurial teams want to work with our brand. Also, the people we attract understand what our brand is about and agree with its values. This creates a virtuous circle. (Quoted in Pisano and Corsi (2012), p. 8.)

The brand also helps to raise capital as it makes the company attractive to partners: they provide the expertise and capital for a joint venture in their area of business (such as insurance or share trading), while Virgin provides the brand image. The early Virgin style of informality and openness remains – ties are rarely worn, denim jeans are common and everybody is on first-name terms.

Business unit autonomy

As the business grew Branson worked at the centre, supported by a small business development group, a press office and advisers on strategy and finance. Having a centre did not mean a centralised operation. Each operating unit was expected to stand alone and to have little contact with head office or other units. Business should be 'shaped around people', Branson believes,

citing his experience of subdividing the record company as it grew. Each new record label was given to up-and-coming managers, creating in-house entrepreneurs who were highly motivated to build a business with which they identified.

The company continues to be a network of operating companies, linked primarily by the Virgin trademark. Virgin Management Ltd (VML) 'manages' the companies, but only in the sense of providing advice and support in conjunction with the sector teams (such as those for Travel or Finance). VML manages Virgin's assets around the world. The company describes the style as a collaborative and supportive relationship between the centre and the businesses. A director:

> Considering all the markets and businesses where we operate, we prefer to run our companies by empowering their management teams and those on the ground. We are a shareholder who adds value, because we are the owners of the Virgin brand and because we reflect the group's long-time experience in different sectors and business models. (Quoted in Pisano and Corsi (2012), p. 9.)

This strategy is expressed operationally in the 'Virgin Charter' – an agreement between Virgin Management Ltd (the holding company) and the subsidiaries. It defines the role of the centre and the subsidiaries in such matters as taxation, legal affairs, intellectual property and real estate.

Central new venture decisions

The company receives many proposals for new ventures, and deciding which of these to invest in has a critical effect on performance: poor choices drain money and distract management attention from profitable ventures – and so destroy value.

In the early years Branson financed new ventures by borrowing, but company policy now is to raise capital either by selling an existing business, or by creating joint ventures – in which another investor puts money into the business in return for shares. A small number have raised capital by listing the company on a stock market, and selling shares to investors.

Deciding whether to invest in a new venture combines subjective and objective methods – with the emphasis on the latter. Mr Murphy:

> Richard is brilliant and very instinctive. Yet now consumers and attitudes move so quickly that we have to be more analytical. We need to combine intuition and qualitative analysis with the real quantitative analysis that says, 'This is your demographic, and this is your profile, and this is where you go next'. (Quoted in Pisano and Corsi (2012), p. 11.)

Mr Murphy, the advisory team and the sector teams try to identify growth areas, basing their investment decisions on financial returns (measured by return on investment, payback time and capital required) AND on a more subjective 'fit with brand' criterion. The staff who make these analyses typically review a potential investment from the customer's perspective, asking how Virgin could improve their experience:

- Is this an opportunity for restructuring the market and creating competitive advantage?
- What are competitors doing?
- Is the customer confused or badly served?
- Is this an opportunity for the Virgin brand?
- Can we add value?
- Will it interact with our other businesses?

New ventures are often steered by managers seconded from other parts of the business, who bring the distinctive management style, skills and experience. Managers in the companies are empowered to run the businesses without VML interfering, but are expected to help one another to overcome problems.

Richard Branson believes that creating discrete legal entities gives people a sense of involvement with, and loyalty to, their unit, as does having the option to buy shares in their business: Virgin has produced many millionaires. Branson does not want his best people to leave the company to start a venture outside; he prefers to make millionaires within.

Virgin.com

During one significant company meeting participants realised that, more by chance than planning, Virgin was in businesses 'that were ideally suited to e-commerce and in which growth is expected to occur – travel, financial services, publishing, music, entertainment'. To exploit this potential the participants decided to streamline several online services (which the businesses had developed autonomously) into a single Virgin website: **Virgin.com**.

By putting all Virgin's business on one site Branson hoped to cross-promote the group's offerings. The site groups these under headings such as online shopping, money, media, leisure and pleasure, travel and tourism, and health. Throughout the group, the company claims that it aims to deliver a quality service by empowering employees, and by facilitating and monitoring customer feedback to continually improve the customer's experience though innovation.

The case outlines recent developments in three of the companies – Virgin Atlantic, Virgin Rail and Virgin Money.

Virgin Atlantic

This was one of Branson's first and most high-profile ventures, launched in 1984 against strong opposition from British Airways. Virgin Atlantic grew successfully (financed in part by selling the profitable record business to EMI) and by 1990, although still a relatively small player, it competed with major carriers on the main routes from London, winning awards for innovation and service. Singapore Airlines held 49 per cent of the venture, selling this to the US carrier Delta Airlines in 2013.

Delta and Virgin now operate the transatlantic routes as a joint venture, each offering four daily flights between London Heathrow and New York JFK. The significance of this is that Virgin's main competitor on that route is British Airways which, in a joint venture with American Airlines, offers twelve flights each day. Business travellers in particular prefer a service with frequent flights, and the BA joint venture had damaged Virgin's position. Craig Kreeger, Virgin Atlantic's CEO since 2013, was confident that the Delta deal, plus the more efficient Dreamliner fleet, which came into service in 2015, will return the business to profit.

Virgin Rail

The main operation of Virgin's rail business is the UK's West Coast Main Line, which it operates under a franchise from the government. It does so in a 51–49 per cent joint venture with Stagecoach, which has an extensive bus, and some rail, operation.

Virgin has operated the line since it was privatised in 1997, and during that time has doubled the number of passengers to 28 million a year. It has earned a good financial return, with an estimated annual operating margin of 6.6 per cent over the term. It also has high customer approval ratings.

In 2012 the franchise was due to end, and in the initial competition Virgin lost the bid for a new 15-year franchise to rival FirstGroup. Sir Richard Branson mounted a fierce attack on the decision, which he believed must have been due to an error in assessing the rival bids. A few weeks after awarding the work to FirstGroup the government announced that the process had indeed been flawed and would be run again. In the meantime Virgin would continue to run the services until at least 2017.

Virgin Money

Virgin had for several years offered financial services online, competing with the established banks in current accounts, savings products and mortgages. In 2011 it entered the branch banking business when it bought Northern Rock bank. This had expanded aggressively by offering competitively priced mortgages, using money it had borrowed in the international markets. After the 2008 financial crisis it ran out of money and was taken over by the UK government.

Virgin bought the bank with funds provided by US billionaire Wilbur Ross, who invested just over £1 billion. The 75 Northern Rock branches that Virgin bought were all in the North East of England, and Virgin made it clear that it had no intention to grow the branch business into other parts of the country. Jayne-Anne Gadhia, chief executive of Virgin Money:

> We want to grow sensibly: we want to service our customers well and couldn't do that if we had hundreds of branches. We plan to create a major new competitor in UK retail banking. The two businesses complement each other well and together will create a strong bank with over 4m customers.

In 2014 the company sold about one third of the company (for £150 million) in an Initial Public Offering (shares are sold to members of the public, and are then traded on the London Stock Exchange). The money received also enabled the bank to make a final repayment to the UK government under the terms of its rescue of the bank.

By 2015 the bank was reporting strong growth in the mortgage business, and planned to launch a digital payment account in 2016.

Aspects of Virgin's context

A diversified business like Virgin operates in many contexts, each with different effects.

- **Virgin Atlantic** is faced by three strong joint ventures on its main routes, and in early 2013 was considering whether to join the Air France-KLM alliance, which in turn is part of the SkyTeam joint venture led by the Franco-Dutch group and Delta. In 2013 Delta Air Lines bought Singapore Airlines' stake in Virgin, and signed a code-sharing agreement with Virgin, which would enable the latter to offer more US destinations. Virgin also acquired the right to fly between Heathrow and Aberdeen/Edinburgh, which it saw as valuable feeder routes for the North Atlantic services.
- **Virgin Rail** faces severe competition in the award of a franchise to run a line, and several train companies have more franchises than Virgin. It competes for passengers with air and coach services, and the service it provides depends partly on the quality of the infrastructure Network Rail provides. Its record on the West Coast Main Line has been mixed, with strong passenger support despite punctuality problems. The line has been profitable for Virgin, but retaining the franchise depends on retaining the support of its partner Stagecoach.
- **Virgin Money** took advantage of the collapse of Northern Rock to acquire a small branch network, and to benefit from high levels of customer dissatisfaction with the large retail banks. These will defend their position. It also faces competition from the rapidly growing Co-operative Bank (Chapter 5 case), and from new entrants such as Metro Bank and the relaunched Tesco Bank.

Current management dilemmas
Protecting the brand

At corporate level the company has many opportunities to expand, but is well aware of the need to protect the Virgin brand, which is a distinctive strategic asset. The dilemma is that it is hard to decide when a company is ready to develop a successful business 'in the Virgin way'. For example, when it bought some health clubs it delayed rebranding them as 'Virgin' until the senior team were convinced that they were ready to take on the name. Joining the SkyTeam Alliance carries similar risks: if passengers have a bad experience with another airline in the alliance, will this diminish their respect for the brand? A more personal dilemma is that the brand has a youthful image, and Branson himself points out that 'having a frontman approaching retirement age could become a problem' (*Financial Times,* 15 October 2012, p. 12).

Deciding direction

On which areas of business should the company focus? Are some areas within the current portfolio more likely to enhance the brand than others, and therefore be candidates for favourable treatment? Are there any new areas that could be candidates for significant investment? Should they do fewer new start-ups, and instead focus on gym, banking and health sectors?

Deciding scale

The company is now investing in fewer, larger investments, and has become quicker to pull out of unsuccessful investments. Gaurav Batra, corporate development and strategy director at VML:

> From 1995 to 2000 we launched 34 new companies; today we do about five investments per year. Start-ups are time-consuming and do not [help much to build the group rapidly] (Pisano and Corsi, 2012, p. 12).

Now it is mainly buying existing companies and working quickly to develop strategy leadership and the brand effect to turn round failing companies quickly. Gordon McCallum, CEO of VML:

> The question we are asking ourselves is: In the next ten years, would we be better placed to create two $5 billion or another ten $1 billion businesses? I would do fewer start-ups unless they have a very clear route to scale and market power . . . and [would instead] focus on our gym, banking and health sectors (Pisano and Corsi 2012, p. 13).

Source: Based on material from Pisano, G.P. and Corsi, E. (2012); INSEAD Case 400-002-1, 'The House that Branson Built: Virgin's entry into the new millennium'; *Financial Times,* 15 December 2008, 18 November 2011, 30 August 2012, 15 October, 2012, 18 February 2013, 25 June 2013, 4 September 2014, 14 November 2014, 29 July 2015; company website.

Part case questions

(a) Relating to Chapters 6 to 9

1 Conduct a SWOT analysis of one of the Virgin brands featured here (Section 6.4).

2 Are the decisions mentioned in the case programmed or non-programmed? Refer to the material on Virgin Rail, and identify an example of the 'dependency' of decisions (Sections 7.3 and 7.4).

3 Having read the case, what sense do you have about the likely features of current strategic planning processes at Virgin Group (the VML level)? (Refer to Sections 8.3 and 8.4.)

4 On balance, does the Virgin story support the planned or the emergent view of strategy?

5 Conduct a five forces analysis of one of the Virgin companies featured here (Section 8.5).

6 Which generic strategies has Virgin Group followed (Sections 8.7 and 8.8)?

7 Why does Branson use joint ventures with other companies to realise the Virgin strategy (Section 8.9)?

8 To what extent has Virgin implemented a marketing orientation? (Refer to Section 9.8.)

9 Where do Richard Branson's publicity stunts fit into the company's marketing strategy?

(b) Relating to the company

1 Visit Virgin's website and comment on how it is now using this to support the businesses.

2 What links the Virgin businesses and what is the role of the centre in relation to them?

3 Access the websites of *The Economist, Financial Times* or BBC News (Business pages) and make notes about how, if at all, the dilemmas identified in the case are still current, and how the company has dealt with them.

4 What new issues appear to be facing the company that were not mentioned in the case?

5 For any one of those issues it faces, how do you think it should deal with it? Build your answer by referring to one or more features of the company's history outlined in the case.

PART 3
EMPLOYABILITY SKILLS – PREPARING FOR THE WORLD OF WORK

To help you develop useful skills, this section includes tasks that relate the themes covered in the Part to six employability skills (sometimes called capabilities and attributes) that many employers value. The layout will help you to articulate these skills to employers and prepare for the recruitment process you will encounter in application forms, interviews and assessment centres.

Task 3.1   Business awareness

If a potential employer asks you to attend an assessment centre or a competency-based interview, they may ask you to present or discuss a current business topic to demonstrate your business awareness. To help you to prepare for this, write an individual or group report on ONE of these topics and present it to an audience. Aim to present your ideas in a 750-word report and/or ten PowerPoint slides at most.

1   Using data from one or more websites or printed sources, outline significant recent developments in Virgin, especially about:

- the range of activities using the Virgin brand;
- developments in any one of these brands – Trains, Money, Atlantic or Health and Fitness;
- the autonomy of the operating companies; and
- strategic direction of the Virgin Group.

Include a summary of commentators' views on Virgin's recent progress.

2   Gather information on the interaction between ONE Virgin company and its competitive environment, including specific examples of new challengers, or new moves by established competitors. What generally relevant lessons can you draw about competition in this sector? Use Chapter 3 (Section 3.4) to structure your answer.

3   Choose another venture capital company that interests you – and which you may consider as a career option. Possibilities could include 3i (**www.3i.com**) or Risk Capital Partners (**www.riskcapitalpartners.co.uk**).

- Gather information from the website and other sources about its structure and operations.
- Give examples of recent public actions, such as buying or selling its investments.
- Which types of new venture does it invest in, and what examples does it give?
- In what ways, if any, have governments and politics influenced the business?
- When you have completed the task, record a short paragraph giving examples of the skills (such as information gathering, analysis and presentation) you have developed from this task. You can transfer a brief note of this to the Table at Task 3.7.

Task 3.2 | Thinking critically

Reflect on the way that you handled Task 3.1, and identify how you exercised the skills of thinking critically (Chapter 1, Section 1.8). For example:

1 Did you spend time identifying and challenging the assumptions implied in the reports or commentaries you read? Summarise what you found then, or do it now.
2 Did you consider the extent to which they took account of the context in which managers are operating? Summarise what you found then, or do it now.
3 How far did they, or you, go in imagining and exploring alternative ways of dealing with the issue?
4 Did you spend time outlining the limitations of ideas or proposals that you thought of putting forward?

When you have completed the task, record a short paragraph giving examples of the thinking skills you have developed from this task. You can transfer a brief note of this to the Table at Task 3.7.

Task 3.3 | Solving problems

Chapter 6 includes ideas on planning to deal with a problem – such as that of completing Task 3.1. Refer to these if you need more guidance on this activity, which invites you to analyse how your team worked on a task.

Use the scales below to rate the way your team planned how it would work on Task 3.1 – circle the number that best reflects your opinion of the discussion.

1 The team used suitable methods to gather sufficient information to create a good plan to complete the task (Section 6.4).

1	2	3	4	5	6	7
Strongly disagree						Strongly agree

2 The team set SMART goals that gave focus to our work on the task (Section 6.5).

1	2	3	4	5	6	7
Strongly disagree						Strongly agree

3 The goals helped to motivate us to achieve the task (Section 6.5).

1	2	3	4	5	6	7
Strongly disagree						Strongly agree

4 The team made a full list of what had to be done to achieve the goals (Section 6.6).

1	2	3	4	5	6	7
Strongly disagree						Strongly agree

5 The team made a suitable implementation plan, and followed it (Section 6.7).

1	2	3	4	5	6	7
Strongly disagree						Strongly agree

6 The team monitored the progress of the plan, and adjusted it accordingly (Section 6.7).

1	2	3	4	5	6	7
Strongly disagree						Strongly agree

When you have completed the task, record a short paragraph giving examples of the planning skills you have developed from this task. You can transfer a brief note of this to the Table at Task 3.7.

Task 3.4   Team working

Chapter 17 includes ideas on team working. This activity helps you use these to analyse how your team worked on Task 3.1.

Use the scales below to rate the way your team worked on this task – circle the number that best reflects your opinion of the discussion.

1 The team was effective in obtaining and using necessary information.

1	2	3	4	5	6	7
Strongly disagree						Strongly agree

2 The team members took on complementary team roles (Section 17.4).

1	2	3	4	5	6	7
Strongly disagree						Strongly agree

3 The team progressed through the stages of team development (Section 17.5).

1	2	3	4	5	6	7
Strongly disagree						Strongly agree

4 The team developed effective working processes that suited the task (Section 17.6).

1	2	3	4	5	6	7
Strongly disagree						Strongly agree

5 The team used their time effectively.

1	2	3	4	5	6	7
Strongly disagree						Strongly agree

6   The team regularly reviewed the ways it was working, and changed these when it would improve performance (Section 17.6).

1	2	3	4	5	6	7
Strongly disagree						Strongly agree

Record three practices that you could use in your next task. If possible, compare your results and suggestions with other members of the team, and agree on practices that would help a team work better.

When you have completed the task, write a short paragraph giving examples of team-working skills (such as observing the team to improve performance) that you have developed from this task. You can transfer a brief note of this to the Table at Task 3.7.

Task 3.5   Communicating

Chapter 16 includes ideas on communicating – and Sections 16.4 and 16.5 are especially relevant to this task. It will help you to analyse how well your team communicated as you worked on Task 3.1.

Use the scales below to rate the way your team communicated during Task 3.1 – circle the number that best reflects your opinion of the discussion.

1   The team handled face-to-face communication well during its meetings (Section 16.4).

1	2	3	4	5	6	7
Strongly disagree						Strongly agree

2   The team communicated effectively by phone, mobile, voicemail and other electronic systems (Section 16.4).

1	2	3	4	5	6	7
Strongly disagree						Strongly agree

3   The team communicated effectively by personal, written methods – letters, email, texting (Section 16.4).

1	2	3	4	5	6	7
Strongly disagree						Strongly agree

4   The team communicated effectively by impersonal written methods – newsletters, online communities (Section 16.4).

1	2	3	4	5	6	7
Strongly disagree						Strongly agree

5 The team adapted between centralised and decentralised communication networks according to the needs of the task (Section 16.5).

1	2	3	4	5	6	7
Strongly disagree						Strongly agree

6 The team communicated its report well to the chosen audience.

1	2	3	4	5	6	7
Strongly disagree						Strongly agree

7 The team experienced no significant barriers to communication, either internally or externally.

1	2	3	4	5	6	7
Strongly disagree						Strongly agree

Record three communication practices that you could use in your next task. If possible, compare your results and suggestions with other members of the team, and agree on practices that would help a team work better.

When you have completed the task, record a short paragraph giving examples of communication skills you have developed from this task. You can transfer a brief note of this to the Table at Task 3.7.

Task 3.6   Self-management

This activity helps you to learn more about managing yourself, so that you can present convincing evidence to employers showing, among other things, your willingness to learn, your ability to manage and plan learning, workloads and commitments, and that you have a well-developed level of self-awareness and self-reliance. You need to show that you are able to accept responsibility, manage time and use feedback to learn.

Reflect on the way that you handled Task 3.1, and identify how you exercised skills of self-management.

1 I effectively planned the time I would spend on each part of the task.

1	2	3	4	5	6	7
Strongly disagree						Strongly agree

2 I tried to balance my commitments and those of other team members across the work, so that all were reasonably busy.

1	2	3	4	5	6	7
Strongly disagree						Strongly agree

3 I think I used my time well.

1	2	3	4	5	6	7

Strongly
disagree

Strongly
agree

4 I tried to ensure that I and others took responsibility for distinct areas of work, to keep moving the task forward.

1	2	3	4	5	6	7

Strongly
disagree

Strongly
agree

5 I often reflected on how I was working on the task to identify possible ways to improve our performance.

1	2	3	4	5	6	7

Strongly
disagree

Strongly
agree

Write down three self-management practices that you could use in your next task. If possible, compare your results and suggestions with other members of the team, and agree on practices that would help a team work better.

When you have completed the task, write a short paragraph giving examples of the self-management practices you have developed from this task. You can transfer a brief note of this to the Table at Task 3.7.

Task 3.7 Recording your employability skills

To conclude your work on this Part, use the summary paragraphs above to record the employability skills you have developed during your work on these tasks, and in other activities. Use the format of the table below to create an electronic record that you can use to combine the list of skills you have developed in this Part, with those in other Parts.

Most of your learning about each skill will probably come from the task associated with it – but you may also gain insights in other ways – include those as well.

Template for laying out record of employability skills developed in this Part

Skills/Task	Task 3.1	Task 3.2	Task 3.3	Task 3.4	Task 3.5	Task 3.6	Other sources of skills
Business awareness							
Thinking critically							
Solving problems							

Skills/Task	Task 3.1	Task 3.2	Task 3.3	Task 3.4	Task 3.5	Task 3.6	Other sources of skills
Team working							
Communicating							
Self-management							

To make the most of your opportunities to develop employability skills as you do your academic work, you need to reflect regularly on your learning and record the results. This helps you to fill any gaps, and provides specific evidence of your employability skills.

PART 4

ORGANISING

Introduction

Part 4 examines how management creates the structure within which people work. Alongside planning the direction of the business, managers need to consider how they will achieve the direction they have chosen. One component is the form of the organisation. This is a highly uncertain area of management as there are conflicting views about the kind of structure to build, and how much influence structure has on performance.

Chapter 10 describes the main elements of organisation structure and the contrasting forms we can observe. Chapter 11 deals with one aspect of that structure, namely its policies on human resource management. These are intended to ensure that employees work towards organisational objectives.

Chapter 12 focuses on how managers can use technology to support their business, specifically information technology and e-business, which have significant implications for organisations and their management. Chapter 13 presents theories of creativity and innovation – practices that are essential if managers are to add value to their resources.

The Part Case is Royal Bank of Scotland, which has gone from being a highly regarded and innovative bank to one that came close to failure. Now owned mostly by the UK government, its managers are trying to rebuild its reputation.

CHAPTER 10
ORGANISATION STRUCTURE

Aim

To introduce the elements that make up an organisation, and consider the link between structure and performance.

Objectives

By the end of your work on this chapter you should be able to outline the concepts below in your own terms and:

1   Outline the links between strategy, organisation and performance
2   Give examples of how managers divide and coordinate work, with their likely advantages and disadvantages
3   Compare the features of mechanistic and organic forms
4   Summarise the work of Woodward, Burns and Stalker, Lawrence and Lorsch and Child, showing how they contributed to this area of management
5   Use the 'contingencies' outlined to evaluate the form of a unit
6   Explain and illustrate the features of a learning organisation
7   Explain alternative methods of coordination, and understand how you can use this to develop the skill of coordinating work
8   Show how ideas from the chapter add to your understanding of the integrating themes

Key terms

The chapter introduces these terms:

organisation structure
organisation chart
formal structure
informal structure
vertical specialisation
horizontal specialisation
formal authority
responsibility
delegation
span of control
centralisation and decentralisation
formalisation

functional, divisional, matrix and
  network structures
outsourcing
mechanistic structure
organic structure
technology
differentiation
integration
contingency theories
determinist
structural choice
learning organisation

Each is a term defined within the text, and in the glossary at the end of the book.

Case study   GlaxoSmithKline (GSK)   www.gsk.com

GSK is one the world's largest pharmaceutical companies, formed in 2000 by the merger of GlaxoWellcome and SmithKlineBeecham. Sales in 2015 were £24 billion – with £14 billion (59 per cent) being in the pharmaceuticals division (medicines to treat serious and chronic diseases). Vaccines accounted for 16 per cent of sales and consumer healthcare (over-the-counter products including Panadol and Lucozade) for 24 per cent.

The company employs over 97,000 staff in 100 countries – including 16,000 in Research & Development. The company has 74 manufacturing sites in 32 countries, with research sites in the UK, US, Spain, Belgium and China.

In 2015 CEO Sir Andrew Witty announced that GSK would reduce its dependence on pharmaceuticals and focus more on vaccines and consumer healthcare. He believed the shift towards these higher-volume markets with steady growth would be more profitable, and that:

> it will not be about 600 million people in Europe and America – [it will] be about those plus the 6 billion in the rest of the world.

Like all pharmaceutical companies, GSK's survival depends on developing new drugs that it can sell profitably. The industry discovers, develops and sells new products – whose patent prevents another company from selling an equivalent for ten years. During this period the company has a monopoly – enabling it to make high profits if the drug sells well. When the patent expires, other companies can copy the formula and sell 'generic' versions cheaply.

Companies such as GSK find it difficult to maintain the flow of new drugs. Diseases that are easy to treat have adequate drugs, and finding new ones is very expensive. It is also harder to obtain approval from regulators. It takes about 12 years from discovering a new formula to the point at which (if approved) it begins to earn an income – and during that time the company is investing money with no return. GSK makes the results of its drugs trials available to the 'Cochrane' group of independent scientists to check its claims about their effectiveness.

Some were critical of the prices GSK set for medicines in emerging countries. It now relates prices to a country's wealth and ability to pay, which has led to significant price reductions. In 2014 the Access to Medicine Index (founded by Bill and Melinda Gates),

© Ben Stansall/AFP/Getty Images

which measures the philanthropic work of drugs companies and their responsiveness to the health needs of emerging markets, ranked GSK top in its annual review.

In the 1960s GSK employed fewer than 1,000 scientists, who worked in a functional structure – chemists, pharmacologists, clinical development and so on. There were few management layers, few projects, and most scientists worked on a single campus. Communication, coordination and the exchange of ideas was easy.

As the number of employees grew rapidly it became clear that the traditional way of organising the business was unsatisfactory. In particular, investors and senior managers were concerned about the high cost and low productivity of research. Scientists now worked on many sites across the world, so communication was difficult and slow – the opposite of that required in a research community.

Sources: Company Annual Report 2011; *British Medical Journal*, 9 March 2013; *Financial Times*, 17 November 2014, p. 20, 7 May 2015, p. 21.

Case questions 10.1

- Visit the company website and note any recent announcements about the development of new medicines or vaccines.
- What type of working environment is likely to encourage scientific creativity?
- What type of working environment is likely to ensure that safety testing and clinical trials required by national regulatory bodies are carried out accurately, consistently and reliably?

10.1   Introduction

Managers at GlaxoSmithKline (GSK) aim to create a context that encourages apparently contradictory behaviours. The company needs a steady flow of new pharmaceuticals that deal with a disease or condition effectively. This depends on encouraging, and paying for, sustained scientific imagination and creativity over many years, in the hope that research teams develop useful products. Those that pass rigorous clinical trials to satisfy national and international regulators that they are safe and effective, and which seem commercially viable, then go into a precisely specified production process. The company needs creativity (in research) and order (in production).

The owner-manager of a new business decides what tasks to do and coordinates them. If the enterprise grows the entrepreneur passes work to newly recruited staff, though the division will be flexible and informal as communication is direct and easy. Informal communication will become less reliable as a business grows, so people begin to introduce some structure – clarifying who does what, and how to share information quickly and accurately. One reason for the success of Virgin Group (a tiny new business in 1971) is the relationship between the central management group and the many companies with which we are familiar.

Those in charge of failing companies often change the structure in the (sometimes forlorn) hope that a new one will work better. Others follow a policy of frequent small changes. The (then) chairman of L'Oréal, the world's biggest beauty company, referred to its

> culture of permanent mini-restructuring. I don't think there has ever been a major restructuring in the whole of L'Oréal's corporate history . . . but there have been hundreds of little ones. What we do is try to live a life of permanent small change to avoid the major disasters. (*Financial Times,* 3 March 2008)

Chapter 2 introduced the work of Max Weber, the first of many scholars and practitioners to observe the work of public and private organisations and use that to build theories about how to design organisations. Managers can draw upon these to help them decide a structure for their business, in their context. They are constantly experimenting and adjusting this – as they find what works, and as conditions change.

The chapter illustrates the main choices they have in deciding how to divide and coordinate work. Coordination is essential to effective management, and the chapter offers an opportunity to begin developing the skill of coordinating work. The chapter contrasts 'mechanistic' and 'organic' forms, and presents theories about when each will be suitable (see Figure 10.1 for an overview). It concludes with ideas on learning organisations.

10.2   Strategy, organisation and performance

Alfred Chandler (1962) traced the evolution of America's largest industrial firms, showing how growth and diversification placed too many demands on centralised structures. As the diversity of products and geographies grew, issues arose which those at the (increasingly remote) centre, without local knowledge, could not handle. His historical analysis of du Pont, General Motors, Standard Oil and Sears, Roebuck showed that they had responded by creating decentralised, divisional structures – an organisational form that many companies use today. It allowed managers at corporate headquarters to provide overall strategic guidance and control, and divisional managers to implement the detail (strategy-shaped structure).

Chandler also shows that structure influenced strategy. A new legal requirement to break Standard Oil into regional companies encouraged one of these – companies, Standard Oil (New Jersey), to expand into foreign markets to increase profits (structure-shaped strategy). Chandler's aim was to study the interaction of strategy and structure as conditions changed. In successive cases he traces how strategies to launch new products or enter new

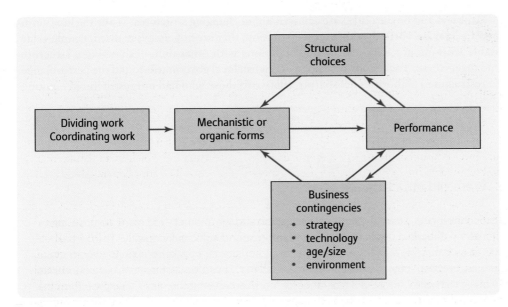

Figure 10.1
Alternative structures and performance

regions strained current structures, and how managers responded by, through trial and error, developing variants of the decentralised divisional form.

Table 10.1 gives examples of visible corporate changes. While senior managers debate these, managers at other levels work on similar issues in their units:

- Should we divide a task into three and give each to one employee, or have them work as a team, responsible for the whole task?
- Should team A do this task, or team B?
- Should that employee report to supervisor A or supervisor B?

Whether the issue is at a multinational business such as Unilever or a small company such as Multi-show Events (see 'Management in practice' feature), the questions are the same – where to commit resources, and how to divide and coordinate the roles of people using them.

Table 10.1 Examples of strategic and organisational decisions

Example	Strategic issue	Organisational issue
Unilever, 2014 www.unilever.com	Slow growth in the margarine and spreads unit (which was run within the Foods Division) has reduced group performance for several years	Created it as a standalone unit with a dedicated management team, who will have autonomy over strategy and investment decisions. Also makes it easier to sell the unit
DixonsCarphone, 2014 www.dixonscarphone.com	Companies agree on a 'merger of equals' to create company with 40,000 employees in 14 countries across Europe	Integrating the two businesses – building common culture between the two brands, especially in merged stores; unifying warehousing and IT systems; securing better deals with suppliers
Top Right Group (previously Emap) 2012 Media www.topright-group.com	Originally a printed magazine company, it had moved into other areas of business, and new CEO wanted these to have more visibility and responsibility	Changed name, split into three companies – events, information services, and the original print media. Central functions (IT, HRM, finance) decentralised into the new businesses

Andrews and Boyne (2012) are cautious about changing structures. While the long-term benefits may be worth the short-term disruption, they are not always realised. People value stable working practices and familiar relations with other units – changing a structure endangers these. Their study of change in English local government found the performance of restructured authorities fell sharply relative to those who had not restructured – noting that:

whether the long-run gains compensate for this remains to be tested in the years ahead. (p. 309)

> **Key ideas**　　**From old structures to new?**
>
> A growing awareness of challenging external forces – globalisation and the internet – led some commentators to predict that traditional, bureaucratic organisations would not respond sufficiently quickly. They predicted (Ashkenas et al. 2002 is an example) that to respond flexibly to customer needs companies would make radical structural changes, creating 'post-bureaucratic' organisations. These would have unclear boundaries (able to work more closely with other firms), a small range of 'core' activities (other firms would perform the rest) and flatter hierarchies (quicker decisions). Many thought staff would have more liberal and emancipated working conditions.
>
> Farrell and Morris (2013) tested empirically the accuracy of these predictions, by gathering evidence from 45 UK organisations (public and private, medium and large). They asked about the recent organisational changes, and their effects on middle managers.
>
> The authors found there had indeed been substantial changes – many had begun to work more collaboratively, discontinue non-core activities, cut staff and reduce management levels. They also found that these changes were usually driven by the need to cut costs, not to improve flexibility or customer responsiveness. Finally, middle managers' work had frequently become more insecure, stressful and demanding – a sharp contrast with predictions about the benefits of post-bureaucratic organisations.
>
> Source: Farrell and Morris (2013).

Organisation structure
'The structure of an organisation [is] the sum total of the ways in which it divides its labour into distinct tasks and then achieves co-ordination among them' (Mintzberg, 1979).

The next section introduces the main tools that people use as they create and recreate their organisation.

10.3　Designing a structure

Organisation structure describes how managers divide, supervise and coordinate work. It gives someone taking a job a reasonably clear idea of what they should do – the marketing assistant should deal with marketing, not finance. The topic relates closely to culture and to human resource management, since the more coherence there is between these three elements the more they will support the strategy.

An organisation chart shows the main departments and senior positions in an organisation and the reporting relations between them.

The organisation chart

Formal structure consists of guidelines, documents or procedures setting out how the organisation's activities are divided and coordinated.

The **organisation chart** shows departments and job titles, with lines linking senior executives to the departments or people for whose work they are responsible. It shows who people report to, and clarifies four features of the **formal structure**:

- tasks – the major activities of the organisation;
- subdivisions – which departments are responsible for which tasks;

- levels – the position of each post within the hierarchy;
- lines of authority – these link the boxes to show who people report to.

Organisation charts give a usually transient summary of tasks and who is responsible for them. Figure 10.2 shows a chart for an aircraft factory that was then part of BAE Systems, a UK defence contractor. There are six departments – design, production engineering, purchasing, inventory, production and human resources. It also shows the chain of command within the factory and the tasks of each department (only some are shown). It includes direct staff such as operators and engineers, and the lines of authority. It does not show the **informal structure** – the many patterns of work and communication that are part of organisational life.

Informal structure
is the undocumented relationships between members of the organisation that emerge as people adapt systems to new conditions and satisfy personal and group needs.

Work specialisation

Within the formal structure managers divide work into smaller tasks for people or departments. They become more expert in these than they could be if they worked on several, and are more likely to suggest improvements. Too much specialisation leads to the negative effects on motivation described in Chapter 15.

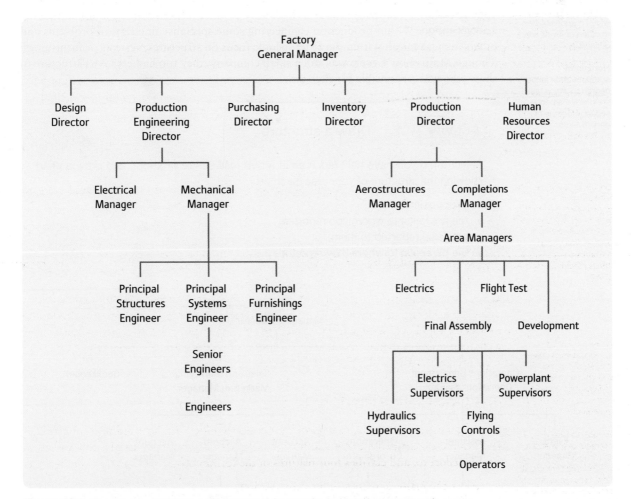

Figure 10.2 The structure within a BAE aircraft factory (www.baesystems.com)

Management in practice   Sales and Marketing   **Multi-show Events**

Multi-show Events employed 11 people providing entertainment and promotional services to large businesses. When Brian Simpson created the business there were two staff – and no structure. He reflected on the process of growth and structure:

> While the company was small thinking about a structure never occurred to me. It became a consideration as sales grew and the complexity of what we offered increased. There were also more people around and I believed that I should introduce a structure so that responsibilities would be clear. It seemed natural to split sales and marketing from the actual delivery and production of events as these were two distinct areas. I felt that by creating 'specialised' departments we could give a better service to clients as each area could focus on their own roles. [Figure 10.3 shows the structure.]
>
> We had to redesign the office layout and introduce a more formal communication process to ensure all relevant information is passed on – I think this structure will see us through the next stage of business growth and development.

Source: Private communication.

Vertical specialisation refers to the extent to which responsibilities at different levels are defined.

Horizontal specialisation is the degree to which tasks are divided among separate people or departments.

Figure 10.2 shows specialisation – design, production and so on. It shows a **vertical specialisation** in that people at each level have distinct responsibilities, and a **horizontal specialisation**. Within production engineering some specialise in electrical problems and others in mechanical: within the latter, people focus on structures, systems or furnishings. Though Multi-show Events was still a small company, they too had created a structure to show who was responsible for each task.

Activity 10.1   Draw a structure

Select a job you have held (such as in a pub, call centre or shop), and draw a chart showing the structure of your area, such as:

- your position;
- the person(s) to whom you reported;
- who else reported to them;
- the person(s) to whom they reported.

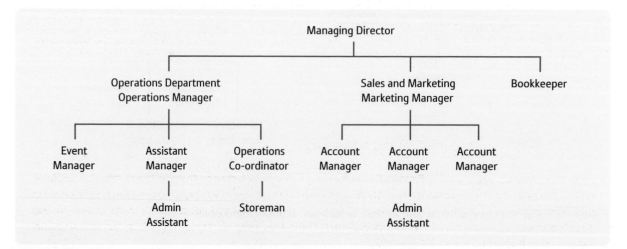

Figure 10.3 The organisation structure at Multi-show Events

Chain of command

The lines of authority show the links between people – who they report to and who reports to them. It shows who they can ask to do work, who they can ask for help – and who will be expecting results from them. Figure 10.2 shows that the production director can give instructions to the aerostructures manager, but not to the electrical manager in production engineering. Figure 10.3 shows the lines of authority in Multi-show Events. In both, people have countless informal contacts that make the system live, and help them to cope with unexpected events.

In allocating **formal authority** managers give people the right to make decisions, allocate resources or give instructions. Formal authority is based on the position, not the person. The production engineering director at BAE has formal authority over a defined range of matters – and anyone else in that job would also have it.

Subordinates comply with instructions because they accept the person has the formal (sometimes called legitimate) authority to make them. An operator in the hydraulics area of final assembly would accept an instruction from the hydraulics foreman, but probably not from the powerplant foreman (they may help as a personal favour, but that is different from accepting formal authority). If managers give instructions beyond their area of formal authority, they meet resistance.

Responsibility is a person's duty to meet the expectations associated with a task. The production director and the hydraulics foreman are responsible for the tasks that go with those positions. To fulfil those responsibilities they require formal authority to manage resources.

Accountability means that people with formal authority over an area are required to report on their work to those above them in the chain of command. The principal systems engineer is accountable to the mechanical manager for the way he or she has used resources: have they achieved what was expected as measured by the cost, quantity, quality or timeliness of the work?

Delegation occurs when people transfer responsibility and authority for part of their work to people below them in the hierarchy. The production director is responsible for all work in that area, and can only do this by delegating. They must account for the results, but pass responsibility and necessary authority to subordinates – and this continues down the hierarchy. Delegating to subordinates enables quicker and better-informed decisions by people familiar with the issue, and may also develop their initiative and sense of responsibility. Some managers are reluctant to delegate, fearing it will reduce their power.

> **Formal authority** is the right that a person in a specified role has to make decisions, allocate resources or give instructions.

> **Responsibility** refers to a person's duty to meet the expectations others have of them in their role.

> **Delegation** occurs when one person gives another the authority to undertake specific activities or decisions.

The span of control

The **span of control** is the number of subordinates reporting to a supervisor. If managers supervise staff closely there is a narrow span of control – the top half of Figure 10.4. If they allow staff more responsibility the supervisor has less to do, so more staff can report to them. The span of control becomes wider, and the structure flatter – the lower half of Figure 10.4.

> A **span of control** is the number of subordinates reporting directly to the person above them in the hierarchy.

Key ideas	Joan Woodward's research

Joan Woodward's study of 100 firms in Essex found great variety between them in the number of subordinates managers supervised (Woodward, 1965). The number of people reporting directly to the chief executive ranged from two to 18, with the median span of control being six. The average span of control of the first line supervisors varied from ten to 90, with a median of 37. Woodward explained the variation by the technological system used (more in Section 10.7, p. 332).

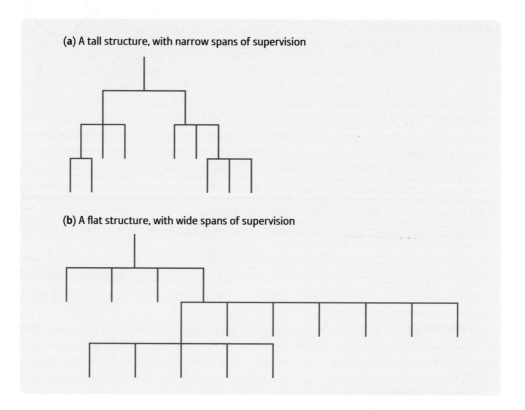

(a) A tall structure, with narrow spans of supervision

(b) A flat structure, with wide spans of supervision

Figure 10.4
Tall and flat
organisation
structures

Centralisation and decentralisation

As an organisation grows, managers divide work vertically, as they delegate decisions to those below them – and so begin to create a hierarchy. Growth brings complexity, but it is usually possible to see three levels – corporate, divisional and operating – such as at The Royal Bank of Scotland (RBS) (www.rbs.com):

- **Corporate:** The most senior group, the Group Board has overall responsibility for controlling the company to ensure its long-term success and for delivering value to shareholders. It approves strategy, monitors performance and maintains external links with regulators and governments.
- **Divisional:** Responsible for implementing policy and allocating budgets and other resources. RBS is (in 2016) organised mainly by three types of customer: Personal and Business Banking (essentially the retail business to 16 million customers); Corporate and International (financial services to UK and international corporations); and Commercial and Private (services to wealth individuals and enterprises). Divisional managers are responsible for meeting targets set by the Board. They represent the division's interests to the Board and monitor performance in the operating units.
- **Operating:** Responsible for delivering services and related technical work. Within the three main divisions there are teams responsible for ensuring that systems and facilities work properly.

Centralisation is when a relatively large number of decisions are taken by management at the top of the organisation.

Decentralisation is when a relatively large number of decisions are taken lower down the organisation in the operating units.

The vertical hierarchy establishes what decisions people at each level can make. This theme is especially relevant in multinationals, which experience constant tension between global consistency and local responsiveness.

Centralisation is when those at the top make most decisions, with managers at divisional level ensuring those at operating level follow the policy.

Decentralisation is when people in divisions or operating units make many of the business decisions. Branch managers in a chain of retail travel agents had considerable freedom over pricing and promotional activities, but were required to follow very tight financial reporting routines. KPMG, the auditing and consulting firm, announced in 2012 that its European division would decentralise more decisions to national offices.

Management in practice

A decentralised structure at Roche
www.roche.com

Roche, based in Switzerland, is one of the world's most successful and profitable pharmaceutical companies. The board appointed a new chief executive – Severin Schwan (a graduate in business and law) who, at the age of 40, has spent his career in the company. The group has a decentralised structure which analysts believe has been a major factor in its success, by encourages each subsidiary to focus their research on specific diseases, while collaborating on marketing. Mr Schwan says teamwork is essential in this knowledge-based business:

> When I toured our labs, I grasped the potential and the enthusiasm of our people. We have to capitalise on that. If you tell your people all the time what to do, don't be surprised if they don't come up with new ideas. Innovative people need air to breathe. Our culture of working together at Roche is based on mutual trust and teamwork. An informal friendly manner supports this: at the same time this must not lead to negligence or shoddy compromises – goals must be achieved and, at times, tough decisions have to be implemented.

Source: *Financial Times*, 4 August 2008, p. 14.
© The Financial Times 2008. All Rights Reserved.

Many organisations display a mix of both. Kering (the owner of many luxury brands, including Gucci) offers its subsidiaries 'freedom within a framework'. The company's 14 brands employ more than 3,300 people in China, but only 100 direct Kering employees. Kering monitors Chinese retailing trends closely, and shares this information with the brands – but the local brand management teams decide if or how to use it. The centre develops strategy, and assists with, for example, property transactions – but brand managers implement the strategy in China (*Financial Times*, 13 June 2013, p. 14).

The issue emerged in the Volkswagen scandal (**Chapter 5**), in that the chief executive of Volkswagen in the United States (where the illegal practices were discovered) had not been part of the group in Germany that developed the technology in question, and knew nothing of it until after the story broke. This tension between centralising and decentralising is common, with the balance at any time reflecting managers' relative power and their views on the advantages of one direction or the other – see Table 10.2.

Formalisation

Formalisation is when managers use written or electronic documents to direct and control employees. These include rules, procedures, instruction manuals, job descriptions – anything that shows what people must do. Operators in call centres use scripts to guide their conversation with customers, ensuring they deal with them consistently and legally.

There is always tension between flexibility and control. People who want to respond to customer needs or local conditions value informal arrangements. Laws intended to protect customers from unsuitable selling methods lead to formal systems, recording procedures and less staff discretion.

Formalisation is the practice of using written or electronic documents to direct and control employees.

Table 10.2 Advantages and disadvantages of centralisation

Factor	Advantages	Disadvantages
Response to change	Thorough debate of issues	Slower response to local conditions
Use of expertise	Concentration of expertise at the centre makes it easier to develop new services and promote best practice methods	Less likely to take account of local knowledge or innovative people
Cost	Economies of scale in purchasing and using common systems (e.g. IT)	Local suppliers may give better value than remote corporate ones
Policy implications	Possibly less risk of local managers acting illegally	Possibly more risk of local managers acting Illegally
Staff commitment	Backing of centre ensures wide support	Staff motivated by more responsibility
Consistency	Provides consistent image to the public – less variation in service standards	Local staff discouraged from taking responsibility – can blame centre

Activity 10.2 Critical reflection on structures

Select an organisation with which you are familiar, or which you can find out about. Gather information about aspects of the structure, such as:

- Does the organisation chart look tall, or flat?
- What evidence is there of high or low levels of formality?
- Which decisions are centralised, and which are decentralised?
- Share your information with colleagues on your course, to increase your awareness of the range of ways in which people have designed structures.

10.4 Dividing work internally – functions, divisions and matrices

Work specialisation divides the larger tasks of an organisation (such as developing new pharmaceuticals) into smaller tasks for designated units (functional, divisional or matrix), within which further specialisation divides those tasks into jobs for individuals. Another approach shares the work among networks of collaborating, but independent, organisations – see Figure 10.5.

Specialisation by function

A **functional structure** is when tasks are grouped into departments based on similar skills and expertise.

When managers divide staff according to profession or function (finance, marketing) they create a **functional structure**: there are six in the BAE chart in Figure 10.2. Figure 10.6 shows a hospital chart, with a functional structure at senior level.

The functional approach can be efficient as people with common expertise work together, and follow a professional career path. It can lead to conflict if functions have different perceptions of organisational goals. Le Meunier-FitzHugh and Piercy (2008) show

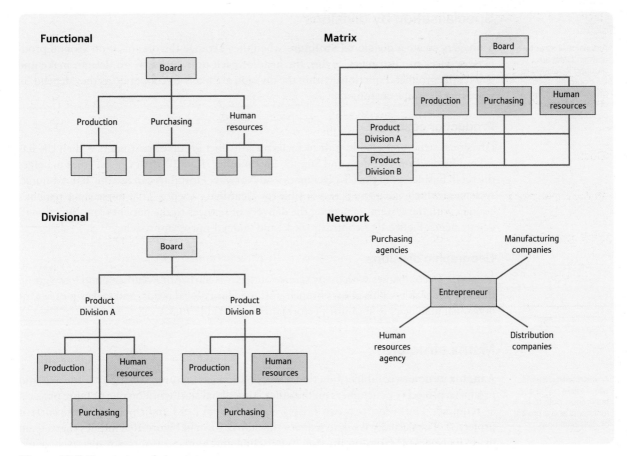

Figure 10.5 Four types of structure

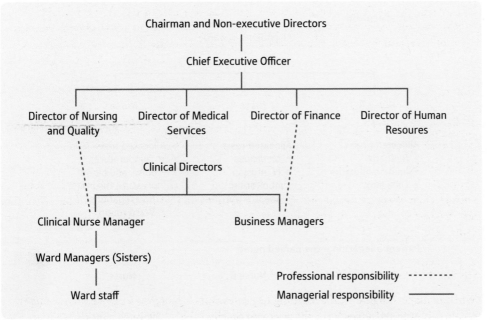

Figure 10.6
Partial organisation structure in a hospital

how staff in sales and marketing experienced this – the former stressing immediate sales, the latter long-term customer relations. Functional staff face conflicts when product managers compete for access to resources (such as IT).

Specialisation by divisions

A **divisional structure** is when tasks are grouped in relation to their outputs, such as products or the needs of different types of customer.

Managers create a **divisional structure** when they arrange the organisation around products, services or customers, giving the head of each unit authority to design, make and deliver the product. Functions within the division are likely to cooperate as they depend on satisfying the same customers.

Product or customer

Divisional structures enable staff to focus on a distinct group of customers – Shell UK has a Trading division (Trading and Supply) and another (Retail North Cluster) that manages the retail businesses in the UK, Denmark and Norway. Hospitals can use the 'named-nurse' system, in which one nurse is responsible for identified patients. That nurse is the patient's contact with the system, managing the delivery of services to the patient from (functional) departments. Figure 10.7 contrasts 'task' and 'named-nurse' approaches.

Geographic divisions

Managers in companies with many service outlets – Waitrose or Weatherspoon – can group them by geography. This allows branch staff to identify local needs, and makes it easier for divisional managers to monitor performance – see Table 10.3.

Matrix structure

A **matrix structure** is when those doing a task report both to a functional and a project or divisional boss.

A **matrix structure** combines functional and divisional structures: function on one axis and products, projects or customers on the other. Functional staff work on one or more projects as required. They report to two bosses – a functional head and the head of the current project(s). They usually work in teams – the matrix form in Figure 10.5 implies that a team made up of people from production, purchasing and human resources respectively could

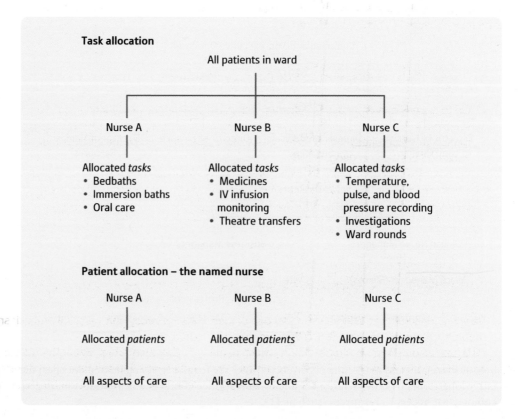

Figure 10.7 Task and named-nurse structures

Table 10.3 Advantages and disadvantages of functional and divisional structures

Structure	Advantages	Disadvantages
Functional	Clear career paths and professional development	Isolation from wider interests damages promotion prospects
	Specialisation leads to high standards and efficiency	Conflict over priorities
	Common professional interests support good internal relations	Lack of wider awareness damages external relations
Divisional	Functional staff focus on product and customer needs	Isolation from wider professional and technical developments
	Dedicated facilities meet customer needs quickly	Costs of duplicate resources
	Common customer focus enables good internal relations	Potential conflict with other divisions over priorities
		Focus on divisional, not corporate, needs

work on Product A, another on Product B and so on. This method sometimes works in organisations that depend on a flow of new products: managers delegate significant responsibility and authority to an identifiable team, which is then accountable for results (Cisco Systems, the case in Chapter 17, is an example, as is Apple – the Part 1 Case).

Others cite situations where matrix structures have not worked, with no clear vision, responsibility, or sense of ownership. When the UK Government merged the Inland Revenue and the Customs service to create HM Revenue and Customs, it chose a matrix structure. This was widely criticised for its complexity, with many suggesting that a traditional hierarchical structure was more suitable for a transaction-processing business such as HMRC, which needs clear lines of communication.

Activity 10.3   Choosing between approaches

- Go to the website of a company that interests you, and gather information about its structure.
- Decide whether it has a functional or a divisional structure – and if the latter, is that based on products or geography?
- If it has international operations, how are they shown in the structure?
- Compare your research with colleagues on your course, and prepare a short presentation summarising your conclusions.

Case study   GlaxoSmithKline – the case continues   www.gsk.com

Senior management at GSK believed that part of their problem with research was the way they organised it. R&D had become large and bureaucratic, which damaged the creative atmosphere in which scientists work best. The company had lost the clear accountability, transparency and personal enthusiasm essential for drug discovery.

The then Chief Executive (Jean-Paul Garnier) concluded that the functional structure was obsolete, while a matrix structure would become too complex. He therefore replaced it with 'Centres of Excellence for Drug Discovery' (CEDDs). Each is focussed on a family of related diseases (such as Alzheimer's or obesity), has a CEO with the authority to initiate and end projects, and employs several hundred scientists. There are only two or three management layers between the CEO and the 'bench' scientists.

The intention was to make decisions more quickly and restore freedom of action to the scientist conducting the research. It also changed the incentive system, to ensure that those who made the discoveries share in the financial rewards. By 2008 it had 12 CEDDs, and the results were promising. When it introduced this divisional structure in 2005 GSK had two products in 'late-stage development'; by 2015 it had over 30.

Sources: Garnier (2008); GSK Annual Report, 2015, p. 6.

Case questions 10.2

- Review this and the earlier instalment of the case, and list which of the structural types mentioned in this and the previous section the company has used.

10.5 Dividing work externally – outsourcing and networks

Creating a structure includes deciding which tasks in the value chain the organisation will do itself, and which it will secure from others – the 'make or buy' decision.

Outsourcing

Outsourcing refers to the practice of delegating selected value chain activities to an external provider.

Outsourcing happens when managers delegate activities in the value chain to external providers – to cut costs or to access expertise. The remaining organisation concentrates on activities such as marketing and integrating the supply chain. Companies routinely outsource transport, distribution and information processing. Franchising (see Section 4.2, p. 116) is a form of outsourcing. New companies, such as innocent drinks (Chapter 2 Case) outsource manufacturing as this saves capital. Many UK public services are outsourced to private companies. Private provision of foster care to children is growing quickly as local authorities reduce costs. The annual cost (in 2014) of placing a child in foster care with a family was about £27,000, compared with £130,000 for placing them in a children's home. The private sector provides about half of all foster care (*Financial Times*, 7 January 2014, p. 20).

One disadvantage of outsourcing is that the company depends on others working to their required standard. When the oil rig on BP's well in the Gulf of Mexico exploded in 2010, the fact that BP neither owned the rig nor employed the contractors did not absolve it of responsibility. A company withdrawing from an area of work will also lose the skills in that area, which may come to matter more.

Collaborative networks

A **collaborative network** is when tasks required by one company are performed by other companies with expertise in those areas.

A **collaborative network** (sometimes called a 'virtual organisation') forms when organisations remain independent but agree to work together in defined areas of work. There is no hierarchical relationship between the players – they work together because they share common goals in some aspects of their business, and hope to gain by contributing their respective skills. The approach is common in high-technology sectors with a large research component – an example, such as that of ARM Holdings, will help to clarify how they can work – see 'Management in practice'.

Management in practice	ARM Holdings www.arm.com

ARM Holdings is a leading designer and supplier of digital electronic products founded at Cambridge in 1990. It has grown from twelve people then to more than 3,000 in 18 countries by 2015.

The founders realised that in a sector with rapid technological development, a new entrant such as ARM could not compete with established companies to manufacture complete IT systems. They decided to concentrate on their strength – designing microprocessors – and to position ARM as an 'enabler' working with other companies. Rather than make things itself, it would be central to an 'ecosystem' of IT design and manufacture. So it had to develop both a business approach and a workplace culture based on collaboration – internally between colleagues and externally with other organisations.

The founders developed a 'Connected Community of Partners' that includes customers and their customers, as well as suppliers and rivals. The vision was to cement ARM's position in the value chain by enabling all stakeholders to collaborate in developing and using microprocessors. There are now about 1,000 companies in the 'Connected Community'.

Source: *Financial Times*, 24 January 2012; ARM Holdings Annual Report 2014.

Miles et al. (2010) review the structural forms outlined in these two sections and draw on their research into collaborative communities to identify their properties:

- **Shared interests**: shared resources or common goals
- **Collaborative values**: willing to share knowledge and contribute to the success of fellow community members, and to seek fairness in contributions and rewards
- **Community-orientated leadership:** focus on facilitating growth sustainability, collaboration and promoting collaborative values and practices
- **Infrastructure to support member collaboration:** systems, processes and norms that support both direct and pooled collaboration among members
- **Expandable resources:** knowledge and other resource pools that all members contribute to and draw from.

Mixed forms

Large organisations typically combine functional, product and geographical structures within the same company – see, for example, BP (Part 2 Case) or RBS (Part 4 Case).

The counterpart of dividing work is to coordinate it, or there will be confusion and poor performance.

Case study	GlaxoSmithKline – the case continues www.gsk.com

A more recent structural innovation is to work more closely with external partners. GSK no longer depends on its own research for new drugs: by 2020 half of the drug discovery projects may be undertaken by external partners. The company's research director estimated that between one-quarter and one-third of GSK's research already involved working with external partners and the CEDD would play a growing role by managing a portfolio of research run by such companies:

In the future we are going to have many more external projects.

In 2010 it announced a further change: a group of 14 scientists would move into a separate company specialising in pain relief. They would take with them the rights to several patents, in exchange for GSK holding an 18 per cent stake in the company. This would enable GSK to reduce overhead costs, while benefiting from the new company's profits. They expect that the scientists will be more highly motivated in their own company than as a small group within a large one.

In 2015 it concluded an agreement with Swiss company Novartis under which the two companies exchanged some products (which better-suited the other company's product range), and created a joint-venture to build their respective businesses in consumer healthcare.

Sources: *Financial Times*, 5 October 2010, 23 October 2014, p.17; Annual Report 2015; Garnier (2008).

Case questions 10.3

- What may be the implications for control of these latest stages in the way the company organises research?
- What may be the effects for individual scientists of outsourcing much of its R&D?

Activity 10.4   Comparing structures

Think of an organisation in which you have worked, or about which you can gather information.

- To which of the four structural forms (Figure 10.5) did it correspond most closely?
- What were the benefits and disadvantages of that approach?
- Compare your conclusions with colleagues on your course, and prepare a list of the advantages and disadvantages of each structure.

10.6   Coordinating work

Those responsible for the divided tasks need to coordinate them. These interdependent individuals achieve this when they act as if they can predict each other's actions – failure occurs when they cannot do so, and act independently. Coordination can be between individuals who are geographically distant, and/or who work for separate organisations.

Direct supervision

A manager can ensure coordination by directly supervising his or her staff to check they are working as expected. The number of people whom anyone can supervise effectively reflects the idea of the span of control – that beyond some (variable) point, direct supervision is no longer sufficient. Geographical separation affects this, though information technology appears to reduce its significance.

Hierarchy

If disputes or problems arise between staff or departments, they can put the arguments to their common boss in the hierarchy, making it the boss' responsibility to reach a solution. At BAE (Figure 10.2), if the engineer responsible for structures has a disagreement with the systems engineer, they can ask the mechanical manager to adjudicate. If that fails they can escalate the problem to the production engineering director – but this takes time. In rapidly changing circumstances (or if they work in different organisations) the hierarchy cannot cope, which delays decisions.

Standardising inputs and outputs

If the buyer of a component specifies exactly what they require, and the supplier meets that, coordination is easy. If staff receive the same training they will need less direct supervision, as their manager can be confident they will work consistently. New staff at Pret A Manger (see p. 50) complete a precise training course before they begin work, which is constantly reinforced.

Rules and procedures

Another method is to prepare rules or procedures, like those in the 'Management in practice' feature. Organisations have procedures for approving capital expenditure, specifying the questions a bid should answer, how people should prepare a case and to whom they should submit it. Software developers face the challenge of coordinating designers working on parts of a project, often in different organisations, so they use strict change-control procedures to ensure that the sub-projects fit together.

Management in practice   **Safety procedures in a power station**

The following instructions govern the steps that staff must follow when they inspect control equipment in a nuclear power station:

1. Before commencing work you must read and understand the relevant Permit-to-Work and/or other safety documents as appropriate.
2. Obtain keys for relevant cubicles.
3. Visually inspect the interior of each bay for dirt, water and evidence of condensation.
4. Visually inspect the cabling, glands, terminal blocks and components for damage.
5. Visually check for loose connections at all terminals.
6. Lock all cubicles and return the keys.
7. Clear the safety document and return it to the supervisor/senior authorised person.

Information systems

Information systems help to ensure that people who need to work in a consistent way have common information, so that they can coordinate their activities. Computer systems and internet applications enable different parts of an organisation, as well as suppliers and customers, to work from common information, helping coordination.

Key ideas   **Coordinating sales and marketing**

Large organisations typically create separate sales and marketing departments, which must then coordinate their work to ensure cooperation, customer satisfaction and profitability. Homberg et al. (2008) concluded (from a survey of German firms in financial services, consumer goods and chemicals) that the best performance was in firms where managers had:

- developed strong structural links between the two functions, especially by using teams, and requiring staff to plan projects jointly; and
- ensured that staff in both functions had high market knowledge – by rotating them between functions to learn about customers and competitors.

Source: Homberg et al. (2008).

Most companies purchase goods and services electronically, ensuring that orders and payments to suppliers flow automatically to match current demand. This coordinates a laborious task where, prior to such technology, mistakes were common.

Direct personal contact

The most human form of coordination is when people talk to each other. Mintzberg (1979) found that people use this method in both the simplest and the most complex situations. There is so much uncertainty in the latter that information systems cannot cope – only direct contact can do this, by enabling people to make personal commitments to each other – see 'Management in practice'.

Management in practice   Coordination in a social service

The organisation cares for the elderly. Someone who had worked there for several years:

Within the centre there was a manager, two deputies, an assistant manager, five senior care officers (SCOs) and 30 officers. Each SCO is responsible for six care officers, allowing daily contact between supervisor and subordinates. While this defines job roles quite tightly, it provides a good communication structure. Feedback is common as there are frequent meetings of the separate groups, and individual appraisals by the SCOs. Staff value this opportunity for praise and comments on how they are doing.

Contact is also common between SCO and care officers during meetings to assess clients' needs – for whom the care officers are directly responsible. Frequent social functions in the department also enhance relations and satisfy social needs. Senior management place controls on the behaviour of care officers, often from legislation or the Health and Safety Executive.

Source: Private communication.

Activity 10.5   Observing coordination

Think of an activity in which you and others have worked together in a coordinated way: it could be in paid or voluntary work, or a social activity. Record your answers to these questions:

- To what extent did someone coordinate the work by direct supervision?
- Was it clear who was in charge, and how they could help coordination?
- Was everyone briefed about the task, and what they were expected to do?
- Were there any written or unwritten rules to follow during the task?
- How was information exchanged between those doing the task?
- What personal contact was possible during the task?
- Compare your conclusions with colleagues on your course, and agree some good coordination practices.

Managers make successive decisions about dividing and coordinating work: these build a structure, which in varying degrees corresponds to a mechanistic or organic form.

10.7   **Mechanistic and organic forms**

Some organisations emphasise the vertical hierarchy by defining responsibilities clearly, taking decisions at the centre, delegating defined tasks and requiring frequent reports. This enables those at the centre to know what is happening and whether staff are working correctly. The organisation presents a uniform image and customers receive consistent treatment. Communication is mainly vertical, as the centre passes instructions down and staff pass queries up. Burns and Stalker (1961) called this a **mechanistic structure**.

Others define tasks broadly and flexibly, use cross-functional teams and base authority on expertise rather than position. Management relies on people nearest the action to find the best solution. Communication is mainly horizontal among those familiar with the task. There may not be an organisation chart, as the division of work is fluid. Burns and Stalker (1961) called this an **organic structure**. Table 10.4 compares the two types of structure.

> A **mechanistic structure** means there is a high degree of task specialisation, people's responsibility and authority are closely defined and decision-making is centralised.

Management in practice   An organic structure at Pixar   www.pixar.com

The company's string of successful movies depends not only on its creative employees, but on how it manages them. Ed Catmull (co-founder of Pixar, and president of Pixar and Disney Animation Studios) has described the 'collective creativity', and how the senior team fosters this. He believes Pixar is unique in the way people at all levels support each other. He describes the daily reviews:

> The practice of working together as peers is core to our culture . . . One example is our daily reviews, or 'dailies', a process for giving and getting constant feedback in a positive way . . . People show work in an incomplete state to the whole animation crew, and although the director makes decisions, everyone is encouraged to comment. There are several benefits. First, once people get over the embarrassment of showing work in progress, they become more creative. Second, directors . . . can communicate important points to the entire crew. Third, people . . . inspire each other to raise their game. Finally, there are no surprises at the end. People's desire to make sure their work is 'good' before they show it [can mean] that their finished version is not what the director wants. The 'dailies' avoid such wasted efforts.

Source: Catmull (2008), p. 70.

Within a large organisation some units correspond to a mechanistic form and others to an organic. A company may have a centralised information system and tightly controlled policies on capital expenditure – while business units have autonomy on research or advertising budgets. Why do managers favour one form of structure rather than another? One (though disputed) view is that it depends on how they interpret contingencies – the situation in which the business works:

> An **organic structure** is one where people are expected to work together and to use their initiative to solve problems; job descriptions and rules are few and imprecise.

> the essence of the contingency paradigm is that organisational effectiveness results from fitting characteristics of the organisation, such as its structure, to contingencies that reflect the situation of the organisation. (Donaldson, 2001, p. 1)

Successful organisations appear to be those in which managers maintain a good fit between contingent (contextual) factors and the structure within which people work. Figure 10.1 showed these contingencies – strategy, technology, age/size and environment.

Table 10.4 Characteristics of mechanistic and organic structures

Mechanistic	Organic
Work on specialised tasks	Contribute experience to common tasks
Hierarchical structure of control	Network structure of contacts
Knowledge located at top of hierarchy	Knowledge widely spread
Vertical communication	Horizontal communication
Loyalty and obedience valued	Commitment to goals valued

Source: Based on Burns and Stalker (1961).

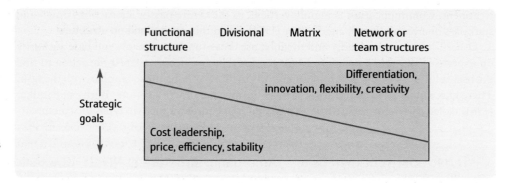

Figure 10.8
Relationship between strategies and structural types

Strategy

Chapter 8 outlined Porter's view that firms adopt one of three generic strategies – cost leadership, differentiation or focus. Those using a cost leadership strategy increase efficiency to keep costs low. A mechanistic structure can support this with defined tasks in an efficient functional structure. A clear hierarchy ensures people work to plan and vertical communication keeps the centre informed.

Those using a differentiation strategy focus on innovation and new products. An organic structure can support this, by enabling ideas to flow easily between people able to contribute, regardless of their function – Pixar is an example.

Figure 10.8 expresses the idea that strategies require appropriate structures. The more the strategy corresponds to cost leadership, the more likely it is that managers will create a functional structure. If the balance is towards differentiation, they are more likely to create a divisional, team or network structure.

Technology

Technology is the knowledge, equipment and activities used to transform inputs into outputs.

Technology refers to the knowledge, tools and techniques used to transform inputs into outputs – buildings, machines, IT systems, and the associated knowledge and procedures.

Joan Woodward (1965) gathered information from 100 UK firms to establish whether structural features such as the span of control or the number of levels in the hierarchy affected performance. The researchers saw no pattern until they analysed companies by their manufacturing process, which showed a relationship between technical complexity and company structure.

- **Unit and small-batch production:** Firms make unique goods to a customer's order. It is similar to craft work, as people and their skills directly shape the process – custom-built cycles, designer furniture, luxury yachts.
- **Large-batch and mass production:** Standard products move along an assembly line, with people complementing the machinery – mobile phones, cars, washing machines.
- **Continuous process:** Material flows through complex technology making the product, as people monitor the process and fix faults – breweries, oil refineries, steel plants.

Different technologies impose different demands. Unit production requires close supervision to ensure staff meet the customer's unique requirements. Supervisors communicate directly with staff to manage the uncertainties of making one-off items – which takes time, so a narrow span of control. Assembly-line work is routine and predictable so a supervisor can monitor more staff: there is a wide span of control. Woodward concluded that successful firms were those where managers had created an organisational form providing the right amount of support for the technology in use.

Technology also delivers services, and managers create structures to shape the way staff interact. When Steve Jobs was at Pixar, he designed the building to maximise inadvertent encounters. At the centre is a large atrium which contains the cafeteria, meeting rooms, bathrooms, and mailboxes. As a result, everyone has strong reasons to go there repeatedly during the course of the workday. It's hard to describe just how valuable the resulting chance encounters are. (Catmull, 2008, p. 71)

Environment

Chapter 3 showed how environments vary in terms of their complexity and dynamism: what does this mean for the structure of firms in those varied environments? Burns and Stalker (1961) compared the structure of a long-established rayon plant in Manchester with the structures of some new electronics companies then being created in the east of Scotland. Both types of organisation were successful – but had different structures.

The rayon plant had clear rules and procedures, tight job descriptions and coordination was primarily through the hierarchy. Tasks were highly specialised – managers defined responsibilities clearly and discouraged people from acting outside of their remit. Those at the centre made most decisions, information flowed up the hierarchy and instructions down.

The small electronics companies had few job descriptions, and procedures were ambiguous and imprecise. Staff were expected to use their initiative and work together to solve problems. Communication was horizontal, rather than vertical (see Table 10.4).

Burns and Stalker (1961) concluded that both forms were appropriate for their contexts. The rayon plant had a stable environment, as its purpose was to supply a steady flow of material to the company's spinning factories. Delivery schedules rarely changed and the technology of rayon manufacture was well known. The electronics companies were in direct contact with their customers, mainly the Ministry of Defence. Demand for products was volatile, with frequent changes in requirements. The technology was new, and in many contracts neither customer nor company knew what the end product would be: it was likely to change during the work.

Case study GlaxoSmithKline – the case continues www.gsk.com

The company's Annual Report for 2011 stated that:

> We have broken up the traditional hierarchical pharmaceutical R&D business model, creating instead smaller units to encourage greater entrepreneurialism and accountability for our scientists.
>
> We are striving to develop new partnerships and approaches, adopting a . . . mindset that is more innovative, open-minded, flexible and consultative. We value the different perspectives other groups can bring to our thinking . . . We are also increasing consultation with patients and payers to ensure the medicines we are developing provide improvements that healthcare systems will value and reward (*GSK Annual Report,* 2011, p. 5).

The same report also explained the international structure of this global business. Consumer healthcare is run as a single unit and support functions such as property and IT are centralised. Pharmaceuticals and vaccines are organised geographically by large regions – for example European pharmaceuticals and vaccines, Japanese P&V and so on.

Geographical units have considerable autonomy in how they work. In 2014 the Chinese authorities fined the company £300 million, after they discovered that GSK's top executive in the country had authorised the payment of bribes to doctors to boost sales. The company apologised for this failure, and vowed to do whatever it could to restore trust in the business.

Source: GSK Annual Report, 2011; *Financial Times*, 26 September 2014, p. 23.

Case questions 10.4

- GSK has had both mechanistic and organic structures: what prompted the change?
- Why may the new structure improve business performance?
- What coordination issues or other risks may arise in the new structure?

	Structure	
	Mechanistic	*Organic*
Uncertain (unstable)	**Incorrect fit:** Mechanistic structure in uncertain environment Structure too tight	**Correct fit:** Organic structure in uncertain environment
Certain (stable)	**Correct fit:** Mechanistic structure in certain environment	**Incorrect fit:** Organic structure in certain environment Structure too loose

Environment is labelled on the left axis.

Figure 10.9 Relationship between environment and structure

Burns and Stalker (1961) concluded that stable, predictable environments would encourage a mechanistic structure. Volatile, unpredictable environments would encourage an organic structure. This recognition that their situation places unique demands on an enterprise was a major step in understanding organisation structure – see Figure 10.9.

Activity 10.6   Comparing mechanistic and organic forms

Think of a department you have worked in, or about which you can gather information.

- Was it broadly mechanistic or organic?
- Why has that form evolved, and is it suitable?
- How does it compare to other departments in the organisation?

Management in practice   Organic problem solving in a mechanistic structure

The organisation I work for has just come through a short-term cash-flow crisis. The problem arose because, while expenditures on contracts are relatively predictable and even, the income flow was disrupted by a series of contractual disputes.

The role culture permeates the head office, and at first the problem was pushed ever upwards. But faced with this crisis all departments were asked for ideas on how to improve performance. Some have been turned into new methods of working, and others are still being considered by the 'ideas team', drawn from all grades of personnel and departments. This was a totally new perspective, of a task culture operating within a role culture – that is, we developed an organic approach. What could be more simple than asking people who do the job how they could be more efficient?

To maintain the change in the long run is difficult, and some parts have now started to drift back to the role culture.

Source: Private communication.

Organisations do not face a single environment. People in each department try to meet the expectations of players in the wider environment, and gradually develop structures that help them to do that. A payroll section has to meet legal requirements on, among other things, salary entitlements, taxation and pensions records. Staff must follow strict rules, with little scope to use their initiative: they work in a mechanistic structure. Staff in product development face different requirements – and will expect to work in a structure that encourages creativity and innovation: they expect to work in an organic structure.

An implication is that coordination between them will be difficult as they work in different ways. Paul Lawrence and Jay Lorsch explored this – see 'Key ideas'.

> **Differentiation** is when the parts of an organisation develop particular attributes in response to the demands posed by their relevant external environments.

Key ideas	**Lawrence and Lorsch: differentiation and integration**

Two American scholars, Paul Lawrence and Jay Lorsch, developed Burns and Stalker's work. They observed that departments doing different tasks face a separate segment of the environment – some relatively stable, others unstable. Lawrence and Lorsch predicted that to cope with these varying conditions departments will develop different structures and ways of working. Those in stable environments would move towards mechanistic forms, those in unstable environments would move towards organic.

Empirical research in six organisations showed that departments did indeed differ in the ways predicted. Those facing unstable environments (research and development) had less formal structures than those facing stable ones (production). The greater the **differentiation** between departments the more effort was needed to integrate their work. Successful firms achieved more **integration** between units by using a variety of integrating devices such as task forces and project managers with the required interpersonal skills. The less effective companies in the uncertain environment used rules and procedures.

Source: Lawrence and Lorsch (1967).

Size and life cycle

Small organisations tend to be informal – people work on several tasks and coordinate by face-to-face contact or direct supervision. Weber (1947) noted that larger organisations had formal, bureaucratic structures: research by Pugh and Hickson (1976) confirmed this. As with the head of Multi-show Events, as managers divide a growing business into units they need more controls such as job descriptions and reporting lines.

> **Integration** is the process of achieving unity of effort among the various subsystems in the accomplishment of the organisation's task.

Management in practice	**Growth and structure in a housing association**

A manager in a housing association, providing affordable housing for those on low incomes, describes how its structure changed as it grew:

> Housing associations have to give tenants and their representatives the opportunity to influence policy. In the early days it had few staff, no clear division of labour and few rules and procedures. It was successful in providing housing, which attracted more government funds, and the association grew. Managing more houses required a more formal structure to support the work. The association no longer served a single community, but several geographical areas. Staff numbers grew significantly and worked in specialised departments. The changes led to concerns amongst both staff and committee that the organisation was no longer responsive to community needs and that it had become distant and bureaucratic.

Source: Private communication from the manager.

This implies that organisations go through stages in their life cycle, with structures adapting to suit. The entrepreneur creates the business alone, or with a few partners or employees. They operate informally with little division of labour and few rules (for a discussion of the unique structural issues facing entrepreneurs in high-technology industries, see Alvarez and Barney (2005)). The owner makes the decisions, so they have a centralised structure. If the business succeeds it will need to raise more capital to finance growth. The owner no longer has sole control, but shares decisions with members of the growing management team. Tasks become divided by function or product, creating separate departments and more formal controls to ensure coordination. Many small companies fail when they expand rapidly but fail to impose controls and systems for managing risks – as an executive of a publishing company that got into difficulties recalled:

> We were editors and designers running a large show, and we were completely over-stretched. Our systems were simply not up to speed with our creative ambitions.

If a business continues to grow, it becomes more bureaucratic with more division of responsibilities and more rules and systems to ensure coordination. Mature, established firms tend to become mechanistic, with a strong vertical system and well-developed controls. More decisions are made at the centre – bringing the danger of slower responses to change and, in some industries, a less competitive position than newer rivals. The managing director of Iris, an advertising agency:

> Iris London is our oldest and our most mature office – about 300 people. When an agency grows to that sort of size . . . it starts to become dysfunctional. You invent admin systems, processes, bureaucracy, and that's countercultural and it stops you being any good, it stops you getting closer to clients and being creative. So we've reorganised around clients [with five groups] of between 30 and 60 people: the creative, the planning, the commercial guys are all sat together, all around dedicated clusters of client type. And that we think will make us more efficient, more effective, more instinctive.

Contingencies or managerial choice?

Contingency theories propose that the performance of an organisation depends on having a structure that is appropriate to its environment.

Contingency theories propose that the most effective structure will depend (be contingent) on the context:

> The organization is seen as existing in an environment that shapes its strategy, technology, size and innovation rate. These contingent factors in turn determine the required structure; that is, the structure that the organization needs to adopt if it is to operate effectively. (Donaldson, 1996, p. 2)

Determinism is the view that the business environment determines an organisation's structure.

Effective management involves formulating a strategy and a structure to support that – by encouraging appropriate behaviour. The emphasis is **determinist** (the form is determined by the environment) and functionalist (the form is intended to support effectiveness). Management's role is to make adjustments to the structure as conditions change – such as by increasing formality as the company grows.

Structural choice emphasises the scope that management has to decide the form of structure, irrespective of environmental conditions.

John Child (2005) disagreed, suggesting that contingency theorists ignore the degree of **structural choice** that managers have. Decisions about structure are not only rational, but also political. The values and interests of powerful groups can influence structure, even if this reduces performance to some degree.

> ### Activity 10.7 Critical reflection – contingency or choice?
>
> Recall some significant changes in the structure of your organisation. Try to establish the reasons for them, and whether they had the intended effects. Do those reasons tend to support the contingency or management choice perspectives?

Case questions 10.5

- Does the GSK example support a contingency or management choice approach?

Another consideration is that the direction of causality is not necessarily from strategy to structure. It is also possible that an organisation with a given structure finds it easier to embark on a particular strategy.

10.8   Learning organisations

The term **learning organisation** is used to describe an organisation that has developed the capacity to continuously learn, adapt and change. In a learning organisation the focus is on acquiring, sharing and using knowledge to encourage innovation.

A **learning organisation** is one that has developed the capacity to continuously learn, adapt and change.

According to Nonaka and Takeuchi (1995), the ability to create knowledge and solve problems has become a core competence in many businesses. In their view, everyone is a knowledge worker – someone dealing with customers quickly knows their likes and dislikes, and their view of the service. Because they are typically in low-paid jobs far from corporate headquarters, this valuable intelligence is overlooked.

Table 10.5 (based on Pedler et al. (1997)) presents a view of the features of an ideal learning organisation – features to which managers can aspire. These features cluster under five headings, shown in Figure 10.10

Table 10.5 Features of a learning organisation

Feature	Explanation
A learning approach to strategy	The use of trials and experiments to improve understanding and generate improvements, and to modify strategic direction
Participative policy making	All members are involved in strategy formation, influencing decisions and values and addressing conflict
Informative	Information technology is used to make information available to everyone and to enable frontline staff to use their initiative
Formative accounting and control	Accounting, budgeting and reporting systems are designed to help people understand the operations of organisational finance
Internal exchange	Sections and departments think of themselves as customers and suppliers in an internal 'supply chain', learning from each other
Reward flexibility	A flexible and creative reward policy, with financial and non-financial rewards to meet individual needs and performance
Enabling structures	Organisation charts, structures and procedures are seen as temporary, and can be changed to meet task requirements
Boundary workers as environmental scanners	Everyone who has contact with customers, suppliers, clients and business partners is treated as a valuable information source
Inter-company learning	The organisation learns from other organisations through joint ventures, alliances and other information exchanges

(continued)

Table 10.5 (*continued*)

Feature	Explanation
A learning climate	The manager's primary task is to facilitate experimentation and learning in others, through questioning, feedback and support
Self-development opportunities for all	People are expected to take responsibility for their own learning, and facilities are made available, especially to frontline staff

Souce: Based on Pedler et al. (1997)

In a learning organisation members share information and collaborate on work activities wherever required – including across functional and hierarchical boundaries. Boundaries between units are either eliminated or are made as porous as possible to enable the flow of ideas and information. Learning organisations emphasise team working, and grant employees a high degree of autonomy. Rather than directing and controlling, managers act as facilitators, supporters and advocates.

Learning depends on information, so there is an emphasis on sharing information among employees in a timely and open manner. This, too, depends on managers creating a structure and culture that encourages people to share information. There is a strong sense of community and mutual trust, so people feel free to share ideas and experiment: they learn without fear of criticism or punishment.

Argyris (1999) distinguished between single-loop and double-loop learning. The classic example of single-loop learning is the domestic thermostat, which, by detecting temperature variations, takes action to correct deviations from a predetermined level. In single-loop learning the system maintains performance at the set level, but is unable to learn that the temperature is set too high or too low. In single-loop learning the question is: 'How can we better achieve that standard of performance?'. In double-loop learning the question

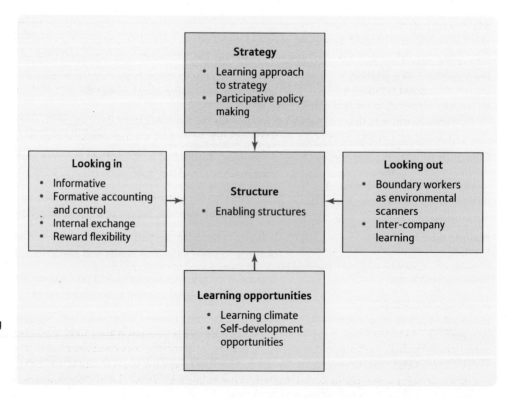

Figure 10.10
Clusters of learning organisation features

Source: Pedler et al. (1997).

becomes: 'Is that an appropriate target in the first place?'. To cope effectively with change, the aim would be to enhance the skills of double-loop learning.

10.9   Integrating themes

Entrepreneurship

Ambos and Birkenshaw (2010) observed the evolution of new ventures. Their multi-year study of nine start-ups (university science-based) found they exhibited one of three 'archetypes' – mutually supporting organisational features – at some time:

- **Aspiration driven** – the desire to build a company; when this archetype dominated, leaders focused on forming the venture and legitimising it to key stakeholders;
- **Market driven** – here the leader(s) focused on market challenges and on meeting the specific needs of their customers; and
- **Capability driven** – here they focused on technology and capability development – turning ideas into prototypes and finding how to turn them into saleable products.

The organisational elements that came together to 'define' these archetypes were specific to new ventures, namely:

- primary driver of action – the issue of most direct concern at the time;
- key stakeholders – the one or two whose support was vital to the next phase;
- key knowledge development – something they needed to develop at the time.

The authors claim their study offers a novel perspective on the evolution of new ventures, as it does not draw on the features of large organisations, but from a common understanding of new ones.

Sustainability

Many senior managers accept that the long-term viability of their business depends on being effective in environmental as well as financial terms. Lawler and Worley (2010) contend that achieving this is not a matter of good intentions, but of locating sustainability within the organisation's strategy and supporting it with suitable structures. They studied companies with good reputations for sustainability to identify how they had ensured that their structures encouraged sustainable behaviour.

One conclusion was that sustainable effectiveness requires an external focus – structures that put as many people as possible in touch with the external environment so that they can experience what is happening and be able to make sound contributions to strategy and operations. General Electric required that each business strengthened its marketing teams, so that managers were more aware of how the environment was changing and how GE had to change to achieve sustainable effectiveness. They also refer to Cisco's 'eco-board', which is accountable for achieving the company's green objectives across the organisation. BP (**Part 2 Case**) is another example of an organisation that has made significant structural changes to ensure that staff report safety and environmental concerns directly to senior management, not to heads of production units with other priorities.

Internationalisation

The growth of multinationals – based in one country but with significant production and sales in many others – continues, as managers see new opportunities beyond their home territory. At the same time they have to defend their position against new entrants from other countries. A perennial topic in multinationals is the balance between global integration and local responsiveness. Bartlett and Ghoshal (2002) show how managers at some firms – such as the Japanese Kao and Matsushita – sought to integrate worldwide operations to achieve global efficiency through economies of scale. Others, including Philips and Unilever, were more sensitive to local differences, permitting national subsidiaries high levels of autonomy to respond to local conditions.

They go on to suggest that as global pressures increased, companies needed to develop a more complex range of capabilities:

> To compete effectively, a company had to develop global competitiveness, multinational flexibility, and worldwide learning capability simultaneously. Building these [capabilities] was primarily an organisational challenge, which required organisations to break away from their traditional management modes and adopt a new organisational model. This model we call the transnational. (p. 18)

They also present evidence and research on the organisational challenges that companies face if they wish to perform effectively in the international economy.

Governance

The financial crisis that began in 2008 showed that many bankers had been taking great risks with the bank funds by investing in loans that were not only very risky, but packaged in such a complex way that others had difficulty understanding them. The bankers' behaviour had been encouraged in part by an incentive structure that rewarded them handsomely for profits, even if these were short-lived. This was not intentional fraud, but a failure to pay enough attention to banks' governance structures.

The Combined Code (2006) gives clear guidance to companies on how to structure their boards to ensure adequate governance and control. This is a voluntary Code of Best Practice, which the boards of companies listed on the London Stock Exchange are expected to follow. It includes guidance on matters such as:

- **The Board:** Every company should be headed by a Board that is collectively responsible for the success of the company;
- **Chairman and chief executive:** There should be a clear division of responsibilities between the running of the Board and the executive responsible [for running the business]. No one individual should have unfettered powers of decision.
- **Board balance:** The Board should include a balance of executive and [independent] non-executive directors so that no individual can dominate the Board's decisions.
- **Board appointments:** There should be a formal, rigorous and transparent procedure for appointing new directors.

Paradoxically, while this Code is widely seen as a valuable aid to corporate governance, all the banks that had to be rescued by the government had complied with the Code.

Summary

1 Outline the links between strategy, structure and performance

- The structure signals what people are expected to do, encourages actions that support strategy, and so enhances performance. A structure may also enable a strategy to emerge that a different structure would have hindered.

2 Give examples of management choices about dividing and coordinating work, with their likely advantages and disadvantages

- Managers divide work to enable individuals and groups to specialise on part of the whole, and so become more skilled. Task division needs to be accompanied by suitable coordination.
- Centralisation brings consistency and efficiency, but also the danger of being slow and out of touch with local conditions. People in decentralised units can respond quickly but risk acting inconsistently.
- Functional forms allow people to specialise and develop expertise and are efficient; but they may be inward looking and prone to conflicting demands.
- Divisional forms allow focus on particular markets of customer groups, but can duplicate facilities.
- Matrix forms try to balance the benefits of functional and divisional forms, but can lead to conflicts over resources.
- Networks of organisations enable companies to draw upon a wide range of expertise, but may involve additional management and coordination costs.
- Coordination can be achieved by direct supervision and personal contact, hierarchy, standardising inputs and outputs, rules and information systems.

3 **Compare the features of mechanistic and organic structures**

- Mechanistic – people perform specialised tasks, hierarchical structure of control, knowledge located at top of hierarchy, vertical communication, loyalty and obedience are valued.
- Organic – people contribute experience to common tasks, network structure of contacts, knowledge widely spread, horizontal communication, commitment to task goals is valued.

4 **Summarise the work of Woodward, Burns and Stalker, Lawrence and Lorsch and John Child, showing how they contributed to this area of management**

- Woodward: appropriate structure depends on the type of production system ('technology') – unit, small-batch, process.
- Burns and Stalker: appropriate structure depends on uncertainty of the organisation's environment – mechanistic in stable, organic in unstable.
- Lawrence and Lorsch: organisational units' organisation faces different environments, which implies there will be mechanistic and organic forms within the same organisation, raising coordination problems.
- John Child: contingency theory is too deterministic – managers have more choice over structure than contingency theories implied.

5 **Use the 'contingencies' believed to influence choice of structure to evaluate the suitability of a form for a given unit**

- Strategy, environment, technology, age/size and political contingencies (Child) are believed to indicate the most suitable form, and the manager's role is to interpret these in relation to their circumstances.

6 **Explain and illustrate the features of a learning organisation**

- Learning organisations are those that have developed the capacity to continuously learn, adapt and change. This depends, according to Pedler et al. (1997), on evolving learning-friendly processes for looking in, looking out, learning opportunities, strategy and structure.

7 **Explain alternative ways to coordinate work, and understand how you can use this to develop the skill of coordinating work**

- Using the coordination methods outlined in the chapter depends on skill, and the chapter provides an opportunity to understand how knowing these methods can help a person develop the skill of coordinating work.

8   **Show how ideas from the chapter add to your understanding of the integrating themes**

● Ambos and Birkenshaw (2010) traced the development of nine new businesses and identified three 'archetypes' – patterns of mutually supporting organisational elements that all firms exhibited – namely that they were driven by aspiration, markets and capabilities.

● Lawler and Worley (2010) showed how an organisation's sustainability intentions can be made more robust and likely to have an effect if they are visibly located in the structure.

● Bartlett and Ghoshal (2002) trace the many dilemmas companies face in creating a structure for their international operations.

● The financial crisis led many to call for tighter systems of governance and control – but many troubled banks already appeared to have such systems in place, which were not used.

Test your understanding

1   What did Chandler conclude about the relationship between strategy, structure and performance?

2   Draw the organisation chart of an organisation or department that you know. Compare it with the structures shown in Figure 10.2, writing down points of similarity and difference.

3   List the advantages and disadvantages of centralising organisational functions.

4   Several forms of coordination are described. Select two that you have seen in operation and describe how they work – and how well they work.

5   Explain the difference between a mechanistic and an organic form of organisation.

6   Explain the term 'contingency approach' and give an example of each of the factors that influence the choice between mechanistic and organic structures.

7   If contingency approaches stress the influence of external factors on organisational structures, what is the role of a manager in designing an organisation?

8   What is the main criticism of the contingency approaches to organisation structure?

9   What examples can you find of organisational activities that correspond to some of the features of a learning organisation, as identified by Pedler et al. (1997)?

10 Summarise an idea from the chapter that adds to your understanding of the integrating themes.

Think critically

Think about the structure of your company, or one with which you are familiar, then make notes on these questions:

● What is the structure – centralised or decentralised; functional or divisional, etc?

● In responding to issues of structure, what **assumptions** about the nature of organisations appear to guide your approach? How do they assume people should coordinate their work?

● What factors in the **context** of the company appear to shape its approach to organising – what kind of environment are you working in, for example? Does the context add to the challenge of coordination?

● Have managers seriously considered whether the present structure is right for the business? Do they regularly compare your structure with that in other companies to look for **alternatives,** including how they achieve adequate coordination?

● What **limitations** can you identify in any of the ideas and theories presented here? For example, can you envisage a situation in which using contingency theory to shape design choices would be unwise?

Develop a skill – coordinating work

Being able to coordinate work among those engaged in a common task is an essential skill, and this exercise should help you develop that.

- **Awareness:** Assess how you typically coordinate the work of people you depend on to complete a task – in your studies, or in social activities (moving smoothly to a new flat requires a lot of coordination, and may suggest other tasks to use here). Do you, for example, assume it will all work out, and leave it to chance? Or do you watch over each stage of the process very closely?

- **Learning:** Read again Sections 10.1 and 10.6 and summarise the main ideas presented there. Why is coordinating fundamental to managing?

- **Analysis:** Review your work on Activity 10.5. What evidence does that provide about the effects of using, or not using, each method of coordination? How did the context seem to shape the method used?

- **Practice:** Identify (on your own or with colleagues) a task in which you need to coordinate several people or enterprises (as before, related to any aspect of life) in the next week or so. Decide which coordination method from Section 10.6 you will use (also recall Activity 10.5), and plan the task accordingly.

  - Follow your plan and record the outcomes. How did your coordination plan work?

  - If possible, compare your work with that of others to see what else you can learn.

- **Application:** Decide on another opportunity to practise this skill within the next week.

Read more

Burns, T. and Stalker, G.M. (1961), *The Management of Innovation,* Tavistock, London.

Homburg, C., Jensen, O. and Krohmer, H. (2008), 'Configurations of marketing and sales: A taxonomy', *Journal of Marketing,* vol. 72, no. 2, pp.133–54.

An account of research into one of the continuing questions in organisation structure, of particular interest to students of marketing.

Lawrence, P. and Lorsch, J.W. (1967), *Organisation and Environment,* Harvard Business School Press, Boston, MA.

Qiao, G. and Conyers, Y. (2014), *The Lenovo Way,* McGraw Hill, New York.

The lead author is a senior manager at the Chinese company that took over IBM's personal computer business in 2005. The company has developed a reputation for skillfully integrating acquisitions – including having an adaptable state of mind.

Woodward, J. (1965), *Industrial Organisation: Theory and practice,* Oxford University Press, Oxford. Second edition 1980.

These three influential books give accessible accounts of the research process, and it would add to your understanding to read at least one of them in the original.

Go online

These websites have appeared in the chapter:
   www.arm.co.uk
   www.gsk.com
   www.roche.com

www.rbs.com
www.unilever.com
www.topright-group.com
www.dixonscarphone.com
www.pixar.com

Visit two of the business sites in the list, and navigate to the pages dealing with corporate news, investor relations or 'our company'.

- What organisational structure issues can you identify that managers in the company are likely to be dealing with? Can you find any information about their likely culture from the website?
- What kind of environment are they likely to be working in, and how may that affect their structure and culture?

CHAPTER 11

HUMAN RESOURCE MANAGEMENT

Aim

To introduce the topic of human resource management and to examine some of the major practices.

Objectives

By the end of your work on this chapter you should be able to outline the concepts below in your own terms and:

1   Understand the contribution of HRM to organisational performance
2   Understand the potential links between strategy and HRM
3   Describe the HRM practices concerned with the flow of people into and through the organisation
4   Describe the HRM practices concerned with reward management
5   Understand how HRM aims to manage workforce diversity
6   Recognise the issues you will face as a potential job seeker, and understand how to develop the skill of preparing for an interview
7   Show how ideas from the chapter add to your understanding of the integrating themes

Key terms

The chapter introduces these terms:

human resource management (HRM) validity
external fit   personality tests
internal fit   assessment centres
job analysis   performance-related pay
competencies   diversity

Each is a term defined within the text, and in the glossary at the end of the book.

In 2015 BMW, whose headquarters are in Munich, was the world's leading premium automobile company, employing about 116,000 people on the BMW, Mini and Rolls-Royce brands. It has 24 production facilities in 13 countries, with a sales network in more than 140 countries. Management has chosen to focus on three premium segments of the international car market, with each of its brands being the market leader in its segment. The BMW corporate Strategy Number ONE expresses the vision to be the leading provider of premium products and premium services for individual mobility.

In 2014 it delivered 2.1 million automobiles to customers, about 8 per cent more than in the previous year: this included 300,000 Minis and 4,000 Rolls-Royce motors. Western Europe is its main market, accounting for about 60 per cent of all BMW cars sold (though China is an increasingly important market for Rolls-Royce). The company manufactures motorcycles and has a joint venture with Rolls-Royce to produce aircraft jet engines. It concentrates on the top-end of the car market, which commands high prices, and has also invested in overseas manufacturing plants – in 2009 it opened a second plant in China.

BMW's business strategy includes providing purchasers with a wide variety of choices about how their car is equipped. The variety of possible combinations is so great that exactly the same car is produced only about once every nine months. The company also emphasises the quality of the product. This combination of variety and quality is a challenge to achieve in a product as complex as the modern car. It requires both advanced technology in manufacturing, and employees who are highly skilled and flexible. Recognising this, the company places great stress on recruiting only the highest-quality workers, with technical and team working skills.

The strategy is supported by its approach to HRM, which derives from, and is highly consistent with, the company's 'six inner values': communication, ethical behaviour to its staff, achievement and remuneration, independence, self-fulfilment and

© Gisela Schober/Getty Images

the pursuit of new goals. This underlying philosophy guides the design of new BMW plants (an open design that makes all operations easy to see, and so helps communication) and the process of introducing new or reformed HRM practices. The company consults widely about these, sharing information on proposals and trying to ensure that successive changes are consistent with each other and build on established policies.

The company provides virtually unprecedented job security. And that is part of the reason why, for many Germans, getting a job at BMW is the ultimate accomplishment. The company's human resource department receives more than two hundred thousand applicants annually (Lawler, 2008, p. 18).

Sources: Lawler (2008); company website.

Case questions 11.1
- What issues concerning the management of people are likely to be raised in a group such as BMW that has rapidly expanded production and distribution facilities?
- How is increased overseas production likely to affect HRM policies?

11.1 Introduction

Activity 11.1 Defining HRM

Before reading on, note down how you would define human resource management. What topics and issues do you think it deals with, and how does it relate to management as a whole? Save your notes and compare them with the topics covered in the chapter as you work.

BMW is a large and successful business in a growing area of the world economy – automobile production. Yet it faces competitive problems stemming from high employment costs in Germany, and strong competitors in its chosen market sectors. Management is attempting to retain the company's position by diversifying the product range and the number of countries in which it manufactures. The company believes that HRM strategy and practices should support its business strategy by providing well-trained and flexible employees.

Such activities are part of a broader change taking place in many companies, where managers are trying to align the way they manage people with their strategy. They aim to develop employees at all levels in ways that will support their strategy. They also seek coherence among the main elements of HRM.

Human resource management refers to all those activities associated with the management of work and people in organisations.

This chapter focuses on some policies and practices intended to influence employee attitudes and behaviour. These practices are commonly referred to as **human resource management (HRM)**, which covers four areas (Beer et al. (1984)):

- employee influence (employee involvement in decision making);
- work systems (work design, supervisory style);
- human resource flow (recruitment, selection and training); and
- reward management (pay and other benefits).

Employee influence and work systems are discussed in Chapters 14 and 15. Consequently, this chapter focuses on human resource flow and reward management. Management designs resource-flow practices to ensure they have the right people available to achieve their goals. Reward management aims to attract, retain and acknowledge employees.

The chapter begins by outlining the emergence of HRM as part of management work. It then presents current practices in the areas of human resource flow and reward management. A prominent HR practice is the selection interview, and preparing for such an event is the focus of the skill development feature.

11.2 HRM and performance

This section outlines the emergence of HRM and how managers expect it to contribute to performance.

From personnel management to HRM

The term 'human resource management' is relatively new, gaining prominence in companies and business schools in the early 1980s. Before then managers institutionalised the way they managed staff by creating personnel departments. Partly influenced by the human relations model (Chapter 2), they believed they could ensure a committed staff by dealing with grievances and welfare. Growing trade union power led management to create departments to negotiate over pay and working conditions.

Personnel management departments typically had limited power, and found it difficult to show that they enhanced organisational performance. Senior management saw them as reactive, self-contained and obsessed with procedures, employee grievances, discipline and trade unions. Their aim was to minimise costs and avoid disruption – and they had little influence on strategy.

Changes in the business world led some observers to propose that issues concerned with managing people should have a higher profile, and especially that line managers should take a larger role. Guest (1987) attributed this to:

- the emergence of globally integrated markets in which competition is severe and where innovation, flexibility and quality are more important than price;
- the economic success during the 1980s of countries that tried to manage employees constructively, such as Japan and West Germany;
- a popular book by Peters and Waterman (1982), which showed that high-performance organisations also had a strong commitment to HRM;
- more educated employees; and
- fewer employees joining trade unions.

Early advocates of HRM proposed that key themes would be integration, planning, a long-run orientation and a link to strategy – believing that together these would improve performance. This reflected the resource-based view of strategy that emphasises the importance of firm-specific resources and competences that are difficult to imitate.

HRM and performance – the empirical evidence

Those advocating HRM aim for a 'win–win' situation for employees and employer: the employees do work that is intrinsically satisfying and financially rewarding, while the organisation is more profitable and secure. Many scholars have tested empirically the extent to which HRM practices affect performance, and Jiang et al. (2012) systematically analysed 116 such studies. They organised their analysis using the model shown in Figure 11.1, which predicts that three groups of HRM practices (enhancing skill, motivation and opportunity) will affect operational and financial outcomes.

These practices are the main elements in most 'High Performance Work Systems'. They do not affect outcomes directly, but through the following mediating variables:

- human capital (knowledge, skill and abilities of employees);
- employee motivation (direction, intensity and duration of their effort);
- voluntary turnover (proportion of employees who quit in a period);

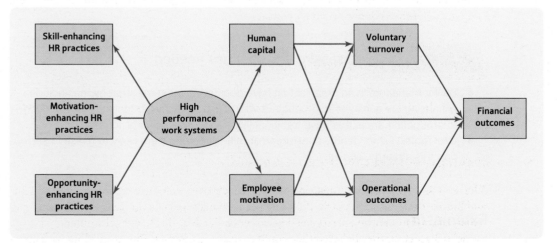

Figure 11.1 Theoretical model of the effects of HPWS on organisational outcomes
Source: Jiang et al. (2012).

Table 11.1 Examples of practices and measures used in Figure 11.1 variables

Variable	Examples of practices and measures
Skill-enhancing practices	Selective recruitment, training, education
Motivation-enhancing practices	Performance-related pay, job security, appraisals, career development, performance management
Opportunity-enhancing practices	Empowerment to use skills, job design, team work, decentralisation, involvement
Human capital	Technical, operational and management skills, educational levels, customer knowledge
Motivation	Motivation, cooperation, helping, organisational citizenship behaviour
Voluntary turnover	Proportion of employees who leave in a period, quit rate
Operational outcomes	Productivity, innovation, customer satisfaction
Financial outcomes	Sales growth, return on assets, overall financial performance

Table 11.1 lists the variables and gives examples of the practices within them.

The analysis by Jiang et al. (2012) concluded that, as expected, certain HRM practices positively affected operational and financial outcomes. The evidence confirmed that skill-enhancing HR practices had a positive effect on human capital (skills), and that motivation-enhancing HR practices had a positive effect on motivation. Both then had positive effects on operational outcomes and hence on financial performance. HRM practices also reduced voluntary turnover, which then enhanced operational and financial performance.

A common theme is that organisations only obtain worthwhile benefits if they take a strategic orientation towards HRM, aiming for a high degree of external and internal fit.

Case question 11.2

- What HRM policies (as listed in Table 11.1) would you expect BMW to use to support the company's 'six inner values' listed in the case?

Activity 11.2   Assessing the changes needed

- Senior managers in an organisation have decided to pursue a strategy that includes enhancing the quality of its products. It will do this partly by introducing team working to production areas that have traditionally been focused on individual work.
- Use Table 11.1 to identify three areas of HRM policy they are likely to revise to support this strategy, and why.

External fit

Chapter 10 showed that organisations develop a structure, which provides the main mechanism through which to deliver their strategy; HRM practices provide some of the tools for this. Figure 11.2 shows this relationship, aiming for a close **external fit** between a firm's business strategy, organisation structure and HRM strategy – and between those and the external environments. For example, Chapter 8 distinguished low-cost and differentiation strategies, which require compatible employee attitudes and behaviours. A low-cost strategy may be best served by paying low wages to a casual labour force. A differentiation strategy, aiming for flexible responses to customer needs, may be best served by imaginative training, team working and shop-floor problem solving.

External fit is when there is a close and consistent relationship between an organisation's competitive strategy and its HRM strategy.

| **Key ideas** | **Human capital and firm performance** |

Crook et al. (2011) studied the relationship between aspects of human capital and firm performance – defining human capital as the explicit and tacit knowledge, skills and abilities embodied in people. They point out that while scholars and practitioners have long assumed that investing in these resources will improve performance, research is equivocal about the relationship. They systematically reviewed the results of 66 empirical studies of the link between human capital and firm performance. They concluded that, as expected, human capital investment has a strong positive effect on firm performance, especially when the human capital concerned is unique to the employing firm (the person is unlikely to take their skills elsewhere). The relationship is also strong when the performance measure used is an operational one, such as quality or sales unit performance, rather than more general measures such as company profits.

Source: Crook et al. (2011).

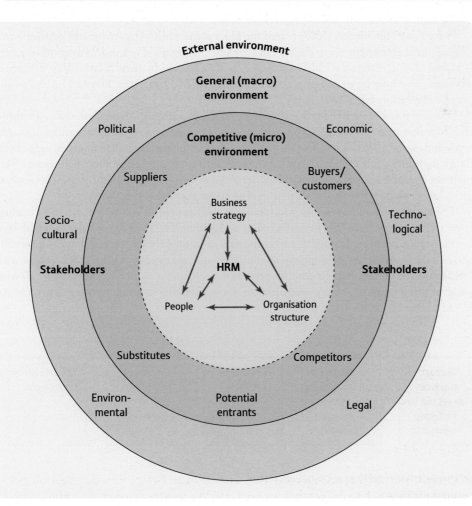

Figure 11.2 Fit between HRM, people, strategy, structure and environment

Source: Fombrun et al. (1984), p. 35.'

Case questions 11.3

- Visit the BMW website and see how the company presents itself and its cars. What image does it convey – what words would you use to describe them?
- To deliver that image, what kind of behaviour would you expect of employees?
- What HRM practices may encourage/discourage that behaviour?

Activity 11.3 Comparing HRM policies

- List the major differences in HRM policies that you would expect to observe between two organisations, one pursuing a low-cost strategy and the other a quality-enhancement strategy. (Use Table 11.1 and related text to assist you.)

Internal fit

Internal fit is when the various components of the HRM strategy support each other and consistently encourage certain attitudes and behaviour.

Organisations are also expected to benefit if their HRM policies achieve **internal fit** in the sense that individual practices complement and reinforce each other. An organisation that encourages team working can support this through a payment system that rewards contributions to the team. Managers will weaken team working if they reward only individual performance, as this will discourage cooperation.

Purcell and Hutchinson (2007) traced the link between HRM practices and performance, paying particular attention to the role of first-line managers. They did so as employee perceptions of, and reaction to, HRM practices will be shaped by their relationship with their manager, and how he or she implements intended HRM practices. Figure 11.3 shows the proposed relationships.

Intended practices are those designed to contribute to strategy. Actual practices are those that first-line managers implement, perhaps adapting them marginally to suit local conditions and expectations. These are the practices that employees see and consider, judge their likely usefulness and fairness – and then form attitudes that shape their behaviour. This includes commitment, task behaviour, discretionary behaviour and other variables such as attendance – which in turn affect financial or economic outcomes.

The team studied 12 organisations (public as well as private sector) known to be leading users of HRM practices. They conducted up to 40 interviews in each organisation with senior managers, first-line managers and employees, and repeated this a year later. The results showed that employees' perceptions of their first-line manager, and their satisfaction with HRM policies, enhanced their commitment, task performance and other variables – all with positive implications for unit performance. Good first-line managers were able to adapt HRM policies to fit local circumstances.

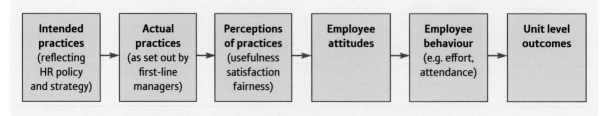

Figure 11.3 The people management–performance causal chain

Source: Based on Purcell and Hutchinson (2007), p. 7.

Critical views of HRM

The view of HRM presented here reflects an assumption that HRM policies can benefit employees as well as employer, since both want the long-term success of the organisation. This is an example of the unitary perspective, introduced in Chapter 2. Others take a pluralist perspective that recognises the legitimacy of different views – between trade unions, between managerial functions, and between managers and trade unions. From this viewpoint it is legitimate for trade unions to disagree with aspects of an HRM policy, even if managers present it as benefitting everyone.

A distinction within HRM itself is between 'hard' and 'soft' approaches (Legge, 2005), in which the former takes a business-led perspective, while the latter sees people as valuable assets whose motivation, involvement and development should have priority over the interests of shareholders.

11.3 What do HR managers do?

Identifying HR roles

Given the range of HR tasks, who does them, and how? This depends on how general managers balance their responsibilities and those of the HR specialists – see 'Key ideas'.

Key ideas · Michael Beer on the general manager's perspective

Michael Beer and his colleagues set out the roles of general managers and of HR specialists, pointing out that many decisions taken by general managers are HRM decisions, even if they do not realise it:

> HRM involves all management decisions and actions that affect the nature of the relationship between the organisation and its employees – its human resources. General managers make important decisions daily that affect this relationship, but that are not immediately thought of as HRM decisions: introducing new technology into the office place in a particular way, or approving a new plant with a certain arrangement of production operations, each involves important HRM decisions. In the long run both the decisions themselves and the manner in which those decisions are implemented have a profound impact on employees: how involved they will be in their work, how much they trust management, and how much they will grow and develop new competencies on the job. (pp. 1–2)

They then advocate their view of the respective roles:

> First, the general manager accepts more responsibility for ensuring the alignment of competitive strategy, personnel policies, and other policies impacting on people. Second, the personnel staff has the mission of [ensuring that] personnel activities are developed and implemented in ways that make them more mutually reinforcing. That is what we mean by the general manager's perspective. (pp. 2–3)

Source: Beer et al. (1984).

To identify how HR managers interpret their role, Caldwell (2003) studied the extent to which HR managers occupied the four roles shown in Figure 11.4:

- **Advisors** – a facilitating role, acting as internal consultants offering expertise and advice to senior managers and line managers.
- **Service providers** – called in by line managers to provide specific HR assistance and support as required. Also provide administrative services to support HR policies such as recruitment, selection and training.

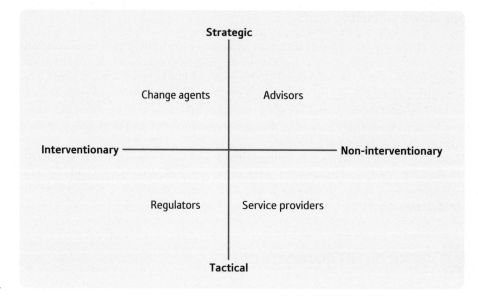

Figure 11.4 Four roles of HR managers.

Source: Caldwell (2003).

- **Regulators** – formulating, disseminating and monitoring the observance of personnel or HR policy and practice, including trade union agreements where relevant.
- **Change agents** – actively promoting proposals for cultural or organisational change, including those related to strategy and business performance.

The most common main role in the 98 organisations he studied was that of advisor, followed by change agents. He also found that HR managers experienced high levels of role ambiguity and role conflict – they were unclear what others expected of them.

Truss and Gill (2009) show how HR managers build the resources they need to do their job by combining structural arrangements with good working relationships. 'Structural arrangements' include:

- providing opportunities to meet with colleagues;
- holding regular meetings of the whole department to discuss policy;
- agreeing personal targets that link staff and departmental objectives;
- seconding staff to line departments;
- taking account of line managers' objectives in deploying HR resources; and
- creating communication mechanisms to link with line managers.

Building 'good working relationships' included:

- sharing positive experiences with line managers;
- ensuring line managers had good contacts with HR practitioners; and
- ensuring HR staff understand organisational needs.

In organisations where HR staff had invested time and effort on these relationships, line managers perceived HR was making an effective contribution to organisational performance. Part of that contribution is through human resource planning.

Activity 11.4   What do HR managers do?

Arrange to talk to someone who works in HRM about their work.

- Use the categories in Figure 11.4 to help analyse what they do, and which of the four categories they spend most time on.
- Use the research by Truss and Gill to analyse how they manage their working relationships with line managers.
- Compare what you have found with others on your course, and summarise your results.

11.4   Human resource planning

Human resource planning is the process through which employers anticipate and meet their needs for staff. It requires estimating the number and type of people the business is likely to require over successive periods, and ensuring they are available.

Forecasting

Large organisations may use complex forecasting techniques to identify their staff requirements – and governments do the same to estimate the likely demand for professional staff who require long training, such as teachers or doctors – Bechet and Maki (1987) describe the methods. Planners use models that typically start with the organisational strategy or with demographic changes that affect demand for services. They forecast the number of staff required to meet those demands and their likely availability – staff in post at the start, together with likely inflows, outflows and internal movements during the planning period. The 'Management in practice' feature shows how McDonald's forecasts short-term demand for staff in its restaurants.

Management in practice   Forecasting staff at McDonald's   www.mcdonalds.co.uk

McDonald's has suffered from the perception that it only offers 'McJobs' – unstimulating jobs with low prospects – and since 2006 has embarked on a campaign to improve its reputation as an employer. It claims to have less labour turnover than competitors, and that when it needs to recruit entry-level 'crew member' positions in the restaurants it can usually select from a large number of unsolicited applicants. Its policy is to promote from within, and claims that more than half the executive team started in the restaurants.

There are seasonal peaks in the demand for labour, and the company has implemented a sophisticated human resource planning software system that enables restaurant managers – who are responsible for recruitment – to plan their staff needs with precision. The software uses data such as past and projected sales figures and labour turnover statistics to forecast the required level of recruitment.

Source: IRS Employment Review 853, 18 August 2006, pp. 42–4.

A limitation of long-term forecasting is the uncertainty of the social and economic environment. For example, attempts to forecast the future demand for nurses (and so for nursing education) struggle to take account of long-term changes in:

- population demographics;
- how that changing population uses health care; and
- how units providing care use nurses.

Since policy makers cannot rely on long-term forecasts of demand, they may be wiser to increase flexibility of supply, so that it is easier to adapt to changes when they happen.

11.5   Job analysis

Job analysis identifies the main constituents of a role, including skills and level of responsibility. It typically leads to a written job description that guides selection, training and performance appraisal. Issues to consider in job analysis include:

- How to collect the data? Possibilities include interviewing current job holders, observing people doing the job and distributing questionnaires.

> **Job analysis** is the process of determining the characteristics of an area of work according to a prescribed set of dimensions.

- Who should collect this data? Should it be those in the job, the supervisor or an internal or external specialist?
- How should the job information be structured and laid out?

The process aims to describe the purpose of a job, its major duties and activities, the conditions under which it is performed and the necessary knowledge, skills and abilities. Jobs are broken into elements that are rated on dimensions such as extent of use, importance, amount of time involved and frequency. Job analysis is made difficult by the volume and complexity of data (McEntire et al. 2006), though online software can overcome this (Reiter-Palmon et al. 2006).

The results of the analysis is a job description, which will usually include these headings:

- job title;
- job purpose;
- job dimensions (e.g. responsibilities for managing budgets or staff);
- organisation chart (who reports to you and who you report to);
- role of department;
- key result areas;
- assignment and review (who allocates and monitors work);
- communication and working relationships (internal and external);
- most challenging part of the job.

Competencies (in HRM) refer to an individual's knowledge, skills, abilities and other personal characteristics required to do a job well.

Rather than thinking about jobs as a set of tasks, HRM practitioners now aim to identify and develop the **competencies** an individual requires to do the job (Kalb et al. 2006). This reflects the need for organisations to be flexible and responsive, from which it follows that they often require employees with broad competencies rather than narrow skills for prescribed tasks.

Team working and job analysis

Team working has implications for job analysis, as the work done by each person may be fluid, especially if managers encourage members to develop a range of skills. As teams work, members develop new skills, so analysis of an individual job soon dates.

Case study   BMW – the case continues   www.bmwgroup.com

Most production staff work in self-managing groups of between eight and 15 members with a high degree of autonomy and clearly defined tasks. Members of the group decide upon each individual's responsibility and how they will move between jobs, as well as making suggestions and decisions about product improvement. Applicants for jobs are screened for their ability to work in a team environment and cooperate with others. Those who are interviewed go through elaborate tests designed to screen out individuals who are not team players.

Each group elects a spokesperson to coordinate activities and to represent them, though they have no power to give orders or impose discipline. Supervisors remain the group's immediate superior

in technical and disciplinary matters, working in an advisory/facilitating role. The supervisor is responsible for proposing and agreeing objectives, presenting progress figures, supporting continuous improvements and ensuring that group members improve their qualifications. Improved product quality and job satisfaction are the aims, leading in turn to greater productivity.

Staff are expected be flexible in terms of time, place and assignment. They can save or overdraw up to 300 hours a year, which enables the company to reduce or increase the labour supply by that amount (for each employee), to cope with temporary changes in demand. BMW offers those nearing retirement the chance to reduce working hours gradually – varying, by mutual consent, with economic conditions. BMW expects staff to be flexible and mobile, moving between plants as requirements change.

Source: Lawler (2008); company website.

Case questions 11.4

- How would the introduction of team working have helped to improve the external fit between HRM and broader strategy?
- To achieve internal fit, what other changes would BMW have needed to make?

Job analysis aims to produce a comprehensive and accurate job description, to inform recruitment and selection.

Activity 11.5 Collect examples of job descriptions or competencies

- Go to the website of an organisation that interests you, and navigate to the pages on careers or current vacancies.
- Try to find examples of job descriptions – compare them with the headings in the text. What factors do they omit, and what do they add?
- Try to find one that includes a statement of competencies required. What does that tell you about the requirements of the job?
- Compare what you find with others on your course, and summarise your results.

11.6 Recruitment and selection

The goal of recruitment is to produce a good pool of applicants for work, while that of selection is to choose the ones most likely to be suitable. The practices employers use may be of particular interest to those seeking jobs.

Recruitment

Options include word of mouth, careers fairs, advertisements, employment agencies and the internet – companies often use Facebook to identify potential recruits based on their interests and personal profiles. Many pay attention to a candidate's presence on social media – see 'Management in practice'.

Management in practice

Recruiters value social media

Brynne Herbert, 30-year-old chief executive of a technology company, comments on their use of social media in recruiting executives:

'do people know that potential employers scour social media presences before interviews? Indeed we do. We judge the quality of your LinkedIn profile and the intellectual quality of your tweets (do you share articles from the *Daily Mail* or from *Harvard Business Review*?)

In fact, when I interview candidates who do not have a social media presence I find it bizarre. What are you doing that is so secretive it merits not having a LinkedIn profile or Twitter account?

When candidates approach me for jobs, I find it even stranger if they have not investigated my social media presence. How should I consider your level of interest in working for our company if you have not figured out that we sell talent mobility software and I support Queens Park Rangers football club?

 Source: *Financial Times*, 29 January 2015.
© The Financial Times 2015. All Rights Reserved.

Selection

This aims to choose the most promising candidates from those that the recruitment phase generates. Managers use methods they hope will minimise:

- **false-positive errors,** where the selection process predicts success in the job for an applicant, who is therefore hired, but who fails; and
- **false-negative errors,** where an applicant who would have succeeded in the job is rejected because the process predicted failure.

As the costs of the latter are not directly experienced by the organisation, managers are more concerned about the former. Selecting the wrong person can cost the organisation dearly and create serious long-term problems.

Zibarras and Woods (2010) show, from a study of almost 600 UK organisations, that informal methods (such as unstructured interviews) are slightly more common than formal ones (structured interviews). The CV is the most commonly used tool, followed by application forms, references and interviews.

Validity occurs when there is a statistically significant relationship between a predictor (such as a selection test score) and measures of on-the-job performance.

Most studies of selection focus on the **validity** of the process, in the sense of its ability to predict future performance. Figure 11.5 shows estimates of the relative accuracy of selection methods, based on the relation between predicted and actual job performance (with zero for chance prediction and 1.0 for perfect prediction).

Management in practice   **Selection for training at RMA Sandhurst**

James Greaves, an officer seconded to Sandhurst, explained the selection process:

The Royal Military Academy Sandhurst takes people from all aspects of British life, and once they meet the minimum educational entrance requirements they enter a two-part selection process. The first lasts a day and a half and consists of psychometric and physical tests to identify individuals who have talents in four domains:

- physical;
- character and personality;
- intellectual; and
- practical ability.

We try to identify these as early as we can for selection for training. The critical one, and probably the most difficult to actually analyse, is the character and personality issue.

We assess them physically, and they have an assault course to go over, you have to run about 600 metres, and during the classroom we look for the ability to perform under pressure, so in a very time-short environment we would look for written assessment and also the ability to stand and think quickly on your feet in front of not only your own peer group (those you're being assessed against) but also a member of the directing staff: he or she sits at the back and asks the questions to see if the individual has what it takes to be trained to become an army officer.

Source: Interview with James Greaves.

Interviews

The interview remains popular as it has low direct costs and can be used for most jobs, despite research showing it has low validity, especially in group interviews (Tran and Blackman, 2006). Interviewer ratings correlate poorly with measures of subsequent performance of the candidates hired (they generate too many false-positive errors). Many interviewers are not good at seeking, receiving and processing the amount and quality of information needed for an informed decision. Some:

- are poorly prepared and ask too many questions of limited value;
- give disproportionate influence to information obtained early in the interview;
- compare applicants with an idealised stereotype;
- give too much weight to appearance and non-verbal behaviour; and make decisions too quickly.

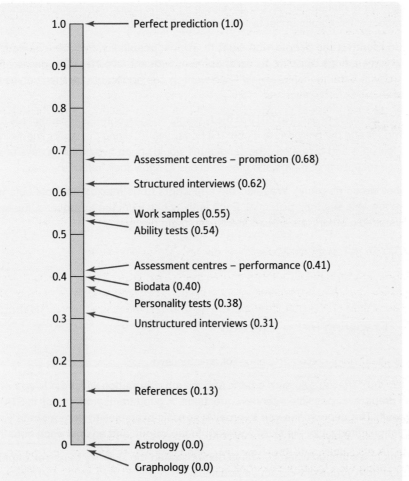

Figure 11.5 The predictive accuracy of selection methods.

Source: Beardwell and Thompson (2014), p. 162.

Aware of these difficulties, and of the need for many employees to be flexible, collaborative and innovative, organisations are themselves using innovative selection processes, in addition to the interview – see 'Management in practice'.

Management in practice   Recruiting for TGI Friday

Jacqui McManus, director of culture and people development at the nationwide restaurant chain TGI Friday, is clear that every aspect of its recruitment activity is a means to an end.

> We are not looking for average people who want to work in hospitality. We are looking for extraordinary people who have a huge appetite to care, connect with and entertain our guests. This doesn't always come across in a traditional interview – we want to see applicants be themselves and let their personalities shine.

As an example, at a recruitment event in 2015 at the National Space Centre, 300 candidates competed for 80 front-of-house, kitchen and bar positions at a new TGI Friday venue. Hiring managers knew what they were after – the 'Friday's feeling' – and to that end the candidates would spend two gruelling days of menu-based impersonations, dance routines and improvised presentations to show their 'gift of the gab'.

> We don't see what we do as 'zany'. We need the applicants to be relaxed and feel safe with us – it's only then that we are able see their potential. Each activity has a unique purpose: some are looking to identify a creative streak, others are around identifying team players.

Source: *People Management*, May 2015, pp. 28–29.

Key ideas   Preparing for an interview

Trought (2012) gives useful guidance on preparing for an interview:

> What will they ask you? The job selection criteria and the job description will provide you with hints and tips you need to prepare for possible interview questions. A good framework to use is STAR: Situation, Task, Action, Result. This encourages you to provide specific examples to demonstrate your skills relevant to the selection criteria. List the skills you want to talk about, and against each note these points:
>
> - **Situation:** Think of a situation when you have demonstrated the skill. Try to use examples from your course and also from your extra-curricular activities.
> - **Task:** What was your aim?

- **Action:** What was your role? What did you do or say?
- **Result:** What was the outcome?

Here are some other possible questions for which you can prepare answers:

- Why do you want to work for (this company)?
- What do you think you can offer?
- What are your strengths and weaknesses?

Source: Trought (2012), pp. 115-116.

Personality tests

Some organisations supplement the interview with more structured methods – especially **personality tests**. These provide a relatively objective measure of the dimensions of someone's personality, and are usually administered online.

They, too, have limitations, and psychologists advise that:

- they should only be used and interpreted by qualified and approved experts;
- an individual's personality may vary with circumstances;
- good performers in the same job may have different personalities.

> A **personality test** is a sample of attributes obtained under standardised conditions that applies specific scoring rules to obtain quantitative information for those attributes that the test is designed to measure.

They will still probably be more accurate than a manager's subjective perception of an applicant – but the Zibarras and Woods (2010) survey cited earlier showed that less than one in five UK organisations used them. Wolf and Jenkins (2006) found that a common reason for testing is to justify a selection decision if someone challenges it.

Assessment centres

Assessment centres use many systematic tests and several assessors to create a comprehensive picture of a candidate's abilities and potential – in areas such as competence, work ethic and emotional intelligence. They have higher validity than interviews, since using many tests and several assessors ensures more accurate predictions of performance. Chamorro-Premuzic (2015) describes their present popularity with companies, and advises applicants to seek opportunities (for example through a careers service) to practise the technique before taking the real thing.

> **Assessment centres** are multi-exercise processes designed to identify the recruitment and promotion potential of personnel.

In uncertain business conditions some organisations build a culture that relies on self-motivated, committed people – and try to ensure they select people with those attributes rather than specific skills for a current job. The Eden Project is an example (www.eden project.com) – see also the 'Management in practice' feature.

Management in practice   Hiring for Hiscox   www.hiscox.co.uk

Kevin Kerridge, Head of Direct and Partnerships at Hiscox (an insurance business), talks about ensuring recruits fit the company:

> When people want to work for Hiscox they have to go through a very rigorous recruitment process and that starts with the HR team doing initial interviews, sifting CVs and doing aptitude tests. If they pass that then the managers who are recruiting for the positions get involved: candidates have at least one, probably two or three interviews with the teams and the managers they'll be working with.
>
> I like to really put people on the spot when they come and work for me so the most important thing is about that energy and drive and that willingness to make a difference. Not just a job but somewhere you

live and breathe the culture of what you're trying to achieve. So I meet them, assess the energy and also set them a task, maybe a presentation on a challenge that I've got. I see the ideas and things that people come up with around those challenges. I think that's a good way of actually testing whether people fit here or not.

Source: Interview with the director.

11.7 Reward management

Table 11.2 summarises some common types of reward system.

Reward management systems aim to align employer and employee objectives, by encouraging action in line with organisational goals. There has been a shift towards flexible and variable reward systems, including:

- from collectively bargained pay towards individual performance systems;
- linking pay systems more directly to business strategy and organisational goals;
- emphasising non-pay items, such as life assurance and childcare vouchers;
- introducing flexible pay components and individualised reward packages.

Developments in pay policies are also linked to changes in work organisation, and the BMW case illustrates both.

Case study   BMW – the case continues   www.bmw.com

The company depends on high performers who are committed to their work and willing to perform well. The pay system is based on fairly rewarding an individual's performance and that of the team. BMW implements this philosophy of performance and reward consistently across all markets and all hierarchical levels. The performance-based element in pay increases with a person's level in the hierarchy. The components of salary are:

- **Fixed salary:** each employee receives a fixed pay of 12 monthly salaries, with no difference between male and female employees. This is assessed and adapted once a year.
- **Company bonus:** the company supplements the fixed pay with a share in company profit – in 2008, for example, this meant that the total pay of most employees amounted to 15 monthly salaries.
- **Individual bonus:** the company also rewards individual performance, the amount depending on an evaluation by their immediate boss.

Source: Company website.

Case questions 11.5

- What external factors may have prompted this review of the payment system at BMW?
- How would it affect the management of the appraisal system?
- What demands would it make on the management information system?

Table 11.2 Reward management systems

Type of system	Basis of calculating reward
Time rate	Hours worked
Payment by results	Quantity of output

(continued)

Table 11.2 Reward management systems (continued)

Type of system	Basis of calculating reward
Skill-based pay	Knowledge and skill
Performance-related pay	Individual performance in relation to agreed objectives
Flexible benefits packages	Selection of benefits (for example, health care or company car) to suit individual's preferences and lifestyles

Performance-related pay

Performance-related pay aims to link a human resource flow activity (performance appraisal) with reward, which brings the risk of expecting the appraisal process to achieve too many objectives. Some organisations have used such arrangements for many years and report positive effects on both individual and organisational performance. At others, the results of performance-related pay have been less impressive. Either there has been little positive impact on organisational performance or the arrangements have been counter-productive for other reasons (Beer and Cannon, 2004). Lawson (2000) noted:

> **Performance-related pay** involves the explicit link of financial reward to performance and contributions to the achievement of organisational objectives.

> the amount of work being undertaken in organisations to modify, change and improve individual performance pay schemes indicates a trend of unhappiness with them. In short, the record of performance-related pay arrangements has been highly variable. (p. 315)

Possible reasons include:

- introducing new pay arrangements without adequate discussion, consultation and explanation;
- performance-related pay fits the circumstances of some firms better than others; it is unlikely to work where there is no trust between employees and managers;
- the review of a person's performance rarely takes sufficient account of the context – such as the difficulty of the task the person was doing.

Management in practice   Performance-related pay: avoiding conflict

In this voluntary organisation the annual appraisal system was used to set a performance-related payment that could be quite substantial. In practice, managers were mainly concerned not to risk de-motivating staff or disrupting working relationships. The appraisal scores therefore always tended to be 'on the overly generous side', which resulted in a substantial increase in salary costs for the organisation – with no obvious improvements to employee motivation, effort or organisational performance.

Source: Interview with manager

Flexible reward systems

More flexible mechanisms for calculating pay have become popular, under labels such as cafeteria benefits, flexible benefits and package compensation. The company offers a compensation package that may include life insurance, medical care or a company car. The benefits for the employer include: aligning reward strategy with business strategies; meeting the requirements of a diverse workforce; and providing value for money. How do employees perceive these arrangements – are the perks designed to help them, or to tie them to the desk? People will view identical perks differently – see 'Key ideas'.

11.8   Equal opportunities and diversity

Much HR work is designed to discriminate between people – at selection, to secure the most suitable candidates, then through appraisal, reward and promotion policies to identify those most likely to meet the demands of more senior jobs.

The essence of equality is to ensure that these essential judgemental processes – selecting some, but not others – are conducted fairly. Unfair discrimination results from people being treated on the basis of limited, and perhaps prejudiced, understanding of the groups to which they belong, rather than on their individual strengths and weaknesses.

The changing workforce

Diversity (at work) refers to differences between individuals at work on any attribute that may evoke a perception that the other person is different from self (Guillame et al., 2013, p. 124).

The workforce in advanced economies is diverse, and the management challenge is to match that **diversity** within organisations. This is both to comply with legal requirements on equal opportunities and to gain a business advantage by matching the social context – there is a 'business case' for diversity. Guillaume et al. (2013) suggest that there is a substantial lack of knowledge about the HRM practices that promote positive outcomes from a diverse workforce. They define workforce diversity very broadly, as 'differences between individuals at work on any attribute that may evoke a perception that the other person is different from self' (p. 124). Clearly this implies an infinite number of attributes, though discussions of managing diversity in organisations tend to focus on those of gender, race, disability and age.

Gender

In the UK, the proportions of men and women in the workforce have been converging, so that 70 per cent of women and 78 per cent of men are recorded as being in the workforce. However, according to Torrington et al. (2008) (upon which this section draws at several points), women continue to be disproportionately concentrated in low-paid work. Equally, pay differentials between men and women have narrowed little, if at all, for many years.

Management in practice

Women in the boardroom

A report by Lord Davies reported that only two companies listed in the FTSE100 index (large companies whose shares are traded on the London Stock Exchange) had an equal number of men and women on their boards. There were only three female chairmen and only five chief executives. In a commentary, Lord Davies pointed to changing social attitudes among young people, who expect to work for companies that have equality in every way, shape or form, as well as increasing acceptance among chairmen that diversity is a business issue.

 Source: *Financial Times*, 29 October 2015, p. 3.
© The Financial Times 2015. All Rights Reserved.

Race

Participation in the workforce in advanced economies is lower among ethnic minority groups than other groups. Those from minority groups who are in employment tend to be disproportionately employed in hotel and catering work rather than in, say, professional and executive work.

People with disability

Those with disability are more likely to be unemployed than their able-bodied contemporaries – and if those working lose their job, it takes them longer to find another.

Age

People are living longer and many who would previously have retired in their mid-60s are still fit and capable of doing paid work. The proportion of people over 65 who are working is rising, while the proportion of those under 25 who are working is falling. There is, however, also evidence that age-bias is deeply ingrained, with many line managers perceiving older workers as being less able to cope with change, training or technology.

Approaches to equality

Torrington et al. (2008) distinguish between 'equal opportunities' and 'diversity' approaches to these issues.

Equal opportunities

The equal opportunities approach seeks to influence behaviour through legislation to prevent discrimination. This approach concentrates on equality of opportunity rather than outcome, and is based on the view that some individuals are discriminated against on the basis of irrelevant views or beliefs about the group to which they belong. The approach therefore tries to ensure that organisations put in place formal procedures to ensure that selection and other processes use fair criteria when deciding whose application to reject.

The weakness of this approach is that the focus is on formal processes, and these cannot be universally standard throughout a complex organisation. Senior management may, in good faith, subscribe to the principles of Equal Opportunities legislation, and expect their staff to put in place procedures to ensure compliance. In a competitive market, staff, facing many other pressures and demands on their time, may sometimes be less than fully diligent in adhering to these policies. Provisions favouring certain groups may also cause resentment among those members of the workforce who do not benefit from them, or who feel they are being disadvantaged in some way.

Managing diversity

The managing diversity approach focuses on individuals, rather than groups, aiming to improve opportunities for all, not only those in minority groups. Separate groups are not singled out for treatment. The central theme of diversity management is that of valuing everyone as individuals, going beyond what is legally required to look for what is positively valued: the focus is on valuing difference.

The approach also presents the economic and business case for valuing difference – that an organisation can benefit from diversity among employees. Ethnically diverse employees may enable it to connect with that community as customers; creating a mutually-supportive working environment may improve relations and reduce disputes within the organisation; and a workforce from diverse backgrounds may enhance the scope for creative approaches to problem solving (see also 'Key ideas).

Key ideas   **A case for diversity**

Diversity is a reality in labour markets and customer markets today. To be successful in working with and gaining value from this diversity requires a sustained, systematic approach and long-term commitment. Success is facilitated by a perspective that considers diversity to be an opportunity for everyone in an organisation to learn from each other how better to accomplish their work. [It also] requires a supportive and co-operative organisational culture as well as group leadership and process skills that can facilitate effective group functioning. Organisations that invest their resource are taking advantage of the opportunities that diversity offers and should outperform those that fail to make such investments.

Source: Kochan et al. (2003), p. 18.

BMW is an example of a company that has followed this approach, as the next part of the 'Case study' shows, with particular reference to enabling older workers to continue to contribute and add value.

Case study   **BMW – the case continues**   www.bmwgroup.com

The BMW group are aware of demographic changes in the workforce, where the birth rate in many Western countries has consistently been lower than the number of deaths, while life expectancy has continued to rise. This ageing workforce affects nations' social security systems and businesses. BMW has formed a project 'today for tomorrow' to help the group adapt to changing demographics, through five areas:

- design of the working environment: ergonomically designed work stations in offices and manufacturing to help avoid physical strain;

- health management and preventive health care: gyms and fitness courses at all plant locations;
- needs-based retirement models: flexible retirement packages that allow individuals to retire early or continue after the age of 65;
- qualifications and skills: the increasing importance of life-long learning; and
- communications: increased awareness of social and corporate changes among managers and associates.

Source: Company website.

Case questions 11.6

- What benefits might BMW gain from a higher proportion of older workers?
- What do you think are the problems associated with an older workforce?
- How might human resource practices change to deal with this?

11.9 Integrating themes

Entrepreneurship

Observing how dependent new enterprises are on the quality of employees, while at the same time being unable to aford significant investment in HR staff, Sheehan (2014) asked whether the use of HR practices has performance benefits for SMEs. Her research team surveyed 336 UK firms with between ten and 250 employees, and at least 18 months old, on their use of a selection of formal HR practices. These included recruitment and selection procedures, performance appraisals, performance-based pay, training and development, and forms of employee consultation. The measures of performance were profitability, innovation and labour turnover.

These benefits were especially pronounced when several HR practices were used in combination, rather than as isolated interventions.

Sustainability

A primary aim of HRM policies has been to align employee and organisational outcomes in terms of economic benefits (sales growth, return on assets). It is equally plausible to envisage HRM supporting other corporate responsibilities – such as the well-being of staff.

Flexibility in pay systems and employment contracts, together with high-performance work practices, raise ethical questions through their effect on employee working hours, stress and work–life balance. Creating organisation structures that facilitate participation, work designs (**Chapter 15**) that enhance employee skills and personal growth and communication systems that increase employee awareness are examples of how HRM practices can broaden the focus of an organisation's sustainability record.

Internationalisation

An international strategy needs to be supported by HRM practices that take account of the international dimensions of employee influence, work systems, human resource flows and reward management.

Companies operating internationally face the dilemma of standardising the HRM practices of overseas subsidiaries towards HQ practices. In contrast, localisation refers to the adoption by overseas subsidiaries of those management practices commonly employed by domestic companies in their respective host countries. Managers are likely to adopt a mixed approach – just as they do in marketing, where promotion and distribution practices are usually localised, even if advertising is standardised across all countries. They need to integrate different approaches into a coherent international HRM strategy, balancing a desire for closer regional or global integration of HRM practices, with the need to make these responsive to probably contradictory local demands. Their workforce will include different national cultures, working physically distant from each other. They will also be working in different management systems, which, as Chapter 4 showed, have implications not only for the overall structure and management of business enterprises, but for the rights and responsibilities of employees.

Sparrow et al. (2004) identify three areas of uncertainty:

- the structures adopted by international companies;
- how multinationals staff and manage their subsidiaries; and
- factors that influence the choice between consistency of HRM practice and adapting it to suit local conditions.

Governance

Corporate governance systems aim to regulate the ownership and control of organisations, in the hope of securing the commitment of stakeholders to the organisation, by regulating their conflicting interests. This is also the aim of modern HRM practices, which have generally replaced the tight control of workers implied by scientific management with attempts to involve workers more fully in planning, organising and conducting production.

Konzelmann et al. (2006) note that corporate governance arrangements still appear to give most attention to shareholder interests. The dilemma is that they are often perceived to give priority to short-term interests, rather than to the long-term interests of the enterprises. These may be best served by developing modern HRM practices that integrate the interests of the organisation and the employees, but may conflict with short-term interests of shareholders. It is also likely that financial interests who are represented in governance arrangements will have little interest or knowledge of HRM practices, and will not see it as their role to comment on these essentially detailed management issues.

Corporate governance arrangements are thus likely to do little, if anything, to support the development of modern HRM practices.

Summary

1 **Understand the contribution of HRM to organisational performance**

- The rise of HRM can be explained by issues such as more globally integrated markets, highly publicised 'companies of excellence', changing composition of the workforce and the decline of trade unions.

2 **Understand the potential importance for organisational performance of HRM**

- The importance of achieving external fit by linking the wider business strategy and HRM strategy.
- Internal coherence among HRM policies is crucial.

3 **Describe the HRM practices concerned with the flow of people into and through the organisation**

- In recent years, due to the need for flexibility, there has been a move away from viewing jobs as a set of tasks to thinking about the set of competencies a person requires to accomplish a job successfully.

4 **Describe some HRM practices concerned with reward management**

- In the search for more flexibility, employers have introduced more individually-determined pay systems and linked pay more closely to organisational goals.

5 **Recognise the issues you will face as a potential job seeker, and understand how to develop the skill of preparing for an interview**

- The chapter has shown ways of anticipating interview questions, and has given the opportunity to practise developing the skill of presenting your skills in a convincing way.

6 **Understand how HRM aims to manage workforce diversity**

- Selection processes may engender greater diversity if they take account of Schneider's Attraction-Selection-Attrition (ASA) model.
- Appraisals can do the same if they guard against the effects of racial bias.
- BMW shows how management employment practices can make the workplace more suitable for older workers.

7 **Show how ideas from the chapter add to your understanding of the integrating themes**

- A recent empirical study in over 300 small UK firms showed that using HR practices improved profitability and innovation, and reduced labour turnover.
- An organisation's HRM practices affect many aspects of employee well-being through their effects on matters such as working hours, stress and work–life balance. These improve the firm's sustainability.
- Companies operating internationally face the dilemma between standardising the HRM practices of overseas subsidiaries towards HQ practices, or favouring localisation, whereby overseas subsidiaries adopt management practices commonly used in that host country.
- Corporate governance arrangements and modern HRM practices are both intended to support the long-term interests of stakeholders. Few of those involved in governance are familiar with HRM (being mainly from finance), so are unlikely to support the development of modern HRM practices.

Test your understanding

1 What are the possible benefits of an organisation adopting a deliberate HRM strategy?

2 What do the terms internal and external fit mean in an HRM context?

3 Summarise the criticism of HRM that it is based on a unitary perspective.

4 What evidence did the chapter include about the effects of HRM on performance?

5 How can the concept of organisational analysis support the recruitment process?

6 What are the main criticisms of personality testing?

7 What are the advantages and disadvantages of performance-related pay?

8 What lessons can you draw from the way BMW has used the payment system to support other aspects of the HRM policy? More generally, summarise the lessons you would draw from the BMW case.

9 Summarise an idea from the chapter that adds to your understanding of the integrating themes.

Think critically

Think about the way your company, or one with which you are familiar, deals with HRM. Then make notes on these questions:

- Which of the issues discussed in this chapter are most relevant to your approach to HRM? Is there a clear and conscious attempt to link HRM with wider strategy? What **assumptions** do people make in your business about the role of HRM? Does the organisation rely heavily on the interview as a recruitment tool – or are they aware of the limitations?

- Are changes in the business **context** affecting staff commitment? May further changes in context (such as greater diversity) affect the validity of the interview?

- Compare your organisation's approach to HRM with that of others, to see what **alternatives** they use. Do they differ on what makes a good interview?

- If there are differences, can you establish the likely reasons, and does this suggest any possible **limitations** in the present approach?

Develop a skill – preparing for an interview

A successful interview technique is essential to your career, and this exercise is about developing one aspect of that skill – presenting your own skills. You may be asked to talk convincingly about your skills – and this will help you prepare for that.

- **Assessment:** Make an assessment of how well you perform in interviews. Do you leave feeling reasonably confident, or that you did not do as well as you might have? What do you think are your main strengths and weaknesses?

- **Learning:** Section 11.6 outlined the interview within a wider recruitment process. Read that section again, paying especial attention to the 'Key ideas' feature (on p. 360), which contains tips on preparing for the interview. How would you distinguish a good interviewee from a poor one? What is the good one likely to do?

- **Analysis:** Consider the possible implications for you of this evidence in Section 11.6. Identify some skills that you are likely to be asked about, or you would like to talk about, in your job interview, AND in which you can demonstrate some ability. List them down the left-hand column, and then make notes under each of the STAR columns in the template below.

Skill	Situation	Task	Action	Result

- **Practice:** Identify ways in which you may be able to practise presenting your skills to an interviewer – ideally work with a colleague on your course who is doing the same thing, and present to each other. Practise presenting each skill, and reflect on the results so that you can learn from the experience.

- **Application:** When you have completed the practice, review what you did, and whether preparing had any effects. Reflect on what you can learn.

  - Decide on another opportunity to practise this skill within the next week.

Read more

Beer, M., Spector, B., Lawrence, P.R., Quinn Mills, D. and Walton, R.E. (1984), *Managing Human Assets,* Macmillan, New York.

A short and very clear text that influenced the popularity of HRM ideas.

Chamorro-Premuzic, T. (2015), 'Ace the assessment', *Harvard Business Review,* vol. 93, no. 7/8, pp. 118–21.

Two recent papers on topical concerns.

Guillaume, Y.R.F., Dawson, J.F., Woods, S.A., Sacramento, C.A. and West, M.A. (2013), 'Getting diversity at work to work: What we know and what we still don't know', *Journal of Occupational and Organisational Psychology,* vol. 86, no. 2, pp. 123–41.

Lawler, E. (2008), *Talent,* Jossey Bass, San Francisco, CA.

A useful analysis of how some managers ensure that policies and practices throughout the organisation help employees develop their abilities, including a chapter on HRM.

Legge, K. (2005), *Human Resource Management: Rhetorics and realities,* (anniversary edition) Macmillan, London.

A critical examination of HRM, emphasising the gap between the ideal and the practice

Go online

Visit the websites of companies that interest you, perhaps as possible places to work. Or you could look at some of those featured in this chapter, such as:

www.bmw.com
www.hiscox.com
www.mcdonalds.co.uk
www.edenproject.com

Navigate to the pages dealing with 'about the company' or 'careers'.

- What do they tell you about working there?
- What do they say about the recruitment and selection process?
- What clues do they give about their appraisal and rewards policies?

CHAPTER 12

INFORMATION SYSTEMS AND E-BUSINESS

Aim

To show how converging information systems can transform organisations if people manage them intelligently.

Objectives

By the end of your work on this chapter you should be able to outline the concepts below in your own terms and:

1 Explain how converging technologies change the ways in which people add value to resources

2 Recognise that, to use these opportunities, managers change both technology and organisation

3 Distinguish between operations information systems and management information systems

4 Illustrate how organisations use the internet to add value by using three types of information system – enterprise, knowledge management and customer relations

5 Understand the relationship between IS, organisation and strategy

6 Explain how IS and organisation interact, and understand how you can use that to help develop the skill of setting a project agenda

7 Show how ideas from the chapter add to your understanding of the integrating themes

Key terms

This chapter introduces these terms:

internet
intranet
extranet
blogs
social networking sites
user-generated content (UGC)
wikinomics
co-creation
Metcalfe's law
information systems management
transaction processing system (TPS)
big data
data
information

process control system
office automation system
management information system
decision support systems
executive information system
e-commerce
e-business
disintermediation
reintermediation
customer relationship management
  (CRM)
enterprise resource planning (ERP)
knowledge management (KM)

Each is a term defined within the text, and in the glossary at the end of the book.

Case study   Google   www.google.com

Sergey Brin and Larry Page founded Google in 1999 and in 2016 it was the world's largest search engine, with the mission: 'to organise the world's information and make it universally accessible and useful'. The need for search services arose as the World Wide Web expanded, making it progressively more difficult for users to find relevant information.

Brin and Page began working on this problem in 1995 as doctoral students in computing science at Stanford University. Page was thinking about ways to rate automatically the quality of websites. He realised that an algorithm was the only way to do this objectively – and that the data to use in the algorithm already existed – but no one was using it. He asked Brin:

> Why don't we use the links on the web to do that?

Page understood that web links were like citations in a scholarly article. It was widely recognised that you could identify which papers were really important without reading them – simply tally up how many other papers cited them in notes and bibliographies (cited in Levy, 2011, p. 17). This insight encouraged Page and Brin (with a group of fellow students) to devise an automatic way to rank every site – by seeing which other sites it linked to AND which sites linked to it. Page called the system PageRank – the basis of Google – as (apart from being his name) it ranks every page on the web. It does not evaluate the page itself, but by seeing how many other people have linked their page to it. This set the basic blocks of web search:

> Search was [and is] a four-step process. First came a sweeping search of all the world's web pages, via a spider [a program that crawled the web for data, visiting a thousand pages simultaneously]. Second was indexing the information [about web links] from the spider's crawl and storing the data on racks of computers known as servers. The third step, triggered by a user's request, identified the pages that seemed best

© Kim Kulish/Corbis/Getty Images

suited to answer that query. That result was known as search quality. The final step involved formatting and delivering the results to the user (Levy, 2011, p. 19).

The PageRank algorithm enables advertisers to deliver a message that is relevant to the results on a page. Advertisers pay a fixed amount, depending on what they have bid for a keyword, each time their ad is viewed: the more they bid, the nearer the top of the page their advertisement will be.

When the company offered shares to the public in 2004, Page warned potential investors that Google was not a conventional company and did not intend to become one. In the interests of long-term stability the share ownership structure was such that the founders owned roughly one third of the shares, but controlled over 80 per cent of the votes.

Source: Based on Harvard Business School case 9-806-105, Google Inc., prepared by Thomas R. Eisenmann and Kerry Herman; Levy (2011).

Case questions 12.1

- What are the inputs and the outputs of the Google business?
- What are the distinctive features of the Google story, set out here?

12.1 Introduction

Google is an organisation founded on data – it gathers, processes and disseminates it from and to millions of people in a way that gives them valuable information. All have different requirements and ways of working, yet Google developed a free search engine that works at astonishing speed to meet their needs. Google survives on income from advertisers – who pay because it identifies customers most likely to respond to their ad when it appears beside the search results. Google (like eBay, Facebook, YouTube and many more) is an example of a company created to use the internet – it is a pure 'e-business' company, whose managers built it around computer-based information systems (IS).

In that sense it differs from companies founded long before the internet but that now depend on it to support the business. Their managers began by implementing relatively simple information systems, which they progressively built, through trial and error, into the complex ones they use today. Traditional businesses such as British Airways, Ford, or Sainsbury's depend on information about each stage of the value-adding process:

- inputs – cost and availability of materials, staff and equipment;
- transformation – delivery schedules, capacity utilisation, efficiency, quality and costs;
- outputs – prices, market share and customer satisfaction.

Their systems gather data about all of these, and feed information to staff working throughout, and beyond, the organisation. Figure 12.1 shows how information systems support these fundamental management processes.

Computer-based information systems can make operations more efficient, change the way people work together and offer new strategic possibilities and threats. Used well, they help managers to add value to resources. Used badly they destroy wealth – when managers invest in an IS project that does not deliver what they expected, and is abandoned or replaced. Flyvbjerg and Budzier (2011) analysed almost 1,500 IS projects and found that, on average, they exceeded their budget by 27 per cent. A few exceeded this – about one in 60 cost double what was expected, and 70 per cent took longer to complete than expected. Many IS projects are now so large that they touch many aspects of the organisation – which greatly increases their risk of failure.

Every manager is affected by the vast changes brought by the internet, as information systems move from background activities (accounting, stock control) into foreground activities (online banking or sponsored websites), which directly involve customers, and then

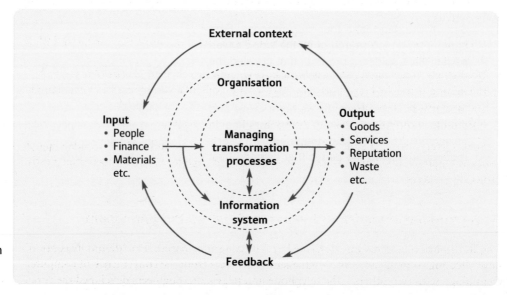

Figure 12.1 The role of information systems in organisations

into activities that customers manage themselves (social networks or music downloads). No organisation is immune: if dissatisfied customers use a popular social networking site to spread bad news about a business, managers need to respond – even if they have never heard of the site. A pressing issue for any company is the extent to which their boards and senior managers have the depth of experience in technology to lead their business successfully in this changing world.

This chapter will show how IS can transform organisations. It shows how traditional businesses progressively widened the role of computer-based systems in managing data about their operations, and how technical developments have led to the convergence of data, voice and vision systems. This led to the phenomenon of co-creating value, in which users not only view content on a site, but also create it. In either case, adding value depends on managing both technological and organisational issues – which the chapter will illustrate with accounts of three widely used systems, and with the link between IS and strategy. Both 'technology' and 'organisation' need to be on the project agenda – which is why that is the topic of the 'Develop a skill' theme at the end of this chapter.

Activity 12.1   Applying the open systems model

Apply the open systems model in Figure 12.1 to an organisation that you know.

- What are the inputs and outputs?
- Describe the transformation process.
- List examples of information systems that provide information about inputs, outputs and transformations.

12.2   Converging technologies – new ways to add value

Using IS to add value to data

Since the 1950s organisations that make and deliver products or services have extended the tasks of computer-based information systems (IS), beginning with routine accounting and stock control systems, then manufacturing and transport, and now covering almost every activity:

- Allied Bakeries use engineering maintenance systems to monitor equipment and plan maintenance;
- UK Vehicle Licensing Agency encourages drivers to pay their road tax online;
- the mining firm Rio Tinto uses driverless trucks, controlled and monitored by computers, to transport iron ore in its mines; and
- most large organisations only accept online job applications.

Such systems are embedded throughout the organisation and still raise management issues as requirements change or new systems become available. Managers then begin costly projects to change or enhance them.

Using convergence to add value to data, sound and vision

The information systems just described are all computer-based. The 'digital disruption' now affecting so many aspects of management follows from the convergence of computer technology with two others – the telephone and television. Engineers developed the three

The **internet** is a web of hundreds of thousands of computer networks linked together by telephone lines and satellite links through which data can be carried.

An **intranet** is a version of the internet that only specified people within an organisation can use.

An **extranet** is a version of the internet that is restricted to specified people in specified companies – usually customers or suppliers.

technologies in different eras, and for many years they worked independently. As the cost of computing power fell, engineers began to use the digital technology at the heart of computing to redesign how telephones transmit voice signals, and how television transmits images. They could then combine the three technologies in a single device – such as your mobile phone. The common language and rules specifying the format in which to send data between devices enabled them to communicate electronically, creating the **internet** (Berners-Lee, 1999). Another relevant term is an **intranet**, a private computer network operating within an organisation by using internet standards and protocols. The opposite is an **extranet**, a network that uses the internet to link organisations with specified suppliers, customers or trading partners.

Linking mobile phones to the internet led to the rapid growth of the 'wireless internet', liberating the computer from the desk top, and enabling people to send and/or receive text, voice and visual data almost wherever they are. This drives change in established businesses (the BBC claims the iPlayer has changed how people watch television, viewing over a million programmes online each day (www.bbc.co.uk)), and enables disruptive new entrants:

- Sky News disrupts print newspapers;
- Amazon disrupts book retailing and many other retail sectors;
- Uber disrupts taxi operators in major cities around the world;
- AirBnB disrupts hotel companies;
- Apple Pay may disrupt established banks' payments systems.

The implication for managers is clear: part of their role is to evaluate, and act on, the threats and opportunities that modern IS brings. Pinkham et al. (2010) provide an overview of how advances in IS enable an organisation's resources to add more value, including through co-creation.

A **blog** is a web log that allows individuals to post opinions and ideas.

Social networking sites use internet technologies that enable people to interact within an online community to share information and ideas.

Producers and consumers co-create value

Individuals using blogs and social network sites are now driving the growth of internet traffic. **Blogs** attract individuals with an interest in the topic to ask questions or express their views in a discussion group. **Social networking sites** have developed from blogs, by providing a communication channel for people who want to share their interests with other members of an online community.

| Management in practice |

Social media gives Topshop fashion a new look
www.topshop.com

According to Tracy Yaverbaum, group director of retail at Facebook,

> The fashion community is known for taking risks and experimenting, and now they are starting to do it in digital.

Fashion brands are embracing social media to reach their customers and fans, [most of whom] will not be attending the London Fashion Show. When Topshop showed its unique collection, it teamed up with Facebook and Instagram to create a 'social catwalk'. It shared at least two key looks from the show on Facebook before they appeared on the catwalk.

Five Instagrammers were given unprecedented access to the show, with their content appearing on Topshop's channels and also in the window of its London flagship store on Oxford Circus.

Sheen Sauvaire, global marketing and communications director at Topshop, says technology is bringing about a revolution in fashion, turning the traditional idea of the catwalk on its head, and forging deeper relationships between the retailer and its customers.

Another company's links with Twitter means customers in the US can buy a selection of the nail colours worn by the models directly from a tweet. In 2014 an internet research company estimated that 29 per cent of online retail sales would take place on smartphones and tablets that year, double the amount in 2013.

 Source: *Financial Times*, 16 September 2014, p. 20.

This digital culture erodes boundaries between producers and consumers. Wikipedia, written by volunteers, quickly became the world's largest encyclopaedia, competing with Encyclopaedia Britannica (www.britannica.com). YouTube claims to hold the world's largest collection of videos, including professional work. Amazon encourages visitors to the site to review books, which others can read before they buy. Media groups encourage readers to write stories for their websites. All are examples of **user-generated content (UGC)** – which users create and place on a site for others to view.

Tapscott and Williams (2006) refer to this as **wikinomics**, a business culture that sees customers not as consumers but as co-creators and co-producers. Smartphones allow people to build and maintain their social relationships through creating and sharing content. They decide how much time or money to spend using content (downloading music, games or professional apps) and how much to spend creating content (uploading photographs, film reviews or texts). Many companies now encourage **co-creation**, through blogs, customer reviews and online communities. They believe this not only enhances customers' experience of, and loyalty to, the brand: it may also add to the engagement of employees, and produce more useful innovations.

Companies are still trying to find how best to manage the co-creation possibilities – which involves, for example, how to integrate the resources of other actors with a firm's own resources, and how to design and monitor the project (Frow et al. 2015). Nevertheless, the more people who join such a community, the more valuable it becomes. This follows from **Metcalfe's law**: 'the value of a network increases with the square of the number of users connected to the network'. The more people who have phones, the more valuable a phone becomes to the next adopter. This 'network effect' encourages more people to use an existing website, and creates barriers for new entrants – who have few users – to attract others. New payment systems face this barrier. Retailers need to install card readers and banks have to put in software to process payments. A new system, like Apple Pay, needs to reach a point where enough users have the cards or apps required, and enough ticket barriers, tills, or websites are willing to accept them, to justify any investment.

Figure 12.2 illustrates the idea. In a traditional economic system producers create products that consumers order, receive and pay for (Figure 12.2a). The alternative is when companies such as Google, Facebook or YouTube provide a platform, customers view the content and may in turn add to that with their own content – a video, a message or a page from another site. They add value to the platform as they provide more information and so enhance its perceived quality. Consumption does not reduce value, but increases it (Figure 12.2b) – see the 'Management in practice' feature.

User-generated content (UGC) is text, visual or audio material that users create and place on a site for others to view.

Wikinomics describes a business culture in which customers are no longer only consumers but also co-creators and co-producers of the service.

Co-creation involves the joint creation of value by the firm and its network of 'actors', such as customers, suppliers and distributors.

Metcalfe's law states that the value of a network increases with the square of the number of users connected to the network.

Management in practice   An online forum in health care

A physician dealing with fertility treatment at the University Hospital Nijmegen, The Netherlands, spent a lot of time informing couples of the pros and cons of the treatments, and in providing emotional support. As an experiment he started an online forum in which his clients (exclusively) share information and anxieties. It also provides relevant medical information. From time to time the doctor and other staff join the sessions. The 'electronic fertility platform' saves a lot of the time the doctor used to spend advising and supporting clients. Clients contribute anonymously to the platform, and so help each other.

Source: Boddy et al. (2009a), p.62.

Figure 12.2
Traditional delivery and customer participation

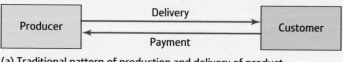

(a) Traditional pattern of production and delivery of product or service, followed by payment by a customer.

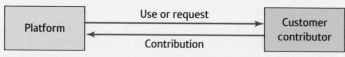

(b) New pattern of consumption by customers, who also contribute to a platform, such as Wikipedia, Google or Linux.

Activity 12.2   Reflect on your use of social networking sites

Consider an occasion when you used a social networking site to interact with an organisation.

- What were the circumstances?
- Did it change your view of the company?
- What could the company do to benefit more from such exchanges?

12.3   Managing the new opportunities to add value

Adding value in traditional delivery systems

The internet evidently challenges established ways of doing business. Combined with political changes, this is creating a wider, often global, market for many goods and services. The challenge for managers is to make profitable use of these possibilities. This includes looking beyond technology – which receives most attention – to the wider organisation. A manager who played a major role in guiding internet-based changes at his company commented:

> The internet is not a technology challenge. It's a people challenge – all about getting structures, attitudes and skills aligned.

The internet affects all aspects of organisational activity, enabling new forms of organisation and new ways of doing business. Established organisations typically go through successive stages in the way they use the internet, which Figure 12.3 illustrates.

The simplest websites provide information, enabling customers to view product or other information; conversely suppliers use their website to show customers what they can offer. Interaction occurs when customers enter information and questions about (for example)

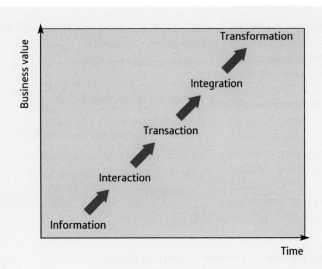

Figure 12.3 Stages in using the internet

a flight for a weekend break. The system then uses the customer information, such as preferred dates and times of travel, to show availability and costs. Conversely, a supplier who sees a purchasing requirement from a business (perhaps expressed as a purchase order on the website) can agree electronically to meet the order. The next stage is to enable transactions, when the customer buys their flight online, and the whole transaction takes place electronically.

A company achieves integration when it links its internal system to the website, so that when a customer goes online to place an order, it automatically passes to internal operating systems that begin the processes (including those at suppliers) required to make and deliver the order. Transformation refers to the situation where a company links internal and external systems, includes customers to product design and engages with online communities.

Case study   Google – the case continues   www.google.com

Google has always been economical in the way it invests in the computer hardware required to collect, store and process data. As a business start-up they were short of money – so instead of buying expensive equipment they bought old and damaged servers at very low cost. They knew some of these would fail – and designed the file system to manage failure by redistributing data instantly from a damaged machine to an available working one.

A feature of the site is the speed at which it returns search results – usually within a second. The company is obsessed with speed, and engineers challenge any refinements that may slow response times. From the start its focus has been on developing 'the perfect search engine', defined by Page as something that 'understands what you mean and gives you back

what you want'. Rather than use a small number of large servers that tend to run slowly at peak times, Google has invested in probably a million smaller servers housed in vast data centres around the world. It gives very little information about the scale, capacity or location of these data centres: since it builds the servers itself, observers believe it is the world's largest computer manufacturer.

Google engineers prototype new applications on the platform; if any of these begin to get users' attention, developers can launch beta [test] versions to see whether the company's vast captive customer base responds enthusiastically. If one of the applications becomes a hit, Google's vast computing resource can make room for it. In the development process Google simultaneously tests and markets them to the user community – testing and marketing are virtually indistinguishable. This creates a unique relationship with consumers, who become an essential part of the development team as new products evolve, and then transition seamlessly from testing to using products as they would any other commercial offering.

The company allows independent developers to share access and create new applications that incorporate elements of the Google system. They can easily test and launch applications and have them hosted in the Google world, where there is an enormous

target audience and a practically unlimited capacity for customer interactions.

Source: Iyer and Davenport (2008); Levy (2011).

Case questions 12.2

● What benefits do you expect Google will gain from this close involvement with developers?

● And what do the developers gain?

● What may be the risks to either Google or the developers?

Adding value through online communities

Millions of people use online platforms to interact socially, and this urge is of great interest to companies. Some create and host customer communities to provide closer links with customers, hoping to learn more about the views and preferences than through conventional market research techniques. They host product discussions – if people are critical, managers want to know this so they can deal with the problem. A users' blog might identify possible new uses for a product, or hint at features the company could add. This is still challenging for companies, who are trying to work out how best to use these opportunities to build a positive image, or at least prevent a negative one – see 'Management in practice'.

Management in practice   Managers learn to use the social web

Bernoff and Li (2008) note that:

> Companies are used to being in control. They typically design products, services and marketing messages based on their . . . view of what people want . . . Now, though, many customers are no longer cooperating. Empowered by online social technologies . . . customers are connecting with, and drawing power from, each other. They're defining their own perspectives on companies and brands, a view that's often at odds with the image a company wants to project. This groundswell of people using technologies to get the things they need from one another, rather than from companies, is now tilting the balance of power from company to customer. (p. 36)

The authors advise managers how they can best respond to this change by 'working with the groundswell' – developing a clear view of how they can use social applications to achieve business goals. Among their examples:

● **'Listening'**: a software company uses an application that allows customers to suggest new features and then vote on them; this helps the company to decide which of the (thousands of) suggestions to develop.
● **'Talking'**: a car company wanted to increase students' awareness of a new model. They created a stunt in which students lived in the car for a week; from there they wrote blogs, posted YouTube videos and contacted thousands of friends through Facebook, greatly increasing awareness of the brand, at a fraction of the cost of traditional publicity methods.
● **'Energising'**: an old and respected company wanted to build enthusiasm among current and new customers for the brand. It hired four enthusiastic customers to act as 'lead ambassadors', whose job was to build an online community of users to exchange ideas and experiences with the product. The size of this community quickly exceeded expectations, and generated a substantial increase in sales.

Source: Bernoff and Li (2008).

Whether a business is in a traditional delivery or co-creation mode, it will only add value if managers look beyond the technology, and towards related organisational issues.

Adding value depends on managing technology AND organisation

Whether the company is an internet-based start-up or an established business, it requires deliberate management action to create the IS infrastructure to engage with the internet. **Information systems management** is the term used to describe the activities of planning, acquiring, developing and using IS, such as Google's network of data centres – and also of making the necessary organisational changes if it is to pay off – see 'Key ideas'.

Any information system includes people and processes as well as hardware and software – as shown in Figure 12.4.

A computer-based student record system illustrates this. The hardware consists of computers and peripherals such as printers, monitors and keyboards. This runs the record system, using software to manipulate the data and to either print the results for each student or send them electronically – which they see as information. The system also requires people (course administrators) to enter data (name and other information about students and their results) following certain processes – such as that one person reads from a list of grades while another keys the data into the correct field on the student's record. Managers of a department might use the output to compare the pass rate of each course – so the record system is now part of the university's management information. Staff will use their knowledge (based on learning and experience) to interpret trends and evaluate their significance.

Figure 12.4 also shows that the hardware and software is part of a wider organisational context, which includes people, working processes, structures and cultures. An IS includes identifiable elements of this context, which affect the outcomes of IS investments just as much as the technological elements. Failure to deal properly with these issues is a major cause of the many IS projects that fail to deliver value (Boddy et al. 2009a; Flyvbjerg and Budzier, 2011).

> **Information systems management** is the planning, acquisition, development and use of these systems.

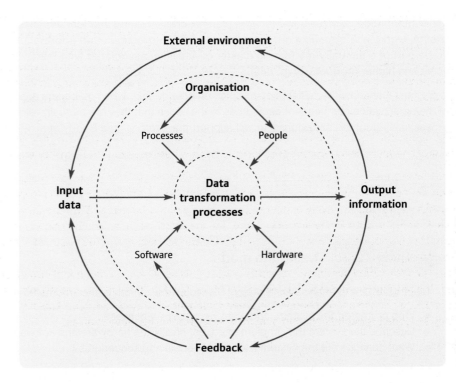

Figure 12.4
The elements of a computer-based IS

Source: Managing Information Systems: Strategy and Organisation, 3rd ed., FT/Prentice Hall, Harlow (Boddy, D., Boonstra, A., and Kennedy, G. 2009) p. 6, Figure 1.1, Copyright © Pearson Education Ltd. 2002, 2005, 2009.

Key ideas	The extroverted firm – complementarities improve productivity

An article in *Management Science* by Tambe et al. (2012) reiterates that effective performance depends on being able to detect and respond to changes in a firm's operating environment. Modern IS enable companies to track customer behaviour (extreme examples being the way Amazon and Google record their customers' key-strokes and analyse this data to optimise their products, processes and marketing), but this data is of no value unless the company can use it. The authors draw on research to suggest that the value of IS investment will be enhanced if companies associate this with decentralised decision making. The logic is that this will enable the firm to respond quickly to the information, through product innovation – see Figure 12.5.

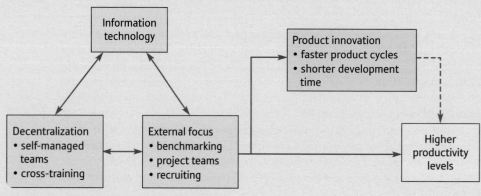

Figure 12.5 The complementarities model
Source: Tambe et al. (2012), p. 844

They tested the model in a survey of over 200 US firms and found that, as expected, firms gain more from IT investments if they capture:

> external information through networks of customers, suppliers, partners and new employees . . . an effective response to external information requires that firms have the mechanisms in place through which to absorb this information, such as self-managing teams, cross training and [decentralised decision making]. Internal workplace organisation, external information practices and information technologies seem to be part of a mutually-reinforcing cluster of activities associated with faster product development cycles and higher productivity (p. 845).

This study is one of many that show the benefits of complementarity or 'fit' – when managers ensure that discrete elements of the organisation complement each other, in the sense that they are mutually reinforcing, sending consistent messages about the behaviour that will support the strategy (see Boddy et al. 2009a for more on this theme).

Source: Tambe et al. (2012).

Activity 12.3	Using the model

Use Figure 12.4 to analyse an IS project that you know, or can gather information about.

- Who promoted the system, and what were their objectives?
- Describe the system they implemented, especially the hardware and software.
- What changes did the system lead to for people and procedures?

- What changes were there for other aspects of the organisation, such as its culture and structure?
- What were the outcomes, and how did they compare with the objectives?
- What can you learn from this case?

12.4   Types of information systems

Table 12.1 illustrates two broad types of IS. Operational IS support the needs of the day-to-day business operations, and how front-line staff and their supervisors work. Management IS typically inform the decisions of middle and senior managers.

Data and information

Both types of systems turn 'data' into 'information'. **Data** refers to recorded descriptions of things, events, activities and transactions – their size, colour, cost, weight, date and so on. It may be a number, a piece of text, a drawing or photograph, or a sound. In itself it may or may not convey **information** to a person. Information is a subset of data that means something to the person receiving it, which they judge to be useful, significant or urgent. It comes from data that have been processed (by people or with the aid of technology) so that they have meaning and value – by linking them to other pieces of data to show a comparison, a sequence of events, or a trend. The output is subjective since what one person sees as valuable information, another may see as insignificant data – depending on their background and interests.

Data are raw, unanalysed facts, figures and events.

Information comes from data that has been processed so that it has meaning for the person receiving it.

Operations information systems

Operations systems provide the information to keep work moving efficiently and include countless applications that staff use routinely.

Transaction processing systems (TPSs) record and process data from customer and supplier transactions, salary and other systems affecting employees, as well as those with banks and tax authorities. A TPS collects data as transactions occur and stores it in a central database, which is then the source of other reports such as customer statements or supplier payments. Such systems help managers to keep track of transactions and their financial implications.

A **transaction processing system (TPS)** records and processes data from routine transactions such as payroll, sales or purchases.

Table 12.1 Types of information systems

Management levels	Generic categories of information systems	Specific types of information systems
Senior managers – managing the business	Management information systems	Executive information
		Decision support
Middle managers – managing managers		Information reporting
Line managers – supervising people doing the work	Operational information systems	Office automation
		Process control
People doing the work		Transaction processing

A process control system monitors and controls variables describing the state of a physical process.

They also need systems to monitor and control physical processes. Breweries, bakeries, refineries and similar operations use **process control systems** to monitor defined variables such as temperature, pressure or flow, compare them with the required state, and adjust as necessary. Staff monitor the systems to check if they need to take further action.

An **office automation system** uses several systems to create, process, store and distribute information.

Office automation systems bring together email, word processing, spreadsheet and many other systems to create, process, store and distribute information. They can also link to TPS or process control systems to make structured decisions. Banks analyse the pattern of a customer's transactions to decide whether to make a loan. Office automation systems streamline the administrative processes of a business, and provide input to other systems.

Management information systems (MIS)

A management information system provides information and support for managerial decision making.

A **management information system (MIS)** provides managers with information for decisions. It is supported by the operations information systems and other sources. Those running production or service facilities constantly face choices about (for example) whether to engage more or fewer staff, arrange schedules or accept a reservation. To increase the chances that their decisions add value they need information about, for example, capacity, orders or available materials. Good information increases their confidence, and information reporting systems help to achieve this, by providing accurate and up-to-date information on the current operation.

Decision support systems help people to calculate the consequences of alternatives before they decide which to choose.

Decision support systems (DSS), sometimes called expert or knowledge systems, help managers to calculate the likely consequences of alternative actions. A DSS incorporates a model of the process or situation, and will often draw data from operational systems. Some examples:

- Businesses use DSS to calculate the financial consequences of investments.
- Banks use knowledge systems to analyse proposed loans. These incorporate years of lending experience and enable less experienced staff to make decisions.
- NHS Direct in the UK uses an expert system to enable nurses in a call centre to deal with calls from patients who would otherwise visit their doctor. It proposes questions, interprets the answers and recommends the advice the nurse should give.

An **executive information system** provides those at the top of the organisation with easy access to timely and relevant information.

Executive information systems are essentially management information systems aimed at the most senior people in the business. Rather than detail, they provide easy access to data from many sources, processed in a way that meets top management requirements.

Activity 12.4	**Collecting examples of applications**

Collect new examples of one operational and one management information system.

- What information do they deal with?
- How do they help people who use them in their work?
- What issues about the design of these systems should managers consider, in view of the growth of social networking and similar technologies?

---

e-commerce refers to the activity of selling goods or services over the internet.

e-business refers to the integration, through the internet, of all an organisation's processes from its suppliers through to its customers.

12.5	**The internet and e-business**

Two commonly used terms are **e-commerce** and **e-business**. The former refers to the simple practice of offering goods and services through a website – which is defined here as e-commerce. A more radical, and now very-widely used way to trade on the internet is what is here called e-business, when companies use a website to manage information about sales, capacity, inventory, payment and so on – and to exchange that information with their suppliers or business customers. Some companies only sell over the internet – see 'Management in practice'.

Management in practice   Asos – online-only fashion   www.asos.com

Nick Robertson founded Asos in 2000 as an online fashion retailer – it is now an international business that is also the largest online-only fashion retailer in the UK. About 700,000 people a day visit the website – most of them 16 to 34-year-olds who are the company's target group of customers. The company's HQ is in Camden, North London, and the fulfilment centre – which receives orders from customers and then packs and delivers the goods to them – is in Hemel Hempstead (about 30 miles north).

The Camden office is where most of the images that appear on the website are produced – including photo shoots (the company photographs 2,000 items a week) and catwalk videos. Keeping the fashion and technology parts of the company under one roof – the company employs 16 designers and 120 people in information systems – enables both sides of the business to learn from each other:

We are a fashion and a technology business.

While many companies discourage blogging or tweeting in the office, Mr Robertson encourages it, as an ideal way to keep in touch with customers and fashion trends:

They're doing what they would be doing anyway, but they're doing it for Asos.

This is no coincidence. Most Asos staff fit the demographic of the company's customers – young, trendy, mainly female. Understanding exactly who its customers are is a great strength. Mr Robertson believes that employing the same types of people as Asos sells to means the company knows how to meet them – as shown by a marketing strategy built upon social networking sites. Teenagers think they have 'discovered' Asos through blogs and tweets, instead of feeling they have responded to a sales pitch.

Sources: *Financial Times*, 22 February 2011; company website.

The internet changes the relationship between a company and its customers and suppliers as electronic systems bypass parts of the supply chain – known as **disintermediation**. Figure 12.6 shows how a manufacturer and a wholesaler can bypass partners to reach customers directly.

Disintermediation
Removing intermediaries such as distributors or brokers that formerly linked a company to its customers.

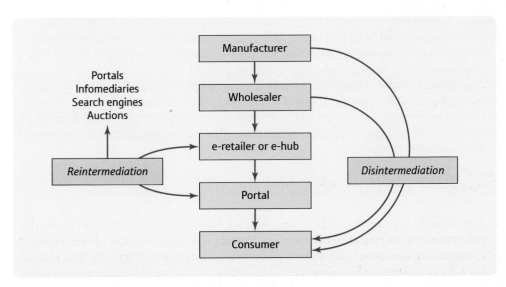

Figure 12.6
Reinventing the supply chain

The benefits of disintermediation are to reduce transaction costs and enable direct contact with customers. Companies can also extend their 'reach' from a local presence to a national or international one. **Reintermediation** is the creation of new intermediaries between customers and suppliers by providing (new) services such as supplier search and product evaluation. Examples are portals such as www.lastminute.com and www.moneyfacts.co.uk, which help customers to compare offers and follow links to their preferred supplier.

Reintermediation
Creating intermediaries between customers and suppliers, providing services such as price comparison and product evaluation.

Three widely used internet applications are customer relationship management, enterprise resource planning and knowledge management.

Customer relationship management (CRM)

Customer relationship management (CRM) The process of maximising the value delivered to the customer through all interactions, both online and traditional. Effective CRM aims to develop one-to-one relationships with valuable customers.

Chapter 9 (**Section 9.5**) introduced the idea of customer relationship, a process by which companies aim to build long-term, profitable relationships with their customers. This involves many organisational changes, and IS play a major role in supporting this. CRM software tries to align business processes with customer strategies to recruit, satisfy and retain profitable customers (Ryals, 2005; Kumar et al. 2006). Figure 12.7 shows three approaches. The first treats all customers in the same way by sending impersonal messages in one direction. The second sends a one-sided, but unique message to each customer, depending on their profile. The third personalises the messages that may lead to real interaction, in the hope of increasing customer loyalty.

Many businesses want to focus on recruiting and retaining valuable, long-term customers and hope CRM will help them to:

- gather customer data swiftly;
- identify and capture valuable customers while discouraging less valuable ones;
- increase customer loyalty and retention by providing customised products;
- reduce costs of serving customers;
- make it easier to acquire similar customers.

The 'Management in practice' feature is an example of this idea in advertising.

Management in practice   Iris and 'The Source'   www.irisnation.com

Iris is a rapidly growing advertising agency, with close relationships with international customers. As an example of the services it offers, Ian Millner, Managing Director describes 'The Source':

A key part of our global relationship with Sony Eriksson is a digital asset management system, that has now been branded The Source. The role of that system is to collect all marketing assets of value, most of which will have been originated by Iris, have it all in one place so that if you're Sony Eriksson in Brazil or in Indonesia or in China, instantly you're able to access marketing materials that have value and relevance for you to use really, really quickly in your marketplace.

So this idea of real time sharing is a key part of working with clients in dynamic and competitive markets, and I think the other bit that comes with that is not only value but also speed to market. It's so important now to be able to do things quickly, so that is a massive asset in our sort of overall strategic relationship with that client but also our anticipation is that there'll be more and more clients now who want that type of agency partner globally.

Source: Interview with Ian Millner.

Maintaining good customer relationships also depends on using their information in a way that they trust – some tools to help analyse such an approach feature in 'Key ideas'.

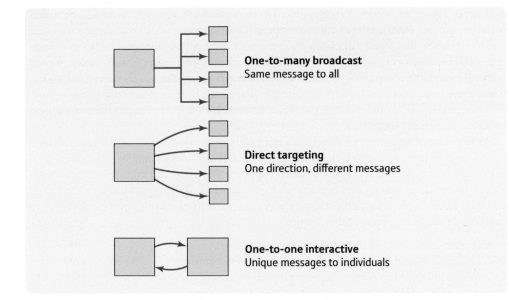

One-to-many broadcast
Same message to all

Direct targeting
One direction, different messages

One-to-one interactive
Unique messages to individuals

Figure 12.7
Communications
methods and
messages

Key ideas   **Do customers trust you with their data?**

Websites have for years been able to track users' online activities and so target advertising precisely. Morey et al. (2015) observe that technological advances, such as incorporating intelligent technology in physical products ('wearables' as well as mobile devices), allow companies to collect new data about customers, especially about their location and behaviour, giving examples from Medtronics and Uber. They claim that customers appreciate the benefits, but are wary of the risks of abuse and security breaches. The authors advocate that companies align their interests with customers', to ensure both benefit.

To assist that analysis, the authors categorise data according to its source, and how the company intends to use it. Three sources are:

● **self-report** – where users have voluntarily given demographic, email address, or work history;
● **digital exhaust** – such as location data or browsing history, created while using mobile devices; and
● **profiling** – derived by combining self-reported data, 'digital exhaust', and possibly other data, to predict a person's interests and behaviour, which is used for marketing.

The authors distinguish three uses of the data:

● **sell to third parties** – such as data about a credit card transaction;
● **facilitate targeted marketing** – using browsing history to shape online advertising; and
● **improve a product or service** – adapting a product to a user's interests, such as allowing a map application to recommend a route from the user's location.

The authors advocate that if companies are transparent about their data sources, and how they use them, customers will be more likely to trust them. They also suggest rewarding customers for using their data.

Source: Morey et al. (2015).

Enterprise resource planning (ERP) systems

Fulfilling a customer order requires that people in sales, accounting, production, purchasing and so on cooperate with each other to exchange information. However, the IS on which they depend were often designed to meet the needs of a single function, and cannot exchange information. Manufacturing will not automatically know the number and types of product

Enterprise resource planning (ERP) An integrated process of planning and managing all resources and their use in the enterprise. It includes contacts with business partners.

to make because their systems are not linked to the systems that process orders. A common solution is to use **enterprise resource planning (ERP)** systems, which coordinate activities and decisions across many functions by creating a system that allows them to exchange information. When a customer places an order this information flows automatically to each relevant part of the company – warehouse, manufacturing, suppliers, accounting and so on. Customer service staff, and often the customer, can track the progress of the order online, from the same, constantly updated, database. Information flows between all functions and levels, as shown in Figure 12.8.

At the heart of an enterprise system is a central database that draws data from and feeds it into applications throughout the company. Table 12.2 shows examples of business processes and functions that enterprise systems support. Managers can implement these modules separately, but gain greater benefits when they are linked through the central database.

ERP systems give management direct access to current operating information and so enable companies to, among other things:

- integrate customer and financial information;
- standardise manufacturing processes and reduce inventory;
- improve information for management decisions across sites;
- enable online links of suppliers' and customers' systems with the internal ones.

Murphy et al. (2012) show that implementing ERP has sometimes led to more centralised, standardised systems with closer monitoring, while in other cases it has had the opposite effect – local decisions, empowerment and more job satisfaction. A consistent theme in such studies is that since an ERP system is likely to require organisational changes, they are high-risk investments. This may explain why Wieder et al. (2006) found no significant

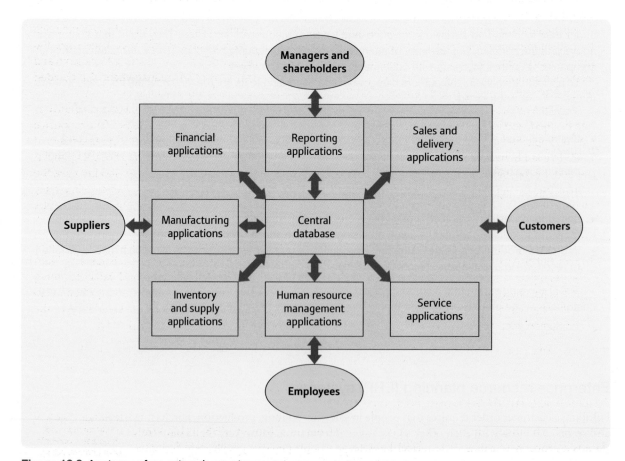

Figure 12.8 Anatomy of an enterprise system.

Table 12.2 Examples of business processes supported by enterprise systems

Financial	Accounts receivable and payable, cash management and forecasting, management information, cost accounting, profitability analysis, profit-centre accounting, financial reporting
Human resources	Payroll, personnel planning, travel expenses, benefits accounting, applicant tracking
Operations and logistics	Inventory management, maintenance, production planning, purchasing, quality management, vendor evaluation, shipping
Sales and marketing	Order management, pricing, sales management, sales planning, billing

differences in performance between adopters and non-adopters of ERP systems. Bozarth (2006) illustrates the complexities of implementing such systems, as does the 'Management in practice' feature of ERP in a hospital.

Management in practice **ERP in a hospital**

Management in this Dutch hospital found it increasingly difficult to maintain many old, functional systems that were unable to exchange data. They were also aware that, like any large hospital, there were many stakeholders from functional units some of whom, especially medical staff, had a high degree of autonomy over their working methods.

Hospital management decided to replace their fragmented IS with an ERP system containing modules for patient management, finance, material, human resources and management information. They knew the project was urgent, as the finance system in particular, on which it depended to send invoices to patients and insurance companies, was close to collapse. As well as approving the project, top management also decided which ERP software to use and appointed external consultants to manage the project.

Very little progress was made in implementing ERP. The external consultants had less experience than they had claimed, and ignored many suggestions and comments from doctors and administrators. The emphasis was on implementing the standard system rapidly, and on adjusting hospital systems to the requirements of ERP. This led to resistance by both groups of hospital staff and as the finance module was not being implemented, the hospital's income declined rapidly, bringing it close to bankruptcy. It only survived because the administrative staff spent a great deal of time checking the invoices the system produced, and creating many by hand. Faced with this crisis, management abandoned the ERP system and instead purchased a separate, stand-alone invoicing system. The authors conclude:

> This paper confirms research that ERP implementation is not only related to the technical features of the system, but also to the way it is implemented and how it affects processes, power, culture and finance . . . Managers must be aware of the ways in which ERP socially affects the established institutional settings. During the initial stages of the implementation process, decisions have to be made about necessary changes to either the system or the organisation, or both. These changes must meet the needs of stakeholders if the implementation of ERP is to be successful and effective (Boonstra and Govers, 2009, p. 190).

Source: Boonstra and Govers (2009).

Knowledge management (KM) systems

'**Knowledge** builds on information that is extracted from data' (Boisot, 1998, p. 12). While data is a property of things (size, price) knowledge is a property of people, which predisposes them to act in a particular way. It embodies understanding, experience and learning,

> **Knowledge** builds on information and embodies a person's prior understanding, experience and learning.

and is either confirmed or modified as people receive new information. Knowledge enables people to add more value to resources, since they can react more intelligently to information and data than those without that experience and learning. Someone with good knowledge of a market will use it to identify significant patterns or trends, and so attach a different meaning to the information than someone without that knowledge.

Managers (especially those employing many skilled professionals) have long wanted to make better use of their employees' knowledge, believing it vital to innovation and the primary source of wealth in modern economies. Staff often believe the knowledge they need to improve performance is within the business – but they cannot find it. **Knowledge management (KM)** refers to attempts to improve the way organisations create, acquire, capture, store, share and use knowledge. This will usually relate to customers, markets, products, services and internal processes, but may also refer to knowledge about relevant external developments.

A **knowledge management portal** provides a single point through which employees can access the many sources of information and knowledge within an organisation.

Managing knowledge is not new – the industrial revolution occurred when people applied new knowledge to manufacturing processes. What is new is the growth of knowledge-intensive businesses employing thousands of professionals around the world. Their work generates knowledge and they also seek it, so face the puzzle of how to access, and renew, the internal stock of potentially useful knowledge about their current work. Developments in IS make it easier for people to share data, information and knowledge irrespective of physical distance. This has encouraged many to implement knowledge management (KM) systems.

The challenge is to decide what knowledge to include: not discriminating clearly leads to unwieldy and useless databases that no one uses – see 'Key ideas' for one view on how to do this.

> **Knowledge management systems** are a type IS intended to support people as they create, store, transfer and apply knowledge.
>
> A **knowledge management portal** provides a single point through which employees can access the many sources of information and knowledge within an organisation.

Key ideas　Identifying which knowledge really matters.

Ihrig and Macmillan (2015) comment that while 'big data' is a fashionable topic, too much focus on that may mean a company neglects to manage other strategically important knowledge assets. These could include their core competences, areas of expertise and intellectual property. They advocate developing a clear understanding of how knowledge contributes to the organisation's success, and then mapping what knowledge they have, which are the most critical assets, and how they should be managed.

The core of their process is to map the firm's knowledge, by asking people what they consider the key dimensions of competitive performance, and what knowledge underpins that. This conversation ideally takes place at several levels of the business, and across functional or divisional boundaries, to identify a relatively small number of critically important knowledge domains. These can then be mapped and analysed to identify characteristics such as whether it is tacit (unstructured) or explicit (structured), and how widely it is diffused around the organisation. It then becomes feasible, they say, to begin interpreting the complex data so available, to identify both gaps which should be filled, and/or new opportunities to exploit the newly-understood knowledge assets.

Source: Ihrig and Macmillan (2015).

Recall the distinction between data, information and knowledge (pp. 383 and 389). Many systems that people refer to as 'knowledge' management systems appear to deal with data and information, rather than knowledge. While computer-based systems are effective at dealing with (structured) data and information, they are still less effective at dealing with (unstructured) knowledge. They are unlikely to replace the learning that takes place through interpersonal contact.

Case study   Google – the case continues   www.google.com

Google has a technocratic culture, in that individuals prosper based on the quality of their ideas and their technological acumen. Engineers are expected to spend 20 per cent of their time working on their own creative projects. The company provides plenty of intellectual stimulation which, for a company founded on technology, can be the opportunity to learn from the best and brightest technologists.

There are regular talks by distinguished researchers from around the world. Google's founders and executives have thought through many aspects of the knowledge work environment, including the design and occupancy of offices (jam-packed for better communication); the frequency of all-hands meetings (every Friday); and the approach to interviewing and hiring new employees (rigorous, with many interviews). These principles suggest an unusually high level of recognition for the human dimensions of innovation. Brin, Page, and Schmidt have taken ideas from other organisations – such as the software firm SAS Institute – that are celebrated for how they treat their knowledge workers.

The investors who had supplied the capital to create the business pressed the founders to build a professional management team. The company was growing rapidly, hiring staff, building data centres and facilities for developers – but the founders were reluctant to appoint a professional CEO. In late 2000

they relented, and appointed Eric Schmidt – who had an excellent reputation as a computer scientist, and in senior management positions at other technology companies. As far as the engineering side was concerned, the founders were keen that the software engineers

> would arrange themselves in pods of three, work on projects, and check in with [the head of engineering]. That struck some of Google's executives as madness. Stacy Sullivan, the head of HR, begged Page and Brin not to go through with it. 'You can't just self-organise!' she told them, 'People need someone to go to when they have problems!' (Levy, 2011, p. 158)

Eventually the 'self-organising' plan faded, and formal management structures evolved.

Source: Levy (2011).

Case questions 12.3

- What are the likely advantages to Google, and to its staff, of these practices?
- Read the Pixar 'Management in practice' (p. 415) and note any similarities and differences between their practices and those of Google.

KM tools can exploit explicit knowledge about previous projects, technical discoveries or useful techniques. But reusing existing knowledge may do less for performance than using it as a step towards creating new knowledge that suits the situation. That creative process depends more on human interaction than on technology. Adding value depends on insight and judgement (Govindarajan and Gupta (2001)):

> effective knowledge management depends not merely on information-technology platforms but . . . on the social ecology of an organisation – the social system in which people operate (made up of) culture, structure, information systems, reward systems, processes, people and leadership (p. 72).

People are more likely to use a KM system if the culture recognises and rewards knowledge sharing.

'Big data'

A potential source of new knowledge that is arousing great interest is the vast amount of information that organisations now collect about individuals' lifestyles and spending habits, especially as they use social media and make online purchases. Every such transaction creates an electronic record, which is useful to the company making the transaction,

Big data describes information of an order of magnitude far greater than has been encountered before. Typically the data comes from social media, or from connected devices including satellites, surveillance cameras and mobile phones.

but if it is combined with data about the person's other transactions, and indeed many aspects of their lives, marketers find this '**big data**' of great value.

Business intelligence refers to software applications that analyse data from a company, and sometimes from other sources such as census or market research surveys. Sometimes called data mining, powerful computers sort unimaginable amounts of data to identify patterns and relationships that may be significant – and in time for managers to be able to respond to it while it is still current. An example would be the exact location of a person with certain food preferences in relation to a restaurant that could satisfy them – so the system sends a promotional offer to their mobile.

> Marketers have long mined consumer information – ranging from public records data about how much a person's house is worth to surveys about whether they are married or have children – to send direct mailings and make telephone pitches to people most likely to buy their products . . . Big data's renewed heft in the advertising industry came . . . as smartphones spread and people digitised their lives.
>
> This not only unearthed a treasure trove of real-time data about individuals, but is also forcing the advertising and marketing industries into new ways of doing business . . . The industry is. . . creating dossiers about individuals based on everything from the information revealed in online dating profiles to the pictures people posted to social networks, the items they put in their online shopping carts, and the television programmes viewed on digital video recorders.
>
> These profiles are now the nexus around which an increasing part of the advertising industry operates. (From an article by Emily Steel in the *Financial Times,* 13 December 2012, p. 19).

Others urge managers to be cautious about the likely returns from investing heavily in such systems:

> The ability to study large trend and patterns is clearly useful. But it is no substitute for getting around the business and asking people, especially frontline staff, what they think is happening.
>
> The data can tell you how many customers you have lost each month, but not necessarily why they have gone. You can do online surveys, which some may bother to complete, but you would learn far more from contacting and talking to some of those lost customers yourself. (From an article by Michael Skapinker, *Financial Times,* 9 May 2013, p. 12)

Activity 12.5 What knowledge do you need for a task?

- Identify for an employee (perhaps yourself) what knowledge they create, acquire, capture, share and use while doing a specified task.
- Identify examples of explicit and tacit knowledge in this example.
- For one of your examples of tacit knowledge: (a) how do they/you obtain that knowledge?; (b) can you envisage how a computer-based IS would be able to provide it?

12.6 IS, strategy and organisation – the big picture

Computer-based IS can contribute to an organisation's strategy, as can any other capability – they are all resources upon which managers draw, provided they do so in a way that the resources align with, complement, each other. This section shows how managers can take a strategic perspective on IS, and on the organisational changes this requires.

Case study   Google – the case continues   www.google.com

The company has rapidly extended the range of services it offers, while remaining rigorously focused on search. Although the headquarters is in California, their mission is to facilitate access to information across the world – more than half of their searches are delivered to users living outside the US, in more than 35 languages. The company invites volunteers to help in translating the site into additional languages.

Beyond its core search and advertising capabilities, the company has embarked on ventures involving online productivity, blogging online payments, social networks, mobile phone operating systems (Android) and many more information domains. It has acquired companies for their apps: Picasa for photo management; YouTube for online videos; DoubleClick for web ads; Keyhole for satellite photos (now Google Earth); Urchin for web analytics (now Google Analytics).

The company acquired YouTube, the video-sharing site, in 2006, as a further extension of its services. Such acquisitions can be seen as a way of growing the business in a way that stays focused on Google's distinctive competence, (developing superior search solutions) and earning revenue from these through targeted advertising. The company has also shown great skill in investing heavily to ensure that all the pieces of the business fit together. This includes educating advertisers about how to use its systems to best effect.

What was once a search company has become an internet, data and software company with boundless ambition and the capacity to deliver a flow of unexpected products (John Gapper, *Financial Times*, 6 June 2013, p. 13).

In late 2015 it created a holding company – Alphabet – to provide a clearer management structure for the whole group. It plans to begin disclosing the profitability (or otherwise) of each business, which will make it easier for investors to value the company, and thus improve their confidence in it.

Source: Company website; *Financial Times*, 27 September 2012, 12 August 2015.

Case questions 12.4

- Referring to Chapter 8 (Strategy), what kind of strategy is Google following?
- What 'strategic direction' (Section 8.6) did the purchase of YouTube represent?
- Visit the website to identify recent strategic developments, and consider what they reveal about the company's strategy for growth.

IS and strategy

Chapter 8 showed that strategy sets the overall direction, and how Porter's five forces model is a useful tool for identifying the competitive forces affecting a business. Figure 12.9 uses the tool to show how IS can become a source of competitive advantage, and Table 12.3 gives examples.

This helps managers to identify ways of using their IS as a source of competitive advantage (or to identify potential threats from others).

Managers also use IS to support their chosen strategy – such as a differentiation or cost leadership. They can use IS to achieve a cost leadership strategy by, for example, using:

- computer-aided manufacturing to replace manual labour;
- stock-control systems to cut inventory; or
- online order entry to cut order processing costs.

They can support a differentiation strategy by using:

- computer-aided manufacturing to offer flexible delivery;
- stock-control systems to extend the range of goods on offer; or
- using online systems to remember customer preferences, and suggest purchases.

They can support a focus strategy by using:

- computer-aided manufacturing to meet unique, non-standard requirements;
- online ordering to allow customers to create a unique product by selecting features.

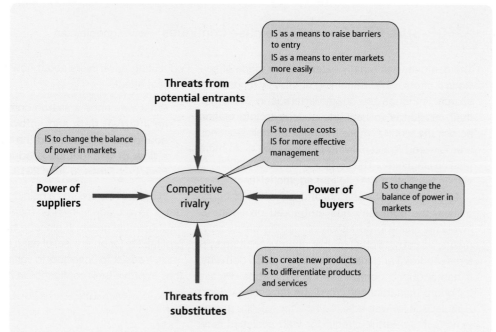

Figure 12.9
How information systems can change competitive forces: Porter's model.

Source: Adapted from Strategy and the internet, *Harvard Business Review,* Vol. 79 (3), pp. 63–78 (Porter, M.E. 2001), Copyright © 2001 by Harvard School Publishing Corporation, all rights reserved, reprinted by permission of Harvard Business Review.

Table 12.3 Using information systems to affect the five forces

Porter's five forces		Examples of information systems support
Threat of potential entrants	Raise entry barriers	Electronic links with customers make it more costly for them to move to competitors, discouraging new entrants
	Entering markets more easily	Bertelsmann, a German media group, entered book retailing by setting up an online store; Virgin offers financial services by using online systems
Threat of substitutes	Creating new products	ApplePay and similar systems are potential substitutes for services run by banks
	Differentiating their products	Retailers use database technology and CRM systems to identify precise customer needs and create unique offers
Bargaining power of suppliers	Increasing power of suppliers	Airlines use yield management systems to track actual reservations against capacity on each flight, and then adjust prices for the remaining seats to maximise revenue
	Decreasing power of suppliers	Online recruitment through a website reduces the need to advertise vacancies in newspapers, reducing their power to earn advertising revenue
Bargaining power of buyers		Buyers can use the internet to access more suppliers, and to compare prices for standard commodities
Intensity of rivalry	Using IS to reduce costs	ERPs enable closer control of manufacturing systems, leading to greater consistency in planning and lower costs
	More effective management	IS provide more detailed information on trading patterns, enabling management to use resources more efficiently

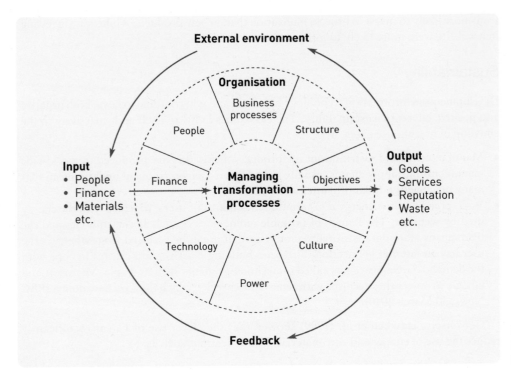

Figure 12.10
Possible action
areas in a plan

IS, strategy and organisation

Managers who wish to use one or more of these applications also need to ensure that
other elements of the organisation complement the information system – as only if it does
is there likely to be a strategic benefit. As noted in Chapter 6, new technology projects
often fail because managers pay too much attention to the technology, and too little to
contextual aspects such as the culture or structure ((Sabherwal et al. 2001; Boddy and
Paton, 2005). Figure 6.6 (repeated here as Figure 12.10) provides a simple reminder of the
organisational issues that are likely to arise when implementing any significant information system.

12.7   Integrating themes

Entrepreneurship

There are few empirical studies of the link between investing by small firms in modern IS
and innovation, but Higon (2012) used data from over 7,500 companies (in all sectors of the
UK economy) with less than 250 employees to test the relationship. The data came from the
2004 national Small Business Survey. She distinguished between five types of IS investment –
PC applications, email, website, e-commerce and R&D systems (such as computer-aided
design), and distinguished whether they were intensive users of each technology or not. IS
can help both product innovation and process innovation, either or both of which is likely
to contribute to long-term performance of the enterprise.

Higon found that investing in R&D applications and in websites had a positive effect on
both product and process innovations, though in different ways. Those investing in R&D

were more likely to invest in process innovation than in new products, while those investing in a website were more likely to innovate in new products.

Sustainability

Developments in information technology have had, and will continue to have, both negative and positive effects on sustainability. The electronics industry itself adds massively to the emission of greenhouse gases, by:

- **Manufacturing and distribution:** the products themselves are produced in worldwide manufacturing supply chains, usually linked by air-freight; frequent updates mean that many machines go to landfill after a few years.
- **Widespread use**: the energy consumption of millions of users, together with the energy used by websites. The launch of portable online devices such as smartphones and the iPad means more data is stored remotely so that it can be accessed from wherever the user has an internet connection. Firms are building massive data centres to cope with the demand. Greenpeace has called on technology giants such as Apple, Microsoft and Google to power these centres with renewable energy – which they are now doing. (BBC News, 30 March 2010).

Conversely, Hawken et al. (1999) showed that the clever use of IT can significantly reduce the use of energy and raw materials by applications such as:

- online meeting facilities, such as video-conferencing or social networking sites, which reduce the need to travel;
- energy management systems to monitor and control energy use in buildings;
- manufacturing planning systems that enhance the design and manufacture of products to minimise the use of energy and raw materials; and
- transport systems that monitor and control engine efficiency to save fuel.

Internationalisation

New technologies enable international business, since firms can disperse their operations round the globe and manage them remotely. The technology enables managers to keep in close touch with dispersed operations and to transfer knowledge between them. Paik and Choi (2005) showed the difficulties in applying technology across national boundaries, in their study of a global management consultancy, with over 75,000 consultants in 40 countries. Like most such firms, the consultancy considers the knowledge of its staff to be a core capability for achieving competitive advantage. To ensure that this knowledge is widely shared, it has spent large sums on KM systems, especially Knowledge Exchange (KX) – a repository of internally generated knowledge about clients, topics, best practices and so on – to which consultants were expected to contribute ideas as they completed projects for clients.

However, the authors found that few East Asian consultants contributed to the database, for three reasons:

- a perception among East Asian consultants that others did not appreciate their regional knowledge;
- a requirement to provide ideas in English; East Asian consultants were conversant in English, but found it time-consuming to translate documents into English; and
- cultural differences – staff in some countries were not motivated to contribute if there was no direct personal incentive, which the global reward system did not take into account.

They conclude that their study shows that global companies seeking a common approach to knowledge management need to make allowances for local cultural differences, as discussed in Chapter 4.

Governance

Advances in information systems technology offer senior managers the promise of greatly improved performance: but many IS projects fail to deliver, and destroy a great deal of wealth. Weill and Ross (2005) believe that the waste of resources this represents could be avoided by better IS governance processes, since:

> without them individual managers resolve isolated issues as they arise, and those individual actions may be at odds with each other. Our study of almost 300 companies around the world suggests that IT governance is a mystery to key decision makers in most companies . . . [yet] when senior managers take time to design, implement and communicate IT governance processes, companies get more value from IT.

They believe that the key issue for managers is to be clear about how they are going to control decisions about investments in IS. This is a multi-stage process in which players at various levels and in many functional areas exercise their power to influence IS decisions. To ensure that these decisions align information systems with wider organisational objectives, IS governance is the practice of allocating decision rights, and establishing an accountability framework for IS decisions.

Summary

1 **Explain how converging technologies change the way people add value to resources**

 - Continuing advances in information systems for processing data have been enhanced by the convergence of systems so that they now integrate data, sound and visual systems.
 - The radical result is that this enables producers and customers to co-create value.

2 **Recognise that, to use these opportunities, managers change both technology and organisation**

 - Established organisations use IS to make radical changes in the services they offer and how they work.
 - They also, as do new internet-based organisations, find ways to benefit from the possibilities of co-creation with customers.
 - Both depend on managing both technical and organisational issues.

3 **Distinguish between operations information systems and management information systems**

 - Operations information systems – such as transaction processing and office automation systems – support processes that keep current work running smoothly.
 - Management information systems – for information reporting, decision support and executive systems, provide managers with information to support decision making.

4 **Illustrate how organisations use the internet to add value by using three types of information system – customer relations, enterprise and knowledge**

 - Internet-based (e-business) systems are systems that operate across organisational boundaries, enabling new relations with business partners and customers.
 - Enterprise systems use a central database to integrate data about many aspects of the business as an aid to planning.
 - Knowledge management systems attempt to improve the ability of an organisation to use the information that it possesses.
 - Customer relations systems aim to capture and process information about each customer, so that products and services can be tailored more closely to individual needs.

5 **Understand the relation between IS, strategy and organisation**

- Computer-based IS can support strategy: each of Porter's five forces are potentially affected by IS, leading to either threats or opportunities.
- Similarly, managers can use IS to support a low-cost, differentiation or niche strategy.
- Whatever strategy they follow, it will be more successful if they ensure that complementary organisational changes are in place – such as ensuring the alignment of strategy and structure, and the appropriate governance structures for the IS function – to ensure, for example, the right balance between central and local provision.

6 **Explain how IS and organisations interact, and understand how you can use that to help develop the skill of setting a project agenda**

- The chapter has shown how successful IS and e-business projects depend on managing organisational as well as technical factors. IS project agendas ideally include both, and the 'Develop a Skill' feature helps develop the skill of setting a project agenda.

7 **Show how ideas from the chapter add to your understanding of the integrating themes**

- Higon (2012) shows that small firms investing in R&D were more likely to focus on process innovation, while those investing in website development were more likely to innovate in new products.
- The rapid spread in the use of IS is both one cause of the unsustainable use of resources, and also part of the solution, by enabling managers to redesign and monitor their processes to minimise resource use.
- While information systems enable managers to monitor and control international operations, to be effective they need to take account of national cultural differences (see Chapter 4), and of how people in different countries interpret and use information.
- Organisations waste huge amounts of money on information systems projects that fail to deliver what was expected, partly because senior managers have not paid sufficient attention to their systems for the governance and control of the IS function.

Test your understanding

1 Explain the significance of information systems to the management of organisations. How do they relate to the core task of managing?

2 Give some original examples of companies using information systems to add value.

3 Identify examples of co-creation, and explain the benefits to company and customer.

4 For what purposes are commercial companies using social networking sites?

5 Draw a sketch to illustrate why computer-based IS are more than just technology.

6 Give examples of how IS can affect at least two of the forces in Porter's model, and so affect the competitiveness of a business.

7 Outline the stages though which organisations go in using the internet, giving an original example of each.

8 What clues does the hospital case in Section 12.5 ('Management in practice' feature on p. 389) show about possible difficulties in using ERP systems?

9 Describe how the five forces model can show the likely effects of IS on strategy.

10 Summarise an idea from the chapter that adds to your understanding of the integrating themes.

Think critically

Think about the main computer-based information systems that you use in your company, or that feature in one with which you are familiar. Then make notes on these questions:

- What examples of the themes discussed in this chapter are currently relevant to your company?
- How, if at all, have these systems altered the tasks and roles of managers, staff or professionals?
- Do you think the business pays too much attention to the technical aspects of IS projects, and not enough to the social aspects? What **assumptions** appear to have shaped managers' views?
- How have changes in the business **context** shaped the applications being implemented? Does that also have implications for the agenda for IS projects?
- Have managers considered **alternatives** to the way they manage IS projects – for example, by greater user or customer involvement? What elements would you want to add?
- What **limitations** can you see in the ideas presented here, especially on the significance of organisational factors?

Develop a skill – setting a project agenda

The success of any major project (not just in IS) depends on identifying the tasks it needs to deal with, and ensuring they are on the project agenda. This exercise should help you develop that.

- **Assessment:** Assess how well you 'set the agenda' when dealing with a large task. Do you, for example, act quickly to get into action, or do you prefer to spend time finding out what it will involve, and making sure you do not overlook something?
- **Learning:** Read again Sections 12.3 and 12.6, looking especially at Figure 12.10. Why would checking the issues in Figure 12.9 help an IS project? Would they not just add to delay and cost?
- **Analysis:** Consider the likely implications of Figure 12.10 for a manager responsible for implementing an IS project.
- **Practice:** Consider the Google case (on your own or with colleagues) and identify where it mentions any of the items in Figure 12.10. How is the way Google dealt with them likely to have affected the outcome? Record what that tells you about setting the agenda for any project (IS or not).
  - Record what you find, and reflect on what you have learned.
  - If possible, compare your work with that of others to see what else you can learn.
- **Application:** Decide on another opportunity to practise this skill on another case or situation.

Read more

Donnelly, C., Simmons, G., Armstrong, G. and Fearne, A. (2015), 'Digital loyalty card "big data" and small business marketing: Formal versus informal or complementary?' *International Small Business Journal,* vol. 33, no. 4, pp. 422–42.

Iyer, B. and Davenport, T. H. (2008), 'Reverse engineering Google's innovation machine', *Harvard Business Review,* vol. 86, no. 4, pp.58–68.

Many insights into the company.

Krotoski, A. (2013), *Untangling the Web: What the Internet is doing for you,* Faber and Faber, London.

A social psychologist's perspective on the interaction between people and the internet, this book gives many valuable insights into how people are using the internet to suit their needs.

Morey, T., Forbath, T. and Schoop, A. (2015), 'Customer data: Designing for transparency and trust', *Harvard Business Review* , vol. 93, no. 5, pp. 96–105.

An empirical study of how companies are using the growing power of information systems.

Tapscott, E. and Williams, A.D. (2006), *Wikinomics: How Mass Collaboration Changes Everything,* Viking Penguin, New York.

Best-selling account of the rise of co-creation.

Go online

These websites are among those that have appeared in the chapter:

www.google.com
www.kpmg.com
www.topshop.com
www.irisnation.com
www.asos.com
www.bbc.co.uk

Visit two of the business sites in the list, or any others that interest you, and answer these questions:

- If you were a potential employee, how well does the website present information about the company and the career opportunities available?
- Evaluate the sites on these criteria, which are based on those used in an annual survey of corporate websites:

  - Does it give the current share price on the front page?
  - How many languages is it available in?
  - Is it possible to email key people or functions from the site?
  - Does it give a diagram of the main structural units in the business?
  - Does it set out the main mission or business idea of the company?
  - Are there any other positive or negative features?

CHAPTER 13
CREATIVITY, INNOVATION AND CHANGE

Aim

To outline theories of creativity and innovation, showing how context affects both.

Objectives

By the end of your work on this chapter you should be able to outline the concepts below in your own terms and:

1 Explain the meanings of creativity and innovation, with examples
2 Explain the management significance of creativity and innovation
3 Illustrate the organisational factors believed to support creativity and innovation
4 Explain how the interaction of change and context affects how people implement an innovation
5 Compare life cycle, emergent, participative and political theories of change
6 Explain the role of stakeholders in managing change, and understand how this will help develop the skill of identifying stakeholders and their interests
7 Show how ideas from the chapter add to your understanding of the integrating themes.

Key terms

The chapter introduces these terms:

creativity
receptive contexts
innovation
non-receptive contexts
open innovation
life cycle

perceived performance gap
emergent
performance imperatives
participative
organisational change
political model

Each is a term defined within the text, and in the glossary at the end of the book.

Case study   Dyson   www.dyson.co.uk

Dyson is a family-owned technology company, and its founder, Sir James Dyson is still active in the business. Following his first success with a bagless vacuum cleaner, the company is dedicated to inventing new things that solve a problem. In 2015 it was working on more new products than ever, with the goal of creating patentable, problem-solving technologies for new categories of product, and then to make them a reality.

The company is based at Malmesbury, Wiltshire, employing (in 2015) 5,500 people across the world, earning an annual revenue of £1.5 billion. It aims to employ 10,500 people by 2020, with annual revenue of £4 billion, and in a Malmesbury site double the present size. This will give more space for research into new product categories, and for the commercial activities.

James Dyson, born in Norfolk in 1947, studied Classics at school, followed by four years at the Royal College of Art, where he focused on furniture and interior design. A chance meeting led to a job designing products for an engineering company, which he left in 1977 to start his own company. Here he designed and made garden equipment: the business was a success, but after a disagreement over its direction with the investors who had financed it, he left – to start another company.

In 1979 he began to design a radically new form of vacuum cleaner and by 1984 (after over 5,000 prototypes) believed he had created a viable product. Five years of development of his radically new 'Cyclone' and bagless design had damaged his finances, with he and his wife depending on her income as an art teacher. He tried to license the design to major UK and European consumer goods companies, but none was interested. He eventually made a deal with a Japanese company, launching the product in 1986, and sales grew quickly: at last he had a success.

His next move was to set up a manufacturing company in the UK to meet demand. Most banks were unwilling to lend money to finance this investment, so he raised it by borrowing against the security of his house. Manufacturing began in 1993, and by 2000 worldwide sales exceeded £3 billion. Dyson machines, which cleaned very efficiently, and were brightly coloured, quickly sold more than the brands that had rejected his licensing offers.

Despite the initial setbacks, he was now a successful and innovative entrepreneur. Growing demand meant that he wanted to expand the factory in Wiltshire, but the local authority and government

© James Dyson Foundation

refused planning permission. Partly for this reason, but also because most components were now manufactured in Asia, he decided in 2002 to move the factory to Malaysia. Design and engineering would remain in Wiltshire, partly to help defend his products against patent infringements, but also to remain close to design talent.

Dyson is market leader by value in Taiwan, Japan and Hong Kong, and has recently entered the Chinese market. Ninety per cent of machines are sold outside of the UK, to customers in 72 countries. In 2015 it opened the first Dyson store, in Tokyo, and plans to open over 1,000 controlled retail spaces and 45 online stores within retailers' websites.

Source: Based on Company website.

Case questions 13.1

- What examples of creativity and innovation has the case mentioned?

- What have been the main challenges in building this creative company to its present position?

- How do you think creativity differs from innovation?

13.1   Introduction

Dyson is an example of a company that lives by creativity – there are many other vacuum manufacturers, and designs are quickly copied – so the company regularly adds new and improved features to distinguish it. The company also uses its creativity to launch new products, such as hand dryers and garden equipment, which will appeal to consumers. The case also shows that creativity itself does not start a business – persistent determination to overcome endless design challenges was clearly vital, but the founder also needed to secure finance and develop a succession of incremental improvements to keep the company in the news. Later sections will show how the company is also innovative in the way it manages staff to encourage a flow of creative ideas, and to turn the best of those into innovative products.

Other technology companies such as Facebook and Google depend equally strongly on innovations to meet customers' ever-rising expectations. The same is true of established businesses – GlasxoSmithKline and GKN both depend on creative work by their scientists and engineers to develop new pharmaceuticals and solve automotive engineering problems. Managers in the public sector face the same challenge: the British Museum has been creative in finding innovative ways to transform its financial position – see Chapter 14 Case study. Innovation that does not focus on the customers' experience will rarely be worth the trouble.

Companies that fail often do so because they have become unable to innovate. Kodak understood the digital imaging technologies that were eventually to destroy the business, but managers were unable to use them in new products to replace the obsolete film and camera businesses. Sony has become vulnerable to new products such as the iPod and the iTunes store. Disruptive shifts in technology, shortening product life cycles and the arrival of new competitors means that in many areas of the economy the primary task of senior managers is to nurture creativity and innovation – even if others do not yet see the need for change.

Implementing radical innovation usually depends on changing established practices and ways of working. Successful businesses learn to manage this as they repeatedly reinvent the business: GKN does this. They succeed in creating a culture in which people see change as the norm – one intervention in a continuing flow – rather than as a disruption after which the stability they prefer will return. Managers cannot leave these activities to chance: they depend on building a setting in which creativity and innovation add value to their changing organisation.

The chapter presents theories about the nature of creativity, innovation and change – which affect both products and processes. It begins by explaining the distinction between creativity and innovation, presents evidence about their sources, and on the organisational factors that influence innovation. Innovative ideas only add value when people implement them, which involves managing stakeholders to secure their support; so the chapter offers an opportunity to begin developing the skill of identifying stakeholders and their interests. Figure 13.1 shows the themes of the chapter.

Activity 13.1   Recording an innovation

Try to identify someone who is familiar with a major change in an organisation, which they are willing to discuss with you. Make notes on these questions and refer to them as you work on the chapter:

- What was the change?
- Why did management introduce it?
- What were the objectives?
- How did management plan and implement it?
- How well did it meet the objectives?
- What lessons have those involved taken from the experience?

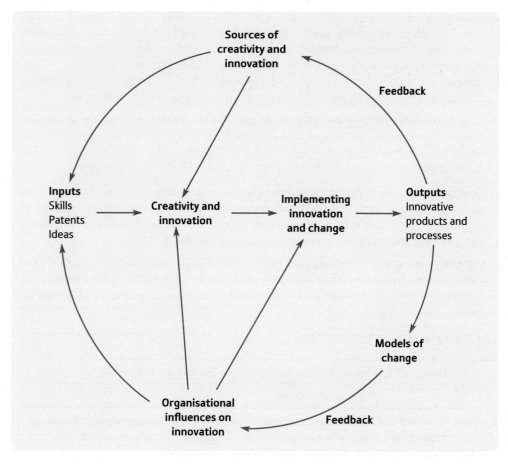

Figure 13.1 An overview of the chapter

Creativity and innovation

Creativity refers to the ability to combine ideas to produce something new and useful – a theme for a film, a new taxi-booking system (Uber), or a system to deliver live theatre performances to cinema audiences (www.nationaltheatre.org.uk). The idea in itself does not add value – people then need to apply it to meet a customer need, or to improve a working process. The innovative organisation is one that encourages creativity and channels it into value-adding outcomes – especially significant in new product development. Google, GKN or The Eden Project are innovative because they take novel ideas and turn them into products or ventures that customers want, or into improved ways of working.

Creativity is the ability to combine ideas to produce something new and useful.

Creativity

Focusing on the characteristics of creative individuals, Sternberg and Lubart (1999, p. 11) note that research consistently shows that creativity depends on six distinct resources converging:

- **intellectual abilities** – the ability to see problems in new ways and so escape from convention, the ability to recognise which ideas are worth pursuing and the ability to persuade others of their value;
- **knowledge** – knowing enough about the field to be able to move it forward, though knowledge sometimes leads to a narrow perspective that obstructs new ideas;
- **style of thinking** – a preference for thinking globally as well as locally – able to recognise which questions are important and which are not;

- **personality** – attributes commonly associated with creativity are a willingness to overcome obstacles, take sensible risks, tolerate ambiguity and be willing to defy convention;
- **motivation** – intrinsic, task-focused motivation is essential to creativity – a focus on, and commitment to, the work being done, rather than potential rewards; and
- **environment** – a context that supports the creative person, if only by providing a forum in which to express ideas, and to encourage their discussion among colleagues.

The 'environment' factor encouraged Amabile et al. (1996) to develop and validate an instrument to assess the organisational stimulants and obstacles to creativity – see Table 13.1.

Amabile and her team (Amabile et al. 1996) conclude that:

Creative ideas from individuals and teams within organisations sow the seeds of successful innovation, [and that their instrument] highlights the psychological context of innovation . . . that can influence the level of creative behaviour displayed in the generation and early development of new products and processes (p. 1178).

Unsworth and Clegg (2010) focused on why employees work creatively, rather than follow established practice. They interviewed 65 design and development engineers in four aerospace factories, whose work was to design solutions to problems identified by

Table 13.1 Factors in KEYS: assessing the climate for creativity

Scale name	Description (partial)	Sample survey item
Stimulant scales		
Organisational encouragement	A culture that encourages creativity through fair, constructive judgement of ideas, reward and recognition of creative work	People are encouraged to solve problems creatively in this organisation
Supervisory encouragement	A supervisor who is a good work model, sets goals appropriately, supports the work group	My supervisor serves as a good work model
Work group support	A diversely skilled group in which people communicate well, are open to new ideas, constructively challenge each other's work	There is free and open communication within my work group
Sufficient resources	Access to appropriate resources including funds, materials, facilities and information	Generally, I can get the resources I need for my work
Challenging work	A sense of having to work hard on challenging tasks and important projects	I feel challenged by the work I am currently doing
Freedom	Freedom in deciding what work to do or how to do it: a sense of control over one's work	I have the freedom to decide how I carry out my projects
Obstacle scales		
Organisational impediments	A culture that impedes creativity through internal political problems, harsh criticism of new ideas, avoidance of risk	There are many political problems in this organisation
Workload pressures	Extreme time pressures, unrealistic expectations for productivity, distractions	I have too much work to do in too little time

Source: Amabile et al. (1996, p. 1166).

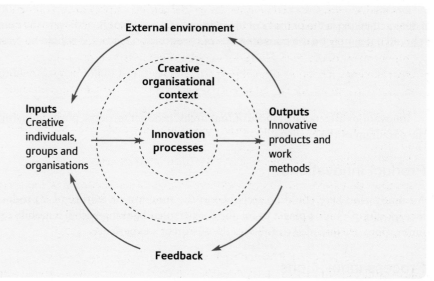

Figure 13.2
Systems view of
innovation

test engineers. They, too, found that the working context influenced staff views about whether the effort of finding a creative solution was worth it: perceptions of context moderated personal inclinations. Management could influence these by making creativity an explicit part of the engineers' role, providing time, resources and a degree of autonomy and creating a supportive culture.

Innovation

In the management context it is useful to think of **innovation** as the process of implementing something new and useful: that is, adding value by incorporating creative solutions in products and/or implementing changes in organisational processes. This is not necessarily major, visible breakthroughs – a flow of incremental improvements can be just as useful to consumers. Laundry detergents show this pattern – moving from powder in a box, to liquid, to concentrated forms, tablets, capsules and many more.

The systems model introduced in Chapter 1 helps to understand how organisations can become more innovative. Figure 13.2 shows that getting the desired outputs (innovative products or work methods) depends on suitable inputs and on suitable ways of transforming those inputs.

Inputs include having creative people and groups who are able to generate novel ideas and methods, but they only flourish in a favourable context. Managers create a context that they hope encourages creative people and the application of their ideas into profitable goods and services. One aspect of that context is encouraging 'design thinking' – see 'Key ideas'.

Innovation is the process of applying or implementing something new and useful.

| **Key ideas** | **Design thinking** |

Gruber et al. (2015) stress the value of 'design thinking' as a tool for innovation, shown by the way companies such as Apple and Dyson have succeeded. They have done this:

by helping to translate technological innovations into products that deliver compelling customer experiences as they have come to dominate their respective industry sectors. By 'design thinking' [they] refer to a human-centred approach to innovation that puts the observation and discovery of human needs at the forefront of the innovation process. It considers not just the technical system constraints but also the sociocultural context.

> At the heart of design thinking is the primacy of the customer or user experience – and the compelling user experience should not simply be the consequence of other design factors, it should be intentional.
>
> Source: Gruber et al. (2015).

Innovations affect one or more of four areas: product, process, positioning (market) and the paradigm of the business.

Product innovations

An innovation here could be a change in the function or feature of a product, such as incorporating a music player or an app for personal banking within a mobile phone. Such innovations are intended to enhance the customer's experience.

Process innovations

Examples are self-service checkouts or online seat reservation systems. Examples in manufacturing would be using robots to assemble cars. Equally important are innovations in management techniques – such as implementing *kaizen* or 'just in time' practices that have influenced management throughout the world (for another example, see 'Management in practice' about Pixar (p. 415).

Case study   Dyson – the case continues   www.dyson.co.uk

Dyson believed the Cyclone captured the market as it was an innovative product that consumers saw as being better than others. Innovation that consumers will value drives the business, and the company clearly invests heavily in the Research, Design and Development Centre in Wiltshire. This supports continuing improvements to the vacuums, and a growing range of other products, which now include a new cordless range of vacuums, as well as dryers, fans, heaters and lighting.

The James Dyson Foundation supports design and technology education, having given substantial sums to the Royal College of Art, Imperial College London and the University of Cambridge. It has 35 research projects with other UK universities. The company also seeks to partner with external expertise to help turn emerging technologies into practice. Mark Taylor heads a team of 150 engineers charged with spotting promising ideas and knowing the right ones to back.

Everyone in the team is responsible for finding new breakthroughs, whether it is home grown or externally sourced, it is all about finding the next generation technologies that we can push forward.

Since design and creativity are the foundations of the company's success, about half of the annual profits are invested in these new ideas. It ensures good use of this money by using a coherent set of practices to encourage the design of high-quality products. Care is taken to recruit only the most talented designers and engineers from university, typically the Royal College of Art, Brunel or Loughborough, and to pay them well.

About 650 engineers, scientists and designers work together, as Sir James believes all can learn from each other. They are located at the centre of the well-designed facility, emphasising the significance of their roles. Teamwork is central to the system, with all engineers and designers being members of frequently changed teams. The culture emphasises dialogue, seen as the foundation of progress. Sir James speaks to employees daily, not just about design but also about marketing and financial issues, and the overall progress of the business.

Source: Company website.

Case questions 13.2

- Visit the Dyson website and read the timeline summarising the company's development.
- Which of the types of innovation mentioned on these pages can you see in the case?

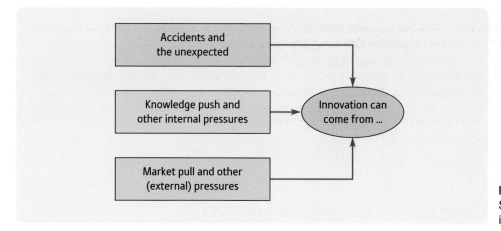

Figure 13.3
Sources of innovation

Position innovations

These are changes in the target market or customer base for a product or service. Amazon has repositioned from its initial bookselling position to provide many other services to business. For many years Lucozade was sold for people recovering from illness – it is now for healthy people engaged in sport. Four-wheel drives were invented for off-road work, and now sell as fashionable family cars.

Paradigm innovations

These are changes in how a whole company presents what it does. Tesco has moved from selling groceries to providing many more of a family's needs – petrol, clothing, financial products (the last providing a synergy as the means to pay for all the others).

13.3   Sources of innovation

Figure 13.3 illustrates the main sources of innovation.

Accidents and the unexpected

Many innovations have been accidental – from Fleming's discovery of Penicillin to the Post-It Note that arose when Art Fry used a recently invented 'sticky but not too sticky' adhesive to keep his book mark in place. This gave him the idea for the Post-It Note which, after a process of design and development, became the familiar product range. The 'Management in practice' feature describes a recent example. The innovative gyro that makes the Segway possible was developed in BAE Systems defence laboratories. Terrorist attacks have led to innovations in safety and security products – such as the biometric scanning device. One of the largest service industries in the world – personal insurance - developed from the need to guard against unexpected events.

Management in practice   **Plugging a 'mole' in the market**   www.magnamole.co.uk

Sharon Wright had her eureka moment while having a phone-line installed in her home. Under pressure for time she offered to help the engineer thread the cable through the wall of her house. To Sharon's surprise the engineer produced a makeshift tool made out of a wire coat-hanger. As well as being difficult to use, Sharon's experience in health and safety management told her this device was unsuitable and hazardous. Market research showed there were no alternative tools available for cable threading.

Within hours she had sketched the design of the Magnamole tool, a plastic rod with a magnet at one end and an accompanying metallic cap for attaching to the wire to be threaded through the wall. She soon had a prototype, and orders followed from large customers around the world.

What is remarkable about Sharon is that she had little knowledge or experience of this area of business, but that did not stop her from taking advantage of a gap in the market.

Source: Company website.

Market pull and other external pressures

No matter how innovative a new product, it will not survive without a market. Before investing significant resources, managers need a sense of the likely need. This is not straightforward: before lightweight digital music players and headphones arrived, sportsmen and women trained without equipment to combat boredom. This technology is now an essential part of a runner's or cyclist's kit, and there are versions for swimmers.

Companies spend heavily to understand changing customer needs – Unilever has several Innovation Centres devoted to just that. Many parts of the UK pub industry are highly innovative: the smoking ban and rapid increases in beer duty has prompted them to look out for new ways to attract customers. Many now offer coffee and breakfast while others take bookings on Twitter, have mystery visitors or offer takeaway food. An industry observer:

they keep surviving and they reinvent themselves.

Key ideas   **Stephen Johnson – environments that favour innovation**

In *Where Good Ideas Come From* (published in 2010) Stephen Johnson presents the idea that environments are the key to understanding innovation:

Some environments squelch new ideas; some environments seem to breed them effortlessly. The city and the Web have been such engines of innovation because, for complicated historical reasons, they are both environments that are powerfully suited for the creation, diffusion, and adoption of good ideas. Neither environment is perfect, by any means. (Think of the crime rates in big cities, or the explosion of spam online.) But both the city and the Web possess an undeniable track record at generating innovation . . . If we want to understand where good ideas come from, we have to put them in context . . .

The argument of this book is that a series of shared properties and patterns recur again and again in unusually fertile environments. I have distilled them down into seven patterns – the more we embrace these patterns [in various activities] the better we will be at tapping our extraordinary capacity for innovative thinking.

Source: Johnson (2010) pp. 16–17.

Regulation changes

The makers of Segway encountered regulatory problems over safety and traffic: regulations often hinder innovation. Other regulations trigger it by requiring change – those on environmental pollution encourage the search for renewable sources of energy. Regulations intended to improve road safety have led to the development of speed cameras and air bags.

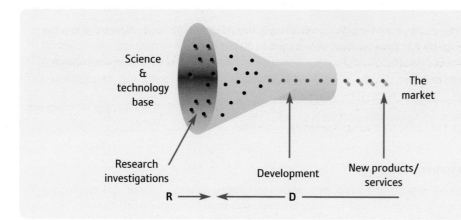

Figure 13.4
A closed innovation model

Source: Chesbrough et al. (2006), p.3.

Co-creation

Chapter 12 showed how innovations in information systems often emerge from collaboration between an organisation and its customers. Ford et al. (2014) note customers assign value by recalling their experience of using products or services, not from their objective nature. This implies that providers who wish to meet customers' expectations need to draw heavily on the latter's knowledge, skills and abilities, and combine these with those of their staff. They describe how Ikea and Disney apply this principle, while stressing that while the concept sounds easy, implementing it is a challenge. There is an example in Chapter 9 (p. 289) showing how Lego uses this method.

Knowledge push – and other internal pressures

Organisations that depend on innovation implement deliberate systems to ensure an adequate flow. Figure 13.4 shows a model of the traditional method – a filter through which people gather, channel and focus ideas before selecting those with most potential. Generating the initial idea is largely random, but thereafter firms try to create a more orderly process. They apply resources to the promising ideas to develop them into something they can implement. The steps look sequential but their duration and complexity varies – some require significant R&D, others a change to the sales effort. Ramirez et al. (2011) describe how Shell uses a process like this – see 'Management in practice'.

Management in practice   Shell's 'Gamechanger2' process   www.shell.com

Since 1998 Shell has used what it calls the Gamechanger process to develop, and select between, innovation projects. In the nine years to 2007, over 2,050 innovation projects were submitted to Gamechanger, and of these 1,950 had been stopped at some point in the gated funnel. 100 were commercial successes. All projects are submitted to one of six 'domains' – 'stepping stones' that show a path from where Shell is now, to several possible futures. The stepping stones reveal areas that Shell needs to explore to realise those futures. Each domain consists of a small set of strategic propositions, and a small number of innovation projects chosen to test those propositions. Proposals must pass a rigorous process before they are accepted into a domain.

For example, the 'bio-fuel' domain could include an ethanol project and an algae project and these projects, together with others in the domain, would give Shell the option to move to a future where fuels are 'grown', not 'mined'.

A strength of the system is believed to be the tight connections it develops between innovation projects and company strategy, as domains ensure staff attend to three concerns – strategic options, opportunities offered by R&D and the company's environment. Since introducing the discipline of the domains in 2003, the proportion of projects surviving the first gate fell from 60 per cent to 30 per cent (more projects were killed off earlier), with no fall in the number of successful outcomes. The system has led to more focused development and the earlier selection of winners.

Source: Ramirez et al. (2011).

Staff as innovators

The Japanese system of *kaizen,* or 'continuous improvement', encourages employees to question work processes and look for incremental improvements in all they do. Suggestion schemes are not new, but the more systematic and proactive approach of the Japanese supported the success of CI. *Kaizen* has been joined by other systems such as total quality management and lean manufacturing (Slack et al. 2013). While differing in emphasis, the common theme is to involve employees in innovation.

Open innovation

Open innovation is based on the view that useful knowledge is widely distributed and that even the most capable R&D organisation must identify, connect to and draw upon external knowledge as a core process in innovation.

Large companies spend significant sums on their R&D laboratories in the hope of finding new products – but they now depend less on this source. The cost of scientific work, the preference of many scientists to create their own research companies and above all the need to present new products quickly is encouraging companies to use '**open innovation**' (Chesbrough et al. 2006). This happens as managers recognise useful knowledge is widely distributed and that they can benefit by drawing upon that wider resource. Figure 13.5 shows this, with the internal technology base being supplemented by an external technology one throughout the process.

GlaxoSmithKline (www.gsk.com) sources half of its new products from external laboratories and Unilever (www.unilever.com) relies on external input for 60 per cent of its innovations – up 25 per cent from when it established an open innovation team in 2009. Roger Leech, Unilever's director of external research:

> We are extremely interested in being able to tap into external sources of new ideas and capabilities. To find solutions in the external world has been extremely important to us, and we are looking at different ways of tapping into that. (*Financial Times,* 11 October 2012)

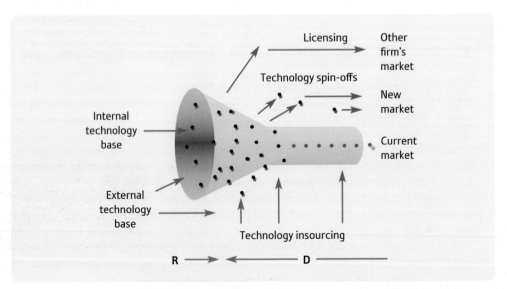

Figure 13.5
An open innovation model

Source: Chesbrough et al. (2006), p. 3.

The method is also a valuable way in which small firms, like ARM Holdings initially, can grow quickly by securing the technology they need from others, rather than investing scarce resources in fixed facilities and high overhead costs. Open innovation can work both ways, as companies transfer their technologies and knowledge to other firms through licensing or joint ventures.

13.4   Organisational influences on innovation

Organisations that depend on innovation aim to create an environment that encourages all staff (not just those with R&D responsibilities) to support a strong flow of successful new things. Figure 13.6 summarises organisational factors that may affect innovation – but that does NOT mean they will all have the same effect (positive or negative) in all circumstances. As in most aspects of management, what works in one context will not necessarily do so elsewhere.

Structure

- A structure (**Chapter 10**) with extensive horizontal communication, team-based working and broadly-defined roles that encourage people to use initiative is more likely to help innovation than a mechanistic form.
- Plentiful resources enable the company to recruit the best staff, and to give them the budget to invest in equipment, conduct trials and experiments, commission research – and be able to absorb the inevitable failures. A successful innovation will take time to introduce and earn revenue – and until then it is draining resources, which the company must sustain.
- Systems to support the innovation process – such as Shell's 'Gamechanger' – increase the chances that innovations occur and support strategy.
- Role-clarity – ensures that the role clearly includes innovation, has few non-essential tasks and rewards those who deliver significant innovations.

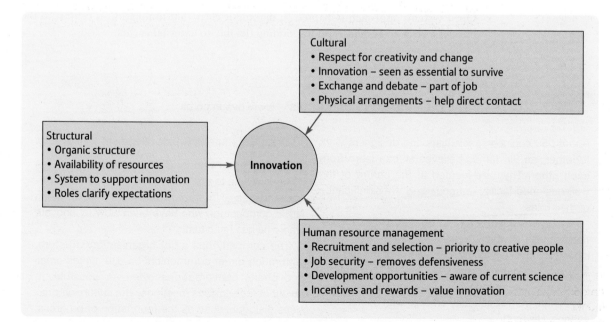

Figure 13.6 Organisation factors that can affect innovation

Key ideas   **Innovation and speed in R&D teams**

One aspect of innovation is the speed at which a research team produces results, especially in developing new products. Pirola-Merlo (2011) found that the context of R&D teams significantly affected performance. An instrument called West's Team Climate for Innovation measures four aspect of a team's context:

- vision (team members share clear and valued objectives);
- participative safety (a non-threatening environment where members can influence decisions);
- task orientation (concern with achieving excellence through high-quality work and critical appraisal); and
- support for innovation (valuing innovation, and supporting work practices). (p. 1077).

The author suggests that an R&D project (lasting months or often years) is not a single innovation event, but a set of (overlapping or sequential) episodes. It is plausible that prior conditions within the team – team climate – influences how they deal with these, and hence the speed and quality of the outcome. Data from 33 R&D teams in four organisations collected over nine months showed that, as predicted, teams with positive ratings on the TCI progressed significantly faster towards project completion, and produced more innovative outcomes, than those with lower ratings.

Source: Pirola-Merlo (2011).

Culture

Innovative organisations tend to have these characteristics:

- Respect and positive encouragement for all types of creativity – Pixar shows that technologists, creative and production staff are equally valued. A culture that discourages ideas or always raises obstacles will soon stop people innovating.
- A willingness to tolerate mistakes – these are inevitable if people are testing unusual ideas to see if they work – it is inevitable that many will not. Trying an idea on a small scale ensures small mistakes and quick learning.
- Value for open debate and criticism of ideas. They encourage people to challenge – but all know they are challenging the idea, not the person.
- Open systems approach (Chapter 2), making it clear that innovation is central to the business, with an emphasis on responding flexibly to external events.

Case study   **Dyson – the case continues**   www.dyson.co.uk

About 650 engineers, scientists and designers work together, as Sir James believes all can learn from each other. They are located at the centre of the well-designed facility, emphasising the significance of their roles.

Dyson considers errors to be part of the innovation process, in which failure is tolerated – innovation inherently involves following a wrong path, and that failure spurs determination to succeed. He aims to create a culture that encourages people to try different things, from which they emerge with useful innovations. His motto:

Creativity + Interactive development = Innovation

He has good relations with the media, always being available to talk to journalists about new products and ideas. Nor does he fear what were his much larger competitors, who have been slow to innovate where he has been fast.

The company has a flat organisation structure, with much direct communication. He avoids email and phone conversations wherever possible, in favour of face-to-face meetings. The culture emphasises dialogue, seen as the foundation of progress.

Designers regularly visit the manufacturing hub in Malaysia to meet the production staff, which he believes must improve the way the two work together.

Source: Company website.

Case questions 13.3

● What examples are there in the case of practices that Dyson hopes will encourage creativity and innovation?

Human resource management

● Ensuring that recruitment identifies innovative and proactive people.
● Training and development – investment to build skills and confidence, to ensure knowledge is current, including the increasing use of online resources available to staff.
● Job security – ensuring people feel secure is likely to encourage innovation; anxiety discourages people from taking career-threatening risks.

Management in practice   **Pixar**   www.pixar.com

Ed Catmull (Catmull, 2008) believes that Pixar's success is due to its work environment, and the close collaboration and interaction between work groups – the technology group that delivers computer graphics tools, the creative department that creates stories and the production group that coordinates the film-making process. Practices include:

● **Getting talented people to work effectively with each other** . . . [by constructing] an environment that nurtures trusting relationships and unleashes everyone's creativity. If we get that right, the result is a vibrant community where talented people are loyal to one another and their collective work. (p. 66)
● **Everyone must be free to communicate with anyone** . . . the most efficient way to deal with numerous problems is to trust people to work out the difficulties directly with each other without having to check for permission. (p. 71)
● **We must stay close to innovations happening in the academic community** . . . we strongly encourage our technical artists to publish their research and participate in industry conferences. Publication may give away ideas . . . but the connection is worth far more than any ideas we may have revealed: it helps us attract exceptional talent and reinforces the belief throughout the company that people are more important than ideas. (p. 71)
● **[Measure progress]** . . . because we're a creative organisation, people [think that what we do can't be measured]. That's wrong. Most of our processes involve activities and deliverables that can be quantified. We keep track of the rates at which things happen, how often something had to be reworked, whether a piece of work was completely finished or not when it was sent to another department . . . Data can show things in a neutral way, which can stimulate discussion. (p. 72).

Source: Catmull (2008).

13.5   Implementing innovation and change

Creativity and innovation only add value when they are implemented – by offering new products or changing the organisation.

Perceived performance gap

A **perceived performance gap** arises when people believe that the actual performance of a unit or business is out of line with the level they desire.

A **perceived performance gap** arises when people believe the performance of a unit or business is out of line with the level they expect. If those responsible for transforming resources into outputs do not meet customer expectations, there is a performance gap. This may lead to other performance gaps emerging – revenue from sales will be insufficient to secure new resources. If uncorrected, the business will fail.

Two aspects of performance dominate much management discussion – what Prastacos et al. (2002) call '**performance imperatives**': the need for flexibility and the need for innovation. Successful businesses develop a high degree of strategic and organisational flexibility, while also being efficient and stable. This apparent paradox reflects the fact that while companies need to respond rapidly, they also need to respond efficiently. They do this by developing stable and predictable processes.

Performance imperatives are aspects of performance that are especially important for an organisation to do well, such as flexibility and innovation.

The other imperative identified by Prastacos et al. (2002) is innovation:

> to generate a variety of successful new products or services (embedding technological innovation), and to continuously innovate in all aspects of the business (p. 58).

The internal context

Chapter 1 introduced the internal context (Figure 1.5, and repeated as Figure 13.7) as the elements within an organisation that influence behaviour. Change begins to happen when sufficient people believe, say, that outdated technology or a confusing structure is causing a performance gap, by inhibiting flexibility or innovation. They notice external or internal events and interpret them as threatening the performance that influential stakeholders expect. This interpretation encourages them to propose changing one or more aspects of the organisation shown in Figure 13.7.

They then have to persuade enough other people that the matter is serious enough to earn a place on the management agenda. Some colleagues will be open to proposals for change, others will ignore them. People initiate change for reasons other than a performance gap – fashion, empire building or a powerful player's personal whim can all play a part. Employees

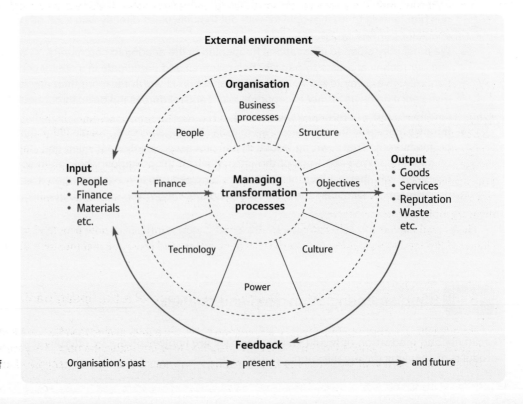

Figure 13.7
Elements of the internal context of management

or trade unions can propose changes in the way things are done to improve working conditions. The need for change is subjective – what some see as urgent others will leave until later. People can affect that process by managing external information – magnifying customer complaints to make the case for change, or minimising them if they wish to avoid change.

Whatever the stated intentions, **organisational change** is an attempt to change one or more of the elements in Figure 13.7.

Change in any of these areas will have implications for others – and these connections sometimes make change more difficult than promoters expected. When retailers introduce an online shopping service alongside their established retail business they need to create a website (technology), decide issues of structure and people (would it be part of the existing stores or a separate unit with its own premises and staff?) and about business processes (how would an order on the website be converted to a box of groceries delivered to the customer's door?). They have to manage these ripples initiated by the main decision. Managers who ignore these ripples achieve less than they expect.

Attempts to innovate a new process will often challenge the prevailing culture – the 'Key ideas' feature shows how one innovative company encountered this challenge.

> **Organisational change** is a deliberate attempt to improve organisational performance by changing one or more aspects of the organisation, such as its technology, structure or business processes.

Key ideas   Introducing Six Sigma to the entrepreneurial culture of 3M

Six Sigma is a method developed to enhance the efficiency of manufacturing and administrative processes. 3M is a successful consumer products company, which during a long history of successful innovation has developed a creative culture. A new chief executive joined 3M from General Motors, and ordered the introduction of Six Sigma to cut costs and improve profits. These potential benefits were enough to silence any initial doubters, but as engineers began to implement the new practices their effects on product innovation became clear: managers questioned the suitability of the technique for 3M.

There was a cultural gap between the technique and the innovative company, and the authors trace a gradual accommodation in both directions. Some cultural beliefs were partially abandoned to accommodate the technique, and some aspects of the technique were shaped to suit the culture. The authors observed what they termed a 'hierarchy of cultural values', in that people were willing to accept some moderate alterations to patterns of thought and value, but were less accommodating towards practices that threatened deeply held beliefs.

Source: Canato et al. (2013).

Context affects the ability to change

While people managing a project aim to change the context, the context within which they work will itself help or hinder them. All of the elements of Figure 12.9 (p. 394) will be present as the project begins, and some of these will influence how people react. Managers will review a proposal from their personal career perspective, as well as that of the organisation. For retailers going online, the existing technology (stores, distribution systems, information systems) and business processes would influence managers' decisions about how to implement the online shopping strategy.

The prevailing culture – shared values, ideals and beliefs – influences how people view change. They tend to welcome a project that fits their culture and resist one that threatens it.

Management in practice   Culture and change at a European bank

While teaching a course to managers at a European bank, the author invited members to identify which of the four cultural types identified in Chapter 2 best described their unit within the bank. They were then asked to describe the reaction of these units to an internet banking venture that the company was introducing.

Course members observed that colleagues in a unit that had an internal process culture (routine back-office data processing) were hostile to the internet venture. They appeared to be 'stuck with their own systems', which were so large and interlinked that any change was threatening. Staff in new business areas of the company (open systems) were much more positive, seeing the internet as a route to new business opportunities.

Source: Data collected by the author.

Receptive contexts are those where features of the organisation (such as culture or technology) appear likely to help change.

Culture is a powerful influence on the success or failure of innovation – see Jones et al. (2005) for evidence of how it affected the acceptance of a new computer system. At some companies the culture encourages change, while elsewhere it encourages caution. Cultural beliefs are hard to change, yet shape how people respond. Managers learn to be guided by these beliefs because they have worked successfully in the past.

Key ideas — Receptive and non-receptive contexts

Pettigrew et al. (1992) sought to explain why managers in some organisations were able to introduce change successfully, while others in the same sector (the UK National Health Service) found it very hard to move away from established practices. Their comparative research programme identified the influence of context on ability to change:

receptive contexts are those where features of the context 'seem to be favourably associated with forward movement [while] . . . in **non-receptive contexts** there is a configuration of features that may be associated with blocks on change' (p. 268).

Their research identified seven contextual factors – conditions that energise change:

1 quality and coherence of policy;
2 availability of key people leading change;
3 long-term environmental pressure – intensity and scale;
4 a supportive organisational culture;
5 effective managerial–clinical relations;
6 cooperative inter-organisational networks;
7 fit between the district's change agenda and its locale.

Together these factors give a widely applicable model of how context affects ability to change.

Source: Pettigrew et al. (1992).

Non-receptive contexts are those where the combined effects of features of the organisation (such as culture or technology) appear likely to hinder change.

The distribution of power also affects receptiveness to change. Change threatens the status quo, and is likely to be resisted by stakeholders who benefit from the way things are. Innovation depends on promoters developing political will and expertise.

The context has a history, and several levels

The present context is the result of past decisions and events. Management implements change against a background of previous events that shaped the context. The promoter of a major project in a multinational experienced this in his colleagues' attitudes:

They were a little sceptical and wary of whether it was actually going to enhance our processes. Major pan-European redesign work had been attempted in the past and had failed miserably. The solutions had not been appropriate and had not been accepted by the divisions. Europe-wide programmes therefore had a bad name. (Boddy, 2002, p. 38)

Beliefs about the future also affect how people react. Optimists are more open to change than those who feel threatened and vulnerable.

The context represented by Figure 13.7 occurs at (say) operating, divisional and corporate levels. People at any of these will be acting to change their context – which may help or hinder those managing change elsewhere. A project at one level may depend on decisions at another about resources, as this manager leading an oil refinery project discovered:

> One of the main drawbacks was that commissioning staff could have been supplemented by skilled professionals from within the company, but this was denied to me as project manager. This threw a heavy strain and responsibility on myself and my assistant. It put me in a position of high stress, as I knew that the future of the company rested upon the successful outcome of this project. One disappointment (and, I believe, a significant factor in the project) was that just before commissioning, the manager of the pilot plant development team was transferred to another job. He had been promised to me at the project inception, and I had designed him into the working operation. (Boddy, 2002, pp. 38–9)

Key ideas   Stakeholders affect change

Chapters 3 and 5 discussed the significance of understanding stakeholders in relation, respectively, to corporate governance and corporate responsibility. Those wanting to implement innovation also benefit from being able to identify and manage influential stakeholders. Boddy (2002) suggests that anticipating the interests of stakeholders likely to be affected by a change helps to spot trouble before it happens, to identify potential allies and to concentrate effort on the most significant players. Important tasks for someone engaged in a change project include:

- identify those with a stake in the change;
- assess their commitment;
- assess their power to help or hinder the change;
- assess their interests, and what they are likely to think or do about it; and
- manage relations with them – to gain support, minimise opposition and generally create an atmosphere favourable to the change.

Source: Boddy (2002).

Acting to change an element at one level will have effects at this and other levels, and elements may change independently. The manager's job is to create a coherent context that encourages desired behaviour, by using their preferred model of change.

13.6   Models of change

There are four complementary models of change, each with different implications for managers – life cycle, emergent, participative and political.

Life cycle

Much advice given to those responsible for managing projects uses the idea of the project **life cycle**. Projects go through successive stages, and results depend on managing each one in an orderly and controlled way. The labels vary, but common themes are:

1 Define objectives.
2 Allocate responsibilities.

Life cycle models of change are those that view change as a process that follows a logical, orderly sequence of activities that can be planned in advance.

3 Fix deadlines and milestones.
4 Set budgets.
5 Monitor and control.

This approach (sometimes called a 'rational–linear' approach) reflects the idea that people can identify smaller tasks within a change and plan the (overlapping) order in which to do them. It predicts that people can make reasonably accurate estimates of the time required to complete each task and when it will be feasible to start work on later ones. People can use tools such as bar charts (sometimes called Gantt charts after the American industrial engineer Henry Gantt, who worked with Frederick Taylor), to show all the tasks required for a project and their likely duration (see the example in Figure 6.7 (p. 199)). These help to visualise the work required and to plan the likely sequence of events.

In the life cycle model, successfully managing change depends on specifying these elements at the start and then monitoring them to ensure the project stays on target. Ineffective implementation is due to managers failing to do this. Figure 13.8 shows the stages in the life cycle of a small project (Lock, 2013) – cyclical because they begin and end with the customer. He emphasises this is an oversimplification of a complex, iterative reality, but that it helps identify where decisions arise:

> Travelling clockwise round the cycle reveals a number of steps or *phases,* each of which is represented by a circle in the diagram. The boundaries between these phases are usually blurred in practice, because the phases tend to overlap. (pp. 8–9)

Many books on project management, such as Lock (2013), present advice on tools for each stage of the life cycle. For some changes the life cycle gives valuable guidance. It is not necessarily sufficient in itself, since in uncertain conditions it makes little sense to plan outcomes in much detail. Better to set the general direction, adapting the target as conditions evolve – which points to an additional theory to represent emergent change.

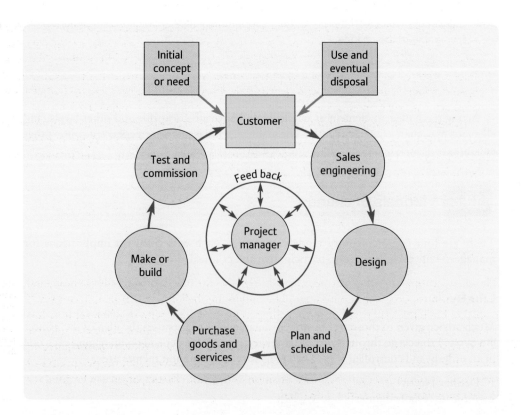

Figure 13.8 A project life cycle

Source: Lock (2013) p. 10.

Activity 13.2   **Critical reflection on the project life cycle**

You may be able to gain some insight into the project life cycle by using it on a practical task. For example:

- If you have a piece of work to do that is connected with your studies, such as an assignment or project, sketch out the steps to be followed by adapting Figure 13.8; alternatively do the same for some domestic, social or management project.
- If you work in an organisation, try to find examples of projects that use this approach, and ask those involved when the method is most useful, and when least useful.
- Make notes summarising how the life-cycle approach helps, and when it is most likely to be useful.

Emergent

Chapter 8 (Section 8.3) showed how Mintzberg (1994) saw strategy as an **emergent** or adaptive process. These ideas apply to change as much as to strategy, since it takes place in the same volatile, uncertain environment. While the life-cycle approach can help implementation, change agents can also use the emergent model to guide them. Choi and Moon (2013) trace how Toyota implemented 'The Toyota Way' – a process innovation that, over many years of incremental change, revolutionised the motor industry (see 'Key ideas').

Emergent models of change emphasise that in uncertain conditions a project will be affected by unknown factors, and that planning has little effect on the outcome.

Key ideas   **Implementing the Toyota way**

The idea of only ordering new stock when existing stock had been used was inspired by a visit to a US supermarket. In the early 1950s Toyota engineers decided to apply the principles to their fledgling car business, without any clear idea of the final shape of the innovation in that context. Rather, they envisaged a series of controlled experiments through which the company continually responded to problems identified during implementation. The 'just-in-time' production method was complemented by a system where employees were empowered to make spontaneous improvements as circumstances changed.

The authors Choi and Moon suggest that innovations depend heavily on how they are implemented since, if done properly, this stage provides ample opportunities to 'rediscover' or refine innovations by observing the distinct ways people use them. They advocate a conscious process of mutual adaptation between innovations and individual users, to realise the full potential of an innovation.

Source: Choi and Moon (2013).

Participative

Those advocating **participative** models stress the benefits of personal involvement in, and contribution to, events and outcomes. The underlying belief is that if people can say 'I helped to build this', they will be more willing to live and work with it, whatever it is. It is also possible that since participation allows more people to express their views the outcome will be better. Ketokivi and Castañer (2004) found that when employees participated in planning strategic change, they were more likely to view the issues from the perspective of the organisation, rather than their own position or function. Participation can be good for the organisation, as well as the individual.

The **participative** model is the belief that if people are able to take part in planning a change they will be more willing to accept and implement the change.

While participation is consistent with democratic values, it takes time and effort and may raise unrealistic expectations. It may be inappropriate when:

- the scope for change is limited, because of decisions made elsewhere;
- participants know little about the topic;
- decisions must be made quickly;
- management has decided what to do and will do so whatever views people express;
- there are fundamental disagreements and/or inflexible opposition to the proposed change.

Participative approaches assume that a sensitive approach by reasonable people will result in the willing acceptance and implementation of change. Some situations contain conflicts that participation alone cannot solve.

Activity 13.3   Critical reflection on participation

Have you been involved in, or affected by, a change in your work or studies?
If so:

- What evidence was there that those managing the change agreed with the participative approach?
- In what way, if any, were you able to participate?
- How did that affect your reaction to the change?

If not:

- Identify three advantages and three disadvantages for a project manager in adopting a participative approach.
- Suggest how managers should decide when to use the approach.

Political

Change often involves people from several levels and functions with different aims and priorities:

> Strategic processes of change are . . . widely accepted as multi-level activities and not just as the province of a . . . single general manager. Outcomes of decisions are no longer assumed to be a product of rational . . . debates but are also shaped by the interests and commitments of individuals and groups, forces of bureaucratic momentum, and the manipulation of the structural context around decisions and changes. (Whipp et al., 1988, p. 51)

Political models
reflect the view that organisations are made up of groups with separate interests, goals and values, and that these affect how they respond to change.

Several analyses of organisational change emphasise a **political model** (Pettigrew, 1985; Pfeffer, 1992a; Buchanan and Badham, 1999). Pettigrew (1985) was an early advocate of the view that change requires political as well as rational (life cycle) skills. Successful change managers create a climate in which people accept the change as legitimate – often by manipulating apparently rational information to build support for their ideas.

Key ideas   Tom Burns on politics and language

Tom Burns (1961) observed that political behaviour in the organisation is invariably concealed or made acceptable by subtle shifts in the language that people use:

> Normally, either side in any conflict, called political by observers, claims to speak in the interests of the corporation as a whole. In fact, the only recognised, indeed feasible, way of advancing political

interests is to present them in terms of improved welfare or efficiency, as contributing to the organisation's capacity to meet its task and to prosper. In managerial and academic, as in other legislatures, both sides to any debate claim to speak in the interests of the community as a whole; this is the only permissible mode of expression. (p. 260)

Source: Burns (1961)

Pfeffer (2010) shows that power and political skill is essential to get things done, since decisions in themselves change nothing – people only see a difference when someone implements them. Projects frequently threaten the status quo: people who have done well are likely to resist the change. Innovators need to ensure the project is put onto the senior management agenda, and that influential people support and resource it. Buchanan and Badham (1999) conclude that the roots of political behaviour:

lie in personal ambition, in organisation structures that create roles and departments which compete with each other, and in major decisions that cannot be resolved by reason and logic alone but which rely on the values and preferences of the key actors. Power politics and change are inextricably linked. Change creates uncertainty and ambiguity. People wonder how their jobs will change, how their work will be affected, how their relationships with colleagues will be damaged or enhanced. (p. 11)

Reasonable people may disagree about means and ends, and fight for the action they prefer. This implies that successful project managers understand they have to develop the political will to build and use their power.

> **Key ideas**   Henry Kissinger on politics in politics
>
> In another work Pfeffer (1992b) quotes Henry Kissinger:
>
> Before I served as a consultant to Kennedy, I had believed, like most academics, that the process of decision-making was largely intellectual and all one had to do was to walk into the President's office and convince him of the correctness of one's view. This perspective I soon realised is as dangerously immature as it is widely held. (p. 31)
>
> Source: Pfeffer (1992b).

The political perspective recognises the messy realities of organisational life. Major changes will be technically complex and challenge established interests. These will pull in different directions and pursue personal as well as organisational goals. To manage these tensions managers need political skills as well as those implied by life cycle, emergent and participative perspectives.

> **Management in practice**   Political action in hospital re-engineering
>
> Managers in a hospital responded to a persistent performance gap (especially unacceptably long waiting times) by 're-engineering' the way patients moved through and between the different clinical areas. This included creating multi-functional teams responsible for all aspects of the flow of the patient through a clinic, rather than dealing with narrow functional tasks. The programme was successful, but was also controversial. One of those leading the change recalled:
>
> I don't like to use the word manipulate, but . . . you do need to manipulate people. It's about playing the game. I remember being accosted by a very cross consultant who had heard something about one of

the changes and he really wasn't very happy with it. And it was about how am I going to deal with this now? And it is about being able to think quickly. So I put it over to him in a way that he then accepted, and he was quite happy with. And it wasn't a lie and it wasn't totally the truth. But he was happy with it and it has gone on.

Source: Buchanan (2008), p. 13.

These perspectives (life cycle, emergent, participative, political) are complementary in that successful large-scale change is likely to require elements of each. Table 13.2 illustrates how each perspective links to management practice.

13.7　Integrating themes

Entrepreneurship

Drucker (1985) comments that 'Entrepreneurs see change as normal and healthy . . . the entrepreneur always searches for change, responds to it, and exploits it as an opportunity (p. 25). He stresses that entrepreneurship is at least as common, and as necessary, in existing business and public services as it is in new ventures, and this is equally true of innovation. Existing businesses depend on innovation just as much as new ventures.

Drucker sets out policies and practices that entrepreneurial management use in established organisations to foster a healthy flow of innovation, one of which is the Business X-Ray – which furnishes the information needed to define how much innovation a business requires, in what areas and within what time frame.

> In this approach a company lists each of its products or services, [and the market each serves] to estimate their position on the product life cycle. How much longer will this product still grow? How much longer will it still maintain itself in the marketplace? . . . When will it become obsolescent? This enables the company to estimate where it would be if it confined itself to managing to the best of its ability what already exists. And this then shows the gap between what can be expected realistically, and what a company still needs to do to achieve its objectives, whether in sales, market standing, or profitability.
>
> That gap is the minimum that must be filled if the company is not to go downhill . . . But innovative efforts . . . have a high probability of failure and an even higher one of delay. A company should have underway at least three times the innovative efforts, which, if

Table 13.2 Perspectives on change and examples of management practice

Perspective	Themes	Example of management practices
Life cycle	Rational, linear, single agreed aim, technical focus	Measurable objectives; planning and control devices such as Gantt charts and critical path analysis
Emergent	Objectives change as learning occurs during the project, and new possibilities appear	Open to new ideas about scope and direction, and willing to add new resources if needed
Participative	Ownership, commitment, shared goals, people focus	Inviting ideas and comments on proposals, ensuring agreement before action, seeking consensus
Political	Oppositional, influence, conflicting goals, power focus	Building allies and coalitions, securing support from powerful players, managing information

successful, would fill the gap. [Hitches and delays are certain in innovation] so to demand innovative efforts which . . . yield three times the minimum results needed is only elementary precaution. (p. 141)

Sustainability

Across the world governments and international agencies are setting targets with the aim of reducing greenhouse gas emissions: an example is that by the European Union to aim for a 20 per cent reduction by 2020. This is a significant opportunity for innovative businesses in developing new technologies that reduce CO_2 emissions. As well as the existing hydro-electric power infrastructure, wind farms are steadily becoming a larger source of electric power in the UK. In addition, significant investment is now being made in marine forms of generation such as wave, tidal and current.

Innovation opportunities are not limited to the generation of power but also arise in infrastructure and especially transport. Hydrogen fuel cells for use in personal vehicles are maturing as a technology, and solar-powered vehicles for public transport are being developed. Unilever is seeking help from companies and universities around the world to help in producing an environmentally friendly detergent – which will work without requiring large quantities of heated water – and more sustainable forms of packaging. More broadly, advocates of what they term 'the circular economy' propose radical innovation in the way economic activity takes place as a route to a sustainable system (Webster et al. 2013).

Internationalisation

Organisations operating internationally will often wish to develop products or process innovations, and are likely to develop these in cross-cultural teams. Cultural diversity in the workplace ideally enables the confluence of ideas from different cultures, and managers may reasonably expect that their combination would lead to creative outcomes. The other possibility is that exposure to people from cultures other than one's own may activate negative emotions, which may inhibit willingness to engage in creative work.

Chua (2013) shows empirically that these negative effects can occur, through the indirect experience of intercultural tensions and conflicts in the immediate social environment. Using data from an online survey, the author shows that while a person's own group may have positive intercultural attitudes, this is not the only relevant variable. The effects of attitudes held by members of their culturally diverse network of contacts, which may include observation of negative intercultural events in other settings, can affect their own attitudes:

If the immediate social environment reeks of intercultural conflicts, individuals' ability to connect ideas from different cultures can be compromised. (p. 1570)

Governance

The financial crisis in 2008 is an example of innovation out of control. Its origins lay in some banks selling mortgages to (sub-prime) customers who could not afford the repayments. The innovation was the way in which the companies making the loans 'packaged' these loans and sold them to other players in the financial supply chain. Innovative bankers converted the original (very dubious) loans into financial products called mortgage-backed securities. These were sold on to hedge funds and investment banks, which saw them as high-return investments. When borrowers started to default on their loans, the value of the investments fell, leading to huge losses. Investors then became nervous about buying any investment linked to mortgages, no matter how high their quality, so that lenders found it increasingly difficult to borrow money in the capital markets – with the familiar results.

Much of the blame was placed on the lack of governance within the banking industry that allowed innovative ideas to be implemented without regard to the risks they posed, or their longer-term consequences. The 'Management in practice' feature gives an example of a bank with very tight governance and control systems.

Management in practice

Governance and control at Santander
www.santander.com

In a speech to the first Santander Conference on International Banking, Emilio Botin, the chairman said:

> Banks must focus on customers, focus on recurring business based on long-term relationships and be cautious in managing risk. You do not need to be innovative to do this well. You do not need to invent anything. You need to dedicate time and attention at the highest level.
>
> Many are surprised to learn that the Banco Santander board's risk committee meets for half a day twice a week and that the board's 10-person executive committee meets every Monday for at least four hours, devoting a large portion of that time to reviewing risks and approving transactions. Not many banks do this. It consumes a lot of our directors' time. But we find it essential and it is never too much.

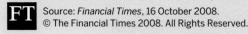 Source: *Financial Times*, 16 October 2008.
© The Financial Times 2008. All Rights Reserved.

Summary

1 **Explain the meaning of creativity and innovation, giving examples**
   - Creativity is the ability to combine ideas and information in unusual ways to create something new and useful. Innovation refers to the processes of implementing such new and useful things into an organisation where they add value.

2 **Explain the management significance of creativity and innovation**
   - As markets' and customers' preferences change with increasing speed, most companies need to be able to encourage creativity and innovation among their staff to meet these market expectations.
     - Product innovation – the changes in the things that the organisation offers for sale.
     - Process innovation – the changes in the process that creates the product.
     - Position innovation – the changes in the way the product is offered or targeted.
     - Paradigm innovation – the changes in how a company frames what it does.

3 **Illustrate the organisational factors believed to support creativity and innovation**
   - Cultural, structural and HR factors influence the context within which creative people work, and which managers can shape.
     - Strategy – innovation is explicitly called for in the corporate strategy.
     - Structure – roles and jobs are defined to aid in innovative behaviour.
     - Style – management empowers the workforce to behave innovatively.
     - Support – IT systems are available to support innovative behaviour.

4 **Explain what the links between change and context imply for those managing a change**
   - A change programme is an attempt to change one or more aspects of the internal context, which then provides the context of future actions. The inherited context can itself help or hinder change efforts.

5 Compare life cycle, emergent, participative and political theories of change

- Life cycle: change projects can be planned, monitored and controlled towards achieving their objectives.
- Emergent: reflecting the uncertainties of the environment, change is hard to plan in detail, but emerges incrementally from events and actions.
- Participative: successful change depends on human commitment, which is best obtained by involving participants in planning and implementation.
- Political: change threatens some of those affected, who will use their power to block progress, or to direct the change in ways that suit local objectives.

6 Explain the role of stakeholders in managing change, and understand how this will help you develop the skill of identifying stakeholders and their interests

- Major change requires the support of stakeholders, and the chapter has provided an opportunity to understand how to develop the skill of identifying stakeholders and their interests.

7 Show how ideas from the chapter add to your understanding of the integrating themes

- Drucker shows how entrepreneurship is as important in large companies as in new ventures, and that all depend on innovation. The example from his books illustrates one practice used to manage innovation in a disciplined way, to ensure an adequate flow of new and useful things.
- The search for sustainable performance offers significant opportunities to innovators who can find ways of reducing the use of energy throughout the value-adding chain.
- International companies often wish to encourage local units to be innovative but cultural differences can impede this.
- The 2008 financial crisis showed the negative side of innovation, when it is not balanced by effective governance and control systems – such as those used by Santander bank, whose managers take risk seriously.

Test your understanding

1 What is the difference between creativity and innovation?
2 Name the four forms of innovation, and briefly describe one of them.
3 What is the significance of the term 'open innovation', as used in the chapter?
4 Outline three organisational influences on innovation, with an example of each.
5 Outline the life cycle perspective on change and explain when it is most likely to be useful.
6 How does it differ from the 'emergent' perspective?
7 What are the distinctive characteristics of a participative approach, and when is it likely to be least successful?
8 What skills are used by those employing a political model?
9 Summarise an idea from the chapter that adds to your understanding of the integrating themes.

Think critically

Think about the way people handle major change in your company, or one with which you are familiar. Then make notes on these questions:

- In implementing change, what **assumptions** about the nature of change in organisations appear to guide the approach? Is one perspective dominant, or do people typically combine several?

- What factors in the **context** appear to shape the approach to managing change – do people appear to consider a range of stakeholder interests when implementing change?
- Has there been any serious attempt to find **alternative** ways to manage major change, such as by dealing differently with stakeholders?
- What **limitations** can you see in the ideas presented here? Is it possible to pay too much attention to stakeholder interests, at the expense of getting the project moving?

Develop a skill – identifying stakeholders and their interests

Those implementing innovations need to manage stakeholders with an interest in the project. The first step is to identify them, and note their interests. This exercise will help you do that.

- **Awareness:** Review how you usually consider stakeholders in relation to a work or social task that you have taken on. Have you ever been aware of forgetting that someone would be affected by your plans for something, and been surprised by their reaction? Or do you always spend time working out who will be involved, and how best you can secure their support?
- **Learning:** Read again Section 13.5 – especially the 'Key ideas' feature (p. 419). You may also want to check back on Sections 3.7 or 5.7. Summarise the main ideas about managing stakeholders, and consider why managing them can affect a project outcome. How might being familiar with using those ideas help your career?
- **Analysis:** Identify a major change project that you can find out about, in which a family member or friend is involved. Ask if they can help you. Alternatively, use the Dyson Case and take Dyson's project to grow the business over the next few years as your focus. Using the stakeholder concept implies understanding who they are, and their interests. How important is their reaction likely to be to the success of the project?
- **Practice:** To answer these questions, draw a stakeholder map. A simple way to do this is to write the name of the project in a circle at the centre of a piece of paper. Draw other circles around the sheet, each representing an individual or group that has a stake in the project. Place the most significant near the centre, the less significant around the edge.
  - For two significant (in your judgement) stakeholders, assess their interests in the project. Do this by considering these questions:
    - What are their main goals, apart from this project?
    - What is the tone of their general relationship with the company – adversarial? supportive? other?
    - What specific behaviour will this project require of them?
    - Are they likely to see this as positive or negative for them?
    - How may they react to defend or advance their interest?
    - What action might the project team consider to influence their support of the project?
    - You can summarise your answers on a grid like this – which is useful when doing this for several stakeholders. Record your notes under these headings:

Stakeholder	Goals?	Current relationship?	What is expected of them?	Positive or negative to them?	Likely reaction?	Ideas for action?

- If possible, compare your map and table with a colleague on your course, noting where they agree and where they differ. Reflect on what you can learn from this, and summarise your conclusions.
- **Application:** Decide on another opportunity to practise this skill within the next week.

Read more

Catmull, E. (2008), 'How Pixar fosters collective creativity', *Harvard Business Review,* vol. 86, no. 9, pp. 64–72.

> The co-founder explains how it works.

Christensen, C. M. and Raynor, M. E. (2003), *The Innovator's Solution: Creating and Sustaining Successful Growth,* Harvard Business School Press, Boston, MA.

> Sets innovation in the context of strategy, combining scholarship and practice to show the benefits of using good theory to guide action.

Johnson, S. (2010), *Where Good Ideas Come From: The Natural History of Innovation,* Allen Lane, London.

> A stimulating look at sources of innovation, including the idea that most significant innovations come not from financially-driven individuals but from creative groups and networks motivated by things other than money.

Tidd, J. & Bessant, J. (2009), *Managing Innovation: Integrating Technological, Market and Organisational Change,* Wiley, Chichester.

> Combines a comprehensive account of innovation theories with many contemporary examples.

Go online

These websites have appeared in this and other chapters:

www.pixar.com
www.gknplc.com
www.magnamole.co.uk
www.gsk.com
www.unilever.com
www.dyson.co.uk
www.nationaltheatre.org.uk
www.shell.com

Visit two of the business sites in the list, and navigate to the pages dealing with corporate news, investor relations or 'our company'.

- What can you learn from the site about recent innovations at the company, either in products or processes?
- Does the site give you a sense of an organisation that is emphasising its innovativeness, or not?
- Does it say anything about how it manages or encourages innovation?

PART 4 CASE
THE ROYAL BANK OF SCOTLAND
www.rbs.co.uk

The company

For many years RBS offered traditional banking services to retail and business customers, mostly in the UK. It took deposits, made loans and provided payment services. During the 1990s the company's senior management took advantage of changes in UK and international banking regulations to widen the scope, and increase the size, of the business. It began to provide more services to UK customers, expand overseas and increase its trading activities – using bank funds to trade in assets on behalf of the bank itself, rather than on behalf of customers.

© Tim Ayers/Alamy Images

In 2007 RBS was innovative and profitable, providing good returns to shareholders. Fred Goodwin became Chief Executive in 1997, and managed a rapid growth in size and profitability. This was publicly recognised in 2004 when he was awarded a knighthood for services to banking. By 2008 RBS was on the point of collapse, and only survived because the UK government invested £45.5 billion in the bank (at about 50 pence a share), in return for an 84 per cent stake in the business. Sir Fred had presided over the biggest bank failure in history.

In 2016 managers and staff were trying to rebuild the business so that the government could sell its shares profitability, returning RBS to private ownership. The shares were worth much less than the price the government had paid for them, implying it would be several years before taxpayers would recover their investment (in a public relations move in 2012, every 10 of the original shares then trading at 25p were converted into one new share valued at 250p). Sir Fred had become so unpopular with the public that there was little opposition when the government arranged to remove his knighthood in 2012.

What happened to bring about this change? Before 2007 the management team, under Goodwin, made many internal changes, including:

- segmenting customers into three groups – retail, commercial and corporate;
- creating new management roles, structures and an aggressive, results-based culture;
- HRM policies to hire more entrepreneurial managers who could deliver the vision of expanding in the UK and overseas, and to base appointment and rewards on achievement and ability.

This transformed the bank, and provided the base for a period of successful growth and acquisitions – and for the later crisis. The table shows the main financial indicators of performance in the two most recent financial years.

Measures of financial performance in year ending 31 December

	2015	2014
Total income (£m)	12,923	15,150
Operating expenses (£m)	(16,353)	(13,859)
Profit (loss) before impairment losses (£m)	(3,430)	1,291
Impairment releases (£m)	727	1352

	2015	2014
Operating loss before tax (£m)	(2703)	2643
Tax (£m)	(23)	(1,909)
Loss from continuing operations (£m)	(2,726)	734

Source: RBS Annual Reports.

Managing to add value

Diversifying the business

Since the early 1990s the bank had diversified from traditional UK banking operations into a range of businesses and countries – so that by early 2008 it had eight 'customer-facing' divisions:

- UK Retail (RBS and Natwest – two divisions)
- Wealth Management (including Coutts Bank)
- Retail Direct (mainly online banking)
- RBS Insurance
- US Retail and Commercial
- Ulster Bank Group
- Corporate Banking and Financial Markets.

These were supported by six Group divisions – Finance, Risk and Internal Audit, Manufacturing, Legal, Strategy and Communications and Human Resources.

Growth by acquisition

RBS gained a reputation for acquiring other financial institutions and integrating them profitably. The most notable of these was the acquisition of NatWest Bank in 2000 – three times the size of RBS at the time. When RBS completed the acquisition, senior management quickly established the 'Integration Programme' to merge the two companies' operations, which it achieved early in 2003. This successful acquisition (Kennedy et al., 2006) enhanced the reputation of Fred Goodwin and his team, though, having made 23 acquisitions since 2000, they claimed they would now on focus on building existing businesses.

However, senior management, supported by the board, completed another deal (in a consortium of banks) in late 2008 – which was disastrous. In the biggest deal in banking history the consortium acquired ABN Amro, a Dutch bank. Many doubted the wisdom of the deal since RBS would need to raise £12 billion to make the purchase, especially as senior management did not conduct a rigorous analysis of ABN Amro before buying it. In 2012 a group of investors claimed the bank's directors had misled them about the financial state of the group. The defendants denied this, arguing that in early 2008 the directors could not have foreseen the economic crisis that occurred later that year.

HRM policies

Goodwin expected the Head of Group HRM to develop policies and cultures that supported his goals. Goodwin's style was highly directive, holding executives personally, and publicly, accountable for their performance. Personal direction was reinforced by a performance management and reward system that reflected the CEO's emphasis on data to guide decisions – reward was closely tied to objective financial measures of the performance of a manager's team. HRM also ran a leadership programme for the top 300 executives to reinforce Goodwin's approach, and to spread it throughout the bank. Martin and Gullan (2012) believe this may have led them to ignore cautionary voices advising against the ABN Amro bid.

Investing to improve efficiency

The bank has for many years developed information technology systems to centralise administration. The clearest example is Manufacturing Division, which deals with routine functions such as clearing cheques and opening accounts – and which has a mechanistic structure. The bank created the division in 1999 by transferring most administrative tasks from the branches to a central location. To select staff for the new division they used personality tests to identify those more comfortable with processes and systems. Those who were more interested in people remained in the branches. The branches themselves had been mechanistic, with staff working on strictly defined tasks. Now they are more organic, with staff trying to meet customers' diverse needs and interest them in other products, within an open layout.

RBS was quick to exploit the opportunities that information technology offered to change the way it dealt with customers. It was an early innovator when it launched Direct Line as one of the first examples of delivering financial services, and later motor insurance, by telephone and online. An online bank complements the services offered by the branches.

In 2012 many customers were unable to access their accounts for several days due to a technical fault during a routine software upgrade. RBS had to pay millions of pounds in compensation to customers.

Trading innovative products

Under Goodwin's leadership the bank built a substantial operation in which traders dealt with complex products, often based on 'sub-prime US mortgages'. These were loans that banks had made to low-income families in the US to buy a home – as with any mortgage, they borrow the money and gradually repay the capital, with interest, over perhaps 25 years. Financial companies devised complex schemes that turned a familiar product into a financial instrument that could be traded on financial markets.

RBS chose to enter this market, not by using the funds of its depositors, but by using short-term loans from other banks. HRM policies, especially those relating to pay and bonuses, encouraged its traders. The FSA report into the collapse of RBS stated that while building up this risky business Goodwin vigorously resisted FSA procedures, which he saw as unnecessary interference. It also found that while the bank claimed to have in place suitable control mechanisms, there was 'a spectacular lack of understanding [about the nature of this business] at the very highest ranks of the bank' (*Financial Times*, 13 December 2011, p. 4). Deteriorating financial conditions (including the collapse of a major US bank) in 2008 reduced confidence among lenders – so that RBS was no longer able to borrow money for this business, many of whose assets were now of little value.

This led to a crisis in October 2008 when the UK government transferred taxpayers' money to RBS so that it could continue trading – and in return received an 83 per cent stake in the company. They demanded management changes, including the dismissal of Sir Fred Goodwin and most of the board. New managers were appointed to rebuild the bank so that it could be returned to private ownership.

Aspects of the RBS context

Competition

RBS is an example of a diversified bank providing a wide range of financial services. It therefore competes not only with other national (such as Barclays) and international (such as HSBC) banks offering a similar range, but also with businesses that focus on just one area (such as Royal Insurance Group or Fidelity Investments). Since the mid-1980s the UK government had encouraged growth of the financial services sector by removing restrictions on who could offer banking services – encouraging many new banks, including those based overseas, to set up in the UK.

Established banks such as RBS also face competition from new entrants including Virgin Money, Metrobank and other smaller specialist lenders (such as Close Brothers), which avoided risky investments during the boom. However, these new entrants face the fact that customers are reluctant to change banks, even when service is poor or expensive.

The authorities also see the risks of competition, which can encourage banks to sell inappropriate products, reward some staff well and in so doing possibly encourage irresponsible behaviour. This in turn encourages government regulation to prevent these perceived abuses.

Regulation

All governments try to regulate banks (and the rest of the financial services sector), hoping that this will ensure they benefit customers and their national economies. Regulators aim to balance the economic benefits of a strong banking sector against the risks to consumers, business and the wider economy if banks' innovative practices and policies fail. They develop guidelines on acceptable practice by banks and apply sanctions against those that breach them.

In 2001 the UK government created the Financial Services Authority (FSA) (www.fsa.gov.uk) with the aim of regulating financial services. All firms providing a financial service must be authorised by the FSA – which sets the standards they must meet, and can act against them if they fail to do so.

The FSA's report into the collapse of RBS acknowledged that there were at least four occasions between 2005 and 2007 when it failed to take a hard enough line:

> They show that the FSA allowed the bank to run high risks with low stocks of capital and liquid assets and left it vulnerable to a loss of investor confidence. These factors reveal how the regulator's 'light touch' approach, emphasising cooperation rather than confrontation, helped RBS down the road to failure. (*Financial Times*, 13 December 2011, p. 4)

In 2012 the UK government announced that it was accepting most of the recommendations of a report from the Independent Commission on Banking (chaired by Sir John Vickers), which sought to protect relatively safe retail banking from riskier investment activities. The government also said that RBS would reduce the size of its investment bank. These reforms mean the deposits of retail consumers and small businesses cannot be used to fund risky trading activities. Implementing them will take many years.

International

Financial services are such an important aspect of modern economies that most countries seek a share of the employment, income and tax revenues that they provide. They compete with each other to attract international firms to their country. This (along with developments in IT that enable the rapid transmission of data across the world) has encouraged many (though not all) financial services companies to become international businesses.

While national governments want to regulate the industry, those in the industry try to shape these decisions in their favour. They imply that if regulations become unfavourable in one country they will move some or all of their operations to those with more favourable conditions. There is constant interaction between financial service firms and national governments over the form and stringency of regulations.

Governments counter this by pressing for common international agreements across the world, or for common regional policies, such as within the European Union. Such international regulations are additional to those that national governments create. The EU announced in 2012 that it would impose a limit on bank bonus levels, possibly limiting them to the same level as salaries. The rules were expected to apply to a relatively small number of staff – senior managers and traders who have significant influence on profits. Banks outside the EU were expected to benefit, as they would find it easier to recruit good senior staff.

Current management dilemmas

The management of RBS is grappling with the challenge of returning the bank to profit, in the face of an EU requirement to reduce the size of the bank (it was required to sell over 300 retail branches by the end of 2013), increase its reserves, reform the pay and bonus system and introduce new systems to balance innovation with control.

Range of services

Stephen Hester replaced Goodwin as Chief Executive, and was himself replaced by Ross McEwan in 2013. He has been trying to rebuild the bank by focusing on its traditional strengths, such as UK retail banking, wealth management and global payments. The investment banking business will be halved in size, and RBS will dispose of other parts of the business such as the Direct Line insurance business, 316 retail branches, some foreign retail assets, weak parts of the investment bank and much of the international business (by 2014 it had already withdrawn from 26 countries).

The focus will be on the UK retail bank, including lending to small businesses. Mr McEwan's plans include opening more small retail branches, including kiosks, in locations that many people pass, such as railway stations and shopping malls. He also plans to invest in refurbishing branches, and improving mobile banking services. He will also reduce head office staff to provide more direct support for branches and customer service.

Pay and bonuses

Despite having had to seek a government bail-out, and to the fury of public and politicians alike, Fred Goodwin insisted that he was entitled to his full pension of over £700,000 a year, due at once although he is only 50. The bank's remuneration committee agreed to Sir Fred's massive payoff as part of the negotiations to remove him – he had a contract.

Others pointed out that bankers' pay during the bubble was too high, but that it would be a mistake for the state to impose pay limits. Finance relies on individuals, and employers compete for their skills. If taxpayers were to get their money back, RBS would need to become profitable, and it was unlikely to do so if it could not pay competitive salaries.

EU rules on bank bonuses have encouraged many banks to raise basic salaries, and to offer valuable non-monetary rewards such as more rapid promotion, fewer time-wasting tasks, less-demanding deadlines and better communications with line managers.

Internal governance

Banks, perhaps more than most organisations, need to balance innovation and control. For years they have attracted very bright graduates from universities and business schools, and encouraged them to develop innovative and profitable products.

RBS itself had all of the formal mechanisms of corporate governance in place – independent non-executive directors, audit and risk committees, remuneration committee. In the years before 2008 none of the people on these boards and committees appears to have been able and willing to stand up to Fred Goodwin. Whatever misgivings they may have had in private, they continued to support the management team in public – 90 per cent of shareholders approved the ABN AMRO deal.

Sources: Kennedy et al., (2006); *Economist,* 14 February 2009, *Financial Times*, 13 October 2008, 13 December 2011, 10 January 2012, 17 January 2012, 14 June 2012, 27 June 2012, 26 April 2013, 28 February 2014, 21 December 2014, 5 January 2015, 18 February 2015; Martin and Gullan (2012); RBS website.

Part case questions

(a) Relating primarily to Chapters 10 to 13

1   Refer to Chapter 7 (Sections 7.6 and Section 7.7). Does this text offer an insight into possible explanations for the troubles at RBS?

2   Which aspects of the bank's operations were mechanistic, and which organic? (Section 10.7)

3   Outline how the HRM practices introduced in the years following Goodwin's arrival contributed to the bank's rise and fall. (Sections 11.6 and 11.7)

4   Describe two examples of the bank using IT to change the way it operates. What organisational changes did it make to support this? (See Sections 12.3 and 12.4)

5   What did it do during the boom years to encourage innovation, especially by traders? What external factors encouraged this risk-taking culture? (Refer to Sections 13.3 and 13.4.)

6   Why do you think the board were unable to influence Fred Goodwin and the senior team – what sources of power did Goodwin possess? (Section 14.6)

(b) Relating to the company

1   Visit the RBS Group website (**www.rbs.com**), including the pages for 'investor relations', and read one or more of the management reports you will find there. Note recent events that add to material in this case.

2   Access the websites of *The Economist, Financial Times* or BBC News (Business pages) and make notes about how, if at all, the dilemmas identified in the case are still current, and how the company has dealt with them.

3   What new issues appear to be facing RBS that the case did not mention?

4   The issue of bank bonuses is still contentious. Summarise how RBS has responded recently to calls for it to limit the rewards to senior staff.

5   What information can you find on the website, or in the annual report, about the company's governance systems, and the issues faced in reaching a balance between innovation and control.

6   What progress has the bank made towards enabling the government to sell its shareholding?

7   For any one of those issues it faces, how do you think it should deal with it? Build your answer by referring to one or more features of the company's history, as outlined in the case.

PART 4
EMPLOYABILITY SKILLS – PREPARING FOR THE WORLD OF WORK

To help you develop useful skills, this section includes tasks that relate the themes covered in the Part to six employability skills (sometimes called capabilities and attributes) that many employers value. The layout will help you to articulate these skills to employers and prepare for the recruitment processes you will encounter in application forms, interviews and assessment centres.

Task 4.1   Business awareness

If a potential employer asks you to attend an assessment centre or a competency-based interview, they may ask you to present or discuss a current business topic to demonstrate your business awareness. To help you to prepare for this, write an individual or group report on ONE of these topics and present it to an audience. Aim to present your ideas in a 750-word report and/or ten PowerPoint slides at most.

1 Using data from one or more websites or printed sources, outline significant recent developments in RBS, especially regarding its:

  ● range of activities (including its international presence);
  ● human resource management policies, including reward systems;
  ● regulation and internal governance; and
  ● progress towards the sale of the government's stake in the business.

2 Gather information on the interaction between RBS and its political and regulatory context, including specific examples of interventions by the regulator to influence the bank, and vice versa. What lessons can you draw from this example of business–government interaction?

3 Choose another financial services company that interests you – and which you may be considering as a career option.

  ● Gather information from the website and other sources about its strategy and structure.
  ● What can you find about the role of HRM policies in supporting the strategy?
  ● How have technological developments affected the business?
  ● How innovative has the company been in products or processes?
  ● What career options does it offer, and how attractive are they?

When you have completed the task, write a short paragraph giving examples of the skills (such as information gathering and presentation) you have developed from this task. You can transfer a brief note of this to the table at Task 4.7.

Task 4.2   Thinking critically

Reflect on the way that you handled Task 4.1, and identify how you exercised the skills of thinking critically (Chapter 1, Section 1.8). For example:

1 Did you spend time identifying and challenging the assumptions implied in the reports or commentaries you read? Summarise what you found then, or do it now.
2 Did you consider the extent to which they took account of the context in which managers are operating? Summarise what you found then, or do it now.
3 How far did they, or you, go in imagining and exploring alternative ways of dealing with the issue?
4 Did you spend time outlining the limitations of ideas or proposals that you thought of putting forward?

When you have completed the task, record a short paragraph giving examples of the thinking skills you have developed from this task. You can transfer a brief note of these to the Table at Task 4.7.

Task 4.3   Solving problems

Chapters 6 and 7 include ideas on problem solving. Refer to these if you need more guidance on this activity, which invites you to analyse how your team worked on Task 4.1.

Use the scales below to rate the way your team worked on this task – circle the number that best reflects your opinion of the discussion.

1 The team defined the problem, and set goals and criteria for the task (Section 6.5).

1	2	3	4	5	6	7
Strongly disagree						Strongly agree

2 The team generated many ideas on how to achieve the goals (Section 6.6).

1	2	3	4	5	6	7
Strongly disagree						Strongly agree

3 The team evaluated the options and made a clear plan for their work.

1	2	3	4	5	6	7
Strongly disagree						Strongly agree

4 The team implemented the plan and monitored progress.

1	2	3	4	5	6	7
Strongly disagree						Strongly agree

A rational approach usually helps people to work through a problem in an orderly way, but sometimes it does not. Reflect on the way that you handled Task 4.1, and identify difficulties you experienced in following the four stages. Note them down, together with possible reasons. Then complete these short tasks:

5   Read Section 6.8 on rational and creative approaches to problem solving, and note which of those you used, or could have used, in this task.
6   Reflect on this model in the light of using it. What are the advantages and limitations of rational and creative approaches? (Chapter 7)
7   Write down three specific problem-solving practices that you could use in your next task. If possible, compare your results and suggestions with other members of the team, and agree practices that would help a team work better.

When you have completed the task, record a short paragraph giving examples of the problem-solving skills you have developed from this task. You can transfer a brief note of these to the Table at Task 4.7.

Task 4.4   Team working

Chapter 17 includes ideas on team working. This activity helps you use these to analyse how your team worked on Task 4.1.

Use the scales below to rate the way your team worked on this task – circle the number that best reflects your opinion of the discussion.

1   The team was effective in obtaining and using necessary information.

1	2	3	4	5	6	7
Strongly disagree						Strongly agree

2   The team members took on complementary team roles (Section 17.4).

1	2	3	4	5	6	7
Strongly disagree						Strongly agree

3   The team progressed through the stages of team development (Section 17.5).

1	2	3	4	5	6	7
Strongly disagree						Strongly agree

4   The team developed effective working processes that suited the task (Section 17.6).

1	2	3	4	5	6	7
Strongly disagree						Strongly agree

5   The team used its time effectively.

1	2	3	4	5	6	7
Strongly disagree						Strongly agree

6 The team regularly reviewed the ways it was working, and changed these when it would improve performance (Section 17.6).

1	2	3	4	5	6	7
Strongly disagree						Strongly agree

Record three practices that you could use in your next task. If possible, compare your results and suggestions with other members of the team, and agree on practices that would help a team work better.

When you have completed the task, write a short paragraph giving examples of team-working skills (such as observing the team to improve performance) that you have developed from this task. You can transfer a brief note of these to the Table at Task 4.7.

Task 4.5   Communicating

Chapter 16 includes ideas on communicating – and Sections 16.4 and 16.5 are especially relevant to this task. It will help you to analyse how well your team communicated as you worked on Task 4.1.

Use the scales below to rate the way your team communicated during Task 4.1 – circle the number that best reflects your opinion of the discussion.

1 The team handled face-to-face communication well during its meetings (Section 16.4).

1	2	3	4	5	6	7
Strongly disagree						Strongly agree

2 The team communicated effectively by phone, mobile, voicemail and other electronic systems (Section 16.4).

1	2	3	4	5	6	7
Strongly disagree						Strongly agree

3 The team communicated effectively by personal, written methods – letters, email, texting (Section 16.4).

1	2	3	4	5	6	7
Strongly disagree						Strongly agree

4 The team communicated effectively by impersonal written methods – newsletters, online communities (Section 16.4).

1	2	3	4	5	6	7
Strongly disagree						Strongly agree

5 The team adapted between centralised and decentralised communication networks according to the needs of the task. (Section 16.5)

1	2	3	4	5	6	7
Strongly disagree						Strongly agree

6 The team communicated its report well to the chosen audience.

1	2	3	4	5	6	7
Strongly disagree						Strongly agree

7 The team experienced no significant barriers to communication, either internally or externally.

1	2	3	4	5	6	7
Strongly disagree						Strongly agree

Record three communication practices that you could use in your next task. If possible, compare your results and suggestions with other members of the team, and agree on practices that would help a team work better.

When you have completed the task, record a short paragraph giving examples of communication skills you have developed from this task. You can transfer a brief note of these to the Table at Task 4.7.

Task 4.6 Self-management

This activity helps you to learn more about managing yourself, so that you can present convincing evidence to employers showing, among other things, your willingness to learn, your ability to manage and plan learning, workloads and commitments, and that you have a well-developed level of self-awareness and self-reliance. You need to show that you are able to accept responsibility, manage time and use feedback to learn.

Reflect on the way that you handled Task 4.1, and identify how you exercised skills of self–management.

1 I effectively planned the time I would spend on each part of the task

1	2	3	4	5	6	7
Strongly disagree						Strongly agree

2 I tried to balance my commitments and those of other team members across the work, so that all were reasonably busy

1	2	3	4	5	6	7
Strongly disagree						Strongly agree

3 I think I used my time well.

1	2	3	4	5	6	7
Strongly disagree						Strongly agree

4 I tried to ensure that I and others took responsibility for distinct areas of work, to keep moving the task forward.

1	2	3	4	5	6	7
Strongly disagree						Strongly agree

5 I often reflected on how I was working on the task to identify possible ways to improve my performance.

1	2	3	4	5	6	7
Strongly disagree						Strongly agree

Write down three self-management practices that you could use in your next task. If possible, compare your results and suggestions with other members of the team, and agree on practices that would help a team work better.

When you have completed the task, write a short paragraph giving examples of the self-management practices you have developed from this task. You can transfer a brief note of these to the Table at Task 4.7.

Task 4.7   Recording your employability skills

To conclude your work on this Part, use the summary paragraphs above to record the employability skills you have developed during your work on these tasks, and in other activities. Use the format of the table below to create an electronic record that you can use to combine the list of skills you have developed in this Part, with those in other Parts.

Most of your learning about each skill will probably come from the task associated with it – but you may also gain insights in other ways – include those as well.

Template for laying out record of employability skills developed in this Part

Skills/Task	Task 4.1	Task 4.2	Task 4.3	Task 4.4	Task 4.5	Task 4.6	Other sources of skills
Business awareness							
Thinking critically							
Solving problems							

Skills/Task	Task 4.1	Task 4.2	Task 4.3	Task 4.4	Task 4.5	Task 4.6	Other sources of skills
Team working							
Communicating							
Self-manage-ment							

To make the most of your opportunities to develop employability skills as you do your academic work, you need to reflect regularly on your learning and record the results. This helps you to fill any gaps, and provides specific evidence of your employability skills.

PART 5

LEADING

Introduction

Generating the effort and commitment to work towards objectives is vital when managing any human activity. One person working alone has only him or herself to motivate. As an organisation grows, management activities become, in varying degrees, separated from the core work activities. The problem of generating effort changes as one person, or one occupational group, now has to secure the willing cooperation and commitment to the task of other people. Those other people may be subordinates, colleagues or those higher in the hierarchy whose support the manager needs to generate and maintain.

How does management secure the effort it needs from others? Chapter 14 examines ideas on influence, while Chapter 15 presents theories about what those others may want from their work. Communication is inherent to management's role of adding value, and Chapter 16 examines this topic.

Teams are an increasingly prominent aspect of organisations, and the motivation and commitment they can generate is often a major influence on performance. Chapter 17 introduces ideas on teams.

The Part Case is the British Heart Foundation, a leading UK medical charity, which is successful in part because of the skill with which it influences many people to support the charity's objectives.

CHAPTER 14
INFLUENCING

Aim

To examine how people influence others by using personal skills and/or power.

Objectives

By the end of your work on this chapter you should be able to outline the concepts below in your own terms and:

1 Distinguish leading from managing, and explain why each is essential to performance

2 Explain why leading and managing both depend on being able to influence others

3 Compare trait, behavioural and contingency perspectives on influencing

4 Outline theories that focus on power (both personal and organisational) as the source of influence

5 Contrast the style and power perspectives, and explain why sharing power may increase it

6 Outline a model of the tactics that people use to influence others, including networking

7 Understand how you can use ideas from the chapter to develop the skill of setting clear goals when planning to influence others

8 Show how ideas from the chapter add to your understanding of the integrating themes

Key terms

The chapter introduces these terms:

influence	initiating structure
leadership	consideration
traits	situational (contingency) models
big five	power
transactional leaders	political behaviour
transformational leaders	delegating
behaviour	networking

Each is a term defined within the text, and in the glossary at the end of the book.

Case study   British Museum   www.britishmuseum.org

In 2015 the British Museum was, for the ninth successive year, the UK's most popular visitor attraction with 6.8 million visitors, up from 6.7 million the previous year. The BM now raises almost half of its income through fund-raising and other activities, with a (diminishing) grant from the government providing the rest.

This was a great change from the position only 12 years earlier. In 2002 it was £6 million in debt, was viewed as not very user-friendly, and was struggling to justify possessing artefacts such as the Elgin Marbles (acquired controversially by Lord Elgin and sold by him to the British Government in 1816). Founded in 1753, the museum has over seven million objects (two million are online) and is internationally recognised for its research and scholarship. However, in 2002 the culture appeared inward-looking, and curators wasted energy competing for funds and other resources. At a time of declining income from government, it was becoming clear that the institution would need to change if it was to retain its position as a leading cultural body.

In 2002 Neil MacGregor (previously Director of the National Gallery) became director, with two main objectives: to change a fragmented organisational culture, and to reaffirm the museum's sense of purpose to internal and external stakeholders.

He focused on the founding ideals of the institution, stressing its role as an encyclopaedic museum that encompasses everyday artefacts as well as art treasures – a collection that a visitor from anywhere in the world could see without charge and build a story about their cultural history.

In creating new exhibitions Mr MacGregor persuaded curators of collections to work together and, in collaboration with the BBC, made a documentary film about the BM. This showed previously unseen aspects of the museum's operations, and emphasised the need for outside links.

He forged close relations with countries such as Iran and China that had no history of cultural links with the West, which led to exchanges and loans of exhibits. He has made the collection available to museums in emerging economies, to reinforce his claim that it is

© Jack Sullivan/Alamy Images

a unique resource for the whole world, and establishing what he called the 'lending library' model.

To strengthen the museum's claim to universal appeal, Mr MacGregor deepened the links with the BBC by devising *A History of the World in 100 Objects,* a radio series showcasing artefacts and civilisations that visitors might normally overlook, using pieces from the collection. This was followed in 2014 by a 30-part radio series *Germany: Memories of a Nation* (accompanying an exhibition of the same name), which had an estimated weekly audience of almost 4 million, and won the 'Radio Programme of the Year' award in 2015.

He cleared the debt that he had inherited within 18 months, and over the following nine years income rose to four times what it was in the year he arrived. The number of visitors is greater than it has ever been.

Sources: Barsoux and Narasimhan (2012); Annual Report and Accounts, 2014–15; *Financial Times,* 16 July 2013, p. 12.

Case questions 14.1

- What examples are there in the case of the people and institutions Mr MacGregor has influenced?

- What, if any, clues are there about the sources of his power to influence them?

- How much of that influence and power depends on one person?

14.1   Introduction

When Neil MacGregor took over the top job at the British Museum it had a large debt, appeared unwelcoming and was unused to change. Although he had the formal authority of being director, he needed to influence many stakeholders for whom that was of no account – potential donors, foreign governments and above all the visiting public. Over the following decade he demonstrated his ability to acquire and use power to great effect – turning the Museum into a successful cultural enterprise.

All managers have to influence others – such as Willie Walsh, Chief Executive at British Airways, persuading staff to accept new working practices. Crossrail managers (Chapter 6) successfully influenced many interest groups – politicians, business leaders, banks, Network Rail – to secure approval for the project in 2009. Sir Alex Ferguson had to influence United's owners, fans, financial interests and star players with big egos – see 'Management in practice'.

Management in practice   Sir Alex Ferguson – influencing genius

Sir Alex Ferguson has more trophies than any manger in football history due, his biographer believes, not to his knowledge of the game or coaching skills, but to his ability to influence. His practices include:

- **Cultivate every interest group inside your company.** Early in his career Sir Alex was sacked for disagreeing with his chairman. He had not grasped that this man's consent was central to his project: 'even if you hate your chairman, you have to find a way of getting on with it', he concluded. Ever since he has worked to keep his club's board, players, fans and sponsors onside. One leader of United's fan base said Sir Alex would chat to him for hours on the phone, keen to know what supporters thought.
- **Gather information everywhere.** A prominent political figure recalled a social gathering at which Sir Alex knew all of those present: 'he calls them all the time, he hoovers up information all the time'.
- **Do not let other people cause you stress.** Asked by the same person how to avoid being overwhelmed by requests from other people he advised: 'You've got to imagine you are putting blinkers on. People want to get into your space. Only you decide who gets into your space. Tell them: I think you can resolve this yourself.'
- **Remember that crises blow over.** Sir Alex has been through many, especially when top players have behaved foolishly. Sir Alex never adjusts his strategy, because he knows crises pass.

Source: Based on material in Kuper (2011).

Influence is the process by which one party attempts to modify the behaviour of others by mobilising power resources.

Whatever their role, people add value to resources by influencing others. The tasks of planning, organising, leading and controlling depend on other people agreeing to cooperate within a web of mutual **influence**. Senior managers influence investors to retain support, sales staff influence customers, a software engineer influences a manager to accept a design. Careers depend on this, and those they are influencing are often more senior, or in other organisations.

In that sense the work of the manager is close to the entrepreneur, implementing new ideas in a hostile or possibly indifferent setting. They often work across functional boundaries, trying to influence people with other priorities.

Figure 14.1 shows the topics in this chapter, beginning by examining why leaders and managers influence others, and presents three 'interpersonal' models (theories) of how they do this – traits, behavioural and contingency. It then presents personal and organisational 'power' theories, and concludes by showing the tactics people use to exert influence, including networking. The figure shows that outcomes depend on method and circumstances and they, in turn, affect the influencer's power. A valuable skill of influencing is to set goals

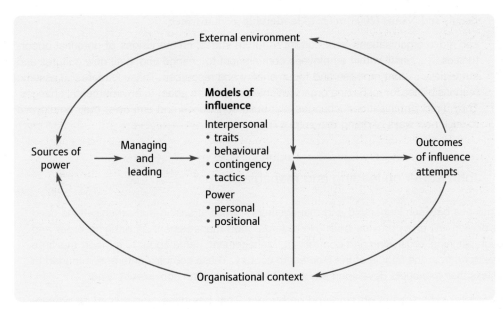

Figure 14.1
An overview
of the chapter

for the end of each influencing event, and the 'Develop a skill' feature is an opportunity to
begin to develop that.

14.2   Managing and leading depend on influencing

Managing and leading

Research and commentary on influencing use the terms 'manager' and 'leader' (and their deriv-
atives) interchangeably. It is worth briefly clarifying the meanings that some attach to these.

Chapter 1 defined a manager as someone who gets things done with the support of
others. Most commentators view an 'effective manager' as one who 'gets things done' to
ensure order and continuity. They maintain the steady state – keeping established systems
in good shape and making incremental improvements. People generally use the term 'effective leader' to denote someone who brings innovation, moves an activity from trouble to
success, makes a difference. They (like Julian Metcalf at Pret A Manger – see 'Management
in practice') do new things, take initiatives, inspire.

Management in practice   Julian Metcalf, founder of Pret A Manger   www.pret.com

Commenting on the leadership of Julian Metcalf, who founded Pret A Manger in 1986 (in 2016 it has about
350 shops), one of his directors said:

> Pret has always been very innovative because our founder, Julian Metcalf, is a true entrepreneur: he
> is here most days and he is really the spirit for all things entrepreneurial here and that is fantastic.
> The benefit of that is that we don't spend months and months and months developing new products,
> we're very quick to turn things around and it's very fast paced here. We have lots of new products and
> upgrades to our ingredients going on month in month out. And people comment when they come here,
> in terms of the pace of change, sometimes it can be hard to keep up with, but it's exciting, and makes
> us feel like a small organisation when in fact we're not.

Source: Interview with the director.

Leadership refers to the process of influencing the activities of others towards high levels of goal setting and achievement.

Bennis and Nanus (2003) refer to **leadership** as that which:

can move organisations from current to future states, create visions of potential opportunities . . . , instil within employees commitment to change and instil new cultures and strategies . . . that mobilise and focus energy and resources. These leaders . . . assume responsibilities for reshaping organisational practices to adapt to environmental changes. They direct organisational changes that build confidence and empower their employees to seek new ways of doing things (p. 17).

Key ideas   **John Kotter on leading and managing**

Kotter (1990) distinguishes between leadership and management – while stressing that organisations need both, and that one person will often provide both. He regards good management as bringing order and consistency – through planning, organising and controlling. 'Management' came about to support the large companies that developed from the middle of the nineteenth century. These complex enterprises tended to become chaotic, unless their managers developed practices to bring order and consistency, and:

to help keep a complex organisation on time and on budget. That has been, and still is, its primary function. Leadership is very different. It does not produce consistency and order . . . it produces movement. (p. 4)

Individuals whom people recognise as leaders create change. Good leadership

moves people to a place in which both they and those who depend on them are genuinely better off, and when it does so without trampling on the rights of others. (p. 5)

Leaders succeed by establishing direction and strategy, communicating it to those whose cooperation they need, and inspiring people. Managing and leading are closely related, but differ in their primary functions – one creates order, the other creates change. Organisations need both.

Source: Kotter (1990).

People work to create change and to create order in varying degrees, so there is no value in a sharp distinction between managing and leading: John Adair quotes a Chinese proverb:

What does it matter if a cat is black or white, as long as it catches mice (Adair, 1997, p. 2).

Managing and leading both depend on influencing others to put in the effort – whether to create order or change.

Targets of influence

People at all levels who want to get something done influence others. Influencing skills at the top (such as in the case of Neil MacGregor) have the most visible effects, shaping the direction of the business or changing the way it operates. People throughout the enterprise have to do the same – even if some have more power than others. The first female practice manager at a City of London legal firm:

The hardest things in management . . . are complicated people issues. Sometimes you realise you can't solve everything. Our assets are the brains and personalities of some highly intelligent people, so there are a huge number of relationship issues. Most of these 250 people are very driven. If you get it right, the commitment is there. But you've got to take a lot of people with you a lot of the time. (*Financial Times,* 15 February 2001, p. 17)

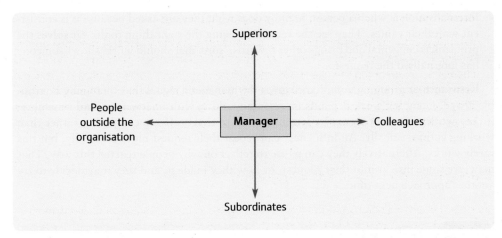

Figure 14.2 Influencing in four directions

Managers and leaders influence others below them in the hierarchy, on the same level, some formally above them – and people outside the organisation: see Figure 14.2. How do managers and leaders try to do this? The following sections aim to answer that question.

Responses to influence

Someone attempting to influence another has an outcome in mind. Kelman (1961) identified three outcomes – compliance, identification and internalisation – to which this section adds a fourth, resistance: see Table 14.1.

- **Resistance** occurs when staff have no commitment to the work, either refusing to do it or doing it grudgingly.
- **Compliance** occurs when 'an individual accepts influence [because they hope] to achieve a favourable reaction' (p. 62). They do what is asked, to avoid trouble – 'I'll do it to keep the peace'.
- **Identification** occurs when someone acts in the way requested because they feel that by doing so they identify with the person making the request – it maintains a desired relationship. They do what they are asked, but without much energy: 'I'll do it – but only because it's you who is asking'.

Table 14.1 Four outcomes of influence attempts

Outcome	Description	Commentary
Resistance	Target opposes the request and actively tries to avoid carrying it out	May try to dissuade the influencer from persisting or seek support to block the influence attempt
Compliance	Target does what is asked, but no more; no enthusiasm, minimal effort	May deliberately let things go wrong, leading to 'I told you so. . . '. Compliance may be enough in some situations
Identification	Target does as requested to maintain valued relationship	Only agreeing because request comes from that person – no wider commitment
Internalisation	Target internally agrees with a request and commits effort to make it work	The most successful outcome for the influencer, especially when task requires a high level of commitment

- **Internalisation** is when a person happily does what they are asked because it is consistent with their values. They see the request as being the right thing to do – it solves the problem, is congenial and brings other rewards: 'sure, that should work' shows someone has internalised the request.

Resistance or grudging compliance gives the manager a signal that there may be trouble ahead. Complex work depends on people working with imagination and flexibility; if they work with customers, the latter soon sense that staff are complying rather than working enthusiastically. An influencer can repeat their request more forcefully, but this rarely works. Alternatively they can pause to reflect on why people reacted this way. That may give some insight into their request, or how they made it, and they may decide to try another approach next time.

14.3 Traits models

> A **trait** is a relatively stable aspect of an individual's personality that influences behaviour in a particular direction.

Many observers have tried to identify the personal characteristics associated with effective leaders. They observed prominent figures to identify enduring aspects of their personality – **traits** – that appeared to explain their success.

The big five

> **The big five** refers to trait clusters that appear consistently to capture main personality traits of leaders: openness, conscientiousness, extraversion, agreeableness and neuroticism.

Researchers found they could group the many observed traits into five clusters (McRae and John, 1992), known as the big five: the left-hand column in Table 14.2 shows the label for each cluster, and the other columns show adjectives describing their extreme positions.

McRae and John (1992) show that each cluster contains six traits. Using these in personality assessments enables researchers to identify the pattern of traits an individual displays, and predict how this will affect performance. Colbert and Witt (2009) note that conscientiousness is the most consistent predictor of work outcomes, probably because such people tend to be dutiful, take care, deal with tasks accurately and persist to overcome difficulties. They also found that supervisors could influence such workers to perform well by emphasising the value of achieving goals, and helping them to do so. Anderson et al. (2008) show that people had more influence when certain big five traits 'fit' the work situation. Extraverts had more influence in a team-orientated consulting firm, while conscientious individuals had more influence in a telecommunications support unit, where staff typically worked alone to solve technical problems.

Table 14.2 The big five trait clusters

Label for cluster	Descriptions of extreme positions in cluster	
Openness	Explorer (O+): creative, open-minded, intellectual	Preserver (O–): unimaginative, disinterested, narrow-minded
Conscientiousness	Focused (C+): dutiful, achievement-orientated, self-disciplined	Flexible (C–): frivolous, irresponsible, disorganised
Extraversion	Extravert (E+): gregarious, warm, positive	Introvert (E–): quiet, reserved, shy
Agreeableness	Adapter (A+): straightforward, compliant, sympathetic	Challenger (A–): quarrelsome, oppositional, unfeeling
Neuroticism	Reactive (N+): anxious, depressed, self-conscious	Resilient (N–): calm, contented, self-assured

James Burns: transactional and transformational leaders

James Burns (1978) distinguished **transactional** and **transformational leaders**. Transactional leaders influence subordinates' behaviour through a bargain. The leader enables followers to reach their goals and those of the leader. If subordinates behave in the way desired by the leader they receive rewards – transactional leaders tend to support the status quo by rewarding subordinates' efforts and commitment.

Transformational (sometimes called charismatic) leaders aim to change the status quo by infusing work with a meaning that encourages followers to raise their aspirations by appealing to higher ideals and moral values. They energise people by articulating an attractive vision for the organisation, reinforcing the values in that vision and empowering subordinates to express new ideas. Another comparison would be that transactional leaders motivate followers to meet their leader's expectations, while transformational leaders motivate followers to exceed them. The two styles are not mutually exclusive – managers will have traits that feature in both styles, but the amount varies, with some being relatively transactional, others relatively transformational.

A **transactional leader** is one who treats leadership as an exchange, giving followers what they want if they do what the leader desires.

A **transformational leader** is a leader who treats leadership as a matter of motivation and commitment, inspiring followers by appealing to higher ideals and moral values.

Key ideas   **How do charismatic leaders gain support?**

Conger and Kanungo (1994) note that people often use the terms 'charismatic' and 'transformational' leadership interchangeably, but suggest that the first term directs attention to leader behaviours, while the second focuses on the effects on followers:

> In essence the two formulations of charismatic and transformational are highly complementary, and study the same phenomenon only from different vantage points. (p. 442).

They developed behavioural scales to measure charismatic leadership, with 25 items in these groups:

- vision and articulation e.g. 'consistently generates new ideas';
- environmental sensitivity e.g. 'recognises barriers that may hinder progress';
- unconventional behaviour e.g. 'uses non-traditional methods';
- personal risk e.g. 'takes high personal risk for the sake of the organisation';
- sensitivity to member needs e.g. 'shows sensitivity to needs and feelings of others';
- not maintaining the status quo e.g. 'advocates unusual actions to achieve goals'.

The full scales have been validated in other scientific studies, and used widely in research on leadership.

While many claim that transformational leadership styles generate higher performance than transactional styles, Garcia-Morales et al. (2008) found that few studies 'trace the causal path of the effects of transformational leadership on performance' (p. 299). They proposed that since knowledge and innovation are vital to performance, perhaps transformational leaders use their charisma and inspiration to encourage practices in these areas. Their study in over 400 Spanish companies confirmed this. Practices associated with transformational leadership, such as allocating resources to develop knowledge and building the skills to use it, did indeed lead to more innovation, which managers believed had enhanced competitive performance.

A limitation of the traits model is that a trait that is valuable in one situation is not necessarily valuable in another. Whatever traits Fred Goodwin had during his early (successful) years as Chief Executive at The Royal Bank of Scotland were still there when he resigned from the almost bankrupt company in 2009. Certain traits are probably necessary for effective leadership, but will not be sufficient for all conditions.

Despite these limitations, the traits model may explain why some people get to positions of influence and others do not. Baum and Locke (2004) note more interest in the personal characteristics of potential leaders, such as those creating new ventures. When people specify traits or personal qualities as part of a selection process they are implicitly assuming that they enhance performance. As two of the foremost scholars of leadership concluded:

> There is no one ideal leader personality. However, effective leaders tend to have a high need to influence others, to achieve; and they tend to be bright, competent and socially adept, rather than stupid, incompetent and social disasters. (Fiedler and House, 1994, p. 111)

Case study   British Museum – the case continues   www.britishmuseum.org

Neil MacGregor had not applied for the job at the Museum. The trustees had invited him to advise them during the appointment process, but they were so impressed by his knowledge and conviction that when the preferred candidate withdrew they offered MacGregor the job. Although still relatively inexperienced, he soon showed that he was both capable and popular. In addition to proven scholarship he displayed a flair for engaging with others – employees, journalists, politicians, viewers and donors.

With support from the Trustees, especially the chairman, Lord Rothschild, he greatly strengthened the museum's administrative and financial processes, and was able to secure significant donations from wealthy supporters. Limits on the funding provided by the government meant that (in common with other museums) it was becoming almost impossible to acquire new objects for the collection at auctions: he concentrated on persuading owners to lend their pieces to the Museum. He has committed the Museum, as the world's largest lender, to sharing its collection and knowledge with the broadest possible audience – shown by the many exhibitions from the collection around the UK.

He had a deep understanding of the history of art, having written books about the collections while director at the National Gallery, and presented their content to a wider public through two successful BBC television series. These showed that he could communicate his knowledge to the general public.

Commentators greeted the news of his appointment enthusiastically, one saying:

> he has the intelligence to build on the museum's strengths, the moral authority to guide it and the charisma to raise the money it desperately needed.

He appointed an experienced manager to take charge of finance and operations. She recalled:

> I got seduced into it by Neil's vision. He had a very powerful sense of what the purpose of the museum is, and I could see there was an important job to be done, both to address issues in the public domain, and to create something (Barsoux and Narasimhan, 2012, p. 6).

Refocusing the Museum on its founding ideals, MacGregor tried to reunite staff around a revived sense of the Museum as an enlightenment institution inspired by humane values, and relevant to the whole world.

Source: Barsoux and Narasimhan (2012); Annual Report and Accounts, 2014–15.

Case questions 14.2

- What features of the transformational leader does MacGregor display?
- How well do you think they fit the type of staff that the Museum employs, and the tasks they do?

Activity 14.1   Which traits do employers seek?

Collect some online job advertisements and recruitment packages. List the traits that the organisations say they value in those they recruit.

14.4   **Behavioural models**

Another set of theories sought to identify the behavioural styles of effective managers. What did they do to influence subordinates that less effective managers did not? Scholars at the Universities of Ohio State and Michigan respectively identified two categories of **behaviour**: one concerned with interpersonal relations, the other with accomplishing tasks.

Behaviour is something a person does that can be directly observed.

Ohio State University model

Researchers at Ohio State University (Fleishman, 1953) developed questionnaires that subordinates used to describe the behaviour of their supervisor, and identified two dimensions – 'initiating structure' and 'consideration'.

Initiating structure refers to the degree to which a leader defines peoples' roles, focuses on goal attainment and establishes clear channels of communication. Those using this approach focused on getting the work done – subordinates should follow the rules and work hard to full capacity. Typical behaviours of this style of leadership included:

Initiating structure is a pattern of leadership behaviour that emphasises the performance of the work and the achievement of production or service goals.

- allocating specific tasks to subordinates;
- establishing standards of job performance;
- informing subordinates of job requirements;
- scheduling work to be done;
- encouraging the use of uniform procedures.

Consideration refers to the degree to which a leader shows concern and respect for followers, looks after them and expresses appreciation (Judge et al. 2004). Such leaders assume that subordinates want to work well and try to make it easier for them to do so. They place little reliance on formal position, with typical behaviours including:

Consideration is a pattern of leadership behaviour that demonstrates sensitivity to relationships and to the social needs of employees.

- expressing appreciation for a job well done;
- not expecting more from subordinates than they can reasonably do;
- helping subordinates with personal problems;
- being approachable and available for help;
- rewarding high performance.

Surveys showed that supervisors displayed distinctive patterns – some scored high on initiating structure and low on consideration, while others scored the reverse. Some were high on both, others low on both. Research into the effects on performance was often inconclusive, but a review of over 130 such studies (Judge et al. 2004) concluded that consideration was more strongly related to follower satisfaction, while initiating structure was slightly more related to leader performance.

University of Michigan model

Researchers at the University of Michigan (Likert, 1961) conducted similar studies and found that two types of behaviour distinguished effective from ineffective managers:

- **Job-centred supervisors** ensured that they worked on different tasks from their subordinates, concentrating especially on planning, coordinating and supplying a range of support activities. These correspond to the initiating structure measures at Ohio.
- **Employee-centred supervisors** combined task-orientated behaviour with human values. They were considerate, helpful, friendly, and engaged in broad supervision rather than detailed observation – similar to what the Ohio group referred to as considerate. Likert (1961) wrote:

Supervisors with the best records of performance focus their primary attention on the human aspects of their subordinates' problems and on endeavouring to build effective work groups with high performance goals. (p. 7)

The leadership grid

Robert Blake and Jane Mouton (1979) developed the managerial grid model to extend and apply the Ohio State research; McKee and Carlson (1999), in association with Blake, continued this work. Figure 14.3 shows various combinations of concern for results (originally 'initiating structure') and concern for people (initially 'consideration') in their (renamed) 'leadership grid'.

The horizontal scale relates to concern for results, from 1 (low concern) to 9 (high concern). The vertical scale relates to concern for people, from 1 (low concern) to 9 (high concern). At the lower left-hand corner (1,1) is the *indifferent* style: low concern for both results and people. The primary objective of such managers is to keep away from active involvement whenever possible. They pass instructions to subordinates, follow the system and make sure that no one can blame them if something goes wrong. They do only enough work to keep their job.

At the upper left-hand corner (1,9) is the *accommodating* style: a low concern for results and a high concern for people. They are very aware of personal feelings, goals and ambitions, and consider how proposed actions will affect their subordinates. This may have negative consequences for others in the workplace, if work is not done on time or to standard.

High concern for results and low concern for people is found in the lower right-hand corner (9,1) – *controlling*. The high concern for results brings determination, focus and a drive for success. Such a manager is usually highly-trained and organised as well as being confident to demand high standards. They believe that efficiency comes from arranging the work so that employees who follow instructions will complete it satisfactorily.

In the centre (5,5) is *status quo*. These managers obtain adequate performance by balancing the need to get work done with reasonable attention to employees' needs. They see a higher level of concern for people or results as too extreme, and act to moderate them by compromises and trade-offs. In the upper right-hand corner (9,9) is the *sound* style, combining a high concern for results with a high concern for people. These managers see no contradiction between combining the two concerns, and encourage performance by creating relationships of trust and respect.

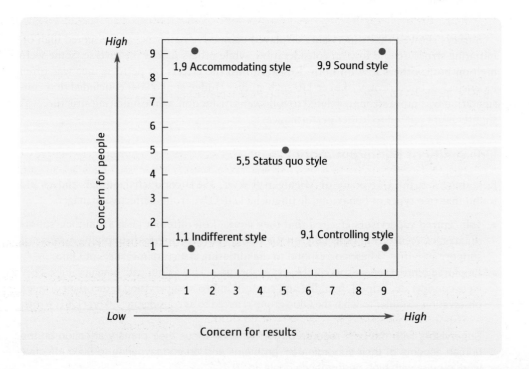

Figure 14.3 The leadership grid

The authors also identified two styles that they labelled *paternalistic* and *opportunistic*, which combined elements of the other five; these are not elaborated on here.

Activity 14.2   Critical reflection on the managerial grid

- Reflect on two managers you have worked with, one effective and one ineffective from your point of view.
- Which of the positions in the grid most closely describe their style? Note some of their typical behaviours.
- What were they like to work for? Does your reflection support or contradict the model? If the latter, what may explain that?

Management in practice

Two leaders' styles

Jeroen Van der Veer, CEO of Shell

Good leadership . . . means being clear about what is weak and what is strong, and where you want to go in the longer term, and having the ability to put it into clear words. The best way for a leader to take a company forward is to have some very simple words about how you would like to change it and the culture of the company.

Kwon Young-Soo, Chief Executive of LG Philips LCD

The company is the world's second-largest flat panel maker, and Mr Young-Soo believes it will thrive on argument:

The era for authoritarian management is gone. When I make a proposal, I want my staff to say 'no' when it does not make sense.

Although the company is a joint venture, its culture, like that of many Korean companies, was based on strict hierarchical structures, reflecting Confucian values. While rising through the ranks of the company he became acutely aware of the importance of internal communication, and since taking over as CEO has encouraged a more open exchange of ideas.

 Source: *Financial Times*, 2 February 2007, p. 19; 10 September 2007.

Many trainers across the world use the grid model to help managers develop towards a '9,9' style. Others question whether that always works: a crisis may require swift action with little time for personal feelings and interests. Situational models offer a possible answer.

Case study   British Museum – the case continues   www.britishmuseum.org

Neil MacGregor's political skills were widely recognised. A senior political figure commented:

When he took over, [the BM] was in the firing line, seen as old-fashioned, isolationist and clearly lined up for more cuts. By treading a very clever political line he has completely turned that around, so it is now a highly favoured institution.

The deputy director of the Museums Association agreed:

He's managed a very sophisticated balancing act between pleasing the public and pleasing the politicians, and still being seen as a world player.

Even internally his political efforts were appreciated. One curator:

On the whole, I think he's been very good for the place. [He has given] everybody working in the place a sense of purpose which we certainly didn't have before. At the same time he has transformed the public's view of what museums are for, and the view of politicians (p. 13).

Source: Barsoux and Narasimhan (2012).

Case questions 14.3

● The traits that are part of Neil MacGregor's personality are becoming clear in the case. What are they?

14.5　Situational (or contingency) models

Situational (contingency) models of leadership attempt to identify the contextual factors that affect when one style will be more effective than another.

Situational models present the idea that managers influence others by adapting their style to the circumstances. Three such models are set out below (Chapter 7 featured a fourth, developed by Vroom and Yetton (1973)).

Tannenbaum and Schmidt's continuum of leadership behaviour

Robert Tannenbaum and Warren Schmidt (1973) saw that leaders had different styles, ranging from autocratic to democratic. Figure 14.4 illustrates these extremes and the positions in between. The leader's choice should reflect three forces:

● **In the manager**: personality, values, preferences and confidence in subordinates.
● **In subordinates**: need for independence, tolerance of ambiguity, knowledge of the problem, expectations of involvement.
● **In the situation**: organisational norms, size and location of work groups, effectiveness of team working, nature of the problem.

House's path–goal model

House (1996) believed that effective leaders help subordinates to identify the path that will raise their performance, and so achieve the rewards they value. He identified four styles:

● **Directive**: letting subordinates know what the leader expects; giving specific guidance; asking subordinates to follow rules and procedures; scheduling and coordinating their work.
● **Supportive**: treating them as equals; showing concern for their needs and welfare; creating a friendly climate in the work unit.
● **Achievement orientated**: setting challenging goals and targets; seeking performance improvements; emphasising excellence in performance; expecting subordinates to succeed.
● **Participative**: consulting subordinates; taking their opinions into account.

House suggested that the appropriate style would depend on the situation – the characteristics of the subordinates and the work environment. If the subordinates have little confidence, the leader should provide coaching and support. If they likes clear direction, the leader should give it. Most skilled professionals expect to use their initiative and resent a directive style: they will respond best to a participative or achievement-orientated leader. The work environment includes the degree of task structure (routine or non-routine), the formal authority system (extent of rules and procedures) and the work group characteristics (quality of team work).

Figure 14.5 summarises the model, which predicts, for example, that:

- a directive style works best when the task is ambiguous and the subordinates lack flexibility – the leader absorbs the uncertainty and shows them how to do the task;

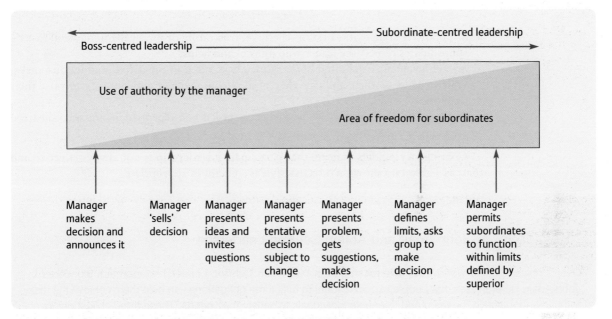

Figure 14.4 The Tannenbaum–Schmidt continuum of leadership behaviour

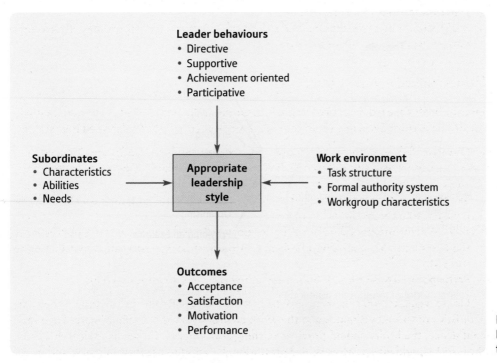

Figure 14.5
House's path–goal theory

Table 14.3 Conditions favouring participative or directive styles

Participative style most likely to work when:	Directive style most likely to work when:
Subordinates' acceptance of the decision is important	Subordinates do not share the manager's objectives
The manager lacks information	Time is short
The problem is unclear	Subordinates accept top-down decisions

- a supportive style works best in repetitive, frustrating or physically unpleasant tasks – subordinates respect the leader who joins in and helps;
- an achievement-orientated style works best on non-repetitive ambiguous tasks, which challenge their ability – they need encouragement and pressure to raise their ambitions;
- a participative approach works best when the task is non-repetitive and the subordinate(s) are confident that they can do the work.

Contingency models indicate that participative leadership is not always effective and that, as Table 14.3 shows, a directive style is sometimes appropriate.

Key ideas   **John Adair and Action Centred Leadership**

Over 2 million people worldwide have taken part in the Action Centred Leadership approach pioneered by John Adair. He proposes that people expect leaders to fulfil three obligations – to help them achieve the task, to build and maintain the team and to enable individuals to satisfy their needs. These three obligations overlap and influence each other – if the task is achieved that will help to sustain the group and satisfy individual needs. If the group lacks skill or cohesion it will neither achieve the task nor satisfy the members. Figure 14.6 represents the three needs as overlapping circles – almost a trademark for John Adair's work. To achieve these expectations the leader performs the eight tasks in the figure.

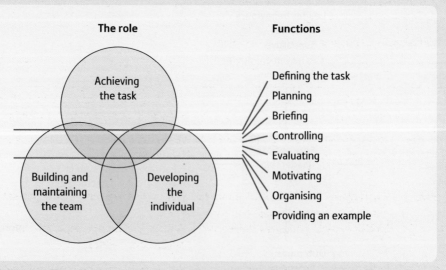

Figure 14.6 Adair's model of leadership functions
Source: Adair (1997, p. 21).

GAINING AND USING POWER **459**

14.6	Gaining and using power

Earlier sections show how people use personal skills to influence others, adapting their methods to the situation. Another perspective is that people use **power** – the ability to produce intended effects – to influence people and events.

Power is the ability to produce intended effects (attributed to Sir Bertrand Russell).

Sources of power

What are the bases of one person's power over another? French and Raven (1959) identified five sources:

- **Legitimate power** flows from the person's formal position. Their job gives them the power, for example, to make capital expenditures, offer overtime, choose a supplier or recruit staff.
- **Reward power** is the ability to reward another if they comply with a request or instruction. The reward can take many forms – pay, time off or interesting work.
- **Coercive power** is the ability to obtain compliance through fear of punishment or harm. It includes reprimands, demotions, threats, bullying language or a powerful physical presence.
- **Referent power,** also called *charismatic* power, is when some characteristics in a person are attractive to others; they identify with them, which gives the charismatic person power.
- **Expertise power** is when people acknowledge someone's knowledge and are therefore willing to follow their suggestions. This knowledge or skill may be *administrative* (how an organisation operates) or *technical* (how to do a task).

Personal and positional sources

Table 14.4 develops the French and Raven list to show that each type of power has a personal and a positional source. The most significant change to the French and Raven model is to show that referent (charismatic) power is not just personal but can also have a positional source (Hales, 2001). Chapter 3 showed how organisations develop distinctive

Table 14.4 Personal and positional sources of power

Power source	Personal	Positional
Coercive	Forcefulness, insistence, determination	Authority to give instructions, with the threat of sanctions or punishment available
Reward	Credit for previous or future favours in daily exchanges	Authority to use organisational resources, including the support of senior people
Expertise:		
Administrative	Experience of the business, whom to contact, how to get things done	Authority to use or create organisational policies or rules
Technical	Skill or expertise relevant to the task	Authority to access expertise, information and ideas across the business
Referent	Individual beliefs, values, ideas, personal qualities	Authority to draw on organisational norms and values

Source: Based on Hales (2001)

cultures and subcultures. When people refer to the prevailing culture in an attempt to influence behaviour ('what I'm asking fits the culture') they are drawing on a positional form of referent power.

Someone who has little access to these sources of power will have less influence than someone with more access. People continually defend their power sources, and try to gain new ones.

Gaining and using positional power

Kanter (1979) showed that someone's position in the organisation affects their power, as it becomes greater if:

- the job-holder rarely needs to seek approval for non-routine decisions;
- the job is central to organisational priorities;
- the job involves mainly external contacts; and
- the job provides opportunities for senior contacts.

The nature of their job thus gives the holder more power to influence others, as subordinates are more likely to agree with a strong and powerful manager than a weak and isolated one. They do so if they believe the manager can engage in **political behaviour** to make things happen: they have 'clout' – weight or political influence. A person's position gives access to the sources of power shown in Table 14.4, and explained further in the following paragraphs.

Political behaviour is 'the practical domain of power in action, worked out through the use of techniques of influence and other (more or less extreme) tactics' (Buchanan and Badham, 1999).

- **Coercive** – the authority to give instructions, with the threat of sanctions or punishment available. A manager working on a high-profile, visible project that people know is important for the company will probably be able to use the hint of senior support or available resources to ensure people accept their instructions. They will probably do even better if they prepare well and present their case convincingly.
- **Reward** – the authority to use organisational resources, including the support of senior people. Someone in a job with a large budget and valuable networks can use these resources, or the promise of them, to exert influence. Managers who choose to be remote and isolated in back-room work will not have that power – and so will have little influence on people or events.
- **Expertise** – **administrative** – the authority to use or create formal organisational policies or rules. This power enables holders of a position to establish rules, procedures or positions that sustain their power – especially if they appoint loyal supporters, or those in their debt, to those positions. In this way they encourage others to act in the way they prefer.

Key ideas   Old and new power

Heimans and Timms (2014) analyse the changing nature of power, and what this may mean for managing. They focus on what they see as the growing tension between 'old' and 'new' power, claiming that old power is enabled by what people or organisations own, know or control. Once institutions based on old power lose that control, they lose their advantage.

In contrast, the authors believe, new power models are enabled by peer coordination and the agency of the crowd. New power flows from tapping into people's growing capacity and desire to participate in ways that go beyond consumption – by, as examples, producing content on Facebook or YouTube, buying and selling temporary accommodation on AirBnB, or contributing knowledge to Wikipedia.

The authors suggest that it is unwise for people and organisations that have prospered under old power to ignore the spread of new models – through which people are seeking to influence events and institutions from which they were formerly excluded.

Source: Heimans and Timms (2014).

- **Expertise – technical** – authority to access expertise, information and ideas across the business. Using this power wisely enables a person to show they know what is happening and that they can secure expert resources if someone needs help. They can use their position, and the contacts that go with it, to build their image as a competent person. This credibility enhances their influence.
- **Referent** – authority to invoke norms and values of the organisational culture. Managers can use their position to influence others by showing that what they propose is consistent with the values and culture of the organisation. They invoke these wider values in support of their proposal.

The more of these sources of power the manager has, the more others will cooperate.

Perceptions of power

Power is only effective if the target of an influence attempt recognises the power source as legitimate and acceptable. If they dispute the knowledge base of a manager, or challenge their positional authority over a matter, the influence attempt is likely to fail. Managers who are successful influencers ensure that they sustain their power sources and take every opportunity to enhance them – see 'Management in practice'.

Management in practice

Marketing brand Me

People should manage their reputation like a brand. The most effective candidates [for promotion] do not leave their image to chance. They work at it, and massage its growth. They know that the best publicists they can have are their immediate staff. They are aware that team members talk about them more than anyone else. So they provide evidence to feed that grapevine . . . Staff need stories about their leader.

Another way to manage your reputation is to manage your boss . . . People keen to manage their reputation should find out what motivates the boss and try to satisfy those goals. If your boss likes punctuality and conscientiousness, turn up on time and work hard. If he or she needs reassurance, give it. If it is power, respond as someone who is less powerful. Why irritate a person who can influence your career path?

 Source: John Hunt, 'Marketing brand Me', *Financial Times*, 22 December 2000.
© The Financial Times 2000. All Rights Reserved.

In a study of 250 managers, Buchanan (2008) found that most believed it was ethical and necessary to engage in political behaviour at work. They worked at (mainly) middle and senior levels in public and private organisations. Respondents frequently saw five behaviours:

- building a network of useful contacts;
- using 'key players' to support initiatives;
- making friends with power brokers;
- bending the rules to fit the situation; and
- self-promotion.

A clear majority agreed that political behaviour was a useful tool to improve organisational effectiveness, and 90 per cent agreed that 'managers who play organisation politics well can improve their career prospects'.

Activity 14.3   Critical reflection on sources of power

- Try to identify at least one example of each of the personal and positional power sources. Examples could come from observing a manager in action (including people in your university or college) or from your reading of current business affairs.
- Can you identify what the person concerned has done to develop their power?
- Have other events helped to build, or to undermine, their power?

'To increase power, share it'

Delegation occurs when one person gives another the authority to undertake specific activities or decisions.

Kanter (1979) also proposed that managers can increase their power by, paradoxically, **delegating** some of it to subordinates. As subordinates carry out tasks previously done by the manager, he or she has more time to build external and senior contacts – which further boost power. By delegating not only tasks but also lines of supply (giving subordinates a generous budget), lines of information (inviting them to high-level meetings) and lines of support (giving visible encouragement), managers develop subordinates' confidence, and at the same time enhance their own power. They can spend more time on external matters, making contacts, keeping in touch with what is happening and so building their visibility and reputation. A weak or fearful manager who fails to delegate, and who looks inward rather than outward, will become increasingly isolated and powerless.

Case study   British Museum – the case continues   www.britishmuseum.org

The British Museum had been set up by an Act of Parliament in 1753, based on a legacy of 70,000 items from the collector Sir Hans Sloane: it was the world's first publicly funded museum. Most of the collection was acquired during the period of the British Empire's greatest power; later international conventions and national legislation banning the export of such antiquities mean it is a collection that can never be reproduced.

While this is a strength, it is also a weakness, as some countries have asked the Museum to return their antiquities – such as the Greek government's claim to the Elgin Marbles. Early in MacGregor's tenure a strongly worded statement by the directors of 18 United States and European museums asserted the importance of the 'universal museum' as a concept, and their right to keep long-held antiquities. The collective defence had emerged at an international meeting of museum directors, allegedly prompted by a 'call for help' from Mr MacGregor.

His willingness to forge links with difficult places paid off, leading to several high-profile loans – for example from Iran – and an exchange deal with China. In 2011 he invited then Prime Minister Gordon Brown to open a sell-out exhibition that attracted over 850,000 visitors, and which obliged the museum to open for 24 hours a day towards the end of its run. There have been several collaborations with national museums from countries with objects in the Museum, enabling them to use them, on loan, for exhibitions in their own country; even the Elgin Marbles could one day be loaned in that way.

Mr MacGregor continued to work closely with the BBC – such as a series of exhibitions about rulers who had changed the world. Each was accompanied by a prime-time TV documentary about the ruler in question – a glossy advert for the exhibition. One observer said:

> Ten years ago, before Neil MacGregor's director-ship, such coordinated publicity was out of the museum's orbit.

He has enthusiastically used the internet as an additional way of enabling members of the public to access the collections. In 2015 the World Conservation and Exhibition Centre opened, which made BM into the world's largest museum, with a critical research programme.

In early 2015 Mr MacGregor announced he would retire the following year. He has been replaced in 2016 by Dr Hartwig Fischer, formerly Director of the Dresden State Art Collections.

Sources: Barsoux and Narasimhan (2012); Annual Report and Accounts, 2011–12, 2014–15.

Case questions 14.4

- Which of the sources of power in Table 14.4 has Neil MacGregor used?
- What has he done to increase his power in the eyes of those he is trying to influence?
- What other forms of authority has he acquired?
- Which of the sources of power in Table 14.4 could staff use?

14.7 Choosing tactics to influence others

Another approach to the study of influence has been to identify directly how managers tried to influence others. An early example of this was work by Kipnis et al. (1980), who identified a set of influencing tactics that managers used in dealing with subordinates, bosses and co-workers. Yukl and Falbe (1990) replicated this work in a wider empirical study, and refined the categories – shown in Table 14.5.

Table 14.5 Influence tactics and definitions

Tactic	Definition
Rational persuasion	The person uses logical arguments and factual evidence to persuade you that a proposal or request is viable and likely to result in the attainment of task objectives
Inspirational appeal	The person makes a request or proposal that arouses enthusiasm by appealing to your values, ideals and aspirations or by increasing your confidence that you can do it
Consultation	The person seeks your participation in planning a strategy, activity or change for which your support and assistance are desired, or the person is willing to modify a proposal to deal with your concerns and suggestions
Ingratiation	The person seeks to get you in a good mood or to think favourably of him or her before asking you to do something

(continued)

Table 14.5 (*continued*)

Tactic	Definition
Exchange	The person offers an exchange of favours, indicates a willingness to reciprocate at a later time, or promises you a share of the benefits if you help accomplish the task
Personal appeal	The person appeals to your feelings of loyalty and friendship towards him or her before asking you to do something
Coalition	The person seeks the aid of others to persuade you to do something, or uses the support of others as a reason for you to agree also
Legitimating	The person seeks to establish the legitimacy of a request by claiming the authority or right to make it or by verifying that it is consistent with organisational policies, rules, practices or traditions
Pressure	The person uses demands, threats or persistent reminders to influence you to do what he or she wants

Source: Based on Yukl and Falbe (1990).

People can draw on the nine tactics to influence subordinates, bosses or colleagues.

Management in practice   Power balances in a charity

I worked for a charity providing advice to small companies in the Middle East. I was newly appointed, and wanted to run some of our courses through two of the business organisations in the region, as this was both fair and would give better results. One of my team members went behind my back, and told one of the organisations that we would only run the courses through them. She also persuaded our chief executive (CEO) that this was the best thing to do: I had no choice but to adhere to the decision.

Being new, almost the only influence tactic I could use with the CEO was *rational persuasion.* The other person had worked there for several years, and had developed close relations with the CEO, and was able to combine *exchange, personal appeal* and perhaps *pressure* to get her way.

Thinking back, and having read Yukl and Falbe's ideas, I realise I could have tried other tactics, such as *coalition* (persuading other team members of the benefits of my view) and *pressure* (threatening not to run the project: this could have worked, because I was the only person there who spoke the local language).

Source: Private communication from the project manager.

Yukl and Tracey (1992) extended the work by examining which tactics managers used most frequently with different target groups. They concluded that managers were most likely to use:

- rational persuasion when trying to influence their boss;
- inspirational appeal and pressure when trying to influence subordinates;
- exchange, personal appeal and legitimating tactics when influencing colleagues.

Lechner and Floyd (2012) found that staff trying to build support for strategic initiatives (such as new product development or acquisitions) combined rational justification, formal authority and informal coalitions. The projects were typically exploratory in nature – that is, they involved developing novel routines or other forms of unfamiliar know-how, which typically have trouble gaining approval. They found that influence attempts using rational

Table 14.6 Types of network

Practitioners	Joined by people with a common training or professional interest, and may be formal or informal
Privileged power	Joined by people in powerful positions (usually by invitation only)
Ideological	Consisting of people keen to promote political objectives or values
People-orientated	Formed around shared feelings of personal warmth and familiarity – friendship groups that people join by identifying with other members
Strategic	Often built to help develop links with people in other organisations

justification had the biggest impact on success, supplemented on occasion by using formal authority. Informal coalitions were only effective in projects that were especially exploratory in nature – but even then they needed the support of formal authority.

14.8   Influencing through networks

Networking refers to 'individuals' attempts to develop and maintain relationships with others [who] have the potential to assist them in their work or career' (Huczynski, 2004, p. 305). Table 14.6 shows several types of network.

Someone active in several networks gains access to contacts and information, which gives them more influence. They know what is happening in their business and use the network to extend their range of contacts in other organisations. Anecdotal evidence that networking is good for a career is supported by Luthans' (1988) research described in Chapter 1. Thomas (2003):

> in management what you know and what you have achieved will seldom be sufficient for getting ahead . . . Knowing and being known in the networks of influence both for what you have achieved and for who you are may be essential if you are to progress (p. 141).

General managers rely heavily on informal networks, especially when working outside the organisation – to make a sale, to gain access to a country's market or to set up a joint venture. Hillman (2005) showed how senior managers increase their influence over the business environment by appointing ex-politicians to their boards of directors. Government policy and regulations bring uncertainty, which managers try to reduce by building close links with politicians and senior officials. She found that firms in heavily regulated industries had more directors with political experience than those in other sectors, and that firms with politicians on their board were associated with better financial performance, especially in heavily regulated industries.

Networking refers to 'individuals' attempts to develop and maintain relationships with others [who] have the potential to assist them in their work or career' (Huczynski, 2004, p. 305).

Key ideas   'To influence, focus on the end of the event'

Whatever sources of power someone draws upon, and whatever tactics they use, they will have more effect if they plan their approach. In particular, they should focus on the event they are planning (email message, one-to-one negotiation, team presentation) to support their attempt at influence, and specify with great clarity what they want to achieve *by the end of* that event. There will be long-term goals to which this event should contribute, but that is more likely to happen if they specify what they want from *this* event.

- **Set the objective (or aim).** Define as clearly and exactly as possible what you want to achieve – what the other person or group will do or say. Some examples:
  - 'The team will have agreed to start work on the new project tomorrow, and have agreed a plan of work.'
  - 'The manager of department X will have agreed to release a named member of staff for this task, and will tell them today.'

These statements are unambiguous, and describe outcomes that are observable – 'yes or no?'.

- **Set success criteria (what will count as success?).** Express what you hope to achieve more precisely by setting measurable targets. These can refer to the result itself, or how people achieve it. Some possible success criteria for the first objective:
  - 'The team members will themselves set out the timetable.'
  - 'They will have made at least three proposals to help the project forward.'
  - 'Tasks will be clearly specified, with names against each.'
  - 'We will have reached agreement within two hours.'

These 'sub-objectives' provide unambiguous measures of progress and what else needs to be done.

- **Plan behaviour.** With clear objectives and success criteria, it is easier to decide what to do or say during the event, taking into account the situation, and the power and interests of those you are attempting to influence.

Source: Boddy (2002), pp. 95–6.

Informal networks are probably becoming more important as a means of influencing:

> As traditional hierarchical structures have given way to flatter and more flexible forms, informal networks have become even more important in gaining access to valuable information, resources, and opportunities. The structure and composition of an individual's network allows him or her to identify strategic opportunities, marshal resources, assemble teams and win support for innovative projects . . . Individuals who hold central positions in informal advice networks enjoy greater influence than those in peripheral positions and receive more favourable performance ratings (Sparrowe and Liden, 2005, p. 505).

The outcome of an influence attempt depends not only on the tactics used but on how well the influencer is able to meet the needs of the person they are influencing – see Chapter 15.

14.9 | Integrating themes

Entrepreneurship

Sir Alex Ferguson spent 26 seasons at Manchester United, and during his tenure the club won almost twice as many trophies as the second-most-successful English club. He was not only team manager, but also played a central role in the development of the club, including the extensive commercial interests. His management style has implications beyond football – and his approach to delegating, described in a recent *Harvard Business Review*, is relevant to entrepreneurs.

> One afternoon (before I went to Manchester United) I had a conversation with my assistant manager. He said, 'I don't know why you brought me here – I don't do anything. I work with the youth team, but I'm here to assist you with the training and with picking the team. That's the assistant manager's job.' At first I said 'No, no, no' but I thought it over for a few days and then said, 'I'll give it a try. No promises'. Deep down I knew he was right. So I delegated the training to him, and it was the best thing I ever did.

It didn't take away my control. My presence and ability to supervise were always there, and what you can pick up by watching is incredibly valuable. Once I stepped out of the bubble, I became more aware of a range of details, and my performance level jumped. Seeing a change in a player's habits allowed me to go further with him: Is it family problems? Money? Is he tired?

I don't think many people fully understand the value of observing. I came to see observation as a critical part of my management skills. (Elberse and Ferguson (2012), p. 124).

Sustainability

A manager wishing to encourage more sustainable performance within their organisation will be engaging on a process of influence – and to achieve their aims they will need to use both interpersonal and positional sources of power to influence others. They will need to gain the support of those above them in the organisation, as well as of other possibly significant stakeholders over whom they have no formal authority – customers, suppliers, bankers and so on. They are likely to meet opposition or indifference from some, as well as enthusiastic support from others – and it is unlikely that, in terms of the Yukl and Falbe (1990) model, they will win the case by rational arguments alone.

They are likely to need to use a range of interpersonal and political strategies, articulated through a suitable combination of tactics. The methods used at The Eden Project may be instructive – see 'Management in practice'.

Management in practice   How people at Eden try to influence   www.edenproject.com

The Eden Project (Chapter 15 Case) aims to help people to re-connect with the natural environment, and Tim Smit (co-founder and chief executive) explains their approach:

We're facing the most incredible challenges over the next 30 years, and I think that's why Eden is so important because to persuade people to change you can't do that with that waggy figure of sanctimony. The only way do to it is to write a story in which people see a better future coming up if we act in a different way: that's been a big weakness of the environment movement is that they get into arguments between themselves about arcane things, and they just leave the general public behind. So I think this storytelling side is vital and that's what we do best. The very creation of Eden is a story. I think we stand for something that makes other people believe in themselves and do stuff – that would be the greatest tribute you could ever pay us if that's what we could achieve.

Source: Interview with Tim Smit.

Internationalisation

The ability to manage internationally depends on being able to influence others in culturally mixed circumstances, where influence tactics that work in one place may be ineffective in another. Cross-cultural studies have found that cultural values (Chapter 4) affect the preferred influence tactics. For example, Fu and Yukl (2000) found that Chinese managers rated coalition formation, giving gifts and favours and personal appeals as more effective – and rational persuasion, consultation and exchange, as less effective, than American managers. The authors noted that these preferences for influencing tactics were consistent with their respective cultural values: for the Chinese with their values of collectivism, feminism and a long-term orientation, and for the Americans with their values of equality, direct confrontation and pragmatism.

There is also evidence that styles of leadership vary between countries. Shao and Webber (2006) found that certain of 'the big five' personality traits associated with transformational leadership behaviour in North America are not evident in China. They attributed this to differences in the prevailing cultures:

> The Chinese culture, characterised as high power distance, high uncertainty avoidance and collectivism, fundamentally reinforces the hierarchical and conformist attributes of the top-down command structure. This structure emphasises a centralised authority and leadership, stability and predictability, which create barriers for the emergence of transformational leaders, who tend to challenge the status quo and raise performance expectations. (p. 943)

Governance

Corporate governance has become prominent in response to recent financial scandals, which have shown that investors take a risk when they entrust their wealth to professional managers, since the latter may manage the business in their personal interest, rather than those of the shareholders.

Mechanisms of corporate governance are the balance against this, as in theory institutional investors (especially) can use their power (either in their votes at shareholder meetings, or by influencing the media) to force companies to reform their governance arrangements. They might advocate changes to the structure and composition of boards to make them more independent of management, or to the way executive pay is decided.

Westphal and Bednar (2008) show that CEOs are not passive in the face of these potentially threatening moves by shareholders. Their survey of some 400 companies shows that CEOs actively used persuasion and ingratiation tactics to deter representatives of institutional investors from using their power to obstruct CEOs' interests. These attempts at influence were generally effective. They note that although institutional investors have the power to impose governance changes, such changes have been adopted slowly. They claim that part of the reason is that CEOs have been able, by using some of the Yukl and Falbe (1990) influence tactics, to deter shareholders from using their power to influence governance systems.

Summary

1 **Distinguish leading from managing, and explain why each is essential to performance**
   - Although both are essential and the difference can be overstated, leading is usually seen as referring to activities that bring change, whereas managing brings stability and order. Many people both lead and manage in the course of their work.

2 **Explain why leading and managing both depend on being able to influence others**
   - Achieving objectives usually depends on the willing commitment of other people. How management seeks to influence others affects people's reaction to being managed. Dominant use of power may ensure compliance, but such an approach is unlikely to produce the commitment required to meet innovative objectives.

3 **Compare trait, behavioural and contingency perspectives on styles of influence**
   - Trait theories seek to identify the personal characteristics associated with effective influencing.
   - Behavioural theories distinguish managers' behaviours on two dimensions, such as initiating structure and consideration.
   - Contingency perspectives argue that the traits or behaviours required for effective influence depend on factors in the situation, such as the characteristics of the employee, the boss and the task.

4 **Outline theories that focus on power (both personal and organisational) as the source of influence**

- The more power a person has, the more they will be able to influence others. Table 14.4 identified sources of power as coercive, reward, expertise (administrative and technical) and referent – all of which can have both personal and organisational dimensions.

5 **Contrast the style and power perspectives, and explain why sharing power may increase it**

- 'Style' perspectives show the range of styles managers can use to influence others, depending on circumstances.
- 'Power' perspectives identify the sources of power that people can draw on to guide their influence attempts.
- Sharing power with subordinates may not only enable them to have more satisfying and rewarding work, but by enabling the manager to have more time to develop senior and external contacts, he or she can then enhance their power more than if they focused on internal matters.

6 **Outline a model of the tactics that people use to influence others, including networking**

- Yukl and Falbe have identified these tactics in attempts to influence others: rational persuasion, inspirational appeal, consultation, ingratiation, exchange, personal appeal, coalition, legitimating and pressure. They have also found that effective influencers vary their tactics depending on the person they are trying to influence. A further line of research identifies the value of building networks as part of effective influencing.

7 **Understand how you can use ideas from the chapter to develop the skill of setting clear goals when planning to influence others**

- Setting 'end of event' goals should help to focus behaviour on achieving them, and so make the influence attempt more successful. The 'Develop a skill' feature helps you understand how to develop that skill.

8 **Show how ideas from the chapter add to your understanding of the integrating themes**

- Entrepreneurs can benefit from the ideas on delegation put forward by Kanter (1982), advocating that leaders pass more power to staff to increase the leader's own power. innocent drinks, Virgin and Google are just a few examples of entrepreneurial companies that influence staff in this way.
- Proposals to add value more sustainably depend on managers being able to influence others over whom they will usually have no formal authority. Like any organisational change, sustainability projects will sometimes meet opposition, so managers or others promoting change will need to use a variety of influencing tactics to achieve their objectives (including methods used in marketing).
- There is accumulating evidence that cultural values affect the influencing tactics used in different countries, and that leadership styles vary between countries.
- Governance and control systems are intended to influence the behaviour of chief executives and senior managers to act in the interests of shareholders. Chief executives do not passively accept such constraints, and the section included evidence of active lobbying to obstruct proposals that the chief executives thought were against their interests.

Test your understanding

1 Why is the ability to influence others so central to the management role?

2 What evidence is there that traits theories continue to influence management practice?

3 What are the strengths and weaknesses of the behavioural approaches to leadership?

4 What is meant by the phrase a '9,9 manager'?

5 Discuss with someone how he or she tries to influence people (or reflect on your own practice). Compare this experience with one of the contingency approaches.

6 Evaluate that theory in the light of the evidence acquired in review question 5 and other considerations.

7 Explain in your own words the main sources of power available to managers. Give examples of personal and institutional forms of each.

8 List the lines of power that Kanter identifies and give an example of each.

9 What does the network perspective imply for someone wishing to be a successful influencer?

10 Summarise an idea from the chapter that adds to your understanding of the integrating themes.

Think critically

Think about the ways in which you typically seek to influence others, and about how others in your company try to exert influence. Then make notes on these questions:

● Thinking of the people you typically work with, who are effective (or less effective) influencers? What do the effective influencers do that others do not – interpersonal skills? power? tactics? Do the prevailing **assumptions** fit with Kanter's view – 'to increase power, share it'?

● What factors in the **context** – including the history of the company or your personal experience – have shaped the way you influence others? How might the context affect how you planned an attempt to influence?

● Have you considered using **alternative** approaches to planning your influence attempts, based on your observations?

● How do you and your colleagues react to Neil MacGregor's approach to revitalising the British Museum? Does it have any **limitations**? Which of his tactics would you try, if you could?

Develop a skill – setting goals to influence others

Setting clear and precise goals is an essential management skill, and is especially valuable when trying to influence others. This focuses on setting clear 'end-of-event' goals.

● **Assessment:** Assess how well you set goals for a meeting – what you want to get out of it. Are you always clear what you want to achieve? Can you express it quickly if someone asks? Or do you wait to see what happens?

● **Learning:** Sections 14.7 and 14.8 introduced ideas on tactics of influencing – all of which will depend on some form of exchange with other people – emails, meetings, presentations etc. Read those sections again, paying especial attention to the 'Key ideas' feature (pp. 465–6), which shows the value of setting clear goals for the end of each such event. Summarise the ideas in these sections. Why is setting clear objectives, success criteria and planning behaviour likely to help you be more influential? How do ideas on goal setting (see Chapters 6 and 8) relate to this?

● **Analysis:** Do you have experience of being at meetings or presentations where the goals were unclear, or when they were very clear? How did either condition affect the outcome? How do you distinguish a clear goal from an unclear one?

- **Practice:** Identify a meeting or similar event you will have soon – to do with your course, or another activity in which you take part. Use the steps in 'Key ideas' (pp. 465–6) to plan your objectives, success criteria and behaviours – and record them in some way. Take part in the event and follow your plan.

- **Application:** When you have completed the work, review how you worked and whether your plan helped you. Reflect on what you can learn.

  Decide on another opportunity to practise this skill within the next week.

Read more

Bennis, W. with Biederman, P.W. (2008), *The Essential Bennis: Essays on Leadership,* Jossey-Bass, San Francisco, CA.

  Brings together some of the most influential essays by this great writer on management.

Elberse, A. and Ferguson, A. (2013), 'Ferguson's formula', *Harvard Business Review,* vol. 91, no. 10, pp. 116–25.

Huczynski, A.A. (2004), *Influencing Within Organisations* (2nd edn), Routledge, London.

  Draws on a wide range of academic research to provide a practical guide to influencing – from how to conduct yourself at a job interview to coping with organisational politics.

Isaacson, W. (2011), *Steve Jobs,* Little, Brown, London.

  Insights into the methods of two people renowned for their abilities to influence others – Sir Alex Ferguson at Manchester United and the late Steve Jobs at Apple.

Maccoby, M. (2015), *Strategic Intelligence: Conceptual Tools for Leading Change,* Oxford University Press, Oxford.

  A concise yet substantial book on leadership, drawing on the author's long and distinguished career as an academic and consultant.

Go online

Visit these websites (or others of similar companies of which you know):

  www.britishmuseum.org
  www.pret.com
  www.edenproject.com

Each of these organisations has tried to develop new approaches to managing and influencing staff, and has, despite some difficult circumstances, survived and prospered. Go to the section on the website about 'careers' or 'our team', and look for clues about the approaches to leadership that the company encourages.

- Use the House model to analyse what conditions may explain their approach.
- Do you find their leadership approach attractive, or not?

CHAPTER 15
MOTIVATING

Aim

To examine theories of behaviour at work and to connect them with management practice.

Objectives

By the end of your work on this chapter you should be able to outline the concepts below in your own terms and:

1 Explain why managers need to understand and use theories of motivation

2 Give examples showing how the context, including the psychological contract, affects motivation

3 Compare behaviour modification, content and process theories

4 Use work design theories to diagnose motivational problems and recommend actions

5 Describe some strategically useful practices such as flexible working and high-performance work systems

6 Show that you can use work design theories to understand how to develop the skill of designing a job that is motivating

7 Show how ideas from the chapter add to your understanding of the integrating themes

Key terms

The chapter introduces these terms:

motivation	hygiene (maintenance) factors
work–life balance	expectancy theory
psychological contract	subjective probability
perceived organisational support	instrumental
organisational citizenship behaviour	valence
perceptions	equity theory
behaviour modification	goal-setting theory
existence needs	intrinsic rewards
relatedness needs	extrinsic rewards
growth needs	job characteristics theory
motivator factors	

Each is a term defined within the text, and in the glossary at the end of the book.

The Eden project is one of the most visited attractions in Europe: over 15 million people have visited it since it opened in 2002. The Annual Report and Accounts for 2014–15 show that the number of visitors in the year rose by five per cent, turnover by £0.5 million, and that it made a financial surplus of £1.4 million. The Commercial Director:

> We believe in profits for a purpose, and our trading surplus will enable us to continue to invest in our education programmes and new partnerships, the visitor destination, and our overseas activities.

© Philip Dubois/Alamy Images

Tim Smit, who co-founded the project, was convinced that people (even those who did not initially like gardens) could be attracted by anecdotes – accessible stories about what they were looking at. He also noticed that people felt very positive about being in well-made, abundant gardens.

This led him to develop the idea of creating a place that looked good, was technically sophisticated, and dedicated to explaining how all life on earth depends on plants. More than that, it could become:

> a place where you started to think about your connection with nature, and whether you might want to get closer to nature again and whether some lessons of life might not be buried in there.

From this vision, Eden has become a globally-recognised brand, generated over £1 billion in revenues for the local economy and employs some 300 staff.

The first task in turning the idea into reality was to persuade people to invest in the project – which would cost about £76 million. Smit approached a leading architect who, after consulting colleagues, agreed to work on the project. Smit:

> So for the next 18 months we had possibly the best design team in the world working for us for nothing. I think the reason Eden came into being was that we formed an enormous gang. There was a bunch of people that were really interested in the idea and we would meet in motorway service stations and in pubs and in people's houses and this just grew as people heard about it. People started leaving their jobs because they became so obsessed with it. And it suddenly had

an inevitability, when we realised we were saying 'when' not 'if' . . . and the dice rolled unbelievably well for us.

> The environment became a big thing, plants are good, people can imagine the Crystal Palace and this is bigger than the Crystal Palace. We said we wanted the biggest in the world, to contain a full-size rainforest, we don't just want some namby-pamby greenhouse. I said we wanted to build a global must-see like the Guggenheim. The tourism people thought we might get 500,000 visitors in the first year: we actually had 1.8 million.

> And in the middle of all that there was a huge fundraising effort to raise the money for what we called the eighth wonder of the world.

In September 2015 it entered into partnership with the Chinese authorities to build a China Eden project.

Source: Interview with Tim Smit; Eden Project website.

Case questions 15.1

Creating Eden has depended on motivating people.

- Which groups of people have featured in the case so far?
- What has Tim Smit wanted these people to do for the Eden Project?
- What clues are there about what motivates them to give their support?

> ### 15.1   Introduction

The Eden Project has captured the public imagination, rapidly becoming one of Europe's most successful visitor attractions and a thriving educational charity. Tim Smit and his colleagues secured the support of talented architects, local agencies, significant funding bodies – and then of staff, visitors and many partner institutions. In good times as well as in bad, charities must raise income and recruit staff to survive; like any business, Eden's management have been thinking up new ways to **motivate** people to continue to support the project enthusiastically.

Motivation refers to the forces within or beyond a person that arouse and sustain their commitment to a course of action.

All organisations need enthusiastic and committed employees who work in a way that supports their goals. This is clearest in service organisations such as Eden, where customers are in direct contact with staff. Culbertson (2009) shows how employee satisfaction affects service quality - but matters just as much in manufacturing or administrative operations. Zara depends on its designers for a constant flow of innovative fashions – and then on thousands of people in the company, and its suppliers, to turn the designs into desirable clothes. Those responsible for delivering public services face a similar challenge to understand the motivation of public servants: are they motivated by similar factors to those in the private sector, or do some distinctive, public-sector values attract people to work in the sector?

Managers want people to work well and occasionally to 'go the extra mile' – doing more than usual to fix a problem or to help a colleague – known as organisational citizenship behaviour. The challenge is to create a context in which people engage willingly with their work to add value. Yet motivation arises within people – so managers need to ensure that people can satisfy their needs through work, bearing in mind that a reward that is attractive to one may not matter to another.

Key ideas   Douglas McGregor – Theory X and Theory Y

Douglas McGregor (1960) set out two views of motivation, Theory X and Theory Y, which he believed represented managers' views about people. To find out which you agree with, complete this questionnaire. Read each pair of statements, and circle the number that best represents your view:

The average person inherently dislikes work	(1 2 3 4 5)	Work is as natural as rest to people
People must be directed at work	(1 2 3 4 5)	People will exercise self-discretion and self-control
People wish to avoid responsibility	(1 2 3 4 5)	People enjoy real responsibility
People feel that achievement at work is irrelevant	(1 2 3 4 5)	People value achievement highly
Most people are dull and uncreative	(1 2 3 4 5)	Most people have imagination and creativity
Money is the only real reason for working	(1 2 3 4 5)	Money is only one benefit from work
People lack the desire to improve their quality of life	(1 2 3 4 5)	People have needs to improve the quality of their life
Having an objective is a form of imprisonment	(1 2 3 4 5)	People welcome objectives as an aid to effectiveness

Add the numbers you circled to give you a score between 8 and 40. If you scored 16 or less, then you agree with Theory X. If you scored 32 or more, then you agree with Theory Y. So what? Managers often wonder how they can motivate staff to higher performance – and use their theory of motivation to decide how to do it. Someone who agrees with Theory X will take a different approach from someone who agrees with Theory Y. McGregor's ideas are a vivid way of illustrating different views on the topic. In practice, most of us combine X and Y views, and so do most jobs – requiring a mix of control and freedom. The skill is to strike the right balance between them.

Money is evidently a major motivator for many people, especially those on low incomes. Others enjoy the work itself – such as Theresa Marshall, a classroom assistant in a city primary school:

> I've found my niche and couldn't be happier – it's no exaggeration to say that I absolutely love my job. My favourite part is helping the children with their reading skills and seeing the pleasure that they can get out of books.

Some enjoy working with physical things or the challenge of designing an innovative product – while others prefer working with people in advisory, sales or customer service jobs. Some are happy to use what skills they have – others stay if they feel they are learning. A manager who recruits staff with little experience or formal qualifications – and gives them skills – says:

> They feel good about themselves because they know they are learning all the time and they gain a sense of self-esteem.

In all situations, managers make assumptions about what staff want – and staff evaluate what is on offer and respond in some way. They also consider how it may affect their **work–life balance**, which is the experience of satisfaction and good functioning at work and at home (Sturges, 2012).

This chapter outlines and illustrates the main theories of human needs – Figure 15.1. How managers interpret the environment shapes what they expect from people – who also

Work–life balance refers to the experience of satisfaction and good functioning at work and at home (Sturges, 2012, p. 1540).

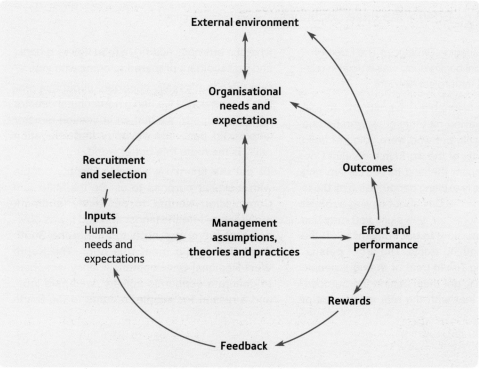

Figure 15.1 An overview of the chapter

have needs and expectations. The next section examines the psychological contract that expresses these mutual expectations. Those that follow introduce four groups of motivational theories – behaviour modification, content, process and work design. Managers implicitly or explicitly draw on their assumptions and theories to implement motivational practices – such as using work design theories to create motivating jobs – the focus of the 'Develop a skill' feature at the end of the chapter.

15.2 Perspectives on motivation – context and the psychological contract

Much behaviour is routine, based on habit, precedent and unconscious scripts. This chapter is concerned with the larger, precedent-setting choices people make at work. For some, work is an occasion for hard, enthusiastic and imaginative activity, a source of rich satisfaction. They are motivated, in the sense that they put effort (arousal) into their work (direction and persistence). Others work grudgingly – it does not arouse their enthusiasm, and is perhaps a way to pass the time until they find something more interesting. Managers consider how to encourage the former and discourage the latter. Theories of motivation, which try to identify factors that energise, channel and sustain behaviour, can inform that consideration. Employees expect more from companies in terms of flexibility, career development and opportunities to contribute. Companies wishing to attract and retain good staff are trying to measure and understand these expectations – and are as concerned about this as they are about what customers expect.

Who are managers trying to motivate? They need to influence (motivate) not only people who report to them – their subordinates – but also senior managers, people in other organisations and customers. Understanding their needs will make it easier.

Case study   Eden – the case continues   www.edenproject.com

Gaynor Coley is Managing Director at The Eden Project, and her financial background was crucial in raising the money that the project needed.

I left a safe, pensionable university job to join Eden in 1997, having met this crew who had no money in the bank, but who were going to build the eighth wonder of the world in a derelict Cornish clay pit. I spent the next three years raising the money: a really exciting period, using all those skills you learn in the City about having a robust business plan, together with skills you may use in fringe theatre - how to get something off the ground when nothing exists. The art of persuasion was putting Tim in front of the right people so he could really get them behind the purpose, then following that with the real mechanics of

what the business needs – a robust plan, a bank, and stakeholders prepared to come with you.

One thing that's really important about this project is teamwork – we had a horticultural director who was superb, we had an education director who could persuade anybody that education really is the route to a better world.

To get the finance we had to identify people with a similar purpose to us. So the Millenium Commission wanted to put really landmark architecture into the landscape and it was obvious that there was nothing else in the South West that would meet this brief. The South West Regional Development Agency was there to generate economic activity, well-paid jobs, and a reason for people to come to the South

West. So they had a different agenda, and part of our task there was to say, 'well, we will fulfil that agenda'. So it was research around what agendas a portfolio of stakeholders had, understanding them and make a pitch relevant to that stakeholder.

Case questions 15.2

- What motivational skills has the managing director demonstrated in raising the funds that Eden required?
- How transferable do you think they would be to other management situations?

Source: Interview with Gaynor Coley.

Those with a critical perspective believe that 'workers need to be influenced to cooperate because of their essential alienation from the productive process' (Thompson and McHugh, 2002, p. 306): employers try to maintain their power over employees, which the latter accept in the absence of realistic alternatives. Staff may even express satisfaction with a new arrangement as a way of coming to terms with the inherent stability of the power structure. As always in management, people see the topic from different perspectives: motivation is not a neutral or value-free subject.

Key ideas   Acknowledge the variety of human needs and aspirations

Lynda Gratton (2011) recalls a study conducted by Tesco that revealed the variety of needs that their employees brought to work:

Once they had collected data about individual employees, they began to combine people with similar aspirations into segments. [They found that] employees' aspirations for work were highly individual . . . Of course some wanted to ascend the corporate hierarchy and to bask in the status of money. However, others wanted more than anything else to have flexible working arrangements that allowed them to occasionally spend time with their children or ageing parents during the day. Some came to work to play and have as much fun as possible, while others didn't much care what they did as long as they got paid fairly.

What is crucial is that we both acknowledge and celebrate the variety of human needs and aspirations . . . By understanding this, we can begin to shift our view of working lives towards [being] more accepting of unique needs, and towards the idea that work can be crafted to acknowledge and meet these needs. (p. 310)

Source: Gratton (2011).

Figure 15.2 illustrates a simple model of human motivation. We all need food, social contact or a sense of achievement, which motivate behaviour to satisfy that need. If the action leads to a satisfactory outcome we experience a sense of reward. The feedback loop shows that we then decide whether the behaviour was appropriate and worth repeating.

The figure also shows that individuals act within a context with immediate and wider elements:

- The job itself – e.g. how interesting, varied or responsible?
- The organisation – e.g. supervision, career prospects, pay?
- The environment – e.g. career threats and opportunities?

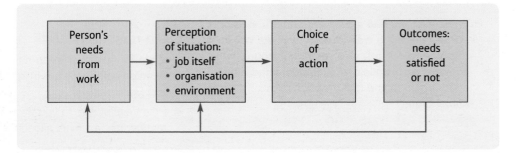

Figure 15.2
Human needs
in context –
the situational
perspective

These affect how people see their job. When jobs are scarce people expect less from work and accept almost any job to pay the mortgage. In better times they are more choosey. In considering this model, remember that:

- we can only infer the needs that matter to someone;
- needs change with age, experience and responsibilities;
- we can often only satisfy one need at the expense of another; and
- the effect of satisfying a need on the future strength of that need is uncertain.

The psychological contract

A psychological contract is the set of understandings people have regarding the commitments made between themselves and their organisation.

The **psychological contract** expresses the idea that each side to an employment relationship has expectations of the other – what they will give and what they will receive. Employers (or their agents, their managers) offer rewards in the expectation they will receive performance. Employees work in the expectation that they will receive rewards they value. Both sides modify these expectations over time, reflecting changing contexts or individual circumstances. There is a constant risk that a contract that satisfied both parties at one time ceases to do so – with consequences for attitudes and behaviour.

Rousseau and Schalk (2000) refer to psychological contracts as

the belief systems of individual workers and their employers regarding their mutual obligations. (p. 1)

Some elements in the contract are written but most are implicit: so the parties may differ about what was promised and what has been delivered. If both are content, they have a positive relationship; if either believes the other has breached the contract, the relationship will suffer.

Guest (2004) proposed the model shown in Figure 15.3 to guide research. A common theme has been to study the effects on behaviour of perceived breaches in the contract.

Perception is the active psychological process in which stimuli are selected and organised into meaningful patterns.

Researchers have studied employees' **perceptions** of the state of the psychological contract with their employer, since business pressures may prompt changes that employees see as breaking the contract. If they do, what are the effects?

Restubog et al. (2007) measured the effects of perceived contract breaches on sales staff in the pharmaceutical industry. Relating their work to Guest's model, they assessed the state of the psychological contract by staff responses to statements such as:

- I have not received everything promised to me in exchange for my contributions.
- Almost all the promises made by my employer during recruitment have been kept thus far.

Organisational citizenship behaviour (OCB) refers to things people do beyond the requirements of their task to help others and to make things run smoothly.

The researchers assessed the effects of perceived breaches in the contract on two of Guest's outcomes (Figure 15.3) – 'job performance' and '**organisational citizenship behaviour**' (**OCB**). These were assessed by supervisors' ratings of the employee on statements such as:

Job performance:

- adequately completes assigned duties;
- fulfils responsibilities specified in the job description; and
- performs tasks that are expected of him/her.

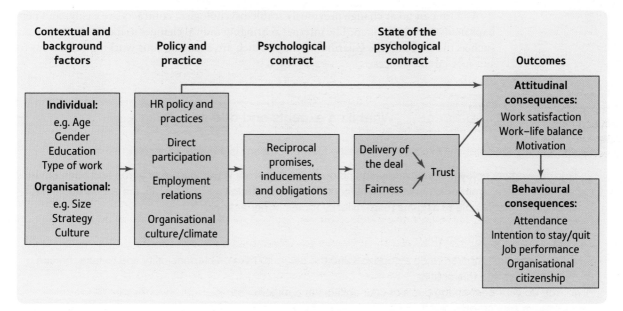

Figure 15.3 A framework for applying the psychological contract to the employment relationship
Source: Based on Guest (2004).

Organisational citizenship (that benefits colleagues):

- helps others who have been absent;
- takes time to listen to co-workers' problems and worries; and
- passes along information to co-workers.

Organisation citizenship (that benefits company):

- attendance at work is above the norm;
- gives advance notice when unable to come to work; and
- adheres to informal rules devised to maintain order.

They found that, as expected, those who believed the contract had been breached were less likely to perform well on the job, and less likely to display organisational citizenship behaviour, though some were more tolerant than others. Another useful concept is **perceived organisational support (POS)** – the beliefs an employee has about the treatment they receive, irrespective of promises made by the organisation. POS forms part of the context of the psychological contract and appears to moderate the effects of breaches (by either side).

Perceived organisational support (POS) refers to the beliefs an employee has about the treatment they receive, irrespective of promises made by the organisation.

Management in practice   'Employees leave managers, not companies'

From the employee's point of view, there is clear evidence that good management rests squarely on four foundations:

- Having a manager who shows care, interest and concern for each employee.
- Knowing what is expected.
- Having a role that fits their abilities.
- Receiving positive feedback and recognition regularly for work well done.

In a Gallup study of performance at unit level, covering more than 200,000 employees across many industries, teams that rated managers highly on these four factors were more productive and more profitable. They also had lower staff turnover and higher customer satisfaction ratings.

Source: *People Management*, 17 February 2000, p. 45.

At a time of great change previously stable psychological contracts are easily, and perhaps inadvertently, broken. The internet is bringing radical changes to media organisations such as the BBC and the Guardian Group, which are changing staff working conditions to suit new circumstances.

Management in practice   What Ikea expects and offers   www.IKEA.com

On the website the company explains that working for the company is a matter of give and take:

> Ikea co-workers enjoy many advantages and opportunities from working in such a free and open environment – but all freedoms are counter-balanced with expectations. For example, the expectation that each co-worker is able to assume responsibility for his or her actions.

What do we expect from you?

- You have the ambition to do a good job and the desire to take on responsibility and to take the consequences that this entails.
- You do your best on the basis of your abilities and experience.
- You are service-orientated and have the customers' best interests at heart.
- You are not status minded, but rather open in your approach to others.

What do we offer you?

- The chance to work in a growing company with a viable business idea.
- The opportunity to further develop your professional skills.
- The opportunity to choose between many different jobs in the company.
- A job with fair and reasonable conditions.
- The chance to assume responsibility following recognised good results, regardless of age.

Source: Company website.

Activity 15.1   Mutual expectations

Identify a time when you were working in an organisation, or think of your work as a student.

- Describe what the organisation expected of you.
- What policies or practices did the organisation use to encourage these?
- What did you expect of the organisation?
- How well did the organisation meet your expectations?
- How did the 'balance' between the two sets of expectations affect your motivation?

The next section outlines a theory that some companies use to influence the actions of staff.

Behaviour modification is a general label for attempts to change behaviour by using appropriate and timely reinforcement.

15.3   Behaviour modification

Behaviour modification refers to a range of techniques developed to treat psychological conditions such as heavy smoking; managers use it to deal with issues such as lateness. The techniques have developed from Skinner's (1971) theory that people learn to see relationships between actions and their consequences, and that this learning guides behaviour. If we receive a reward for doing something, we tend to do it again; if the consequences are unpleasant, we do not.

Behaviour modification techniques focus on observable behaviours, not attitudes and feelings.

> In promoting safety . . . we did not dwell on accident-prone workers or probe for personality or demographic factors, none of which can be changed. Instead we focused on the organisation and what it can do to rearrange the work environment. (Komaki, 2003, p. 96)

This includes specifying what people should do, measuring actual behaviour and identifying the consequences that people experience. If the influencer sees the behaviour as undesirable, he or she tries to influence the person by changing the consequences – rewarding or punishing them.

Komaki (2003) explains how she and her colleagues used the method in a bakery to encourage safe working practices. They worked with management to design these steps:

- **Specify desired behaviour:** This included defining very precisely the safe working practices that were required – such as walking round conveyor belts, how to sharpen knives, using precise terms when giving instructions.
- **Measure desired performance:** Trained observers visited the site and recorded whether workers were performing safely by following the specified behaviours.
- **Provide frequent, contingent, positive consequences:** In this case, the positive consequence was feedback, in the form of charts showing current accident figures, which were much lower than previous levels.
- **Evaluate effectiveness:** Collecting data on accident levels and comparing these with earlier data. In this case people were now working more safely, and the number of injuries had fallen from 53 a year to ten.

Practitioners emphasise that several principles must be used for the method to work (Komaki et al. 2000):

- payoffs (benefits) must be given only when the desired behaviour occurs;
- payoffs must follow very soon after the behaviour, to strengthen the behaviour – reward link;
- desirable behaviour is likely to be repeated if reinforced by rewards;
- reinforcement is more effective than punishment, as punishment only temporarily suppresses behaviour;
- repeated reinforcement can lead to permanent change in behaviour in the desired direction.

Management in practice — Behaviour modification in a call centre

In our call centre staff are rewarded when behaviour delivers results in line with business requirements. Each month staff performance is reviewed against a number of objectives such as average call length, sales of each product and attention to detail. This is known as Effective Level Review and agents can move through levels of effectiveness ranging from 1 to 4, and gain an increase in salary after six months of successful reviews. Moving through effective levels means that they have performed well and can mean being given other tasks instead of answering the phone. The role can become mundane and repetitive so the opportunity to do other tasks is seen as a reward for good performance. Thus it reinforces acceptable behaviour.

Conversely staff who display behaviour that is not desirable cannot move through these levels and repeated failure to do so can lead to disciplinary action. This can be seen as punishment rather than behaviour modification. People can become resentful at having their performance graded every month, particularly in those areas where it is their line manager's perception of whether or not they have achieved the desired results.

Source: Private communication from the call centre manager.

Above all, advocates stress the need to reward desirable behaviours, not take them for granted. Rewards can take the form of individual action (a word of praise or thanks) or organisational practices (shopping vouchers for consistently good timekeeping). Supporters believe the approach encourages management to look directly at what makes a person act in a desirable way, and to ensure those rewards are available. It depends on identifying rewards the person will value (or punishments they will try to avoid). Theories that attempt to understand these are known as content theories of motivation.

15.4 Content theories of motivation

Most writers on this topic have tried to identify human needs so that they can use this knowledge to influence behaviour. Frederick Taylor (Chapter 2) believed that people worked for money and that they would follow strict working methods if management rewarded them financially. Chapter 2 also showed how Mary Parker Follett and Elton Mayo identified other human needs, such as being accepted by a group. Abraham Maslow developed a theory incorporating these and other needs.

Activity 15.2   Was Taylor wrong?

Many managers believe that money is a powerful incentive.

- Find someone who works for an organisation where incentives or commissions make up a significant part of that person's pay and ask how that affects his or her behaviour.
- Are there are any negative effects?

Abraham Maslow – a hierarchy of needs

Maslow was a clinical psychologist who developed a theory of human motivation to help him understand the needs of his patients. He stressed the clinical sources of the theory and that it lacked experimental verification, though he was aware that Douglas McGregor (Section 15.1) had used the theory to interpret his observations of people at work.

Maslow proposed that individuals experience a range of needs, and will be motivated to fulfil whichever is most powerful at the time (Maslow, 1970). What he termed lower-order needs are dominant until they are at least partially satisfied. Normal individuals would then turn their attention to satisfying needs at the next level, so that higher-order needs would gradually become dominant. He suggested these needs formed a hierarchy: the middle column of Table 15.1 shows this, while the others indicate how they can be satisfied at work and away from it.

Physiological needs are those that must be satisfied to survive – food and water particularly. Maslow proposed that if all the needs in the hierarchy are unsatisfied then the physiological needs will dominate: people will focus on obtaining the necessities of life.

Once the physiological needs were sufficiently gratified a new set of needs would emerge, which he termed *safety needs* – the search for

> security; stability; dependency; protection; freedom from fear, anxiety and chaos; need for structure, order, law, limits . . . and so on. (Maslow, 1970, p. 39)

People then concentrate on satisfying these to the exclusion of others by seeking a stable, regular job with good working conditions, reasonable pay and other benefits. They resent sudden or random changes in job prospects.

Table 15.1 How Maslow's needs can be satisfied on and off the job

Ways to satisfy on the job	Hierarchy of needs	Ways to satisfy off the job
Opportunities for personal growth, wider challenges	Self-actualisation	Education, hobbies, community activities
Recognition, thanks, more responsibilities	Esteem	Approval of family, friends and community
Relations with fellow workers, customers, supervisors	Belongingness	Acceptance by family, friends, social groups
Safe work, well-designed facilities, job security	Safety	Freedom from violence, disturbance, pollution
Basic salary, warmth	Physiological	Food, oxygen, water

Belongingness needs would follow the satisfaction of safety needs:

[If] both the physiological and the safety needs are fairly well gratified, there will emerge the love and affection and belongingness needs . . . now the person will feel keenly the absence of friends . . . and will hunger for affectionate relations with people in general. (p. 43)

People satisfy them through friends and family, and at work through being accepted into a congenial and trusted team. They may object if new work patterns disrupt such relationships – and welcome change that brings them closer to people they know and like.

Maslow observed that most people have *esteem needs* – self-respect and the respect of others. Self-respect comes from a sense of achievement, competence, adequacy and confidence. People also seek the respect of others – prestige, status, recognition, attention. They satisfy this by taking on challenging tasks to show they are good at their job and can accomplish something worthwhile.

Key ideas   **Research on organisation-based self-esteem**

Pierce and Gardner (2004) reviewed research on organisation-based self-esteem (OBSE) – esteem influenced by a person's experience at work. System-imposed controls through narrow division of labour, rigid hierarchy, centralisation, standardisation and formalisation imply that individuals cannot self-regulate and self-control. Conversely, systems that allowed higher levels of self-expression and personal control were likely to enhance OBSE. They reviewed over 50 studies and concluded that they:

support the claim that an individual's self-esteem, formed around work and organisational experiences, may well play a significant role in shaping employee intrinsic motivation, attitudes . . . and behaviours. (p. 613)

Structures that provide opportunities for self-direction and self-control promote OBSE, as do signals to employees that they 'make a difference around here'. They also noted that

adverse role conditions (such as role ambiguity), anticipated organisational change, job insecurity, discrimination and harassment . . . undermine experiences of self-worth. (p. 613)

Source: Pierce and Gardner (2004).

Maslow used the term *self-actualisation* to refer to the desire for self-fulfilment and for realising potential:

At this level, individual differences are greatest. The clear emergence of these needs usually rests upon some prior satisfaction of the physiological, safety, love, and esteem needs. (pp. 46–7)

People seeking self-actualisation look for work with personal relevance, doing things that matter to them, or which help them discover new talents. Intelligent staff usually want others to recognise their expertise and then leave them alone to get on with their work. They like complexity, challenge and problem solving, and forming networks with like-minded people.

Management in practice   A new manager at a nursing home

Jean Parker was appointed manager of a nursing home for the elderly. Recent reports by the Health Authority and Environmental Health inspectors had been so critical that they threatened to close the home. Jean recalls what she did in the first eight months:

My task was to make sweeping changes, stabilise the workforce and improve the reputation of the home. I had no influence on pay, and low pay was one of the problems. To motivate staff I had to use other methods. Staff facilities were appalling – the dining areas were filthy, showers and some toilets were not working, there were no changing rooms and petty theft was rife. Given the lack of care and respect shown to staff it is little wonder that care given to residents was poor, and staff were demotivated. They turned up to work, carried out tasks and went home. There had been little communication between management and staff. My approach was to work alongside the staff, listen to their grievances, gain their trust and set out an action plan.

The first steps were easy. The staff room was cleaned and decorated, changing rooms and working showers and toilets were provided. Refreshments were provided at meal breaks. Police advice was sought to combat petty theft and lockers were installed in each area. The effect of these changes on staff commitment was astounding. They felt somebody cared for them and listened. In turn, quality of care improved and staff started to take pride in the home, and bring in ornaments and plants to brighten it.

I then started to hold monthly meetings to give management and staff an opportunity to discuss expectations. Policies and procedures were explained. Notice boards displaying 'news and views' were put up. A monthly newsletter to residents and relations was issued. Staff took part enthusiastically in fund-raising activities to pay for outings and entertainment. This gave them the chance to get to know residents in a social setting, and was a break from routine. A training programme was introduced.

Some staff did not respond and tried to undermine my intentions. Persistent unreported absence was quickly followed by disciplinary action. By the end of the year absenteeism was at a more acceptable level, many working problems were alleviated, and the business started to recover.

Source: Private communication and discussions with the manager.

Maslow did *not* claim that the hierarchy was a fixed or rigid scheme. His clinical experience suggested that most people had these needs in about this order, but he had seen exceptions – people for whom self-esteem was more important than love. For others creativity took precedence, seeking self-actualisation even though their basic needs were not satisfied. Others had such low aspirations that they experienced life at a very basic level.

Nor did he claim that as people satisfy one need, another emerges. Rather, that most normal people feel their needs are partially satisfied and partially unsatisfied. A more accurate description of the hierarchy would be in terms of decreasing percentages of satisfaction at successive levels. So a person could think of themselves as being, say, 85 per cent satisfied at the physiological level and 70 per cent at the safety level (the percentages are meaningless). A higher-level need does not emerge suddenly – a person gradually becomes aware of a need they could now attain.

In summary, Maslow believed that people are motivated to satisfy needs that are important to them at that point in their life, and offered a description of them. The strength of a need depends on the extent to which lower needs have been met. Most people seek to satisfy physiological needs first, after which the others become operative. Self-actualisation is fulfilled last and least often, although he had observed exceptions.

How does Maslow's approach compare with Skinner's? Skinner believed that positive reinforcement motivates people to repeat that behaviour, to receive the rewards again. Maslow believed that people would seek to satisfy their needs by acting in a particular way. Both believed that to change behaviour it is necessary to change the situation. Skinner advocated positive reinforcement to satisfy needs after an activity. Maslow implied providing conditions that enable to people to satisfy their needs from the activity.

Activity 15.3   Critical reflection on the theory

- Which of the needs identified by Maslow did Jean Parker's changes at the nursing home help staff to satisfy?
- Do your studies and related activities on your course satisfy needs identified by Maslow?
- What evidence can you gather from your colleagues on the relative importance to them of these needs?

Clayton Alderfer – ERG theory

Doubting the empirical support for the hierarchy of motives proposed by Maslow, Alderfer developed another approach (Alderfer, 1972). He developed and tested his theory by questionnaires and interviews in five organisations – manufacturer, bank, school and two colleges. He identified three primary needs, towards which a person can feel satisfied or frustrated.

Existence needs include the physiological and material desires – hunger and thirst represent deficiencies in existence needs; pay and benefits are ways to meet material needs.

Relatedness needs involve relationships with significant others – family, colleagues, bosses, team members, subordinates, or regular customers. People satisfy relatedness needs by sharing thoughts and feelings in the hope of acceptance, confirmation and understanding.

Growth needs impel a person to be creative or to have an effect on themselves and their surroundings. People satisfy them by engaging with problems that use their existing or new skills: using talents fully brings a sense of completeness.

Figure 15.4 compares Alderfer's formulation of needs with Maslow's. Alderfer proposed that his three categories are active in everyone, although in varying degrees of strength. Unlike Maslow, he found no evidence of a hierarchy of needs, though he did find that if

> **Existence needs** reflect a person's requirement for material and energy.
>
> **Relatedness needs** involve a desire for relationships with significant other people.
>
> **Growth needs** are those that impel people to be creative or to produce an effect on themselves or their environment.

Maslow's categories	Alderfer's categories
Self-actualisation Esteem – self-confirmed	Growth
Love (belongingness) Esteem – interpersonal Safety – interpersonal	Relatedness
Safety – material Physiological	Existence

Figure 15.4
Comparison of the Maslow and Alderfer categories of needs

higher needs are frustrated, lower needs become prominent again, even if they have already been satisfied.

Both theories are hard to test empirically as it is difficult to establish whether a person has satisfied a need. One of the very few empirical tests (Arnolds and Boshoff, 2002) concluded that top managers were primarily motivated by growth needs, while frontline staff were primarily motivated by existence and relatedness needs. There was also some evidence that satisfying growth needs could also increase the motivation of frontline staff, by enhancing their self-esteem.

Case study   Eden – the case continues   www.edenproject.com

Tim Smit on the reasons for Eden:

Of course we have to give people a good day out, a cup of tea they enjoy, and all that. But I think we have actually struck a vein which has got deeper and more important to us as a society, which is people are not just looking for leisure: what many are looking for is a purpose in their lives, and I think the combination of a great day out, with something meaningful, learning about your environment, learning about your relationship with nature, was a killer proposition. That's why I think we get the numbers we do.

The mission of Eden has changed and developed over the years, but I think there's a seed of an idea that's never gone away and that is about how important it is for us as human beings to understand our relationship with nature. We aren't independent of it: we are dependent on it and part of it. So we give visitors a narrative which is about 'let's protect the habitat of the plants we rely on: coffee, tea, sugar, the things we use in our everyday life'. It's about understanding humans' place in nature, understanding that human ingenuity is going to be the thing that provides really good solutions to challenges as well as to some of the poor behaviour.

We think about how we operate, how we do business, and we believe that what you do is really, really important. So the authenticity of the welcome that you get when you come here, the authenticity of how we treat our suppliers, is what I think lies behind the strength of the Eden brand.

Source: Interview with Tim Smit.

Case questions 15.3

- What human needs is Eden seeking to satisfy?
- How attractive do you think you would find Eden if you worked there, and for what reasons?

David McClelland – affiliation, power, achievement

McClelland (1961) and his colleagues identified three categories of human need that individuals possess in different amounts:

- affiliation – to develop and maintain interpersonal relationships;
- power – to have control over one's environment;
- achievement – to set and meet standards of excellence.

McClelland believed that, rather than being arranged in a hierarchy, individuals possess each of these possibly conflicting needs, which motivate their behaviour when activated. McClelland used the Thematic Apperception Test to assess how significant these categories were to people. The research team showed people pictures with a neutral subject and asked them to write a story about it. The researchers coded the stories and claimed these indicated the relative importance to the person of the affiliation, power and achievement motives.

You can assess your scores on these motives by completing Activity 15.4.

> ## Activity 15.4   Assessing your needs
>
> - From each of the four sets of statements below, choose the one that is most like you:
>   1. (a) I set myself difficult goals, which I attempt to reach.
>   (b) I am happiest when I am with a group of people who enjoy life.
>   (c) I like to organise the activities of a group or team.
>   2. (a) I only completely enjoy relaxation after the successful completion of exacting pieces of work.
>   (b) I become attached to my friends.
>   (c) I argue zealously against others for my point of view.
>   3. (a) I work hard until I am completely satisfied with the result I achieve.
>   (b) I like to mix with a group of congenial people, talking about any subject that comes up.
>   (c) I tend to influence others more than they influence me.
>   4. (a) I enjoy working as much as I enjoy my leisure.
>   (b) I go out of my way to be with my friends.
>   (c) I am able to dominate a social situation.
>
> Now add your responses as follows:
>
> - The number of (a) responses ( ) Achievement
> - The number of (b) responses ( ) Affiliation
> - The number of (c) responses ( ) Power
>
> This exercise will give you an insight into McClelland's three types of motive and into your preference – indicated by the area with the largest score.
> Compare your answers with others in your class. Discuss whether the results are in line with what you would have expected, given what you already know of each other.

Frederick Herzberg – two-factor theory

While Maslow and McClelland focused on individual differences in motivation, Herzberg (1959) related motivation to the nature of a person's work. He developed his theory from interviews with 200 engineers and accountants about their experience of work. The researchers asked them to recall a time when they had felt exceptionally good about their job, and then the events preceding those feelings. The researchers then asked respondents to recall a time when they had felt particularly bad about work, and the background to that. Analysis showed that when respondents recalled good times they frequently mentioned one or more of:

- achievement;
- recognition;
- work itself;
- responsibility;
- advancement.

They mentioned these much less frequently when describing the bad times. When talking about the bad times they most frequently recalled these factors:

- company policy and administration;
- supervision;
- salary;
- interpersonal relations;
- working conditions.

Motivator factors are those aspects of the work itself that Herzberg found influenced people to superior performance and effort.

Hygiene (or maintenance) factors are those aspects surrounding the task that can prevent discontent and dissatisfaction but will not in themselves contribute to psychological growth and hence motivation.

They mentioned these much less frequently when describing the good times.

Herzberg concluded that factors associated with satisfaction describe people's relationship to what they were doing – the nature of the task, the responsibility or recognition. He named these '**motivator factors**', as they seemed to influence people to put on more effort. The factors associated with dissatisfaction described conditions surrounding the work – such as supervision or company policy. He named these '**hygiene**' or ('**maintenance**') **factors** as they served mainly to prevent dissatisfaction, not to encourage performance. Figure 15.5 illustrates the results.

Herzberg concluded that satisfaction comes from within, through doing a task that brings a sense of achievement, recognition or of other motivator factors. Managers cannot require motivation, though they can destroy it by some thoughtless act. Herzberg (1968) wrote about what he termed 'Kick in the Ass' management:

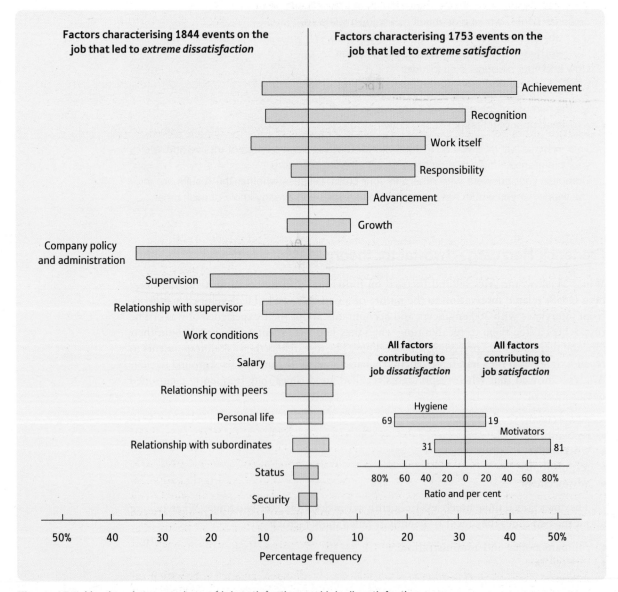

Figure 15.5 Herzberg's comparison of job satisfaction and job dissatisfaction scores

If I kick my dog . . . he will move. And when I want him to move again what must I do? I must kick him again. Similarly, I can change a person's battery, and then recharge it, and recharge it again. But it is only when one has a generator of one's own that we can talk about motivation. One then needs no outside stimulation. One wants to do it.(p. 55)

| Management in practice | Gamma Chemical (part 1) – a focus on hygiene factors |

Gamma Chemical purchased another chemical company that had recently failed, and re-employed 30 of the 40 employees. While there was no overt dissatisfaction, management found it hard to motivate staff. They showed no initiative or creativity, and no commitment to the new company or its goals. Yet the company had:

- increased the salaries of the re-employed staff;
- improved working conditions and provided better equipment;
- placed people in positions of equal status to their previous jobs;
- operated an 'Open Door' policy, with supervisors easily approachable;
- offered security of employment and a no-redundancy policy.

Other aspects of practice included:

- no structured training or development programmes;
- the small unit restricted opportunities for career advancement;
- people had little responsibility as management made decisions;
- there was no clear connection between individual work and company performance.

Source: Private communication and discussions with the manager.

| Activity 15.5 | Critical reflection on Herzberg's theory |

- Comment on Gamma Chemical's assumptions about motivating the re-engaged staff.
- Evaluate the empirical base of Herzberg's research. What reservations do you have about the wider applicability of the theory?
- Gather evidence of other changes in working practice, and decide whether it supports or contradicts Herzberg's theory.

Herzberg believed that motivation depends on whether a job is intrinsically challenging and provides opportunities for recognition. He linked motivation with ideas about job design, and especially the motivational effects of job enrichment. Evidence that is partly consistent with Herzberg's work comes from Sauermann and Cohen (2010), who gathered data from 1,700 PhD-level scientists and engineers on motivational factors and performance (as measured by the number of recent patent applications in which they were named as inventor). The authors found a strong and robust relationship between individuals' desires for income, independence and intellectual challenge and the number of patent applications. Those motivated by jobs with security or responsibility were not so productive.

There are many examples where management has redesigned people's jobs with positive effects. Few, if any, of these experiments were the result of knowing about Herzberg's theory, but their effects are often consistent with its predictions. Section 15.6 has more on this.

| Key ideas | Douglas McGregor Theory X and Theory Y |

Douglas McGregor had a significant influence on our understanding of how the assumptions managers make influence their practice. He distinguished the assumptions of what he called Theory X from those of Theory Y.
Theory X assumptions:

- The average human being has an inherent dislike of work, and will avoid it if at all possible.
- People must therefore be coerced, controlled and directed to get them to put in adequate effort.
- The average human being wishes to avoid responsibility, has little ambition and favours security above all else.

Theory Y assumptions:

- The expenditure of physical and mental effort in work is as natural as play or rest.
- People will exercise self-control and self-direction towards goals to which they are committed.
- The average human being learns to accept responsibility.
- Imagination, ingenuity and creativity are widely, not narrowly, spread in the population.

Significantly different management practices follow from Theory X and Theory Y assumptions.

Source: McGregor (1960).

| 15.5 | Process theories of motivation |

Process theories try to explain why people choose one course of action to satisfy a need rather than another. A person who needs a higher income could satisfy it by, say, moving to another company, applying for promotion or investing in training. What factors will influence their choice?

 ## Expectancy theory

Expectancy theory
states that motivation depends on a person's belief in the probability that effort will lead to good performance, and that good performance will lead to them receiving an outcome they value (valence).

Vroom (1964) tried to answer that question with what he termed the **expectancy theory** of motivation. It focuses on the thinking processes people use to achieve rewards. Stuart Roberts is studying a degree course in Chemistry and has to submit a last assignment. He wants an A for the course, and so far has an average of B+. His motivation to put effort into the assignment will be affected by (a) his expectation that hard work will produce a good piece of work, and (b) his expectation that it will receive a grade of at least an A. If he believes he cannot do a good job, or that the grading system is unclear, his motivation will be low.

The theory assumes that individuals:

- have different needs and so value outcomes differently;
- make conscious choices about their actions;
- choose the action most likely to achieve an outcome they value.

Subjective probability
(in expectancy theory)
is a person's estimate of the likelihood that a certain level of effort (E) will produce a level of performance (P) that will then lead to an expected outcome (O).

There are three components in the theory. First, the person's expectation (or **subjective probability**) that effort (E) will result in some level of performance (P):

$$(E \rightarrow P)$$

This will be affected by how clear they are about their role and the training and support available. If Stuart Roberts understands what the assignment requires and is confident in his ability to do a good job, his $(E \rightarrow P)$ expectancy will be high.

Second, the person's expectation that performance will be **instrumental** in leading to an outcome (O):

$$(P \rightarrow O)$$

How confident is the person that achieving the target will produce the reward? This depends on how clear the appraisal and reward systems are, and their experience of them. A clear grading system, which Stuart understands and knows that staff apply consistently, will mean he has a high $(P \rightarrow O)$ expectancy. If he has found the system unpredictable this expectancy would be low.

The third component is the **valence or value (V)** that the individual attaches to a particular outcome.

This term is the power of the outcome to motivate that individual – how keen Stuart is to get a good degree. So the value of V varies between individuals, reflecting their unique pattern of motivational needs (as suggested by the content theories). Someone who values money and achievement would place a high valence on an outcome that was a promotion to a distant head office. He or she would try to work in a way that led to that. Such an outcome would be less welcome (have a much lower valence) to a manager who values an established pattern of relationships or quality of life in the present location.

In summary:

$$F = (E \rightarrow P) \times (P \rightarrow O) \times V$$

in which F represents the force exerted, or degree of motivation a person has towards an activity. Expectations reflect their personality and their experience of organisational practices, as shown in Figure 15.6.

Using the multiplication sign in the equation signifies that both beliefs influence motivation. If a person believes that however hard they try they will be unable to perform well, they will not be motivated to do so (so $E \rightarrow P = 0$). The same applies for $(P \rightarrow O)$. A low score in either part of the equation, or in V, will lead to low effort, regardless of beliefs about the other part.

A criticism of the theory is that it implies a high level of rational calculation, as people weigh the probabilities of various courses of action. It also implies that managers estimate what each employee values, and try to ensure that motivational practices meet them. Neither calculation is likely to be made that rationally, which may diminish the model's practical value.

However, it is useful in recognising that people vary in their beliefs (or probabilities) about the components in the equation. It shows that managers can affect these beliefs by redesigning the factors in Figure 15.6. If people are unclear about their role, or receive weak feedback, the theory predicts that this will reduce their motivation.

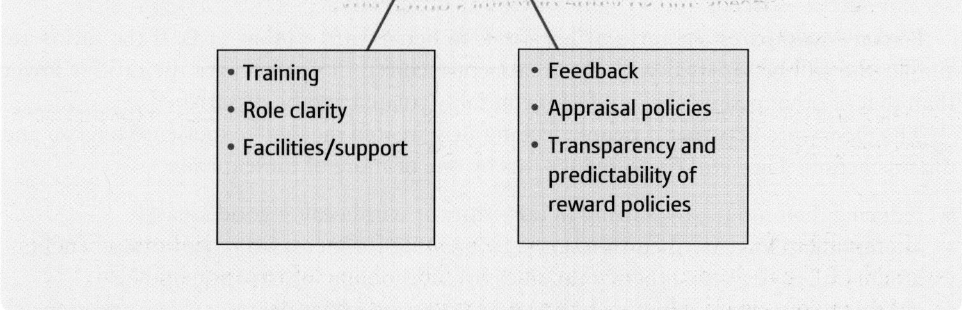

Instrumentality is the perceived probability that good performance will lead to valued rewards, measured on a scale from 0 (no chance) to 1 (certainty).

Valence is the perceived value or preference that an individual has for a particular outcome.

$$F = (E \rightarrow P) \times (P \rightarrow O) \times V$$

- Training
- Role clarity
- Facilities/support

- Feedback
- Appraisal policies
- Transparency and predictability of reward policies

Figure 15.6 Organisational practices affecting subjective probabilities

Management in practice   **Employee ownership at Child Base Nurseries**
www.childbasepartnerships.com

Mike Thompson established Child Base Nurseries in 1989, and the company now operates (in early 2016) 450 nurseries in the Midlands and South of England. Being a network helps staff development, as the nursery nurses can move up a career change – the company's operations director began as a nursery worker. The company is privately owned by the employees, who can buy shares from the Thompson family holding – which is now down to about 28 per cent. The family can only sell their shares to the Employee Benefit Trust, which administers the share scheme. The company's legal rules make it clear that Child Base is established for the benefit of employees – past, present and future. In 2015 it was recognised as one of the *Sunday Times* '100 Best Companies to work for'.

Mr Thompson believes strongly in the principle of employee ownership – he could have made more money by selling his shares in the business to external investors. He says:

You get where you are in business because of other people. Why not put the business back in the hands of the people who helped build it?

Source: *Financial Times*, 22 April 2009.

The theory predicts that managers can influence motivation by these practices:

- establishing the rewards people value;
- identifying and communicating performance requirements;
- ensuring that reasonable effort can meet those requirements;
- supporting the person's effort;
- ensuring a clear link between performance and reward;
- providing feedback to staff on their performance.

It also links insights from the content theories of motivation with organisational practice.

J. Stacey Adams – equity theory

Equity theory argues that perception of unfairness leads to tension, which then motivates the individual to resolve that unfairness.

Equity theory is associated with J. Stacey Adams (a behavioural scientist working at the General Electric Company) who published (Adams, 1963) the idea that fairness in comparison with others influences motivation. People like to be treated fairly and compare what they put into a job (effort, skill, knowledge, etc.) with the rewards they receive (pay, recognition, satisfaction, etc.). They express this as a ratio of their input to their reward. They also compare their ratio with the input-to-reward ratio of others whom they consider their equals. They expect management to reward others in the same way, so expect the ratios to be roughly equal. The formula below sums up the comparison:

$$\frac{\text{Input (A)}}{\text{Reward (A)}} : \frac{\text{Input (B)}}{\text{Reward (B)}}$$

Person A compares the ratio of her input to her reward to that of B. If the ratios are similar she will be satisfied with the treatment received. If she believes the ratio is lower than that of other people she will feel inequitably treated and be dissatisfied.

The theory predicts that if people feel unfairly treated they will experience tension and dissatisfaction. They will try to reduce this by one or more of these means:

- reducing their inputs, by putting in less effort or withholding good ideas;
- attempting to increase their outcomes, by pressing for increased pay or other benefits;
- attempting to decrease others' outcomes by withholding information and help;
- changing their comparison, by basing it on someone where inequity is less pronounced;
- increasing their evaluation of the other person's output so the ratios are in balance.

As individuals differ, so will their way of reducing inequity. Some will try to rationalise the situation, suggesting that their efforts were greater or lesser than they originally thought them to be, or that the rewards are reasonable. For example, a person denied a promotion may decide that the previously desired job would not have been a good move after all. Members may put pressure on other members of the team whom they feel are not pulling their weight.

Case study   Eden – the case continues   www.edenproject.com
Tim Smit on work at Eden:

To work at Eden you've got to be interested in a lot of stuff. You've got to be prepared to catch people when they fall, because people are trying stuff all the time, and you've got to be prepared for the unexpected because part of the way we work is almost deliberately create chaos by doing more stuff than we've possibly got time to do, which means more junior members have more chance to become leaders because the senior ones can't do it all.

One of the things I think is very special about Eden is that the letters after your name don't make any difference. It's what you can do . . . Sure the Finance Director's got to be an accountant and all that sort of stuff, but in the wider scheme of things, to be an Eden person you've got to be optimistic and smiley and damned hard working.

Gayle Conley adds:

We try not to be prescriptive about defining talent and we try to encourage people to take individual responsibility for their own career path here as much as we can help them to a career path.

Jess Ratty speaks about her work:

I began at Eden as a waitress when I was 16 years old with no qualifications: I'm now 24 and the Press Officer. So I've worked in about eight departments and worked my way up through the company. I think Eden's been a fantastic opportunity for me – the ethos and the way you don't have to have a degree – you know they'll give people a chance . . . after working as a waitress I moved to the Stewards team where I learnt a lot about dealing with people. I worked in plant sales, learning a lot about different plants, which was great to learn at 18. Then I worked in retail, the product side of things, and was then picked up by the design team . . . and after a few more jobs one of the managers said 'do you want to go for the job of communications assistant?' And I thought, 'people actually believe in me, they want me to do a job they think I'll be good at!'

Sources: Interviews with the staff members.

Case questions 15.4

- Consider how the company has helped to generate positive attitudes among members of staff.

- Analyse these accounts using Herzberg's theory – which of his 'motivating factors' do staff refer to?

Clearly the focus and the components of the comparisons are highly subjective, although the theory has an intuitive appeal. The subjective nature of the comparison makes it difficult to test empirically, and there has been little formal research on the theory in recent years (though see Mowday and Colwell, 2003). There is, however, abundant anecdotal evidence that people compare their effort/reward ratio with that of other people or groups.

Locke and Latham – goal-setting theory

The best-known advocates of **goal-setting theory** are Locke and Latham (Locke, 1968; Locke and Latham, 1990, 2002), and the theory has four main propositions:

Goal-setting theory argues that motivation is influenced by goal difficulty, goal specificity and knowledge of results.

1 **Challenging goals** lead to higher levels of performance than easy goals. Difficult goals are sometimes called 'stretch' goals because they encourage effort, to stretch ourselves.

Beyond a point this effect fades – if people see a goal as being impossible, their motivation declines.

2 **Specific goals** lead to higher levels of performance than vague goals. We find it easier to adjust behaviour when we know exactly what the objective is, and what others expect us to do.

3 **Participation** in goal setting can improve commitment to those goals, since people have a sense of ownership and are motivated to achieve them. If management explains and justifies the goals, without inviting participation, that can also increase motivation.

4 **Knowledge of results** of past performance – receiving feedback – is necessary to motivation. It is motivational in itself, and contains information that may help people attain the goals. Seijts and Latham (2012) advocate that managers should set learning goals as well as task goals, to help staff develop.

An attraction of goal-setting theory is the directness of the practical implications, including:

- **Goal difficulty**: set goals that are hard enough to stretch employees, but not impossible.
- **Goal specificity**: set goals in clear, precise and, if possible, quantifiable terms.
- **Participation**: allow employees to take part in setting goals, to increase ownership and commitment.
- **Acceptance**: if goals are set by management, ensure they explain and justify them.
- **Feedback**: provide information on performance to encourage employees to adjust.

Individual and contextual variables moderate the relationship between goal difficulty and performance. A confident person with a high need for achievement will respond more positively to a challenging goal than someone with less confidence or a lower need for achievement. The degree of perceived organisational support will also affect how people respond – as does the degree of trust that staff have in their manager: see Crossley et al. (2013).

While challenging goals often lead to higher performance, tying pay to pre-set targets for sales and profit can lead to poor and/or fraudulent behaviour. This can include booking sales that have not been made, gaining sales by heavy price-cutting that means the business loses money, or persuading customers to make investments that are against their interests.

| 15.6 | Designing work to be motivating |

Extrinsic rewards are valued outcomes or benefits provided by others, such as promotion, a pay increase or a bigger car.

Intrinsic rewards are valued outcomes or benefits that come from the individual, such as feelings of satisfaction, achievement and competence.

People value both **extrinsic** and **intrinsic rewards**. Extrinsic rewards are those that are separate from the task, such as pay, security and promotion. Intrinsic rewards are those that people receive as they do the task itself – using skills, sensing achievement, doing satisfying work. Recall that a central element in scientific management was the careful design of the 'one best way' of doing a piece of manual work. Experts analysed how people did the job and identified the most efficient method, usually breaking the job into many small parts. Such work provided few, if any, intrinsic rewards – and Taylor's system concentrated on providing clear extrinsic rewards.

Fragmented work is boring to many people, who become dissatisfied, careless and frequently absent. The ideas from Maslow, Herzberg and McGregor prompted attempts to enable people to satisfy higher-level needs at work, on the assumption that they would work more productively if they could experience intrinsic rewards (motivators in Herzberg's terms) as well as extrinsic ones (Herzberg's hygiene factors). Many refer to this as 'job enrichment'.

Job characteristics theory

Hackman and Oldham (1980) built on these ideas to develop and test empirically an approach to the design of work that focused on characteristics of employees' jobs. Their aim was to build into jobs the attributes that offer intrinsic motivation, and so encourage effort. **Job characteristics theory** predicts that the design of a job will affect internal motivation and work outcomes, with the effects being mediated by individual and contextual factors. Figure 15.7 shows the model, with the addition of implementing concepts in the left-hand column. The model provides guidance on how to design enriched jobs that satisfy employees' higher-level needs.

> **Job characteristics theory** predicts that the design of a job will affect internal motivation and work outcomes, with the effects being mediated by individual and contextual factors.

The model identifies three psychological states that must be present to achieve high motivation. If any are low, motivation will be low. The three states are:

- **Experienced meaningfulness**: the degree to which employees perceive their work as valuable and worthwhile. If workers regard a job as trivial and pointless, their motivation will be low.
- **Experienced responsibility:** how responsible people feel for the quantity and quality of work performed.
- **Knowledge of results**: the amount of feedback employees receive about how well they are doing. Those who do not receive feedback will care less about the quality of their performance.

Management in practice   Enriching the work of a software engineer

A skilled software engineer found that others were expecting him to help them out on too many routine tasks, and this was preventing him from developing new skills – so he became disengaged from the work he enjoyed. He discussed the problem with his manager, who responded effectively in that he:

- made the engineer responsible for two junior engineers who could share the load;
- assigned him to visit customers (previously done by a customer engineer);
- authorised him to plan how to meet customers' needs.

The engineer said:

After these changes, I experienced total fulfilment. I was aware of the customers' problems. And by contacting them directly I knew what they needed. I also saw directly how our solutions helped them.

Source: Private communication from the engineer.

These psychological states are influenced by five *job characteristics*:

- **Skill variety**: the extent to which a job uses a range of skills and experience.
- **Task identity:** whether a job involves a complete operation, with a clear beginning and end.
- **Task significance:** how much the job matters to colleagues and/or the wider society.
- **Autonomy:** how much freedom a person has in deciding how to do the work.
- **Feedback:** the extent to which a person receives feedback.

The extent to which a job contains these elements can be calculated using a tested instrument, and then the scores used to calculate the motivating potential score. Figure 15.7 presents the model schematically.

The model also shows how to increase the motivating potential of a job, by using one or more of five 'implementing concepts':

- **Combine tasks:** Rather than divide work, staff can combine tasks to use their skills and complete more of the whole task. An order clerk could receive orders from a customer and arrange transport and invoicing instead of other people doing this.
- **Form natural workgroups:** Instead of a product passing down an assembly line with each worker performing one operation, a group may share the tasks to assemble the whole product.

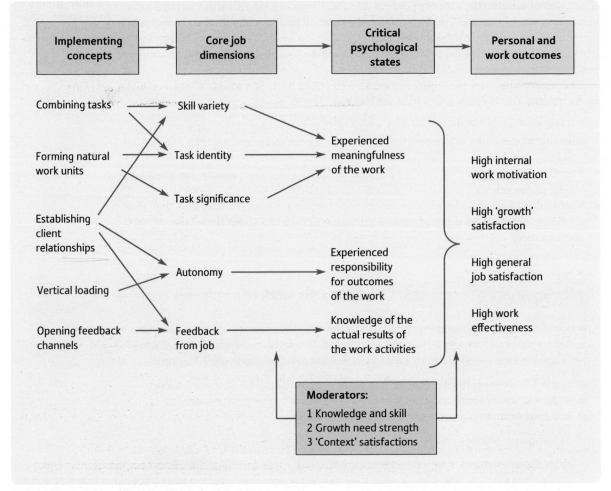

Figure 15.7 The job characteristics model
Source: Adapted from Hackman and Oldham (1980).

- **Establish customer relations:** Instead of doing part of the job for all customers, staff look after all the requirements of some customers, with whom they build closer relationships.
- **Vertical loading:** Operators could take responsibility for checking the quantity and quality of incoming materials and reporting any problems.
- **Open feedback channels:** Staff could attend meetings at which customers explain their requirements, and how earlier work has, or has not, met these.

Finally, the Hackman–Oldham model specifies three moderating influences:

- **Knowledge and skill** – a person's ability to do the work.
- **Growth-need strength** – the extent to which an individual desires personal challenges, accomplishment and learning on the job.
- **'Context' satisfaction** – pay and other conditions.

Key ideas   Meaningful work leads to positive outcomes

Many research teams have used the job characteristics model to test empirically the effects of the variables on work outcomes. Humphrey et al. (2007) conducted a meta-analysis of 259 such studies, doing so in a way that enabled them both to test the validity of the model, and to extend it.

They found that the five motivational characteristics shown in Figure 15.7 were positively related to job satisfaction, growth satisfaction, internal work motivation and positive job performance, and were negatively related to absenteeism. They also found that experienced meaningfulness was a particularly significant mediating factor – if people feel that their work is valuable, this has a positive effect on their motivation.

The team extended the original model by showing that social factors (such as support and opportunities for interaction outside the organisation) and work context factors (physical demands and working conditions) also affected outcomes, alongside the characteristics of the work itself.

Source: Humphrey et al. (2007).

Many managers, such as those at Gamma Chemical (see 'Management in practice'), have changed the kind of work they expect employees to do. This has not usually been to provide more interesting jobs, but in response to business conditions. Nevertheless, such changes often support what the theory predicts. This was also supported by quantitative analysis by Wood et al. (2012) of data from the UK's Work Employment Relations Survey 2004, which found that

enriched job design had significantly positive effects on financial performance, productivity [and] quality. [It also had a significant negative effect on absenteeism]. (p. 435)

Management in practice	Gamma Chemical (Part 2) – a focus on motivating factors

After taking control, Gamma Chemical made these changes to working arrangements:

- introduced a cross-training programme to improve job diversity and individual growth;
- created problem-solving teams from natural work units to give operators a sense of ownership and achievement;
- expected operators to make more decisions, increasing individual authority and accountability;
- introduced an appraisal system that shows operators how their function affects company performance.

Management believed these changes had resulted in 20 per cent more output and 50 per cent less wastage.

Source: Private communication and discussions with the manager.

15.7 Motivating by flexible and high-performance work practices

Lawler (2008) shows how organisations can gain strategic advantages by the way they organise their employees (their 'human capital'). Two broad sets of practices that organisations use are flexible working and high-performance work systems.

Flexible work practices

Most organisations operate some form of workplace flexibility. Whyman et al. (2015) distinguish three forms of flexibility:

- **Numerical**: adjusting the number of employees or their working hours through practices such as part-time working, overtime, shifts, job sharing, or zero-hours contracts.
- **Functional**: adjusting the content of people's jobs, or how they are expected to perform them, through practices such as autonomy, team working, training and job enrichment.
- **Cost**: managers begin adjusting pay so that part of it is related to performance over a period, usually by paying a bonus if this meets the performance targets.

All such schemes will have unique and specific intentions, but common ones are to improve employees' work–life balance and enhance job satisfaction or commitment. These in turn may bring benefits to the organisation through, among other things, lower turnover and higher productivity.

High-performance work practices

High-performance work practices (HPWP) refer to systems in which a bundle of practices (including one or more forms of flexible working) are integrated to encourage employees to identify with organisational goals, and to encourage them to meet those goals. These include:

High-performance work practices (HPWP) refer to systems in which a bundle of practices are integrated to encourage employees to identify with organisational goals, and to encourage them to meet those goals.

- enhancing employment security;
- selective recruitment;
- new reward packages, usually increasing wages;
- better communication on plans and performance;
- participation of employees in decisions;
- more team work, often with considerable autonomy; and
- training and skill development.

These are not widely introduced as free-standing policies, but as parts of an integrated system, in which each is expected to support and strengthen the effects of the others. innocent drinks (Chapter 2) and BMW (Chapter 11) show what is possible – as does the 'Management in practice' feature.

Management in practice	Managing nurses at Western General Hospital

A nurse manager at the Western General Hospital in a large city commented on managing the staff:

The service has been trying to be more responsive to the needs of patients by delegating power and responsibility to local level. Nurses have recognised the benefits to patients if they work by patient allocation rather than by task allocation. This has developed into the 'named nurse' concept, which incorporates four of the five core dimensions of the job characteristics model. The nurse assesses needs, plans, implements and evaluates the care of their patients – offering skill variety, task identity, task significance and autonomy. Perhaps even the feedback element is provided from the evaluation stage of each patient's care.

The recently appointed nurse managers are enthusiastic, and this has filtered down to staff. They are gradually becoming aware of the move from Theory X to Theory Y style of management. They appreciate that at last their skills and experience are being recognised and used.

Information flows more freely and openly. Decisions are made only after discussion with the staff who will be affected by the outcome. Nurses in the wards are aware of their allocated budgets and what they are spending. Recruitment of staff is now done by existing staff, where previously managers decided whom to appoint.

Source: Private communication from a senior nurse in the hospital.

The evidence of the effects of HPWPs varies – though Combs (2006) found a positive relationship between HPWP and performance. This is supported by a longitudinal study by Tregaskis et al. (2013) in a large UK engineering business, in which a comprehensive programme of HPWP was introduced to enhance performance. Interviews and objective measures showed that staff regarded the changes as positive (though there was some evidence of greater stress), and that productivity and safety had improved.

> ### 15.8   Integrating themes

Entrepreneurship

Barringer and Ireland (2010) identify three motivations for entrepreneurs setting up their business – to be independent, to pursue an idea and to make money.

- **Independence:** Many who start their business do so having become frustrated with working for someone else. Perhaps a strong need for achievement, or for esteem, motivates them to follow a course of action that, despite the risks (or perhaps because of them), will enable them to satisfy those needs. Some feel constrained in another organisation from doing work of the quality or scale they think is possible, and going into business on their own is a way to achieve this.
- **Pursue an idea:** People who are naturally alert and aware of what is happening around them readily see ideas for new products and services, and have an urge to implement these ideas, rather than talk about them. Someone with an idea in an established business may be able to persuade them to take it on – but established businesses are often surprisingly resistant to new ideas. In this case an innovator's idea will remain unfulfilled – so a proportion of them take the risk of creating a new venture to put their idea into practice.
- **Make money:** A third reason to start a new business is the prospect of making money – which in some areas of business is clearly substantial. This motivation is often secondary to the other two – good to have as a result of the effort, but not the underlying driver. This is best seen in consumer electronics, where a succession of successful entrepreneurs have maintained that while they value the financial rewards they were more focused on satisfying customers with superior products or services – confident that if they did that, the financial rewards would follow.

Sustainability

Organisations in many sectors of the economy now include measures of sustainable performance as part of their strategy, and depend on their staff to achieve them. To what extent are staff motivated to do so?

Lawler (2008) believes that a characteristic of high-performing organisations is that they ensure their strategy is practical by involving people from all parts of the business in the process of formulating it. This enables them to take account of many perspectives and sources of information, not only about the external environment and the customers, but about the ability of the organisation to deliver the strategy. Equally, the reward system will align personal rewards with the strategy by, for example, rewarding people for their contribution to sustainability. The 'Management in practice' feature gives an example.

> ### Management in practice   Bonuses depend on sustainability   www.dsm.com
>
> The Dutch life sciences company DSM has begun linking top management pay to targets such as the reduction of greenhouse gas emissions, energy use and the introduction of environmentally friendly products. Feike Sijbesma, Chief Executive, said DSM would focus on the triple bottom line – people, profits and planet:
>
> **Sustainability is the key driver of our whole strategy. Pay is the ultimate expression of your values.**
>
> Half of DSM's short-term bonus will be determined by the number of environmentally friendly products it introduces and whether it reduces energy consumption. The other half will be determined by financial targets such as sales and cash flow.
>
> Source: *Financial Times*, 24 February 2010.

Internationalisation

The growing significance of managing internationally sits uncomfortably with the fact that the theories outlined were developed in the United States. Do they apply to people working in other countries? Hofstede (1989) articulated the 'unspoken cultural assumptions' present in Douglas McGregor's Theory X and Theory Y:

> . . . in a comparative study of US values versus those dominant in ASEAN countries, I found the following common assumptions on the US side and underlying both X and Y:
>
> 1 Work is good for people.
> 2 People's capacities should be maximally utilised.
> 3 There are 'organisational objectives' that exist apart from people.
> 4 People in organisations behave as unattached individuals.
>
> These assumptions reflect value positions in McGregor's US society; most would be accepted in other western countries. None of them, however, applies in ASEAN countries. Southeast Asian assumptions would be:
>
> 1 Work is a necessity but not a goal in itself.
> 2 People should find their rightful place in peace and harmony with their environment.
> 3 Absolute objectives exist only with God. In the world, persons in authority positions represent God so their objectives should be followed.
> 4 People behave as members of a family and/or group. Those who do not are rejected by society.
>
> Because of these different culturally determined assumptions, McGregor's Theory X and Theory Y distinction becomes irrelevant in Southeast Asia. (p. 5)

Hofstede's work in Chapter 4 showed marked differences in national cultures. These are likely to influence the relative importance that people in those countries attach to the various motivational factors. People in Anglo-Saxon countries tend to display a relatively high need for achievement, strong masculinity scores and low uncertainty avoidance. This is not the norm in other cultures.

Governance

One controversial theme in the corporate governance debate is that of executive pay – where large salaries and bonuses paid to executives, even those in failing firms, has been the target of public and political criticism. Shareholders, too, have been active in some high-profile cases, trying to reduce or eliminate what they see as excessive payments to senior managers.

Boards face the need to attract and retain qualified and experienced staff, yet need to find ways to structure incentives so that they discourage short-term or risky behaviour by senior managers, and instead support long-term returns to shareholders. These moves may also forestall public pressure for stricter legislation limiting base pay, bonuses and other executive benefits.

Setting realistic goals for performance-based plans is difficult in uncertain economic times, making it harder to set profitability and growth targets in business plans, which are the basis of compensation plans. Compensation committees are being asked to approve a wider range of targets, which are moving from traditional measures such as revenue growth and earnings per share to ones based on the growth of working capital and cash flow. These changes aim to align variable pay with business strategy, and especially to encourage participants to take a long-term perspective.

Summary

1 **Explain why managers need to understand and use theories of motivation**

- People depend on others within and beyond the organisation to act in a particular way, and understanding what motivates them is critical to this. Motivation includes understanding the goals that people pursue (content), the choices they make to secure them (process) and how this knowledge can be applied to influence others (including through work design).

2 **Show how the context, including the psychological contract, affects motivation**

- Social changes affect the people managers try to motivate, so they may need to adapt their approach to suit.
- The relationship between employer and employee is expressed in the psychological contract, which needs to be in acceptable balance for effective performance.

3 **Understand behaviour modification and content and process theories of motivation**

- Behaviour modification attempts to explain how people can influence the behaviour of others by using appropriate and timely reinforcement.
- Content theories seek to understand the needs that human beings may seek to satisfy at work, and include the work of Maslow, Alderfer and Herzberg as well as of earlier observers such as Taylor and Mayo.
- Expectancy theory explains motivation in terms of valued outcomes and the subjective probability of achieving those outcomes.
- Equity theory explains motivation in terms of perceptions of fairness by comparison with others.
- Goal-setting theory believes that motivation depends on the degree of difficulty and specificity of goals.

4 **Use work design theories to diagnose motivational problems and recommend actions**

- People are only motivated if the job meets a need that they value – providing appropriate content factors leads to satisfaction and performance.
- Herzberg suggests that motivation depends on paying attention to motivating as well as hygiene factors.
- Jobs can be enriched by increasing skill variety, task identity, task significance, autonomy and feedback.

5 **Describe some strategically-useful practices, such as flexible working and high-performance work systems**

- Lawler (2008) shows how the workforce can be a source of strategic advantage, and that successful companies attribute this to practices, such as flexible working and high-performance work systems, which build on theories of motivation.

6 **Show how you can use ideas from the chapter to understand how to develop the skill of designing a job that is motivating**

- Evidence is accumulating that jobs consistent with work design theories can satisfy human and financial criteria, so the 'Develop a skill' feature is an opportunity to practise designing a motivating job.

7 **Show how ideas from the chapter add to your understanding of the integrating themes**

- Entrepreneurs are believed to be motivated by factors including a desire for independence, to put ideas into practice and financial reward, as well as being a way of expressing their self-identity.
- Like any strategy, that of building a more environmentally sustainable performance depends on people working with commitment to achieve it. Whether they do so will

depend on aligning their motivation with that of the sustainability goal – the section includes examples of how some organisations try to achieve this.

● Hofstede notes that discussion about McGregor's Theory X and Theory Y is based on observations in Western societies – which are unlikely to apply in emergent economic powers.

● Using spectacular levels of pay and bonus to motivate skilled (and highly mobile) professional staff has attracted criticism from many outside the industries concerned. A job for governance is to balance those views against those who believe that in a market economy they need to pay the market rate.

Test your understanding

1 Outline the basic assumptions of McGregor's Theory X and Theory Y.

2 Describe the psychological contract. What are you expecting (a) from an employer in your career and (b) from an employer who provides you with part-time work while you are studying?

3 Which three things are pinpointed when using behaviour modification?

4 How does Maslow's theory of human needs relate to the ideas of Frederick Taylor?

5 How does Alderfer's theory differ from Maslow's? What research lay behind the two theories?

6 What was your score on the McClelland test? How did that compare with others' scores?

7 Explain the difference between Herzberg's hygiene and motivating factors.

8 Explain the difference between E–P and P–O in expectancy theory.

9 What are the five job design elements that may affect a person's satisfaction with their work?

10 Give an example of an implementing concept associated with each element.

11 Summarise an idea from the chapter that adds to your understanding of the integrating themes.

Think critically

Think about the ways in which you typically seek to motivate other people (staff, colleagues or those in other organisations) and about your organisation's approach to motivation. Then record your answers to these questions:

● Thinking of the people you typically work with, who are effective and who are less effective motivators? What do the effective people do that enables them to motivate others? Do they seem to take a mainly Theory X or mainly Theory Y approach? Do their **assumptions** seem to be broadly correct, or not?

● What factors in the **context,** such as the history of the company or your experience, have shaped the way you motivate others, and your organisation's approach to motivation? Are jobs consciously designed to be motivating?

● Have people put forward **alternative** approaches to motivating, based on evidence about other companies, especially regarding the way jobs are designed?

● What **limitations** can you identify in any of these motivational theories? For example, might they be equally suitable in hi-tech and low-tech working environments?

Develop a skill – design a motivating job

Being able to shape the nature of someone's job (in quite small, day-to-day activities) can help to motivate the person, and so improve your work as well.

- **Assessment:** Assess how much consideration you give to adjusting the elements of a person's job – which can happen as you and some friends design an outing together, when planning a charity event, or perhaps in your part-time job. Do you think deliberately about the job, or do you just leave it to them, or follow the way it has always been done?

- **Learning:** Section 15.6 and Section 15.7 introduced ideas on designing jobs to be motivating. Read those sections again, paying special attention to the 'Management in practice' feature (p. 498), which shows how a nurse manager in a hospital was able to relate recent changes to these theories. Summarise the ideas in these sections. Why is paying attention to practices such as combining tasks or forming natural work units likely to enhance motivation?

- **Analysis:** Do you or people you know have experience of working at a boring or, alternatively, satisfying job? Can you identify what factors in the job caused that? From what you now know, what opportunities were there to have made a boring job more satisfying? What, if anything, prevented that?

- **Practice:** Think about your current job, or a recent one. Describe it using the five core job dimensions. If you cannot describe a job of your own, use one with which you are familiar, such as that of a friend or family member.

  - Now think about the personal and work outcomes as described in Figure 15.7, and consider how the job dimensions affected the work outcomes.

  - Finally, record in some way which of the core dimensions of the job you have studied could be re-designed to improve work outcomes (even if these were already quite positive).

- **Application:** When you have completed the work, review how you worked, and whether your ideas would be likely to make a difference. Reflect on what you can learn. If possible, share your work with a colleague on the course, and note what you have learned. Decide on another opportunity to practise this skill within the next week.

Read more

Culbertson, S.S. (2009), 'Do satisfied employees mean satisfied customers?', *Academy of Management Perspectives,* vol. 23, no. 1, pp. 76–7.

Shows the link between employee satisfaction and customer responses – also relevant to marketing.

Gratton, L. (2011), *The Shift: The Future of Work is Already Here,* Collins, London.

A challenging synthesis of many contemporary ideas about the changes affecting working lives.

Herzberg, F. (1959), *The Motivation to Work,* Wiley, New York.

Maslow, A. (1970), *Motivation and Personality* (2nd edn.), Harper & Row, New York.

The original accounts of these influential works are unusually readable books showing organisations and research in action.

Locke, E.A. and Latham, G.P. (2002), 'Building a practically useful theory of goal setting and task motivation: A 35-year odyssey', *American Psychologist,* vol. 57, no. 9, pp. 705–17.

Review by the founders of goal-setting theory, including the results of many empirical studies.

McGregor, D. (1960), *The Human Side of Enterprise,* McGraw-Hill, New York.

Go online

Visit the websites of companies that interest you, perhaps as possible places to work:

www.edenproject.com
www.greatplacetowork.co.uk
www.gore.com
www.timpson.co.uk
www.ikea.com
www.dsm.com
www.childbasepartnerships.co.uk
www.irisnation.com

Navigate to the pages dealing with 'about the company' or 'careers'.

- What do they tell you about working there? What seem to be the most prominent features?
- What motivational needs do they seem to be aiming to meet? Would they meet your needs?

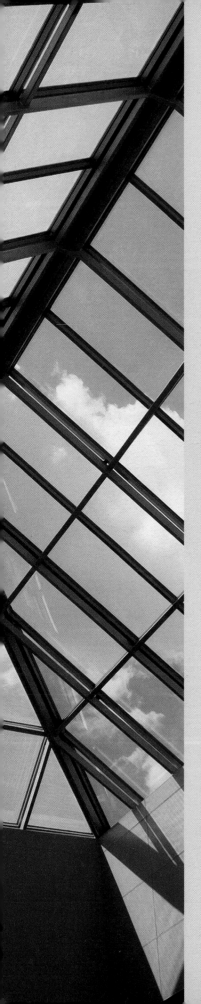

CHAPTER 16
COMMUNICATING

Aims

To describe and illustrate the processes of communicating in organisations, and how these can help or hinder performance.

Objectives

By the end of your work on this chapter you should be able to outline the concepts below in your own terms and:

1 Explain the role of communicating in the manager's job
2 Identify and illustrate the elements and stages in the communication process
3 Use the concept of information richness to select a communication channel
4 Compare the benefits of different communication networks
5 Show how communication practices interact with strategy, structure and power
6 Outline some essential interpersonal communication skills
7 Consider how communication interacts with strategy and the wider context
8 Explain the tasks in making an effective presentation, and understand how you can use this approach to develop your presentation skills
9 Show how ideas from the chapter add to your understanding of the integrating themes

Key terms

The chapter introduces these terms:

communication	non-verbal communication
message	selective attention
encoding	stereotyping
decoding	channel
noise	information richness
feedback	information overload

Each is a term defined within the text, and in the glossary at the end of the book.

Case study   Facebook   www.facebook.com/facebook

In early 2016 Facebook was the world's largest online social network with over 1.3 billion users. These post over 65 million updates a day and share more than four billion pieces of content every week. It has expanded far beyond its American roots, with 70 per cent of users being outside the United States. The 2012 sale of shares in the company signalled clearly that what had begun as a university stunt was now influencing how people and businesses communicate: it was moving from entrepreneurial business start-up to a mature corporate power.

Mark Zuckerburg founded the site to allow users to create a profile page about themselves and what they were doing, and to share this information with friends and acquaintances. Other students at Harvard claim the original idea, and that they hired Zuckerburg to write the software; the contestants reached a legal settlement with the company.

Facebook opened the site in 2004, initially only to people with a university or secondary school email account – though from 2007 it admitted members of the public. Mr Zuckerberg's goal was, and remains, to connect as much of the world's population as possible via the network and then to persuade them to use it as their main route to the internet. People in their teens and early twenties quickly started to use the site, leading to a rapid growth in users. They have alternative social sites – such as Twitter, Tumblr, Snapchat and WhatsApp (which Facebook bought in 2014). Some analysts believe that as older people join, it may become less attractive to younger users. A 2013 survey reported that 40 per cent of Facebook US users aged 18–29 expected to spend less time on the site that year, compared with 1 per cent who expected to spend more.

As users and their 'friends' share information about themselves, they create data that is of great interest to companies who wish to sell goods and services to this relatively young group of consumers. A manager at one brand said:

Facebook is now much bigger than a social network – it's a communication platform.

Facebook earns revenue by meeting advertisers' requirements, but knows that users may object to intrusive advertising that has breached their privacy. It seeks a balance between hoarding data that advertisers crave and ensuring users are still willing to share information online. In 2014 it changed its privacy policy, by stating that the default position for new users would now be to share posts with friends, rather than all users. These issues also interest governments – the

© Josh Edelson/AFP/Alamy Images

US Congress and the European Commission are both observing the company's activities closely in relation to privacy and competition issues.

The company has used some of its growing revenues to buy other companies, including WhatsApp and Instagram, and developed its own Messenger system. It is also working on a new website called 'Facebook at Work' to allow users to chat with colleagues, connect with professional contacts and collaborate over documents. This will bring it into competition with Google Drive, Microsoft Office and LinkedIn.

Sources: Kirkpatrick (2010); *Financial Times*, 17 May 2013, p.19, 23 May 2014, p.1 and 19 November 2014, p. 17.

Case questions 16.1

- If you use Facebook (or similar), what changes, if any, has it made to the way you communicate?

- What aspects of using Facebook to communicate with close friends (a) enhance the process and (b) diminish the process?

16.1   Introduction

Facebook (and similar sites) have become widely accepted tools for communicating, representing a dramatic and permanent change in people's ability to communicate with others. They make people's personal relationships more visible and quantifiable, and have become channels for news and of influence. Managers at Facebook itself face communication challenges – they need (among other things) to communicate the attractions of working at the company to potential staff, ensure rapid and accurate communication among their software developers and between them and other functions, and to understand what people want and expect from Facebook. They also watch for information on developments at potentially competing sites.

Stewart (1967) and Mintzberg (1973) both found that managers spend most of their time communicating. Even when they are not interacting directly with others, such as when they are reading or writing, those activities in themselves are forms of communication. The success of pharmaceutical company GlaxoSmithKline depends on intense communication between research teams, clinical trial staff, regulators and marketers as they develop new drugs. Those in service organisations such as The Eden Project want staff to communicate ideas and suggestions – and to understand company policy. Professionals caring for the sick need to communicate accurate and timely information, often in stressful conditions; failure is often due, at least in part, to poor communication.

Even with the technologies now available, people continue to experience ineffective communication. Computer-based tools do not replace the need for human interaction. Company-wide information systems make it easy for geographically separated people to exchange messages – but how they interpret those messages depends on their relationship:

> Technology won't make messages more useful unless we build personal relationships first. The message will get through more easily if the recipient has some pre-existing relationship with the sender' (Rosen, 1998).

Until people meet they cannot develop the mutual trust and shared knowledge essential for effective communication. This is especially true when mutual understanding depends on context.

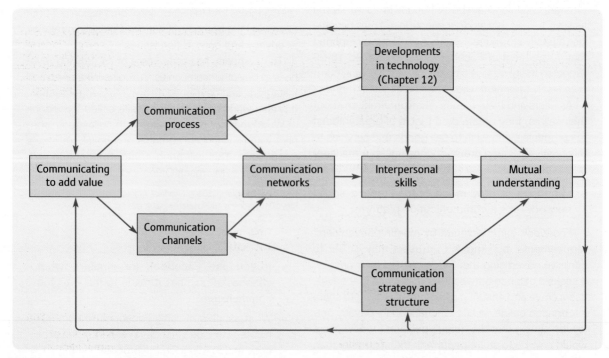

Figure 16.1 An overview of the chapter

It is easy to underestimate communication problems. A professional in a utility business wrote to the author:

> The majority of managers within [the business] consider themselves to be effective communicators. Staff have a different perspective, and a recent staff survey rated communications as being very poor, with information being top down, no form of two-way communications and managers only hearing what they want to hear.

This chapter begins by showing how communication is essential to managing, and then outlines the generic steps in any exchange of messages. People communicate through one or more channels (or media), whose respective usefulness depends on the situation; the same is true of alternative forms of communication networks. Interpersonal communication depends on using identifiable skills to achieve mutual understanding, and these are the focus of the 'Develop a skill' feature. Figure 16.1 provides an overview.

16.2   Communicating to add value

We base our understanding of the world on information and feelings that we receive and send. People at all levels of an organisation communicate about:

- inputs – e.g. the availability of materials or equipment;
- transformation – e.g. about capacity or quality; and
- outputs – e.g. customer complaints or advertising policy.

Information about an order needs to flow accurately to all the departments that will help to satisfy it – and then between departments as the task progresses. People communicate information up and down the vertical hierarchy, and horizontally between functions, departments and other organisations. Figure 16.2 shows how communication supports these value-adding processes.

What is communication?

Communication happens when people share information to reach a common understanding. Managing depends on conveying and interpreting messages clearly so that people can work together. Speaking and writing are easy: achieving a common understanding is not.

Communication is the exchange of information through written or spoken words, symbols and actions to reach a common understanding.

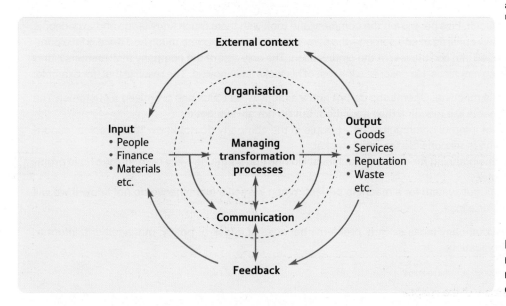

Figure 16.2 The role of communication in organisations

Background and personal needs affect our ability to absorb messages from those with different histories, but until people reach a common understanding, they have not completed the communication episode.

| Activity 16.1 | Collecting symbols and actions |

The definition of communication refers to words, symbols and actions. Try to identify examples of symbols and actions that communicate a message to you. Some clues:

- *Symbols*: someone's style of dress or manner, or the appearance of the entrance to your college or university.
- *Actions*: someone taking time to offer directions to a visitor or looking bored during a meeting; interrupting someone.

How communicating adds value

Communication features in every chapter – influencing others, working in teams, giving marketing information to a designer, interpreting financial data or posting a job vacancy on the website. It is by communicating ideas that people add value through innovation, quality, delivery and cost. *Innovation* depends on good information about customer needs and relevant discoveries – which comes from communication with the scientific community. Embodying ideas in products requires communication within cross-functional teams, and with suppliers and customers. Enhancing quality depends on everyone understanding what quality means to the customer – without communication there is no quality. Another measure of performance is *delivery* – supplying customers with what they expect, when they expect it. That is only possible if people communicate accurate, reliable and timely information up and down the supply chain.

| Management in practice | Communication failure in a small Dutch company |

The company was founded in 1881 and the present owner is one of the fourth generation of the family. The company trades and manufactures packaging machines and employs 16 people. Someone who has recently joined the company said:

> Last year was difficult. Five people left the company and took with them much knowledge and experience. The company really consists of one person – the owner. He does not delegate much and there is little communication between him and the rest of the organisation. The only part of the company that interests him is the game of selling machines. He describes the rest of his tasks as annoying. The result is that, for example:
>
> 1. When we sell a machine, Operations do not know exactly what Sales has promised a customer. The customer expects the machine they specified, but do not always get it.
> 2. There is lack of internal communication – people in the company do not know their precise responsibilities or who is responsible for which tasks.
> 3. There is no time planning for ordered machines. No one knows the delivery date that we have promised a customer.
> 4. There is no budget system for a machine project. When we sell a machine we do not know if we will make a profit or a loss.
>
> All together, the company faces serious problems because of a lack of policy, management, information and communication.

Source: Private communication from the manager.

Case study   Facebook – the case continues   www.facebook.com/facebook

About 85 per cent of the company's revenue comes from advertising (with a rapidly growing share of that coming from ads on mobile devices), so a major challenge has been to persuade enough advertisers to use the site. Initially these were major global brands such as Unilever, Nestlé, Ford and Coca-Cola, but a much wider range of consumer goods companies now use the site. Advertisers track the connections between the site's users – and then aim appropriate advertisements based on the information users reveal.

A company wanting to attract users will typically:

1 Set up a Facebook page containing messages about the brand.
2 Buy advertisements on Facebook to encourage people to visit the company's page, click on the 'like' button and become 'fans' who then receive updates on the brand's products and the comments of other fans through their personal newsfeeds.
3 Install a game or other activity on the page that fans will offer to play with their friends, so they too visit the page – if they become 'fans' they will in turn draw their friends to the page.
4 The company then has access to all the information about the preferences, activities and attitudes of each member of this growing network, to whom it can send precisely targeted adverts.

This information about social connections and affinities excites advertisers:

They have a consumer database of interests and actions and feelings and thoughts, Nichola Mendelsohn, president of the Institute of Practitioners of Advertising, an industry grouping, says about the company. It gives us a huge amount of scope.

The ability to tailor and target marketing messages so finely is something of which advertisers had only dreamt. . . and could be the key to keeping them spending. (From an article by April Dembosky, *Financial Times,* 31 January 2012, p. 11)

Case questions 16.2

In terms of Figure 16.3, advertisements may represent 'noise' in the communication process.

- Have you found this to be a significant aspect of your experience in using the medium?
- What dilemmas does that 'noise' pose for Facebook?

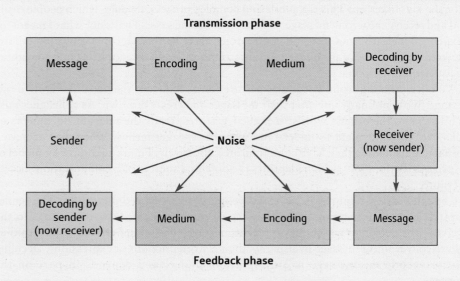

Transmission phase

Message → Encoding → Medium → Decoding by receiver

Sender

Noise

Receiver (now sender)

Decoding by sender (now receiver) ← Medium ← Encoding ← Message

Feedback phase

Figure 16.3 The communication process

The performance of modern communication systems depends on an adequate fit between the system and its context (structure, culture and so on). Technically sophisticated systems only add value if those responsible manage familiar human issues – see 'Management in practice' feature.

Management in practice   **Three responses to smartphones**

MacCormick et al. (2012) studied the use of smartphones in an international investment bank, to establish how their use affected employee engagement – the extent to which people were mentally, emotionally and physically connected to their work. While the ability of smartphones to enable communication between colleagues irrespective of time or place can have positive effects, they can also lead to overload and stress. At the other extreme people may react to being over-connected by declining the offer of a smartphone, not recharging it and not answering it out of normal hours.

Through two sets of intensive interviews with 21 senior executives (repeated after a five-year interval) they identified three types of user:

- Dynamic connectors (functional engagement) who used the devices in ways that increased their autonomy, control and flexibility, and appeared to produce benefits for the organisation such as improved coordination, collaboration and responsiveness.
- Hyper-connectors non-stop work (disengagement) who used the devices in ways that led to burnout, workaholic/addiction and work – life conflict; and for the organisation led to shallow and superficial communication, sending emails when face-to-face contact would be easier and competing to see who had the most emails in a day.
- Hypo-connectors (disengagement) who intentionally resisted connectivity, reflecting fears of being over-connected, loss of control and potential addiction, and for the organisation signs that they were out of contact, unavailable and disinterested.

Source: MacCormick et al. (2012).

16.3   The communication process

The message is what the sender communicates.

We communicate whenever we send a **message** to someone and as we think about what he or she says in return. This is a subtle and complex process, through which people easily send and receive the wrong message. Whenever someone says: 'That's not what I meant' or 'I explained it clearly, and they still got it wrong' there has been a communication failure. We waste time when we misunderstand directions, or cause offence by saying something the listener misinterprets.

We infer meaning from words and gestures and then from the person's reply to our message. We continually interpret their messages and create our own. As colleagues talk, each listens to the other's words, sees their gestures, reads the relevant documents or looks over the equipment to understand what the speaker means. When they achieve a mutual understanding they have communicated effectively. Figure 16.3 shows a model of the process (Berlo, 1960), which identifies the potential sources of communication success or failure.

Communication requires at least two people – a sender and a receiver. The sender initiates the communication when they try to transfer ideas, facts or feelings to the receiver – the person to whom they send the message. The sender **encodes** the idea they wish to convey into a message by using symbols – words, actions or expressions. Deciding how to encode the message is an important choice, and depends in part on the purpose:

Encoding is translating information into symbols for communication.

- Is it to convey specific and unambiguous information?
- Is it to raise an open and unfamiliar problem, and a request for creative ideas?
- Is it to pass on routine data, or to inspire people?

THE COMMUNICATION PROCESS

Key ideas **Accurate encoding**

Five principles help to encode a message accurately:

- **Relevancy:** make the message significant by carefully selecting the words, symbols or gestures.
- **Simplicity:** make it simple by using as few words, symbols and gestures as possible.
- **Organisation:** organise it into clear points, and complete each one before starting the next.
- **Repetition:** repeat key points twice when speaking – people often do not hear or understand first time.
- **Focus:** concentrate on essentials and avoid unnecessary detail.

The message is the tangible expression of the sender's idea. The sender chooses the communication medium – email, face-to-face meeting or letter – to transmit the coded message. The receiver **decodes** the symbols contained in the message, and tries to reconstruct the sender's idea. Coding and decoding can be sources of communication failure as the sender and receiver have different knowledge, experience and interests. Receivers also evaluate a message by their knowledge of the sender. These 'filters' interfere with the conversion of meaning to symbols and vice versa and, along with other distractions and interruptions, are referred to as **noise**. Dimbleby and Burton (2006) identify three filters – within individuals (psychological filters), within the message (semantic filters) and within the context (mechanical filters).

> **Decoding** is the interpretation of a message into a form with meaning.

> **Noise** is anything that confuses, diminishes or interferes with communication.

The final stage is when the receiver responds to the message by giving **feedback** to the sender. This turns one-way communication into two-way. The flow of information between parties is continuous and reciprocal, each giving feedback that allows the sender to know that the receiver has received and understood the message as intended.

> **Feedback** (in communication) occurs as the receiver expresses his or her reaction to the sender's message.

Effective communicators understand it is a two-way process, and positively encourage feedback. They do not rely only on making their message clear, but also encourage the receiver to respond – a nod, a question that implies understanding, a quick email acknowledgement. Without that, the sender cannot know if they have communicated effectively.

Assume communication is going to fail, and put time and effort into preventing that.

Key ideas **Quality of information**

The quality of information depends on four criteria:

1 **Accuracy:** People need to know they can rely on information – that a sales report is an accurate account of sales, that a report of a conversation is true.
2 **Timeliness:** Information is only useful if it is available in time. A manager who needs to keep expenditure within a budget requires cost information frequently enough to be able to act on unfavourable trends.
3 **Quantity:** Most managers receive more information than they can interpret and use, suggesting that some available technologies may damage performance unless they think carefully about how they use them.
4 **Relevance:** This depends on a person's tasks and responsibilities and again requires managers to evaluate critically which of the information they receive is essential.

Non-verbal communication

Interpersonal communication includes **non-verbal communication**, sometimes called body language, which can have more impact on the receiver than the verbal parts. Signals include tone of voice, facial expression, posture and appearance – these provide most of the impact in face-to-face communication.

> **Non-verbal communication** is the process of coding meaning through behaviours such as facial expression, gestures and body postures.

Small changes in eye contact, raising eyebrows or a directed glance while making a statement add to the meaning that the sender conveys. A stifled yawn, an eager nod, a thoughtful flicker of anxiety gives the sender a signal about the receiver's reaction. Gestures and body position give strong signals: leaning forward attentively, moving about in the chair, hands moving nervously, gathering papers or looking at the clock – all send a message. Skilled communicators use non-verbal cues to detect that someone is worried, even if they do not speak out.

Positive non-verbal feedback helps to build relations within a team. A smile or wave to someone at least acknowledges they exist. Related to a task it indicates approval in an informal, rapid way that sustains confidence. Negative feedback can be correspondingly damaging. A boss who looks irritated by what the staff member sees as a reasonable enquiry is giving a negative signal, as is one who looks bored during a presentation.

Management in practice   Virtual teams at Cisco   www.cisco.com

Cisco Systems supplies much of the physical equipment that supports the internet, and most design teams contain staff working in facilities across the world. One team member said:

> It means you have to be a bit more careful when it comes to communication. Most of the time you have to use email and instant messaging to discuss issues, which means there can be misunderstandings if you're not careful. When you interact in person you use things like facial expression and hand gestures – none of these are available when emailing so you have to state your arguments more clearly.

Source: Private communication.

As with any interpersonal skill, some people are better at interpreting non-verbal behaviour than others. The sender of a spoken message can benefit by noting the non-verbal responses to what they say. If they do not seem appropriate (raised eyebrows, an anxious look), the speaker should pause and check that the receiver has received the message that the sender intended.

Perception

Selective attention is the ability, often unconscious, to choose from the stream of signals in the environment, concentrating on some and ignoring others.

Perception is the process by which individuals make sense of their environment by selecting and interpreting information. We receive more information than we can absorb, and **selective attention** keeps us sane. We actively notice and attend to a fraction of the available information, filtering it according to the strength of the signal and our knowledge of the sender.

When people observe information they interpret it, and react to it, uniquely. This 'perceptual organisation' arranges incoming signals into patterns that give meaning to data – relating it to our interest, the status of the sender or the benefits of attending to it. Experience, social class and education affect the meanings people attach to information.

Activity 16.2   Understanding communication practices

- Think of an example where communication between two or more people failed. Note down why you think that happened, using the model in Figure 16.3.
- Use Figure 16.3 to analyse the communication process of someone using Facebook. Note how it differs from face-to-face communication.
- Email is widely used in business: list the advantages and disadvantages of that medium compared with face-to-face communication.

A common form of perceptual organisation is **stereotyping**. 'They always complain' or 'You would expect people from marketing to say that' are signs that someone is judging a message not by its content but by their assumptions about the group to which the sender belongs. If these are inaccurate they will misinterpret a message. Perceptual differences are natural, but interfere with communication and mean that senders cannot assume that receivers attach the same meaning to a message as they intended.

> **Stereotyping** is the practice of consigning a person to a category or personality type on the basis of their membership of some known group.

Case study

Facebook – the case continues
www.facebook.com/facebook

As Facebook has become the dominant online social network in many countries, demand for services that allow businesses to exploit this huge number of potential customers has grown rapidly. To help it compete with other online players such as Google and Apple for online advertising, the company is developing tangible guidelines for marketers, and appointing staff to work closely with select advertisers. Carolyn Everson, Vice-President of Global Marketing for Facebook:

> **We know we have to become easier to work with.**

Independent social media management companies also help advertisers to target their messages for local markets. In return for a fee, they ensure their clients' advertisements appear in people's news feeds, or between personal updates from friends and family. So a user who 'likes' McDonald's will see a promotion for a local favourite, while a user in another part of the country will see one for a different, and locally more relevant, product. One said:

> **We work collaboratively with McDonald's to harness their 18 million fans and manage their locations around the US.**

Companies track user responses to a campaign automatically through software embedded in the system. This allows them to increase their understanding of user behaviour on Facebook, and to track how the social network is changing the way people hear about new brands and products. Facebook itself is helping to promote these reports, and doing its own research, to convince brands of the importance of spending on social media marketing campaigns.

By 2013 the company was able to report that a growing number of people were now accessing Facebook through their smartphones (rather than their desktops). This followed the company's decision the previous year to allow advertisers to place their messages into the news feed, directly in the customer's line of vision. This made the ads more valuable to advertisers.

In 2014 it began using its databases to target advertising at users who are viewing other websites and mobile apps – until then, adverts would only appear when the user was on Facebook. This enabled it to challenge Google, which dominated this market for display ads.

 Sources: *Financial Times*, 29 July 2011, p. 17, 7 May 2013, p. 15, 26 July 2013, p. 19, 30 September 2014, p. 19.
© The Financial Times 2011, 2013, 2014. All Rights Reserved.

Case questions 16.2

- Use Figure 16.3 to analyse how advertisers try to ensure they communicate their messages effectively on Facebook (the medium).
- How may they ensure accurate encoding?
- How do they gather feedback on receivers' responses to their message?

16.4 | Selecting communication channels

The model of communication in Figure 16.3 shows the steps that people take to communicate effectively. The process fails if either sender or receiver does not encode or decode the symbols of the message in the same way. Selecting the wrong communication **channel**

> A **channel** is the medium of communication between a sender and a receiver.

also leads to difficulty: sending a message that requires subtle interpretation as a written instruction, with no chance for feedback, is not good practice.

Lengel and Daft (1988) developed the idea of **information richness** to compare the capacity of channels to promote common understanding: see Figure 16.4.

The richness of a medium (or channel) depends on its ability to:

Information richness refers to the amount of information that a communication channel can carry, and the extent to which it enables sender and receiver to achieve common understanding.

- handle many cues at the same time;
- support rapid two-way feedback; and
- establish a personal focus for the communication.

Face-to-face communication

Face-to-face discussion is the richest medium, as both parties can pick up many cues (concentration, eye contact, body movements, facial expression) in addition to spoken words. This brings a better understanding of the nuances of meaning; someone who had started a business:

> I find the best way to communicate with people is very simply to talk to them and to be upfront and honest and forthright with as much information as you possibly can.

Managers spend much of their time in face-to-face communication – quick, spontaneous and enriched by non-verbal signals. It takes place in one-to-one conversation (face-to-face), through meetings of several people, or when someone addresses an audience at a conference. 'Management by wandering around' is a widely used and effective communication technique as managers gain direct insights into what is happening, which reports from supervisors may filter.

Management in practice   A communications app at BA

Maria da Cunha, Director of People and Legal, says staff engagement is at the heart of the recovery in performance and profits at BA since 2014:

> We are challenging people to find different ways of doing things, and to improve productivity and efficiency. And for that we need highly engaged staff – people who, in times of disruption, are willing to [go the extra mile]. The research shows that a good relationship between someone and their manager is the greatest driver of that.

The company is putting these ideals into innovative practice with a new communications app being used by about 3,000 front-line managers, guiding them on some essential communication practices that easily get lost in the bustle of a global business. The initial users were managers in charge of teams of staff at the airfields, driving passenger buses or on refuelling duties. With teams mobile, and alternating day and night shifts, it is difficult for managers and staff to communicate face-to-face.

The app, held on the manager's iPad, shows (amongst many more pieces of information) who is on the team, and working that day. A prompt alerts the manager to an event they should know about – an employee's birthday, or a long-service anniversary. These are simple things, but they prompt a conversation between people, and show a basic recognition. The app makes people more visible, and ensures managers are talking to their team regularly.

Source: *People Management*, December 2015, pp. 20–2.

Despite the benefits of face-to-face communication, it takes time and becomes more difficult when managers and staff are spread out. The 'Management in practice' feature shows how technology can overcome this.

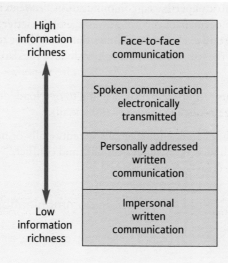

Figure 16.4 The Lengel–Daft media richness hierarchy

Source: Lengel and Daft (1988).

Videoconferencing at Cisco Systems

When Cisco Systems held its annual summit in May 2009 for its top 3100 executives, no one flew to the group's headquarters in California. Instead staff in China, India and the UK gathered in front of high definition screens in conference rooms, and communicated via instant messaging.

The company saved millions of dollars that had been spent on previous events – and found that interaction improved. Managers and directors responded live to some of the more than 10,000 questions posed electronically, with many more being archived for follow-up sessions.

Cisco is not alone, as many more companies with far-flung operations are using similar communication technologies. Nokia, Siemens, IBM and Proctor and Gamble have all made savings on travel costs.

 Source: *Financial Times,* 26 May 2009.
© The Financial Times 2009. All Rights Reserved.

Spoken communication electronically transmitted

This is the second-highest form of communication in terms of media richness. Although when we use a telephone or mobile we cannot see the non-verbal expressions or body language, we can pick up the tone of voice, the sense of urgency or the general manner of the message, as well as the words themselves. Feedback is quick so both parties can check for understanding.

Voicemail systems and answering machines can supplement telephone systems. Many organisations use message recording systems to pass customers to the right department, offering options from which they choose. Such systems reduce costs but annoy customers, especially when they want to speak to a human being.

Personally addressed written communication

Personally addressed written communication has an advantage in that, being addressed personally, it tends to demand the recipient's attention. It also enables the sender to phrase the message in a way that they think best suits the reader. If both parties express their meanings accurately, and seek and offer feedback, they can reach a high level of (recorded) mutual understanding.

Email has replaced most paper-based communication between individuals and within organisations. It has the 'permanent record' advantage of the letter, while instant delivery allows people to complete an exchange in minutes that could have taken days. Mobile texting is likely to overtake the use of email, though both have the disadvantages of:

- lack of body language;
- adding many recipients to the 'copy' box, leading to overload; and
- organisations sending unsolicited messages (junk mail).

Byron (2008) finds that people sending emails (intentionally or not) communicate emotions, increasing the likelihood of misunderstanding and conflict.

Activity 16.3   Critical reflection on communication methods

- Think of a task you have done with a small group of people, either at work or during your studies.
- How did you communicate with each other? List all the methods used, noting the advantages and disadvantages of each.

Impersonal written communication

This is the least information-rich medium – but is suitable for sending a message to many people. Newsletters, emails, company websites and routine computer reports are lean media because they are impersonal and do not encourage response. Managers use them to send a simple message about the company to widely dispersed employees and customers. They also use them to disseminate rules, procedures, product information and news about the company, such as new appointments. The medium also ensures that instructions are communicated in a standard form to people in different places, and that there is a record. The ease with which electronic messages can be sent to large numbers of people leads to **information overload**, when people receive more information than they can read, let alone deal with adequately.

Information overload arises when the amount of information a person has to deal with exceeds their capacity to process it.

Each channel has advantages and disadvantages. If the message is to go to many people and there is a significant possibility of misunderstanding, a structured medium is likely to work best. If it is an unusual problem that needs the opinion of several other people, then a face-to-face discussion will be more effective. Lengel and Daft (1988) found that the preferred medium depended on how routine the topic was:

> Managers used face-to-face [communication] 88 per cent of the time for non-routine communication. The reverse was true for written media. When they considered the topics [were] routine and well-understood, 68 per cent preferred . . . written modes. (p. 227)

Management in practice   Communicating during change at Provident

Provident is a long-established insurance company that depends heavily on agents who visit people in their homes to discuss their needs, deliver cash and collect repayments. It has had to make major changes in the business, and knew it was essential to gain staff support. New communication methods helped to achieve this. They included a regular radio chat show with the managing director and other senior leaders answering staff questions, and weekly in-office 'huddles' to keep staff up to date on how the business is doing and what their immediate goals should be to keep improving performance.

Source: *People Management*, February 2015, pp.18–19.

Case study — Facebook – the case continues — www.facebook.com/facebook

The company competes fiercely with Google for talented staff (it employs many former 'Googlers') and maintaining morale is essential to continued success. The Director of Human Resources (Robyn Reed) recalled that the company faced a severe communication crisis soon after it opened. It was now growing rapidly and attracting the attention of other computing and media companies – some of whom were openly interested in buying Facebook. Staff noted that Mark Zuckerburg was holding many meetings with outsiders – and feared he was planning to sell the company. Zuckerburg did not realise that staff were becoming increasingly unhappy. Reed says:

> The morale of the executives was imploding . . . The rumour mill was churning and Mark wasn't communicating with anyone about what was really happening. The team was close to mutiny. (Kirkpatrick, 2010, pp. 162–3).

She decided to confront him, with the result that:

> he agreed to start seeing an executive coach to get lessons on how to be an effective leader, holding more one-on-one meetings with senior executives, bringing the entire staff together for an 'all-hands' meeting [and then taking] the executive team to an off-site meeting where they could talk about goals and establish better communication channels. [He also] started doing a better job explaining where he thought the company was going (Kirkpatrick, 2010, pp. 164–65).

By 2013 the company employed over 4,000 people, and management realised that this would threaten the intense communication between developers that was the basis of its strength. Practices included:

- building orange footbridges to link the several buildings on the site at Menlo Park in California, to encourage staff to wander among them;
- installing automatic doors to further break the sense of separation between buildings;
- encouraging staff to have lunch with a randomly selected person from another group;
- allowing engineers to change their work teams regularly;
- requiring new staff to encourage 'boot camp' training sessions where people with different skills are forced to bond and then encouraged to remain in close personal contact; and
- monthly 'hackathons' where staff work all night with engineers from other disciplines on a problem outside of their normal work.

The biggest challenges with a company growing fast is that, as you add more people, you stop knowing each other and communicating with each other. The communication starts going up and down silos, says Pedram Keyani, director of engineering for site integrity. Hackathons really help to break that down. (From an article by Gillian Tett, *Financial Times*, 4 April 2013, p. 11).

Sources: *New York Times*, 27 May 2009; Kirkpatrick (2010); *Financial Times*, 4 April 2013.

Case questions 16.3

- What evidence is there in the case about the communication channels that Facebook developers use?
- Which of the communication channels did Zuckerburg and his colleagues use in this part of the case?

Activity 16.4 — Assessing university communications

List the communications channels that your university or college uses to send you information about these aspects of your course:

- changes to rooms, timetables, or dates;
- reading lists and other study materials;
- ideas and information intended to stimulate your thinking and to encourage learning;
- your academic performance;
- advice on what courses to take.

Were the methods appropriate or not? What general lessons can you draw?

Online communities

Online communities use electronic systems to enable communication between geographically dispersed individuals with mutual interests. Some of the forms they take:

- social exchange, to share personal and family news – Facebook;
- individual creativity and self-promotion – YouTube;
- open-source software developments – Linux;
- company-supported user interaction – innocent drinks, Zara;
- offering information to others, and updating others' contributions – Wikipedia;
- media-hosted news and commentary sites – BBC or *Financial Times* blogging;
- internal/knowledge management – used within companies to share information.

Managers in many companies are actively considering how best to engage with social network sites. They represent a shift from vertical to horizontal communication on the web. Where until now most organisational communication has been transmitted downward from sender to receiver, the receivers – individual web users – now have tools they can use to talk to each other. These consumer-focused devices hold threats and opportunities.

Companies that want to make use of the medium take several paths. Some feature positive stories, which their authors hope will be picked up by other sites: if they are, this makes the site more visible. innocent drinks (www.innocentdrinks.com) encourages staff and customers to share information and ideas about current projects or marketing ideas, as well as to chat socially. They can also highlight articles or other information, enabling instant access across the company.

Other companies use social network sites for recruitment, identifying suitable candidates and contacting former employees. News services such as the BBC and political candidates use them to reach new audiences, to interact with present audiences and to gather and form opinion.

16.5 Communication networks

The grapevine

The grapevine is the spontaneous, informal system through which people pass gossip and rumour. It happens throughout the organisation and across all hierarchical levels as people meet in the corridor, by the photocopier, at lunch, on the way home. The information that passes along the grapevine is usually well ahead of the information in the formal system. Grosser et al. (2012) define gossip as evaluative (positive, negative or neutral) comments about other individuals known to the gossipers. They distinguish it from rumour, which is communication about actual or anticipated events – what orders the company has won or lost, who has applied for another job, who has been summoned to explain their poor results to the directors.

The grapevine does not replace the formal system, but passes a different kind of information – qualitative rather than quantitative, ideas rather than agreements. As it is uncensored and reflects the views of people as a whole rather than of those in charge of the formal channels, it probably gives a truer picture of the diversity of opinions than the formal system. The gossip and rumours might be wrong or incomplete, as those passing gossip and good stories of disasters in department X may have their own agenda, such as promoting department Y. The grapevine is as much a vehicle for political intrigue as any formal system.

The grapevine can be a source of early information about what is happening, which allows those affected but not yet formally consulted to begin preparing their position.

Communicating in groups and teams

To understand how people in a group communicate, members need to have some tools to analyse the patterns of interaction. Shaw (1978) conducted a laboratory experiment to identify which communication processes groups used, and how they affected task performance – see Figure 16.5. Autocratic leadership was associated with the wheel, and a democratic style with the all channel structure. Shaw noted that in centralised networks (chain, wheel and 'Y') groups had to go through someone at the centre of the network to communicate with others, which led to unequal access. In the decentralised networks (circle and all-channel) information flowed freely and equally between members.

Different tasks require different communication and Figure 16.6 illustrates two patterns. In a centralised network information flows to and from the person at the centre, while in the decentralised pattern more of the messages pass between those in the network. If the task is simple, the centralised pattern will work adequately. An example would be to prepare next year's staff budget for the library when there are to be no major changes. The person at the centre can exchange familiar, structured information with section heads.

If the task is uncertain the centralised structure will obstruct performance. Imagine a team is developing a new product rapidly in conjunction with suppliers and customers. Because of the novelty of the task, unfamiliar questions will arise, which group members can only solve in an acceptable time by exchanging information rapidly. As organisations grow they supplement informal methods with more formal ones to communicate downwards, upwards and horizontally – see Figure 16.7.

Communicating downwards

Managers communicate downwards when they try to coordinate units' activities by issuing instructions or procedures about, for example:

- new policies, products or services;
- budget changes or any changes in financial reporting and control systems;
- new systems and procedures;
- appointments and reorganisations.

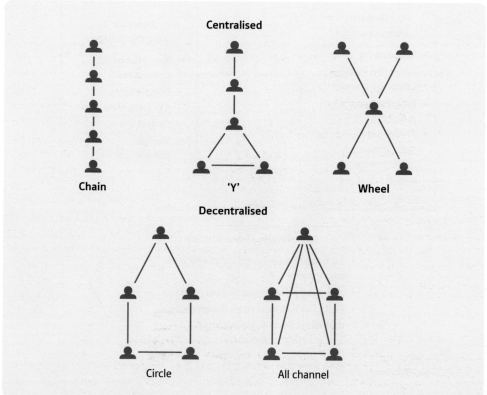

Figure 16.5
Centralised and decentralised communication networks in groups
Source: Shaw (1978).

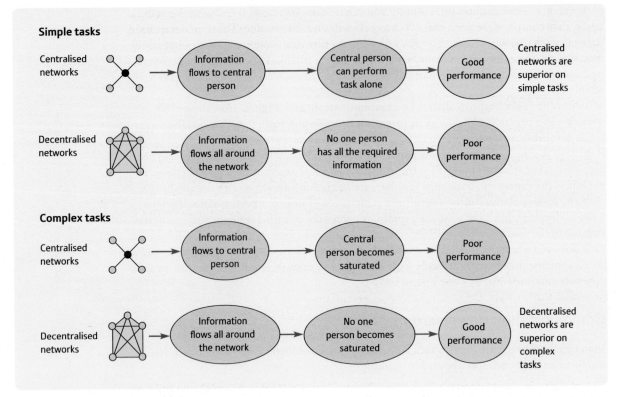

Figure 16.6 Communication structure and type of task

Source: Based on Baron and Greenberg (1997).

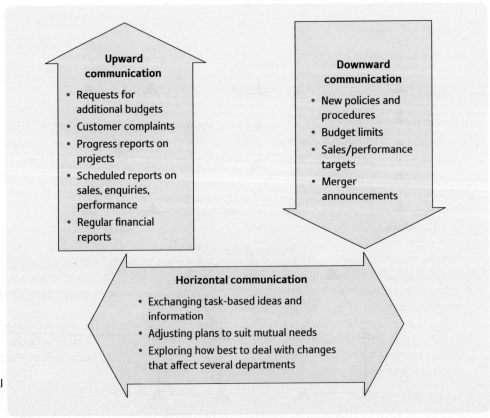

Figure 16.7
Directions of formal communications in organisations

If the downward communication inhibits comments or responses, the sender will be unclear how receivers reacted to the message. If it is unclear, people will interpret it in ways that suit them, perhaps making things worse. Managers can avoid this by checking a draft with one or two colleagues, to ensure that what it says is what they mean.

Team briefings

Team briefings are a popular way of passing information rapidly and consistently throughout the organisation – Blakstad and Cooper (1995) quote the results of a survey of 915 companies in which 57 per cent of respondents rated team briefings as the most common method of communicating with employees. Under this method senior management provides a standard message and format, and briefs the next level in the hierarchy. Those managers then brief their subordinates following the same format, and this continues down the organisation. Addressing small groups with a common structure enables managers to:

- deliver a consistent message;
- involve line managers personally in delivering the message;
- deliver the message to many people quickly;
- reduce the possible distortions by 'the grapevine';
- enable staff to ask questions.

Communicating upwards

Companies can install systems that encourage employees to pass on views and ideas to managers. In small organisations this is usually fairly easy as the owner-manager is likely to be close to the action and so aware of employees' ideas. As the business grows the layers of the hierarchy can easily break the flow. Unless they create mechanisms to allow information to move upwards, their boards may be acting on the wrong information.

Key ideas	Why senior managers ignore vital information

Sidney Finkelstein has studied the causes of corporate failure – one of which is when managers fail to recognise and act on vital information. He found that this was not usually due to incompetence or idleness, but to a combination of circumstances that made them unreceptive to information that mattered. These included:

- **Undirected information:** when staff are slow to recognise the importance of new information, do not take it seriously, or do not know who could act on the information.
- **Missing communication channels:** when there are no formal links between people receiving the information and those who need to act on it. This also happens if channels are blocked – a subordinate reports a problem to a boss, but cannot pass it elsewhere if the boss takes no action.
- **Missing motives:** when employees do not share vital information because there is no incentive – fearing ridicule or displeasure if they bring bad news. If the payment system encourages competition between divisions, there will be no incentive to share information.
- **Missing oversight:** when senior managers assume that the information they receive is correct, without checking that this is the case. The Royal Bank of Scotland Board readily accepted good news in the years before the financial crisis – unaware of the danger that someone may have been deliberately hiding news of severe problems.

Source: Finkelstein (2003).

Employee opinion surveys

Some companies conduct regular surveys among their employees to gauge their attitudes and feelings towards company policy and practice. They may also seek views on current issues, or about possible changes in policy or practice. The surveys can be valuable both as a general indicator of attitudes and as a way to identify issues that need attention. Many specialists offer to conduct such surveys for companies, usually through an online, web-based system – see, for example, *Personnel Today* – www.personneltoday.com.

Suggestion schemes

These are devices by which companies encourage employees to suggest improvements to their job or other aspects of the organisation. Employees usually receive a cash reward if management accepts their idea.

Activity 16.5   Researching opinion surveys

Gather some evidence from a company about its experience of using employee opinion surveys or suggestion schemes.

- What are their purposes?
- Who designs them and interprets the results?
- What have the benefits been?

Formal grievance procedures

These set out the steps to be followed when an individual or group is in dispute with the company. An employee who has been penalised by a supervisor for poor timekeeping may disagree with the facts as presented or with the penalty imposed. The grievance procedure states how the employee should set about pursuing a claim for a review of the case. Similar procedures now exist in colleges and universities, setting out how a student with a grievance about their assessment can appeal against their results to successively higher levels of the institution.

Horizontal communication

Horizontal communication crosses departmental or functional boundaries, usually connecting people at broadly similar levels. Computer-based information systems have greatly increased the speed and accuracy with which routine information can pass between departments. As a customer places an order, modern systems can quickly pass the relevant information to all the departments that will play a part in meeting it, making production a much smoother and more predictable process.

Management in practice

An online tyre service   www.blackcircles.com

Michael Welch founded Blackcircles when he was 22. Customers order their tyres online or by phone, then drive to a garage where the tyres will have been delivered ready for fitting. He claims to sell tyres for about 40 per cent less than high street retailers – being able, amongst other things to stock a greater range of tyres ready for delivery than would be possible for any single garage. He has also cut his cost of acquiring a new customer from £12 in 2006 to about 12p now – mainly through alliances with bigger brands such as Tesco, the AA and Barclaycard:

Two years ago we communicated with 400,000 potential customers through partnerships. Last year it was 4m and this year it will be 22m . . . the more communication with potential customers, the more sales we make, and the lower our cost of acquisition is – and therefore we can invest that back in the price.

 Source: *Financial Times*, 8 April 2009; company website.
© The Financial Times 2009. All Rights Reserved.

Much horizontal communication is about less routine, less structured problems: when several functions cooperate to introduce new products or systems, people communicate frequently. They exchange information on the current state of affairs so that each can contribute to the project as required.

This also includes communication with other organisations – especially suppliers, customers or partners in collaborative projects. Modern technology makes it technically much easier to pass information between people irrespective of where they are – and this can be used to improve the quality of service. Organisational factors are sometimes a barrier to implementing such systems, especially functional, structural and professional boundaries.

16.6   Interpersonal skills for communicating

If communication was perfect the receiver would always understand the message as the sender intended. That rarely happens, as people interpret information from their perspectives, and their words fail to express feelings or emotions adequately. Power games affect how people send and receive information, so we can never be sure that the message sent is the message received. Breakdowns and barriers can disrupt any communication chain.

Communication skills for senders

The ideas presented in this section suggest some practices that are likely to improve anyone's interpersonal communication skill.

Send clear and complete messages

The subject, and how the sender views it, is as much part of the communication process as the message itself. The sender needs to compose a message that will be clear to the receiver, and complete enough to enable both to reach a mutual understanding. This implies anticipating how others will interpret the message, and eliminating potential sources of confusion – providing a specific example usually helps to make the point more clearly.

Encode messages in symbols the receiver understands

Senders need to compose messages in terms that the receiver will understand – avoiding the specialised language (or jargon) of a professional group when writing to an outsider. Similarly, something that may be read by someone whose native language is different should be written in commonplace language, and avoid the clichés or local sayings that will confuse them.

Select a medium appropriate for the message

The sender should consider how much information richness a message requires, and then choose the most appropriate medium, taking into account any time constraints. The main factor in making that choice is the nature of the message, such as how personal it is or how likely it is that the receiver may misunderstand it.

Select a medium that the receiver monitors

Receivers prefer certain media and pay more attention to messages that come by a preferred route. Some dislike over-formal language, while others dislike casual terms in written documents. Putting a message in writing may help understanding, but others may see it as a sign of distrust. Some communicate readily by email, others are reluctant.

Avoid noise

Noise refers to anything that interferes with the intended flow of communication, which includes multiple – sometimes conflicting – messages being sent and received at the same time. If non-verbal signals are inconsistent with the words, the receiver may see a different meaning in your message from what was intended. Noise also refers to the inclusion in a message of distracting or minor information that diverts attention from the main business. Communication suffers from interruptions that distract both parties and prevent the concentration essential to understanding.

| Key ideas | Seven practices for effective presentations |

- **Be clear about who the receiver is.** What is their state of mind? What assumptions are they likely to bring? What are they feeling in this situation?
- **Know your objective.** What do you want to accomplish by the end of the meeting? (See Chapter 14, p. 470 'Develop a skill' for ideas on this). Decide what you want them to do, and work back from there.
- **Make time to practise.** Practise until you can confidently deliver it in a conversational way, ready to improvise if a good opportunity arises.
- **Review the message before you say it.** Think about it from the receivers' point of view. Do you need to clarify some elements?
- **Use words that are familiar to the audience.** Use examples and illustrations that come from their world.
- **If they do not seem to understand you, clarify the message.** Ask questions, repeat your message using different words and examples.
- **Use specific examples and stories** to illustrate your presentation. You will sense interest rising as soon as you enter into a good example.

Communication skills for receivers

Pay attention

Busy people are often overloaded and have to think about several things at once. Thinking about their next meeting or a forthcoming visit from a customer, they become distracted and do not attend to messages they receive. In face-to-face communication the sender will probably notice this, and that in turn will affect their further actions.

Be a good listener

Communication experts stress the importance of listening. While the person sending the message is responsible for expressing the ideas they want to convey clearly, the receiver also has responsibilities for the success of the exchange. Listening involves actively attending to what is said, and gaining as accurate a picture as possible of the meaning the sender wished to convey.

Many people are poor listeners. They concentrate not on what the speaker is saying but on what they will say as soon as there is a pause.

> ## Key ideas — Six practices for effective listening
>
> - **Stop talking,** especially that internal, mental, silent chatter. Let the speaker finish. Hear them out. It is tempting in a familiar situation to complete the speaker's sentence and work out a reply. This assumes you know what they are going to say: you should instead listen to what they are actually saying.
> - **Put the speaker at ease** by showing that you are listening. The good listener does not look over someone's shoulder or write while the speaker is talking. If you must take notes, explain what you are doing. Take care, because the speaker will be put off if you look away or concentrate on your notes instead of nodding reassuringly.
> - Remember that your **aim is to understand** what the speaker is saying, not to win an argument.
> - Be aware of your **personal prejudices** and make a conscious effort to stop them influencing your judgement.
> - Be alert to **what the speaker is not saying** as well as what they are. Very often what is missing is more important than what is there.
> - **Ask questions.** This shows that you have been listening and encourages the speaker to develop the points you have raised. It is an active process, never more important than when you are meeting someone for the first time – when your objective should be to say as little and learn as much as possible in the shortest time.

Be empathetic

Receivers are empathetic when they try to understand how the sender feels, and try to interpret the message from the sender's perspective, rather from their own position. A junior member of staff may raise a problem with a more senior colleague, which perhaps reflects their inexperience. The senior could be dismissive of the request, indicating that the subordinate ought to know how to deal with the situation. An empathetic response would take account of the inexperience, and treat the request with a greater understanding.

Supportive communication

Whetten and Cameron (2011) propose that people learn the skills of supportive communication – that which seeks to preserve a positive relationship between the communicators while still dealing with the business issues. There are eight principles, shown in 'Key ideas'.

> ## Key ideas — Whetten and Cameron – supportive communication
>
> - **Problem orientated, not person orientated**
>   A focus on problems and issues that can be changed rather than people and their characteristics.
>
> | Example: | 'How can we solve this problem?' | Not: | 'Because of you there is a problem.' |
> |---|---|---|---|
>
> - **Congruent, not incongruent**
>   A focus on honest messages in which verbal messages match thoughts and feelings.
>
> | Example: | 'Your behaviour really upsets me.' | Not: | 'Do I seem upset? No, everything's fine.' |
> |---|---|---|---|

- **Descriptive, not evaluative**
  A focus on describing an objective occurrence, your reaction to it, and offering an alternative.

  | Example: | 'Here is what happened, here is my reaction, here is a suggestion that would be more acceptable.' | Not: | 'You are wrong for doing what you did.' |

- **Validating, not invalidating**
  A focus on statements that communicate respect, flexibility and areas of agreement.

  | Example: | 'I have some ideas, but do you have any suggestions?' | Not: | 'You wouldn't understand, so we'll do it my way.' |

- **Specific, not global**
  A focus on specific events or behaviours, avoiding general, extreme or vague statements.

  | Example: | 'You interrupted me three times during the meeting.' | Not: | 'You're always trying to get my attention.' |

- **Conjunctive, not disjunctive**
  A focus on statements that flow from what has been said and facilitating interaction.

  | Example: | 'Relating to what you've just said, I suggest . . . ' | Not: | 'I want to say something (regardless of what you have just said).' |

- **Owned, not disowned**
  A focus on taking responsibility for your statements by using personal ('I') words.

  | Example: | 'I have decided to turn down your request because . . . ' | Not: | 'Your suggestion is good, but it wouldn't get approved.' |

- **Supportive listening, not one-way listening**
  A focus on using a variety of responses, with a bias towards reflective responses.

  | Example: | 'What do you think are the obstacles standing in the way of improvement?' | Not: | 'As I said before, you make too many mistakes: you're just not performing.' |

Source: Whetten, D.A. and Cameron, K.S., *Developing Management Skills*, 8th edition (2011), © 2011. Reprinted by permission of Pearson Education, Inc., Upper Saddle River, NJ.

They believe that following these principles ensures greater understanding of messages, while at the same time making the other person feel accepted and valued. As such they can be effective tools for achieving mutual understanding.

16.7   Communication and strategy – the wider context

Strategy

Argenti et al. (2005) show how managers can apply the themes of this chapter to strategic performance. They suggest that while there are adequate models for developing strategies, less attention has been paid to communicating. Citing examples of corporate disasters that show the damage that poor communication of strategy does to a company's reputation, they propose that managers ensure a close link between communication practices and strategy, quoting Michael Dell:

> I communicate to customers, groups of employees and others, while working on strategy. A key part of strategy is communicating it. Communication is key to operations and an integral part of the process. (p. 84)

Their research enabled them to develop a framework for strategic communication, shown in Figure 16.8, comprising iterative loops between elements of a strategy and the constituencies likely to be affected.

They claim that putting the approach into practice requires an integrated, multilevel approach, linking communication functions with relevant stakeholder groups and the channels most likely to be suitable for each topic and group. They stress that while the approaches shown in Table 16.1 can be tailored to each stakeholder group, the messages need to be consistent with each other and with the intended strategy.

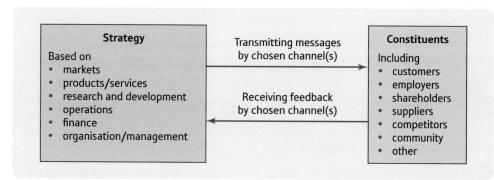

Figure 16.8 The framework for strategic communication

Source: Based on Argenti et al. (2005).

Table 16.1 Elements of a strategic approach to communications

Communication functions	Objectives	Constituencies		Channels
		Primary	Secondary	
Media relations	Public relations, crisis management	All constituents	Media	Press releases, interviews
Employee communications	Internal consensus building	Employees	Customers, families	Public meetings, memos. newsletters
Financial communications	Transparency, meeting financial expectations	Investors	Analysts, media	Conference calls, CEO, CFO
Community relations	Image building	Communities	NGOs media	Events, speeches, philanthropy
Government relations	Regulatory compliance, meeting social expectations	Regulators	Media customers	Lobbying efforts, one-to-one meetings
Marketing communications	Driving sales, building image	Customers	All key constituencies	Advertising, promotions

Source: Based on Argenti et al. (2005)

Structure

Organisations are typically divided into units that focus on their particular part of the task. In hierarchical, mechanistic structures (see Chapter 10) most information passes vertically between managers and subordinates. This sometimes creates a 'silo' mentality, in which people focus too much on local interests and priorities and not enough on other players. They forget that others may be affected by what they are doing – and fail to communicate with them.

Structural factors also affect the ability of staff to use technology to support information flow between organisations, or between professional groups. The units within a care system are separated by boundaries that distinguish and protect them from others. Functional boundaries are particularly apparent between health and social care, but there are also structural and professional divisions within each discipline. At whatever level of analysis, boundaries demarcate a unit from its environment, defending it from others (e.g. by helping to protect its budget) and providing an interface for interactions with others (e.g. by exchanging resources). The 'Management in practice' feature shows how these boundaries can impede the use of new communication technologies.

| Management in practice | Communication barriers in healthcare |

Boddy et al. (2009b) report on a study into the limited progress in implementing electronic systems in healthcare ('e-health'). Many available systems permit information to pass between professional staff irrespective of their physical or organisational location. Progress has been slow, and a research team sought to establish the nature of the barriers. One respondent commented:

> There's some disjointedness in the system which creates a lot of friction and slower progress [than is desirable].

Another illustrated this by referring to a system that had been approved for use nationally, but which health boards had been slow to implement. During that time a rival package had appeared, which many people had started to use in preference to the one that the NHS was promoting.

A common theme was that health board autonomy led to different strategies towards e-health, and to incompatible local systems. This was partly due to different technologies, but also because people adapt working practices to fit the technology: both forces inhibit acceptance of national systems. One said:

> We've sorted out [a national solution], but then our lab system won't feed the correct data. A lot of it's to do with the fact that the UK has multiple systems for doing exactly the same thing, which is ludicrous. Some boards have put money into e-health and others haven't.

Source: Boddy et al. (2009b)

Power

Information has great value. Those who possess it have something others do not have and may need or want. Sole ownership of information can also be used to boost or protect a person's status or the significance of his or her role. Access to information and the means of communicating it to others is a source of power. People may hoard it rather than share it, and use it at the most opportune moment. Those with access to inside information have both prestige and power.

16.8   Integrating themes

Entrepreneurship

In his book *Innovation and Entrepreneurship* (Drucker, 1985), Peter Drucker discusses entrepreneurship in both start-up companies and in established businesses. He presents widely relevant examples of management practices that foster an entrepreneurial spirit within established businesses. Writing of a perennially successful entrepreneurial business supplying health-care products he notes one practice in particular that is important in the larger company. This is:

> a session – informal but well-prepared – in which a member of the top management group sits down with the junior people from research, engineering, manufacturing, marketing, accounting and so on. The senior opens the session by saying: I'm here to listen. I want to hear from you what your aspirations are, but above all, where you see opportunities for this company, and where you see threats. And what are your ideas for us to try to do new things, develop new products . . . what questions do you have about the company, its policies, its position in the marketplace?

These sessions (he concludes):

> are an excellent vehicle for upwards communications, the best means to enable juniors, and especially professionals, to look up from their narrow specialties and see the whole enterprise . . . Above all, these sessions are one of the most effective ways to instil entrepreneurial vision throughout the company. (p. 145)

Sustainability

Moving towards a more sustainable economy depends on communicating information about both the problem and the solutions being proposed. Being controversial, issues of structure and power are bound to influence the communication process, which those wishing to promote sustainable performance need to take into account.

They could use the Argenti et al. (2005) model to help ensure that they exchange information with relevant constituencies, and so come up with a sustainability strategy that is both environmentally worthwhile and commercially viable.

Equally, they could check their communications practices against the communications model to ensure that they pay adequate attention to all the elements of the communication process. People vary in their understanding of the topic, and practice should reflect this.

Internationalisation

Liu et al. (2010) developed and tested a method of measuring what they call the Quality of Communications Experience (QCE) and examined the effect of this in simulated international negotiations. As they point out:

> managers and professionals at all levels work and interact with people from different cultural backgrounds. Employees travel round broader regions while their jobs remain headquartered in one place . . . [so] it becomes more important to be aware of cultural differences and to be able to interact effectively with people from other cultures. (p. 469)

To test the empirical support for this they developed an instrument to measure the dimensions of QCE and then tested this in a series of experimental situations. QCE is an individual-level variable, that depends heavily on the behaviour and reactions of the other party to the interaction – similar to the reactions people are likely to experience in normal activities.

Three dimensions make up QCE:

- **Clarity** – the extent to which each party understands the meaning of what the other is trying to communicate (sample item (out of five) – 'I understood what the other side was saying').
- **Responsiveness** – the extent to which each party sees the other as responding in an appropriate way – ideas of coordination or reciprocity that shape our experience of social interaction (sample item (out of five) – 'the other side responded to my questions and requests quickly during the interaction').
- **Comfort** – the experience of positive feelings experienced during the exchange (sample item (out of five) 'the other side seemed comfortable talking with me').

They hypothesised that QCE would be lower during interactions across cultures than it would be during interactions between people from the same cultures, and also that a higher degree of QCE would lead to better outcomes from the interaction. Their evidence supported these predictions – and also implied that negotiators may be able to adapt their approach to negotiations to take account of the other party's communication pattern.

Governance

High-profile scandals, mistakes and quality failures place an organisation's reputation at risk – possibly destroying in weeks what managers have taken years to build. Governance arrangements could include a regular review of how senior managers handle communications in the face of bad publicity. How customers and members of the public view an event is substantially influenced by how managers handle communications about it. Toyota experienced this in early 2010, when a series of faults led the company to recall millions of vehicles in many countries. The company was widely perceived to have handed the episode badly, causing more damage to the reputation of the brand than was necessary – especially when the media became interested in the topic. Mattila (2009) shows the importance of anticipating (inevitable) damaging publicity from unintentional events by having comprehensive and tested communications strategies in place.

Governance and control arrangements, however robust they appear, depend on people exchanging information – both sending and paying attention to it. The communication models in this chapter highlight the barriers to the effective transmission of information about, for example, risky business being done. Structural and political factors, as well as interpersonal ones, often prevent information reaching those who require it – and/or prevent them from acting on it.

Summary

1 **Explain the role of communicating in the manager's job**

- People at all levels of an organisation need to add value to the resources they use, and to do that they need to communicate with others – about inputs, the transformation process and the outputs. It enables the tasks of planning, organising, leading and controlling.
- It also enables managers to perform their informational, decisional and interpersonal roles.

2 **Identify and illustrate the elements and stages in the communication process**

- Sender, message, encoding, medium, decoding receiver and noise.

3 **Use the concept of information richness to select a communication channel**

In descending order of information richness, the channels are:
- face-to-face communication
- spoken communication electronically transmitted
- personally addressed written communication
- impersonal written communication.

4 **Compare the benefits of different communication networks**

- Centralised networks work well on structured, simple tasks, but are less suitable for complex tasks as the centre becomes overloaded.
- Decentralised networks work well on complex tasks, as information flows between those best able to contribute. On simple tasks this is likely to cause confusion.

5 **Outline some essential interpersonal communication skills**

- Send clear and complete messages.
- Encode messages in symbols the receiver understands.
- Select a medium appropriate for the message.
- Include a feedback mechanism in the message.
- Pay attention.
- Be a good listener.

6 **Show how communication interacts with strategy, structure and power**

- Argenti et al. (2005) have advocated that managers develop coherent arrangements for communicating with key constituencies in formulating strategy, identifying the functions, objectives and channels to use.
- An organisation's structure has a significant effect on the flow of communication between units, and the same applies to the exchange of information between organisations. While technology enables easier communication, structures can impede the flow in practice.

7 **Explain the tasks in making an effective presentation, and understand how you can use this approach to develop your presentation skills**

- The chapter outlined practices that help make an effective presentation, and the 'Develop a skill' feature at the end of this chapter offers a chance to practise that skill.

8 **Show how ideas from the chapter add to your understanding of the integrating themes**

- Drucker reports an example of a communication practice that he found very effective as a way of instilling entrepreneurial vision throughout a company.
- Proposals for sustainability depend on effective communication with many constituencies, which have varying interests towards the topic. Those promoting such projects could use the Argenti et al. (2005) model to guide them.
- Communication between those managing internationally is an opportunity for enriching the range of ideas and contributions available, provided those conducting the dialogue can overcome a common human anxiety about differences.
- Governance and control systems depend on accurate information being sent and attended to by those who should act on it. The ideas in this chapter show how structural and political factors can block the flow of information through a governance system.

Test your understanding

1 Explain why communication is central to managing.

2 Draw a diagram of the communication process, showing each of the stages and elements. Then illustrate it with a communication episode you have experienced.

3 How does feedback help or hinder communication?

4 What is non-verbal communication, and why is it important to effective communication?

5 What do you understand by the term 'information richness', and how does it affect the choice of communication method?

6 What is team briefing?

7 Name three practices that can improve interpersonal communication skill.

8 Outline Argenti's model of strategic communications.

9 Give examples of the way in which the structure of an organisation can affect communication.

10 Show how ideas from the chapter add to your understanding of the integrating themes.

Think critically

Think about the ways in which you typically communicate with others, and about communication in your organisation, or one with which you are familiar.

• Thinking of the people you typically work with, who are effective and who are less effective communicators? What do the effective communicators do?

• What **assumptions** about the communication process (Figure 16.3) seem to guide how (a) you and (b) the people you work most closely with typically communicate?

• What factors in the history or current **context** of the organisation may have shaped communication practices? What significance does the organisation give to how people present ideas to others?

• Have people put forward **alternative** communication practices, based on evidence from elsewhere?

• What **limitations** can you identify in any of these communication theories? For example, do you find the Lengle–Daft model a helpful way of choosing a channel?

Develop a skill – presenting ideas to an audience

Being able to make an effective presentation is a vital management skill – during the selection process and thereafter throughout your career. This exercise should help you develop that.

• **Assessment:** Assess how well you make a presentation to an audience. Do you, for example, find that an audience is evidently interested in what you are saying, and becomes actively involved by asking questions? Or do they seem to lose interest before you have finished? Recall a presentation that seemed to work well – what did the speaker do?

• **Learning:** Read again Section 16.6, especially the 'Key ideas' feature on 'Seven practices for effective presentations' (p. 526).

• **Analysis:** Consider the possible implications for you of these ideas. Why should preparation help what should seem spontaneous and relaxed? Think of a good (or poor) presentation you have seen. Which of the ideas in Section 16.6 were present, or absent?

- **Practice:** Identify (preferably with one or two colleagues on your course) a presentation you are likely to have to make, either during your course (for example, 'Make a presentation on the strengths and weaknesses of X's Theory'), or when you attend an interview (such as 'Explain in five minutes why you want to work here').

  - Follow the steps in 'Key ideas', and make your presentations to each other.
  - Reflect on your presentations when you have finished, and note what you have learned.

- **Application:** Decide on another opportunity to practise this skill within the next week.

Read more

Burton, G. (2013), *Presenting: Deliver presentations with confidence,* Collins, London.

Detailed introduction to all aspects of making a good presentation.

Finkelstein, S. (2003), *Why Smart Executives Fail: And what you can learn from their mistakes,* Penguin, New York.

Fascinating account of the sources of communication failure in public and private organisations.

Goffman, E. (1959), *The Presentation of Self in Everyday Life,* Doubleday, New York.

A classic (and short) work that gives many insights into interpersonal communications.

Kirkpatrick, D. (2010), *The Facebook Effect,* Virgin Books, New York.

Detailed account of the early years, with good insights into the management issues that members of the company had to resolve as it grew.

Whetten, D.A. and Cameron, K.S. (2011), *Developing Management Skills,* Prentice Hall International, Upper Saddle River, NJ.

Extended discussion of interpersonal communication skills, with useful exercises.

Go online

These websites have appeared in the chapter:

www.facebook.com/facebook
www.cisco.com
www.innocentdrinks.com
www.blackcircles.com
www.personneltoday.com

Visit two of the sites, or others that interest you, and navigate to the pages dealing with recent news, press or investor relations.

- In what ways is the company using the website to communicate information about inputs, outputs and transformation processes?
- Is it providing a one-way or a two-way communication process?

CHAPTER 17
TEAMS

Aim

To outline the significance of teams and how they develop.

Objectives

By the end of your work on this chapter you should be able to outline the concepts below in your own terms and:

1 Distinguish the types of teams in organisations
2 Use a model to analyse the composition of a team
3 Identify the stages of team development and explain how teams move between them
4 Identify specific team processes and explain how they affect performance
5 Evaluate the outcomes of a team for the members and the organisation
6 Outline how their context influences team performance
7 Explain the elements of team processes and understand how you can use these to help you develop the skill of observing a team
8 Show how ideas from the chapter add to your understanding of the integrating themes

Key terms

This chapter introduces these terms:

formal teams	team
informal groups	preferred team role
self-managing team	team-based rewards
virtual teams	observation
structure	content
working groups	concertive control

Each is a term defined within the text, and in the glossary at the end of the book.

Case study   Cisco Systems   www.cisco.com

Cisco Systems is a company at the heart of the internet. It develops and supplies the physical equipment and software that allows data to travel over the internet, and also provides support services to companies to improve their use of the network. A group of scientists from Stanford University founded Cisco in 1984 and its engineers have focused on developing internet protocol (IP)-based networking technologies. The core areas of the business remain the supply of routing and switching equipment, but it is also working in areas such as home networking, network security and storage networking.

The company employs over 70,000 staff around the world, developing new systems and working with customers to implement and enhance their network infrastructure. Most projects are implemented by staff from several sites working as virtual teams, in the sense that they are responsible for a collective product but work in physically separate places.

The company created a team to coordinate the testing and release of a new version of a complex piece of software that monitors the performance of the many elements in a network. When the product was released a few months later, the members of the team were free to work on other projects. The team had eight members, drawn from four sites and three countries:

Name	Location	Role
Steve	Raleigh, North Carolina	Project coordinator
Richard	Cumbernauld, Scotland	Development manager
Graham	Cumbernauld, Scotland	Development engineer
Eddie	Cumbernauld, Scotland	Development engineer
Rai	Austin, Texas	Test engineer
Silvio	Austin, Texas	Test engineer
Jim	Raleigh, North Carolina	Network architect
Gunzal	Bangalore, India	Release support engineer

The role of the coordinator was to ensure the smooth operation of the team and to monitor actual progress

© Mario Proenca/Bloomberg/Getty Images

against the challenging delivery schedule. The software was developed in one of the company's European plants – development engineers wrote the code and passed it to test engineers. They were responsible for rigorous testing, and reporting problems so that the development engineers could fix them.

The network architect has extensive knowledge of the network hardware that the software would manage, and supervised the development and testing of the software to ensure it worked efficiently with the hardware. The release support engineer dealt with the logistics of software release, such as defining each version and ensuring deliverables were available to the manufacturing departments at the appropriate times.

Each member worked full-time on the project, though they never met physically during its lifetime. All members took part in a weekly conference call, and also a daily call attended by the coordinator, development manager and a member of the test team. Communication throughout the team was mainly by email, with some instant messaging.

Source: Communication from members of the project team.

Case questions 17.1

- What challenges would you expect a team that never meets will face during its work?

- In what ways may it need to work differently from a conventional team?

- What kinds of team does Cisco use in Hackman's typology? (See Section 17.2.)

17.1 Introduction

Managers at Cisco use teams extensively to deliver products and services to customers. The people with the skills it needs to deliver a unique customer's project are widely dispersed around the organisation but need to work together. Teams bring them together for the duration of a project – they then disperse and re-form in different combinations to work on their next project. The company also uses teams for internal projects, where staff from several functions and locations work together to solve an operational problem, such as improving a financial or marketing system.

People at work have always developed loyalties among small groups of fellow workers and there are well-documented examples of industries where work was formally organised in small, self-managing teams (Trist and Bamforth, 1951). Teams are common in research-based organisations such as Dyson or GlaxoSmithKline, where scientists and engineers from several disciplines work together on a common project. Manufacturing firms such as BMW (www.bmw.com) or GKN (www.gkn.com) organise staff in teams. Some work across organisations – as when BAA created integrated teams from suppliers, consultants, contractors and BAA staff to design and deliver Terminal 5 at London's Heathrow Airport. Teams bring together those with different experiences and perspectives to solve difficult problems – see 'Key ideas'.

Key ideas **Teams at work**

A review of research on teams by Salas et al. (2008) sets the scene:

Teams have become the strategy of choice when organisations are confronted with complex and difficult tasks. Teams are used when errors lead to severe consequences; when the task complexity exceeds the capacity of an individual; when the task environment is ill-defined, ambiguous and stressful; when multiple and quick decisions are needed; and when the lives of others depend on the collective insight of individual members. Teams are used in aviation, the military, healthcare, financial sectors, nuclear power plants, engineering problem-solving projects, manufacturing and countless other domains.

Source: Salas et al. (2008).

While Salas et al. (2008) are correct about the wide use of teams, forming one does not mean it will necessarily work well. Some, such as that at Cisco, work to high standards and levels of achievement, while others waste time and other resources, destroying rather than adding value. Despite their popularity, evidence about their benefits is mixed – perhaps because the diverse backgrounds that make a team worthwhile also make it harder for members to work together. Figure 17.1 helps to explain this variation, showing teams as an open system. The main inputs are the team members themselves – so composition affects performance. Members need to learn to work together; the processes they use will also affect performance.

The chapter begins by outlining the types of team you may encounter (including 'virtual' teams), which leads to a definition. You will then learn about the composition of teams, their stages of development, internal processes and how context also affects performance. A final section examines the outcomes of teams. Learning to observe a team helps people to become more effective team members, so the 'Develop a skill' feature at the end of the chapter focuses on that.

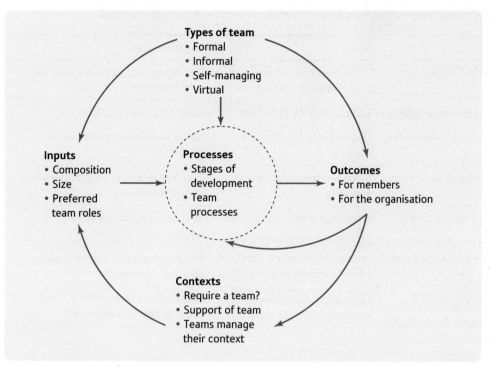

Figure 17.1 An overview of the chapter

17.2   Types of team

Teams have many functions and take many forms – with implications for their members.

Functions of teams

Hackman (1990) identified seven team functions, and Table 17.1 summarises the risks and opportunities associated with each.

Some of these functions (performing groups, task forces) imply the teams (such as that at Cisco) are likely to be temporary, while others may be relatively stable and long-lived. Temporary teams embody unique challenges relating to pace of team development and divided loyalties. These are becoming common in new product development, media production and R&D, which frequently rely on temporary creative teams to perform the organisation's primary process.

Table 17.1 Hackman's classification of team types and their associated risks and opportunities

Type	Risks	Opportunities
Top management teams – to set organisational directions	Underbounded; absence of organisational context	Self-designing; influence over key organisational conditions
Task forces – for a single unique project	Team and work both new	Clear purpose and deadline
Professional support groups – providing expert assistance	Dependency on others for work	Using and honing professional expertise
Performing groups – playing to audiences	Skimpy organisational supports	Play that is fuelled by competition and/or audiences
Human service teams – taking care of people	Emotional drain; struggle for control	Inherent significance of helping people
Customer service teams – selling products and services	Loss of involvement with parent organisation	Bridging between parent organisation and customers
Production teams – turning out the product	Retreat into technology; insulation from end users	Continuity of work; able to hone team design and product

Source: Hackman (1990), p. 489.

The types of team identified by Hackman take several forms – formal or informal, self-managing or virtual.

Formal teams

A **formal team** is one that management has deliberately created to perform specific tasks to help meet organisational goals.

Managers create **formal teams** as they shape the organisation's basic structure, and allocate specific tasks to them. Vertical 'teams' consist of a manager and his or her subordinates within a single department or function. The manager and staff in the treasury department of a bank, or the senior nurse, nursing staff and support staff in a unit of the Western General Hospital, are formally constituted into (possibly several) vertical teams, as is a team leader and his or her staff in a BT call centre. In each case, senior managers created them to support their goals.

Horizontal teams consist of staff from roughly the same level, but from several functions. The Cisco team is an example, formed to release new software. In Hackman's typology, these task forces (often called cross-functional teams) deal with non-routine problems that require knowledge from several professions.

Informal groups

An **informal group** is one that emerges when people come together and interact regularly.

Informal groups are a powerful feature of organisational life. They develop as day-to-day activities bring people into contact – and they discover common sporting or social interests. Work-related informal groups arise when people exchange information and ideas: staff using a software package may begin to share problems or tips. Those in separate departments dealing with the same customer may pass information to each other to avoid misunderstandings, even though this is not a requirement. Informal groups may develop in opposition to management – people who believe they are being unfairly treated may come together to express their dissatisfaction.

Self-managing teams

A **self-managing team** operates without an internal manager and is responsible for a complete area of work.

Self-managing teams are responsible for a complete area of work, and operate without close supervision. Members are responsible for doing the work but have a high degree of autonomy in how they do it: they manage themselves, including planning, scheduling and

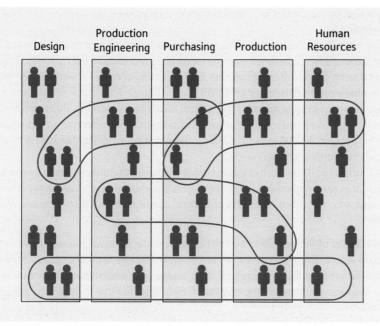

Figure 17.2 Horizontal and vertical teams in an engineering company

assigning tasks among members. They also establish the pace of work, make operating decisions, work out how to overcome problems and manage quality. They are likely to have a considerable influence over selecting new employees – as happens at BMW.

Key ideas	Informal networks: the company behind the chart

According to Krackhardt and Hanson (1993):

> If the formal organisation is the skeleton of the company, the informal is the central nervous system. This drives the collective thought processes, actions and reactions of the business units. Designed to facilitate standard modes of production, management create the formal organisation to handle easily anticipated problems. When unexpected problems arise, the informal organisation becomes active. Its complex web of social ties form every time colleagues communicate and solidifies over time into surprisingly stable networks. Highly adaptive, informal networks move diagonally and elliptically, skipping entire functions to get work done.

> The authors suggest that these informal networks can either foster or disrupt communication processes. They recommend that managers try to understand them in order to make use of their strengths, or to adjust aspects of the formal organisation to complement the informal.

Source: Krackhardt and Hanson (1993), p. 104.

Virtual teams

Modern communications technologies enable and encourage people to create **virtual teams**, in which the members are physically distant for most of the time, even though they are expected to deliver a collective outcome. Virtual teams use computer technology to link members – smartphones, email, videoconferencing and online discussion. They can perform all the functions of a team that is in the same place, but lack the face-to-face interaction and discussion that helps working relationships. While virtual teams bring expertise together without the expense of travel, they require careful management to ensure the benefits of team working are retained. Practices include ensuring that some regular (or at least initial)

Virtual teams are those in which the members are physically separated, using communications technologies to collaborate across space and time to accomplish their common task.

face-to-face contact occurs, and that members resolve issues of roles, working methods and conflict management.

Many of the teams in Cisco are like this, with the added challenge that they work across national boundaries. The growth of international business means that people frequently work in teams drawn from different nations and cultures, and this form of remote working raises new challenges (Zander et al. (2013)). At a superficial level differences of time zone create problems of managing working hours, lunch breaks and holiday cycles. Larger difficulties arise from likely differences among team members, reflecting inevitable differences in their respective 'home' units regarding the goals of a project, attitudes to sharing knowledge and differences in motivation.

Dixon and Panteli (2010) note that while communication technology enables the growth of virtual teams, it is now embedded in the work of team members who work together in the same place – and who are often members of several collocated and virtual teams. Modern technologies:

> expand the abilities of individuals to switch between multiple tasks and teams with minimal overhead and effort. Even, therefore, where team members are collocated, increasingly they are also simultaneously members of other teams with whom they interact using communication technology. This, on the one hand, reduces the face-to-face interactions with their collocated colleagues but, on the other hand, increases connectivity and interaction with geographically dispersed colleagues (p. 1179).

Activity 17.2 Reflect on an experience of team working

Recall times when you have been part of a team.

- Which of the seven types listed by Hackman have you experienced? Do you agree with his comments on the risks and opportunities of those types? If not, what were they?
- Which of the other types have you experienced? Record the circumstances, as you will be able to use this during the chapter.
- If possible, compare your notes with other members of your course.

17.3 Crowds, groups and teams

The teams described in the previous section were not random collections of people. A crowd in the street is not usually a team: they are there by chance, and will have little if any further contact. What about the staff in a supermarket or in the same section of a factory? They are not a crowd: they have some things in common, and people may refer to them as a team. Compare them with five people designing some software for a bank, each of whom brings distinct professional skills to their collective discussions of the most suitable design, or with seven students working together on a group assignment. They have a **structure** to handle the whole process, work largely on their initiative and move easily between tasks, helping each other as needed.

Structure is the regularity in the way a unit or group is organised, such as the roles that are specified.

Activity 17.3 Crowds, groups and teams

Note down a few words that express the differences between the examples given. Do some sound more like a group or a team than others?
Consider a Davis Cup tennis or Ryder Cup golf team, in which most of the action takes place between individual participants from either side. No significant coordination occurs between the members during a match.

- In what ways would such teams meet the above definition?
- Can you think of other examples of people who work largely on their own but are commonly referred to as a team?

In normal conversation we use the words 'group' and 'team' to mean the same thing, and this book follows that usage. However, some distinguish between the two, and it is useful to be aware of this to avoid confusion. Katzenbach and Smith's (1993) definition of a team illustrates this: 'A small number of people with complementary skills who are committed to a common purpose, performance goals, and working approach for which they hold themselves mutually accountable' (p. 45). A few people working together may do so very amiably and productively, but may be quite loosely associated with each other – they may not think of themselves as having a shared purpose, may not use a common method of working, and may not see themselves as mutually accountable. They may exchange normal social courtesies and perhaps exchange task advice and information. But they are accountable for their work as individuals. In many situations such '**working groups**' will meet the required performance standards, as long as members do their job competently. **Teams** use collective discussion, debate and decision to deliver 'collective work products' – something more than the sum of individual efforts.

The essential point is that whether we use the term 'group' or 'team', they differ in their outcomes – some will perform well, and others will fail. The practical task is not to debate what to call them, but to understand the causes and consequences of differences in performance. As long as people are aware of this distinction they should use whichever term seems suitable. It is what groups and teams do that matter, not what they are called. Katzenbach and Smith's (1993) definition suggests some criteria against which to evaluate features of a team.

> A **working group** is a collection of individuals who work mainly on their own but interact socially and share information and best practices.

> A **team** is 'a small number of people with complementary skills who are committed to a common purpose, performance goals, and approach for which they hold themselves mutually accountable' (Katzenbach and Smith, 1993).

Small number

More than about 12 people find it hard to operate as a coherent team. It becomes harder to agree on a common purpose and the practicalities of where and when to meet become tricky. Most teams have between two and ten people – with between four and eight probably being most common.

Complementary skills

Teams benefit from having members who, between them, share *technical, functional* or *professional* skills relevant to the work. A team implementing a computer network requires at least some members with technical skills; one developing a retail strategy needs some with strategy or marketing expertise.

Second, a team needs people with *problem-solving* and *decision-making* skills. These enable members to approach a task systematically, using appropriate techniques. Finally, a team needs people with *interpersonal* skills to hold it together. Members' attitudes and feelings towards each other and to the task change as work continues. This may generate conflict so the team needs someone who can manage this.

Common purpose

Teams cannot work unless members invest time and effort to clarify and understand their common purpose. They need to express this in clear performance goals upon which members can focus their time and energy. A common purpose helps members to communicate, since they can interpret and understand their contributions more easily.

Common approach

Teams need to decide how they will work together to accomplish their purpose. This includes deciding who does what, how the group should make decisions and how to deal with conflict. The common approach includes integrating new members into the team, and generally working to promote the mutual trust necessary for success.

Mutual accountability

A team cannot work as one until its members willingly hold themselves to be collectively and mutually accountable for the outcomes. As members do real work towards a common purpose, commitment and trust usually follow. If one or more members are unwilling to accept this collective responsibility, the team will not become fully effective.

Activity 17.4   Using the definition to analyse a team

Recall a team of which you have been a member. Alternatively, arrange to gather information for this activity from someone who has experience of team working in an organisation.

- To what extent do you feel the team was effective?
- To what extent did it meet the five criteria listed in the definition?
- Can you identify how meeting these criteria, or not doing so, affected performance?
- If possible, compare your evidence with other members of your course.

17.4   Team composition

Figure 17.1 shows that one factor in team performance is its composition, which Bell (2007) defines as the configuration of member attributes (e.g. number, abilities, demographics, personality, values, attitudes) in a team. These have a powerful influence on team processes and outcomes, and her review of 89 studies confirmed that agreeableness, conscientiousness, experience and a preference for team work all had positive effects on performance. A team of self-centred stars will be a disaster.

As team members work on the task, their unique attributes lead them to take on distinct roles. Teams need balance, and two relevant ideas are the distinction between task and maintenance roles, and Belbin's research on team roles.

Task and maintenance roles

Some people focus on the task, on doing the job, on meeting deadlines. Others put their energy into keeping the peace and holding the group together. Table 17.2 summarises the two.

Teams need both roles, and skilful managers try to ensure that both are present.

Meredith Belbin – team roles

Meredith Belbin and his colleagues systematically observed several hundred teams performing a task, and concluded that each member tended to behave in a way that corresponded to one of nine roles. The balance of these roles affected how well a team performed.

Table 17.2 Summary of task and maintenance roles

Emphasis on task	Emphasis on maintenance
Initiator	Encourager
Information seeker	Compromiser
Diagnoser	Peacekeeper
Opinion seeker	Clarifier
Evaluator	Summariser
Decision manager	Standard setter

Key ideas   **Belbin's research method**

Henley School of Management based much of its training on inviting managers to work in teams of up to ten on exercises or business simulations. The organisers had observed that some teams achieved better objective results than others – irrespective of the abilities of the individual members as measured by standard personality and mental tests. The reasons were unclear – why did some teams of individually able people perform less well than teams composed of less able people?

Belbin conducted a study in which observers, drawn from course members, used a standard procedure to record the types of contribution that members made. Team members voluntarily took psychometric tests, and team performance led to a quantifiable result. The researchers formed teams of members with above-average mental abilities, and compared their performance with the other teams. The 'intelligent' teams usually performed less well. Of 25 such teams only three were winners, and the most common position was sixth in a league of eight. The explanation lay in the way they behaved, typically spending time in debate, arguing for their point of view to the exclusion of others. These highly intelligent people were good at spotting flaws in others' arguments, and became so engrossed in these that they neglected other tasks. Failure led to recrimination. The lesson was that behaviour (rather than measured intelligence) affected group performance.

Source: Belbin (1981).

The researchers noted that some people were creative, full of ideas and suggestions. Others were concerned with detail, ensuring the team dealt with all aspects of the job, while others kept the team together. Table 17.3 lists the nine roles identified by Belbin (2010), who saw that winning teams had members who took on a balance of roles that differed from the balance in less successful ones.

Winning teams had an appropriate balance, such as:

- a capable coordinator;
- a strong plant – a creative and clever source of ideas;
- at least one other clever person to act as a stimulus to the plant;
- a monitor–evaluator – someone to find flaws in proposals before it was too late.

Ineffective teams usually had a severe imbalance, such as:

- a coordinator with two dominant shapers – since the shapers will not allow the coordinator to take that role;
- two resource investigators and two plants – since no one listens or turns ideas into action;
- a completer–finisher with monitor–evaluators and implementers – probably slow to progress, and stuck in detail.

Table 17.3 Belbin's team roles

Role	Typical features
Implementer	Disciplined, reliable, conservative and efficient. Turns ideas into practical actions
Coordinator	Mature, confident, a good chairperson. Clarifies goals, promotes decision making, delegates well
Shaper	Challenging, dynamic, thrives on pressure. Has the drive and courage to overcome obstacles
Plant	Creative, imaginative, unorthodox. Solves difficult problems
Resource investigator	Extravert, enthusiastic, communicative. Explores opportunities. Develops contacts
Monitor–evaluator	Sober, strategic and discerning. Sees all options, judges accurately
Team worker	Cooperative, mild, perceptive and diplomatic. Listens, builds, averts friction, calms the waters
Completer	Painstaking, conscientious, anxious. Searches out errors and omissions. Delivers on time
Specialist	Single-minded, self-starting, dedicated. Provides knowledge and skills in rare supply

Source: Belbin (2010).

Preferred team roles are the types of behaviour that people display relatively frequently when they are part of a team.

Belbin did not suggest that all teams should have nine people, each with a different **preferred team role**. His point was that team composition should reflect the task:

> The useful people to have in a team are those who possess strengths or characteristics that serve a need without duplicating those that are already there. Teams are a question of balance; what is needed is not well-balanced individuals but individuals who balance well with one another. In that way human frailties can be underpinned and strengths used to full advantage. (Belbin, 1981, p. 77)

Trainers use the model widely to enable members to evaluate their preferred roles. They also consider how the balance of roles within a team affects performance. Some managers use it when filling vacancies. A personnel director joined a new organisation and concluded that it employed few 'completer–finishers'. Management started initiatives and programmes but left them unfinished as they switched to something else. She resolved that in recruiting new staff she would try to bring at least one more 'completer–finisher' to the senior team.

Management in practice   Using Belbin's roles in film-making teams

Hollywood had experienced a shift from long-term jobs to short-term project teams. With their highly skilled freelance staff who come together for a brief period to carry out specific tasks and then disband, film making offers a model for the future of work in the wider world. Angus Strachan has been using Belbin's model to help film directors manage expensive production teams more effectively:

> Managing film teams requires a mature coordinator who can handle creative people with delicate egos and strong opinions . . . A good unit production manager is a strong monitor–evaluator, someone who can carefully analyse the overall situation and make the big calls. The second assistant director needs to be a strong completer–finisher, passing on accurate information that enables the unit production manager to keep abreast of the situation . . . A successful assistant director also needs to be a good communicator and organiser who has the flexibility to adjust schedules – in Belbin's terms to take on the resource investigator role.

Source: Angus Strachan, 'Lights, camera, action', *Personnel Management*, 16 September 2004, pp. 44–6.

However, there is no evidence that companies use the model when forming teams from existing staff. Managers typically form teams on criteria of technical expertise, departmental representation, or who is available. How the team processes will work is a secondary consideration. This is understandable, but in doing so managers make the implicit assumption that people will be able and willing to cover roles if one seems to be lacking. Whether managers use the theory or not, it implies that anyone responsible for a team may find the work goes better if they put effort into securing the most suitable mix of members.

The performance of a team is also affected by how well it moves through distinct stages of development, and by the team processes the members establish.

Case study   Cisco – the case continues   www.cisco.com

Recalling the roles within the team, Steve said:

> My job was mainly to ensure that everything in the virtual team runs smoothly – often just a matter of arranging and coordinating meetings, but also encouraging some kind of creative spark that'll help discussion along. Gunzal takes his time to make decisions, but when he does, he's usually correct. Eddie is very systematic in his work, and very hard working.

Another commented:

> I'd say Graham is often the one who comes up with original ideas, while Jim has an incredible range of contacts within the company, and can usually find the right person to go to. Rai is very precise in everything he does and it's very important that he receives the correct information from the engineers. If they don't explain something properly he's good at going back to ask for more information.

Source: Communication from members of the project team.

Case questions 17.2

- Which of the Belbin roles can you identify among the members of the team?
- Are any of the roles missing, and how may that have affected team performance?

Activity 17.5   Critical reflection on team composition

Evaluate a team you have worked with using Belbin's team roles.

- Which roles were well represented, and which were missing?
- Did that affect how the team worked?
- Which of the roles most closely matches your preferred role?
- What are the strengths and weaknesses of Belbin's model to the manager?

17.5   Stages of team development

Putting people into a team does not mean they perform well immediately, as teams need to learn to work together. Some never perform well. Tuckman and Jensen (1977) developed a theory that groups potentially pass through five stages of development, shown in Figure 17.3.

Forming

Forming is the stage at which members choose, or are told, to join a team. Managers may select them for their functional and technical expertise or for some other skill. They come together and begin to find out who the other members are, exchanging fairly superficial

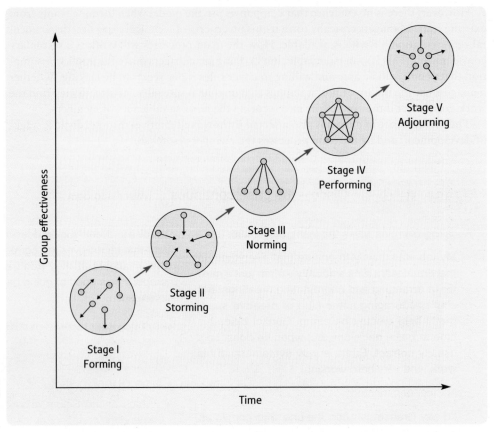

Figure 17.3 Stages of team development

information about themselves, and beginning to offer ideas about what the group should do. People are trying to make an impression on the group and to establish their identity with other members.

Storming

Conflicts may occur at the storming stage, so it can be an uncomfortable time for the group. As the group begins the actual work members begin to express differences of interest that they withheld, or did not recognise, at the forming stage. People realise that others want different things, have other priorities and, perhaps, have hidden agendas. Different personalities emerge, with contrasting attitudes towards the group and how it should work. Some experience conflicts between their time with the group and other duties. Differences in values and norms emerge.

Some groups never pass this stage. There may be little open conflict and members may believe the group is performing well – but may be deluding themselves. If the group does not confront disagreements it will remain at the forming or storming stage and do no significant work. Performance depends on someone doing or saying something to move the group to the next stage.

Norming

Here the members begin to accommodate differences and establish adequate ways of working together. They develop norms – expected ways to behave – about how they should interact, handle the task, deal with differences. People create or clarify roles and responsibilities. They may establish a common language to allow members to work effectively.

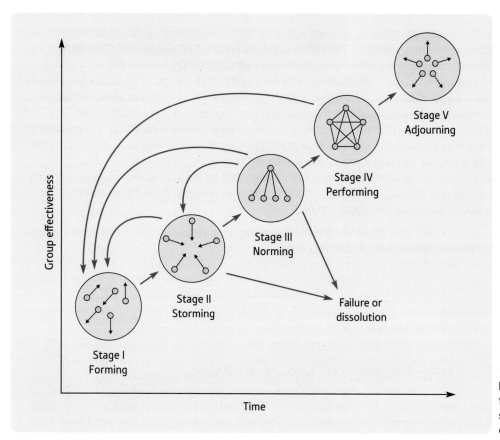

Figure 17.4 Modified model of the stages of team development

Performing

Here the group is working well, gets on with the job to the required standard and achieves its objectives. Not all groups get this far.

Adjourning

The team completes its task and disbands. Members may reflect on how the group performed and identify lessons for future tasks. Some groups disband because they are clearly not able to do the job, and agree to stop meeting.

A team that survives will go through these stages many times. As new members join, as others leave, or as circumstances change, tensions arise that take the group back to an earlier stage. A new member implies that the team should revisit, however briefly, the forming and norming stages to bring the new member psychologically into the team and communicate how they should behave. The process will be more like Figure 17.4 than the linear progression implied by the original theory.

Key ideas	Managing the virtual team life cycle

Furst et al. (2004) noted the benefits of virtual teams in eliminating boundaries of time and space, but also found that they more often fail than succeed. To explain this they tracked the evolution of six virtual teams in a company, using the Tuckman and Jensen model. They found that virtual teams faced additional problems at each stage of the model, compared to those working in the same place.

- **Forming** is more difficult, and takes longer, as there is less frequent communication, especially the informal chat between workers who meet regularly. This reduces the speed at which people make friendships and increases the risk of forming false impressions or stereotypes about other team members.
- **Storming** can also be more fraught, as the absence of frequent non-verbal clues increases the risks of misunderstanding. Disagreements can be exacerbated or prolonged if people do not respond quickly to electronic communication – even if caused by differences in working times or poor technology.
- **Norming** in virtual teams needs to clarify how to coordinate work, how to communicate and how quickly to respond to requests. The process of norming itself is made more complex with electronic communication, as it is harder to try out ideas tentatively and to see reactions.
- **Performing** depends on sharing information, integrating ideas and seeking creative solutions. The challenges of virtual working at this stage include competing pressure from local assignments, losing focus and the fear of a failure that would damage a career.

The authors use their analysis to suggest what those managing a virtual team could do at each stage to increase the chances of virtual teams reliably adding value.

Source: Furst et al. (2004).

Case study　　Cisco – the case continues　　www.cisco.com

Members of the team commented on the way the team developed. A common issue was the problem of scheduling meetings:

> I've always found in virtual teams that when the team is first formed it isn't really getting any serious work done (unless we're under severe time pressure), it's about getting everyone together so they at least have some knowledge of the others in the team. (Steve)

Another said:

> It was strange when we first started working together, because we didn't push on and get any testing or fixing done straight away. Steve was really pushing for us all to spend a few hours in conference calls getting to know each other and how we were all going to work together. We took our time to get into the actual work that was required. (Graham)

Other reflections included:

> I had a few discussions with Steve . . . he wanted us to spend most of our time in conference meetings with the rest of the team, while my engineers already had a good understanding of the work that was needed and just wanted to get on with it. But Steve is the team lead so we had to go along with his approach. (Richard)

> It's weird having to form such a close relationship with someone [when] you don't even know what they look like. But as we're using IM [Instant Messenger] just about every day you get used to it. I think you sometimes have to make an extra effort to talk directly to people, just to keep the relationship going. Sometimes it'd be easier for me to email Rai, but I phone him, just so we can have a bit of a chat. (Eddie)

> It means you have to be a bit more careful when it comes to communication. Most of the time you have to use email and IM to discuss issues, which means there can be misunderstandings if you're not careful. When you interact in person you use things like facial expression and hand gestures – none of these are available when emailing so you have to state your arguments more clearly. (Jim)

Source: Communication from members of the project team.

Case questions 17.3

- Relate these accounts to the stages of team development.
- What examples of forming, storming and norming does the case contain?

17.6 Team processes

Effective teams, often with the help of coaches, develop processes that help them complete their tasks. These include a common approach, patterns of communication and observing team practices.

Common approach

The outcome of an effective 'norming' stage is that members agree both the administrative and social aspects of working together. This includes deciding who does which jobs and how the group should make decisions. The common approach includes:

- agreeing the purposes of the team, and the outputs it will deliver;
- how to achieve that purpose – gathering information, deciding what has to be done, creating a plan;
- integrating new members;
- setting, and keeping to, agendas and timetables;
- recording what has been agreed;
- specifying who is to do what;
- agreeing dates and times of team meetings.

Team members need to control their meetings effectively – whether face to face or at a distance – conducting them in a way that suits the purpose of the task. Table 17.4 is an example of advice widely available about effective and ineffective meetings.

Stachowski et al. (2009) showed the benefits of developing a 'common approach'. They wanted to know whether patterns of interaction in a crisis affected performance, and assessed this by observing crews responsible for running nuclear power plants. The researchers observed and recorded crews' interaction patterns during regular training sessions, when the crews (each with between three and six members) took part in a simulated crisis. Crews were rated as being effective or ineffective by analysis of their information exchanges.

The analysis showed statistically significant differences: effective crews had fewer interaction patterns than less effective ones (i.e. they followed a similar routine to cope with many circumstances, rather than frequently changing routines); fewer team members featured in the response patterns; and exchanges were short and concise. While the research site was unique, the conclusion that some teams develop methods that work better than others applies widely.

Table 17.4 Five tips for effective meetings

Meetings are likely to succeed if:	Meetings are likely to fail if:
they are scheduled well in advance	they are fixed at short notice (absentees)
they have an agenda, with relevant documents available in advance	they have no agenda or papers (no preparation, lack of focus, discussion longer)
they have a start and finish time, and follow a schedule (approximate) of times for each item	they are of indefinite length (talk drifts), time is lost and important items are not dealt with (delay, and require a further meeting)
decisions and responsibilities for action are recorded and circulated within 24 hours	decisions lack clarity (misunderstanding what was agreed, delay, reopening issues)
they keep subgroups or members of related teams informed of progress	the team is not aware of work going on in other teams that is relevant to its work

Table 17.5 Categories of communication within a group

Category	Explanation
Proposing	Putting forward a suggestion, idea or course of action
Supporting	Declaring agreement or support for an individual or their idea
Building	Developing or extending an idea or suggestion from someone else
Disagreeing	Criticising another person's statement
Giving information	Giving or clarifying facts, ideas or opinions
Seeking information	Seeking facts, ideas or opinions from others

Categories of communication

Group members depend on information and ideas from others to do tasks; a useful skill is to identify the kind of contribution that people make and whether this helps performance. Table 17.5 shows six categories of group communication, which enables an observer to analyse how a group uses time, and how this affects performance. A group that devotes most of its time to proposing ideas and disagreeing with them will not perform well. A group that spends time proposing and building, using their listening skills, will perform better.

Observing the team

Observation is the activity of concentrating on how a team works rather than taking part in the activity itself.

Content is the specific substantive task that the group is undertaking.

Members can develop the skill of assessing how well a team is performing a task, and an especially useful skill is to develop the ability to **observe** a group. This means concentrating on the process (what people say or do) rather than on the **content** of the immediate task. They work slightly apart from the team for a short time and keep a careful record of what members say or do, how other members react and how that affects performance. At the very least, members can reflect on these questions at the end of a task:

- What did people do or say that helped or hindered the group's performance?
- What went well during that task, which we should try to repeat?
- What did not go well, which we could improve?

With practice, members are able to observe what is happening as they work on the task. They can do this more easily if they focus on specified behaviours, perhaps adapted from those in Table 17.5.

17.7   Outcomes of teams – for the members

Acceptance by a group meets a widely held human need – Mary Parker Follett (Chapter 2) observed the social nature of people and the benefits of cooperative action. She saw the group as an intermediate institution between the solitary individual and the abstract society, and believed that it was through the group that people organised cooperative action:

> Early psychology was based on the study of the individual; early sociology was based on the study of society. But there is no such thing as the 'individual', there is no such thing as 'society'; there is only the group and the group-unit – the social individual. Social psychology must begin with an intensive study of the group, of the selective processes which go on within it, the differentiated reactions, the likenesses and the unlikenesses, and the spiritual energy which unites them. (Quoted in Graham, 1995, p. 230)

Likert (1961) developed this theme of organising work in groups. He observed that effective managers encouraged participation by group members in all aspects of the job, including setting goals and budgets, controlling costs and organising work. Individuals became members of a team who were loyal to each other and who had high levels of team-working skills. Likert maintained that these groups were effective because of the principle of supportive relationships. He agreed with Maslow that people value a positive response from others, which helps to build and maintain their self-esteem. Social relationships at work serve the same purpose, especially when people spend much of their time in a group. Managers in effective organisations had deliberately linked such groups to ensure people had overlapping membership of more than one group: 'each person . . . is a member of one or more functioning workgroups that have a high degree of group loyalty, effective skills of interaction and high performance goals' (Likert, 1961, p. 104). Figure 17.5 shows the principle.

Key ideas   **Mary Parker Follett and Japanese management**

According to Tokihiko Enomoto, Professor of Business Administration at Tokai University, Japan:

Follett's work has become part of our teaching on management, and is well known to quite a number of . . . managers in our government institutions and business organisations. Much of what Follett says about individuals and groups reflects to a substantial extent our Japanese view of the place of individuals in groups, and by extension their place in society . . . She sees individuals not as independent selves going their separate ways, but as interdependent, interactive and interconnecting members of the groups to which they belong. This is something close to the Japanese ethos. We can fully agree with Follett when she writes that 'the vital relation of the individual to the world is through his groups'.

Source: Quoted in Graham (1995), pp. 242–3.

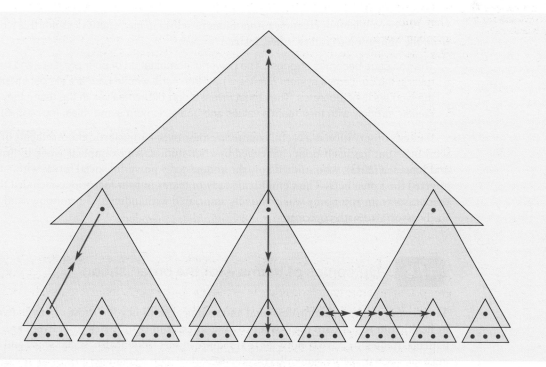

Figure 17.5 Likert's principle of supporting relationships

Note: The arrows indicate the linking-pin functions, both vertical and horizontal – as in cross-functional teams.

Source: Adapted from Likert (1967), p. 50.

These ideas continue to influence practice. As members overcome problems they build mutual trust and confidence. They benefit from the buzz of being in a team, and of 'being part of something bigger than myself'. Recent empirical work by Ellemers et al. (2013) confirms the many positive outcomes of teams. They show that a person who feels they are included in a team, and that their contribution is valued, have positive feelings about the team. They are therefore willing to contribute more to the common task.

There is a counter-view, which is valuable in showing that not all teams have that positive outcome – and that some can subject their members to what Barker (1993) refers to as a system of **concertive control**. This was not imposed by management, but arose as workers negotiated a consensus among themselves. He studied an electronic components company whose founders organised the 90 manufacturing staff (two-thirds of them women) into self-managing teams. Each was responsible for part of the product range and were able to decide how they would work together. An example of concertive control occurred when the late delivery of components meant that a team would miss a delivery target. To recover the position the team agreed to work late and also to accommodate the external commitments of some members. This set a precedent for the way members would behave:

Concertive control is when workers reach a negotiated consensus on how to shape their behaviour according to a set of core values.

> I work my best at trying to help our team to get stuff out the door. If it requires overtime, coming in at five o'clock and spending your weekend here, that's what I do. (Barker, 1993 p. 422)

Members rewarded those who conformed by making them feel part of the team. They punished those who had 'bad' attitudes. The norms evolved from a loose system that workers 'knew' to a tighter system of objective rules. One explained:

> Well we had some disciplinary thing. We had a few certain people who didn't show up on time and made a habit of coming in late. So the team got together and kind a set some guidelines and we told them, you know, 'If you come in late the third time and you don't do anything to correct it, you're gone.' That was a team decision that this was a guideline that we follow. (p. 426)

Barker concludes that creating autonomous or self-managed teams does not free workers from the obligation to follow rules. Instead:

> The iron cage becomes stronger. The powerful combination of peer pressure and rational rules in the concertive system creates a new iron cage whose bars are almost invisible to the workers it incarcerates. They must invest a part of themselves in the team: they must identify strongly with their team's values and goals, its norms and rules. (pp. 435–6)

Barker's observation is a useful counter to some over-enthusiastic endorsements of team working – but has itself been challenged by later studies. An example is work by Jønsson and Jeppesen (2013), who studied how the undoubtedly powerful social forces within teams affected their members. Their empirical study of teams in four factories concluded that in these cases team autonomy was positively associated with individual autonomy, and negatively associated with coercion.

17.8   Outcomes of teams – for the organisation

Teams can bring together professional and technical skills beyond those of any individual. In health and social care there is a growing interest in team work to deliver care, since patients' frequently have conditions that require inputs from health, social work and housing professionals. More generally, the ability to deal with a customer may require exchanging ideas among several professionals, which is easier if they are part of a recognised team:

When representatives from all of the relevant areas of expertise are brought together, team decisions and actions are more likely to encompass the full range of perspectives and issues that might affect the success of a collective venture. Multidisciplinary teams are therefore an attractive option when individuals possess different information, knowledge, and expertise that bear on a complex problem. (Van Der Vegt and Bunderson, 2005, p. 532)

Teams can bring both high efficiency and high-quality jobs by:

- providing a structure within which people work together;
- providing a forum in which issues can be raised and dealt with – rather than being ignored;
- enabling people to extend their roles, perhaps increasing responsiveness and reducing costs;
- encouraging acceptance and understanding by staff of a problem and the solution proposed; and
- promoting wider learning by encouraging reflection, and spreading lessons widely.

Management in practice   Teamwork pays off at Louis Vuitton   www.vuitton.com

The French company Louis Vuitton is the world's most profitable luxury brand. The success of the company is attributed to a relentless focus on quality, a rigidly controlled distribution system and ever-increasing productivity in design and manufacture. Eleven of the thirteen Vuitton factories are in France: although they could move to cheaper locations, management feels more confident about quality control in France.

Employees in all Vuitton factories work in teams of between 20 and 30 people. Each team, such as the ones at the Ducey plant in Normandy, works on one product, and members are encouraged to suggest improvements in manufacturing. They are also briefed on the product, such as its retail price and how well it is selling, says Stephane Fallon, who runs the Ducey factory. 'Our goal is to make everyone as multi-skilled and autonomous as possible', says team leader Thierry Nogues.

The team work pays off. When the Boulogne Multicolour (a new shoulder bag) prototype arrived at Ducey, workers who were asked to make a production run discovered that the decorative metal studs caused the zipper to bunch up, adding time and effort to assembly. The team alerted factory managers, and technicians quickly moved the studs a few millimetres away from the zipper. Problem solved.

Source: *Business Week*, 22 March 2004.

Teams can also obstruct performance. The discussion that generates new perspectives takes longer than it would take for an individual to make a decision. If a team strays onto unrelated issues or repeats a debate it loses time. Opponents of a decision can prolong discussion to block progress. Some teams allow one member to dominate, such as the formal leader in an organisation where people do not challenge authority. A technical expert may take over if others hesitate to show their lack of knowledge or to ask for clear explanations. If any of these things happen, being on the team will probably be a dissatisfying and unproductive experience. It may produce a worse result, and be more costly, than if one person had dealt with the issue.

As J. Richard Hackman, an authority on teams, told an interviewer:

I have no doubt that a team can generate magic. But don't count on it (quoted in Coutu and Beschloss, 2009, p. 100).

In one of his books Hackman (1990) proposed three criteria against which to evaluate a team – shown in Table 17.6.

Table 17.6 Criteria for evaluating team effectiveness

Criteria	Description
Has it met performance expectations?	Is the group completing the task managers gave to it – not only the project performance criteria, but also measures of cost and timeliness?
Have members experienced an effective team?	Is it enhancing their ability to work together as a group? Have they created such a winning team that it represents a valuable resource for future projects?
Have members developed transferable team-work skills?	Are members developing team-work skills that they will take to future projects?

Source: Based on Hackman (1990).

17.9 Teams in context

Does the task require a team approach?

Despite their potential benefits, teams are not always worth the cost, since they may represent an expensive solution to a simple problem. The usefulness of teams depends on the task:

- **simple puzzles of a technical nature** can be done effectively by competent staff working independently;
- **familiar tasks with moderate degrees of uncertainty** need some sharing of information and ideas, but the main requirement is reasonable cooperation and coordination between people;
- **a high degree of uncertainty and relatively unknown problems** require high levels of information sharing and deep interpersonal skills to cope with the 'shared uncertainty'.

If the task requires people to work together to create joint work products beyond what an individual could do, then the cost of creating a team will be worthwhile.

Does the context support the team?

Aspects of a team's context affect how it performs. The 'Management in practice' feature gives an example of a team in trouble, partly because of contextual factors.

Management in practice   A community mental health team

The management of a health care unit decided to reduce the number of hospital places and increase resources for community care. As part of the change a resource centre was established containing multidisciplinary teams, each with about 30 staff, to provide a 24-hour service for the severely mentally ill in the community. The service would use a team approach with a flattened hierarchy and greater mutual accountability, and this was supported by many team-building and similar activities.

It soon became clear that many staff could not cope with the extra responsibility and shared decision making. The job is difficult and sometimes dangerous, since people's lives are at stake. Management therefore changed the system to clarify the role of each member of staff and to give a clearer structure of authority and management. It also recognised that, while team working may be an ideal, it needs to be supported by broader management structures and practices.

Source: Communication from a manager in the service.

For a team to meet the criteria in Table 17.6 it needs to deal with all the areas of Figure 17.1 – composition, internal processes and contextual support. The latter matters because otherwise it will depend too much on internal team practices and personal enthusiasm – which may not be sufficient in a hostile context. A manager should also attend to wider organisational conditions such as:

- the availability of **team-based rewards**;
- information systems to support the task and provide feedback on progress; and
- available education and training, including coaching and guidance.

These will often strengthen the benefits of skilled and enthusiastic members.

Team-based rewards are payments or non-financial incentives provided to members of a formally established team and linked to the performance of the group.

Activity 17.6   **Critical reflection on teams**

Recall some teams of which you have been a member.

- Which of the advantages and disadvantages have you observed?
- When teams have performed well, or badly, can you relate that to ideas in this chapter, such as the stages of group development, or to Belbin's team roles?

17.10   **Integrating themes**

Entrepreneurship

Scholars researching entrepreneurship have usually concentrated on the individual founder – their traits, skills, social background and so on. These are clearly relevant to performance, but so too is the team of people that the founder builds, possibly at the start-up phase, but certainly if it grows and needs to raise further capital for expansion.

Forbes et al. (2006) point out that the pressure to build an entrepreneurial team comes from the venture capitalists who provide the initial funding. Whether they decide to invest or not is influenced by their view of the founder, and also of the management team he or she assembles. Forbes et al. (2006) note that research on top management teams routinely shows how their composition affects performance. They therefore studied the processes of recruiting additional members to entrepreneurial teams – a significant decision in that it materially alters the resources available to the founder. Among the issues they examined were how the addition of a new member affected existing team processes and the conflicting criteria used in recruiting them. For example, did the founder recruit someone able to fill identifiable resource gaps, or did they recruit mainly on personality – looking for someone with whom they had empathy – irrespective of technical skills?

Sustainability

Building Terminal 5 at London Heathrow provided the airport's owner, BAA, with an opportunity to set new standards in environmental sustainability – and also with a novel way of using teams to deliver the project. Some of the early decisions – such as the requirement only to use timber approved by the Forest Stewardship Council and to avoid using polyvinyl chloride (PVC) – will deliver environmental sustainability to BAA for many years. Early in the process the company created an environmental assessment team of external professionals to help the project team develop a robust sustainability framework. This included challenging targets for the terminal in areas such as energy, water, pollution control and waste management.

These targets (or requirements) then became part of the brief of the teams created to deliver the 16 projects and 147 separate sub-projects to design and build the terminal – which they did, on time and in budget (Wolstenholme et al. 2008). The director of capital projects at BAA attributes much of this success to the system of integrated teams. These were not formed in the conventional way (by gathering representatives of relevant companies or disciplines) but by selecting only individuals with the right skill sets for the activity in hand, irrespective of employer. It was seen as a virtual organisation, using skills from consultants, contractors, suppliers and necessary skills from BAA themselves. Their work was supported by a novel form of contract that encouraged teams to focus on delivering their part of the project to the customer and not, as is often the case in construction, trying to blame another company for any difficulties. The achievement of individual team milestones were celebrated, and supported by an award scheme that acknowledged exceptional performance – including those that helped meet the sustainability targets.

Internationalisation

A common feature of internationalisation is that companies create multinational or global teams to work on projects or regular activities. Such teams are often 'virtual', in the sense that although they are working on a common task they are physically separated and span different time zones. Their dominant means of communication is usually through computer-based systems such as emails and videoconferencing.

Virtual teams face all the challenges of team performance that face teams that are located in the same place, and in addition they need to overcome the difficulties of working with those from different cultures. Their transitory nature means that members may be part of several such teams simultaneously, limiting their ability to build close relationships with members of any particular one. Finally, virtual meetings lack the physical cues present in face-to-face meetings, which makes it more difficult for members to give and respond to the non-verbal cues that prevent misunderstanding.

Zander et al. (2013) identify three major challenges facing those leading global virtual teams:

- **Goal alignment:** Team members will be working in their local organisation unit, to whose priorities they will be subject, as well as in the global team. This implies the team will embody significant differences in priorities, potentially delaying progress.
- **Knowledge sharing:** Members will come from diverse cultures, one dimension of which will be their beliefs about the wisdom of sharing knowledge widely or narrowly – even though members nominally belong to the same organisation.
- **Motivation:** As with goals, members will have different degrees of commitment to the project, reflecting organisational as well as personal interests. Members' motivational needs are harder to identify in a virtual than in a face-to-face environment.

Governance

Whatever the structure and form of governance arrangements, these will be directed at monitoring and controlling those responsible for areas of work – frequently members of senior teams. A significant challenge here is that successful groups take on a life of their own, and can become increasingly independent of the organisation that created them. As members learn to work together they generate enthusiasm and commitment – and become harder to control. The team may divert the project to meet goals that they value, rather than those of the sponsor. As experts in the particular issue, they can exert great influence over management by controlling or filtering the flow of information to the organisation as a whole, so that their goals become increasingly hard to challenge.

Chapter 7 (Section 7.7) examined the concept of groupthink, which occurs when members become so attached to a group that they suppress dissenting views so as not to jeopardise their acceptance by the other members. A common feature of groups that have succumbed to this condition is their inability to consider a range of alternatives rationally, or to see the likely consequences of the choice they made. This, at the same time, makes some external governance arrangement all the more necessary, and also all the more challenging to put into practice.

Summary

1 **Distinguish the types of teams used by organisations**
   - As management faces new expectations about cost and quality, many see teams as a way of using the talents and experience of the organisation more fully to meet these tougher objectives.
   - Hackman's typology shows the opportunities and challenges faced by top teams, task forces, professional support, performing, human service, customer service and production teams respectively.

2 **Use a model to analyse the composition of a team**
   - Belbin identified nine distinct roles within a team and found that the balance of these roles within a team affected performance. The roles are: implementer, coordinator, shaper, plant, resource investigator, monitor–evaluator, team worker completer, specialist.

3 **Identify the stages of team development and explain how a team moves between them**
   - Forming, storming, norming, performing and adjourning. Note also that these stages occur iteratively as new members join or circumstances change.

4 **Identify specific team processes and explain how they affect performance**
   - Effective teams develop a common approach and working methods, develop skills in several types of communications and are skilled in observation and review, enabling them to learn from their experience.

5 **Evaluate the outcomes of a team for the members and the organisation**
   - Members benefit from being part of a social group, from meeting performance expectations, from experiencing an effective team and developing transferable team-work skills.
   - The organisation can benefit from the combination of skills and professions, though the evidence of the links to organisational success are mixed.

6 **Outline the contextual factors that influence team performance**
   - Teams are not necessary suitable for all tasks.
   - Teams need to be supported by suitable payment systems and by education and training, and by relevant technologies.
   - Teams themselves can act to manage their boundaries effectively.

7 **Explain the elements of team processes and understand how you can use these to help you develop the skill of observing a team**
   - Observing the processes that affect the performance of a team or any other meeting is a widely-useful management skill, and the chapter has provided an opportunity to develop this.

8 **Show how ideas from the chapter add to your understanding of the integrating themes**
   - Adding an additional member to the top team is a critical decision for those founding new ventures, when they need to balance resource requirements with personal empathy in choosing a candidate.

- Designing and constructing Terminal 5 at Heathrow to meet new standards of sustainability is an example of how well-managed teams from diverse professional backgrounds can contribute.
- Teams working internationally face additional challenges in that they lack the nuances that come from regular face-to-face interaction.
- Teams that are effective face the danger that as their success increases they become resistant to criticism – the members believe their own propaganda. This makes it harder for governance systems to control those teams that need it most.

Test your understanding

1 What are the potential benefits of team work to people and performance?

2 How many stages of development do teams go through? Use this model to compare two teams.

3 List the main categories of behaviour that can be identified in observing a group.

4 Compare the meaning of the terms 'task' and 'maintenance' roles.

5 Evaluate Belbin's model of team roles. Which three or four roles are of most importance in an effective team? What is your preferred role?

6 Give examples of the external factors that affect group performance. Compare the model with your experience as a group member.

7 What are the potential disadvantages of teams?

8 Summarise an idea from the chapter that adds to your understanding of the integrating themes.

Think critically

Think about your experience of teams, and about the ways in which your organisation uses teams. Then make notes on these questions:

- Thinking of the teams in which you have worked, what **assumptions** seem to have guided those who created them? What have you observed in the effective teams that did not happen in the less effective?
- Considering both examples, did you observe anything about their respective **context** that may have affected whether they worked or not?
- Have you observed other teams, in different situations, that used **alternative** working methods based on practice in other companies?
- What **limitations** can you identify in any of these team theories, or in your organisation's approach to using teams? Have you observed teams that were clearly an unsuitable way of dealing with the issue?

Develop a skill – observing team processes

Observing the processes that affect the performance of a team or any other meeting is a widely used management skill, and this exercise will help you develop it.

- **Assessment:** Make an assessment of how well you observe what goes on in a meeting. Do you focus entirely on completing the task (content) or do you pay at least as much attention to what people say and do (process), and how this affects the team's progress?
- **Learning:** Section 17.5 (stages of team development) and Section 17.6 (team processes) are both relevant to this skill. Read them again, paying special attention to the sub-sections on 'categories of communication

and 'observing the team'. Summarise the ideas about how teams work in these sections. Why may understanding team process (by being able to observe them accurately) further your career?

- **Analysis:** Consider the possible implications for you of this evidence in Section 17.5 and Section 17.6. Recall the work you did on Activity 17.4, as it is an example of the topics you may want to note when observing a team.

- **Practice:** Identify a team or group (such as tutorial or project group) of which you are a member. Use the next suitable meeting (e.g. *not* one where you are responsible for the main presentation) and concentrate not on the task, but on observing the processes. Use Table 17.5 as a template, and as you listen to the discussion, allocate each comment to one or other of the categories, by placing a tick or other mark in that category.

  - When the task is finished, add up the number of contributions in each category. Can you identify how that distribution helped or hindered the group's progress? Also make notes on the three questions in the section 'Observing the team' **(p. 552).** If possible, share what you have observed with the group members.

  - Reflect on the experience of observing, and consider what you can learn from the experience.

- **Application:** Decide on another opportunity to practise this skill within the next week.

Read more

Belbin, R.M. (2010), *Team Roles at Work,* (2nd edition) Butterworth/Heinemann, Oxford.

A new edition of a book about the experiments that led Belbin to develop his model of team roles – with many more useful observations on team working.

Coutu, D. and Beschloss, M. (2009), 'Why teams DON'T work', an interview with J. Richard Hackman, *Harvard Business Review* , vol. 87, no. 5, pp. 98–105.

An interview with Hackman, whose work features in the chapter, in which he develops the point made here that teams require members to put in effort and develop skills if a team is to work.

De Rond, M. (2012), *There is an I in Team,* Harvard Business Review Press, Cambridge, MA.

Draws on examples from sport and business to explore the challenges of managing teams made up of highly ambitious creative individuals.

Dixon, K.R. and Panteli, N. (2010), 'From virtual teams to virtuality in teams', *Human Relations,* vol. 63, no. 8, pp. 1177–97.

Zander, L., Zettinig, P. and Mäkelä, K. (2013), 'Leading global virtual teams to success', *Organisational Dynamics,* vol. 42, no. 3, pp. 228–37.

Two articles about the challenges of working in virtual teams, and (in Dixon and Panteli) on the changing relationship between virtual and collocated teams.

Go online

These websites have appeared in this and other chapters:

www.cisco.com
www.vuitton.com
www.bmw.com
www.gkn.com

Each has tried to develop new approaches to using teams – encouraging staff to share ideas and experience, as well as gaining personal satisfaction from them. Try to gain an impression from the site (perhaps under the careers/working for us section) of what it would be like to work in an organisation in which teams are a prominent feature of working.

PART 5 CASE
BRITISH HEART FOUNDATION
www.bhf.org.uk

The organisation

In 1961 a group of medical professionals wanted to raise funds for research into the causes, diagnosis, treatment and prevention of heart disease. They created the British Heart Foundation, which has grown into the UK's largest independent funder of cardiovascular research, raising £147 million in the 2014–15 financial year. It uses this to fund the work of scientists in UK universities, on projects to prevent heart disease and to care for those recovering from it.

The BHF's current strategy sets out its mission as being to win the fight against heart and respiratory disease, and its vision of a world in which people do not die prematurely or suffer from heart and circulatory disease. It is driven by the research that it funds, and identifies six areas of work to support that:

- **Support**: we will make sure patients and their families receive the best possible support, information and care;
- **Grow income**: we will deliver an ambitious programme of activity to raise more money to power our life-saving work;
- **World-class organisation**: we will ensure that every part of the charity is well-led, effective and promotes the spirit and value of 'Fight for Every Heartbeat';
- **Listen, influence, engage**; Everything we do will be informed by the needs and views of patients and key stakeholders;
- **Prevention**: We will promote cardiovascular health and the prevention of cardiovascular disease;
- **Survival**: We will lead the fight to ensure more people survive a heart attack or cardiac arrest.

The income to support these activities came, in 2014–15, from four sources:

- legacies (41 per cent) – when supporters leave money to the BHF in their will;
- fund-raising (37 per cent) – including high-profile national events such as the London-to-Brighton cycle ride, the Mending Broken Hearts appeal and volunteers collecting donations;
- retail (20 per cent) – BHF is the largest charity retailer in the UK, with 730 shops;

© Jack Sullivan/Alamy Images

- investments (2 per cent) – income from investments in shares and other financial assets.

The BHF accounts for over half of the cardiovascular research in the UK, and has played a major role in the development of heart science. A director said:

> We are there for heart patients in terms of care, in terms of setting up nursing programmes, and defibrillator programmes to help with emergency life skills in the community. We're also there in terms of prevention, helping people to stay well if they've had a heart attack, and trying to prevent them getting a heart attack in the first place. But principally, and the words run through the stick of rock that is the British Heart Foundation, we are a research charity. We spend more on medical research than any other single entity, including the government, so we are

there to try and unlock the key to heart disease: why it is that someone can smoke for eighty years, drink like a fish and live to be a hundred: and somebody else who lives a heart-healthy life can be afflicted with heart disease in their thirties? We're trying to unlock that key. So that's the BHF.

BHF supports research mainly through providing finance to scientists in UK universities – in the 2014–15 financial year it awarded £81.8 million for research, including 218 new grants. It also funds almost one hundred individual fellowships to support the work of distinguished scientists and has helped to build and equip several major research facilities. In addition to research, it spent £31.9 million on 'prevention, survival and support activities. This all depends on continually raising money, as the then Chief Executive Peter Hollins said:

> Although set up for altruistic purposes, the only way [BHF can achieve its vision] is if you're successful at raising money – and to be successful at raising money you've got to have really good financial information. So we're pretty meticulous about monitoring trends in the income we get from every single bit of the organisation. Most people coming into the British Heart Foundation from a commercial organisation, as I did myself, will recognise our financial structure.
>
> As well as raising money and funding research, the BHF has an educational role, in advising individuals on healthy life-styles and how to avoid heart disease. It also seeks new ways to care for people with heart disease, and if something works cost-effectively, passing it to the NHS in the hope they will implement it.

Managing to add value

Monitoring income and costs

The chief executive:

> The money the BHF raises involves a lot of hard work by a lot of dedicated people. People do all sorts of things for us, climb mountains, cross deserts, organise tea parties: so we've got a moral obligation to make sure that money is properly used – everybody needs to understand that and make sure they're behaving accordingly. We expect everybody in the organisation to be financially literate, and to look for opportunities to save money.
>
> The financial ratio that guides us more than anything else is whether the money we've got coming in is broadly matching what we're spending. That apart, a ratio I look at very closely is our cost to income ratio. In other words, I look at how much of the income that we raise actually gets to the

coalface? Because people do all sorts of extraordinary things to raise money for us, and what they want to see is as much of that money getting to charitable purpose as possible. They don't want to see money being spent on buildings or administration or executive salaries. So looking at how much of our income is spent on that is probably the most critical ratio as far as I'm personally concerned.

The BHF finance teams pay close attention to income and expenditure. On the former they have a range of familiar income measures, such as monthly management accounts that staff analyse in what they call a quite 'intrusive' way to understand what lies behind a set of figures. Does a positive or negative figure reflect a temporary factor, or the beginning of a trend? They spend a lot of time forecasting short -, medium - and long-term income, and the factors affecting them.

An example is legacies – their main source of income. If these were to stop growing or begin to fall, this would have a have a major impact on the charity. The average time between someone making a will and dying is about seven years. So BHF tracks measures of legacy intent and legacy interest, and uses sophisticated statistical techniques to forecast the amount of income they are likely to receive from legacies in seven years time – similar to an actuarial valuation of a pension scheme.

Such financial planning matters, because BHF commits to long-term programmes of research – which it needs to be confident it can sustain. So staff make thorough statistical analysis of income and expenditure trends to understand accurately the present position and what the outcome for the year is likely to be. The trustees (similar to the board of directors in a commercial business) expect the chief executive and the finance director to give them timely and accurate advice on what the year as a whole is going to look like.

Retailing success

The chief executive:

> We have won a number of awards for the success of our charity retailing operation, and the question is, how do we do it? The answer is actually very simple, we are more professional than everybody else. Those leading our retail operation have been professional retailers and they have decided to come into the British Heart Foundation quite frequently for some family reason – a member of the family has been touched by heart disease. They're professional retailers, they come to the British Heart Foundation and we have generated a terrific feeling of professionalism and team work. I'm very proud of our retail operation – it's the best in the sector. I think we've got an ethos and belief in

ourselves that feeds on itself; I'm convinced it'll go from strength to strength.

Protecting the reputation

Betty McBride, Director of Policy and Communications:

BHF is very conscious of the value of a positive reputation. We are our reputation because people need to trust our advice. They need to understand that when we say things, we say them because they are evidence-based statements. They come to us for help, and our reputation is the only thing that keeps us in people's minds and keeps them seeing us as being the one-stop shop for heart health.

So our reputation is everything, and protecting our reputation is a significant part of not only my job, but everybody's job, and brand is a word that is thought about and said by people across the foundation. It isn't just something that sits in my office and with my, sort of, communications and multimedia team; actually people understand how important our reputation, and therefore our brand, is. So you get a workforce and a volunteer force who understand that our good name and the things that we stand for are everything to us.

We take a two-layered approach to managing our brand and reputation. [As well as the evidence base you'd expect from a medical research charity] we have a brand-tracker system: twice a year we ask a representative sample of people – what do they think of us? What do they think about our brand? How are we performing against our brand values? How are we performing against their aspirations and hopes for us? We also have an independent look at our brand via a charity brand-tracker service that we buy into. And we have our own online panel of about three thousand people who give us feedback. So that's the first element of managing our brand and reputation.

The second is a very strong internal communication strategy so that we are constantly telling our teams about who the British Heart Foundation is, who it aspires to be, and what they need to do in order to row for team BHF.

Simon Hopkins, the Finance Director, explains how this allies with his area of responsibility:

Motivation's about translating for people how the work that they do is fundamental and pivotal to the work that the scientists and the campaigners, and the other people at the frontline of the charity do. Having a vision and a strategy gives my teams, all of whom are in analytical roles, a 'line of sight' to the [bigger purpose of BHF] and shows them how our priorities in financial analysis translate into the organisation's priorities.

This year we produced a graphical strategy document for use with staff, showing each of the six BHF operating priorities and showing our objectives as a division under them. Whether it's providing heart health statistics or ten-year financial models – we demonstrate how generating these helps BHF grow its research capacity: it says 'the better we are at financial forecasting, the more aggressively we can invest in research'. And I use the word 'aggressively' advisedly. The better we produce incisive statistics about differences in heart health around the UK, the better that our campaigners and prevention care professionals can target really explicit and incisive campaigns to remove those inequalities. So analysis leads to decisions, and decisions lead to differences in peoples' lives, and my people respond absolutely to that.

And the other important thing is that when there are site visits or when visiting professors come to head offices to give a talk, I make sure that people from the procurement team, the internal audit team, the accounts payable team, attend those events because it brings the science to life. And without fail, whenever I've had a member of staff who's gone on a site visit, or to a talk by an eminent cardiologist who's in the building, those people come to their desks reinvigorated because they've re-established and revalidated their connection with the cause. Using those kind of motivational things are really, really important.

Managing staff

The chief executive:

In recruitment and selection we look for people who've not just accepted what's come to them, but who've taken a different direction, done something that's innovative. We look for evidence that they've been part of a team – have caused a group of people to do something which is worthwhile and that actually matters.

In a charity it's extremely hard to give people financial incentives. To the extent that we've got incentives they are mainly around recognising people and giving them more responsibility. We expect a lot of people – I always say I want everybody to go home tired at the end of the week because we expect that level of commitment. So in the absence of financial incentives it is very much around recognition. We make it absolutely crystal-clear to people what it is we're trying to achieve, and giving them recognition when they do that.

We also have internal development programmes where people get to work with other people from around the organisation, and help each other learn and grow as managers and potential managers.

We also move people between the teams. We move everybody round a bit and we find that that is an incentive – people know that good work and demonstrating a continual improvement ethic will bring some good broadening opportunities. That ends up on their CV, and a good CV, by definition does the right thing for you. We're very keen on helping people grow a very well-rounded and impressive CV.

Staff commented on BHF's attitude towards ideas, which is to welcome them and be positive – they are things to nurture. People embrace change in an open-minded fashion, though that does not make it easy – but having an organisation that has been involved in some major innovations in the treatment of heart disease helps the innovative culture to permeate the charity.

Communicating

BHF were quick to adopt social media as part of their communication strategy, and see many benefits. Betty McBride:

Social media has been a revolution that has freed us up to do wonderful things in a really cost-effective way. We did a campaign involving Vinnie Jones teaching the world to press hard and fast on the chest, so you could save someone who'd had a cardiac arrest in front of you. We paid a lot of money to put the video on television but it was picked up on YouTube and we used social media channels – Facebook, Twitter – to 'blow on the flames of social media'. That worked – two and a half million people viewed our Vinnie Jones video on YouTube. Now, we couldn't pay for that kind of interaction with the public, so social media, for us, has made an enormous difference in the way that we communicate.

It has also meant that we can have really bespoke communities – groups of people who become online members of a community. It can be as big as 3,000 for broader issues, but it also can be something much narrower – you could have something as small as two or three hundred people with a special interest who connect to each other through Facebook or our online communities.

Sometimes you realise that you have to stick to your guns and continue what you're doing. But when you know why people don't like it if you have to continue, you can encourage people to understand the reasons behind your work. One quite

delicate example is that as a medical research charity we fund research involving animals. Now, we have to do that because there is no alternative to a beating heart, so we do fund work involving animals. But when people complain to us, I like to be able to speak to them about what we do, and we always find that by being straightforward with people they appreciate what we do. We often get responses which say: 'actually, I don't agree with what you do but thank you for responding to me and thank you for telling me why you do it'. Audiences react really well to that kind of response.

Aspects of BHF's context

Charities inevitably compete with each other for resources – income in all its forms, and the support of volunteers. The retail outlets compete with other retailers and with other charity shops – including for donations of things to sell.

The recession may be reducing the available money people wish to give to charities in general. Against that, the recession is an opportunity, as more people come into the shops and it is easier and cheaper to secure shop space as the recession drives some store chains out of business.

The efforts of the UK government to cut the budget deficit has reduced the money available to charities – the amount of government grant-giving has reduced very significantly and that affects some charities very badly – but has so far had little direct effect on BHF.

Management dilemmas
Ensuring funding resilience

The BHF mix of funding streams may protect it from the worst effects of reductions in government spending as it does not rely on that for funds. However, cuts in government funding to universities and related organisations may lead to requests that the BHF steps in to fill those gaps. The chief executive:

That's a really important issue for us – we've got a responsibility towards our donors to make sure that the money we spend is discharging our mission, which is really a catalytic one, finding new ways of doing things – not simply filling holes that the government has decided it can't afford to fill anymore.

Acceleration and deceleration

The finance director:

Most of our funds go to run discrete programmes, projects and campaigns, so we have a lot of discretion and can accelerate or decelerate should we need to, quite dynamically. There's a real key thing, probably the single most important part of my job is to make sure we get that balance right between resilience and acceleration. Why do I talk about acceleration? We don't want to beat heart disease in ten or twenty years' time, we want to beat it tomorrow. So there's something that says we should go as fast as we can, as long as the quality of research, the science talent, is there. It's my job to define the capacity for speed in the organisation. That is the single most important measure that I work to.

Developing staff

The finance director again:

It's vital that we continue to adapt the organisation to meet changing conditions, all of which depends on our staff. To help BHF and to make their jobs more intrinsically rewarding we will create more specialised, more focused and probably a lot more interesting jobs for people within my own division, so we've told them that. And people's response has been pretty positive, because they're thinking we'll grow, we'll develop as individuals if we support this change, we'll have greater focus and we'll be able to specialise. We've told them what's in it for them (better CV) and we can see the results of engaging people like that.

Part case questions

(a) Relating to Chapters 14 to 17

1 The case mentions 'influence' or 'persuasion' at several points. List the examples you find, and consider whether the same influence methods are likely to work for each of them. Why may they differ? (Section 14.2)

2 Identify two specific examples of BHF trying to influence another person, group or institution, and decide which approach to influence they used. (Sections 14.5, 14.6, 14.7, 14.8)

3 How do they motivate staff, and which theories of motivation do these methods relate to most closely? (Sections 15.4, 15.5 and 15.6)

4 Identify at least three groups with whom BHF needs to communicate. What communication channels do they use with each? (Sections 16.4, 16.5)

5 Social media has clearly worked well. Would it work equally well for all those receiving BHF communication? If not, why not? (Section 16.4)

(b) Relating to the BHF

1 Visit the BHF website (www.bhf.org.uk) and read one or more of the management reports, including the Annual Report, you will find there. Note recent events that add to material in this case, such as major stories about fundraising or research.

2 What new issues is BHF facing that the case did not mention?

3 What part does reputation play in managing the charity? Recall the 'twin-track' approach they take and summarise what they do under each track.

4 Why is financial management and forecasting so important to a non-commercial organisation?

PART 5
EMPLOYABILITY SKILLS – PREPARING FOR THE WORLD OF WORK

To help you develop useful skills, this section includes tasks that relate the themes covered in the Part to six employability skills (sometimes called capabilities and attributes) that many employers value. The layout will help you to articulate these skills to employers and prepare for the recruitment process you will encounter in application forms, interviews and assessment centres.

Task 5.1   Business awareness

If a potential employer asks you to attend an assessment centre or a competency-based interview, they may ask you to present or discuss a current business topic to demonstrate your business awareness. To help you to prepare for this, write an individual or group report on ONE of these topics and present it to an audience. Aim to present your ideas in a 750-word report and/or ten PowerPoint slides at most.

1. Using data from one or more websites or printed sources, outline significant recent developments in the British Heart Foundation, especially regarding:

   - fund-raising and grant-giving performance in the last year (from the website **www.bhf.org.uk** go to the page 'About BHF' and then access the Annual Report and Accounts);
   - changes in government or regulatory practices that have affected BHF;
   - changes in how management organise and manage the charity;
   - its use of social media to communicate with donors; and
   - its internal governance arrangements.

2. Choose another major charity or not-for profit organisation that interests you – and which you may consider as a career option. Gather information from the website and other sources about what it does and how it is organised.

   - What can you find about the role of teams in the organisation?
   - How innovative has it been in motivating donors and supporters, and in raising funds?
   - What career options does it offer, and how attractive are they?
   - Evaluate its communication practices, using a model from Chapter 16.

When you have completed the task, record a short paragraph giving examples of the skills (such as information gathering, analysis and presentation) you have developed from this task. You can transfer a brief note of these to the Table at Task 5.7.

Task 5.2   Thinking critically

Reflect on the way that you handled Task 5.1, and identify how you exercised the skills of thinking critically (Chapter 1, Section 1.8). For example:

1 Did you spend time identifying and challenging the **assumptions** implied in the reports or commentaries you read? Summarise what you found then, or do it now.
2 Did you consider the extent to which they took account of the **context** in which managers are operating? Summarise what you found then, or do it now.
3 How far did they, or you, go in imagining and exploring **alternative** ways of dealing with the issue?
4 Did you spend time outlining the **limitations** of ideas or proposals that you thought of putting forward?
5 When you have completed the task, record a short paragraph giving examples of the thinking skills you have developed from this task. You can transfer a brief note of these to the Table at Task 5.7.

Task 5.3   Solving problems

Chapter 6 includes ideas on planning to deal with a problem – such as that of completing Task 5.1. Refer to these ideas if you need more guidance on this activity, which invites you to analyse how your team worked on a task.

Use the scales below to rate the way your team planned how it would work on Task 5.1 – circle the number that best reflects your opinion of the discussion.

1 The team used suitable methods to gather sufficient information to create a good plan to complete the task **(Section 6.4)**.

1	2	3	4	5	6	7
Strongly disagree						Strongly agree

2 The team set SMART goals that gave focus to our work on the task **(Section 6.5)**.

1	2	3	4	5	6	7
Strongly disagree						Strongly agree

3 The goals helped to motivate us to achieve the task **(Section 6.5)**.

1	2	3	4	5	6	7
Strongly disagree						Strongly agree

4 The team made a full list of what had to be done to achieve the goals **(Section 6.6)**.

1	2	3	4	5	6	7
Strongly disagree						Strongly agree

5 The team made a suitable implementation plan, and followed it **(Section 6.7).**

1	2	3	4	5	6	7
Strongly disagree						Strongly agree

6 The team monitored the progress of the plan, and adjusted it accordingly **(Section 6.7).**

1	2	3	4	5	6	7
Strongly disagree						Strongly agree

When you have completed the task, record a short paragraph giving examples of the planning skills you have developed from this task. You can transfer a brief note of these to the Table at Task 5.7.

Task 5.4   Team working

Chapter 17 includes ideas on team working. This activity helps you use these to analyse how your team worked on Task 5.1.

Use the scales below to rate the way your team worked on this task – circle the number that best reflects your opinion of the discussion.

1 The team was effective in obtaining and using necessary information.

1	2	3	4	5	6	7
Strongly disagree						Strongly agree

2 The team members took on complementary team roles **(Section 17.4).**

1	2	3	4	5	6	7
Strongly disagree						Strongly agree

3 The team progressed through the stages of team development **(Section 17.5).**

1	2	3	4	5	6	7
Strongly disagree						Strongly agree

4 The team developed effective working processes that suited the task **(Section 17.6).**

1	2	3	4	5	6	7
Strongly disagree						Strongly agree

5 The team used its time effectively.

1	2	3	4	5	6	7
Strongly disagree						Strongly agree

6 The team regularly reviewed the ways it was working, and changed these when it would improve performance (**Section 17.6**).

1	2	3	4	5	6	7
Strongly disagree						Strongly agree

Record three practices that you could use in your next task. If possible, compare your results and suggestions with other members of the team, and agree on practices that would help a team work better.

When you have completed the task, write a short paragraph giving examples of team-working skills (such as observing the team to improve performance) you have developed from this task. You can transfer a brief note of these to the Table at Task 5.7.

Task 5.5   Communicating

Chapter 16 includes ideas on communicating – and Sections 16.4 and 16.5 are especially relevant to this task. They will help you to analyse how well your team communicated as you worked on Task 5.1.

Use the scales below to rate the way your team communicated during Task 5.1 – circle the number that best reflects your opinion of the discussion.

1 The team handled face-to-face communication well during its meetings (**Section 16.4**).

1	2	3	4	5	6	7
Strongly disagree						Strongly agree

2 The team communicated effectively by phone, mobile, voicemail and other electronic systems (**Section 16.4**).

1	2	3	4	5	6	7
Strongly disagree						Strongly agree

3 The team communicated effectively by personal, written methods – letters, email, texting (**Section 16.4**).

1	2	3	4	5	6	7
Strongly disagree						Strongly agree

4 The team communicated effectively by impersonal written methods – newsletters, online communities (**Section 16.4**).

1	2	3	4	5	6	7
Strongly disagree						Strongly agree

5 The team adapted between centralised and decentralised communication networks according to the needs of the task **(Section 16.5).**

1	2	3	4	5	6	7
Strongly disagree						Strongly agree

6 The team communicated its report well to the chosen audience.

1	2	3	4	5	6	7
Strongly disagree						Strongly agree

7 The team experienced no significant barriers to communication, either internally or externally.

1	2	3	4	5	6	7
Strongly disagree						Strongly agree

Record three communication practices that you could use in your next task. If possible, compare your results and suggestions with other members of the team, and agree on practices that would help a team work better.

When you have completed the task, record a short paragraph giving examples of communication skills you have developed from this task. You can transfer a brief note of these to the Table at Task 5.7.

Task 5.6   Self-management

This activity helps you to learn more about managing yourself, so that you can present convincing evidence to employers showing, among other things, your willingness to learn, your ability to manage and plan learning, workloads and commitments, and that you have a well-developed level of self-awareness and self-reliance. You need to show that you are able to accept responsibility, manage time and use feedback to learn.

Reflect on the way that you handled Task 5.1, and identify how you exercised skills of self-management.

1 I effectively planned the time I would spend on each part of the task.

1	2	3	4	5	6	7
Strongly disagree						Strongly agree

2 I tried to balance my commitments and those of other team members across the work, so that all were reasonably busy.

1	2	3	4	5	6	7
Strongly disagree						Strongly agree

3 I think I used my time well.

1	2	3	4	5	6	7
Strongly disagree						Strongly agree

4 I tried to ensure that I and others took responsibility for distinct areas of work, to keep moving the task forward.

1	2	3	4	5	6	7
Strongly disagree						Strongly agree

5 I often reflected on how I was working on the task to identify possible ways to improve my performance.

1	2	3	4	5	6	7
Strongly disagree						Strongly agree

Write down three self-management practices that you could use in your next task. If possible, compare your results and suggestions with other members of the team, and agree on practices that would help a team work better.

When you have completed the task, write a short paragraph giving examples of the self-management practices you have developed from this task. You can transfer a brief note of these to the Table at Task 5.7.

Task 5.7 Recording your employability skills

To conclude your work on this Part, use the summary paragraphs above to record the employability skills you have developed during your work on these tasks, and in other activities. Use the format of the table below to create an electronic record that you can use to combine the list of skills you have developed in this Part, with those in other Parts.

Most of your learning about each skill will probably come from the task associated with it – but you may also gain insights in other ways – include those as well.

Template for laying out record of employability skills developed in this Part

Skills/Task	Task 5.1	Task 5.2	Task 5.3	Task 5.4	Task 5.5	Task 5.6	Other sources of skills
Business awareness							
Thinking critically							
Solving problems							

Skills/Task	Task 5.1	Task 5.2	Task 5.3	Task 5.4	Task 5.5	Task 5.6	Other sources of skills
Team working							
Communicating							
Self-management							

To make the most of your opportunities to develop employability skills as you do your academic work, you need to reflect regularly on your learning and record the results. This helps you to fill any gaps, and provides specific evidence of your employability skills.

PART 6
CONTROLLING

Introduction

Any purposeful human activity needs control if it is to achieve what is intended. From time to time you check where you are in relation to your destination. The sooner you do this, the more confident you are of being on track. Frequent checks ensure you take action quickly enough to avoid wasting time, effort and resources.

An owner-manager can often keep control by observing directly what is going on, and using their experience to decide what, if any, corrective action they should take. As the organisation grows, so does its complexity. It becomes increasingly difficult to know the current position as work goes on simultaneously in many places. Work activity, objectives and measures differ across the organisation, making it harder for senior managers to understand which areas are working well, and which are not.

To help them exercise control, managers use many systems and techniques. Chapter 18 introduces operations management as a source of control and discusses the concept of controlling the quality of products and services. Chapter 19 explores generic methods of control and performance management, showing how they can enable the enterprise to monitor and adjust activities to ensure they support stated objectives. Chapter 20 investigates finance as another form of control, showing the main financial measures used to assess performance.

The Part Case is Tesco, Britain's largest retailer, which illustrates many approaches to controlling an ever-expanding business, and how a lack of control can lead to trouble.

CHAPTER 18
MANAGING OPERATIONS AND QUALITY

Aim

To introduce the organisation as a set of linked operational processes working together to deliver a product that conforms to a predefined quality standard.

Objectives

By the end of your work on this chapter you should be able to outline the concepts below in your own terms and:

1 Define the term operations management
2 Describe the transformation process model of operations management
3 Show how operations management can contribute to competitiveness
4 Identify different forms of operational activity
5 Define the term quality in the operational context
6 Explain the idea of assessing quality systematically, and understand how you can use this to develop the skill of assessing what customers mean by quality
7 Show how ideas from the chapter add to your understanding of the integrating themes

Key terms

This chapter introduces these terms:

operations management
transformation process
craft system
factory production
operations strategy
supply chain management

just-in-time inventory systems
span of processes
break-even analysis
layout planning
total quality management (TQM)

Each is a term defined within the text, and in the glossary at the end of the book.

Case study   Zara   www.zara.com

Inditex is the world's biggest clothes retailer (as measured by sales), and the largest brand within the group is Zara. Amancio Ortega (who retired as Chairman of Inditex in 2011) formed the company with Rosalia Mera in 1975. Mr Ortega had begun working as a delivery boy for a shirt-maker and in 1963, when still in his 20s, he started supplying clothes to wholesalers. In 1975 a German customer cancelled a large order, so the firm opened its first Zara retail shop in La Coruña, Spain – simply as an outlet for cancelled orders. The experience taught Ortega the importance of the 'marriage' between the operations of production and retailing. This guided the company's evolution – Miguel Diaz, a senior marketing executive:

> It is critical for us to have five fingers touching the factory and the other five touching the customer. (Ferdows et al. 2004, p. 106)

The company had six stores by 1979 and opened them in all major Spanish cities during the 1980s. In 1988 the first international Zara store opened in Porto, Portugal, followed by New York (1989) and Paris (1990). The company is now a worldwide business with over 2,000 stores in 2016. Its international presence shows that national frontiers do not prevent people from sharing a single fashion culture.

Zara claims to move with society, reflecting the ideas, trends and tastes that society creates. It also moves fast:

> it keeps to a time period between the decision to produce a garment and the moment it is ready for the consumer that no one else has ever achieved: an average of two weeks for any of the shops in [all of the countries where they operate]. Its main competitors' times lie between 40 days for H&M and over 60 for Benetton, to mention only those which. . . get anywhere near the Inditex times. (Badia, 2009, p. 130)

Zara designers link closely with the public. Information travels continuously from the stores to the design teams, transmitting the demands and concerns of the market. The close integration of activities – design, production, logistics and sales (through the Zara stores) – means it is flexible and fast in adapting. In 2014 it began to introduce Radio Frequency Identification (RFID) technology – each garment is alarmed with a unique code at the logistics centre, which enables staff in the stores to respond instantly

© Edificio Inditex

to a customer request about availability – in the store, at another store, or online. This is a recent example of the group's drive for continuous innovation. It takes great care over the stores' design, window displays and interior decor, and locates them in the best sites of major shopping districts.

Management created the Inditex Group 1985 as the holding company for their businesses, including Zara – which accounts for 65 per cent of group sales. In 2016 Inditex employed over 137,000 people in 88 countries, selling through 6,700 stores. The Zara website alone has over 1 million daily visits, while 23 million people follow the brand on Facebook. Sales in 2014 were €18.1 billion, from both bricks-and-mortar stores and the online sales platform – which was available in 27 countries.

Sources: Ferdows et al. (2004); Badia (2009); company website; Inditex Annual Report, 2014.

Case question 18.1
Good operations management is based on process consistency.

- What do you think are the major managerial challenges in setting up an operations system to serve a fast-moving and fickle market such as fashion?

18.1 Introduction

Zara depends on good operational systems. It offers new designs quickly to catch the latest fashion trend and aims to sell them in large quantities – so they must be of a consistent quality to ensure customers buy again. It is an integrated fashion business: Zara staff design, manufacture, distribute and sell most of the products. Two factors are critical to Zara's success: the creative ability to catch the mood of the customer with interesting and exciting designs, and the operational capability to design, manufacture and distribute goods quickly and efficiently. Neither factor can exist alone – it needs both good design AND good operational processes.

Adding value in any business needs good operational systems – the activities required to deliver products and services. For example, an airline flight depends on coordinating many separate but linked operating systems to ensure the aircraft is cleaned, maintained, fuelled, crewed and in the right place for passengers to board. Similar challenges confront charities engaged in humanitarian emergencies – famines, droughts, earthquakes or floods. They need to source food, water and medical supplies from around the world and deliver them quickly and efficiently to their destination – a huge logistical challenge.

Large organisations employ a chief operating officer (COO) to ensure smooth day-to-day running of current operating processes and to implement new ones to improve the efficiency and effectiveness with which they use resources. Operational failure destroys value – the BP oil spill in 2010, a computer failure at RBS in 2012 – both cost the companies significant amounts of money as well as damaging their reputations.

The chapter begins by introducing the basic concepts and language of operations management, which you will be able to use in any sector of the economy. It then explains what a 'product' is in services and manufacturing respectively and outlines the activities of operations. It concludes by exploring the meaning of quality and how to manage it.

18.2 What is operations management?

System and process

We live in a world of systems that shape our personal lives, our transport, our security, our work. The system that is our society 'manages' our lives – bringing safety and economy by removing many random events, and allowing better use of time and energy. Organisations also benefit from consistency and predictability, so creating effective systems is the central challenge of operations management.

The operations challenge

Operations management is all of the activities, decisions and responsibilities of managing the production and delivery of products and services.

Slack et al. (2013) define **operations management** as the activities, decisions and responsibilities of managing the production and delivery of products and services.

The way to do this is to implement systems and processes that are:

- repeatable – can be done over and over again;
- consistent – produce the same result every time;
- reliable – do not break down randomly.

The standard of performance now required against each criterion is growing because of:

- increased competition in an international economy;
- more complex activities as customers expect products with more functions;

- tighter regulations to control pollution; and
- legislation on employment and working conditions.

Process therefore need also to be:

- efficient – producing most output for least input;
- competitive – at least as good as others in the same business; and
- compliant – with relevant legislation.

Case question 18.2

- Do you think the current tendency towards globalisation will help or hinder Zara's success?

The transformation process

The first step in achieving an efficient, process-based organisation is to understand the work of the organisation as a **transformation process** that turns inputs (resources) into outputs.

Figure 18.1 models the transformation process. It shows inputs entering the operational processes of the organisation, which transforms them into an output – the product or service to be sold. There are two types of input:

- **transforming** resources are the elements that carry out the transformation; and
- **transformable** resources are the elements that the process transforms into the product.

Transforming resources are:

- facilities – buildings, equipment/tools and process technology;
- staff – people involved in the transformation process;
- capital – to buy materials and pay for facilities and staff.

> The **transformation process** refers to the operational system that takes all of the inputs (raw materials, information, facilities, capital and people) and converts them into an output product to be delivered to the market.

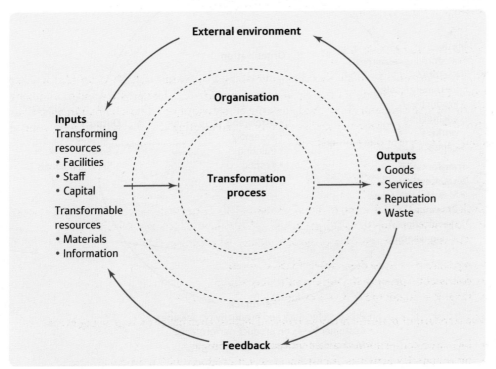

Figure 18.1
The transformation process

Transformable resources are:

- materials such as metal, wood or plastic, which change to become components of the final product such as cars, buildings or phones;
- information such as design specifications, assembly instructions, scientific concepts or market intelligence. Information, such as design specifications, can inform the transformation process and itself become part of the output – when raw data becomes a published report.

The transformation process includes the feedback system that monitors performance on specified dimensions, and records deviations from standards. This ensures the process performs in a repeatable, reliable and consistent manner.

There are two types of feedback:

- Feedback that is internal to the process and ensures it results in a consistent product. This feedback is generally quantitative and monitors specified aspects of the product or process, e.g. the number of units produced, dimensions such as weight, or measurements such as oven temperature. Any deviation indicates it requires remedial action.
- Feedback that is external to the transformation process ensures the product is accepted by the market and satisfies the customer. This type of feedback can be either qualitative (how the customer enjoyed the product) or quantitative (how many people bought it).

Figure 18.2 illustrates the transformation process for the manufacture of a motor car.

The nature of products

It is common to associate the term 'product' with something tangible – a physical artefact that can be seen, held and used. Until recently this was generally correct as most of what was bought and sold took a physical or tangible form. However, the growth of the service

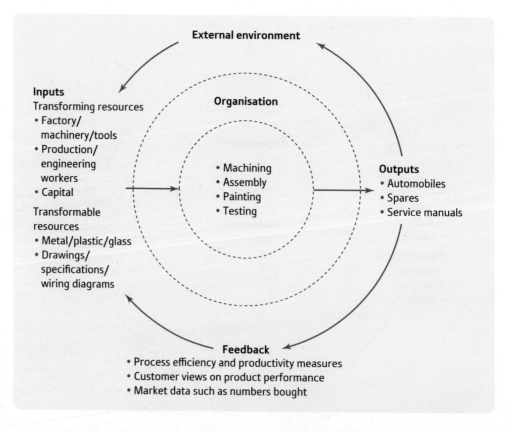

Figure 18.2 A manufacturing transformation

sector means the term is now often applied to intangibles such as financial services, holidays, health care or legal advice. A mortgage is no less a product than a car or a watch; it is designed for a purpose, sold, paid for and used. Operations managers see the 'production' process of these intangible products in the same way as the production process of tangible products – inputs, processes and feedback loops.

In restaurants the product is the experience of the meal. Although eating out is considered a service, it combines the physical product (the meal), the service experience that staff provide and the ambience of the surroundings.

The distinction between physical product and service delivered is therefore becoming blurred. Few physical products are sold without some form of service package. For operations managers this means that the transformation process model applies as much to restaurants, banks, schools and hospitals as it does to factories. Figure 18.3 illustrates a transformation process for a typical service – education.

Service delivery and the customer

While the transformation process applies to both goods and services, there are differences. The main one is that in service delivery the customer is present during the process, and is indeed one of the raw materials that is transformed – a student from non-graduate to graduate, a customer with untidy hair to one with styled hair or a patient with a disease to one who is cured. The presence of the customer has consequences for operations:

- Randomness – the process needs to be able to handle the randomness that the customer brings.
- Heterogeneity – that randomness leads to inconsistencies in the service delivered, as each customer may have a slightly different experience: a dining experience will be affected by the atmosphere created by other customers.

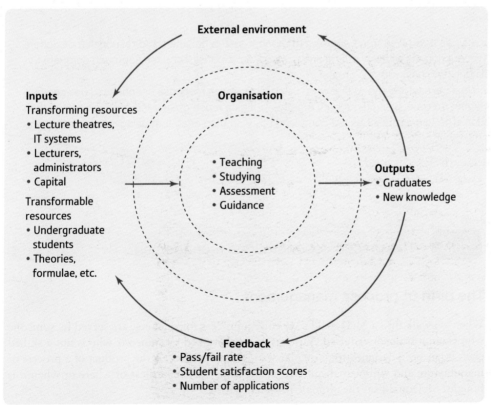

Figure 18.3
An educational
transformation

- Intangibility – the nature of the service experience makes it difficult to ensure service quality. It is more difficult to measure the service experience than the utility or functionality of a physical product.
- Perishability – services are difficult to store; an unused hotel room loses that revenue for ever, as the next night is a different revenue opportunity.

Activity 18.1   Service operations

- If you have ever sought legal advice then consider, from a customer's perspective, how can a lawyer ensure consistency, reliability and repeatability in the process of delivering legal services.

Key ideas   Designing transformation with the customer in mind

Cachon and Swinney (2011) develop and compare alternative production systems in the fashion industry, taking into account their likely effects on 'strategic' consumer behaviour. This refers to the consumer's decision to buy a fashion item now at full price, or to wait until the end-of-season sale for a bargain – if it is still available. The company's operations processes will affect that choice, and so its revenue.

A 'fast fashion' system has two components:

- **Short production and distribution lead times,** closely matching supply with uncertain demand ('quick response'). Firms achieve this by combining local production with modern information systems that continuously monitor sales and inventory levels (to reduce the risk of selling surplus stock cheaply).
- **Highly fashionable, trendy product design** ('enhanced design'). Firms achieve this by carefully monitoring consumer tastes and incorporating ideas into their designs very rapidly (to increase the consumer's willingness to pay full price).

Fast fashion is costly, as it requires trend spotters to monitor tastes, talented and responsive designers and expensive local production. As with any operations strategy, firms considering the approach compare the benefits (greater willingness to pay) with the greater costs.

The authors' mathematical analysis shows that while using either quick response or enhanced design bring benefits in terms of higher revenue, using them both together brings a much greater increase in revenue than using either in isolation. The two approaches are complementary, in the sense that using one increases the benefits from using the other.

Source: Cachon and Swinney (2011).

18.3   The practice of operations management

The birth of process management

When we walk into a McDonald's we enter a process for queuing, are served by someone who is not a trained waiter and purchase a meal cooked by someone who is not a skilled chef. It has been designed to particular standards of quality, is the product of a process of manufacture and will be made in exactly the same way regardless of where or when it is bought. McDonald's is the ultimate in systemisation.

Process design is often associated with F.W. Taylor and scientific management. In the late 19th century the United States was experiencing rapid industrialisation. Skilled workers were scarce, so Taylor's methods aimed to solve this by making the attributes of the worker almost irrelevant. Taylor and his supporters believed in 'rationalism' – the view that if one understands something one should be able to state it explicitly and write a rule for it. Taylor's objective in applying rules and procedures to work was to replace uncertainty with predictability. By applying this thinking to the process of manufacturing, it would become more reliable, consistent and repeatable.

Management in practice   Disney's 'production' of cartoons

At the age of 21 Walter Elias (Walt) Disney moved to Hollywood and opened a movie studio. In *The Magic Kingdom* Steven Watts (2001) describes Disney's attempts to apply the techniques of mass production to the art of making cartoons. Disney had great admiration for Henry Ford and introduced an assembly line at the studio. Like all production lines this system employed a rigorous division of labour. Instead of drawing entire scenes, artists were given narrowly defined tasks, meticulously sketching and inking characters while supervisors looked on with stopwatches timing how long it took to complete each activity.

During the 1930s this 'production' system resembled that of an automobile plant. Hundreds of young people were trained and fitted into the machine for 'manufacturing' entertainment. While this was labelled the 'Fun Factory' the working conditions on the assembly line were not always fun for the workers, with operations management methods leading to employee dissatisfaction and strikes.

Source: Watts (2001).

Before Taylor, work was based on the **craft system**, where individuals controlled the work process because their skill and knowledge told them what to do and how to do it. This left managers and owners who were trying to implement **factory production** with little control over production methods or levels of output. To take full advantage of the possibilities of mechanisation and the factory system, all of the activities within a particular transformation process had to be fully understood by those who controlled the organisation.

Although Taylor worked mainly in the steel industry, his ideas became the basis of operations management today. Henry Ford used them to design the production line system that came to dominate manufacturing, from where they spread to the service sector.

While Taylor's principles raised efficiency they could also have negative effects for those doing the work, and hence for long-term performance. Separating planning and organising work from doing it, while at the same time implementing detailed process rules for the worker to follow with little discretion, diminished the worker's skills and disrupted the craft system. This meant the worker no longer had the knowledge or skill to ensure the quality of the product, which depended more on the quality of the manufacturing process than on the worker's skills. The design of the process was paramount, as a poorly designed process would produce a poor product.

> The **craft system** refers to a system in which the craft producers do everything. With or without customer involvement they design, source materials, manufacture, sell and perhaps service. The craft system is based on workers with the embodied knowledge, skill and experience to carry out all necessary activity.

> **Factory production** is a process-based system that breaks down the integrated nature of the craft worker's approach and makes it possible to increase the supply of goods by dividing tasks into simple and repetitive processes and sequences that could be done by unskilled workers and machinery on a single site.

Activity 18.2   Taylor's processes

- Observe the organisations that you come into contact with in your daily life. Try to identify the processes that they use. Can you find any that are not underpinned in some way by Taylor's principles?

Management in practice   Sunseeker   www.sunseeker.com

From modest beginnings in a shed to a workforce of 2,000 working in modern shipyards, Sunseeker is the leading brand of yacht for the very rich. While the products are at the cutting edge of quality and technology, the company remains committed to crafts skills. Although much of the work in design and manufacturing is done by computers and machinery, Sunseeker claims the basis of its success is the skill of the artisans who form and polish the woods, metals and glass that produce the work of art that is a Sunseekeer yacht.

Production is a subtle blend of machine-produced fabrication using the best that process management can offer, and hand-assembly and detail finishing where the human influence on product quality cannot be matched.

Sunseeker admits that you can build a quality boat without the traditional craftsmanship it relies on – but, it says, it wouldn't be Sunseeker . . .

Source: Company website.

Activity 18.3   Craft versus factory

- Consider the manufacture of high-quality products such as a Sunseeker yacht, a Rolls-Royce motor car or a Rolex watch. In each of these products consider which parts of the manufacturing process are best done by machines and which parts are best done by hand.

Operations strategy

Operations strategy defines how the function will support the business strategy by ensuring the organisation has the resources and competences to meet market requirements.

Chapter 8 looked at strategy as the process of setting an organisation's direction. The business creates and delivers products through its operations, so it also needs an **operations strategy** to define how the function will support the business strategy, by ensuring the organisation has the resources and competences to meet market requirements. It clarifies the primary purposes and characteristics of the operations processes, and designs systems to achieve these.

Management in practice   Linn Products   www.linn.co.uk

Linn Products was established in 1972 by Ivor Tiefenbrun (who retired as chairman in 2011). Born in Glasgow, he was passionate about two things – engineering and listening to music. When he couldn't buy a hi-fi good enough to satisfy him he decided to make one himself. In 1972 Linn introduced the Sondek LP12 turntable, the longest-living hi-fi product still in production anywhere in the world and still the benchmark by which all turntables are judged. The Linn Sondek LP12 turntable revolutionised the hi-fi industry, proving categorically that the source of the music is the most important component in the hi-fi chain. Linn then set out to make the other components in the hi-fi chain as revolutionary as the first, setting new standards of performance with each new product.

Today, Linn is an independent, precision-engineering company uniquely focused on the design, manufacture and sale of complete music and home-theatre systems for customers who want the best. Linn systems can be found throughout the world in royal residences and on luxury yachts. In 2012 it received the Queen's Award for Enterprise and Innovation, and launched the Kiko music system.

At Linn, operations is an integrated process, from product development through to after-sales service. Company staff design all aspects of the products and control all the key processes. Linn believes everything can be improved by human interest and attention to detail. So the same person builds, tests and packs a complete product from start to finish. They take all the time necessary to ensure every detail is correct. Only then will the person responsible for building the product sign their name and pack it for despatch. Every product can be tracked from that individual to the customer, anywhere in the world. Linn systems are sold only by selected retailers who have a similar commitment to quality.

Source: Company website.

Activity 18.4   Searching for excellence

- While most organisations strive for excellence in some way or other, consider the operational challenges in actually becoming and remaining a world leader.

Case study   Zara – the case continues   www.zara.com

What sets Zara apart from many of its competitors is what it has done with its business information and operations processes. Rather than trying to forecast demand and producing to meet that (possible) demand, it concentrates on reacting swiftly to (actual) demand:

> The shops act as aerials, detecting the directions and preferences of the market in every specific area . . . [the shop managers are a vital link in the organisation as the experts in sensing trends]. The boss of each shop therefore acts as a leader [providing information which central departments process continuously, which] is made completely available to suppliers, including on-line access. From the early days the group has received and treated its suppliers more like partners than mere occasional suppliers (Badia, 2009, p. 88).

A distinctive aspect of the operation is the close link between stores and headquarters:

> Store managers hold daily staff meetings to discuss local trends, such as which colour of pastel trousers are selling well in Dubai, or what hemlines are in Bogota – information which is

then fed back to headquarters (*Financial Times*, 23 May 2011, p. 23).

Most clothes suppliers take three months to develop the styles for a season's range and the same again to set up the supply chain and manufacturing processes. Zara does this in weeks by:

- making decisions faster with better information;
- running design and production processes concurrently;
- holding stocks of fabric that can be used in several lines;
- distributing products efficiently.

The company's operations strategy is clearly directed at speed – ensuring the shortest time between the design idea and the garment reaching the stores.

Sources: Ferdows et al. (2004); Badia (2009); company website.

Case question 18.3

- Investigate the operational strategy of another large clothing retailer, such as Marks & Spencer. Can you identify any differences?

The four Vs of operations

Although all operations systems transform inputs into outputs, they differ on four dimensions:

- **Volume**: how many units they produce of each type of product. Consumer goods are examples of high-volume production, supported by investment in special facilities, equipment and process planning.

- **Variety:** how many types (or versions) of a product are manufactured in the same facility. Fashion houses and custom car makers use more hand tools and highly skilled staff to enable the flexibility required to make a variety of unique products.
- **Variation in demand:** how the volume of production varies with time. Facilities at holiday resorts cope with wide variations in throughput depending on the time of year.
- **Visibility:** the extent to which customers see the manufacturing or delivery process. This applies mainly in services, where the presence of the customer is vital to the process.

The four Vs help to define operations strategy. By deciding on the type of operation it will be – what volume, how much variety, how volume will vary and how visible it will be, managers can begin to design the operations processes.

18.4   **Operations processes**

Production systems

For production operations these decisions translate into two main considerations: volume of product and flexibility of the operations system – its ability to cope with changes in volume and/or variety. Hayes and Wheelwright (1979) propose that a single manufacturing system cannot efficiently produce different volumes of a variety of products. If a high volume is required consistently and reliably, then the manufacturing system must be arranged to produce only one product. If several products are required then the system must be more flexible to cope with their multiple requirements. Hayes and Wheelwright categorise four types of production operation – see Figure 18.4.

Project systems

These exist at the low-volume end of the spectrum and deal with the manufacture of very small numbers of product – often only single units. This entails many interdependent parallel operations of long duration to achieve an output. Examples include construction projects such as oil rigs, dams and skyscrapers, in which thousands of operations accumulate to complete one product over several years. The defining feature of this

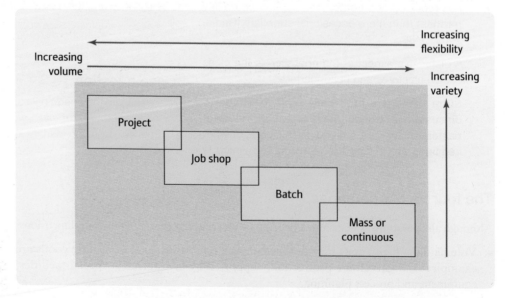

Figure 18.4 The product–process matrix

Source: Based on Hayes and Wheelwright (1979).

system is that the product is built in one place with all the resources brought to it and all the activities going on around it. The product will not move until it is complete, and sometimes not at all.

Job-shop systems

These are also relatively low-volume, producing special products or services to customer specifications with little likelihood that any product will be repeated. In a manufacturing context a tool room that makes special tools and fixtures is a classic example, as is a tailor who makes made-to-measure clothes to customer requirements. Such low-volume systems tend to use general-purpose equipment worked by skilled staff. They exhibit a high degree of flexibility but have high unit costs.

Batch operations

These are possibly the most common systems in use today. Many distinct products are produced as required. One of the distinctive features of such systems in comparison to job-shop systems is that, since orders are repeated from time to time, it becomes worthwhile to spend time planning and documenting the sequence of processing operations, employing work study techniques, providing special tooling and perhaps some automation. There will be a mix of skilled, semi-skilled and unskilled labour in this type of system.

Mass production and continuous flow manufacturing

This type is used where demand for a single product is sufficiently high to warrant the installation of specialised automatic production lines. With their high rates of output and low manning levels, unit costs are typically very low. Such systems generally have little flexibility. Where the entities produced are discrete items, such as cars or mobile phones, the term 'mass production' is used; where the entity is not discrete, such as chemicals like petroleum or other substances such as cement, then the term 'continuous production' is used.

Service systems

In service delivery operations the product–process matrix does not adequately cater for the fourth V – Visibility; the presence of the customer in the process and the potential for diversity and randomness this brings will defeat the best-designed processes. Figure 18.5 shows a similar model that helps to categorise service processes.

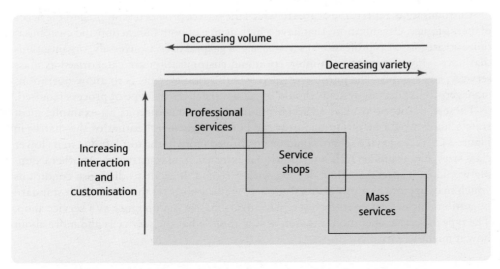

Figure 18.5
Service process types

Professional services

These are high-contact operations where customers may spend a lot of time in the process. These services provide high levels of customisation and are adaptable to individual customers' needs. As a result the operational system relies on skilled and knowledgeable people rather than high levels of automation. Typical examples of these are legal services or health care.

Service shops

These offer lower levels of customer contact and less customisation to deal with larger volumes of customers with similar needs. Examples include most restaurants and hotels, high-street banks and many public services. Essentially the customer is buying a standard service that may be slightly customised to their needs. While people are still part of the process they tend to have limited skills and knowledge, and less discretion while working within a more rigid process.

Mass services

These provide standard customer transactions, very limited contact time and little or no customisation: the emphasis is on automation and repetition. Staff will be low skilled and follow set procedures, much like the staff on a production line, and the processes may be highly automated. Typical mass services include supermarkets, call centres and mass transport systems. For example, in a railway station staff can sell tickets but have no discretion to offer customised journeys or make decisions beyond the scope of the process.

Activity 18.5 **Cutting up craft skills**

- Consider a service such as a surgical operation. Do you think that routine surgery could be carried out by more scientifically managed methods where, for example, the person that performs the operation is not a qualified surgeon, but is trained to carry out a single procedure?

It is important to note that in the service sector, 'interaction' (how much the customer can intervene in the process) is not the same as 'contact time'. A lecture to a large number of students is high in 'contact' but comparatively low in 'interaction': so high duration of contact does not always mean a more interactive service.

'Customisation' reflects the degree to which the service provided is tailored to the needs of the customer. Organisations that have a high degree of both interaction and customisation are categorised as professional services, e.g. legal practices. Conversely, organisations that have a low degree of both interaction and customisation are categorised as mass services, e.g. schools. The purpose of such classification systems is to allow operations managers to decide how systems should be set up to deliver the type of process required.

These classifications exist as a continuum. Using education as an example, most state schools would be positioned near the bottom right-hand corner of the matrix in Figure 18.5. A fee-paying school could be positioned more to the top-left due to its lower class sizes, more support staff and additional extra-curricular activities. Another example would be a specialist clinic dealing with rare and difficult-to-diagnose conditions which may operate as a professional service, while a hospital that deals with standard operations such as cataracts or hip replacements may be set up more as a service shop. The type of service operation is therefore less about what the service is and more about how it might be provided.

18.5   Process design

Span of processes: make or buy?

When Henry Ford developed his moving assembly-line method of producing the Model T car, he chose to 'own' all stages of production, i.e. the widest possible span of processes. Ford's company owned the rubber plantations that supplied the raw materials for the tyres, the forests that supplied the wood for the wheels and the iron mines, steel plants, foundries, forges, rolling mills and machine shops that manufactured the engine and other components. Its ownership of the complete span of processes even extended to a shipping line and a railway to transport materials and product.

No car manufacturer today has such a wide **span of processes**, as specialism is the key to efficient operations. The skills required to produce parts differ from those required to assemble them into the car – so it is more efficient for a dedicated supplier to make them. Direct control of the operation is largely replaced by managing the several independent companies who make up the supply chain. As the performance of a company's internal operations depends substantially on the quality and timeliness of what it buys from suppliers, many now put considerable effort into **supply chain management**. This usually involves developing close working relationships with a small number of suppliers who show that they are able and willing to re-design the way they work to meet the customer's requirements – in exchange for long-term commitments by the customer to the supplier.

This is equally true in the service sector, where, in a service such as airline travel, a company may decide to focus on long flights between hub airports, leaving other airlines to provide the feeder flights. Likewise, the catering service and maintenance activity might be outsourced to specialist suppliers.

> The **span of processes** is the variety of processes that a company chooses to carry out in-house.

> **Supply chain management** refers to managing the sequence of suppliers providing goods and services so that the independent organisations work collaboratively for mutual gain.

Activity 18.6   The supply chain

- Consider a consumer product such as a bicycle – choose a popular model from one of the larger brands. Investigate its manufacturing process by drawing a supply chain map that includes all of the companies that are involved in the manufacture of this one item.

Process selection

Having identified strategically which type of operation you want to create in relation to the four Vs, what you want to do within your operation and what you want to buy-in from a specialist supplier, the question then to be answered is what process configuration to implement.

The answer to this question may not be straightforward. The simplest case would be where the various processes required are already owned by the company, and there is enough free capacity to meet the forecast demand. In this case a simple **break-even analysis** may help in making the choice. For each of the process sequences to be compared, the fixed and variable costs are determined. Fixed costs are those, such as special tooling costs, that are required to set up the processes and are independent of the volume of output. Variable costs are those, such as direct labour and material costs, that vary in direct proportion to the volume of output. Figure 18.6 shows how the total costs of three process sequences (A, B and C) change with volume of output, alongside the associated revenue.

> A **break-even analysis** is a comparison of fixed versus variable costs that will indicate at which point in volume of output it is financially beneficial to invest in a higher level of infrastructure.

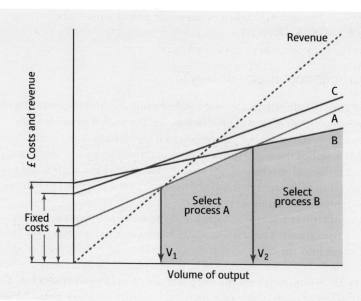

Figure 18.6
Break-even
analysis

This shows that, for quantities below V_1, none of the process sequences recover their costs; for quantities between V_1 and V_2, process sequence A is the most economical; for quantities greater than V_2, process B becomes the least costly. In this example process sequence C is uncompetitive at all levels of output.

Case study   Zara – the case continues   www.zara.com

Zara designs all its products in-house – about 40,000 items per year from which 10,000 are selected for production. The firm encourages a collegial atmosphere among its designers, who seek inspiration from many sources such as trade fairs, discotheques, catwalks and magazines. Extensive feedback from the stores also contributes to the design process.

The designers for women's, men's and children's wear sit in different halls in a modern building attached to the headquarters. In each of these open spaces the designers occupy one side, the market specialists the middle, and the buyers (procurement and production planners) occupy the other side. Designers first draw out design sketches by hand and then discuss them with colleagues – not just other designers but also the market specialists and planning and procurement people. This process is crucial in retaining an overall 'Zara style'.

The sketches are then redrawn where further changes and adjustments, for better matching of weaves, textures and colours, are made. Critical decisions are made at this stage, especially regarding selection of the fabric. Before moving further through the process, it is necessary to determine whether the new design could be produced and sold at a profit. The next step is to make a sample, a step often completed manually by skilled tailors located in the small pattern and sample-making shops co-located with the designers. If there are any questions or problems, the tailors walk over to the designers to discuss and resolve them on the spot.

The final decision on what to produce is normally made by agreement between the designer and colleagues from marketing, procurement and production.

Sources: Ferdows et al. (2004); company website.

Layout planning is the activity that determines the best configuration of resources, such as equipment, infrastructure and people, that will produce the most efficient process.

Facility layout

In addition to the sequence of the processes, consideration must also be given to their physical layout in relation to each other. **Layout planning** is an important issue because operational efficiency will be affected by the chosen layout's effects on the following factors:

- amount of inter-process movement of materials and/or customers;
- health and safety of staff and customers;
- levels of congestion and numbers of bottlenecks;
- utilisation of space, labour and equipment;
- levels of work-in-progress inventory required.

In the layout of service operations there may be other factors to consider, as a result of the customers' participation in the processes:

- Maximum product exposure – in the layout of retail stores, basic purchases and check-out stations are often positioned remote from the shop entrance, obliging the customer to walk past displays of other more-profitable products, which they may be enticed to buy.
- The 'ambience' of the physical surroundings – décor, noise levels, music, temperature and lighting may affect the customers' judgement of the service, how long they stay and how much they spend.
- The customers' perception of waiting times.

The reason for the inclusion of the word 'perception' in this last point is best illustrated by an example. An airline experienced a high level of complaints from its passengers about the waiting time in the baggage-reclaim area. The airline's solution was to re-direct baggage to the carousel furthest from the arrival gates. Though passengers had to walk further, and the baggage took just as long to arrive, the customers' perceptions were that the waiting time had been reduced.

Layout planning occurs at three levels of detail:

- Layout of departments on the site. For example, in a public house this would concern the sizing and positioning of the public bar, the lounge bar, toilets, kitchen and storeroom within the confines of the building used.
- Layout within departments. Continuing with the bar example, this would address the sizing and positioning of customer seating areas, the drinks counter, the food counter, slot machines, public telephone, passageways, etc.
- Layout of workplaces. For the bar counter this would determine the detailed layout of pumps for draught beers and other drinks, cash registers, sinks, shelves for bottled beers, spirits, wines and soft drinks, etc.

There are four well-established forms of facility layout: fixed-position, process, product and cell.

Fixed-position layout

This configuration is typically used for low-volume, project-type operations where the product being produced is massive, and movement of the material from process to process is impossible or impractical. Bridges, oil rigs and office buildings fall into this category so the processes required come to the site.

In the service sector, football stadiums, theatres, cinemas and lecture rooms are all examples of fixed-position layouts, where the service that is the performance is presented in one place for communal attendance.

Process layout

This form of layout is used when there is no dominant flow pattern, and is particularly appropriate for job shop and small-batch operations. Figure 18.7 is a schematic representation of a process layout, showing three (of many) job process sequences.

By bringing similar process types together in departments, the advantages of flexibility and concentration of process expertise are gained. The disadvantages are: long delivery times, high levels of materials handling and transport, relatively high levels of work-in-progress inventory, low equipment utilisation and consequent high unit costs. Scheduling

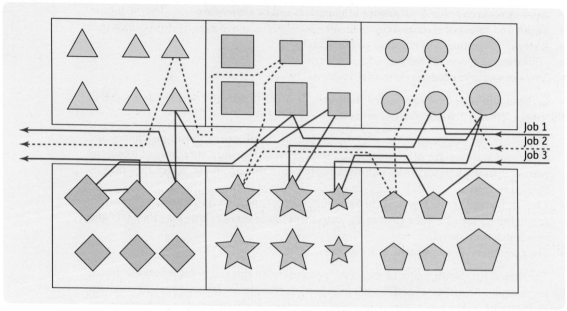

Figure 18.7 Process Layout

of many jobs with different process routes through a process layout while monitoring their progress are among the most challenging tasks for operations managers.

Many service operations adopt the process layout, but, instead of material movements, customers move from department to department; common examples include supermarkets, department stores, museums, art galleries and libraries.

Product layout

This form of layout is used when the demand for a single product is sufficiently high to warrant truly continuous operation, or mass production for discrete items such as cars, mobile phones, ball-point pens and confectionery, and process systems for 'fluids' such as oil products, sugar and cement. It is possible to have an automatic production line specially designed to incorporate not only the sequence of processes, but also an automatic transport system to move the product from process to process, in unison. With such a system there is no need for expensive work-in-progress between processes, less floor space is required and throughput time for a particular item is very short. Figure 18.8 shows this.

However, although such systems deliver very low unit costs, they are vulnerable because of the absence of work-in-progress buffers: if one process fails, very quickly the whole line comes to a halt. Since only a single product type is produced, the challenge for the operations manager is to balance the level of output with the anticipated level of customer demand. When an imbalance occurs it is often reported in the business press; for example, computer components, such as memory chips, seem to be in a perpetual flux of over-supply and shortage. Automobile companies also are guilty of overproducing and then storing cars until they are sold. As a car buyer this is an important consideration, as the 'new' car that you buy may not be new at all but may have been 'stored' in a car park for a year or more before it is sold.

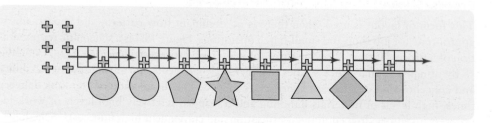

Figure 18.8
Product layout

Applications of the product layout are less common in service operations, but the following display some of its characteristics: self-service cafeteria, student registration, automatic mail sorting and some hospital diagnostic procedures.

Cell or group layout

Cell or group layout is suitable for many small- to medium-batch operations, and is especially useful when management wants to reduce the time it takes to get the product to the consumer. In a cell layout, a product is made by a small group of staff physically close to each other, who are able to move quickly from making one product to making another as demand changes. In contrast, setting up a mass-production assembly line takes a lot of time, and is equally time-consuming to change. Consumer electronics groups, such as Sony, often use the cell system as it enables them to respond quickly to changes in consumer demand. Service operations that exhibit some of the cell layout's attributes include car tyre/exhaust/battery replacement outlets and island-layout self-service cafeterias.

Case study   Zara – the case continues   www.zara.com

Zara manufactures approximately 50 per cent of its products in factories in what the company calls its 'proximity' – Spain, Portugal and Morocco – with another 35 per cent coming from Asia. This is unusual at a time when many clothing companies source most of their products from Asia.

Many of the outside suppliers have offices close to Zara's headquarters. With its relatively large and stable orders, Zara is a preferred customer for most suppliers, who give priority to Zara orders and are generally more responsive.

The make/buy decisions are usually made by the procurement and production planners. The key criteria for making these decisions are required levels of speed and expertise, cost-effectiveness and availability of sufficient capacity. Such decisions are made carefully, paying great attention to minimising the risks associated with achieving the correct workmanship and speed of supply.

For its in-house production, half of all fabrics are purchased un-dyed to allow faster response to mid-season colour changes.

The purchased fabric is then cut by machine. A typical factory has three or four cutting machines with long tables where typically 30 to 50 layers of fabric are laid out under a top paper layer. The cutting pattern is generated by the Computer Aided Design system (which automatically minimises fabric waste), checked by skilled operators and then drawn by the machine onto the top layer (so that cut pieces can be identified later). After a final visual check by the operator, the machine then cuts the multiple layers

into hundreds of small pieces. Operators then pack each piece into a separate clear plastic bag to be sent to sewing subcontractors.

Zara uses subcontractors for all sewing operations. Subcontractors themselves often collect the bagged-up cut pieces, along with appropriate components (such as buttons and zippers) in small trucks. There are some 500 sewing subcontractors close to La Coruña, many working exclusively for Zara. The company closely monitors their operations to ensure quality, compliance with labour laws and adherence to the production schedule. Zara believes that outsourcing a highly labour-intensive operation, like sewing, allows its own factories to remain more focused and provides more flexibility to change production volumes quickly. Subcontractors bring back the sewn items to the same factory, where each piece is inspected. Finished products are placed in plastic bags, labelled and sent to the distribution centre.

Completed products procured from outside suppliers are also sent directly to the distribution centre and Zara controls their quality by sampling batches of these.

Sources: Ferdows et al. (2004); company website.

Case questions 18.4

- Is Zara a craft or a factory system?
- Review the information about the manufacturing system Zara uses and list its advantages and disadvantages.

18.6   The main activities of operations

Providing goods and services to a customer depends on five key operations activities, and these provide a useful way of describing and analysing an organisation's operations system (Sprague, 2007). These activities are:

- capacity;
- standards;
- materials;
- scheduling;
- control.

None of these activities operates alone but combine to form an operations system.

Capacity

Capacity is the ability to yield an output – it is a statement of the ability of the numerous resources within an organisation to deliver to the customer. Defining capacity depends on identifying the main resources required to deliver a saleable output – staff, machinery, materials and finance. Capacity is limited by whichever resource is in shortest supply – a hospital's capacity to conduct an operation will be determined by some minimum number of specifically competent surgeons, nurses and related professionals. In service organisations all aspects of capacity may be visible to the customer – they can see the quality of staff, and the state of the physical equipment and resources.

Standards

Standards relate to either quality or work performance. Quality standards are embedded in the specification of the product or service delivered to the customer. Work-performance standards enable managers to estimate and plan capacity by providing information on the time it takes to do something. One of the advantages that low-cost airlines have established is that the time it takes them to turn round an aircraft between landing and take-off is much lower than for conventional airlines. This enables them to fly more journeys with each aircraft – significantly increasing capacity at little cost.

Materials

Just-in-time inventory systems schedule materials to arrive precisely when they are needed on a production line.

A vital aspect of the operations function is to ensure an adequate supply of the many material resources needed to deliver an output. One of the dilemmas is that holding stocks of materials, called inventory, is expensive – it ties up working capital, incurs storage costs and in changing markets there is a risk that stocks become outdated because of a change in model. Too much material can be as problematic as too little. Materials management is particularly important in manufacturing systems where the cost of raw materials and components, all of which may become obsolete if fashions change, are significant. Many companies have invested in developing **just-in-time inventory systems** that are intended to deliver supplies exactly when they are needed – see 'Management in practice'.

Management in practice   Smith and Nephew – inventory for surgery

Smith and Nephew (an orthopaedics company) hired an executive from Federal Express (parcel delivery) to improve its operations and reduce the cost of holding stocks of parts. The problem arises from the fact that when S&N sells an artificial hip or knee to a surgeon, it also provides a suite of ancillary instruments as well as joints of different sizes in case the original choice does not fit as well as it should. While the hip replacement alone may cost $10,000, there could easily be $250,000 of additional hips and specialist tools in an operating room to implant the replacement. The chief executive of S&N:

> We have to get a couple of hundred thousand dollars worth of inventory, including instruments and tools to do the surgery, plus all the right implants to the right customer and the right surgical suite every single time without fail. It's a huge logistical challenge for us.

Source: *Financial Times*, 15 March 2010, p. 18.

Scheduling

This is the function of coordinating the available resources by time or place – specifying which resources need to be available and when in order to meet demand. It begins with incoming information about demand and its likely impact on capacity. Service, productivity and profitability depend on matching supply with demand. Capacity management generates supply; scheduling links demand with capacity. It can be carried out over several time periods. Aggregate scheduling is done for the medium term, and is closely associated with planned levels of capacity: as airlines plan their future fleets, which they need to do several years ahead, they make judgements about both their capacity and the likely demand (translated into frequency of flights on particular routes). Master scheduling deals with likely demand (firm or prospective orders) over the next few months, while dispatching is concerned with immediate decisions, for example about which rooms to allocate to which guests in a hotel.

Control

Control is intended to check whether the plans for capacity, scheduling and inventory are actually working. Without control, there is little point in planning, as there is no mechanism then to learn from the experience. There are generally four steps in the control process:

- setting objectives – setting direction and standards;
- measuring – seeing what is happening;
- comparing – relating what is happening to what was expected to happen;
- acting – taking short-term or long-term actions to correct significant deviations.

Only through control can immediate operations be kept moving towards objectives, and lessons learned for future improvements.

18.7 Quality

What is quality?

In addition to the factors that govern the design of effective and efficient operations systems, features of the product or service that is being delivered must also be considered – especially price and quality.

For undifferentiated products such as transport, consumer goods such as cleaning products or services such as fast food, the price will be paramount as many customers will reason that cheapest is best. The price the customer is charged is governed largely by the cost the company incurs in producing the product or service. That in turn is largely driven by the efficiency of the operation. Therefore if low cost is important, the operational processes – how they are sequenced, the automation and tooling and the people who work within them – must all be designed with low cost in mind. This may mean compromising on the quality of the product by offering a basic service or product as opposed to a more comprehensive or functional one.

Quality appears difficult to quantify as it depends on the product, the application and the subjective views of the person making the assessment. As Crosby (1979) wrote:

> The first erroneous assumption is that quality means goodness, or luxury or shine, or weight. The word 'quality' is used to signify the relative worth of things in such phrases as 'good quality', 'bad quality' . . . Each listener assumes the speaker means what he or she, the listener, means by the phrase . . . This is precisely the reason we must define quality as conformance to requirements if we are to manage it. If a Cadillac conforms to the requirements of a Cadillac then it is a quality car, if a Pinto conforms to the requirements of a Pinto then it is a quality car. Don't talk about poor quality or high quality, talk about conformance and non-conformance. (p. 14)

Crosby's proposal moves the definition of quality from a term that is nebulous and difficult to define to a set of more tangible measures.

Key ideas   Product quality

The quality of products and services is based on the requirements of the customer. Therefore any product, as long as it does what the customer wants, can be considered a quality product. The most important activity is therefore to define and understand precisely what the customer is expecting and set up operations to deliver exactly that.

Six features help to define quality in terms of what customers expect:

- **Functionality** – what the product does. Where price is less of a consideration, products that do more may be more attractive. This is especially true with technology-based products such as the iPhone, where functionality is the prime consideration in choice: users see a product that does more as being of higher quality than one that does less.
- **Performance** – how well it does what it is meant to do. This element will feature more strongly in higher-value, 'statement' products such as a Porsche car, where top speed and acceleration are considered important. A product that is faster, more economical, stronger or easier to use will be seen as higher quality than others that are not. A higher-performance product is seen as a higher-quality product.
- **Reliability** – the consistency of performance over time. Are the promises made to the customer honoured correctly and in the same way over many occasions? A more reliable product is seen as a higher-quality product.
- **Durability** – how robust it is. This may feature more on products that are used a lot, such as tools and equipment, or products that operate in a harsh environment. Climbing equipment needs to be resistant to breakage. A more durable product is seen as a higher-quality product.
- **Customisation** – how well the product fits the need. This is more relevant in products where additional features may be added to the core functions in products, such as a mobile phone, or in financial services. The more a product or service fits exactly to a customer's need the higher quality it is seen to be.
- **Appearance** – how the product looks. This is important not only to convey the correct image, such as a well-decorated house or a highly polished car, but also where appearance affects the utility of the product such as a website where a clear layout affects how easy it is to use. A product that looks good is considered a higher-quality product.

The customer's perception of quality will combine some or all of these factors: each can contribute to the quality standard the customer desires.

Case study   Zara – the case continues   www.zara.com

The middle-aged mother buys clothes at Zara because they are cheap, while her teenage daughter buys there because they are in fashion. The matching of both low cost and acceptable quality is a winning combination. Like any other industry, low cost in the clothing industry is obtained by having efficient and streamlined operational processes. Quality is more subjective; with garments, quality is defined more by the design or 'look' that the customer wants to be seen wearing rather than the quality of the construction. Most of these garments are destined to have a short life as they will be discarded or relegated to the back of the cupboard when fashion changes. This means aspects of manufacturing quality such as durability and robustness will be of little importance to the customer, so long as a certain standard is reached.

Case question 18.5

● Consider the concept of fashion. What does quality actually mean? Think of specific factors that define the quality of fashion.

Additional dimensions of service quality

All of the elements mentioned apply to both products and services and are commonly labelled the 'tangibles'. In service operations intangible features affect perceptions of quality:

● **Responsiveness** – willingness to help a customer and provide prompt service. While applicable to all service encounters, this element is most powerful in a less-structured service environment where there is more opportunity for the customer to request something at random that maybe outside the normal scope of the operation. A high-class restaurant may be expected to be more responsive than a fast-food outlet, where the customer would not think to request an alteration to the meal on offer.

● **Assurance** – ability of the operation to inspire confidence. This element is most easily illustrated in provision of professional services: in a dental surgery the ambience of the surroundings, the equipment and the knowledge and expertise of the staff make the customer feel secure.

● **Empathy** – understanding and attentiveness shown to customers. Here the focus is mainly on the skills of the staff, their awareness of others and ability to communicate effectively. This is most easily seen in relation to the emergency services, where empathy with the victim is both a key feature of the service experience and a critical factor in the effective performance of the task.

Order-winning and order-qualifying criteria

A good way to determine the relative importance of each quality element is to distinguish between order-winning criteria and order-qualifying criteria (Hill, 1992).

● Order-winning criteria are features that the customer regards as the reason to buy the product or service. Improving these will win business.
● Order-qualifying criteria will not win business, but may lose it – if they are not met they will disqualify the product or service from consideration.

Quality management

Quality depends on operational systems. Theory and techniques about managing quality were developed first in the manufacturing sector, but are now also used in the service sector.

In manufacturing, craftspeople tend to take pride in their work and continuously strive to improve their mastery of the craft. During the evolution of the factory system the craft system suffered as management subdivided the work process into smaller tasks performed by different people. This had two detrimental effects on quality. Firstly, no single person was responsible for the whole process, so the pride in work that was evident in the craft system and was the basis of quality was removed. Secondly, craft skills were eroded and the consequence of this was that the capability of the individual to build quality into a product was lost. In essence, process management removed quality assurance from the remit of production staff, in effect taking the responsibility for producing quality products away from manufacturing workers. To remedy this situation attempts were made to 'build' quality into the process with more and more detailed and comprehensive processes used for the manufacture of each product. This, however, had only limited success.

The problem of production quality was not fully grasped until the mid to late 20th century with pioneers such as Juran (1974), Deming (1988) and Feigenbaum (1993), working to develop philosophies and methods. Although developed initially in the West, it was the Japanese who had most success as they applied the lessons widely and conscientiously. They also recognised the fundamental truth of craft production, which is that the person who performs the transformation is the best person to ensure quality. The Japanese quality revolution was therefore based on placing the responsibility for quality with the worker. History has thus come full circle, with individuals taking pride in doing quality work and striving to make regular improvements in the production process.

| **Key ideas** | **Principles of total quality management (TQM)** |

- **Customer focus:** the aim is to meet the needs and expectations of customers.
- **Comprehensive:** covers all parts of the organisation.
- **Inclusive:** includes every person in the organisation and across the supply chain.
- **Measurement:** tracks all costs affecting quality, especially those of failures and of getting things right first time.
- **Methods:** clear systems and procedures to support quality, implemented by teams.
- **Continuous:** developing the idea of continuous, incremental improvement.

Source: Based on Slack et al. 2013, pp. 548–9.

Total quality management (TQM) is a philosophy of management that is driven by customer needs and expectations and focuses on continually improving work processes.

Although there were many people involved in the search for quality and many systems developed, the principles are best encapsulated in the system of **total quality management (TQM)**. This advocates that a constant effort to remove waste adds value – see 'Key ideas'. Some of these wastes are obvious – scrapped material and lost time through equipment failure – but other wastes come through bad systems or poor communications and may be more difficult to find and measure. Progressive, small improvements reduce costs as the operational process uses resources more effectively. Crosby (1979) introduced the idea that 'quality is free': it is getting it wrong that costs money.

Quality systems and procedures

Kaynak (2003) surveyed much of the empirical research on quality to identify four sets of management practices that had, collectively, been shown to enhance manufacturing and service quality.

- **Quality data and reporting:** This refers to the extent to which quality data, is collected, recorded and used for quality improvement purposes. This can include internal data, such as statistical process control, but also information about the quality of incoming materials from suppliers, and their responsiveness to requests from the company.

- **Supplier quality management:** Quality depends heavily on the performance of suppliers, so many observers advocate that to achieve high quality, companies should develop close working relationships with a small number of careful selected suppliers. They also advise that these relationships should aim to be for the long term, to enable suppliers to develop ever-closer understandings of the needs of the customer, and vice versa.
- **Product/service design:** This refers to practices such as the clarity of product/service specification procedures; thoroughness of new product/service reviews before offering to market; engaging suppliers and customers in the design of products; and meeting customers' expectations. This activity may create opportunities to save cost, time and waste – waste being the use of resources that do not add value for the customer.
- **Process management:** This refers to the amount of systematic documentation of internal processes, reliability of quality processes, inspections of incoming materials and of work in-process and the stability of production schedules and work distribution. That in itself is likely to depend on a quality culture that has top management support (Baird et al. 2011).

Kaynak and Hartley (2008) suggested that companies that develop effective practices in these four areas are likely to see improved quality, less inventory and better financial performance.

| 18.8 | **Integrating themes** |

Entrepreneurship

Entrepreneurial companies thrive in part by enabling talented and creative people to imagine and design new products that deviate from the norm. They depend on a culture in which individuals have considerable creative freedom. Yet such entrepreneurial activities must be integrated in some way with the organisations strategy, partly through the work of operations managers. Yet the control-related structures, policies, procedures and systems of operations management appear to be at odds with the entrepreneurial spirit.

This conflict is illustrated in Lashinsky's (2012) account of Apple in the years following Steve Jobs' return to create the business we know today. Jobs was the visionary, Cook the taskmaster. He joined Apple in 1998 when Jobs knew that the company's operations were broken, and that fixing them did not interest him.

The new recruit quickly closed all of Apple's factories, opting instead to [outsource] manufacturing. The goal was to strengthen Apple's balance sheet by cutting down on the wasteful practice of [storing more components than were needed]. (p. 95).

Then:

He took over sales, which before Apple opened its retail locations . . . meant selling through retailers. Next he took on customer support . . . and when the iPhone came out, Cook spearheaded negotiations with wireless carriers around the world. Released from worrying over whether customer service was operating smoothly or if retail outlets were receiving inventory to match customer demand, [Jobs was able to dream of new products and how to market them] and move on to the next task while his orders were being implemented. (pp. 96–7)

Cook (CEO since 2012) is responsible for Apple's operational excellence, which has given it the 'dynamic capability' to be simultaneously innovative and efficient.

The two ways a company makes money are by growing revenues and cutting costs. Apple does both, and the operations machinery that Cook built is the engine that drives down costs while enabling the products that lead to growth. (p. 99)

Sustainability

All pollution is caused in some way by an operational failure. Whether it is a poorly designed process producing more waste than necessary or the result of an accident, the cause is an inadequate operations process. Fabbe-Costes et al. (2014), writing in a special issue of the *International Journal of Operations and Production Management* on sustainable operations management, point out that many practitioners now regard the topic as a mainstream concern.

As managers encounter external pressure to run a more sustainable business, they aim to rearrange their operations to improve their 'triple bottom line' (Figure 1.7) of people, planet and profits. This depends on reviewing the affects of all aspects of operations – including product design, sourcing, production, transportation models, stock policies and many more. Although operations managers can work to increase the efficiency of processes and reduce waste in operations within their direct control, a great deal of waste occurs elsewhere in their supply chain – 'upstream' in their suppliers, and 'downstream' as their product is moved towards the final consumer – so that aspect too becomes part of their agenda.

Internationalisation

Section 18.7 showed that TQM as an approach to managing quality has both social and technical dimensions, which need to be managed in a coherent way if companies are to achieve the full benefits. The social aspect focuses on leadership, teamwork, involvement in decisions and training. The technical aspect emphasises improving production methods and developing systematic processes to constantly improve the delivery of goods and services to customers. While the social and the technical need to be handled together, it appears that most problems that prevent full use of the approach lie in the social area, especially those relating to culture. An organisation that, for example, lacks a tradition of team work or acceptance of innovation is likely to find that these aspects of its culture inhibit acceptance of TQM.

The same principles are worth considering from an internationalisation perspective. As overseas operations increase, companies face growing pressure to manage quality in a consistent way across the whole enterprise, irrespective of where it is located. Studies of how they do this has led to inconclusive results, falling broadly into two groups. One sees a move towards 'convergence', as companies respond to universal pressures on quality by adopting uniform systems across their operations. The opposite 'culture specific' view is that even though managers face universal pressures to improve performance, these will be moderated locally by aspects of the culture unique to that nation.

Vecchi and Brennan's study (2011) found considerable evidence for the culture-specific view, in that the extent of adoption of the principles of quality management clearly varied between the countries in their study – some were more receptive to the ideas than others – and that these differences were systematically related to known dimensions of national cultures. To take just one example from a complex paper, they expected, and found, that countries with high 'uncertainty avoidance' scores would be receptive to quality programmes, since these in part involve the formalisation of practices intended to reduce uncertainty and error.

Governance

Safety and quality standards are now more prevalent than ever. In addition to umbrella organisations such as the International Standards Organisation (ISO) and the British Standards Institute (BSI), all industries have specific bodies – such as the Civil Aviation Authority (CAA) for airline safety and the Food Standards Agency (FSA), which is concerned with food and how it is sold and labelled.

As more standards are introduced and business becomes more highly regulated it is the responsibility of the operations staff to design processes that are compliant in how they operate. There have been many high-profile cases where industrial accidents, such as the Cyanide gas leak in Bhopal caused by Union Carbide or the radiation leak at the 3 mile Island Nuclear Generating facility operated by Metropolitan Edison, have led to serious disasters. These examples were the result of process failure. Operations personnel must become aware of the governance regulating all operational activity as any contravention, while probably not news worthy, will have some detrimental effect on the business, the customer or the environment.

Summary

1 **Define the term operations management**
   - Operations management is the activities, decisions and responsibilities of managing the production and delivery of products and services.
   - This includes responsibility for people, process and product.

2 **Describe the transformation process model of operations management**

   Transformation process is the organisational system that takes inputs:
   - Facilities
   - Staff
   - Finance
   - Raw materials
   - Information

   and transforms these into output products – either tangible goods or intangible services that can be sold in the market.

3 **Show how operations management can contribute to the competitiveness of the organisation**
   - By designing and implementing systems and processes that are repeatable, consistent, reliable, efficient and compliant with the legislation that governs the overall environment.
   - By creating an operations system that is aligned with the goals of the organisation in terms of Volume of output, Variety of product, Variation in demand and Visibility of process.

4 **Identify different forms of operational activity**
   - Managing the capacity of the transformation process.
   - Setting process and product standards to be adhered to within the transformation process.
   - Managing the materials pipeline into and through the transformation process.
   - Scheduling of the required resources to be used in the transformation process.
   - Controlling the activities within the transformation process.

5 **Define the term quality and describe features that can be used to quantify it**
   - Quality means conformance to the requirements of the customer.
   - Product or service quality can be described in relation to functionality, performance, reliability, durability, customisation and appearance.

6 **Explain the idea of assessing quality systematically, and understand how you can use this to develop the skill of assessing what customers mean by quality**
   - Identifying what customers regard as 'quality' is an essential part of the operations function, so the chapter provides an opportunity to begin to develop that skill.

7 **Show how ideas from the chapter add to your understanding of the integrating themes**
   - The operations system at Apple is an example of how managers can develop a business that is both innovative and efficient.
   - All waste is the result of an operations failure, so performance depends on changing operations to reduce waste both within the immediate process and across the supply chain.
   - Implementing a quality system is a social as well as a technical task, so those implementing TQM or other systems in an international business are likely to find that some aspects are more consistent with, and so acceptable to, local cultures than others.
   - Operations staff work in an increasingly regulated environment, so need to focus on designing processes that are not only efficient and sustainable, but which comply with regulatory and control systems.

Test your understanding

1 Review some consumer goods, such as mobile phones, cars and kitchen appliances. Identify the service elements attached to the purchase of these products.

2 Discuss why variation in the inputs to the transformation process is a bad thing. Which of the five inputs is likely to be subject to most variation and which to least?

3 Why is control over quality at source so important?

4 How does service quality differ from manufacturing quality?

5 Why is delivery reliability more important than delivery speed?

6 Describe and discuss the importance of the demand/supply balance.

7 Discuss why it is impossible to have a single production system that is equally efficient at all volumes of throughput.

8 Describe the differences between product, process and cell layouts.

9 Discuss the concepts of order winners and order qualifiers.

10 Summarise an idea from the chapter that adds to your understanding of the integrating themes.

Think critically

Think about the ways in which a company you are familiar with deals with operational issues such as capacity, scheduling, quality or cost. Then make notes on these questions:

- What **assumptions** do people make in your business about the role of operations? Is it, for example, seen as central to success, or as a secondary activity? What part to customers' views on quality play?

- What is the dominant view about how changes in the business **context** affect operations, and the need for operational change? Again, are changes in customer expectations about quality monitored systematically?

- Can you compare your organisation's approach to operations with that of colleagues on your course, especially those in similar industries, to see what **alternatives** others use?
- If there are differences in approach, can you establish the likely reasons, and does this suggest any possible **limitations** in the present approach?

Develop a skill – assessing what customers mean by quality

Understanding what customers regard as 'quality' is an essential part of the operations function, so this exercise helps you begin to develop that skill.

- **Assessment:** Assess how aware you are of what counts as 'quality', in a product or service you use. Do you instinctively think of it as being related to price, or packaging, or a familiar brand – or do you feel it is very subjective and hard to manage?
- **Learning:** Section 18.7 introduced theories of product and service quality. Read that section again, paying special attention to the 'Key ideas' feature (p. 596), which describes six features of product quality, and the sub-section on additional considerations when assessing service quality (p. 597). Summarise the main idea presented in this feature. Why is this significant for managers?
- **Analysis:** Consider the six product features and the three extra service ones. Which of them will probably be the easiest to monitor and assess in practice? How do you think organisations do this? What if customers make widely contrasting assessments on one or more of these quality criteria?
- **Practice:** Identify a product or service you use regularly, and whose quality matters to you. Make an initial subjective assessment of the quality of the product or service, and record that. Now use the criteria in Section 18.7 to assess the quality of the product systematically, and record your assessment.
  - Compare what you have found with colleagues on your course, and comment on what you learned from using these factors to assess quality systematically.
- **Application:** When you have completed the work, review it, and what you can learn from it about understanding customers' quality requirements.
  - Decide on another opportunity to practise this skill within the next week.

Read more

Crosby, P. (1979) *Quality is Free,* McGraw Hill, New York.

A classic text detailing the basics of quality management and showing how it all started.

Lowson, R.H. (2002) *Strategic Operations Management: The New Competitive Advantage,* Routledge, London.

An established comprehensive and authoritative text specialising in operations strategy and its philosophies and techniques.

Slack, N., Brandon-Jones, A. and Johnston, R. (2013), *Operations Management* (7th edn.), Pearson, Harlow.

Covers all of the main current topics in operations management.

Sprague, L. (2007) 'Evolution of the field of operations management,' *Journal of Operations Management,* vol. 25, no. 2, pp. 219–38.

A brief but comprehensive summary of the field of operations management from a historical perspective.

Go online

These are some of the websites that have appeared in the chapter:

www.zara.com
www.sunseeker.com
www.linn.co.uk
www.apple.com

Visit two of the websites in the list (or any other company that interests you) and navigate to the pages dealing with the products and services they offer. This is usually the first one you see, but in some it may be further in.

- What messages do they give about the nature of the goods and services they offer? What challenges are they likely to raise for operations in terms of their emphasis on, for example, quality, delivery or cost? What implications might that have for people working in the company?

- See if you can find any information on the site about the operating systems, or how they link with their suppliers.

CHAPTER 19
CONTROL AND PERFORMANCE MEASUREMENT

Aim

To show why control is one of the four tasks of managing, and how the design of control and measurement systems can help organisations to meet their goals.

Objectives

By the end of your work on this chapter you should be able to outline the concepts below in your own terms and:

1 Define control and explain why it is an essential activity in managing

2 Describe and give examples of the generic control activities of setting targets, measuring, comparing and correcting

3 Discuss strategies and tactics used to gain and maintain control

4 Explain how the choice of suitable measures of performance can help in managing the organisation

5 Explain why those designing performance measurement and control systems need to take account of human reactions to managerial control

6 Explain the tasks in creating a control system, and understand how you can use this approach to develop your skill at monitoring progress on a task

7 Show how ideas from the chapter add to your understanding of the integrating themes

Key terms

This chapter introduces these terms:

balanced scorecard	key performance indicators (KPIs)
control process	management by objectives
control system	organisational performance
corrective action	output measure
efficiency	process measure
effectiveness	range of variation
input measure	standard of performance

Each is a term defined within the text, and in the glossary at the end of the book.

Case study · Performance measurement in the NHS

NHS Foundation Trusts (often called Foundation Hospitals) are at the cutting edge of the government's commitment to devolution and decentralisation of public services and are at the heart of a patient-led NHS. They are not subject to direction from Whitehall. Instead, local managers and staff working with local people have the freedom to develop services tailored to the particular needs of their patients and local communities. (*A Short Guide to NHS Foundation Trusts*)

Foundation Trusts were introduced in 2004, and by early 2016 there were 152 NHS Foundation Trusts (NHSFTs). They were intended to be a new type of organisation, established as independent, not-for-profit public benefit corporations with accountability to their local communities rather to central government. The secretary of state for health was to have no direct powers of direction over NHSFTs, although they were to remain firmly part of the NHS. They exist to provide and develop health care services in a way that is consistent with NHS standards and principles: free care based on need, not ability to pay.

NHSFTs were to have greater freedoms and flexibilities to manage their affairs, for example in freedom from central control, freedom to access capital sources, and freedom to invest surpluses (Harradine and Prowle, 2012, p. 217).

The intention of this change was to devolve decision making from central government to local communities, so that hospitals were more responsive to their needs. They were an important part of the government's agenda to create a patient-led NHS in England, and would bring significant change to the control of Foundation hospitals.

Those with Foundation status are accountable locally to a board of governors and nationally to Monitor, the independent regulator of NHS Foundation Trusts (**www.monitor-nhsft.gov.uk**). This form of control should allow each hospital more autonomy to use its income to provide relevant care and services for its geographical area.

Hospitals are among the most complex of organisations. They employ a large number of highly skilled staff, use very sophisticated technology, operate extremely complex processes and often deal in life or death situations. They also have limited budgets, and

© Christopher Furlong/Getty Images

the issue of their performance and value for money has been a matter of concern to all governments for many years. Central to the issue of performance is that of control.

Foundation hospitals represent a shift in philosophy from centralised, 'one size fits all', directive control by government to a more decentralised, customised and empowered form of control. Hospitals are responsible for managing their income in an attempt to create a market-like environment in the hope that empowered managers will be better able to intelligently allocate resources to areas of most need and behave more efficiently.

Limited resources mean that some form of budgeting system is essential, though

health professionals often see the budgeting system as a tool of administrative control aimed at constraining NHS expenditure and their ambitions to improve services (Harradine and Prowle, 2012, p. 219).

Sources: *A Short Guide to NHS Foundation Trusts* (2005), Department of Health Publications; Harradine and Prowle (2012).

Case questions 19.1

- What are the likely benefits of control in a hospital?
- What sources of information would a control system be able to use?

19.1 | Introduction

Effective public organisations add value, in part, by implementing and controlling processes that are consistent, repeatable and reliable. Doing so enables them to achieve standards that their stakeholders expect – and legislation requires public organisations to report to their regulators on how their performance compares with targets. Mid-Staffordshire Hospitals Trust required all of its hospitals, including Stafford Hospital, to provide such measures. These are intended to show how well it is using resources and to draw attention to areas for improvement. All hospitals do this – beds are scarce and expensive resources that incur surprisingly high daily costs for the hospital, so hospitals invest in bed management systems to ensure that patients leave as soon as they are able to, freeing the resource for others. They monitor how many patients attend clinics to ensure that they provide the right number, and that they deliver value for money.

Designing and using a performance measurement system is often controversial, given the diversity of stakeholders with an interest in both the measures and in service performance. Some see it as a way to exert central control over local institutions if, for example, units' performance is published in league tables. Others see it as a necessary element in public accountability, where services are required to report annually on what they have achieved with public money. Others again see performance measurement as a useful tool guiding frontline managers to focus on organisational priorities.

Commercial businesses face similar demands from their stakeholders – especially their investors. Public companies such as Shell or Apple publish annual reports that review performance and make estimates for the year to come; private companies such as the Virgin Group do not make their reports public, but its shareholders receive regular reports on the performance of the part of the group in which they have invested. Measuring performance is central to **control**, which shows whether a unit is performing in the way people expected.

All managers exercise control as they transform input resources into output products and services. No matter how thoroughly they plan their objectives and how to meet them, unforeseen internal and external events will intervene. Managers therefore need to supplement planning with controlling – checking that work is going to plan, and if necessary taking corrective action. The sooner they note deviations, the easier it is to bring performance into line. This applies at all levels – a senior nurse responsible for the flow of patients in the Accident and Emergency department, a consultant responsible for the quality of work in an operating theatre or a general manager responsible for overall hospital performance.

Control has many positive meanings, standing for order, predictability or reliability. If things are under control employees are clear about what they are expected to do and customers know what standard of product they will receive. Control is an essential part of organisational life; it helps to ensure that the cooperative work of many resources adds value. An absence of control implies uncertainty, chaos, inefficiency and waste. As control depends on influencing people's behaviour, designing a control system is not a technical process, but one that needs to take account of human and contextual factors.

The chapter begins by describing what managerial control is and the strategies and tactics that can be used to achieve it. It then goes on to discuss how to measure an organisation's performance. The last section introduces a human perspective on control and discusses how control and performance measurement affects employees.

> **Control** is the process of monitoring activities to ensure that results are in line with the plan and acting to correct significant deviations.

The control process

The **control process** is intended to support the achievement of objectives. Managers design **control systems** for different activities – especially finance but also marketing, operations, HRM and many more. Although their degree of formality and explicitness varies, the control process incorporates four elements, shown in Figure 19.1 – setting targets, measuring performance, comparing this with the standard and taking action to correct any significant gap between the two.

Setting targets

Targets provide direction and a **standard of performance** to aim for. The standard will itself affect achievement – people will ignore standards that are too high as unattainable, or too low as not being worthwhile. Some measures are generic, widely used and relevant to most management situations, such as employee satisfaction or absence, costs against budget, or sales against target. Managers will also use measures that are unique to their activity and area of responsibility – pages of advertising booked or students recruited.

Some aspects of performance can be measured in objective and quantifiable terms – such as sales, profit or return on assets. Equally important aspects of performance (product innovation, flexibility, company reputation or service quality) are more subjective and here managers look for acceptable qualitative measures.

Measuring – the tools of control

Control requires that performance can be measured against a target. Table 19.1 shows the sources of information people can use to measure performance, and their advantages and disadvantages; combining them gives a more reliable picture than relying on one alone.

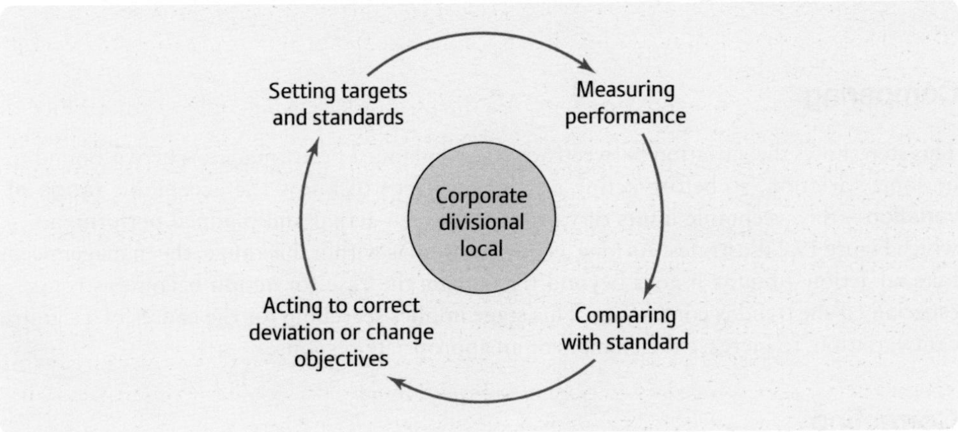

The **control process** is the generic activity of setting performance standards, measuring actual performance, comparing actual performance with the standards and acting to correct deviations or modify standards.

A **control system** is the way the elements in the control process are designed and combined in a specific situation.

Standard of performance is the defined level of performance to be achieved, against which an operation's actual performance is compared.

Figure 19.1 The control process

Table 19.1 Common sources of information for measuring performance

	Advantages	Disadvantages
Personal observation	Gives first-hand knowledge, information is not filtered, shows the manager is interested	Subject to personal bias, time consuming, obtrusive – people see what is happening
Oral reports	Quick way to get information, allows for verbal and non-verbal feedback	Information is filtered, no permanent record
Written reports	Comprehensive, and can show trends and relationships, easy to store and retrieve	Time to prepare, may ignore subjective factors
Online information systems	Rapid feedback, often during the process	Information overload, may be stressful to staff

Management in practice

Can you trust what is reported?

Chris Finlayson is CEO of BG Group, a global oil and gas producer. He worked for Shell for 30 years, including several years as head of exploration for the company's Russian interests, including the Sakhalin Liquified Natural Gas project. This experience taught him that one of the challenges of leadership is that you cannot know the detail of every project. The pipeline infrastructure for Sakhalin 2 alone comprises 300 km of offshore pipes and 1600 km of onshore pipework.

That said, every two or three months he visited Sakhalin and, together with the project's CEO, made sure that what was being reported to them was accurate. The trick is to know when to dive down into the detail and head off problems, he says.

You have to stay at a sufficiently high level to understand what is going on right across the business, while having a sense of intuition [to know] there is something here that makes me worried.

 Source: From an article in the *Financial Times*, 30 December 2013, p. 12.

Comparing

The **range of variation** sets the acceptable limits within which performance can vary from standard without requiring remedial action.

This step shows the variation between actual and planned performance. There is bound to be some variation, so before acting a manager needs to know the acceptable **range of variation** – the acceptable limits of variation between actual and planned performance – which Figure 19.2 illustrates. As long as the variation is within this range, the manager need take no action – but as it goes beyond that range, the case for action becomes stronger, especially if the trend is continuing. This stage implies searching for the causes of a significant variation, to increase the chances of an appropriate response.

Correcting

Corrective action aims to correct problems to get performance back on track.

The final step is to act on significant variations – either to correct future performance or to revise the standard. Attempts to bring performance up to the required standard could involve any aspects of the transformation process and involves taking **corrective action** such as redesigning a process, resetting a machine or cutting prices to sell excess stocks. This may mean dealing with longer-term issues of design, quality or skill.

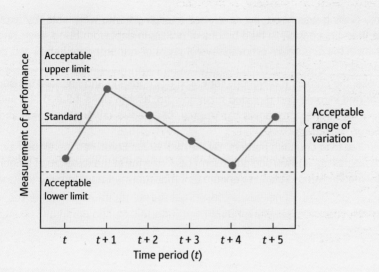

Figure 19.2
Defining the acceptable range of variation

Assessing control systems

Consider the course you are studying. With your fellow students, analyse how your performance on the course is controlled by answering these questions:

- **What standards of performance are you expected to achieve?**
  - Who sets the standards?
  - Are they clear or ambiguous?
- **How is your performance measured?**
  - Do you know what the criteria are?
  - How often is performance measured?
- **Who compares your performance with the standard?**
  - Is this done publicly?
  - Is the comparison objective or subjective?
- **What happens if your performance is not up to standard?**

  - What feedback do you get?
  - Is it useful?

Management in practice **Enron – a lack of control**

The Enron scandal, revealed in October 2001, eventually led to the bankruptcy of the Enron Corporation, an energy company based in Texas, and the dissolution of its auditor, Arthur Andersen, one of the largest accountancy partnerships in the world.

Enron was formed in 1985 after the merger of Houston Natural Gas and InterNorth. By 1992, Enron was the largest merchant of natural gas in North America. In an attempt to achieve further growth, Enron pursued a diversification strategy. By 2001 it had become a conglomerate owning and operating gas pipelines, pulp and paper mills and electricity and water supplies. The corporation also traded in financial markets for products and services.

When Chief Executive Jeffrey Skilling was hired, he developed executives who were able, by exploiting accounting loopholes and poor financial control, to hide billions of dollars in debt from failed deals and projects. The roots of the scandal lay in the accumulation over several years of inappropriate habits and values, which finally spiralled out of control.

From late 1997 until its collapse, the primary motivations for Enron's accounting and financial transactions seem to have been to keep reported income and reported cash flow up, asset values inflated and liabilities hidden. These practices led not only to the company's bankruptcy, but also to criminal charges, and then prison sentences, for several Enron managers.

The lack of control was not limited to accounting matters. By the mid-1990s Enron had developed a culture that encouraged innovation and risk taking: it rewarded short-term performance at the expense of longer-term success. There were few control mechanisms in place to ensure that managers were performing in a sensible and professional manner.

Source: McLean and Elkind (2003).

19.3 Strategies for control – mechanistic or organic?

Managers design a control system using their assumptions about how it will affect behaviour. Rules and procedures clan be implemented to give people precise and unambiguous directions on how to perform tasks and deal with unusual events. Alternatively they can be written in broader terms leaving more discretion to staff. Procedures may cover all aspects of work or a small number of critically important activities. Controls may emphasise conformity or encourage creativity.

If such decisions are made consistently and coherently, this suggests that managers are taking a strategic approach to control, in the sense that they have a clear understanding of its purposes and how to implement it. Two opposing strategies are mechanistic and organic, terms introduced in Chapter 10.

Mechanistic control refers to the extensive use of rules and procedures, top-down authority, written job descriptions and other formal methods of influencing people to act in desirable ways. Organic control refers to the extensive use of flexible authority, relatively loose job descriptions and more reliance on self-control. Each approach will work well in a situation to which it is suitable. Table 19.2 compares the two approaches.

Table 19.2 Examples of mechanistic and organic controls

Tools	Mechanistic control	Organic control
Supervision	Stress on following procedures and plans	Stress on encouraging learning and creativity
Organisation structure	Top-down authority, emphasis on position power, detailed job descriptions	Dispersed authority, emphasis on expert power, flexible job descriptions
Rules and procedures	Detailed, on many topics	Broad, on as few topics as practicable
Machinery	Information on performance used by supervisors to check on staff	Information on performance used by staff to learn and improve
Cultural	Encourages conformity, focus is on controlling individuals	Encourages creativity and innovation, promotes freedom

Which strategy to choose?

Chapter 10 contrasted mechanistic and organic structures, and introduced the theory that choice of form reflects one or more contingencies. It showed that organisations often combine both approaches, using mechanistic forms in stable, predictable areas, and organic for more uncertain areas. The same applies to the choice of control systems. John Child (2005) proposed contingency factors that could affect this choice – namely competitive strategy, importance of innovation and employee expertise – shown in Table 19.3.

Tactics for control

Defining the strategy is the first step in creating a coherent control system, which then requires support from a set of relevant practices – each of which can contribute in the right circumstances.

Direct supervision

In small organisations or units most control is by direct supervision as the owner or unit head can see directly what is happening. They can personally inspect and report on progress, quickly see if it is in line with the plan and act if necessary. Done with enthusiasm and sensitivity this method is very effective – if people use it clumsily staff will find it intrusive and overbearing.

Organisation structure

Most organisations set out what people are expected to do by giving them job descriptions that allocate the person's tasks and responsibilities. These can be very narrowly and specifically defined, or they can be broad and defined in general terms. They may also establish with whom the job holder is expected to communicate, and the boundaries of their responsibility. This is a form of control as it constrains people – by specifying what they can or cannot do, and what output standards they should achieve. Similarly organisations can be centralised, with control being held at the top, or decentralised with control spread throughout the structure.

Rules and procedures

As organisations become too large for personal control, managers develop rules and procedures to control activities and alert senior people to significant deviations. Rules establish acceptable behaviour and levels of performance and so are a way of controlling the workforce. They can guide people on how to conduct the business, how to perform the tasks, how to apply for equipment or what to do when a customer places an order.

Table 19.3 Contingencies and choice of control strategies

Contingency	Control strategy likely to be appropriate	
	Mechanistic, use of rules, procedures and machinery to measure quantitative output	Organic, use of HRM and cultural controls stressing self-managing teams, and qualitative output measures
Competitive strategy	Cost leadership	Differentiation
Importance of innovation	Low	High
Employee expertise	Low	High

Management by objectives

Management by objectives is a system in which managers and staff agree their objectives, and then measure progress towards them periodically.

Some organisations use a system of **management by objectives** to exercise control. Here managers throughout the hierarchy agree their goals for the following period. The approach is partly based on goal-setting theory, which predicts that the level of difficulty of a goal will affect the effort people put into achieving it. The key is that workers should focus on the outcome to be achieved and therefore must be given the latitude to achieve it by a variety of methods as they see fit.

Control through machinery

In this method machines or information systems are designed to control, directly or indirectly, what people do. Direct technological controls occur where the machine directs what people do or say. Assembly lines transport the object being made along a moving conveyor, with operators performing a short task to add another piece to the product, with almost no scope to alter the way they work. The machine sets the speed of work, time spent on each task is short and workers have little if any influence over their tasks. The scripts in a call centre that specify the questions to ask, how to respond to customer questions and how to close the conversation, have a similar controlling effect on the way a person works. In process industries such as brewing, computer sensors capture information on process performance, compare it with set criteria and, if needed, automatically adjust the equipment to keep the process in line with the plan.

Human resource management control

The processes of HRM discussed in Chapter 11 can support the control process. Selection and training procedures ensure that the number and type of recruits fit the profile of attitudes, social skills and technical competence that support wider objectives, and that new staff are trained to follow the company's ways of working. The appraisal and reward system can encourage behaviour that supports business objectives. The behaviour of employees can be controlled by offers of rewards if people comply with management policies, and of penalties if they do not.

Key ideas	Barker on concertive control

Barker (1993) notes three broad strategies that have evolved as organisations seek to control members' activities. The first is 'simple control', the direct, authoritarian and personal control of work by bosses, best seen in nineteenth-century factories and in small family-owned companies today. The second is 'technological control', in which control emerges from the physical technology, such as in the assembly line found in traditional manufacturing. Third and most familiar is 'bureaucratic control', where control follows from the hierarchically-based social relations in the organisation, and the rules that reward compliance and punish non-compliance.

Technological control resulted not only from technological advances but also from worker alienation from the authoritarianism that can arise in simple control. But technological control via the assembly line also led to worker dissatisfaction. Bureaucratic control, with its emphasis on rational–legal rules, hierarchical monitoring and rewards for compliance was developed to counter the problems of technological control.

Bureaucracy too has problems – the main one being an inability to respond quickly to changing conditions. Many companies have sought to overcome these problems by introducing a greater degree of self-control through the use of self-managing teams.

Barker's research in one company showed how team members developed values and norms about good team behaviour, and put pressure on members, especially new members, to follow them. This form of concertive control was not only stronger than many bureaucratic controls, but was also less visible, as team members accepted it as the normal way to do things.

Source: Barker (1993).

Values and beliefs

Another approach to control aims to ensure that members of the organisation meet management requirements by encouraging internal compliance rather than relying on external constraint. A unit that develops a strong culture with which staff can identify will help to control their actions. Extensive socialisation and other practices encourage them to act in ways that are consistent with the dominant values and beliefs. This may be positive, but can sometimes be oppressive and constraining.

Activity 19.2 Examples of control tools

- From your experience of organisations – a part-time job or the university – identify examples of each of these approaches to control.
- What are their advantages and disadvantages in the situation where they are used?

Case study NHS – the case continues

Foundation Trusts work within a context that affects their managers' roles. Although hospital managers are legally responsible to their trust's Board of Governors, some have doubted whether the latter will be able to control hospital management, which is heavily influenced by powerful medical professionals. These have a tradition of autonomy and resistance to outside interference with their professional judgements.

They will also face challenges from the evolving policy context affecting the health service. For example, trusts that increase the services they deliver (to defined quality standards) receive more funding, and vice versa. They therefore have a strong incentive to attract patients and deliver a higher volume of service. In addition, many services in an area are commissioned by groups of general practitioners, for which trusts compete to provide at an agreed price. So trusts need to achieve a balance between three objectives:

- delivering health services, in terms of quantity and quality, in line with contractual arrangements agreed with commissioners;
- maintaining a financial balance over the accounting period; and
- developing and implementing a plan for changing the delivery of health services to maintain longer-term sustainability (Harradine and Prowle, 2012, p. 219).

Case questions 19.2

- Why do you think professionals such as doctors resist managerial control?
- What are the implications of having three objectives for the control process, and for the sources of information that managers can use?
- Which aspects of a hospital's work are likely to suit mechanistic controls, and which organic?

Management in practice Creativity and control at Apple www.apple.com

All organisations use a mix of control tactics, many combining mechanistic and organic strategies. A simple example of this can be seen in organisations that both design and manufacture products. Apple is renowned for introducing innovative high-tech products, in a culture that allows innovation to flourish. The success of the company is built on the excellence of this design and development capability. Ideas cannot be 'manufactured' by process or thought of 'to order', therefore the control strategy used for R&D workers is organic, with knowledge workers working within a flexible and supportive environment.

However, the products are manufactured using a mechanistic approach. Each unit must be exactly the same, with each manufacturing process designed to be completely consistent and reliable. Control of quality is critical, with manufacturing tolerances sometimes specified in microns (millionths of a meter) and process defect rates of less than one in a million. Cleanliness is vital, with 'clean rooms' ensuring contaminants are minimised. To achieve this workers must fit into the process with no deviation tolerated, as any unplanned activity will lead to a process failure.

Control of cost in volume manufacturing is critical, with companies such as Apple manufacturing their products in low-wage countries, using many of the principles of scientific management, within a strict cost-control system. People doing exactly what they are told is the key to production efficiency in this system.

Sources: Gamble et al. (2004); company website.

Activity 19.3   **Control and operational efficiency**

- From a manufacturing control point of view, are lower-skilled and poorly educated workers more suitable than highly skilled and better-educated workers?
- Which do you think will be easier to control?

19.4   **How do you know you are in control?**

Once the strategy for guiding the control system has been decided and the tactics to be used for controlling the organisation selected, some mechanism for setting standards and monitoring performance must be implemented. This depends on measuring key variables regularly.

Types of performance measurement

Performance measurement refers to quantifying the efficiency and effectiveness of an action.

Feedback is essential to check that systems are consistently reliable, and depends on **performance measurement** – quantifying the efficiency and effectiveness of an action – checking progress against defined parameters at the beginning, during, or at the end of the process (Barrows and Neely, 2012). Figure 19.3 illustrates these in relation to a car journey.

Input measures

An **input measure** is an element of resource that is measured as it is put in to the transformation process.

Think of the journey as a 'process' of travelling from one place to another. The driver can re-fuel the car before the journey. If they then measure what they put in and what is left at the end, and do some arithmetic, they can calculate the fuel efficiency of the car. In organisational terms this may mean measuring the amount of material that is input to the process then working to reduce the waste so that less is needed. A more sophisticated **input measure** may be the skill of the workers, since a better worker may result in a more efficient process.

Process measures

Instruments can measure speed during the journey to tell us whether we are moving fast enough to arrive as planned. Moving too quickly means arriving too soon, with the associated reduction in fuel efficiency; moving too slowly means the danger of being late. In

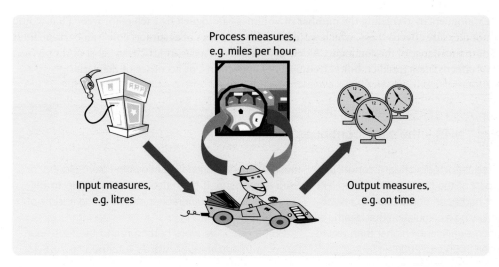

Process measures,
e.g. miles per hour

Input measures,
e.g. litres

Output measures,
e.g. on time

Figure 19.3 Types of performance measure

organisational terms, **process measures** may be the heat of an oven, the flow rate of liquid in a pipe or the speed of rotation of a machine. In all cases deviation from the norm will indicate possible sub-optimal performance. Another process measure is health and safety – the number and type of accidents occurring during a process, against a target of zero.

A **process measure** is a measurement taken during an operational process that provides data on how the process is performing.

Output measures

This is the activity of measuring the quantity of output for a definable area of work – whether for a unit or the business as a whole. In relation to our car journey this may be the arrival time or total fuel used. In an operational process this may simply be the number of units produced: is it on target or not? It may be a dimension: is a 100 gram bar of chocolate actually 100 grams. If more, then too much chocolate has been given and profit reduced; if less, the customer is receiving less than the advertised amount and the company is in trouble. Other popular **output measures** are financial metrics, such as labour and materials cost.

An **output measure** is a measurement taken after an operational process is complete.

The measures taken in our car journey should show us how to alter the process the next time to improve either fuel consumption or on-time performance. The same is true in operational processes. The measures taken should provide information that allows the control system to be adjusted to achieve a better outcome and so optimise efficiency.

Performance measures are required to calculate how efficiently or effectively our organisation is operating. While both these terms are sometimes used interchangeably, in fact they have very different meanings.

Efficiency

Efficiency is often thought of as 'doing things right'. It is a measure of output divided by the inputs needed to produce the output. It is widely used to show how productively a process is working, and how well people have managed it – more output for fewer inputs is better since that implies that value is being added to the resources. A simple measure of output would be sales revenue (number sold × price), while input can be measured by the cost of acquiring and transforming resources into the output. An increase in the ratio of output to input indicates an increase in efficiency. Managers are under constant pressure from shareholders or taxpayers to produce their output more efficiently, by using fewer resources.

Efficiency is a measure of the inputs required for each unit of output.

Effectiveness

Effectiveness is often thought of as 'doing the right things'. It is a measure of how well the outcomes of a process relate to the broader objectives of the unit – that is, how well the process supports the achievement of broader goals. A library can measure the efficiency of its

Effectiveness is a measure of how well an activity contributes to achieving organisational goals.

cataloguers by recording the number of volumes catalogued by each employee. That would not measure effectiveness, which would require measures of accuracy, consistency, timeliness or maintenance of the catalogue. A delivery service can measure efficiency (cost of the service) or effectiveness (predictability, frequency of collections, or accuracy of deliveries).

Case study   NHS – the case continues

In 2009 the NHS regulator published a report into Stafford Hospital, part of the Mid-Staffordshire NHS Foundation Trust. It had been undertaken to investigate the hospital following a calculation that deaths at the hospital had been significantly higher than would be expected between 2005 and 2008.

The report placed some of the blame on the performance measurement system. One performance metric was the Accident and Emergency four-hour waiting-time target. Staff told the Healthcare Commission that there was a lot of pressure on them to meet this target. Several doctors recounted occasions where managers had asked them to leave seriously ill patients to treat minor ailments so the target could be met. One had been asked to leave a heart-attack patient being given life-saving treatment.

Nurses reported leaving meetings in tears after being told their jobs were at risk after breaching the target. And the report concluded patients were sometimes 'dumped' into wards near A&E with little nursing care, so the targets could be met.

The four-hour target, which in simple terms aims to ensure that patients are treated and either admitted or sent home within four hours, at first glance seems reasonable. However, on further consideration it is complicated to enforce. Patients' conditions and circumstances differ widely, including some whom it would be dangerous to discharge quickly – such as those with chest pains or recovering from alcohol or drug overdoses; it may also not be suitable to discharge elderly or vulnerable patients in the middle of the night.

Some hospitals were getting round the four-hour target with observation wards attached to A&E to which patients could be admitted. Others refused to accept patients into their A&E departments from the ambulance so that the 'four hour clock' would not start ticking.

Unthinkingly trying to meet this simple but ultimately misconceived target seriously damaged patient care.

Source: 'Learning and Implications from the Mid-Staffordshire NHS Foundation Trust, Monitor – Independent Regulator of NHS Foundation Trusts', Final Report – 5 August 2009.

Case questions 19.3

- Which types of performance measures listed in the text does the hospital appear to have used?
- What alternative approaches to measuring performance may have produced a more satisfactory outcome – bearing in mind the three possibly conflicting targets hospital managers may be balancing?

19.5   How to measure performance?

Choosing performance measures

There are five generic performance objectives – quality, speed, dependability, flexibility and cost. Each can be expressed in more detailed measures, such as level of complaints or delivery times, or aggregated into composite measures such as customer satisfaction scores. The composite measures usually have more strategic relevance, indicating such things as how a product is performing in the market. The more detailed measures tend to have more operational relevance, such as how a process or a person is performing. Detailed measures are usually monitored more closely and more often – in some cases highly mechanised processes are monitored by sensors hundreds of times a second. Companies use multiple

Table 19.4 Aggregating performance measures

Composite measures	Customer Satisfaction		Agility		Resilience
Generic measures	Quality	Dependability	Speed	Flexibility	Cost
Examples of detailed measure	Defects per unit Customer returns Scrap rate	Mean time between failures Lateness	Delivery time Throughput	Range of functionality Number of options	Raw material cost Labour cost

Source: Adapted from Slack et al. (2013), p. 607.

measures to build a picture of how they are performing, much like a doctor will check blood pressure, heart rate and cholesterol level rather than relying on any one measure to guide their diagnosis. Table 19.4 shows how detailed performance measures can be aggregated into composite ones.

There are two problems with devising useful performance measures. The first is that of achieving a balance between having too few measures (straightforward and simple to use) and having too many (comprehensive but difficult to manage). Managers aim for a compromise by ensuring that there is at least a clear link between the measures chosen and the strategic objectives of, for example, marketing, operations and finance. If good quality is the main reason that customers buy the product then they place more emphasis on implementing measures that ensure the quality rather than cheapness of the product. The most important measures are called **key performance indicators (KPIs)**

The second is the problem of setting performance targets that do not create the wrong behaviours as employees try to find ways around them so that the target is met but to the detriment of the overall operation. Here common sense must be applied and the consequences of each target must be thoroughly considered in tandem with the overall control strategy that is in place. In the NHS four-hour case, the key to the successful operation of the A and E department is in the skill of the staff, the quality of the support infrastructure and equipment and providing the frontline doctors and nurses with the flexibility to do their job the best way that they see fit. Instead of using an output measure of a four-hour waiting time, implementing input measures such as skills matrices combined with process measures such as equipment availability will, if used correctly, ensure the best people are supported by the best equipment. This should reduce waiting times and also improve care quality.

The five indicators are composites of many smaller measures. Quality is a composite of many process measures that ensure that the product produced is exactly as it should be. Speed is an aggregate of how quickly materials are moved between processes, and how effectively machines and staff work to complete each process.

One criticism of performance measures is the tendency to focus on the 'easy to measure' things such as finance and units of output, while avoiding more complex ones such as customer satisfaction and quality of staff. The more difficult to measure aspects are sometimes the most useful. In design and development work ensuring that employees have the skills and knowledge to do their jobs will do more for effectiveness than measuring the output of a deficient employee. Likewise, measuring customer satisfaction and loyalty will be more useful than measuring revenue, since a satisfied customer will return and so generate more revenue.

> **Key performance indicator (KPI)** are a summarised set of the most important measures that inform managers how well an operation is achieving organisational goals.

The balanced scorecard

Kaplan and Norton (1992) noted that while

> traditional financial performance measures worked well for the industrial era . . . they are out of step with the skills and competencies companies are trying to master today. (p. 71)

Financial measures are essential but carry the hazard that short-term targets may encourage practices that damage long-term performance – for example by postponing investment in equipment or customer service. They found that senior executives recognised that no single measure could provide a clear performance target or focus attention on the critical areas of the business. Rather, they wanted a balanced presentation of both financial and operational measures. Their research enabled them to devise a **balanced scorecard** – a set of measures that gives a fast but comprehensive view of the business. It includes financial measures that tell the results of actions taken, and complements these with measures of customer satisfaction, internal processes and innovation – measures that drive future financial performance.

It allows managers to view performance comprehensively, by answering these questions:

1   How do customers see us? (customer perspective);
2   What must we excel at? (internal perspective);
3   Can we continue to improve and create value? (innovation and learning perspective);
4   How do we look to shareholders? (financial perspective).

The scorecard illustrated in Figure 19.4 brings together in a single management report many elements of a company's agenda, such as the need to be customer orientated, to shorten response time, improve quality or cut the time taken to launch a new product. It also guards against the dangers of working in isolation, as it requires senior managers to consider all the important operational measures together. They can then judge whether improvement in one area may have been achieved at the expense of another.

Kaplan and Norton (1993) advocate that companies spend time identifying, for each of the four measures, the external and internal factors that are important and developing suitable measures of performance. For example, under the customer heading, they may believe that customers are concerned about time, quality, performance, service and cost. They should therefore articulate goals for each factor, and then translate these goals into specific measures.

The approach has been widely adopted (Neely and Al Najjar, 2006), but despite its popularity, Akkermanns and Oorschot (2005) point out that it should be applied critically by asking:

> The **balanced score-card** is a performance measurement tool that looks at four areas: financial, customer, internal processes and innovation and learning, which contribute to organisational performance.

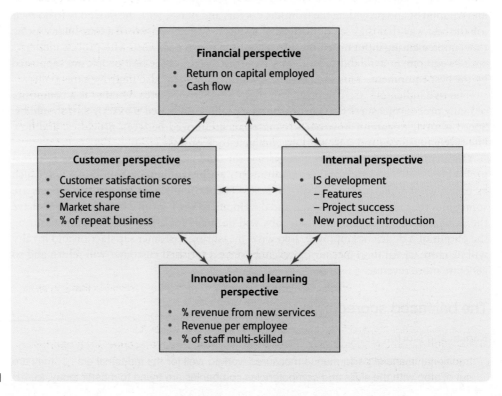

Figure 19.4 The balanced scorecard

- Are the selected measures the right ones?
- Should there be more, or fewer?
- At what levels should performance targets be set?

Perspectives in detail

Each perspective of the balanced scorecard can in itself be considered an aggregate measure. It is important to understand what each perspective is there to represent and the detailed measures that could be used in each to provide meaningful information.

Innovation and learning perspective

This set of measures should indicate how intangible assets such as people and information are supporting the organisation. The objective is to ensure the company is managing its intangibles in the correct way and it should describe people performance such as skills, talent and know-how with measures such as training logs and attendance, and information performance with measures such as data accuracy and IT fault logging.

Internal perspective

This perspective indicates whether the company is doing the right things in the right way. The objective here is to ensure the correct processes are being used effectively and efficiently. Measures may be productivity, machine down-time or part scrap rates.

Customer perspective

This perspective indicates whether the customer is getting what they want. The objective is to ensure the customer is happy with the product or service. The measures therefore represent customer satisfaction such as product in-service performance or number of customer complaints.

Financial perspective

This perspective indicates how well the company is performing financially. Therefore the objective is to represent shareholder value. Here measures can simply be profit-, cost- or revenue-related.

Figure 19.5 illustrates a simple balanced scorecard for an airline. Here they are keen to ensure that the performance of the process for preparing the aircraft for its next flight is as efficient as possible. There are two things worth noting that illustrate the power of this measurement tool. First, if the measures in the learning and growth and the internal perspectives are correct (i.e. the activity is carried out by skilled people and the process is operating as it is supposed to) then there will be less delays so hopefully the customer will be happier with the travel experience. Second, if the turnaround process is carried out efficiently then the profit should go up as the cost goes down. This illustrates not only the importance of choosing the correct measures but also of how achieving well-chosen measures in the learning and growth and internal perspectives should mean that the measures in the customer and the financial perspectives are easier to meet (Kaplan and Norton, 2004; 2008).

Activity 19.4   Starting a balanced scorecard

Begin to develop a balanced scorecard for activities within an organisation that you are familiar with.

- Create measures and targets under each of the four headings.
- Comment on the strengths and weaknesses of the balanced scorecard for performance measurement.

	Objective	Measurement	Target
Financial	• Increase profit • Grow revenue	• Time aircraft in air • Fuel bill	X% £Y
Customer *Attract and retain customers*	• Increase on-time flights • Reduce time on-ground	• Ranking • Repeat custom	1st 100%
Internal *Fast ground turnaround*	• Reduce refuelling time • Reduce baggage loading time	• On-time arrival • On-time departure • Loading time • Fuelling time	100% 100% X min Y min
Learning *Strategic job families e.g., ramp agent*	• Upskill people • Create IT support system	• Staff availability • Delays due to human error • Data errors	100% 0 0

Figure 19.5 Airline performance measurement

Organisational performance is the accumulated results of all the organisation's work processes and activities.

Such measures of **organisational performance** show how well managers have conducted their role of adding value to the resources they have used in their area of responsibility.

Designing performance feedback systems

Greve (2010) reviews examples of how managers use performance feedback systems and offers suggestions on their design.

- Goals should reflect the organisational strategy, and provide clear guidance for those who are working in rapidly changing circumstances. The hierarchy of goals should also reflect the organisational structure.
- Aspiration levels (level of goal difficulty) should provide a reasonable degree of stretch (a suggestion supported by most research on goal setting) and reflect external requirements and internal capabilities.
- The frequency of performance feedback should be such as to ensure that the signals about performance are as strong and unambiguous as possible, and not distorted by incidental events or other 'noise' in the system. Doing so should ensure that any indications of a need to change are reliable and can be used credibly to set out a new direction.

Case study   NHS – the case continues

An inquest into the mid-Staffordshire Hospital Trust by Monitor found failings in several areas. From a performance measurement and control perspective the two most relevant were: 1) a lack of clarity on the standards that should be achieved as the threshold for gaining Foundation status; and 2) that Monitor itself – the regulatory body – must revise its view of what information is required as evidence that performance standards are being achieved.

There were two further observations of particular interest to performance measurement. In a conclusion entitled 'Figures preferred to people' the inquiry found that performance data was often given more weight than the opinions of those involved and that performance systems did not bring to light the serious and systemic failures in the hospital – despite this being the purpose of the performance measurement system.

Another conclusion entitled 'A focus on systems not outcomes' indicated that staff were focusing too much on the process and not enough on the standard of care, even though that was the intention of the process.

In February 2013 the final report of the public inquiry into the Stafford Hospital failings was published. It built upon the 2009 report, confirming the main findings – such as that Trust management had ignored patients' complaints, that the regional health authority were too quick to trust the hospital's

management and national regulators were not challenging enough. The report recommended making it a criminal offence to hide information about poor care, and reaffirmed that many patients had been let down by a culture that put cost-cutting and target-chasing ahead of the quality of care.

In 2014 the responsibilities of Mid-Staffordshire Trust were transferred to two other Trusts, it ceased to exist, and Stafford Hospital was given a new name.

Sources: 'Learning and Implications from the Mid-Staffordshire NHS Foundation Trust', Monitor – Independent Regulator of NHS Foundation Trusts Final Report – 5 August 2009. *Report of the Mid-Staffordshire NHS Foundation Trust Public Inquiry,* chaired by Robert Francis QC (2013), The Stationery Office, London.

Case question 19.4

- Discuss the difference between a public sector organisation and a private sector company. Do you think that the threat of going out of business tends to make it easier to implement performance measurement systems in a private sector company?

19.6   Human considerations in control

Control systems are intended to influence people to act in ways that support the organisational objectives and so reflect the assumptions that those who designed the systems have about the people they are trying to control. The more accurate these assumptions are, the more likely the control system will support business objectives.

People have personal and local objectives that they seek to achieve in addition to, or perhaps in place of, the stated objectives of the organisation. Chapter 15 discussed how people seek to satisfy their human needs at work and how they will evaluate a control system in part by asking whether it helps or obstructs them in meeting those needs. How they react will reflect their interests and their interpretation of the situation – which may be different from the interests of those establishing the controls.

Control is also a political process in which powerful individuals and groups seek to dominate others. People may oppose a control system not for its intrinsic features, but for what it implies about their loss of power relative to another group, or because they feel it will restrict their ability to use their initiative and experience. Therefore while there is a clear operational perspective on control or, put another way, a neutral aspect of keeping actions in line with goals, control is also closely tied to ideas about motivation, influence and power.

While effective control depends on suitable control and performance measurement systems, these systems in turn depend on how people see them. Control is only effective when it influences people to act in the way intended by those designing the system, who therefore need to take into account the likely reactions of those being controlled.

Problems with formal control systems

Lawler (1976) identified three potential problems with formal control systems.

First, management controls lead to 'rigid bureaucratic behaviour'. Most people prefer to act in ways that make them look good to others, so we tend to concentrate on activities that are measured. If the consequences of a poor assessment are severe, then people will tend to focus their efforts on those parts of the job that are assessed, and ignore those that are not. This is exemplified in the NHS case, where managers were keen to 'look good' by meeting their assigned targets. The standards tell people what they have to do to perform well and perhaps to gain promotion; these behaviours may not necessarily be in the best interests of the business as a whole. Sales staff in a store paid a bonus on the volume of sales may focus on generating sales, perhaps using high-pressure tactics that secure a single sale but discourage the customer from coming again. Or they may focus on sales at the expense of checking stock or maintaining the display areas – especially if these are not assessed as part of the control system. Other examples could be reluctance to work outside one's own area of responsibility, concentrating on meeting sub-unit goals rather than those of the enterprise as a whole, or accepting minimum standards as long as they exceed the target.

Second, controls may encourage people to supply inaccurate information. The more important the measure, the more likely it becomes that people will distort information to enhance recorded performance. The bargaining that surrounds payment by results or a commission payment system is an example. Line managers and employees will have different views about the fairness of a particular piece rate, and the latter will often give invalid data on the complexity of the work or the time it requires to overcome a difficulty, to ensure a more favourable rate.

Third, people may resist a system that they feel threatens their satisfaction or in some way undermines their ability to meet their psychological needs from work. Table 19.6 illustrates this by showing how a control system can have either positive or negative effects on a person's ability to satisfy their human needs. Controls can encourage both positive and negative behaviour – positive by encouraging commitment, enthusiasm and higher ambition, negative if they lead people to be fearful and defensive.

Table 19.5 Performance standards based on the competing values framework

Value	Criteria of effectiveness	Examples of performance measures
Rational goal	Attaining goals	Achievement of objectives, task completion
	Output quantity	Sales, profits, productivity, efficiency
	Output quality	Reliability, responsiveness, reputation
Internal process	Efficiency and costs	Operating costs, productivity, efficiency
	Continuity, smooth workflow	Coordination; adequacy, quality and distribution of information
Human relations	Employee satisfaction	Quality of working life, absenteeism, turnover
	Interpersonal relations	Trust, community relations, conflict resolution
	Involvement	Participation, empowerment
Open systems	Resources: quantity	Finance, physical assets, contracts won
	Resources: quality	Skills, knowledge base, quality of clients
	Competitive position	Reputation in industry, evidence of leadership
	Adaptation	Ability to cope with uncertainty, flexibility
	Innovativeness	Technological and administrative innovation

Sources: Based on Quinn et al. (2003) and Harrison (2005).

Table 19.6 Possible effects of control systems on human needs

Maslow's categories of human needs	Controls may support satisfaction	Controls may hinder satisfaction
Self-actualisation	Feedback encourages higher performance, accepting new challenges	Controls may limit initiative, autonomy, ability to experiment and discover
Esteem	Publishing successes builds recognition, self-confidence; reputation with colleagues and senior managers	Publishing failure damages esteem, undermines reputation; inaccurate information also damaging
Belongingness	Team-based assessments can support bonding and team development	Individual rewards may breed competition and damage cooperation
Security	Knowledge of how performance is assessed gives certainty	Controls that leave expectations unclear undermine security; information seen as threat
Physiological	Help focus effort and meet performance requirements	Controls highlight poor performance and threaten job

Competing values and performance measurement

Organisations, and units within them, develop unique cultures that are likely to shape their views on performance measurement. The competing values framework (Quinn et al. 2003) provides a tool for anticipating and managing this. The four 'competing values' represent ways of analysing effectiveness: Table 19.5 lists these and illustrates performance measures (drawing on Harrison, 2005) consistent with each.

Activity 19.5   Assessing the human effects of a control system

Consider a control system at work, or where you are studying.

- Have they had any effects similar to those that Lawler identified?
- How did that affect the way people reacted to the system?
- How could management have redesigned the controls to avoid those effects?

19.7   Integrating themes

Entrepreneurship

The potential benefits of performance management systems to support decisions and learning are as relevant to small entrepreneurial businesses as they are to large corporations, but small businesses may be deterred from making good use of the idea by, among other things, resource limitations, lack of awareness or a cultural bias again formal systems. Garengo and Bititci (2007) sought to establish the factors affecting the use of performance management among small firms, and concluded that the main factors were the nature of their governance arrangements, and their information systems. Table 19.7 illustrates their research.

The authors identified three forms of governance arrangement, which they labelled:

- **Traditional family firm** – capital held by the entrepreneur and a small number of their family members. The owners make the decisions, and the board of directors has only a 'service' role.
- **Open family firm** – entrepreneur manages the business, and other shareholders not involved in management. Board of directors exerts some control over entrepreneur.
- **Managerial company** – shareholders not involved in management – manager(s) run the business in conjunction with the board, which takes a strategic role.

In relation to Table 19.7, companies A and B (managerial companies) are both managed by managers who have no shareholdings in the business – so the shareholders and their board expect the managers to use a performance management system to keep them informed about the business. Companies C (open family company) and D (traditional family company) are both managed by entrepreneurs, and use PMS using basic financial and manufacturing data – largely based on the entrepreneurs' knowledge of their business.

Sustainability

Many companies now publish formal reports on their environmental policies and performance, seeing it as in their business interests do so. A commitment to measure environmental performance motivates managers to be more analytical and disciplined about their operating processes – less pollution tends to mean a more efficient process. They also believe that the positive public relations gained by socially responsible companies will make the company more attractive to customers and potential employees.

Riccaboni and Leone (2010) describe the case of Procter & Gamble, who have built the issue of sustainability into the organisation through four themes:

Table 19.7 PMS characteristics and scope of companies in study

Scope of PMS	Characteristics of performance management system		
	Basic	Advanced	Excellent
	Not responsive	Responds to internal change	Responds to internal and external change
	Not systematic	Data reflects needs, some communication	As advanced, plus check data quality
	Not integrated	Partial integration	Fully integrated
Traditional – focus on financial performance			
Dual – financial and one other measure (e.g. market share)	Company D		
Partially balanced – financial and several other measures		Company C	
		Company B	
Balanced – all relevant measures			Company A

- delight the customer with sustainable innovations;
- improve the environmental profile of its operations;
- develop social responsibility programmes; and
- equip P&G workers to build sustainability thinking into their everyday work.

They conclude that by doing this the company have gone a long way to making sustainability issues part of the 'business as usual' of the organisation.

Internationalisation

While communications technology supports the internationalisation of management, this still has consequences for performance management and control of international businesses. Dispersed companies have all the control issues of local companies but some are amplified.

There is a strategic issue about how much central control to impose, and how much to encourage local autonomy and responsiveness. If part of the reason for success has been the ability of local companies to act entrepreneurially, then implementing a control system that imposes greater central control would be counter-productive.

For reasons of remoteness, head office has comparatively few opportunities to use direct control and supervision, which is often a very effective means. Instead it has to rely more on rules and procedures, and a range of formal financial and output controls. An alternative is to try to develop strong cultural controls, which influence people to act in ways that align with corporate aims, irrespective of their location.

As Chapter 4 showed, countries have developed substantially different management systems, as well as differences of national culture. These factors will affect very significantly how people respond to control systems, as well as raising difficult issues of comparability between the reports for different countries, and the interpretations to be placed upon them.

Governance

Walton (1985) noted that managers have to choose between a strategy based on imposing control and one based on eliciting commitment. He suggests the latter is consistent with recognising employees as stakeholders in the organisation, and is likely to lead to higher performance, especially in situations requiring them to use imagination and creativity. He concludes that organisations should develop a culture of commitment if they are to meet customer expectations with respect to quality, delivery and market changes.

This perspective on stakeholder thinking has expanded to include the customer in the organisational performance management system. This is most common in industries such as defence and construction, where large and complex projects are carried out and there needs to be a high degree of interaction along the supply chain throughout the duration of the relationship. Here it is important to establish common inter-company performance measures that govern behaviour in-line with commonly accepted objectives.

Summary

1 **Define control and explain why it is an essential activity in managing**
   - Control is the counterpart of planning and is the process of monitoring activities to ensure that results are in-line with the plan and taking corrective action if required.
   - Organisational control ensures that operational processes remain consistent, repeatable and reliable.

2　**Describe and give examples of the generic control activities of setting targets, measuring, comparing and correcting**

- Setting targets gives direction to an activity and sets standards of acceptable performance.
- Measuring involves deciding what measures to use, and how frequently.
- Comparing involves selecting suitable objects for comparison, and the time period over which to do it.
- Correcting aims to rectify a deviation from plan either by altering activities or changing the objectives.

3　**Discuss strategies and tactics used to gain and maintain control**

- Control systems exist on a spectrum where the extremes are mechanistic and organic.
- Mechanistic approaches are likely to be suitable in stable environments or in support of cost leadership strategies.
- Organic approaches are likely to be suitable in unstable environments or in support of differentiation strategies.
- Organisations can use a combination of direct supervision, organisational structure, rules and procedures, management by objectives, machinery, HRM practice and values and beliefs to maintain control.

4　**Explain how the choice of suitable measures of performance can help in managing the organisation**

- Managers can use either input, process or output measures to control the organisation.
- The balanced scorecard supplements measures of financial performance with those of customer satisfaction, internal process and innovation and growth, which all play a part in an overall assessment of performance.
- Control systems must be matched to the overall model that the organisation is being managed with in relation to the competing values framework.

5　**Explain why those designing performance measurement and control systems need to take account of human reactions**

- Control depends on influencing people, so is only effective if it takes account of human needs.
- Controls can encourage behaviour that is not in the best interests of the organisation.
- Controls can encourage people to supply the system with inaccurate information.
- People will resist controls that they feel threaten their ability to satisfy their needs from work.

6　**Explain the tasks in creating a control system, and understand how you can use this approach to develop your skill at monitoring progress on a task**

- Being able to control a task helps to ensure it is completed on time and within budget, and that it adds value to the resources used. One part of control is to monitor progress during the work, and the chapter has included an exercise to help you develop that skill.

7　**Show how ideas from the chapter add to your understanding of the integrating themes**

- The extent to which small businesses use performance measurement appears to be strongly influenced by their governance systems, as well as the nature of their information systems.
- While more companies are reporting on their sustainability record, they will only make a difference when they include sustainability criteria in their routine management control systems, so that it becomes part of 'business as usual' for staff.
- Remoteness makes it difficult for international companies to exercise genuine control over distant units, however sophisticated the information technology; cultural controls may be more effective.
- Governance and control systems need to be supported by a culture of commitment if they are to affect behaviour at the operating level.

Test your understanding

1. Explain why control is important.
2. Is planning part of the control process?
3. Describe the four steps in the control process.
4. Explain how the balanced scorecard was an improvement on earlier performance measurement systems.
5. Give an original example of a measure in each quadrant of the balanced scorecard.
6. Explain how input, process and output measures differ.
7. Explain why the competing values framework can help in designing a control and performance management system.
8. What are the implications for those designing a control system of Lawler's work on control?
9. Summarise an idea from the chapter that adds to your understanding of the integrating themes.

Think critically

Think about the way your company, or one with which you are familiar, seeks to control performance. Review the material in the chapter, and perhaps visit some of the websites identified. Then make notes on these questions:

- What examples of the themes discussed in this chapter are currently relevant to your company? What types of controls are you most closely involved with? Which of the techniques suggested do you and your colleagues typically use, and why? What techniques do you use that are not mentioned here?
- In responding to these issues, what **assumptions** about the nature of control appear to guide your approach? Do the assumptions take account of, say, the competing values framework, or the balanced scorecard?
- What factors in the **context** of the company appear to shape your approach to control – is the balance towards a mechanistic or an organic approach, and is that choice suitable for the environment in which you are working?
- What **alternative** approaches to control have you identified in your work on this chapter? Would any of them possibly make a useful contribution to your organisation?
- Has the chapter highlighted any possible **limitations** in the control systems used in your organisation? Have you considered, for example, if there is too much control, or too little? Have you compared your control processes with those in other companies?

Develop a skill – monitoring progress on a task

Being able to control a task helps to ensure it is completed on time and within budget, and that it adds value to the resources used. One part of control is to monitor progress during the work, and this exercise should help you develop that skill.

- **Awareness:** Assess how well you 'monitor progress' when you are doing some work – either on your own, or when working with others. Do you, for example, focus on doing the work itself, with little regard to the time it is taking, or whether you are doing what you were expected to? Or do you instinctively make regular checks on progress, or that work is going to plan?
- **Theory:** Read again Section 19.2, especially the work you did on Activity 19.1 ('Assessing control systems', p. 611). Summarise the main ideas in the section. Why is being in control of a task likely to help a manager?

- **Analysis:** What are the potential problems in setting a target – and why is it an essential step in control? Think of a situation in which you felt that work was being well, or poorly, controlled. What were the effects on (a) your motivation and (b) your performance? Which of the ideas in Section 19.2 were present, or absent?

- **Practice:** Identify (on your own or with colleagues) a task that you need to undertake, either in your studies or in other aspects of your life (in a job, a fundraising event, a social event you are organising).

  - Develop a simple control process, using Figure 19.1 to guide you.

  - Use this to monitor progress as you and/or other people work on the task.

  - Keep records of how this helps you manage the task, and how it helps you to take corrective action if necessary.

  - Record what you find, and reflect on what you have learned about control.

- **Application:** Decide on another opportunity to practise this skill within the next week.

Read more

Barrows, E. and Neely, A. (2012), *Managing Performance in Turbulent Times: Analytics and Insight,* John Wiley & Sons, Hoboken, NJ.

> Modern and comprehensive introduction to the topic, covering public and private sectors.

Kaplan, R.S. and Norton, D.P. (1992) 'The balanced scorecard: measures that drive performance', *Harvard Business Review,* vol. 70, no. 1, pp. 71–9.

> The original writing on balanced scorecards as performance management tools.

Kaplan, R.S. and Norton, D.P. (2008) *The Execution Premium: Linking strategy to operations for competitive advantage,* Harvard, Boston, MA.

> Brings balanced scorecards, performance measurement and management control right up to date, linking them all to show how they can be used to create competitive advantage.

Go online

These websites illustrate the themes of the chapter, and those in the Part Case:

> **www.apple.com**
> **www.tesco.com**
> **www.monitor-nhsft.gov.uk**

Visit any company website and go to the section in which the company reports on its performance:

- What financial measures do they report on most prominently?

- From the chairman's and/or chief executive's reports, what other measures have they been using to assess their performance?

CHAPTER 20

FINANCE AND BUDGETARY CONTROL

Aim

To show why organisations need finance, where it comes from, how its use should be controlled and why financial measures are critical indicators of performance.

Objectives

By the end of your work on this chapter you should be able to outline the concepts below in your own terms and:

1 Describe the role of the finance function in management

2 Interpret basic financial reports

3 Explain the difference between profit and cash

4 Appreciate the importance of financial results in evaluating performance

5 Explain how budgets are important as a management control mechanism

6 Discuss the differences between functional and project-based budgeting

7 Explain the significance of the profit and loss statement, and use this to help you develop the skill of reading a profit and loss statement

8 Show how ideas from the chapter add to your understanding of the integrating themes

Key terms

This chapter introduces the following ideas:

capital market	fixed (long-term) assets
limited liability company	current assets
shareholders	liabilities
cash flow statement	shareholders' funds
assets	work breakdown structure
profit and loss statement	cost breakdown structure
balance sheet	

Each is a term defined within the text, as well as in the glossary at the end of the book.

BASF is one of the world's leading chemical companies, with subsidiaries in more than 80 countries, and customers across the world. The head office and main chemical processing complex is at Ludwigshafen, Germany. The company's portfolio is arranged into five segments: Chemicals, Performance Products, Functional Materials & Solutions, Agricultural Solutions and Oil & Gas.

BASF wants to contribute to a sustainable future and has embedded this in its corporate purpose: "We create chemistry for a sustainable future". The company does so by creating chemistry for its customers and society and by making the best use of available resources. BASF's shares are listed in the Dow Jones Sustainability Index. Research and development is at the heart of the group's efforts to retain its competitive position.

BASF has successfully developed highly integrated processing plants to use resources and materials to maximum advantage. Waste and by-products are used as inputs to other processes. Pipe networks facilitate efficient, safe and environmentally friendly transfer of resources. They describe this integration as 'Verbund'. BASF operates six of these sites as well as approximately 340 additional production sites worldwide.

As an energy-intensive company, BASF is committed to energy efficiency and global climate protection. The Verbund system minimises undesirable emissions, but also benefits BASF customers. The BASF Group maintains close relationships with its customers to find mutually beneficial solutions to their problems. Reward systems for employees are based on the employees' individual performance and are closely related to the company's success.

© BASF

A summary of the BASF operating (profit) report for year ended 31 December 2015 is:

	€ millions
Sales	70,449
Less Cost of sales	51,372
Gross profit on sales	19,077
Less Selling expenses	8,062
Less General and administrative expenses	1,429
Less Research and development expenses	1,953
Less Other items	2,085
Operating profit before tax (PBT)	5,548
Less Taxation	1,247
Less Minority interests	314
Net income	3,987

Source: Company Annual Report, 2015.

Case questions 20.1

- What was the company's profit in the year to 31 December 2015?
- What proportion of its sales revenue was spent on research and development?

20.1 Introduction

In the financial year that ended on 31 December 2015 BASF made a net profit of €3,987 million from its activities. This 'headline' figure is a very crude measure of the effectiveness with which the managers have run the company over the year. The problem for investors is how to assess this performance. Is it consistent with the stated targets of the company? Does the way it has been achieved bode well for the future by, for example, investing in research that will bring returns in later years? Investors will also want to know how these broad summary figures relate to the work of managers and staff within the firm – are they motivated and organised in ways that encourage them to produce good returns in the future?

Similar questions arise about the annual report of any firm. Investors and financial analysts continually evaluate a company's financial performance against its objectives and against comparable businesses. They try to judge its prospects, and how effectively managers are doing their jobs. Much of the information in the report is qualitative and subjective, designed to create a favourable impression and positive expectations.

Chapter 1 described organisations as aiming to add value to the resources they use. It is crucial to the success of an organisation that it has the appropriate resources and that these are well managed to achieve the results that stakeholders expect. Most companies depend on people in the external environment for the funds they need to grow the business. The main source of information for people outside the business who wish to assess its performance and prospects is the company's annual report to shareholders. This contains a great deal of financial and other data – but is more subjective than at first appears. It is important to know how financial performance is measured, and the assumptions that people make in constructing the figures. It is also important to know how these financial measures relate to the performance of those working within the firm.

The chapter begins by explaining why companies need the capital market and how they communicate with it. A major link in that process is the annual report, so the chapter then explains important parts of that document. The chapter goes on to show how these figures, which are intended mainly for investors outside the organisation, influence and are themselves influenced by processes of internal planning and control. It finishes by looking inside the company at how financial targets are planned for and achieved.

20.2 The world outside the organisation

The pressures on companies to perform

Many people reading this book will be expecting to start a career that they hope will provide an income to support an attractive lifestyle. Few will be thinking about retirement or the need to support themselves after their working lives have ended. This may be a sombre subject to introduce, but it is fundamentally important to understanding the financial environment in which organisations operate.

Activity 20.1 Identifying shareholders

- Go to the companies' websites and access the annual report and accounts for Marks & Spencer (**www.marksandspencer.com**) and Mothercare (**www.mothercare.com**) for the year ended 31 March 2015 (click on 'Investor Relations'). What can you discover about the shareholders in the companies?

Investment companies such as pension funds and life assurance companies expect to pay their investors an acceptable income or lump sum when they retire. The funds can only do this if they invest contributions successfully, and investors naturally expect their premiums to be invested profitably by fund managers. These companies compete with each other, and the rewards for success and consequent growth in contributions from investors are high. There is pressure on the fund managers to perform well by identifying good investment opportunities, which is also in the investors' best interests as eventual pensioners. The fund managers will be looking for good investment opportunities in companies that are profitable and well managed. To attract money into a business to enable it to expand, management needs to demonstrate to the capital market that it is profitable and successful or that it has plans that are very likely to mean that it will become profitable and successful.

This is what fund managers in the **capital market** expect, and this external market pressure directly affects the organisation and all employees. There may be some periods of low or negative profitability (losses) and the capital markets accept that, but continual losses will eventually lead to failure, as a company will simply run out of money and fail to meet its financial obligations. So the pressures to perform that managers and employees feel originate outside the organisation. However, as many employees are investors and all are future pensioners dependent on the performance of fund managers, those pressures serve their long-term interests (Coggan, 2002).

> The **capital market** comprises all the individuals and institutions that have money to invest, including banks, life assurance companies and pension funds and, as users of capital, business organisations, individuals and governments.

Within an organisation it is unlikely that managers, apart from those at the top, will feel the direct pressure from outside. Yet this external pressure affects what top managers expect of those below them. These expectations pass down the organisation so all staff experience them in some way, even if indirectly. The pressures can be considerable as the senior managers expect to be rewarded with the opportunity to purchase shares in the company at a favourable price (known as share, or stock, options), which can lead to dubious practices and fraud to enhance the share price. Financial regulators have sought to prevent this by proposals to improve corporate governance and the quality of financial reporting, but their powers are limited.

Raising capital

If you have looked at the annual report of M&S or Mothercare you will have discovered that investment management companies rather than individuals are major shareholders. Such companies are one of the many sources from which large organisations raise capital.

A principal way in which a large public company (a public limited company or PLC) can raise money is by issuing shares to people and institutions that respond to a share issue. The main benefit is to enable companies to finance large-scale activities. The shareholders appoint the directors who are ultimately responsible for managing the company. A shareholder is entitled to vote at general meetings in accordance with the number of shares owned. Once the shareholders have paid for their shares in full they cannot generally be required to pay more money into the company, even if it fails.

The affairs of companies are governed by company law, in some countries administered by a government body such as the Securities and Exchange Commission in the United States, and by the body governing the share market, such as the Bourse in France and the Stock Exchange in the United Kingdom. Before a company can invite the public to subscribe for shares it has to be registered with the national financial regulators and meet their requirements. The first step after registration is to issue a prospectus that explains the history of the company, what it plans to do as a business and what it plans to do with the money raised. However, if the business is small it may still be a limited liability company but will not be able to invite the public to buy shares. The promoters will contribute their own money, most likely in a sufficient amount to ensure that they have control (more than 50 per cent of the shares). The amount of capital available to the company in these circumstances will be limited to the money the founders can afford to contribute. They may also go to a bank to seek finance, but the willingness of a bank to lend will also depend on the amount sub-scribed by the shareholders. Banks, fund managers and investors will contribute only if they believe that it is a sound, well-managed business that is likely to make a profit. Investors have many investment opportunities, and will not invest in a company that will not reward them for the risk they are taking. The amount of return they expect will reflect the risk – the greater the risk, the greater the required return they will expect.

Activity 20.2   Borrowing money

- Find out the interest rate at which you could borrow money to (a) buy a car, (b) buy a house or (c) spend on your credit card. Can you explain what you discover?

A limited liability company has an identity and existence in its own right as distinct from its owners (shareholders in Europe, stockholders in North America). A shareholder has an ownership right in the company in which the shares are held.

Shareholders are the principal risk takers in a company. They contribute the long-term capital for which they expect to be rewarded in the form of dividends – a distribution from the profit of the business.

Being a **limited liability company** gives a business access to large amounts of capital, but at the same time allows some protection to **shareholders**, as they are not liable for the debts of the business in the event of its financial failure. This limited liability means that investors can contribute capital knowing that only this, and not their other assets, is at risk. This risk is why investors expect a higher return than they would receive if they put their money in a bank or in government securities, where the risk is virtually zero. But the limited liability means that the risk is controlled and so allows investors to accept riskier investments than they otherwise would.

20.3   Reporting financial performance externally

Because a company has access to capital in this limited liability form there has to be regula-tion to protect investors. The Companies Act is the principal instrument of control within the United Kingdom, with the addition of the Stock Exchange for those listed as public companies. A most important requirement is to provide information about the performance of the business from time to time (Elliott and Elliott, 2015). The capital markets, and indeed anyone who is considering investing in a company, need to understand how the company is performing: financial measures provide a company 'health check' showing how well management is running the company. This health check is detailed most comprehensively in the company's annual report. Among other things the annual report includes financial information of three distinct types: the cash flow statement, the profit and loss (or income) statement and the balance sheet.

Activity 20.3   Reading an annual report

- Access the annual report through the website of a company that interests you. List the main kinds of information that you find in it, for example financial, product, people and management.

A cash flow statement shows the sources from which cash has been generated and how it has been spent during a period of time.

Cash flow statement

The easiest to understand of the three statements is the cash flow, which shows where cash has come from and how it has been spent. Below is a simplified summary of the **cash flow statement** for M&S for the year ended 31 March 2015.

	£ millions
Net cash inflow from operating activities	
Cash generated from operating activities	1349.1
Payment of taxation	(71.1)
Net cash flow from operating activities	1278.0
Cash flows from investing activities	
Capital expenditure, proceeds on property disposals and financial investment	(658.4)
Interest received	9.3
Net cash (outflow) on investing activities	(649.1)
Cash flows from financing activities	
Interest paid	(115.3)
Other debt financing	(259.3)
Equity dividends paid	(280.7)
Other equity financing	40.8
Net cash (outflow) from financing activities	(614.5)
Net cash inflow from all activities above	14.4
Effect of exchange rate changes	(2.3)
Opening net cash	175.7
Net closing cash	187.8

In the ordinary course of successful business it might be expected that the cash received from trading (selling products or services) would be greater than the cash spent to purchase components, supplies, labour, energy and all the other resources combined to secure the sales. The cash surplus could then be reinvested to help finance expansion and some of it paid to the shareholders as dividend on their investment. Their original shareholder contribution remains in the company, however, as part of the continuing capital base. In the case of M&S there was an increase in cash of £14.4 million after paying dividends, making interest payments and investing in new assets, as well as disposing of some existing **assets**.

Assets are the property, plant and equipment, vehicles, stocks of goods for trading, money owed by customers and cash; in other words, the physical resources of the business.

The idea of a cash surplus being the essential requirement for success is appealing but unfortunately too simplistic. Taking as an example a motor vehicle manufacturer, a car has to be designed and tested, components sourced from suppliers, production lines prepared and cars distributed to dealers before any of the cars can be sold – so there will be very heavy cash outflows before cash starts to come in. This process may take a couple of years. In some industries, such as pharmaceuticals and chemicals, investments in continuing research and development may take ten years or longer before cash begins to flow back, and then only if the research is successful.

Much the same thing occurs in new technology-based service companies such as eBay, since they have to invest heavily in building their website and in advertising to make people aware that they exist before cash begins to flow in. It would be highly unlikely in these conditions for the business to show a cash surplus while it is making such heavy investment.

Activity 20.4   Measuring R&D expenditure

- Look at the annual report for BASF (**www.basf.com**), Siemens (**www.siemens.com**), Solvay (**www.solvay.com**) or any large manufacturing business, and find out what it tells you about research and development. List the projects that the report mentions. What does the report say about the length of time before the projects will be profitable?

It is impossible to draw sensible conclusions about the company's financial performance on the basis of cash flow alone. Not only is the annual surplus or deficit influenced by major investment, but other infrequent events, such as a major restructuring exercise following a new strategy, could also distort the impression.

The profit and loss statement

A profit and loss statement reflects the benefits derived from the trading activities of the business during a period of time.

The **profit and loss statement** (or income statement) is designed to overcome the limitations of a cash flow statement. However, cash has the important characteristic of complete objectivity; cash flows can be observed, measured and verified, while profit measures are subjective.

The profit after taxation and the profit retained in the business are quite different from the cash surplus reported in the cash flow statement. This is because the profit statement is not based on cash but on business transactions that (a) may result in cash transactions in the future, or (b) reflect cash transactions from previous periods. For example, sales include credit sales that approved customers may pay for later and cost of goods sold will include the purchase of some goods that will be paid for in the next financial year.

Case questions 20.2

Refer to the summary income statement for BASF.

- Calculate the gross profit as a percentage of sales.
- Calculate the operating profit before tax as a percentage of sales.

Activity 20.5   Calculating and comparing profit

Look at the annual report of a company in a similar line of business to M&S.

- Calculate the gross profit in a recent year as a percentage of sales.
- Calculate the profit before tax as a percentage of sales.
- How does the company compare on these measures against M&S?
- Is there a major difference in the items in the profit statements of the two companies?

Depreciation

Depreciation is one major cause of the difference between cash flow and profit. Think about the investments mentioned in relation to motor vehicle production; apart from occasional modifications, the same basic model may be produced and sold for several years. So, in order to judge the profit accruing in any year, the initial investment to develop the design and make the cars may be spread over the life of the investment and be subtracted from sales revenue in each year. This process is called depreciation. The idea is simple, but accountants have to make several estimates before they can measure the annual amount.

Depreciation is based on the original cost of the investment, including set-up and training, less the expected scrap value at the end of its life. Hence an estimate must be made of the life of the investment, the residual value and the initial cost, all of which are open to conjecture. To make matters worse there are at least four methods of spreading the cost over the lifespan. The simplest is to allocate an equal amount each year. But assets may also be periodically revalued to take account of changes in their fair value (the present value of expected future cash flows, or the expected market price less selling costs if it were to be sold), which then becomes the base for calculating depreciation.

Credit

Most products are not sold for cash but on credit, sometimes for an extended period of time. A retail store might offer generous credit terms in order to promote sales – 'nothing to pay for six months' or 'easy terms over nine months' are familiar promotional devices. Suppose that the company's financial year ends on 31 December and that a customer is buying a product at the end of October on nine months' credit of equal monthly payments. Should the company report the full value of the sale, the three instalments that the customer has paid, or nothing until the bill has been paid for in full? It is usual practice to report the full amount; this is reasonable because the business has a legal contract that forces the customer to pay. Experience shows that not all customers will pay in full, so there will be bad debts: accountants have to estimate the level of these before arriving at profit.

Warranty claims

If a problem arises with a product sold under warranty it will be replaced or fixed, but at a cost to the manufacturer. The cost of repairing under warranty has to be estimated because warranty claims may not be made within the same financial year as the sale.

Management in practice   Volkswagen emissions scandal

Volkswagen admitted in September 2015 that it had fitted software designed to cheat emissions tests for nitrogen oxides in 11 million diesel vehicles worldwide. Around 508,000 VW cars, 393,000 Audis, 132,000 Skodas, 80,000 VW commercial vehicles and 77,000 Seats in the UK are affected by the scandal. VW car sales fell by 20 per cent in November compared to the same month in 2014.

Volkswagen has set aside €6.7 billion (£5 billion) to deal with the controversy; it is thought by some analysts that the company may choose to sell off some of its luxury brands such as Lamborghini and Bentley, providing an opportunity for Volkswagen to raise the kind of money that is expected to be needed to pay the fines likely to be assessed by courts and regulators internationally.

Analysts are predicting a 'grim few years ahead' for the company.

Source: Based on a Press Association report, 30 December 2015.

These are simple examples of subjectivity in profit measurement to illustrate that the measure of profit cannot be said to be totally accurate. It is an approximation. Nevertheless, it is the main indication of trading performance measured in financial terms. The question remains, how well does profit reflect good performance? To evaluate this, profit needs to be related to the amount of investment in the business; how much investment was required to make the profit?

Measuring periodic performance

Both the cash flow and the profit statements relate to a period of time – conventionally a financial or trading year. It is usual for large organisations also to produce brief reports on their performance quarterly or half-yearly.

Just how much profit is desirable has to be considered in relation to the investment in a business. Therefore a measure of investment is needed with which to compare periodic profit. If an investor can invest in risk-free government securities for a guaranteed minimum return, an investment in a risky company that does not offer at least the same expectation of reward would not be considered. So you would expect the return, or ratio of profit to investment, to be higher for a risky than for a risk-free investment. People assess the rate of return they require from one investment by comparing alternative investment opportunities and their rates of return.

How can the investment base be measured? The obvious base is the amount of the initial investment. If you deposit money in a bank deposit account it will attract interest. At the end of the year you can measure the rate of return by expressing the interest earned for the year as a percentage of the initial investment. If you leave the interest in the account the following year, the investment base would be increased by the amount of interest reinvested. The initial investment plus the interest you earned in the first year now becomes a part of the capital base, as you chose not to withdraw it. The investment base can grow over time. Much the same happens in a business. Profit is generated, some is distributed as a cash dividend, and the balance, usually the larger proportion, is retained in the business to finance expansion.

A simple measure of the capital base with which to compare profit appears to be the amount of capital originally contributed plus profit that is retained and added each year to the base.

Another way to look at it, for large companies listed on the Stock Exchange, is to relate the profit or earnings per share to the share price. This approach recognises that a successful business will grow and develop a good reputation reflecting the result of professional management and reliable, high-quality products. If you own shares in such a company you would expect the value of those shares to increase with the success of the business. You would continue to hold the shares only as long as the return, based on the price at which you could sell the shares in the market, is at least equal to that from an alternative investment with similar risk.

The balance sheet

A **balance sheet** shows the assets of the business and the sources from which finance has been raised.

The annual report that shows the capital base of a business is the **balance sheet**. The BASF balance sheet at 31 December 2015 is shown in the next instalment of the case study.

Case study   **BASF Group – the case continues**   www.basf.com

Group balance sheet as at 31 December 2015

Assets	€ millions	
Intangible (patents, licences, goodwill)	12,537	
Property, plant and equipment (at cost after depreciation deducted)	25,260	
Financial assets	8,473	
Total long-term assets		46,270
Current assets		
Inventories	9,693	
Accounts receivable from customers and others	9,516	
Other liquid assets (including cash)	5,357	
Current assets		24,566
Total assets		70,836
Shareholders' equity	31,545	
Long-term liabilities	25,055	
Accounts payable and other short-term liabilities	14,236	
Total equity and liabilities		70,836

The balance sheet reveals two separate but related aspects of the business.

First are the assets categorised as either **fixed (long-term) assets** or **current assets**. These include the physical resources such as property, buildings, machinery, computers, stocks (or inventories) of raw materials, work in progress and completed products, money owed by customers and cash.

Second are the **liabilities** or the sources of finance that have enabled the business to acquire its assets. Finance (or capital) comes from shareholders by way of contributions for shares when they are first issued, together with retained profits from successful operations as previously explained. This is the shareholders' capital (or **shareholders' funds**). In addition there will usually be money borrowed from a bank and possibly from other sources as well. The sum total of the shareholders' funds and liabilities will equal (or balance with) the amount of assets. The former represents the source from which the finance has been raised. The latter shows the destination or the physical resources in which the capital has been invested. Assets and liabilities are divided into two categories: current, applying to those that are expected to be traded within a year, and non-current, expected to remain in the business longer than a year.

The shareholders are the main risk takers and the profit is attributable to them. Therefore, to measure the efficiency with which the funds are used, it is usual to measure the *rate of return on equity* – the profit after tax divided by shareholders' funds.

Fixed (long-term) assets are the physical properties that the company possesses – such as land, buildings, production equipment – which are likely to have a useful life of more than one year. There may also be intangible assets such as patent rights or copyrights.

Current assets can be expected to be cash or to be converted to cash within a year.

Liabilities of a business as reported in the balance sheet are the debts and financial obligations of the business to all those people and institutions that are not shareholders, e.g. a bank, suppliers.

Shareholders' funds are the capital contributed by the shareholders plus profits that have not been distributed to the shareholders.

Case question 20.3

- Refer to the summary financial information for BASF. Calculate the rate of return (after tax) on equity (shareholders' funds).

Share values

While the numbers reflected in the statements discussed are one method of gauging the performance of a company, there is another way of approaching the question of performance measurement: the share price. If you were thinking of buying shares in a company, you would consider the likely future returns in relation to the price you would have to pay for them. You would compare investment opportunities and attempt to choose the one that offers the best return for whatever degree of risk you were prepared to accept. The return you expected would be an estimate of future dividends plus the likely growth in the share price, and you would relate this to the price you would have to pay to buy the shares. If the potential investment offered a greater expected return than shares you already held (assuming the same degree of risk), not only would you be interested in buying the new shares, but you would also be inclined to sell your existing shares to buy new ones in order to increase your return. It would be rational for all investors in this position to behave in the same way.

So the measure of performance that shareholders adopt will not be directly related to the company's financial reports, but more to the financial markets. They will be comparing expected returns with the prices of shares in the market. This does not mean that financial reports from companies do not serve any useful purpose. They do, because they provide information that helps the traders to assess the likely returns from these companies and, above all, provide information about past performance and recent financial position; ultimately about the risk inherent in their investments. While share prices in the market are influenced by buying and selling pressure, the expectations that give rise to those pressures come in part from the financial reports.

The directors and senior managers of a company have to keep track of what is going on in the markets relevant to their business. Some are specific to their own activities, and some general – the capital and labour markets. Their performance is being evaluated all the time and they need to know what the buyers and sellers in the financial markets are thinking.

Financial managers will be watching the share price. They have to convert external pressures from the market into pressure for internal action. In particular, companies whose shares do not offer returns consistent with those of competitors are likely to become takeover targets with bids from stronger, more efficient performers. Unexpected movements in share price might signal activity in the market that directors ought to know about. If another company is actively buying their shares in the market and so raising the price, this might indicate they are planning a takeover bid. If a large shareholder is selling shares, thus pushing the price down, does this mean performance in the company has fallen short of expectations? In both circumstances the directors need to know about market activities to plan their response.

20.4   Managing financial performance internally

Gaining financial control of the business

Most managers and employees can do little on their own to influence externally reported performance measures. Nevertheless, everything that happens in the business will have some financial impact. So companies need systems to ensure that the financial consequences of decisions are understood internally and that the operational plan is adhered to. An organisation cannot wait until the accountant prepares a financial report at the end of the year to see whether it has been profitable or not – by then it is too late. Profit does not just happen, it has to be planned for and then operations controlled to ensure the plan is executed (Horngren et al. 2012). The main control mechanism is called budgeting.

Activity 20.7   Preparing a budget

- Prepare a simple cash budget for your own finances for next month. You will need to consider the cash you have available from savings in the past, how much cash you expect to receive during the month and what you plan to spend.

The budgeting process usually begins at the top level when the directors set budgetary targets for business performance. Simple top-level targets often set are for revenue (sales) and profit. These targets need to be translated into other targets that have meaning at the operating levels.

Management in practice   GKN group objectives   www.gkn.com

This company operates in a range of markets including automotive, aerospace and powder metallurgy, so the corporate objectives must be relevant to all the divisions to provide an overall direction. A few of its strategic objectives set out in 2014:

- to be the leader in its chosen markets;
- to achieve a rate of growth above that of the market;
- to achieve a group profit margin of 8–10 per cent;
- return on invested capital of 20 per cent.

Note the third and fourth bullet points – here the top management are setting clear financial targets in relation to profit margins and return on investment, and these will be the basis of the budgeting system as it flows down through the organisation.

Source: Company website.

Budgeting by department

Companies are typically structured into departments such as purchasing, design, production and human resources. Each is independently managed yet they must be coordinated to ensure that all work to achieve the required corporate financial targets. Each function has control over certain parts of the financial jigsaw. Production will have control over the cost of manufacturing activities; purchasing must negotiate prices for supplies of material or components; sales will be responsible for generating revenue; and human resources may be responsible for agreeing salaries. Although managed independently, each depends on the others. The simplest example of this interdependence is in production volumes and the costs associated with economies of scale. Manufacturing costs will vary depending on how well sales do their job. More sales mean larger production volumes and so lower costs per unit.

Manufacturing budgets are based on projected sales, but these are hard to predict so the outcome will vary from the plan. Yet without a plan there is no sense of direction or clarity of purpose. The process of budget preparation in itself is a useful exercise but it should be done as part of the larger business planning process that enables the parts of the organisation to relate their activities to each other. Business planning is a valuable coordination device helping to achieve the focus of the whole company on the same objectives.

The simplest budgets are those that are allocated by function, as shown in Table 20.1. In this method, cost is allocated to cover the work carried out within the functional areas.

Some budgets are less specific and need to be spread across the organisation, normally as a proportion allocated to each function or area. Examples of these are the:

- **overhead budget** – showing the consumption of resources that cannot be identified with particular functions, e.g. energy and utilities, directors fees.
- **capital budget** – showing planned spending on new equipment, buildings and acquisitions of other companies.

Once each budget is negotiated and agreed, it becomes part of the operational control system. Each budget will be allocated to a responsible senior manager who will typically distribute it throughout their subordinate managers. For example, a production director may split the budget between the machining budget held by the machining manager and the assembly budget held by the assembly manager.

Project budgeting

Setting budgets for departments allows an analysis of their costs over a period, but not for a product or activity; a design department may require the production department to build prototypes, or purchasing to buy material for testing. If each department is allocated a yearly budget then it will be difficult to see how much was actually spent on the activities that comprised the design work for a product. Project-based costing tries to overcome this, by using the product (or project) life span shown in Figure 20.1.

Table 20.1 Functional budget allocation

Budget	Function	Cost or revenue-bearing activities
Sales	Sales and marketing	Sale of product to customer
Materials and parts	Purchasing	Buying parts and material from suppliers
Design and Development	Design	Engineering, prototype building, testing, analysis
Manufacturing	Production	Assembly, testing, inspection, packing

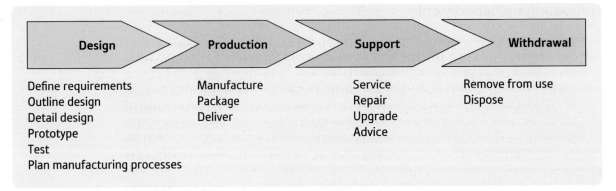

Figure 20.1 A product life span

Each phase of the product's life span must have a budget, and will also require input from other units. This method of budgeting breaks the work into packages that are not necessarily based in one department. This is called a **work breakdown structure** (Grey and Larson, 2008). The mechanism for budgeting and cost collection is called the **cost breakdown structure** and this is based on allocating cost to the packages of work in the work breakdown structure. This means costs can be analysed by work activity rather than by organisational unit.

Project-based costing systems are used by companies that have several products, each following its own life cycle: a car company will typically have some models in development, some in production and some no longer made, but which still require support and service. Departments will be working on all of these, and allocating their costs not only to the product but to the activity. Figure 20.2 shows a small extract from a cost breakdown structure for an aircraft design and build programme.

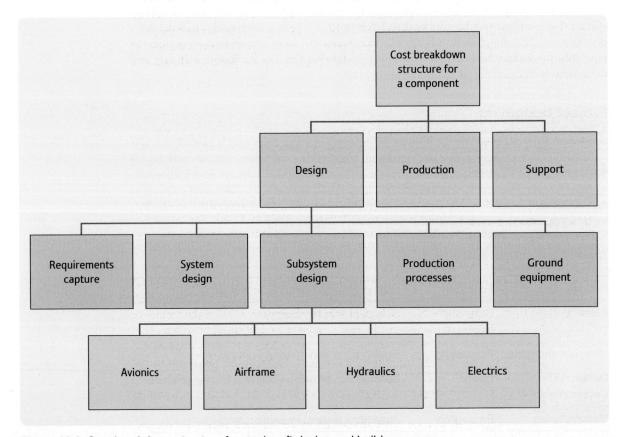

Figure 20.2 Cost breakdown structure for an aircraft design and build programme

Costs will be allocated to the activity rather than the function, and each function will have a budget for work on that activity.

For example, planning production processes may be carried out by production engineering, who are part of the production function – but they have to do this work during the development phase of the project so that the production processes are ready to allow production to begin. Another example is the activity of clarifying exactly what the finished product is expected to do, and so what inputs will be required from each function during its design and production. This work can only be done by staff from across marketing, design and engineering and production functions, as doing the work correctly requires skills from each area. It is important to understand the cost of each activity so that on completion lessons can be learned for the next product.

While project management methodology, of which cost breakdown structures are a part, is commonly thought of in relation to large products such as buildings and oil rigs, it is useful in any industry where functions 'overlap' on phases of activity. A mobile phone, though small and inexpensive, still has to be designed before it can be produced in volume and the same cross-functional cooperation (and cost management) is needed. Cost breakdown structures are especially useful in very integrated forms of organisation, such as matrix structures or project teams made up of people from several functions.

The issues of accounting across periods of time (mentioned previously) are also eased with activity-based cost allocation using a cost breakdown structure. It is critical that a budget is set for each phase so that the company knows whether it has overspent or not before moving onto the next phase. Design and development phases are typically all cost and no income. In some cases, especially the design of a unique product for a specific customer, the customer pays instalments towards the cost as the design progresses. In the defence industry the government pays as contractors complete specified stages of work.

When product is in full production there is less need for a cost breakdown structure, as costs are generated mainly by the manufacturing function. But even here, should a problem arise due to a design flaw, design staff must intervene to solve it and the costs of this be shown as part of the design cost. An example of this is shown in the 'Management in practice' feature describing the Toyota recall. In this example a design problem was uncovered after many cars had been produced and sold. The cost to rectify is not a production or service cost but is part of the design cost.

20.5   Other budgeting considerations

Employee performance

The budgeting process in an organisation can have a significant influence on managers' behaviour. If the process is authoritarian and unthinking it will lead to suboptimal performance. The pressure to meet budget may be translated into action that is against long-term interests – as when a salesperson institutes a price increase in the coming month to achieve a short-term sales target without regard to the longer-term risks of losing customers.

In some organisations the immediate reaction to employees who fail to achieve budget is negative. Poor budgetary adherence may not be the employee's fault so before taking action it is important to check first whether the budget was intelligently set and if the employee had the resources to achieve it. Consistent failure to achieve budget should first lead to a review of the budget to ensure that the targets are fair and achievable. Only then should there be an attempt to take remedial action to improve an activity. The successful use of budgets depends on those affected, managers and staff alike, developing a sense of ownership towards them. As conditions change, the budget should be revised so that it continues to be credible.

A budget is, in essence, short term – usually for no more than one year. Nevertheless it has to be set in a longer-term context and be consistent with the strategic direction.

Expenditures towards long-term investments in research and development, product and market development, new plant and equipment or even the acquisition of other businesses have to be included in the short-term budget, and cash requirements in the cash budget.

Decision making

The one certainty in any organisation is that conditions will change. The budget cannot be revised every time minor changes occur or fresh opportunities arise. An organisation has to be flexible and responsive. Frequently opportunities arise that require prompt action – for example, a special order for a normal product or service that is to be sold at a low promotional price into a new market. In these circumstances the normal measurement of the average cost of producing and delivering the service may be an inappropriate starting point for computing potential profit. Many of the costs will not change as a result of accepting this opportunity: there will be no further research and development, no requirement to increase productive capacity (assuming that capacity is available) and, possibly, little added labour cost. In these conditions consideration need only be given to the costs that will increase directly as a result of choosing to accept this order: delivery, materials or additional resources consumed.

Suppose that Osram has an opportunity to make and sell electric light bulbs to a new retailer. The decision-making process may be as follows:

- Is there enough manufacturing capacity without having to reduce normal production? If so, there is no need to take account of any additional capital costs.
- Are additional employees required or will existing employees have to work longer? If so, the extra costs will be attributable to this order; otherwise there are no added labour costs.
- Do the bulbs need different packaging? In this case there may be design and printing costs as well as costs of packaging material. The set-up costs will have to be included.

The important issue is to identify costs that are directly traceable and attributable to this opportunity. The normal average cost of producing light bulbs may be irrelevant, since that includes the cost of research and development, capital equipment and administrative overheads, which will not necessarily increase with this order.

Undoubtedly the retailer is looking for a special price, lower than that which Osram might normally charge. If this price exceeds the identified cost it may be an attractive opportunity. Suppose that the normal selling price is 80 cents and that the usual cost is made up (per unit) as follows:

	Cents
Labour	10
Materials	20
Packaging	5
Delivery	3
Overheads	25
	63
Contribution to profit	17
	80

The retailer wants to buy lamps at 60 cents. If we establish that Osram's overheads will not increase, that labour costs will be 8 cents, materials 20 cents and packaging 10 cents, then the appropriate cost per unit will be 38 cents. If additional delivery is $100 per journey for up to 10,000 light bulbs, the design and set-up costs for printing the packaging are $10,000 and the order is for 100,000 bulbs, is it acceptable to sell at 60 cents?

		Cents
Unit costs:	Labour	8
	Material	20
	Packaging	10
		38

	$
Cost for 100,000	38,000
Delivery cost	1,000
Design, set-up	10,000
Relevant cost	49,000
Revenue	60,000
Contribution to profit	11,000

This appears to be an acceptable sales opportunity as long as it does not erode Osram's normal market and as long as the existing customers do not expect the normal price to be lowered.

It is one of the main jobs of the cost or management accountant to process financial information quickly in order to assist managers to take decisions of the kind described above.

Routine information for managers

Another aspect of internal financial measurement is more routine. Unlike the system of financial reporting for the organisation as a whole, which is geared to the needs of the capital market, internal information has to be related to the needs of the managers. They will be interested in financial measurements related to their own area of responsibility. For example, a marketing manager will need information about groups of products, brands, customers, regions and marketing areas. In research and development, costs accumulating for each project might be compared with research progress to date. This approach runs right through the value chain, recognising that value can be added from research, development and design, through to distribution and customer service. It is not just the manufacturing process or service delivery process that adds value and requires measurement.

20.6   Integrating themes

Entrepreneurship

The most critical requirement for new ventures is to raise capital. This is not only necessary for survival in itself, but can often bring new skills into the business if investors require the entrepreneur to strengthen their management resources as one of the conditions of investing. Ventures typically seek this investment in a series of rounds, each providing capital for the near future: successive rounds typically draw resources from existing investors, plus a few new ones.

Hallen and Eisenhardt (2012) examined how entrepreneurs form ties efficiently with members of the venture capital community. Efficient tie formation happens when the approach leads to a completed tie, is arranged with little time and effort and results in ties with a desired partner.

This matters since, otherwise, raising capital consumes an excessive amount of the entrepreneur's time.

They found that the venture executives themselves (rather than members of the investor community) play a central role in fund-raising – although the latter often advise on strategies and identify possible additional investors. They identify two strategies. The first is to use existing strong ties – which have already been activated and proved satisfactory for investors who are willing to invest in further rounds. The second, and essential to firms without the track record that enables them to use existing ties, is to use 'catalysing strategies' – an approach that is available to many firms. This involves entrepreneurs offering opportunities and inducements that make their venture attractive to investors. Research with nine ventures in the online security industry identified components of these 'catalysing strategies', including:

- **casual dating** – informal but deliberate, repeated meetings about the venture with a few potential partners; not at first seeking investments, but asking for advice about the venture;
- **amplifying signals of progress** – especially by timing approaches around positive 'proof-points', such as a major customer paying for a product, to show the venture is making progress;
- **scrutinising interest** – actively seeking confirmation of the potential partner's genuine degree of interest in the venture; and
- **crafting alternatives** – signalling that the venture has alternative routes to finance available, as an inducement to encourage a desired partner to commit.

The authors' research showed that ventures that used one or more of these tactics were able to form ties more efficiently than those who used other approaches.

Sustainability

To understand the environmental impact of an organisation, and how it should perform more sustainably, some form of measurement must be made. Environmental and sustainability accounting have been receiving increasing attention as a vehicle for this (Lamberton, 2005). Grey (1993) identified three methods:

1 Sustainable cost is a measure of the (hypothetical) cost of restoring the earth to the state it was in prior to an organisation's impact.
2 Natural capital inventory accounting involves the recording of stocks of natural capital over time, with changes in stock levels used as an indicator of the (declining) quality of the natural environment. There are four types of natural capital: 1) critical – the ozone layer, tropical hardwood, etc.; 2) non-renewable/non substitutable – oil, petroleum and mineral products; 3) non-renewable/substitutable – waste disposal, energy usage and; 4) renewable – plantation timber, fisheries.
3 Input–output analysis that accounts for the physical flow of materials and energy inputs, and product and waste outputs in physical units. It aims to measure all material inputs to the process, and outputs of finished goods, emissions, recycled materials and waste for disposal.

By using a combination of these techniques some attempt can be made by companies to control their operational performance in a sustainable way.

Internationalisation

Different legal systems, industry financing, taxation systems, structure of the accounting profession, language and traditions mean that financial reporting varies between countries. France, Germany, Portugal, Spain and Japan have historically required compliance with a rigid national framework for financial reporting (Alexander and Nobes, 2013). This is now changing as international financial reporting standards (IFRS) are being introduced in more than 140 countries including all the G20 countries, having started the process in 2005.

IFRS should help to overcome the difficulties of comparing the financial performance of companies in different countries and promote their access to international capital markets.

As organisations develop stronger alliances and cooperative arrangements, at both the strategic and operational levels, the role of the accountant is expanded beyond the limits of the organisation within which he or she works. Cooperation in the supply chain can result in improved performance for both organisations involved. For example, to achieve benefits of cost reduction and/or improved profitability through quality improvement, there has to be an open relationship and trust between the organisations. Accountants play a role in this cooperation by advising on the financial consequences for both organisations (Atkinson et al. 2007).

Governance

The report by the then Financial Services Authority (now the Prudential Regulation Authority) into the failure of the Royal Bank of Scotland contains many lessons for those responsible for the governance of both the financial and the wider aspects of a business. The report concludes that the bank did not do things that were particularly unusual at the time, but that it took them to greater extremes. It had made a successful acquisition of NatWest, which led the bank's senior managers become overconfident in their ability to complete successful mergers They did very little due diligence on ABN Amro before making their disastrous bid for the company, and no one on the board appears to have challenged the wisdom of this bid.

This sense of optimism pervaded RBS, and was reinforced by financial incentives that encouraged the CEO and his senior colleagues to concentrate on increasing revenue, profits and assets, rather than on capital, liquidity and the quality of assets (including those represented by the many very risky loans the bank made). The 17 directors on the board appear to have been affected by 'groupthink' – the tendency to value membership of the team above the exercise of critical, independent commentary. They were relatively lacking in financial experience, and were the kind of people who were unlikely to go against the consensus of their colleagues. The board failed to monitor the bank's overall exposure to risk, and hence did not appreciate how vulnerable it was to a change in market sentiment.

The report also notes that shareholders did little or nothing to protect their interests – agreeing to a rights issue to support the risky ABN Amro acquisition, which only exacerbated the scale of their eventual loss.

Summary

1 **Describe the role of the finance function in management**
   - It must choose between investment opportunities.
   - Shareholders expect management to invest in projects to add shareholder value.
   - Management requires adequate financial information.
   - The finance function offers a system for assessing the financial consequences of decisions in a relatively objective way.
   - Management is required to communicate financial information about the company to actual and prospective shareholders through the financial reports.

2 **Interpret basic financial reports**
   - Operating profit, EBIT and net profit as a proportion of sales is a useful basis for comparing firms in the same industry and for each firm through time.
   - All measures of performance based on accounting numbers are subject to the opinions of those who prepare them.

3 **Explain the difference between profit and cash**
- Profit is based on accounting interpretation of financial data.
- Cash flow measures actual cash transactions and is less subject to opinion than profit.
- In most businesses a financial plan will show expected sales, costs, resources needed to fulfil the plan, a cash forecast and an expected balance sheet.

4 **Appreciate the importance of financial results to evaluate performance**
- Owners and shareholders, and the capital market generally, exercise significant influence over managers.
- The capital markets' reaction to reports of financial performance affects the ability of the company to raise capital.
- Financial information also helps to measure management performance internally – actual revenue and expenditure can be compared with the budget.
- Financial information can help control the management of projects, to ensure that what is spent corresponds to what has been planned.

5 **Explain how budgets are important as a financial control mechanism**
- Budgets support the overall operational plan by providing focus and a financial coordination mechanism.
- Budgets ensure that the financial targets set at the top level are flowed down through the organisation to allow each manager to understand his/her responsibilities.

6 **Discuss the difference between functional and project-based budgeting**
- A functional budget is allocated to a functional manager and defines the cost of all the activities that are carried out within that function.
- A project budget is set using a cost breakdown structure that allocates cost to a phase of the project and activity rather than to a function in the management structure.
- The project budget is more flexible, allowing a greater level of analysis to be carried out on the cost of each activity and cost over a time period.

7 **Explain the significance of the profit and loss statement, and use this to help you develop the skill of reading a profit and loss statement**
- The ability successfully to read and interpret a P&L statement can have a significant impact on your career, and the chapter provides an opportunity for you to develop that skill.

8 **Show how ideas from the chapter add to your understanding of the integrating themes**
- While companies have historically been required by shareholders to report on performance in financial terms, techniques of sustainability accounting are emerging that enable them to report performance on sustainability criteria in an increasingly objective way.
- To ensure comparability in the financial reports of companies operating in different jurisdictions, each with unique financial reporting requirements, common international financial reporting standards are now emerging.
- Pressure from powerful shareholders for high short-term returns on their investments encouraged much of the excessive risk taking that has, in turn, been the main stimulus for tighter regimes of governance and control.

Test your understanding

1 Why do companies have to make a profit? Check the website for Marks & Spencer plc (**www.marksand spencer.com**). What do the directors have to say about profit and recent performance?

2 How is profit measured?

3   Explain why profit is different from cash. Look up any company report to see if you can explain the main difference between profit and cash for the company.

4   What does a balance sheet tell us about an organisation? What can you discover about the activities of BASF (**www.basf.com**) from its balance sheet?

5   Can you explain how the external pressures on a company to generate a profit are translated into internal planning systems? Explain how this occurs in M&S. What is the purpose of a budget?

6   How does a budget operate as a control mechanism?

7   Explain why the financial information prepared for external purposes is not necessarily appropriate for managers.

Think critically

Think about the ways in which your company, or one with which you are familiar, deals with financial reporting and management accounting matters. Then make notes on these questions:

- What examples of the issues discussed in this chapter struck you as being relevant to practice in your company?

- Is the budget-setting process conducted fairly, and in a reasonably participative way? Are those who must meet the budgets adequately involved in setting them?

- What **assumptions** seem to be reflected in the way budgets are set?

- What factors such as the history or current **context** of the company appear to influence the way the company handles these financial and budgeting processes? Does the current approach appear to be right for the company in its context?

- Has serious attention been given to **alternative** approaches to budgeting within the company?

- To what extent are people in your organisation aware of the **limitations** of financial measures of performance? Have they acted to take account of this by, for example, considering some kind of balanced scorecard approach?

Develop a skill – reading a profit and loss statement

The ability successfully to read and interpret a P&L statement can have a significant impact on your career, so this exercise is about that.

- **Assessment:** Make an assessment of how well you can understand a P&L statement by accessing the annual report of any major company that you have heard about recently – following the business news on the BBC is an excellent way of keeping in touch with what is going on in the business world in terms of company results. Find the P&L statement and notes; study them and ask yourself how well you can interpret what they really mean.

- **Learning:** Section 20.3 dealt with the P&L statement. Read that section again, then summarise the main points about the P&L statement.

- **Analysis:** Consider the possible implications for the company of their P&L Statement.

- **Practice:** Then compare your views with those of analysts and commentators reported in the financial news.

- **Application:** Reflect on your own analysis and that reported by the professional commentators. What do you learn from this?

    - Decide on another opportunity to practise this skill within the next week.

Read more

Horngren, C.T., Datar, S.M. and Rajan, M. (2012), *Cost Accounting* (14th edn), Prentice Hall, Harlow.

A standard text that covers all areas of the topic in great detail.

Lamberton, G. (2005), 'Sustainability accounting – a brief history and conceptual framework,' *Accounting Forum,* vol. 29, no. 1, pp. 7–26.

A summary of the area of sustainability and accounting.

Larson, E. and Grey, C. (2010), *Project Management: The Management Process,* McGraw-Hill/Irwin, New York.

A broad overview of project management and control of costs.

Ross, S., Westerfield, R. and Jordan, B. (2012), *Fundamentals of Corporate Finance* (10th edn) McGraw-Hill/Irwin, New York.

A sound introduction to principles of corporate finance.

Go online

These websites contain material relevant to the chapter:

www.basf.com
www.siemens.com
www.gkn.com
www.solvay.com
www.mothercare.com
www.marksandspencer.com

Visit the websites in the list, or for any other company that interests you, and navigate to the pages that include their annual report or investor relations (see also 'recent trading statements'). Sometimes they may include 'presentations to analysts' (who advise fund managers on investment decisions).

- What kind of information do they include in these pages, and what messages are they trying to present to the financial markets? If performance has been poor, what reasons do they give, and what do they promise to do about it? What implications might that have for people working in the company?

- You could keep the most recent trading statement, and then compare it with the next one, which will be issued in a few months.

- Gather information from the media websites (such as **www.ft.com**) that relates to the companies you have chosen. What stories can you find that indicate something about the financial performance of those companies?

PART 6 CASE

TESCO

www.tesco.com

In 2016 Tesco was the UK's largest private sector employer, with over 300,000 staff in about 3,000 stores. It had experienced trading difficulties for several years and a new senior management team was attempting to recover its once-dominant position. While the UK accounts for over two-thirds of sales, it is also one of the world's largest retailers, with a presence in Europe and Asia and a joint venture in China. Attempts to enter overseas markets have delivered very mixed results, and some shareholders continue to challenge this aspect of management strategy.

Jack Cohen founded Tesco in 1919 as a grocery stall, opening the first store in 1929. He was aware that supermarkets had been successful in the United States and tried to introduce the idea to the United Kingdom. He opened small self-service stores in 1948, followed by his first self-service supermarket in 1956. The company grew rapidly by acquisition during the 1960s, taking advantage of the abolition of the Retail Price Maintenance Act in 1964. This had prohibited retailers from selling goods at prices below those that suppliers specified. Abolition allowed Tesco and similar chains to compete aggressively with established retailers (mainly small, family-owned grocers) on price. Tesco's size enabled it to buy products from food manufacturers more cheaply than smaller rivals.

The business prospered and in 1997 Terry Leahy became CEO, having previously been marketing director. Growth accelerated as management increased the scale and scope of the business, by opening more and larger stores, and offering more services including:

- non-food items, especially home wares and clothing;
- fuel retailing, through an alliance with Esso;
- financial services, now delivered through Tesco Bank;
- mobile and home telephone products, and broadband.

In early 2015 the new CEO, Dave Lewis (who had joined the previous October), presented the company's results for the last financial year. These showed a decline in sales, profits and in the dividend payable to shareholders. He had earlier revealed that the company had overstated profits in the previous year by £250 million, which the Financial Conduct Authority was investigating.

Shareholders looked to the new CEO to develop a new and more profitable strategy for the business. The table below shows some financial indicators of performance in the last two years.

© Mike Booth/Alamy Images

Financial performance indicators for the year to the end of February each year

	2015	2014
Group revenue (£m)	69,654	70,894
Trading profit (£m)	1,390	3,315
Earnings per share (p)	9.42	32.05
Dividend per share (p)	1.16	14.76
Return on capital employed (%)	4.1	13.6

Sources: Company Annual Reports 2014, 2015.

Managing to add value

Diverse formats

As the UK stores widened the range of products available, the company also diversified the way it delivered these to customers. The physical stores took one of six formats:

1 Tesco Homeplus – larger store for all DIY and home electrical products;
2 Tesco Onestop – small neighbourhood shop;
3 Tesco Express – local stores selling fresh food, wines, beers and spirits;
4 Tesco Metro – larger stores in city centres offering a range of food, including sandwiches and ready-meals;
5 Tesco Superstore – even larger stores offering a wide range of food and non-food products;
6 Tesco Extra – very large, edge-of-town stores offering the widest range of food and non-food products.

Almost two-thirds of the cost of delivering products to UK supermarkets comes from taking goods the last mile to stores. This cost has increased as chains have increased the number of convenience (Onestop and Express) stores: these earn higher margins than large stores, but cost more to stock. Online grocery sales are also more expensive than large physical stores, as they incur costs of assembling a customer's order and delivering it to them. In 2013 the company decided it no longer required many of the sites it had bought for new stores. It had done so when property values were higher, so disposing of them will bring a loss of about £800 million.

Clubcard

In 1994 Tesco launched its Clubcard scheme, which has over 11 million active holders. Shoppers join the scheme by completing a simple form with some personal information, and their purchases earn vouchers based on the amount they spend. Every purchase is electronically recorded, and the data analysed to identify their shopping preferences. This is then used to design a package of special offers that are most likely to appeal to that customer, mailed to them quarterly. Each mailing brings more business.

The scheme was devised and is run by Dunnhumby, a data analysis business that is owned by Tesco. They analyse the data to identify the kind of person the Clubcard holder is – whether they have a new baby, young children, whether they like cooking, and so on. Each product is also ascribed a set of attributes – expensive or cheap? An ethnic recipe or a traditional dish? Tesco own-label or an upmarket brand? The information on customers, shopping habits and product attributes is used to support all aspects of the business.

The database is believed to be the largest holding of personal information about named individuals within the UK. This information has informed some strategic decisions, such as the move into smaller store formats and the launch of the internet shopping site. It also shaped the development and sale of Tesco mobile phones, pet insurance and the 'Finest' food range.

The company has also launched Tesco TV, an online video service similar to Lovefilm, which will be available free to Clubcard holders, enabling them to access films and TV shows on the site. It hopes advertisers will use the site to send video ads to customers, based on the information about them in the Clubcard database.

Key performance indicators

To help in controlling such a large and diverse business, Leahy implemented the concept of the balanced scorecard, adapting the idea and calling it the Steering Wheel:

> This tool helped us to clarify our vision and strategy; to communicate and link our strategic objectives and targets; to plan and set clear targets; and to improve learning and feedback from the shop floor. The very act of creating the Steering Wheel forced the senior management team to agree not just broad-brush strategic statements, but what delivering them would mean in practice . . . it bought a new discipline and consensus to managing business, day in, day out. Above all the Steering Wheel was practical and simple . . . it could be applied to each and every part of the business, every division and every store . . . [and] eventually linked to the individual targets and performance of stores – and then, at a lower level still, the teams within that store. (Leahy, 2012, p. 185)

The Steering Wheel had the four balanced scorecard quadrants (customer, operations, people, finance) plus 'community', each containing eight performance indicators.

In 2015 the new CEO reported that while the Steering Wheel had served the company well, it had become too complicated, with over 40 measures. It has been replaced by six simple performance indicators, shown in the table.

Key performance indicators, and scores in 2014/2015 financial year

Indicators	Measure	Scores 2014/2015
Customers recommend us and come back time and again	Customer survey and spend	Down 2.5% on year before

Colleagues rec- ommend us as a great place to work and shop	Survey of staff	70% good place to work 77% good place to shop
We build trusted partnerships with suppliers	Survey of suppliers	58% satisfied
Grow sales	£69,6547m	Down 1.3%
Deliver profits	£1,390m	Down 57.5%
Improve operat- ing cash flow	£1,860m	Down 59.6%

Source: Tesco PLC Annual Report and Financial Statements, 2015.

As with the Steering Wheel, responsibility for delivering the KPIs is delegated to the relevant business unit. Every Tesco store has its own set of KPIs with specific deliverables ranging from strategy to day-to-day work. The KPIs are measured regularly, and quarterly reports go to the board to help monitor the performance of the business. The summary report for the company is sent to all store managers, and shared with staff.

Tesco online

Process, roles, discipline – these are things that irritate people who are in a hurry to see their bold, revolutionary idea become reality . . . At Tesco, whenever we had a great new idea, or wanted to launch a major initiative, we focussed forensically not just on what we wanted to do, but on how we were actually going to achieve it. And perhaps one of the best examples of an audacious, well-executed plan was the launch of Tesco.com, today the world's largest online food business. (Leahy, 2012, p. 161)

Leahy goes on to explain the origins of **Tesco.com** in 1995, which arose from a chance visit with a senior colleague to a trade exhibition on the future of retailing – at which the computer-based ideas appeared, at the time, to be quite farfetched. Leahy and his colleague saw that the fundamental ideas behind the vision would make life easier for customers. So they decided to go ahead quickly with a small project that did not require Board approval. The project team set out to create an e-commerce service from their existing stores, with staff picking the customer's order from the shelves and passing it to the van for delivery.

Those first few years were a classic example of learning on the job, and the benefits of starting a big project with small, careful first steps. Using the information we had gained about how customers behaved online, we rapidly reworked our deliberately loose process, gradually firming it up and turning it into a stable system as new patterns of behaviour became more certain and predictable. (Leahy, 2012, p. 169).

Overseas operations

Since the mid-1990s the company has been investing overseas, and by 2013 was active in 14 countries. Over half of the group's space is now overseas, and its strategy reflects the lessons learned in developing that business, including:

- be flexible – each market is unique and requires a different approach;
- act local – local customers, cultures and suppliers require a local approach: very few members of the Tesco International team are expatriates;
- keep focus – to be the leading local brand takes years to achieve.

It opened in Eastern Europe and in Asia, the latter growing especially quickly. Sir Terry Leahy had launched a US venture in 2004, with a plan for up to 10,000 convenience outlets. The chain began trading in 2007, and has had difficulty establishing a significant presence in the US market. By 2012 the US business had lost about £800m since 2007, and was closed in 2012. It also left Japan, where it had also failed. Some believe the losses incurred overseas destroyed funds that could have been used to strengthen the UK stores' response to tougher competition.

Over-reporting profits

Late one Friday in September 2014 a member of Tesco's finance team chose to raise concerns over certain half-year profit figures. These concerns rapidly passed to Dave Lewis, the (very) new Chief Executive, who made further investigations over the weekend and alerted the Financial Conduct Authority. On Monday the company announced that it had suspended four executives, launched an accounting investigation, and admitted that the half-year profit was overstated by £250 million.

The errors related to 'commercial income', which the company (in common with other supermarkets) receives from suppliers. When they reach deals with suppliers, this includes a price for the goods. But suppliers try to motivate the supermarkets to sell more of their products with cash payments known as rebates if they sell a certain volume of goods in future periods, or by helping the stores to fund new promotions. If the supermarket's income in the current accounting period is below expectations, they may be tempted to include these agreed rebates as current income, though it is, in effect, 'borrowing' this income from the future period. This action makes current profits larger than they really are.

Several commentators observed that the Board was taken by surprise – despite one analyst querying earlier how the company could report that margins were stable when costs were rising faster than gross income. Others noted the company's incentive scheme at the time, in which 50 per cent of top executives' bonus payments depended on the level of trading profit.

In early 2016 an industry regulator (the Groceries Code Adjudicator) found Tesco guilty of serious breaches of industry rules, as it had deliberately delayed payments due to suppliers, to make its finances look better. One simple practice was to delay payments due to suppliers on credit notes before key financial reporting periods (so that the company appeared to have more cash than it would if it paid these debts to suppliers). If a supplier pursued the matter, Tesco might hint that this would reduce their chances of future orders.

Aspects of Tesco's UK context

Competition

Tesco is a diversified retailer providing a wide range of products and services. In the UK, which accounts for two-thirds of its sales and most of its profits, the most obvious competitors are the other three major supermarket chains, which together control about two-thirds of the market. The retail stores also compete with discount retailers Aldi and Lidl – whose combined market share has been growing by almost 2 per cent a year since 2010, while that of the 'big four' has declined by the same amount. Tesco also competes with independent local shops, and with businesses that focus on one area of its product range, such as HSBC in financial services or BP in petrol retailing. Economic conditions affect all retailers, as recession and uncertain job prospects encourage shoppers to buy less and to seek out cheaper brands – reducing store revenues.

Online shopping

A major change affecting most parts of the retail sector is the growth of online shopping. About 3 per cent of retail sales were made online in 2005, and this had grown to 15 per cent by 2015. Clearly well-known sites such as Amazon have done very well from this, but the main winners from the growth of online shopping have been well-established retailers, rather than unknown new entrants to the industry. Shoppers prefer to buy online from brands they already know.

Online shopping is especially popular for non-food items, and the proportion of these sold online is growing rapidly. Some specialist retailers, such as Mothercare

and HMV, suffered especially badly from online competition. The winners from the growth of online shopping appeared to be the larger chains that could offer customers the option to order online and then to collect from a conveniently located physical store. One analyst observed:

> Customers crave convenience, so larger retailers with multi-channel capabilities, enabling online orders to be picked up in store, stand to gain market share from less tech-savvy rivals. (*Financial Times,* 27 October 2012, p. 17)

Global retailing

Consumer habits may be converging towards global brands, especially as those in emerging economies develop tastes for Ikea furniture or Scotch whisky. But for basic food and drink needs, local habits prevail. After 20 years in which some major national retailers have tried to expand overseas, the dream of building a global grocer is dying. There have been some successes, such as Carrefour in Brazil, Walmart of the US in Mexico and Tesco in South Korea, but no chain has yet built itself into a truly global player. Investors query if it would be better for food retailers to curtail their global ambitions, and concentrate instead on delivering value to shareholders by defending their position at home. As one said:

> Better management at home is more important than sticking flags around the world to try to build an empire. Maybe shareholders don't want an empire. They just want attractive returns. (From an article by Andrea Felstead, *Financial Times,* 6 January 2012, p. 9)

Retail space

By 2015 it was clear that all the big supermarket chains were becoming very cautious about opening large stores. UK shoppers are changing their buying patterns – buying more online, at smaller convenience stores, or at Aldi and Lidl. The big stores have cut their store opening plans, and have written down the value of their property assets. To the extent that they are opening stores, most are smaller convenience stores: some larger ones have been closed or divided so that other retailers can take over some of the space.

Current management dilemmas

As Dave Lewis began to rebuild the business that had performed poorly for several years, he and his management team had to decide where to focus their investment budget – regaining competitiveness, balancing online and store sales, and how much to invest overseas.

Regaining competitiveness

Tesco, like other retailers, faces competition from discounters Aldi and Lidl, which offer comparable quality more cheaply, though with a smaller range of products. This implies finding ways to reduce prices to match theirs. One option could be to be more flexible on pricing – offering a more limited range and fewer facilities at stores that are close to the discounters. Where the discounters are less of a challenge, the focus on price may be less important.

Strengthening the balance sheet

In 2014/15 the company made a profit of £1.3 billion, compared with debt of over £22 billion – which the CEO, Dave Lewis, acknowledged was a significant burden. It had also committed to allocate £270 million each year to reduce the pension fund deficit. There are several ways to raise money to reduce debt, such as selling assets (e.g. more of the overseas businesses) or raising cash from shareholders. It had already announced the closure and sale of 43 stores, including seven superstores and six Homeplus non-grocery outlets. Mr Lewis had offered Dunnhumby for sale, but after being unable to secure a suitable price, had withdrawn it from sale. His preferred method for reducing debt is 'self-help' – generating cash from the business, and using that to pay off debt. It will also reduce head office space and cut costs in central functions and store management.

Rebuilding trust and transparency

The company acknowledges that it needs to overcome the reputational damage caused by the discovery that it had been over-reporting profits. It has responded by:

- appointing new management who focus on securing favourable costs from suppliers, rather than relying on commercial income from suppliers for promoting their products;
- implementing a Code of Business Conduct, supported by a company-wide training programme;
- promoting a 'speak-up' culture with a strong focus on ethics and compliance – these factors are now key measures in staff performance management and reward systems.

It has also removed sweets from the check-outs in all stores, and organises a national collection of food for distribution to those in need, through the Trussell Trust and other charities.

Overseas strategy

Some observers have questioned the value of expanding overseas, especially when the core UK operation was struggling to make a profit. They advocate a more vigorous pruning of the foreign businesses. The Japanese and US businesses were sold in 2012 and 2013 respectively, followed by that in South Korea in 2015. It has reduced its stake in China by merging its stores with a state-controlled company, which will own 80% of the venture.

However, in 2014 it announced that it would make a 'modest' re-entry to the US market by opening seven franchised stores selling its clothing brand, F&F.

Sources: *Financial Times*, 5 September 2011, p. 19, 13 January 2012, p. 19, 28 June 2013, p. 16, 3 October 2013, p. 22, 15 April 2014, 9 January 2015, 22 September 2015, p. 23; The Times, 27 January 2016, pp. 38–39; company website.

Part case questions

(a) Relating to Chapters 18 to 20

1 Adapt Figures 18.2 and 18.3 (pp. 580 and 581) to analyse the transformation process in Tesco, especially to identify and list examples of transforming and transformable resources.

2 What types of operations processes are referred to, or implied, in the case? (Section 18.4)

3 Give an example of how each activity of operations will be used in Tesco. (Section 18.6)

4 What issues does Tesco face in meeting customers' expectations of quality? (Section 18.7)

5 How has Clubcard helped Tesco to control the business? What other benefits has it gained? (Section 19.2)

6 What benefits do you expect the company will have gained from using the Steering Wheel, and its simpler replacement? (Section 19.4)

7 What evidence is there of the company taking account of the human aspects of control? (Section 19.6)

8 What can you discover about the movement of the Tesco share price over the past year and the reasons for this? (Section 20.2)

9 What can you discover about shareholders trying to influence company management? Access this information from the websites of *The Economist, Financial Times* or BBC News (Business pages).

(b) Relating to the company

Visit the Tesco website, including the pages on 'investor relations'. Note recent events that add to material in this case.

1 Which, if any, of the dilemmas identified in the case are still current, and how has the company dealt with them?

2 What is Tesco's relative performance in the most recent trading period? Which competitors have gained and lost share? Access this information from the websites of *The Economist, Financial Times* or BBC News (Business pages).

3 What new issues appear to be facing the company that were not mentioned in the case?

4 For any one of those issues it faces, how do you think it should deal with it? Build your answer by referring to one or more features of the company's history, as outlined in the case.

PART 6

EMPLOYABILITY SKILLS – PREPARING FOR THE WORLD OF WORK

To help you develop useful skills, this section includes tasks that relate the themes covered in the Part to six employability skills (sometimes called capabilities and attributes) that many employers value. The layout will help you to articulate these skills to employers and prepare for the recruitment processes you will encounter in application forms, interviews and assessment centres.

Task 6.1   Business awareness

If a potential employer asks you to attend an assessment centre or a competency-based interview, they may ask you to present or discuss a current business topic to demonstrate your business awareness. To help you to prepare for this, write an individual or group report on ONE of these topics and present it to an audience. Aim to present your ideas in a 750-word report and/or ten PowerPoint slides at most.

1 Using data from the company website and business sites such as *The Economist, Financial Times* or BBC News (Business pages), outline significant recent developments in Tesco, especially regarding their:
   - range of activities (including their international presence);
   - financial performance and movements in the share price;
   - growth of their online offering;
   - key performance indicators; and
   - current policy on where they focus investment.

Include a summary of commentators' views on the firm's recent progress.

2 Gather evidence on the interaction between Tesco and its competitors, including specific examples of recent moves by Tesco and ONE competitor. Compare their respective financial performance over recent periods, and show how this may have influenced management strategies. What generally useful lessons can you learn from your analysis of competition in this market?

3 Choose another retail company that interests you – and which you may consider as a career option.
   - Gather information from the website and other sources about its strategy and structure.
   - What can you find about the role of specific policies designed to support the strategy?
   - How does management appear to control the business? What key performance indicators do they measure?

- How have technological developments in online sales or social media affected the business?
- What career options does it offer, and how attractive are they?

When you have completed the task, record a short paragraph giving examples of the skills (such as information gathering, analysis and presentation) that you have developed from this task. You can transfer a brief note of these to the Table at Task 6.7.

Task 6.2   Thinking critically

Reflect on the way that you handled Task 6.1, and identify how you exercised the skills of thinking critically (Chapter 1, Section 1.8). For example:

1 Did you spend time identifying and challenging the **assumptions** implied in the reports or commentaries you read? Summarise what you found then, or do it now.
2 Did you consider the extent to which they took account of the **context** in which managers are operating? Summarise what you found then, or do it now.
3 How far did they, or you, go in imagining and exploring **alternative** ways of dealing with the issue?
4 Did you spend time outlining the **limitations** of ideas or proposals that you thought of putting forward?

When you have completed the task, record a short paragraph giving examples of the thinking skills you have developed from this task. You can transfer a brief note of these to the Table at Task 6.7.

Task 6.3   Solving problems

Chapter 6 includes ideas on planning to deal with a problem – such as that of completing Task 6.1. Refer to these if you need more guidance on this activity, which invites you to analyse how your team worked on a task.

Use the scales below to rate the way your team planned how it would work on Task 6.1 – circle the number that best reflects your opinion of the discussion.

1 The team used suitable methods to gather sufficient information to create a good plan to complete the task (Section 6.4).

1	2	3	4	5	6	7
Strongly disagree						Strongly agree

2 The team set SMART goals that gave focus to our work on the task (Section 6.5).

1	2	3	4	5	6	7
Strongly disagree						Strongly agree

3 The goals helped to motivate us to achieve the task (Section 6.5).

1	2	3	4	5	6	7
Strongly disagree						Strongly agree

4 The team made a full list of what had to be done to achieve the goals (Section 6.6).

1	2	3	4	5	6	7
Strongly disagree						Strongly agree

5 The team made a suitable implementation plan, and followed it (Section 6.7).

1	2	3	4	5	6	7
Strongly disagree						Strongly agree

6 The team monitored the progress of the plan, and adjusted it accordingly (Section 6.7).

1	2	3	4	5	6	7
Strongly disagree						Strongly agree

When you have completed the task, record a short paragraph giving examples of the planning skills you have developed from this task. You can transfer a brief note of these to the Table at Task 6.7.

Task 6.4   Team working

Chapter 17 includes ideas on team working. This activity helps you use these to analyse how your team worked on Task 6.1.

Use the scales below to rate the way your team worked on this task – circle the number that best reflects your opinion of the discussion.

1 The team was effective in obtaining and using necessary information.

1	2	3	4	5	6	7
Strongly disagree						Strongly agree

2 The team members took on complementary team roles (Section 17.4).

1	2	3	4	5	6	7
Strongly disagree						Strongly agree

3 The team progressed through the stages of team development (Section 17.5).

1	2	3	4	5	6	7
Strongly disagree						Strongly agree

4 The team developed effective working processes that suited the task (Section 17.6).

1	2	3	4	5	6	7
Strongly disagree						Strongly agree

5 The team used its time effectively.

1	2	3	4	5	6	7
Strongly disagree						Strongly agree

6 The team regularly reviewed the ways it was working, and changed these when it would improve performance (Section 17.6).

1	2	3	4	5	6	7
Strongly disagree						Strongly agree

Record three practices that you could use in your next task. If possible, compare your results and suggestions with other members of the team, and agree on practices that would help a team work better.

When you have completed the task, write a short paragraph giving examples of team-working skills (such as observing the team to improve performance) that you have developed from this task. You can transfer a brief note of these to the Table at Task 6.7.

Task 6.5 Communicating

Chapter 16 includes ideas on communicating – and Sections 16.4 and 16.5 are especially relevant to this task. It will help you to analyse how well your team communicated as you worked on Task 6.1.

Use the scales below to rate the way your team communicated during Task 6.1 – circle the number that best reflects your opinion of the discussion.

1 The team handled face-to-face communication well during its meetings (Section 16.4).

1	2	3	4	5	6	7
Strongly disagree						Strongly agree

2 The team communicated effectively by phone, mobile, voicemail and other electronic systems (Section 16.4).

1	2	3	4	5	6	7
Strongly disagree						Strongly agree

3 The team communicated effectively by personal, written methods – letters, email, texting (Section 16.4).

1	2	3	4	5	6	7
Strongly disagree						Strongly agree

4 The team communicated effectively by impersonal written methods – newsletters, online communities (Section 16.4).

1	2	3	4	5	6	7
Strongly disagree						Strongly agree

5 The team adapted between centralised and decentralised communication networks according to the needs of the task (Section 16.5).

1	2	3	4	5	6	7
Strongly disagree						Strongly agree

6 The team communicated its report well to the chosen audience.

1	2	3	4	5	6	7
Strongly disagree						Strongly agree

7 The team experienced no significant barriers to communication, either internally or externally.

1	2	3	4	5	6	7
Strongly disagree						Strongly agree

Record three communication practices which you could use in your next task. If possible, compare your results and suggestions with other members of the team, and agree on practices that would help a team work better.

When you have completed the task, record a short paragraph giving examples of communication skills you have developed from this task. You can transfer a brief note of these to the Table at Task 6.7.

Task 6.6 Self-management

This activity helps you to learn more about managing yourself, so that you can present convincing evidence to employers showing, among other things, your willingness to learn, your ability to manage and plan learning, workloads and commitments, and that you have a well-developed level of self-awareness and self-reliance. You need to show that you are able to accept responsibility, manage time and use feedback to learn.

Reflect on the way that you handled Task 6.1, and identify how you exercised skills of self-management.

1 I effectively planned the time I would spend on each part of the task.

1	2	3	4	5	6	7
Strongly disagree						Strongly agree

2 I tried to balance my commitments and those of other team members across the work, so that all were reasonably busy.

1	2	3	4	5	6	7
Strongly disagree						Strongly agree

3 I think I used my time well.

1	2	3	4	5	6	7
Strongly disagree						Strongly agree

4 I tried to ensure that I and others took responsibility for distinct areas of work, to keep moving the task forward.

1	2	3	4	5	6	7
Strongly disagree						Strongly agree

5 I often reflected on how I was working on the task to identify possible ways to improve my performance.

1	2	3	4	5	6	7
Strongly disagree						Strongly agree

Write down three self-management practices that you could use in your next task. If possible, compare your results and suggestions with other members of the team, and agree on practices that would help a team work better.

When you have completed the task, write a short paragraph giving examples of the self-management practices you have developed from this task. You can transfer a brief note of these to the Table at Task 6.7.

Task 6.7 | Recording your employability skills

To conclude your work on this Part, use the summary paragraphs above to record the employability skills you have developed during your work on these tasks, and in other activities. Use the format of the table below to create an electronic record that you can use to combine the list of skills you have developed in this Part, with those in other Parts.

Most of your learning about each skill will probably come from the task associated with it – but you may also gain insights in other ways – include those as well.

Template for laying out record of employability skills developed in this Part

Skills/Task	Task 6.1	Task 6.2	Task 6.3	Task 6.4	Task 6.5	Task 6.6	Other sources of skills
Business awareness							
Thinking critically							
Solving problems							
Team working							
Communicating							
Self-management							

To make the most of your opportunities to develop employability skills as you do your academic work, you need to reflect regularly on your learning and record the results. This helps you to fill any gaps, and provides specific evidence of your employability skills.

GLOSSARY

Administrative management is the use of institutions and order rather than relying on personal qualities to get things done

The **administrative model of decision making** describes how people make decisions in uncertain, ambiguous situations

Agency theory seeks to explain what happens when one party (the principal) delegates work to another party (the agent)

Ambiguity is when people are uncertain about their goals and how best to achieve them

Arbitrariness (of corruption) is the degree of ambiguity associated with corrupt transactions

Assessment centres are multi-exercise processes designed to identify the recruitment and promotion potential of personnel

Assets are the property, plant and equipment, vehicles, stocks of goods for trading, money owed by customers and cash: in other words, the physical resources of the business

The **balanced scorecard** is a performance measurement tool that looks at four areas: financial, customer, internal processes and innovation, which contribute to organisational performance

A **balance sheet** shows the assets of the business and the sources from which finance has been raised

Behaviour is something a person does that can be directly observed

Behaviour modification is a general label for attempts to change behaviour by using appropriate and timely reinforcement

Big data describes information of an order of magnitude far greater than has been encountered before. Typically the data comes from social media, or from connected devices including satellites, surveillance cameras and mobile phones

The **big five** refers to trait clusters that appear consistently to capture main personality traits: openness, conscientiousness, extraversion, agreeableness and neuroticism

A **blog** is a Web log that allows individuals to post opinions and ideas

Bounded rationality is behaviour that is rational within a decision process that is limited (bounded) by an individual's ability to process information

A **brand** is a product or service whose [features] differentiate it in some way from other products or services designed to meet the same need

A **break-even analysis** is a comparison of fixed versus variable costs that will indicate at which point in volume of output it is financially beneficial to invest in a higher level of infrastructure

Bureaucracy is a system in which people are expected to follow precisely defined rules and procedures rather than to use personal judgement

A **business plan** is a document that sets out the markets the business intends to serve, how it will do so and what finance they require

The **capital market** comprises all the individuals and institutions that have money to invest, including banks, life assurance companies and pension funds and, as users of capital, business organisations, individuals and governments

A **cash flow statement** shows the sources from which cash has been generated and how it has been spent during a period of time

Centralisation is when a relatively large number of decisions are taken by management at the top of the organisation

Certainty describes the situation when all the information the decision maker needs is available

A **channel** is the medium of communication between a sender and a receiver

Co-creation involves the joint creation of value by the firm and its network of 'actors' such as customers, suppliers and distributors

Collectivism 'describes societies in which people, from birth onwards, are integrated into strong, cohesive ingroups which . . . protect them in exchange for unquestioning loyalty' (Hofstede, 2005, p. 76)

Communication is the exchange of information through written or spoken words, symbols and actions to reach a common understanding

Competences are the skills and abilities that an organisation uses to deploy resources effectively – systems, procedures and ways of working

Competencies (in HRM) refer to an individual's knowledge, skills, ability and other personal characteristics required to do a job well

A **competitive environment (or context)** is the industry-specific environment comprising the organisation's customers, suppliers and competitors

Competitive strategy explains how an organisation (or unit within it) intends to achieve competitive advantage in its market

Complexity theory is concerned with complex dynamic systems that have the capacity to organise themselves spontaneously

Concertive control is when workers reach a negotiated consensus on how to shape their behaviour according to a set of core values

Consideration is a pattern of leadership behaviour that demonstrates sensitivity to relationships and to the social needs of employees

Content is the specific substantive task that the group is undertaking

Contingencies are factors such as uncertainty, interdependence and size that reflect the situation of the organisation

Contingency theories propose that the performance of an organisation depends on having a structure that is appropriate to its environment

Control is the process of monitoring activities to ensure that results are in line with the plan and acting to correct significant deviations

The **control process** is the generic activity of setting performance standards, measuring actual performance, comparing actual performance with the standards and acting to correct deviations or modify standards

A **control system** is the way the elements in the control process are designed and combined in a specific situation

Core competences are the activities and processes through which resources are deployed to achieve competitive advantage in ways that others cannot imitate or obtain

Corporate governance refers to the rules and processes intended to control those responsible for managing an organisation

Corporate responsibility refers to the awareness, acceptance and management of the wider implications of corporate decisions

Corrective action aims to correct problems to get performance back on track

Corruption is the use of entrusted power for private gain

A **cost breakdown structure** is a system for categorising and collecting costs that allows cost to be attributed and analysed by activity rather than function

A **cost leadership strategy** is one in which a firm uses low price as the main competitive weapon

The **craft system** refers to a system in which the craft producers do everything. With or without customer involvement they design, source materials, manufacture, sell and perhaps service

Creativity is the ability to combine ideas in a unique way to produce something new and useful

Critical success factors are those aspects of a strategy that must be achieved to secure competitive advantage

Critical thinking identifies the assumptions behind ideas, relates them to their context, imagines alternatives and recognises limitations

Culture is the set of values, beliefs, norms and assumptions that are shared by a group and that guide their interpretations of, and responses to, their environments

Cultural intelligence is when a person is skilled and flexible about understanding a culture, and learns as they interact with it

Current assets can be expected to be cash or to be converted to cash within a year

A **customer-centred organisation** is focused upon, and structured around, identifying and satisfying the demands of its customers

Customer relationship management (CRM) The process of maximising the value delivered to the customer through all interactions, both online and traditional

Customer satisfaction is the extent to which a customer perceives that a product matches their expectations

Customers are individuals, households, organisations, institutions, resellers and governments that purchase products from other organisations

Data are raw, unanalysed facts, figures and events

Decentralisation is when a relatively large number of decisions are taken lower down the organisation in the operating units

A **decision** is a specific commitment to action (usually a commitment of resources)

Decision criteria define the factors that are relevant in making a decision

Decision making is the process of identifying and defining problems and opportunities, and making plans to resolve them

Decision support systems help people to calculate the consequences of alternatives before they decide which to choose

A **decision tree** helps someone to make a choice by progressively eliminating options as additional criteria or events are added to the tree

Decoding is the interpretation of a message into a form with meaning

Delegation occurs when one person gives another the authority to undertake specific activities or decisions

Demands are human wants backed by the ability to buy

Determinism is the view that the business environment determines an organisation's structure

Differentiation is when the parts of an organisation develop particular attributes in response to the demands posed by their relevant external environments

Differentiation strategy consists of offering a product or service that is perceived as unique or distinctive on a basis other than price

Disintermediation is the process of removing intermediaries, such as distributors or brokers, that formerly linked a company to its customers

Diversity (at work) refers to differences between individuals at work on any attribute that may evoke a perception that the other person is different from self

A **divisional structure** is when tasks are grouped in relation to their outputs, such as products or the needs of different types of customer

Dynamic capabilities are an organisation's abilities to renew and recreate its strategic capabilities to meet the needs of a changing environment

E-business refers to the integration, through the Internet, of all an organisation's processes from its suppliers through to its customers

E-commerce refers to the activity of selling goods or service over the internet

Economies of scale are achieved when producing something in large quantities reduces the cost of each unit

Effectiveness is a measure of how well an activity contributes to achieving organisational goals

Efficiency is a measure of the inputs required for each unit of output

Emergent models of change emphasise that in uncertain conditions a project will be affected by unknown factors, and that planning has little effect on the outcome

Encoding is translating information into symbols for communication

Enlightened self-interest is the practice of acting in a way that is costly or inconvenient at present, but which is believed to be in one's best interest in the long term

Enterprise resource planning (ERP) is a computer-based planning system that links separate databases to plan the use of all resources within the enterprise

Entrepreneurs are people who see opportunities in a market, and quickly mobilise resources to deliver the product or service profitably

Equity theory argues that perception of unfairness leads to tension, which then motivates the individual to resolve that unfairness

Escalating commitment is a bias that leads to increased commitment to a previous decision, despite evidence that it may have been wrong

Ethical audits are the practice of systematically reviewing the extent to which an organisation's actions are consistent with its stated ethical intentions

Ethical consumers are those who take ethical issues into account in deciding what to purchase

Ethical decision-making models examine the influence of individual characteristics and organisational policies on ethical decisions

Ethical investors are people who only invest in businesses that meet specified criteria of ethical behaviour

Ethical relativism is the principle that ethical judgements cannot be made independently of the culture in which the issue arises

Exchange is the act of obtaining a desired object from someone by offering something in return

An **executive information system** provides those at the top of the organisation with easy access to timely and relevant information

Existence needs reflect a person's requirement for material and energy

Expectancy theory argues that motivation depends on a person's belief in the probability that effort will lead to good performance, and that good performance will lead to them receiving an outcome they value (valence)

The **external environment (or context)** consists of elements beyond the organisation – it combines the competitive and general environments

External fit is when there is a close and consistent relationship between an organisation's competitive strategy and its HRM strategy

An **extranet** is a version of the internet that is restricted to specified people in specified companies – usually customers or suppliers

Extrinsic rewards are valued outcomes or benefits provided by others, such as promotion, a pay increase or a bigger car

Factory production is a process-based system that breaks down the integrated nature of the craft worker's approach and makes it possible to increase the supply of goods by dividing tasks into simple and repetitive processes and sequences that could be done by unskilled workers and machinery on a single site

Feedback (in systems theory) refers to the provision of information about the effects of an activity

Feedback (in communication) occurs as the receiver expresses his or her reaction to the sender's message

Femininity pertains to societies in which social gender roles overlap

Five forces analysis is a technique for identifying and listing those aspects of the five forces most relevant to the profitability of an organisation at that time

Fixed (long-term) assets are the physical properties that the company possesses – such as land, buildings, production equipment – which are likely to have a useful life of more than one year. There may also be intangible assets such as patent rights or copyrights

A **focus strategy** is when a company competes by targeting very specific segments of the market

Foreign direct investment (FDI) is the practice of investing shareholder funds directly in another country, by building or buying physical facilities, or by buying a company

Formal authority is the right that a person in a specified role has to make decisions, allocate resources or give instructions

Formalisation is the practice of using written or electronic documents to direct and control employees

Formal structure consists of guidelines, documents or procedures setting out how the organisation's activities are divided and coordinated

A **formal team** is one that management has deliberately created to perform specific tasks to help meet organisational goals

Franchising is the practice of extending a business by giving other organisations, in return for a fee, the right to use your brand name, technology or product specifications

Functional managers are responsible for the performance of an area of technical or professional work

A **functional structure** is when tasks are grouped into departments based on similar skills and expertise

The **general environment (or context)** (sometimes known as the macro-environment) includes political, economic, social, technological, (natural) environmental and legal factors that affect all organisations

General managers are responsible for the performance of a distinct unit of the organisation

Global companies work in many countries, securing resources and finding markets in whichever country is most suitable

Globalisation refers to the increasing integration of internationally dispersed economic activities

A **goal (or objective)** is a desired future state for an activity or organisational unit

Goal-setting theory argues that motivation is influenced by goal difficulty, goal specificity and knowledge of results

Groupthink is 'a mode of thinking that people engage in when they are deeply involved in a cohesive in-group, when the members' striving for unanimity overrides their motivation to realistically appraise alternative courses of action' (Janis, 1972)

Growth needs are those that impel people to be creative or to produce an effect on themselves or their environment

Heuristics are simple rules or mental short-cuts that simplify making decisions

High-context cultures are those in which information is implicit and can only be fully understood by those with shared experiences in the culture

High-performance work practices (HPWP) refer to systems in which a bundle of practices are integrated to encourage employees to identify with organisational goals, and to encourage them to meet those goals

Horizontal specialisation is the degree to which tasks are divided among separate people or departments

Human relations approach is a school of management that emphasises the importance of social processes at work

Human resource management (HRM) refers to all those activities associated with the management of work and people in organisations

Hygiene (or maintenance) factors are those aspects surrounding the task that can prevent discontent and dissatisfaction but will not in themselves contribute to psychological growth and hence motivation

An **ideology** is a set of integrated beliefs, theories and doctrines that helps to direct the actions of a society

The **illusion of control** is a source of bias resulting from the tendency to overestimate one's ability to control activities and events

People use an **incremental model** of decision making when they are uncertain about the consequences. They search for a limited range of options, and policy unfolds from a series of cumulative small decisions

Incremental innovations are small changes in a current product or process that bring a minor improvement

Individualism pertains to societies in which the ties between individuals are loose

Influence is the process by which one party attempts to modify the behaviour of others by mobilising power resources

An **informal group** is one that emerges when people come together and interact regularly

Informal structure is the undocumented relationships between members of the organisation that emerge as people adapt systems to new conditions and satisfy personal and group needs

Information comes from data that has been processed so that it has meaning for the person receiving it

Information overload arises when the amount of information a person has to deal with exceeds their capacity to process it

Information richness refers to the amount of information that a communication channel can carry, and the extent to which it enables sender and receiver to achieve common understanding

Information systems management is the planning, acquisition, development and use of these systems

Initiating structure is a pattern of leadership behaviour that emphasises the performance of the work in hand and the achievement of production or service goals

Innovation is the application or implementation of something new and useful

An **input measure** is an element of resource that is measured as it is put in to the transformation process

Instrumentality is the perceived probability that good performance will lead to valued rewards, measured on a scale from 0 (no chance) to 1 (certainty)

The **internal environment (or context)** consists of those elements of the organisation or unit within which a manager works, such as people, culture, structure and technology

An **intranet** is a version of the internet that only specified people within an organisation can use

Intangible resources are non-physical assets such as information, reputation and knowledge

Integration is the process of achieving unity of effort among the various subsystems in the accomplishment of the organisation's task

The **interaction model** is a theory of change that stresses the continuing interaction between the internal and external contexts of an organisation, making the outcomes of change hard to predict

Internal fit is when the various components of the HRM strategy support each other and consistently encourage certain attitudes and behaviour

International management is the practice of managing business operations in more than one country

The **internet** is a web of hundreds of thousands of computer networks linked together by telephone lines and satellite links through which data can be carried

Intrinsic rewards are valued outcomes or benefits that come from the individual, such as feelings of satisfaction, achievement and competence

Job analysis is the process of determining the characteristics of an area of work according to a prescribed set of dimensions

Job characteristics theory predicts that the design of a job will affect internal motivation and work outcomes, with the effects being mediated by individual and contextual factors

A **joint venture** is an alliance in which the partners agree to form a separate, independent organisation for a specific business purpose

Just-in-time inventory systems schedule materials to arrive precisely when they are needed on a production line

Key performance indicators are a summarised set of the most important measures that inform managers how well an operation is achieving organisational goals

Knowledge builds on information and embodies a person's prior understanding, experience and learning

Knowledge management systems are a type of IS intended to support people as they create, store, transfer and apply knowledge

Layout planning is the activity that determines the best configuration of resources, such as equipment, infrastructure and people, that will produce the most efficient process

Leadership refers to the process of influencing the activities of others towards high levels of goal setting and achievement

A **learning organisation** is one that has developed the capacity to continuously learn, adapt and change

Liabilities of a business, as reported in the balance sheet, are the debts and financial obligations of the business to all those people and institutions that are not shareholders, e.g. a bank, suppliers

Licensing is when one firm gives another firm the right to use assets such as patents or technology in exchange for a fee

Lifecycle models of change are those that view change as an activity that follows a logical, orderly sequence of activities that can be planned in advance

A **limited liability company** has an identity and existence in its own right as distinct from its owners (shareholders in Europe, stockholders in North America). A shareholder has an ownership right in the company in which the shares are held

Line managers are responsible for the performance of activities that directly meet customers' needs

Linear systems are those in which an action leads to a predictable reaction

Low-context cultures are those where people are more psychologically distant so that information needs to be explicit if members are to understand it

Management is the activity of getting things done with the aid of people and other resources

Management as a distinct role develops when activities previously embedded in the work itself become the responsibility not of the employee, but of owners or their agents

Management as a universal human activity occurs whenever people take responsibility for an activity and consciously try to shape its progress and outcome

Management by objectives is a system in which managers and staff agree their objectives, and then measure progress towards them periodically

A **management information system** provides information and support for managerial decision making

A **manager** is someone who gets things done with the aid of people and other resources

A **market offering** is the combination of products, services, information or experiences that an enterprise offers to a market to satisfy a need or want

Market segmentation is the process of dividing markets comprising the heterogeneous needs of many consumers into segments comprising the homogeneous needs of smaller groups

Marketing is the process by which organisations create value for customers in order to receive value from them in return

The **marketing environment** consists of the actors and forces outside marketing that affect the marketing manager's ability to develop and maintain successful relationships with its target consumers

A **marketing information system** is the systematic process for the collection, analysis and distribution of marketing information

The **marketing mix** is the set of marketing tools – product, price, promotion and place – that an organisation uses to satisfy consumers' needs

Marketing orientation refers to an organisational culture that encourages people to behave in ways that offer high-value goods and services to customers

Masculinity pertains to societies in which social gender roles are clearly distinct

A **matrix structure** is when those doing a task report both to a functional and a project or divisional boss

A **mechanistic structure** means there is a high degree of task specialisation, people's responsibility and authority are closely defined and decision-making is centralised

The **message** is what the sender communicates

A **metaphor** is an image used to signify the essential characteristics of a phenomenon

Metcalfe's law states that the value of a network increases with the square of the number of users connected to the network

Mindfulness is the ability to pay attention in a reflective and creative way to cues in cross-cultural situations

A **mission statement** is a broad statement of an organisation's scope and purpose, aiming to distinguish it from similar organisations

A **model (or theory)** represents a complex phenomenon by identifying the major elements and relationships

Motivation refers to the forces within or beyond a person that arouse and sustain their commitment to a course of action

Motivator factors are those aspects of the work itself that Herzberg found influenced people to superior performance and effort

Multinational companies are managed from one country, but have significant production and marketing operations in many others

Needs are states of felt deprivation, reflecting biological and social influences

A **network structure** is when tasks required by one company are performed by other companies with expertise in those areas

Networking refers to behaviours that aim to build, maintain and use informal relationships (internal and external) that may help work-related activities

Networking refers to 'individuals' attempts to develop and maintain relationships with others [who] have the potential to assist them in their work or career' (Huczynski, 2004, p. 305)

Noise is anything that confuses, diminishes or interferes with communication

Non-linear systems are those in which small changes are amplified through many interactions with other variables so that the eventual effect is unpredictable

A **non-programmed (unstructured) decision** is a unique decision that requires a custom-made solution when information is lacking or unclear

Non-receptive contexts are those where the combined effects of features of the organisation (such as culture or technology) appear likely to hinder change

Non-verbal communication is the process of coding meaning through behaviours such as facial expression, gestures and body postures

Observation is the activity of concentrating on how a team works rather than taking part in the activity itself

An **office automation system** uses several systems to create, process, store and distribute information

Offshoring is the practice of contracting out activities to companies in other countries who can do the work more cost-effectively

Open innovation is based on the view that useful knowledge is widely distributed and that even the most capable R&D organisation must identify, connect to and draw upon external knowledge as a core process in innovation

An **open system** is one that interacts with its environment

Operational plans detail how the overall objectives are to be achieved, by specifying what senior management expects from specific departments or functions

Operational research is a scientific method of providing (managers) with a quantitative basis for decisions regarding the operations under their control

Operations management is the activities, decisions and responsibilities of managing the production and delivery of products and services

Operations strategy defines how the function will support the business strategy by ensuring the organisation has the resources and competences to meet market requirements

Optimism bias is a human tendency to see the future in a more positive light than is warranted by experience

An **organic structure** is one where people are expected to work together and to use their initiative to solve problems; job descriptions and rules are few and imprecise

An **organisation** is a social arrangement for achieving goals that create value

An **organisation chart** shows the main departments and senior positions in an organisation and the reporting relations between them

Organisation structure 'The structure of an organisation [is] the sum total of the ways in which it divides its labour into distinct tasks and then achieves co-ordination among them' (Mintzberg, 1979)

Organisational citizenship behaviours refer to things people do beyond the requirements of their task to help others and to make things run smoothly

Organisational change is a deliberate attempt to improve organisational performance by changing one or more aspects of the organisation, such as its technology, structure or business processes

Organisational performance is the accumulated results of all the organisation's work processes and activities

Organisational readiness refers to the extent to which staff are able to specify objectives, tasks and resource requirements of a plan appropriately, leading to acceptance

An **output measure** is a measurement taken after an operational process is complete

Outsourcing refers to the practice of delegating selected value-chain activities to an external provider

The **participative model** is the belief that if people are able to take part in planning a change, they will be more willing to accept and implement that change

A **perceived performance gap** arises when people believe that the actual performance of a unit or business is out of line with the level they desire

Perceived organisational support (POS) refers to the beliefs an employee has about the treatment they receive, irrespective of promises made by the organisation

Perception is the active psychological process in which stimuli are selected and organised into meaningful patterns

Performance measurement refers to quantifying the efficiency and effectiveness of an action

Performance imperatives are aspects of performance that are especially important for an organisation to do well, such as flexibility and innovation

Performance-related-pay involves the explicit link of financial reward to performance and contributions to the achievement of organisational objectives

A **person culture** is one in which activity is strongly influenced by the wishes of the individuals who are part of the organisation

A **personality test** is a sample of attributes obtained under standardised conditions that applies specific scoring rules to obtain quantitative information for those attributes that the test is designed to measure

Pervasiveness (of corruption) represents the extent to which a firm is likely to encounter corruption in the course of normal transactions with state officials

PESTEL analysis is a technique for identifying and listing the political, economic, socio-cultural, technological, environmental and legal factors in the general environment most relevant to an organisation

Philanthropy is the practice of contributing personal or corporate wealth to charitable or similar causes

Planning is the iterative task of setting goals, specifying how to achieve them, implementing the plan and evaluating the results

A **policy** is a guideline that establishes some general principles for making a decision

Political behaviour is 'the practical domain of power in action, worked out through the use of techniques of influence and other (more or less extreme) tactics' (Buchanan and Badham, 1999)

Political models reflect the view that an organisation consists of groups with different interests, goals and values, which affect how they act

Political risk is the risk of losing assets, earning power or managerial control due to political events or the actions of host governments

Power is the ability to produce intended effects (attributed to Sir Bertrand Russell)

A **power culture** is one in which people's activities are strongly influenced by a dominant central figure

Power distance is the extent to which the less powerful members of organisations within a country expect and accept that power is distributed unevenly

Preferred team roles are the types of behaviour that people display relatively frequently when they are part of a team

Prior hypothesis bias results from a tendency to base decisions on strong prior beliefs, even if the evidence shows that they are wrong

A **procedure** is a series of related steps to deal with a structured problem

A **process control system** monitors and controls variables describing the state of a physical process

A **process measure** is a measurement taken during an operational process that provides data on how the process is performing

The **product life cycle** suggests that products pass through the stages of introduction, growth, maturity and decline

A **profit and loss statement** reflects the benefits derived from the trading activities of the business during a period of time

A **programmed (or structured) decision** is a repetitive decision that can be handled by a routine approach

Project managers are responsible for managing a project, usually intended to change some element of an organisation or its context

A **psychological contract** is the set of understandings people have regarding the commitments made between themselves and their organisation

Radical innovations are large, game-changing developments that alter the competitive landscape

The **range of variation** sets the acceptable limits within which performance can vary from standard without requiring remedial action

The **rational model of decision making** assumes that people make consistent choices to maximise economic value within specified constraints

Real goals are those to which people give most attention

Receptive contexts are those where features of the organisation (such as culture or technology) appear likely to help change

Reintermediation involves creating intermediaries between customers and suppliers, providing services such as price comparison and product evaluation

Relatedness needs involve a desire for relationships with significant other people

Relational resources are intangible resources available to a firm from its interaction with the environment

Representativeness bias results from a tendency to generalise inappropriately from a small sample or a single vivid event

Responsibility refers to a person's duty to meet the expectations others have of them in their role

Risk refers to situations in which the decision maker is able to estimate the likelihood of the alternative outcomes

A **role** is the sum of the expectations that others have about the responsibilities of a person occupying a position

A **role culture** is one in which people's activities are strongly influenced by clear and detailed job descriptions and other formal signals as to what is expected of them

A **rule** sets out what someone can or cannot do in a given situation

Satisficing is the acceptance by decision makers of the first solution that is 'good enough'

Scenario planning is an attempt to create coherent and credible alternative stories about the future

Scientific management is a school of thought that attempted to create a science of factory production

Selective attention is the ability, often unconscious, to choose from the stream of signals in the environment, concentrating on some and ignoring others

Self-awareness refers to a person's understanding of their preferred reaction to people and situations

A **self-managing team** operates without an internal manager and is responsible for a complete area of work

Shared value is creating economic value in a way that also creates value for society by addressing its needs and challenges

Shareholders are the principal risk takers in a company; they contribute the long-term capital for which they expect to be rewarded in the form of dividends – a distribution from the profit of the business

Shareholders' funds are the capital contributed by the shareholders plus profits that have not been distributed to the shareholders

Social networking sites use internet technologies that enable people to interact within an online community to share information and ideas

A **socio-technical system** is one in which outcomes depend on the interaction of both the technical and social subsystems

A **span of control** is the number of subordinates reporting directly to the person above them in the hierarchy

The **span of processes** is the variety of processes that a company chooses to carry out in-house

Staff managers are responsible for the performance of activities that support line managers

Stakeholders are individuals, groups or organisations with an interest in, or who are affected by, what the organisation does

Standard of performance is the defined level of performance to be achieved against which an operation's actual performance is compared

Stated goals are those that are prominent in company publications and websites

Stereotyping is the practice of consigning a person to a category or personality type on the basis of their membership of some known group

Strategic misrepresentation is where competition for resources leads planners to underestimate costs and overestimate benefits, to increase the likelihood that their project gains approval

Strategic capabilities are the capabilities of an organisation that contribute to its long-term survival or competitive advantage

A **strategic plan** sets out the overall direction for the business, is broad in scope and covers all the major activities

A **strategic business unit** consists of a number of closely related products for which it is meaningful to formulate a separate strategy

Strategy is about how people decide to organise major resources to enhance performance of an enterprise

Structural choice emphasises the scope that management has to decide the form of structure, irrespective of environmental conditions

Structure is the regularity in the way a unit or group is organised, such as the roles that are specified

Subjective probability (in expectancy theory) is a person's estimate of the likelihood that a certain level of effort (E) will produce a level of performance (P), which will then lead to an expected outcome (O)

Subsystems are the separate but related parts that make up the total system

Supply chain management refers to managing the sequence of suppliers providing goods and services so that the independent organisations work collaboratively for mutual gain

Sustainability refers to economic activities that meet the needs of the present population while preserving the environment for the needs of future generations

A **SWOT analysis** is a way of summarising the organisation's strengths and weaknesses relative to external opportunities and threats

A **system** is a set of interrelated parts designed to achieve a purpose

A **system boundary** separates the system from its environment

Tangible resources are the physical assets of an organisation such as plant, people and finance

A **target market** is the segment of the market selected by the organisation as the focus of its activities

A **task culture** is one in which the focus of activity is towards completing a task or project using whatever means are appropriate

A **team** is 'a small number of people with complementary skills who are committed to a common purpose, performance goals, and approach for which they hold themselves mutually accountable' (Katzenbach and Smith, 1993)

Team-based rewards are payments or non-financial incentives provided to members of a formally established team and linked to the performance of the group

Technology is the knowledge, equipment and activities used to transform inputs into outputs

The **theory of absolute advantage** is a trade theory that proposes that by specialising in producing goods and services that they can produce more efficiently than others, and then trading them, nations will increase their economic wealth

Total quality management (TQM) is a philosophy of management that is driven by customer needs and expectations and focuses on continually improving work processes

A **trait** is a relatively stable aspect of an individual's personality, which influences behaviour in a particular direction

A **transaction** occurs when two parties exchange things of value to each other at a specified time and place

A **transaction processing system (TPS)** records and processes data from routine transactions such as payroll, sales or purchases

A **transactional leader** is one who treats leadership as an exchange, giving followers what they want if they do what the leader desires

The **transformation process** is the operational system that takes all of the inputs (raw materials, information, facilities, capital and people) and converts them into an output product to be delivered to the market

A **transformational leader** is a leader who treats leadership as a matter of motivation and commitment, inspiring followers by appealing to higher ideals and moral values

Transnational companies operate in many countries and delegate many decisions to local managers

The **triple bottom line** is the idea that organisations can assess their performance on social and environmental criteria as well as financial ones

Uncertainty is when people are clear about their goals, but have little information about which course of action is most likely to succeed

Uncertainty avoidance is the extent to which members of a culture feel threatened by uncertain or unknown situations

Unique resources are resources that are vital to competitive advantage, and which others cannot obtain

User-generated content (UGC) is text, visual or audio material that users create and place on a website for others to view

Valence is the perceived value or preference that an individual has for a particular outcome

Validity occurs when there is a statistically significant relationship between a predictor (such as a selection test score) and measures of on-the-job performance

Value is added to resources when they are transformed into goods or services that are worth more than their original cost plus the cost of transformation

A **value chain** 'divides a firm into the discrete activities it performs in designing, producing, marketing and distributing its product. It is the basic tool for diagnosing competitive advantage and finding ways to enhance it'. (Porter, 1985)

Vertical specialisation refers to the extent to which responsibilities at different levels are defined

Virtual teams are those in which the members are physically separated, using communications technologies to collaborate across space and time to accomplish their common task

Wants are the form that human needs take as they are shaped by local culture and individual personality

Wikinomics describes a business culture in which customers are no longer only consumers but also co-creators and co-producers of the service

A **work breakdown structure** is a system for categorising work activity based on phases or packages of work rather than the responsibility of the function that is performing the work

A **working group** is a collection of individuals who work mainly on their own but interact socially and share information and best practices

Work–life balance refers to the experience of satisfaction and good functioning at work and at home.

REFERENCES

Adair, J. (1997), *Leadership Skills,* Chartered Institute of Personnel and Development, London.

Adams, J.S. (1963), 'Towards an understanding of inequity', *Journal of Abnormal and Social Psychology,* vol. 67, no. 4, pp. 422–36.

Adler, P.S. and Borys, B. (1996), 'Two types of bureaucracy: Enabling and coercive', *Administrative Science Quarterly,* vol. 41, no. 4, pp. 422–36.

Akkermanns, H.A. and van Oorschot, K.E. (2005), 'Relevance assumed: a case study of balanced scorecard development using system dynamics', *Journal of the Operational Research Society,* vol. 56, no. 8, pp. 931–41.

Alderfer, C. (1972), *Existence, Relatedness and Growth: Human needs in organisational settings,* Free Press, New York.

Alexander, D. and Nobes, C. (2013), *Financial Accounting: An International Introduction,* Financial Times/Prentice Hall, Harlow.

Alvarez, S.A. and Barney, J.B. (2005), 'How do entrepreneurs organise firms under conditions of uncertainty?', *Journal of Management,* vol. 31, no. 5, pp. 776–93.

Amabile, T.M., Conti, R., Coon, H., Lazenby, J. and Herron, M. (1996), 'Assessing the work environment for creativity', *Academy of Management Journal,* vol. 39, no. 5, pp. 1154–84.

Amaral, L.A.N. and Uzzi, B. (2007), 'Complex systems: A new paradigm for the integrative study of management, physical, and technological systems', Management Science, vol. 53, no. 7, pp. 1033–5.

Ambec, S. and Lanoie, P. (2008), 'Does it pay to be green? A systematic overview', *Academy of Management Perspectives,* vol. 22, no. 4, pp. 45–62.

Ambos, T.C. and Birkinshaw, J. (2010), 'How do new ventures evolve? An inductive study of archetype changes in science-based ventures', *Organisational Science,* vol. 21, no. 6, pp. 1125–40.

Anderson, C., Spataro, S.E. and Flynn, F.J. (2008), 'Personality and organisational culture as determinants of influence', *Journal of Applied Psychology,* vol. 93, no. 3, pp. 702–10.

Andrews, R. and Boyne, G. (2012), 'Structural change and public service performance: the impact of the reorganisation process in English local government', *Public Administration,* vol. 90, no. 2, pp. 297–312.

Ansoff, H.I. (1965), *Corporate Strategy,* Penguin, London.

Antorini, Y.M., Muniz, A.M. and Askildsen, T. (2012), 'Collaboration with customer communities: lessons from the Lego Group', *MIT Sloan Management Review,* vol. 53, no. 3, pp. 73–9.

Argenti, P.A., Howell, R.A. and Beck, K.A. (2005), 'The strategic communication imperative', *MIT Sloan Management Review,* vol. 46, no. 3, pp. 83–9.

Argyris, C. (1999), *On Organisational Learning,* (2nd edn) Blackwell, Oxford.

Arnolds, C.A. and Boshoff, C. (2002), 'Compensation, esteem valence and job performance: an empirical assessment of Alderfer's ERG theory', *International Journal of Human Resource Management,* vol. 13, no. 4, pp. 697–719.

Ashkenas, R., Ulrich, D., Jick, T. and Kerr, S. (2002), *The Boundaryless Organisation: Breaking the Chains of Organisational Structure,* (3rd edn) Jossey-Bass, San Francisco.

Atkinson, A.A, Kaplan, R.S., Matsumara, E.M. and Young, M.S. (2007), *Management Accounting* (6th edn), Financial Times/Prentice Hall, Harlow.

Babbage, C. (1835), *On the Economy of Machinery and Manufactures,* Charles Knight, London. Reprinted in 1986 by Augustus Kelly, Fairfield, NJ.

Badia, E. (2009), *Zara and her Sisters: The Story of the World's Largest Clothing Retailer,* Palgrave Macmillan, Basingstoke.

Baird, K., Hu, K.J. and Reeve, R. (2011), 'The relationships between organisational culture, total quality management practices and operational performance', *International Journal of Operations and Production Management,* vol. 31, no. 7, pp.789–814.

Barkema, H.G., Xiao-Ping, C., Gerard, G., Yadong, L., and Tsui, A.S. (2015), 'West meets East: New concepts and theories', *Academy of Management Journal,* vol. 58, no. 2, pp. 460–79.

Barker, J.R. (1993), 'Tightening the iron cage: Concertive control in self-managing teams', *Administrative Science Quarterly,* vol. 38, no. 3, pp. 408–37.

Barringer, B.R. and Ireland, R.D. (2010), *Entrepreneurship: Successfully Launching New Ventures,* Pearson Prentice-Hall, Upper Saddle River, NJ.

Barrows, E. and Neely, A. (2012), *Managing Performance in Turbulent Times: Analytics and Insight,* John Wiley & Sons, Hoboken, N.J.

Baron, R.A. and Greenberg, J. (1997) *Behaviour in Organisations,* Pearson Education, Upper Saddle River, NJ.

Barsoux, J. and Narasimhan, A. (2012), *Restoring the British Museum,* Case No. IMD – 3 – 2230, published by IMD, Geneva.

Barthélemy, J. (2006), 'The experimental roots of revolutionary vision', *MIT Sloan Management Review,* vol. 48, no. 1, pp. 81–4.

Bartlett, C.A. and Ghoshal, S. (2002), *Managing Across Borders: The Transnational Solution,* Harvard Business School Press, Boston, MA.

Baum, J.R. and Locke, E.A. (2004), 'The relationship of entrepreneurial traits, skill and motivation to subsequent venture growth', *Journal of Applied Psychology,* vol. 89, no. 4, pp. 587–98.

Beardwell, J. and Thompson, A. (2014), *Human Resource Management: A Contemporary Approach,* (7th edition) FT/Prentice Hall, Harlow.

Bechky, B.A. and Okhuysen, G.A. (2011), 'Expecting the unexpected? How SWAT officers and film crews handle surprises', *Academy of Management Journal,* vol. 54, no. 2, pp. 239–61.

Bechet, T.P. and Maki, W.R. (1987), 'Modelling and forecasting focusing on people as a strat resource', *Human Resource Planning,* vol. 10, no. 4, pp. 209–17.

Beer, M., Spector, B., Lawrence, P.R., Quinn Mills, D. and Walton, R.E. (1984), *Managing Human Assets,* Macmillan, New York.

Beer, M. and Cannon, M.D. (2004), 'Promise and peril in implementing pay-for-performance', *Human Resource Management,* vol. 43, no. 1, pp. 3–48.

Belbin, R.M. (1981), *Management Teams: Why they succeed or fail,* Butterworth/Heinemann, Oxford.

Belbin, R.M. (2010), *Team Roles at Work,* (2nd edition) Butterworth/Heinemann, Oxford.

Bennis, W. and Nanus, B. (2003), *Leaders: Strategies for Taking Charge,* HarperCollins, New York.

Berle, A.A. and Means, G.C. (1932), *The Modern Corporation and Private Property*, The Macmillan Company, New York.

Berlo, D.K. (1960), *The Process of Communication: An introduction to theory and practice,* Holt, Rinehart & Winston, New York.

Berners-Lee, T. (1999), *Weaving the Web,* Orion, London.

Bernoff, J. and Li, C. (2008), 'Harnessing the power of the oh-so-social web', *MIT Sloan Management Review,* vol. 49, no. 3, pp. 36–42.

Biggs, L. (1996), *The Rational Factory,* The Johns Hopkins University Press, Baltimore, MD.

Blackwell, E. (2008), *How to Prepare a Business Plan,* Kogan Page, London.

Blake, R.R. and Mouton, J.S. (1979), *The New Managerial Grid,* Gulf Publishing, Houston, TX.

Blakstad, M. and Cooper, A. (1995), *The Communicating Organisation,* Institute of Personnel and Development, London.

Bloom, N., Sadun, R. and Van Reenen, J. (2012), 'Does management really work?', *Harvard Business Review,* vol. 90, no. 11, pp. 76–82.

Boddy, D. (2002), *Managing Projects: Building and leading the team,* Financial Times Prentice Hall, Harlow.

Boddy, D. and Paton, R.A. (2005), 'Maintaining alignment over the long-term: lessons from the evolution of an electronic point of sale system', *Journal of Information Technology,* vol. 20, no. 3, pp. 141–51.

Boddy, D., Boonstra, A., and Kennedy, G. (2009a), *Managing Information Systems: Strategy and Organisation,* (3rd edition) Financial Times/Prentice Hall, Harlow.

Boddy, D., King, G., Clark, J.S., Heaney, D. and Mair, F. (2009b), 'The influence of context and process when implementing e-health', *BMC Medical Informatics and Decision Making,* vol. 9, no. 9.

Boiral, O. (2007), 'Corporate greening through ISO 14001', *Organisation Science,* vol. 18, no. 1, pp. 127–46.

Boisot, M.H. (1998) *Knowledge Assets: Securing competitive advantage in the information economy,* Oxford University Press, Oxford.

Bond, S.D., Carlson, K.A. and Keeney, R.L. (2008), 'Generating objectives: Can decision makers articulate what they want?', *Management Science,* vol. 54, no. 1, pp. 56–70.

Bondy, K. and Starkey, K., (2014), 'The dilemmas of internationalisation: Corporate social responsibility in the multinational corporation', *British Journal of Management,* vol. 25, no. 1, pp. 4–22.

Boonstra, A. and Govers, M.J.G. (2009), 'Understanding ERP system implementation in a hospital by analysing stakeholders', *New Technology, Work and Employment,* vol. 24, no. 2, pp. 177–93.

Bozarth, C. (2006), 'ERP implementation efforts at three firms', *International Journal of Operations & Production Management,* vol. 26, no. 11, pp. 1223–39.

Bremmer, I. (2014), 'The new rules of globalisation', *Harvard Business Review,* vol. 92, no. 1/2, pp. 103–7.

Brinckmann, J., Grichnik, D. and Kapsa, D. (2010), 'Should entrepreneurs plan or just storm the castle? A meta-analysis on contextual factors impacting the business planning–performance relationship in small firms', *Journal of Business Venturing,* vol. 25, no. 1, pp. 24–40.

Brookfield, S.D. (1987), *Developing Critical Thinkers,* Open University Press, Milton Keynes.

Buchanan, D. and Badham, R. (1999), *Power, Politics and Organisational Change: Winning the turf game,* Sage, London.

Buchanan, D.A. (2008), 'You stab my back, I'll stab yours: Management experience and perceptions of organisation political behaviour', *British Journal of Management,* vol. 19, no. 1, pp. 49–64.

Burgers, J.H., Van Den Bosch, F.A.J. and Volberda, H.W. (2008), 'Why new business development projects fail: Coping with the differences of technological versus market knowledge', *Long Range Planning,* vol. 41, no. 1, pp. 55–73.

Burgess, N. and Currie, G. (2013), 'The knowledge brokering role of the hybrid middle level manager: The case of healthcare', *British Journal of Management,* vol. 24, supplement S1, pp. S132–42.

Burns, J.M. (1978), *Leadership,* Harper & Row, New York.

Burns, T. (1961), 'Micropolitics: mechanisms of organisational change', *Administrative Science Quarterly,* vol. 6, no. 3, pp. 257–81.

Burns, T. and Stalker, G.M. (1961), *The Management of Innovation,* Tavistock, London.

Burton, G. (2013), *Presenting: Deliver presentations with confidence,* Collins, London.

Byron, K. (2008), 'Carrying too heavy a load? The communication and miscommunication of emotions by email', *Academy of Management Review,* vol. 33, no. 2, pp. 309–27.

Cachon, G.P. and Swinney, R. (2011), 'The value of fast fashion: Quick response, enhanced design, and strategic consumer behaviour', *Management Science,* vol. 57, no. 4, pp. 778–95.

Cadbury, A. (1992), 'Report of the Committee on the Financial Aspects of Corporate Governance', Gee and Co. Ltd, London.

Caldwell, R. (2003), 'The changing roles of personnel managers: Old ambiguities, new uncertainties', *Journal of Management Studies,* vol. 40, no. 4, pp. 983–1004.

Canato, A., Ravasi, D. and Phillips, N. (2013), 'Coerced practice implementation in cases of low cultural fit: Cultural change and practice adaptation during the implementation of Six Sigma at 3M', *Academy of Management Journal,* vol. 56, no. 6, pp. 1724–53.

Carroll, A.B. and Buchholtz, A.K. (2015), *Business and Society: Ethics and Stakeholder Management,* (9th edition) Cengage Learning, Andover.

Carroll, A.B. (1999), 'Corporate social responsibility', *Business and Society,* vol. 38, no. 3, pp. 268–295.

Catmull, E. (2008), 'How Pixar fosters collective creativity', *Harvard Business Review,* vol. 86, no. 9, pp. 64–72.

Chamorro-Premuzic, T. (2015), 'Ace the assessment', *Harvard Business Review,* vol. 93, no. 7/8, pp. 118–121.

Chandler, A.D. (1962), *Strategy and Structure,* MIT Press, Cambridge, MA.

Chandra, A. and Kaiser, U. (2014), 'Targeted advertising in magazine markets and the advent of the internet,' *Management Science,* vol. 60, no. 7, pp. 1829–43.

Chesbrough, H., Vanhaverbeke, W. and West, J. (eds.) (2006), *Open Innovation: Researching a New Paradigm,* Oxford University Press, Oxford.

Child, J. and Tsai, T. (2005), 'The dynamic between firms' environmental strategies and institutional constraints in emerging economies: Evidence from China and Taiwan', *Journal of Management Studies,* vol. 42, no. 1, pp. 95–125.

Child, J., Chung, L. and Davies, H. (2003), 'The performance of cross-border units in China: a test of natural selection, strategic choice and contingency theories', *Journal of International Business Studies,* vol. 34, no. 3, pp. 242–54.

Child, J. (2005), *Organisation: Contemporary Principles and Practice,* Blackwell Publishing, Oxford.

Choi, J.N. and Moon, W.J. (2013), 'Multiple forms of innovation implementation: The role of innovation, individuals, and the implementation context', *Organisational Dynamics,* vol. 42, no. 4, pp. 290–7.

Christensen, C.M. and Raynor, M.E. (2003), *The Innovator's Solution: Creating and Sustaining Successful Growth,* Harvard Business School Press, Boston, Mass.

Chua, R.Y.J. (2013), 'The costs of ambient cultural disharmony: Indirect intercultural conflicts in social environment undermine creativity', *Academy of Management Journal,* vol. 56, no. 6, pp.1545–77.

Clissold, T. (2014), *Chinese Rules: Mao's Dog, Deng's Cat and Five Timeless Lessons from the Front Lines in China,* Harper Collins, London.

Coeurderoy, R., Cowling, M., Licht, G. and Murray, G. (2012), 'Young firm internationalisation and survival: Empirical tests on a panel of 'adolescent' new technology-based firms in Germany and the UK', *International Small Business Journal,* vol. 30, no. 5, pp. 472–92.

Coggan, P. (2002), *The Money Machine,* Penguin, Harmondsworth.

Cohen, M.D., March, J.G. and Olsen, J.P. (1972), 'Garbage can model of organisational choice', *Administrative Science Quarterly,* vol. 17, no. 1, pp. 1–25.

Colbert, A.E. and Witt, L.A. (2009), 'The role of goal-focused leadership in enabling the expression of conscientiousness', *Journal of Applied Psychology,* vol. 94, no. 3, pp. 790–6.

Coll, S. (2012), *Private Empire: ExxonMobil and American Power,* Allen Lane/Penguin, London.

Combs, J., Liu, Y., Hall, A. and Ketchen, D. (2006), 'How much do high-performance work practices matter? A meta-analysis of their effects on organisational performance', *Personnel Psychology,* vol. 59, no. 3, pp. 501–28.

Confederation of British Industry and Universities UK (2009), *Future Fit: Preparing Graduates for the World of Work,* CBI, London.

Conger, J.A. and Kanungo, R.N. (1994), 'Charismatic leadership in organisations: perceived behavioural attributes and their measurement', *Journal of Organisational Behaviour,* vol. 15, no. 5, pp. 439–52.

Cooke, S. and Slack, N. (1991), *Making Management Decisions* (2nd edition) Prentice Hall, Hemel Hempstead.

Corfield, R. (2009), *Successful Interview Skills,* Kogan Page, London.

Cornelius, P., Van de Putte, A. and Mattia, R. (2005), 'Three decades of scenario planning at Shell', *California Management Review,* vol. 48, no. 2, pp. 92–109.

Coutu, D. and Beschloss, M. (2009), 'Why teams DON'T work', an interview with J. Richard Hackman, *Harvard Business Review,* vol. 87, no. 5, pp. 98–105.

Crook, T.R., Todd, S.Y., Combs, J.G., Woehr, D.J. and Ketchen, D.J. (2011), 'Does human capital matter? A meta-analysis of the relationship between human capital and firm performance', *Journal of Applied Psychology,* vol. 96, no. 3, pp. 443–56.

Crosby, P. (1979), *Quality is Free,* McGraw-Hill, New York.

Crossley, C.D., Cooper, C.D. and Wernsing, T.S. (2013), 'Making things happen through challenging goals: Leader proactivity, trust, and business-unit performance', *Journal of Applied Psychology,* vol. 98, no. 3, pp.540–549.

Culbertson, S.S. (2009), 'Do satisfied employees mean satisfied customers?', *Academy of Management Perspectives,* vol. 23, no. 1, pp. 76–7.

Cyert, R. and March, J.G. (1963), *A Behavioural Theory of the Firm,* Prentice Hall, Englewood Cliffs, NJ.

Czarniawska, B. (2004), *Narratives in Social Science Research,* Sage, London.

Davenport, T.H. and Harris, J.G. (2005), 'Automated decision making comes of age', *MIT Sloan Management Review,* vol. 46, no. 4, pp.83–9.

Deal, T.E. and Kennedy, A.A. (1982), *Corporate Culture: The rites and rituals of corporate life,* Addison-Wesley, Reading, MA.

Deming, W.E. (1988), *Out of the Crisis,* Cambridge University Press, Cambridge.

Devinney, T.M. (2009), 'Is the socially responsible corporation a myth? The good, the bad, and the ugly of corporate social responsibility', *Academy of Management Perspectives,* vol. 23, no. 2, pp. 44–56.

de Rond, M. (2012), *There is an I in Team*, Harvard Business Review Press, Cambridge, MA.

de Wit, B. and Meyer, R. (2004). *Strategy: Process, Content and Context, an International Perspective,* International Thomson Business, London.

de Wit, B. and Meyer, R. (2010), *Strategy Synthesis: Resolving Strategy Paradoxes to Create Competitive Advantage* (concise edition), Cengage Learning, Andover.

Dimbleby, R. and Burton, G. (2006), *More Than Words: An introduction to communication*, (4th edition) Routledge, London.

Dixon, K.R. and Panteli, N. (2010), 'From virtual teams to virtuality in teams', *Human Relations,* vol. 63, no. 8, pp. 1177–97.

Doganis, R. (2006), *The Airline Business,* (2nd edition) Routledge, London.

Donaldson, L. (1996), *For Positivist Organization Theory,* Sage London.

Donaldson, L. (2001), *The Contingency Theory of Organizations,* Sage, London.

Donnelly, C., Simmons, G., Armstrong, G. and Fearne, A. (2015), 'Digital loyalty card 'big data' and small business marketing: Formal versus informal or complementary?' *International Small Business Journal,* vol. 33, no. 4, pp. 422–42.

Drucker, P.F. (1974 *Management: Tasks, Responsibilities, Practices*, Harper, New York.

Drucker, P.F. (1985), *Innovation and Entrepreneurship*, (2nd edition) Butterworth-Heinemann, Oxford.

Drummond, H. (1996), *Escalation in Decision-Making,* Oxford University Press, Oxford.

Duncan, R.B. (1972), 'Characteristics of organisational environments and perceived environmental uncertainty', *Administrative Science Quarterly,* vol. 17, no. 3, pp. 313–28.

Eccles, R.G., Ioannou, I., and Serafeim, G., (2014), 'The impact of corporate sustainability on organisational processes and performance', *Management Science,* vol. 60, no. 11, pp. 2835–57.

Edvardsson, B. and Enquist, B. (2009), *Values-based Service for Sustainable Business: Lessons from IKEA,* Routledge, London.

Edvardsson, B. and Enquist, B. (2002), 'The IKEA saga: How service culture drives service strategy', *Services Industries Journal,* vol. 22, no. 4, pp. 153–86.

Elberse, A. and Ferguson, A. (2013), 'Ferguson's formula', *Harvard Business Review,* vol. 91, no. 10, pp. 116–25.

Ellemers, N., Sleebos, E., Stam, D. and de Gilder, D. (2013), 'Feeling included and valued: How perceived respect affects positive team identity and willingness to invest in the team', *British Journal of Management,* vol. 24, no. 1, pp. 21–37.

Elliott, B. and Elliott, J. (2015), *Financial Accounting and Reporting*, (10th edition) Financial Times/Prentice Hall, Harlow.

Engau, C. and Hoffmann, V.H. (2011) 'Effects of regulatory uncertainty on corporate strategy – an analysis of firms' responses to uncertainty about post-Kyoto policy', *Environmental Science and Policy*.

Fabbe-Costes, N., Roussat, C., Taylor, M. and Taylor, A. (2014) 'Sustainable supply chains: a framework for environmental scanning practices', *International Journal of Operations and Production Management,* vol. 34, no. 5, pp. 664–94.

Farrell, C. and Morris, J. (2013), 'Managing the neo-bureaucratic organisation: lessons from the UK's prosaic sector', *International Journal of Human Resource Management,* vol. 24, no. 7, pp. 1376–92.

Fayol, H. (1949), *General and Industrial Management,* Pitman, London.

Feigenbaum, A.V. (1993), *Total Quality Control,* McGraw-Hill, New York.

Ferdows, K., Lewis, M.A. and Machuca, J.A.D. (2004), 'Rapid-fire fulfilment', *Harvard Business Review,* vol. 82, no. 11, pp. 104–10.

Fiedler, F.E. and House, R.J. (1994), 'Leadership theory and research: a report of progress', in C.L. Cooper and I.T. Robertson (eds.), *Key Reviews of Managerial Psychology,* Wiley, Chichester.

Financial Reporting Council (2006), *The Combined Code on Corporate Governance*, FRC, London.

Finkelstein, S. (2003), *Why Smart Executives Fail: and what you can learn from their mistakes,* Penguin, New York.

Finkelstein, S., Whitehead, J. and Campbell, A. (2009), 'How inappropriate attachments can drive good leaders to make bad decisions', *Organisational Dynamics,* vol. 38, no. 2, pp. 83–92.

Fleishman, E.A. (1953), 'The description of supervisory behaviour', *Journal of Applied Psychology,* vol. 37, no.1, pp. 1–6.

Flyvbjerg, B. (2008), 'Curbing optimism bias and strategic misrepresentation in planning: Reference class forecasting in practice', *European Planning Studies,* vol. 16, no. 1, pp. 3–21.

Flyvbjerg, B. and Budzier, A. (2011), 'Why your IT project may be riskier than you think', *Harvard Business Review,* vol. 89, no. 9, pp. 23–5.

Follett, M.P. (1920), *The New State: Group organisation, the solution of popular government,* Longmans Green, London.

Forbes, D.P., Borchert, P.S., Zellmer-Bruhn, M.E. and Sapienza, H.J. (2006), 'Entrepreneurial team formation: An exploration of new member addition', *Entrepreneurship: Theory & Practice,* vol. 30, no. 2, pp. 225–48.

Ford, R.C., Edvardsson, B., Dickson, D. and Enquist, B. (2012), 'Managing the innovation co-creation challenge: Lessons from service exemplars Disney and IKEA, *Organisational Dynamics,* vol. 41, no. 4, pp. 281–90.

Fox, A. (1974), *Man Mismanagement,* Hutchinson, London

Freeman, R.E. (1984), *Strategic Management: A Stakeholder Approach,* Pitman, Boston.

French, J. and Raven, B. (1959), 'The bases of social power', in D. Cartwright (ed.), *Studies in Social Power,* Institute for Social Research, Ann Arbour, MI.

Friedman, M. (1962), *Capitalism and Freedom,* University of Chicago Press, Chicago.

Friedman, T. (2005), *The World is Flat: A Brief History of the Globalised World in the 21st Century,* Penguin/Allen Lane, London.

Frow, P., Nenonen, S., Payne, A. and Storbacka, K. (2015), 'Managing co-creation design: A strategic approach to innovation', *British Journal of Management,* vol. 26, no. 3, pp. 463–83.

Fu, P.P. and Yukl, G. (2000), 'Perceived effectiveness of influence tactics in the United States and China', *Leadership Quarterly*, vol. 11, no. 2, pp. 252–66.

Furst, S.A., Reeves, M., Rosen, B. and Blackburn, R.S. (2004), 'Managing the life cycle of virtual teams', *Academy of Management Executive,* vol. 18, no. 2, pp. 6–20.

Gabriel, Y. (2005), 'Glass cages and glass palaces: Images of organisation in image-conscious times', *Organisation,* vol. 12, no. 1, pp. 9–27.

Gamble, J., Morris, J. and Wilkinson, B. (2004), 'Mass production is alive and well: the future of work and organisation in east Asia', *International Journal of Human Resource Management,* vol. 15, no. 2, pp. 397–409.

García-Morales, V.J., Lloréns-Montes, F.J. and Verdú-Jover, A.J. (2008), 'The effects of transformational leadership on organisational performance through knowledge and innovation', *British Journal of Management,* vol. 19, no. 4, pp. 299–319.

Garengo, P. and Bititci, U. (2007), 'Towards a contingency approach to performance measurement: an empirical study in SMEs', *International Journal of Operations and Production Management,* vol. 37, no. 8, pp. 802–25.

Garnier, J-P. (2008), 'Rebuilding the R&D engine in big pharma', *Harvard Business Review,* vol. 86, no. 5, pp. 68–76.

Garvin, D.A. (2013), 'How Google sold its engineers on management', *Harvard Business Review,* vol. 91, no. 12, pp. 74–82.

Gebhardt, G., Carpenter, G.S. and Sherry, J.F. (2007), 'Creating a market orientation', *Journal of Marketing,* vol. 70, no. 4, pp. 37–55.

Germain, D. and Reed, R. (2009), *a book about innocent*, Penguin, London.

Gilbreth, F.B. (1911), *Motion Study: A method for increasing the efficiency of the workman,* Van Norstrand, New York.

Gilbreth, L.M. (1914), *The Psychology of Management,* Sturgis & Walton, New York.

Glaister, S. and Travers, T. (2001), 'Crossing London: Overcoming the obstacles to CrossRail', *Public Money & Management,* vol. 21, no. 4, pp. 11–17.

Govindarajan, V. and Gupta, A.K. (2001), 'Building an effective global business team', *MIT Sloan Management Review,* vol. 42, no.4, pp. 63–71.

Graham, P. (1995), *Mary Parker Follett: Prophet of management,* Harvard Business School Press, Boston, MA.

Grant, R.M. (2003), 'Strategic planning in a turbulent environment: evidence from the oil majors', *Strategic Management Journal,* vol. 24, no. 6, pp. 491–517.

Gratton, L. (2011), *The Shift: The Future of Work is Already Here,* Collins, London.

Grey, C.F. and Larson, E.W. (2008), *Project Management: The management process,* McGraw-Hill/Irwin, New York.

Grey, R. (1993), *Accounting for the Environment,* Chapman, London.

Greenwood, R.G., Bolton, A.A. and Greenwood, R.A. (1983), 'Hawthorne a half century later: Relay assembly participants remember', *Journal of Management,* vol. 9, Fall/Winter, pp. 217–31.

Greve, H.R. (2010), 'Designing performance feedback systems to guide learning and manage risk', *Organisational Dynamics,* vol. 39, no. 2, pp. 104–14.

Grosser, T.J., Lopez-Kidwell, V., Labianca, G. and Ellwardt, L. (2012), 'Hearing it through the grapevine: Positive and negative workplace gossip', *Organisational Dynamics,* vol. 41, no. 1, pp. 52–61.

Gruber, M., de Leon, N., George, G. and Thompson, P. (2015), 'Managing by design', *Academy of Management Journal,* vol. 58, no. 1, pp. 1–7.

Guest, D.E. (1987), 'Human resource management and industrial relations', *Journal of Management Studies,* vol. 24, no. 5, pp. 502–21.

Guest, D.E. (2004), 'The Psychology of the employment relationship: An analysis based on the psychological contract', *Applied Psychology,* vol. 53, no. 4, pp. 541–55.

Guillaume, Y.R.F., Dawson, J.F., Woods, S.A., Sacramento, C.A. and West, M.A. (2013), 'Getting diversity at work to work: What we know and what we still don't know', *Journal of Occupational and Organisational Psychology,* vol. 86, no. 2, pp. 123–41.

Guler, I. (2007), 'Throwing good money after bad? Political and institutional influences on sequential decision making in the venture capital industry', *Administrative Science Quarterly,* vol. 52, no. 2, pp. 248–85.

Guthrie, D. (2006), *China and Globalisation: The Social, Economic and Political Transformation of Chinese Society,* Routledge, London.

Hackman, J.R. (1990), *Groups that Work (and Those that Don't),* Jossey-Bass, San Francisco, CA.

Hackman, J.R. and Oldham, G.R. (1980), *Work Redesign,* Addison-Wesley, Reading, MA.

Hales, C. (2001), *Managing Through Organisation,* Routledge, London.

Hales, C. (2005), 'Rooted in supervision, branching into management: Continuity and change in the role of first-line manager', *Journal of Management Studies,* vol. 42, no. 3, pp. 471–506.

Hall, E. (1976), B*eyond Culture,* Random House, New York, NJ.

Hallen, B.L. and Eisenhardt, K.M. (2012), 'Catalysing strategies and efficient tie formation: How entrepreneurial firms obtain investment ties', *Academy of Management Journal,* vol. 55, no. 1, pp. 35–70.

Hamm, S. (2007), *Bangalore Tiger,* McGraw-Hill, New York.

Handy, C. (1993), *Understanding Organisations*, (4th edition) Penguin, Harmondsworth.

Hassard, J.S. (2012), 'Rethinking the Hawthorne Studies: The Western Electric research in its social, political and historical context', *Human Relations,* vol. 65, no. 11, pp. 1431–61.

Harradine, D. and Prowle, M. (2012), 'Service line reporting in a National Health Service Foundation Trust: An initial assessment', *Public Money and Management,* vol. 32, no. 3, pp. 217–24.

Harrison, M. (2005), *Diagnosing Organisations: Methods, Models and Processes* (3rd edition), Sage, London.

Hartley, J. (2008) (ed.), *Managing to Improve Public Services,* Cambridge University Press, Cambridge.

Harvey, J.B. (1988), 'The Abilene Paradox: The management of agreement', *Organisational Dynamics,* vol. 17, no. 1, pp. 17–43.

Hawken, P., Lovins, A.B. and Lovins. L.H. (1999), *Natural Capitalism: The next industrial revolution,* Earthscan, London.

Hayes, R.H. and Wheelwright, S.C. (1979), 'Link manufacturing process and product lifecycles', *Harvard Business Review,* vol. 57, no. 1, pp. 133–40.

Healey, M.P., Hodgkinson, G.P., Whittington, R. and Johnson, G. (2015), 'Off to plan or out to lunch? Relationships between design characteristics and outcomes of strategy workshops', *British Journal of Management,* vol. 26, no. 3, pp. 507–28.

Heath, M.T.P. and Chatzidakis, A. (2012), 'Blame it on marketing': consumers' views on unsustainable consumption', *International Journal of Consumer Studies,* vol. 36, no. 6, pp. 656–67.

Heimans, J. and Timms, H. (2014), 'Understanding "new power"', *Harvard Business Review,* vol. 92, no. 12, pp. 48–56.

Hendy, D. (2013), *Public Service Broadcasting,* Palgrave Macmillan, Basingstoke.

Henriques, D.B. (2011), *Bernie Madoff: The Wizard of Lies,* Oneworld Publications, New York.

Heracleous, L. (2013), 'Quantum strategy at Apple Inc', *Organisational Dynamics,* vol. 42, no. 2, pp. 92–9.

Herzberg, F. (1959), *The Motivation to Work,* Wiley, New York.

Herzberg, F. (1968), 'One more time: how do you motivate employees?', *Harvard Business Review,* vol. 46, no. 1, pp. 53–62.

Higón. D.A. (2012), 'The impact of ICT on innovation activities: Evidence for UK SMEs', *International Small Business Journal,* vol. 30, no. 6, pp. 684–99.

Hill, C.W.L. and Jones, T.M. (1992), 'Stakeholder-Agency Theory', *Journal of Management Studies,* vol. 29, no. 2, pp. 131–54.

Hillman, A.J. (2005), 'Politicians on the board of directors: Do connections affect the bottom line?', *Journal of Management,* vol. 31, no. 3, pp. 464–81.

Hodgkinson, G.P., Whittington, R., Johnson, G. and Schwarz, M. (2006), 'The role of strategy workshops in strategy development processes: Formality, communication, co-ordination and inclusion', *Long Range Planning,* vol. 39, no. 5, pp. 479–96.

Hodgson, J. and Drummond, H. (2009), 'Learning from fiasco: what causes decision error and how to avoid it', *Journal of General Management,* vol. 35, no. 2, pp. 81–92.

Hofstede, G. (1989), 'Organising for cultural diversity', *European Management Journal,* vol. 7, no. 4, pp. 390–397.

Hofstede, G. (1991), *Cultures and Organisations: Software of the mind,* McGraw-Hill, London.

Hofstede, G. and Hofstede, G.J. (2005), *Cultures and Organisations: Software of the Mind,* (2nd edition) McGraw-Hill, New York.

Homburg, C., Jensen, O. and Krohmer, H. (2008), 'Configurations of marketing and sales: A taxonomy', *Journal of Marketing,* vol. 72, no. 2, pp. 133–54.

Homburg, C., Wieseke, J. and Bornemann, T. (2009), 'Implementing the marketing concept at the employee–customer interface: The role of customer need knowledge', *Journal of Marketing,* vol. 73, no. 4, pp. 64–81.

Horngren, C.T., Foster, G. and Datar, S.M. (2012), *Cost Accounting*, (14th edition) Financial Times/Prentice Hall, Harlow.

House, R.J. (1996), 'Path–goal theory of leadership: lessons, legacy and a reformulation', *Leadership Quarterly,* vol. 7, no. 3, pp. 323–52.

House, R.J., Hanges, P.J., Javidan, M., Dorfman, P.W. and Gupta, V. (2004), *Culture, Leadership and Organisations: The GLOBE study of 62 Societies,* Sage, Thousand Oaks, CA.

Huczynski, A.A. (2004), *Influencing Within Organisations*, (2nd edition) Routledge, London.

Humphrey, S.E, Nahrgang, J.D. and Morgeson, F.P. (2007), 'Integrating motivational, social, and contextual work design features: A meta-analytic summary and theoretical extension of the work design literature', *Journal of Applied Psychology,* vol. 92, no. 5, pp. 1332–56.

Ihrig, M. and Macmillan, I. (2015), 'Managing your mission-critical knowledge', *Harvard Business Review,* vol. 93, no. 1/2, pp. 80–7.

Isaacson, W. (2011), *Steve Jobs,* Little, Brown, London.

Iyengar, S.W. and Lepper, M.R. (2000), 'When choice is demotivating: can one desire too much of a good thing?', *Journal of Personality and Social Psychology,* vol. 79, no. 6, pp. 995–1006.

Iyer, B. and Davenport, T.H. (2008), 'Reverse engineering Google's innovation machine', *Harvard Business Review,* vol. 86, no. 4, pp. 58–68.

Jackson, L. (2014), 'Participating publics: Implications for production practices at the BBC' in Glowacki, M. and Jackson, L. (eds.), *Public Media Management for the 21st Century,* Routledge, London.

Janis, I.L. (1972), *Victim of Groupthink*, Houghton-Mifflin, Boston, MA.

Janis, I.L. (1977), *Decision Making: A psychological analysis of conflict, choice and commitment,* The Free Press, New York.

Javidan, M. and Bowen, D. (2013) 'The 'global mindset' of managers: What it is, why it matters, and how to develop it', *Organisational Dynamics,* vol. 42, no. 2, pp. 145–55.

Jiang, K., Lepak, D.P., Jia J. and Baer, J.C. (2012) 'How does Human Resource Management Influence Organisational Outcomes? A Meta-Analytic investigation of mediating mechanisms', *Academy of Management Journal*, vol. 55, no. 6, pp. 1264–294.

Johns, G. (2006), 'The essential impact of context on organisational behaviour', *Academy of Management Review,* vol. 31, no. 2, pp. 386–408.

Johnson, G. and Tellis, G.J. (2008), 'Drivers of success for market entry into China and India', *Journal of Marketing,* vol. 72, no. 1, pp. 1–13.

Johnson, G., Whittington, R., Scholes, K., Angwin, D. and Regner, P. (2014), *Exploring Strategy,* (10th edition) Pearson, Harlow.

Johnson, S. (2010), *Where Good Ideas Come From: the Natural History of Innovation,* Riverhead Books, New York.

Johnson, G., Langley, A., Melin, L. and Whittington, R. (2007), *Strategy as Practice: Research Directions and Resources,* Cambridge University Press, Cambridge.

Jones, D.A., Willness, C.R. and Madey, S. (2014), 'Why are job seekers attracted by corporate social performance? Experimental and field tests of three signal-based mechanisms', *Academy of Management Journal,* vol. 57, no. 2, pp. 383–404.

Jones, O. (2000), 'Scientific management, culture and control: a first-hand account of Taylorism in practice', *Human Relations,* vol. 53, no. 5, pp. 631–53.

Jones, R. and Rowley, J. (2011), 'Entrepreneurial marketing in small businesses: A conceptual exploration', *International Small Business Journal,* vol. 29, no. 1, pp. 25–36.

Jones, R.A., Jimmieson, N.L. and Griffiths, A. (2005), 'The impact of organisational culture and reshaping capabilities on change implementation success: The mediating role of readiness for change', *Journal of Management Studies,* vol. 42, no. 2, pp. 361–86.

Jønsson, T. and Jeppesen, H.J. (2013), 'Under the influence of the team? An investigation of the relationship between team autonomy, individual autonomy and social influence within teams', *International Journal of Human Resource Management,* vol. 24, no. 1, pp. 78–93.

Judge, T.A., Piccolo, R.F. and Ilies, R. (2004), 'The forgotten ones? The validity of consideration and initiating structure in leadership research', *Journal of Applied Psychology,* vol. 89, no. 1, pp. 36–51.

Juran, J. (1974), *Quality Control Handbook,* McGraw-Hill, New York.

Kahneman, D. (2011), *Thinking, Fast and Slow,* Penguin/Allen Lane, London.

Kaplan, S. (2011), 'Strategy and PowerPoint: An inquiry into the epistemic culture and machinery of strategy making', *Organisation Science,* vol. 22, no. 2, pp. 320–46.

Kalb, K., Cherry, N., Kauzloric, R., Brender, A., Green, K., Miyagawa, L. and Shinoda-Mettler, A. (2006), 'A competency-based approach to public health nursing performance appraisal', *Public Health Nursing,* vol. 23, no. 2, pp. 115–124.

Kanter, R.M. (1979), 'Power failure in management circuits', *Harvard Business Review,* vol. 57, no. 4, pp. 65–75.

Kaplan, R.S. and Norton, D.P. (1992), 'The Balanced Scorecard – Measures that Drive Performance', *Harvard Business Review,* vol. 70, no.1, pp. 71–9.

Kaplan, R.S. and Norton, D.P. (2004), *Strategy Maps: converting intangible assets to tangible outcomes,* Harvard Business School Press, Boston, MA.

Kaplan, R.S. and Norton, D.P. (2008), *The Execution Premium: linking strategy to operations for competitive advantage,* Harvard Business School Press, Boston, MA.

Katzenbach, J.R. and Smith, D.K. (1993), *The Wisdom of Teams,* Harvard Business School Press, Boston, MA.

Kaynak, H. (2003), 'The relationship between total quality management practices and their effects on firm performance, *Journal of Operations Management,* vol. 21, no. 4, pp. 405–435.

Kaynak, H. and Hartley, J.L. (2008) 'A replication and extension of quality management into the supply chain', *Journal of Operations Management,* vol. 26, no. 4, pp. 468–89.

Keaveney, P. and Kaufmann, M. (2001), *Marketing for the Voluntary Sector,* Kogan Page, London.

Kelman, H.C. (1961), 'Processes of Opinion Change', *Public Opinion Quarterly,* vol. 25, no. 1, pp. 57–78.

Kennedy, G., Boddy, D. and Paton, R. (2006), 'Managing the aftermath: lessons from The Royal Bank of Scotland's acquisition of NatWest', *European Management Journal,* vol. 24, no. 5, pp. 368–79.

Kersley, B., Alpin, C., Forth, J., Bryson, A., Bewley, H., Dix, G. and Oxenbridge, S. (2006), *Inside the Workplace:* *Findings form the 2004 Workplace Employment Relations Survey,* Routledge, London.

Ketokivi, M. and Castañer, X. (2004), 'Strategic planning as an integrative device', *Administrative Science Quarterly,* vol. 49, no. 3, pp. 337–65.

Khaneman, D. and Tversky, A. (1974), 'Judgement under uncertainty: Heuristics and biases', *Science,* vol. 185, pp. 1124–31.

Khanna, T. (2014), 'Contextual intelligence', *Harvard Business Review,* vol. 92, no. 9, pp.58–68.

Kiechel, W. (2012), 'The management century', *Harvard Business Review,* vol. 90, no. 11, pp. 62–75.

King, G., O'Donnell, C., Boddy, D., Smith, F., Heaney, D. and Mair, F.S. (2012), 'Boundaries and e-health implementation in health and social care', *BMC Medical Informatics and Decision Making,* vol. 12, no. 10.

Kipnis, D., Schmidt, S.M. and Wilkinson, I. (1980), 'Intra-organisational influence tactics: explorations in getting one's way', *Journal of Applied Psychology,* vol. 65, no. 4, pp. 440–52.

Kirby, M.W. (2003), *Operational Research in War and Peace: The British Experience from the 1930s to the 1970s,* Imperial College Press, London.

Kirkman, B.L., Lowe, K.B. and Gibson, C.B. (2006), 'A quarter century of Culture's Consequences: a review of empirical research incorporating Hofstede's cultural values framework', *Journal of International Business Studies,* vol. 37, no. 3, pp. 285–320.

Kirkpatrick, D. (2010), *The Facebook Effect,* Virgin Books, New York.

Kirsch, D., Goldfarb, B. and Gera, A. (2009), 'Form or substance: the role of business plans in venture capital decision making', *Strategic Management Journal,* vol. 30, no. 5, pp. 487–515.

Klein, G. (1997), *Sources of Power: How people make decisions,* MIT Press, Cambridge, MA.

Klein, G.D. (2011), 'Creating cultures that lead to success: Lincoln Electric, Southwest Airlines, and SAS Institute', *Organisational Dynamics,* vol. 41, no. 1, pp. 32–43.

Kleiner, A. (2003), *Who Really Matters: The core group theory of power, privilege and success,* Doubleday, New York.

Knapp, M.L. and Hall, J.A. (2002), *Non-verbal Communication in Human Interaction,* Thomson Learning, London.

Kochan, T.A. et al. (2003), 'The effects of diversity on business performance: Report of the diversity research network', *Human Resource Management,* vol. 42, no. 1, pp. 3–21.

Komaki, J. (2003), 'Reinforcement theory at work: enhancing and explaining what workers do', in L.W. Porter, G.A. Bigley and R.M. Steers (eds), *Motivation and Work Behaviour* (7th edn), Irwin/McGraw-Hill, Burr Ridge, IL.

Komaki, J.L., Coombs, T., Redding, T.P. and Schepman, S. (2000), 'A rich and rigorous examination of applied behaviour analysis research in the world of work', in C.L. Cooper and I.T. Robertson (eds), *International Review of Industrial and Organisational Psychology,* Wiley, Chichester, pp. 265–367.

Konzelmann, S., Conway, N., Trenberth, L. and Wilkinson, F. (2006), 'Corporate governance and human resource management', *British Journal of Industrial Relations,* vol. 44, no. 3, pp. 541–67.

Kotler, P. and Keller, K.L. (2014), *Marketing Management,* (14th edition) Pearson Education, Harlow.

Kotler, P., Armstrong, G., Wong, V. and Saunders, J. (2008), *Principles of Marketing*, (5th European edition) Financial Times/Prentice Hall, Harlow.

Kotter, J.P. (1990), *A Force for Change: How leadership differs from management,* The Free Press, New York.

Kotter, J.P. and Heskett, J. (1992), *Corporate Culture and Performance,* Free Press, New York.

Krackhardt, D. and Hanson, J.R. (1993), 'Informal networks: the company behind the chart', *Harvard Business Review,* vol. 71, no. 4, pp. 104–11.

Kumar, N. (2006), 'Strategies to fight low-cost rivals', *Harvard Business Review,* vol. 84, no. 12, pp. 104–12.

Kumar, V., Venkatesan, R. and Reinartz, W. (2006), 'Knowing what to sell, when, and to whom', *Harvard Business Review,* vol. 84, no.3, pp. 131–7.

Kumar, V., Jones, E., Venkatesan, R. and Leone, R.P. (2011), 'Is market orientation a source of sustainable competitive advantage or simply the cost of competing?', *Journal of Marketing,* vol. 75, no. 1, pp. 16–30.

Kumar, V. (2015), 'Evolution of marketing as a discipline: What has happened and what to look out for', *Journal of Marketing,* vol. 79, no. 1, pp. 1–9.

Kuper, S. (2011), *The Football Men: Up Close with the Giants of the Modern Game,* Simon and Schuster, London.

Lamberton, G. (2005), 'Sustainability accounting – a brief history and conceptual framework,' *Accounting Forum,* vol. 29, no. 1, pp. 7–26.

Lashinsky, A. (2012), *Inside Apple,* John Murray (Publishers), London.

Latham, G.P. and Locke, E.A. (2006), 'Enhancing the benefits and overcoming the pitfalls of goal setting', *Organisational Dynamics,* vol. 35, no. 4, pp. 332–40.

Lawler, E.E. (1976), 'Control systems in organisations', in Dunnette, M.D. (ed.) *Handbook of Industrial and Organisational Psychology,* Rand-McNally, Chicago.

Lawler, E.E. (2008), *Talent*, Jossey-Bass, San Francisco, CA.

Lawler, E.E. and Worley, C.G. (2010), 'Designing organisations for sustainable effectiveness', *Organisational Dynamics,* vol. 39, no. 4, pp. 265–27.

Lawrence, P. and Lorsch, J.W. (1967), *Organisation and Environment,* Harvard Business School Press, Boston, MA.

Lawson, P. (2000), 'Performance-related pay', in R. Thorpe and G. Homan (eds.), *Strategic Reward Systems,* Prentice Hall, Harlow.

Leahy, T. (2012) *Management in 10 Words,* Random House, London.

Lechner, C. and Floyd, S.W. (2012), 'Group influence activities and the performance of strategic initiatives', *Strategic Management Journal,* vol. 33, no. 5, pp. 478–95.

Legge, K. (2005), *Human Resource Management: Rhetorics and realities,* (Anniversary edition) Macmillan, London.

Leidecker, J.K. and Bruno, A.V. (1984), 'Identifying and using critical success factors', *Long Range Planning,* vol. 17, no.1, pp. 23–32.

Le Meunier-Fitzhugh, K. and Piercy, N.F. (2008), 'The importance of organisational structure for collaboration between sales and marketing', *Journal of General Management,* vol. 34, no. 1, pp. 19–35.

Lengel, R.H. and Daft, R.L. (1988), 'The selection of communication media as an executive skill', *Academy of Management Executive,* vol. 11, no. 3, pp. 225–32.

Levitt, T. (1965), 'Exploit the product life cycle', *Harvard Business Review,* vol. 43, no. 6, pp. 81–94.

Levitt, T. (1960), 'Marketing myopia', *Harvard Business Review,* vol. 38, no. 4, pp. 45–56.

Levitt, T. (1983), 'The globalisation of markets', *Harvard Business Review,* vol. 61, no. 3, pp. 92–102.

Levy, S. (2011), *In the Plex: How Google Thinks, Works and Shapes our Lives,* Simon and Schuster, New York.

Li, J. and Kozhikode, R.K. (2012), 'Organisational learning of emerging economy firms: The case of China's TCL Group', *Organisational Dynamics,* vol. 40, no. 3, pp. 214–21.

Liberman-Yaconi, L., Hooper, T. and Hutchings, K. (2010), 'Towards a model of understanding strategic decision-making in micro-firms', *Journal of Small Business Management,* vol. 48, no. 1, pp. 70–95.

Likert, R. (1961), *New Patterns of Management,* McGraw-Hill, New York.

Likert, R. (1967), *The Human Organisation: Its Management and Value,* McGraw-Hill, New York.

Lindblom, C.E. (1959), 'The science of muddling through', *Public Administration Review,* vol. 19, no. 2, pp. 79–88.

Lister, B. (2008), 'Heathrow Terminal 5: enhancing environmental sustainability', *Proceedings of the Institution of Civil Engineers – Civil Engineering,* vol. 161, no. 5, pp. 21–4.

Liu, L. A., Chua, C.H. and Stahl, G.K. (2010), 'Quality of communication experience: Definition, measurement, and implications for intercultural negotiations', *Journal of Applied Psychology,* vol. 95, no. 3, pp. 469–87.

Lloyd, C. and Payne, J. (2014), 'It's all hands-on, even for management': Managerial work in the UK café sector', *Human Relations,* vol. 67, no. 4, pp. 465–88.

Lock, D. (2013), *Project Management* (10th edition), Gower, Aldershot.

Locke, E.A. (1968), 'Towards a theory of task motivation and incentives', *Organisational Behaviour and Human Performance,* vol. 3, pp. 157–89.

Locke, E.A. and Latham, G.P. (1990), *A Theory of Goal Setting and Task Performance,* Prentice-Hall, Englewood Cliffs, NJ.

Locke, E.A. and Latham, G.P. (2002), 'Building a practically useful theory of goal setting and task motivation – A 35-year odyssey', *American Psychologist,* vol. 57, no. 9, pp. 705–17.

Lorenz, A. (2009), *GKN: The Making of a Business,* Wiley, Chichester.

Lorsch, J.W. (1986), 'Managing culture: the invisible barrier to strategic change', *California Management Review,* vol. 28, no. 2, pp. 95–109.

Lovallo, D. and Kahneman, D. (2003), 'Delusions of success', *Harvard Business Review,* vol. 81, no. 7, pp. 56–63.

Luchs, M.G., Naylor, R. W., Irwin, J.R. and Raghunathan, R. (2010), 'The sustainability liability: Potential negative effects of ethicality on product preference', *Journal of Marketing,* vol. 74, no. 5, pp. 18–31.

Luthans, F. (1988), 'Successful vs effective real managers', *Academy of Management Executive,* vol. 11, no. 2, pp. 127–32.

MacCormick, J.S., Dery, K. and Kolb, D.G. (2012), 'Engaged or just connected? Smartphones and employee engagement', *Organisational Dynamics,* vol. 41, no. 3, pp. 194–201.

Magretta, J. (2013), *What Management Is (How it works, and why it's everyone's business),* (2nd edition) Profile Books, London.

Mahajan, V. (2012), *The Arab World Unbound: Tapping into the power of 350 Million Consumers,* Jossey-Bass, San Francisco, CA.

Mallin, C.A. (2013), *Corporate Governance,* (4th edn) Oxford University Press, Oxford.

March, J.G. (1988), *Decisions and Organisations,* Blackwell, London.

Martin, G. and Gullan, P.J. (2012) 'Corporate governance and strategic human resources management (SRHRM) in the UK financial services sector: the case of the Royal Bank of Scotland', *International Journal of Human Resource Management,* vol. 23, no. 16, pp. 3295–314.

Martin, J. (2002), *Organisational Culture: Mapping the terrain,* Sage, London.

Maslow, A. (1970), *Motivation and Personality* (2nd edition), Harper & Row, New York.

Matten, D. and Moon, J. (2008), "Implicit' and 'Explicit' CSR: A conceptual framework for a comparative understanding of corporate social responsibility', *Academy of Management Review,* vol. 33, no. 2, pp. 404–24.

Mattila, A.S. (2009), 'How to handle PR disasters? An examination of the impact of communication response type and failure attributions on consumer perceptions', *Journal of Services Marketing,* vol. 23, no. 4, pp . 211–18.

Mayo, E. (1949), *The Social Problems of an Industrial Civilisation,* Routledge and Kegan Paul, London.

McClelland, D. (1961), *The Achieving Society,* Van Nostrand Reinhold, Princeton, NJ.

McCrae, R.R. and John, O.P. (1992), 'An introduction to the five-factor model and its applications', *Journal of Personality,* vol. 60, no. 2, pp. 175–215.

McEntire, L.E., Dailey, L.R., Holly, K. and Mumford, M. (2006), 'Innovations in job analysis: Development and application of metrics to analyse job data', *Human Resource Management Review,* vol. 16, no. 3, pp. 310–23.

McGregor, D. (1960), *The Human Side of Enterprise,* McGraw-Hill, New York.

McKee, R.K. and Carlson, B. (1999), *The Power to Change,* Grid International, Austin, Texas.

McLean, B. and Elkind, P. (2003), *The Smartest Guys in the Room,* Penguin, London.

Melancon, S. and Williams, M. (2006), 'Competency-based assessment centre design: a case study', *Advances in Human Resource Management,* vol. 8, no. 2, pp. 283–314.

Micklethwait, J. and Wooldridge, A. (2003), *The Company: A short history of a revolutionary idea,* Weidenfeld and Nicolson, London.

Miles, R.E., Snow, C.C., Fjeldstad, O.D., Miles, G. and Lettl, C. (2010), 'Designing organisations to meet 21st-century opportunities and challenges', *Organisational Dynamics,* vol. 39, no. 2, pp. 93–103.

Miller, S., Wilson, D. and Hickson, D. (2004), 'Beyond planning: strategies for successfully implementing strategic decisions', *Long Range Planning,* vol. 37, no. 3, pp. 201–18.

Mills, C. and Pawson, K. (2012), 'Integrating motivation, risk-taking and self-identity: A typology of ICT enterprise development narratives', *International Small Business Journal,* vol. 30, no. 5, pp. 584–606.

Mintzberg, H. (1973), *The Nature of Managerial Work,* Harper & Row, New York.

Mintzberg, H. (1975), 'The manager's job: Folklore and fact', *Harvard Business Review,* vol. 53, no. 4, p.49–61.

Mintzberg, H. (1979), *The Structuring of Organisations,* Prentice Hall, Englewood Cliffs, NJ.

Mintzberg, H. (1994), *The Rise and Fall of Strategic Planning,* Prentice Hall International, Hemel Hempstead.

Mohrman, S.A. and Worley, C.G. (2010), 'The organisational sustainability journey: Introduction to the special issue', *Organisational Dynamics,* vol. 39, no. 4, pp. 289–94.

Morey, T., Forbath, T. and Schoop, A. (2015), 'Customer data: Designing for transparency and trust', *Harvard Business Review,* vol. 93, no. 5, pp. 96–105.

Morgan, G. (1997), *Images of Organisation,* Sage, London.

Morgan, N.A., Vorhies, D.W. and Mason, C.H. (2009), 'Market orientation, market capabilities, and firm performance', *Strategic Management Journal,* vol. 30, no. 8, pp. 909–20.

Moritz, M. (2009), *Return to the Little Kingdom,* Duckworth Overlook, London.

Mowday, R.T. and Colwell, K.A. (2003), 'Employee reactions to unfair outcomes in the workplace: the contribution of Adams' equity theory to understanding work motivation', in L.W. Porter, G.A. Bigley and R.M. Steers (eds), *Motivation and Work Behaviour* (7th edn), Irwin/McGraw-Hill, Burr Ridge, IL.

Mumford, E. (2006), 'The story of socio-technical design', *Information Systems Journal,* vol. 16, no. 4, pp. 317–42.

Murphy, G.D., Chang, A. and Unsworth, K. (2012), 'Differential effects of ERP systems on user outcomes—a longitudinal investigation', *New Technology, Work and Employment*, vol. 27, no. 2, pp. 147–62.

Neely, A. and Al Najjar, M. (2006), 'Management learning not management control: The true role of performance measurement', *California Management Review,* vol. 48, no. 3, pp. 101–14.

Newell, S. (2006) 'Selection and assessment', in Redman, T. and Wilkinson, A. (eds) *Contemporary Human Resource Management,* Financial Times/Prentice-Hall, Harlow, pp. 65–98.

Nissen, C.S. (2014), 'Public service media management face old and new challenges' in Glowacki, M. and Jackson, L. (eds.), *Public Media Management for the 21st Century,* Routledge, London.

Nonaka, I. and Takeuchi, H. (1995), *The Knowledge Creating Company,* Oxford University Press, New York.

Nutt, P.C. (2002), *Why Decisions Fail: Avoiding the blunders and traps that lead to debacles,* Berrett-Koehler, San Francisco, CA.

Nutt, P.C. (2008), 'Investigating the Success of Decision Making Processes', *Journal of Management Studies,* vol. 45, no. 2, pp. 425–55.

O'Cass, A. and Ngo, L.V. (2011), 'Examining the firm's value creation process: A managerial perspective of the firm's value offering strategy and performance', *British Journal of Management,* vol. 22, no. 4, pp. 646–671.

O'Connell, J.F. and Williams, G. (2005), 'Passengers' perceptions of low cost airlines and full service carriers', *Journal of Air Transport Management,* vol. 11, no. 4, pp. 259–72.

Ogbonna, E. and Harris, L.C. (1998), 'Organisational culture: it's not what you think', *Journal of General Management,* vol. 23, no. 3, pp. 35–48.

Ogbonna, E. and Harris, L.C. (2002), 'Organisational culture: a ten-year, two-phase study of change in the UK food retailing sector', *Journal of Management Studies,* vol. 39, no. 5, pp. 673–706.

Ogbonna, E. and Harris, L.C. (2014), 'Organisational cultural perpetuation: A case study of an English Premier League football club', *British Journal of Management,* vol. 25, no.4, pp. 667–686.

O'Gorman, C., Bourke, S. and Murray, J.A. (2005), 'The nature of managerial work in small growth-orientated businesses', *Small Business Economics,* vol. 25, no. 1, pp. 1–16.

Ordanini, A., Rubera, G. and Sala, M. (2008), 'Integrating Functional Knowledge and Embedding Learning in New Product Launches: How Project Forms Helped EMI Music', *Long Range Planning,* vol. 41, no. 1, pp. 17–32.

Orlitzky, M., Schmidt, F. and Rynes, S. (2003), 'Corporate social and financial performance: A meta-analysis', *Organization Studies*, vol. 24, no. 3, pp. 403–441.

Paik, Y. and Choi, D. (2005), 'The shortcomings of a standardised global knowledge management system: The case study of Accenture', *Academy of Management Executive,* vol. 19, no. 2, pp. 81–84.

Papke-Shields, K.E., Malhotra, M.K. and Grover, V. (2006), 'Evolution in the strategic manufacturing planning process of organisations', *Journal of Operations Management,* vol. 24, no. 5, pp. 421–39.

Parada, P., Alemany, L. and Planellas, M. (2009), 'The internationalisation of retail banking: Banco Santander's journey towards globalisation', *Long Range Planning,* vol. 42, no. 5–6, pp. 654–77.

Parker, D. and Stacey, R. (1994), *Chaos, Management and Economics: The implications of non-linear thinking,* Hobart Paper 125, Institute of Economic Affairs, London.

Parker, L.D. and Ritson, P.A. (2005), 'Revisiting Fayol: Anticipating contemporary management', *British Journal of Management,* vol. 16, no. 3, pp. 175–94.

Parry, E. and Tyson, S. (2008), 'An analysis of the use and success of online recruitment methods in the UK', *Human Resource Management Journal,* vol. 18, no. 3, pp. 257–74.

Pedler, M., Burgoyne, J. and Boydell, T. (1997), *The Learning Company: A Strategy for Sustainable Development,* (2nd edition) McGraw-Hill, London.

Peloza, J. (2006), 'Using corporate social responsibility as insurance for financial performance', *California Management Review,* vol. 48, no. 2, pp. 52–72.

Pentland, A. (2013), 'Beyond the echo chamber', *Harvard Business Review,* vol. 91, no. 11, pp. 80–6.

Peters, T.J. and Waterman, D.H. (1982), *In Search of Excellence,* Harper & Row, London.

Petersen, J.A., Kushwaha, T. and Kumar, V. (2015), 'Marketing communication strategies and consumer financial decision making: The role of national culture', *Journal of Marketing,* vol. 79, no. 1, pp. 44–63.

Pettigrew, A. (1985), *The Awakening Giant: Continuity and change in Imperial Chemical Industries,* Blackwell, Oxford.

Pettigrew, A., Ferlie, E. and McKee, L. (1992), *Shaping Strategic Change,* Sage, London.

Pfeffer, J. (2010), *Power: Why Some People Have It and Others Don't,* Harper Business, New York.

Pfeffer, J. (1992a), *Managing with Power,* Harvard Business School Press, Boston, MA.

Pfeffer, J. (1992b), 'Understanding power in organisations', *California Management Review,* vol. 34, no. 2, pp. 29–50.

Pfeffer, J. and Sutton, R.I. (2006), 'Evidence-based management', *Harvard Business Review,* vol. 84, no. 1, pp. 62–74.

Pfeffer, J. and Sutton, R.I. (2006), *Hard Facts, Dangerous Truths and Total Nonsense,* Harvard Business School Press, Boston, MA.

Pierce, J.L. and Gardner, D.G. (2004), 'Self-esteem within the work and organisational context: A review of the organisation-based self-esteem literature', *Journal of Management,* vol. 30, no. 5, pp. 591–622.

Pierce, L. and Snyder, J. (2008), 'Ethical spillovers in firms: Evidence from vehicle emissions testing', *Management Science,* vol. 54, no. 11, pp. 1891–903.

Pinkham, B.C., Picken, J.C. and Dess, G.G. (2010), 'Creating value in the modern organisation: The role of leveraging technology', *Organisational Dynamics,* vol. 39, no. 3, pp. 226–39.

Pinto, J. (1998), 'Understanding the role of politics in successful project management', *International Journal of Project Management,* vol. 18, no. 2, pp. 85–91.

Pirola-Merlo, A. (2010), 'Agile innovation: The role of team climate in rapid research and development', *Journal of Occupational and Organisational Psychology,* vol. 83, no. 4, pp. 1075–84.

Pisano, G.P. and Corsi, E. (2012), *Virgin Group: Finding New Avenues for Growth,* Harvard Business School case 9-612-070.

Porter, M.E. (1980), *Competitive Strategy,* Free Press, New York.

Porter, M.E. (1985), *Competitive Advantage: Creating and sustaining superior performance,* Free Press, New York.

Porter, M.E. (1994), 'Competitive strategy revisited: a view from the 1990s', in P. B. Duffy (ed.), *The Relevance of a Decade,* Harvard Business School Press, Boston, MA.

Porter, M.E. (2008), 'The five competitive forces that shape strategy', *Harvard Business Review,* vol. 86, no. 1, pp. 78–93.

Porter, M.E. and Kramer, M.R. (2011), 'Creating shared value', *Harvard Business Review,* vol. 89, no. 1/2, pp. 62–77.

Prahalad, C.K. and Lieberthal, K. (2003), 'The End of Corporate Imperialism', *Harvard Business Review,* vol. 81, no. 8, pp. 109–17.

Prastacos, G., Soderquist, K., Spanos, Y. and Van Wassenhove, L. (2002), 'An integrated framework for managing change in the new competitive landscape', *European Management Journal,* vol. 20, no. 1, pp. 55–71.

Purcell, J. and Hutchinson, S. (2007), 'Front-line managers as agents in the HRM-performance causal chain: theory, analysis and evidence', *Human Resource Management Journal,* vol. 17, no. 1, pp. 3–20.

Pye A. (2002), 'Corporate directing: governing, strategising and leading in action', *Corporate Governance – an International Review,* vol. 10, no. 3, pp. 153–62.

Quinn, J.B. (1980), *Strategies for Change: Logical incrementalism,* Irwin, Homewood, IL.

Quinn, R.E., Faerman, S.R., Thompson, M.P. and McGrath, M.R. (2003), *Becoming a Master Manager,* (3rd edition) Wiley, New York.

Ramírez, R., Roodhart, L. and Manders, W. (2011), 'How Shell's domains link innovation and strategy', *Long Range Planning,* vol. 44, no. 4, pp. 250–270.

Rangan, K., Chase, L. and Karim, S. (2015), 'The truth about CSR', *Harvard Business Review,* vol. 93, no. 1/2, pp. 40–9.

Reiter-Palmon, R., Brown, M., Sandall, D., Bublotz,C. and Nimps, T. (2006), 'Development of an O*Net web-based job analysis and its implementation in the US Navy: Lessons learned', *Human Resource Management Review,* vol. 16, no. 3, pp. 294–309.

Restubog, S.L.D., Bordia, P. and Tang, R.L. (2007), 'Behavioural outcomes of psychological contract breach in a non-western culture: The moderating role of equity sensitivity,' *British Journal of Management,* vol. 18, no. 4, pp. 376–86.

Riccabone, A. and Leone, E.L. (2010), 'Implementing strategies through management control systems: the case of sustainability', *International Journal of Productivity and Performance Management,* vol. 59, no. 2, pp. 130–44.

Roberts, C. (2014), 'Strategy migration in a changing climate', *Harvard Business Review,* vol. 92, no. 5, p. 42.

Roberts, P. and Dowling, G. (2002), 'Corporate reputation and sustained superior financial performance', *Strategic Management Journal,* vol. 23, no. 12, pp. 1077–93.

Roberts, J., McNulty, T. and Stiles, P. (2005), 'Beyond agency conceptions of the work of the non-executive director: Creating accountability in the boardroom', *British Journal of Management,* vol. 16, Supplement 1, pp. S5–S26.

Rodriguez, P., Uhlenbruck, K. and Eden, L. (2005), 'Government corruption and the entry strategies of multinationals', *Academy of Management Review,* vol. 30, no. 2, pp. 383–96.

Roeder, M. (2011), *The Big Mo: Why Momentum Now Rules Our World,* Virgin Books, London.

Roethlisberger, F.J. and Dickson, W.J. (1939), *Management and the Worker,* Harvard University Press, Cambridge, MA.

Ronen, S. and Shenkar, O. (1985), 'Clustering countries on attitudinal dimensions – A review and synthesis', *Academy of Management Review,* vol. 10, no. 3, pp. 435–54.

Rosen, S. (1998) 'A lump of clay', *Communication World,* vol. 15, no. 7, p. 58.

Rosenzweig, P. (2013), 'What makes strategic decisions different?', *Harvard Business Review,* vol. 91, no. 11, pp. 88–93.

Rousseau, D.M. and Schalk, R. (2000), *Psychological Contracts in Employment: Cross-national perspectives,* Sage, London.

Rugman, A.M. (2005), *The Regional Multinationals,* Cambridge University Press, Cambridge.

Rugman, A.M. and Hodgetts, R.M. (2003), *International Business,* FT/Prentice Hall, Harlow.

Rumelt, R.P. (2011), *Good Strategy/Bad Strategy: the difference and why it matters,* Profile, London.

Ryals, L. (2005), 'Making customer relationship management work: the measurement and profitable management of customer relationships', *Journal of Marketing,* vol. 69, no. 4, pp. 252–61.

Sabherwal, R., Hirschheim, R. and Goles, T. (2001), 'The dynamics of alignment: insights from a punctuated equilibrium', *Organisation Science,* vol. 12, no. 2, pp. 179–97.

Sahlman, W.A. (1997), 'How to write a great business plan', *Harvard Business Review,* vol. 75, no. 4, pp. 98–108.

Salas, E., Cooke, N.J. and Rosen, M.A. (2008), 'On teams, teamwork, and team performance: Discoveries and Developments', *Human Factors,* vol. 50, no. 3, pp. 540–47.

Sauermann, H. and Cohen, W.M. (2010), 'What makes them tick? Employee motives and firm innovation', *Management Science,* vol. 56, no. 12, pp. 2134–53.

Schaefer, A. (2007), 'Contrasting institutional and performance accounts of environmental management systems: Three case studies in the UK water & sewerage industry', *Journal of Management Studies,* vol. 44, no. 4, pp. 506–35.

Schein, E. (2010), *Organisational Culture and Leadership,* (4th edition) Jossey-Bass, San Francisco, CA.

Schwartz, B. (2004), *The Paradox of Choice,* Ecco, New York.

Senge, P., Smith, B., Kruschwitz, N., Laur, J. and Schley, S. (2008), *The Necessary Revolution: How individuals and organisations are working together to create a sustainable world,* Nicholas Brealey Publishing, London.

Shao, L. and Webber, S. (2006), 'A cross-cultural test of the 'five factor model of personality and transformational leadership', *Journal of Business Research,* vol. 59, no. 8, pp. 936–44.

Shaw, E. (2006), 'Small firm networking: An insight into contents and motivating factors' *International Small Business Journal,* vol. 24, no. 1, pp. 5–29.

Shaw, M.E. (1978), 'Communication networks fourteen years later', in Berkowitz, L. (ed.), *Group Processes,* Academic Press, London.

Sheehan, M. (2014), 'Human resource management and performance: Evidence from small and medium-sized firms', *International Small Business Journal,* vol. 32, no. 5, pp. 545–70.

Simms, A. and Boyle, D. (2010), *Eminent Corporations: The Rise and Fall of Great British Brands,* Constable, London

Simon, H. (1960), *Administrative Behaviour,* Macmillan, New York.

Skinner, B.F. (1971), *Contingencies of Reinforcement,* Appleton-Century-Crofts, East Norwalk, CT.

Slack, N., Brandon-Jones, A. and Johnston, R. (2013), *Operations Management*, (7th edition) Pearson, Harlow.

Smith, A. (1776), *The Wealth of Nations,* ed. with an introduction by Andrew Skinner (1974), Penguin, Harmondsworth.

Smith, J.H. (1998), 'The enduring legacy of Elton Mayo', *Human Relations,* vol. 51, no. 3, pp. 221–49.

Søderberg, A-M. (2015), 'Recontextualising a strategic concept within a globalising company: A case study on Carlsberg's 'Winning Behaviours' strategy', *International Journal of Human Resource Management,* vol. 26, no. 2, pp. 231–57.

Sparrow, P., Brewster, C. and Harris, H. (2004), *Globalising Human Resource Management,* Routledge, London.

Sparrowe, R.T. and Liden, R.C. (2005), 'Two routes to influence: Integrating leader-member exchange and social network perspectives', *Administrative Science Quarterly,* vol. 50, no. 4, pp. 505–35.

Sprague, L. (2007), 'Evolution of the field of operations management', *Journal of Operations Management,* vol. 25, no. 2, pp. 219–38.

Spriegel, W.R. and Myers, C.E. (eds.) (1953), *The Writings of the Gilbreths,* Irwin, Homewood, IL.

Stachowski, A.A., Kaplan, S.A. and Waller, M.J. (2009), 'The benefits of flexible team interaction during crises', *Journal of Applied Psychology,* vol. 94, no. 6, pp. 1536–43.

Stern, N. (2009), *A Blueprint For a Safer Planet: How to manage climate change and create a new era of progress and prosperity,* The Bodley Head, London.

Sternberg, R.J. and Lubart, T.I. (1999), 'The concept of creativity: Prospects and paradigms' in Sternberg R.J. (ed.), *Handbook of Creativity,* Cambridge University Press, Cambridge.

Stewart, R. (1967), *Managers and their Jobs,* Macmillan, London.

Stiles, P. (2009), 'The changing nature of the Japanese business system and its impact on Asia', *Long Range Planning,* vol. 42, no. 4, pp. 427–38.

Stott, P. A. (2010), 'Detection and attribution of climate change: a regional perspective', *Wiley Interdisciplinary Reviews – Climate Change,* vol. 1, no. 2.

Sturges, J. (2012), 'Crafting a balance between work and home', *Human Relations,* vol. 65, no. 12, pp. 1539–59.

Sull, D.N. (2007), 'Closing the gap between strategy and execution', *MIT Sloan Management Review,* vol. 48, no. 4, pp. 30–8.

Sull, D., Homkes, R. and Sull, C. (2015), 'Why strategy execution fails – and what to do about it', *Harvard Business Review,* vol. 93, no. 3, pp. 57–66.

Swartz, M. and Watkins, S. (2002), *Power Failure: The rise and fall of Enron,* Aurum, London.

Tambe, P., Hitt, L.M. and Brynjolfsson, E. (2012), 'The extroverted firm: How external information practices affect innovation and productivity', *Management Science,* vol. 58, no. 5, pp. 843–59.

Tannenbaum, R. and Schmidt, W.H. (1973), 'How to choose a leadership pattern: should a manager be democratic or autocratic – or something in between?', *Harvard Business Review,* vol. 37, no. 2, pp. 95–102.

Tapscott, D. (2009), *Grown Up Digital: How the Net Generation is Changing Your World,* McGraw-Hill, New York.

Tapscott, D. and Williams, A.D. (2006), *Wikinomics: How Mass Collaboration Changes Everything,* Viking Penguin, New York.

Taras, V., Steel, P. and Kirkman, B.L. (2011), 'Three decades of research on national culture in the workplace: Do the differences still make a difference?', *Organisational Dynamics,* vol. 40, no. 3, pp. 189–98.

Tayeb, M.H. (1996), *The Management of a Multicultural Workforce,* Wiley, Chichester.

Taylor, F.W. (1917), *The Principles of Scientific Management,* Harper, New York.

Taylor, J.W. (2008), 'A comparison of univariate time series methods for forecasting intraday arrivals at a call centre', *Management Science,* vol. 54, no. 2, pp. 253–65.

Teece, D.J. (2009), *Dynamic Capabilities and Strategic Management,* Oxford University Press, Oxford.

Teerikangas, S. and Very, P. (2006), 'The culture–performance relationship in M&A: From yes/no to how', *British Journal of Management,* vol. 17, no. S1, pp. S31–S48.

Thomas, A.B. (2003), *Controversies in Management: Issues, debates and answers,* (2nd edition) Routledge, London.

Thomas D.C. and Inkson, K. (2009), *Cultural Intelligence: Living and Working Globally,* Berret-Koehler Publishers, Inc. San Francisco.

Thompson, J.D. (1967), *Organisations in Action,* McGraw-Hill, New York.

Thompson, P. and McHugh, D. (2002), *Work Organisations: A Critical Introduction,* Palgrave, Basingstoke.

Timpson, J. (2010), *Upside Down Management: A Common Sense Guide to Better Business,* Wiley, Chichester.

Torrington, D., Hall, L., Taylor, S. and Atkinson, C. (2008), *Human Resource Management,* (8th edition) Pearson, Harlow.

Tran, T. and Blackman, M. (2006), 'The dynamics and validity of the group selection interview', *Journal of Social Psychology,* vol. 146, no. 2, pp. 183–201.

Tregaskis, O., Daniels, K., Glover, L., Butler, P. and Meyer, M. (2013), 'High performance work practices and firm performance: A longitudinal case study', *British Journal of Management,* vol. 24, no. 2, pp. 225–44.

Trevino, L.K. and Weaver, G.R. (2003), *Managing Ethics in Business Organisations: Social Scientific Perspectives,* Stanford University Press, Stanford, Ca.

Trist, E.L. and Bamforth, K.W. (1951), 'Some social and psychological consequences of the Longwall Method of coal getting', *Human Relations,* vol. 4, no. 1, pp. 3–38.

Trompennaars, F. (1993), *Riding the Waves of Culture: Understanding cultural diversity in business,* The Economist Books, London.

Trought, F. (2012), *Brilliant Employability Skills,* Prentice Hall, Harlow.

Truss, C. and Gill, J. (2009), 'Managing the HR function: the role of social capital', *Personnel Review,* vol. 38, no. 6, pp. 674–95.

Tuckman, B. and Jensen, N. (1977), 'Stages of small group development revisited', *Group and Organisational Studies,* vol. 2, pp. 419–27.

Turner, M.E. and Pratkanis, A.R. (1998), 'Twenty-five years of groupthink theory and research: lessons from an evaluation of the theory', *Organisational Behaviour and Human Decision Processes,* vol. 73, no. 2, pp. 105–15.

Unsworth, K.L. and Clegg, C.W. (2010), 'Why do employees undertake creative action? *Journal of Occupational and Organisational Psychology,* vol. 83, no. 1, pp. 77–99.

Van der Heijden, K. (1996), *Scenarios: The art of strategic conversation,* Wiley, Chichester.

Van der Vegt, G.S. and Bunderson, J.S. (2005), 'Learning and performance in multidisciplinary teams: The importance of collective team identification,' *Academy of Management Journal,* vol. 48, no. 3, pp. 532–47.

Vecchi, A. and Brennan, L. (2011), 'Quality management: a cross-cultural perspective based on the GLOBE framework', *International Journal of Operations and Production Management,* vol. 31, no. 5, pp. 527–53.

Vogel, D. (2005), *The Market for Virtue: The Potential and Limits of Corporate Social Responsibility,* Brookings Institution Press, Washington, D.C.

Vroom, V.H. (1964), *Work and Motivation,* Wiley, New York.

Vroom, V.H. and Yetton, P.W. (1973), *Leadership and Decision-making,* University of Pittsburgh Press, Pittsburgh, PA.

Walton, E.J. (2005), 'The persistence of bureaucracy: A meta-analysis of Weber's model of bureaucratic control', *Organisation Studies,* vol. 26, no. 4, pp. 569–600.

Walton, R.E. (1985), 'Work innovations at Topeka: After six years', *Journal of Applied Behavioural Science,* vol. 13, no.3, pp. 422–33.

Wang, T and Bansal, P. (2012), 'Social responsibility in new ventures: profiting from a long-term orientation', *Strategic Management Journal,* vol. 33, no.10, pp.1135–1153.

Watson, T.J. (1994), *In Search of Management,* Routledge, London.

Watts, S (2001), *The Magic Kingdom: Walt Disney and the American Way of Life,* Houghton-Mifflin, Boston, MA.

Weber, M. (1947), *The Theory of Social and Economic Organisation,* Free Press, Glencoe, IL.

Webster, K., Bleriot, J. and Johnson, C. (2013), *A New Dynamic: Effective Business in a Circular Economy,* Ellen MacArthur Foundation, Cowes.

Weill, P. and Ross, J. (2005), 'A matrixed approach to designing IT governance', *MIT Sloan Management Review,* vol. 46, no. 2, pp. 26–34.

Westphal, J.D. and Bednar, M.K. (2008), 'The Pacification of Institutional Investors', *Administrative Science Quarterly,* vol. 53, no. 1, pp. 29–72.

Whetten, D.A. and Cameron, K.S. (2011), *Developing Management Skills,* (8th edition) Prentice Hall International, Upper Saddle River, NJ.

Whipp, R., Rosenfeld, R. and Pettigrew, A. (1988), 'Understanding strategic change processes: some preliminary British findings', in A. Pettigrew (ed.), *The Management of Strategic Change,* Blackwell, Oxford.

Whitley, R. (1999), *Divergent Capitalisms: The Social Structuring and Change of Business Systems,* Oxford University Press, Oxford.

Whittington, R., Molloy, E., Mayer, M. and Smith, A. (2006), 'Practices of strategising/organising: broadening strategy work and skills', *Long Range Planning,* vol. 39, no. 6, pp. 615–29.

Whyman, P.B., Baimbridge,M.J., Buraimo, B.A. and Petrescu, A.I. (2015), 'Workplace flexibility practices and corporate performance: Evidence from the British private sector, *British Journal of Management,* vol. 26, no. 3, pp. 347–64.

Wieder, H., Booth, P., Matolcsy, Z.P. and Ossimitz, M-L. (2006), 'The impact of ERP systems on firm and business process performance', *Journal of Enterprise Information Management,* vol. 19, no. 1, pp. 13–29.

Williams, K., Haslam, C. and Williams, J. (1992), 'Ford vs Fordism: the beginnings of mass production?' *Work, Employment and Society,* vol. 6, no. 4, pp. 517–55.

Willoughby, K.A. and Zappe, C.J. (2006), 'A methodology to optimise foundation seminar assignments', *Journal of the Operational Research Society,* vol. 57, no. 8, pp. 950–6.

Wolf, A. and Jenkins, A. (2006), 'Explaining greater test use for selection: the role of HR professionals in a world of expanding regulation', *Human Resource Management Journal,* vol. 16, no. 2, pp. 193–213.

Wolff, H-G. and Moser, K. (2009), 'Effects of networking on career success: A longitudinal study', *Journal of Applied Psychology,* vol. 94, no. 1, pp. 196–206.

Wolstenholme, A., Fugeman, I. and Hammond, F. (2008), 'Heathrow Terminal 5: delivery strategy', *Proceedings of the Institution of Civil Engineers – Civil Engineering,* vol. 161, no 5, pp. 10–15.

Wood, S., Van Veldhoven, M., Croon, M. and de Menezes, L. M. (2012), 'Enriched job design, high involvement management and organisational performance: The mediating roles of job satisfaction and well-being', *Human Relations,* vol. 65, no. 4, pp. 419–45.

Woodward, J. (1965), *Industrial Organisation: Theory and practice,* Oxford University Press, Oxford (2nd edn 1980).

Worley, C.G., Feyerherm, A.E. and Knudsen, D. (2010), 'Building a collaboration capability for sustainability: How Gap Inc. is creating and leveraging a strategic asset', *Organisational Dynamics,* vol. 39, no. 4, pp. 325–34.

Yeow, H., Nicholson, D., Bryant, C. and Westbury, M. (2012), 'Achieving more for less at Canary Wharf Crossrail station, London', *Civil Engineering,* vol. 165, no. 5, pp. 50–7.

Yip, G.S. (2003), *Total Global Strategy II,* Pearson Education, Upper Saddle River, NJ.

Yukl, G. and Falbe, C.M. (1990), 'Influence tactics in upwards, downward and lateral influence attempts', *Journal of Applied Psychology,* vol. 75, no. 2, pp. 132–40.

Yukl, G. and Tracey, J.B. (1992), 'Consequences of influence tactics used with subordinates, peers and the boss', *Journal of Applied Psychology,* vol. 77, no. 4, pp. 525–35.

Zander, L., Zettinig, P. and Mäkelä, K. (2013), 'Leading global virtual teams to success', *Organisational Dynamics,* vol. 42, no. 3, pp. 228–37.

Zenger, T. (2013), 'What Is the theory of your firm?' *Harvard Business Review,* vol. 91, no. 6, pp. 72–8.

Zibarras, L. D. and Woods, S. A. (2010), 'A survey of UK selection practices across different organisation sizes and industry sectors', *Journal of Occupational and Organisational Psychology,* vol. 83, no. 2, pp. 499–511.

INDEX